TREASURES NEW AND OLD
RECENT CONTRIBUTIONS TO MATTHEAN STUDIES

SOCIETY
OF BIBLICAL
LITERATURE

SBL

SYMPOSIUM SERIES

Gail R. O'Day, Editor

Number 1

TREASURES NEW AND OLD
RECENT CONTRIBUTIONS TO MATTHEAN STUDIES

edited by
David R. Bauer and Mark Allan Powell

David R. Bauer
Mark Allan Powell
editors

Treasures New and Old

Recent Contributions to
Matthean Studies

Scholars Press
Atlanta, Georgia

Treasures New and Old
Recent Contributions to Matthean Studies

edited by
David R. Bauer
Mark Allan Powell

Library of Congress Cataloging in Publication Data
Treasures new and old : recent contributions to Matthean studies /
David R. Bauer, Mark Allan Powell, editors
    p.   cm.—(Symposium series ; no. 1)
  Includes bibliographical references and indexes.
  ISBN 0-7885-0220-4 (alk. paper). — ISBN 0-7885-0221-2 (pbk. :
alk. paper)
  1. Bible. N. T. Matthew—Criticism, interpretation, etc.
I. Bauer, David R. II. Powell, Mark Allan, 1953– . III. Series:
Symposium series (Society of Biblical Literature) ; no. 1.
BS2575.2.T74   1996
226.2'06—dc20   95-51504
                                 CIP

Printed in the United States of America
on acid-free paper

For

Jack Dean Kingsbury

and

Charles H. Talbert

with gratitude for their initiative and leadership

Contents

Contributors

Janice Capel Anderson
University of Idaho
Moscow, Idaho

David R. Bauer
Asbury Theological Seminary
Wilmore, Kentucky

Margaret E. Dean
Phillips Graduate Seminary
Tulsa, Oklahoma

David E. Garland
Southern Baptist Theological Seminary
Louisville, Kentucky

Donald A. Hagner
Fuller Theological Seminary
Pasadena, California

Amy-Jill Levine
Vanderbilt Divinity School
Nashville, Tennessee

Ulrich Luz
University of Bern
Switzerland

Mark Allan Powell
Trinity Lutheran Seminary
Columbus, Ohio

Russell Pregeant
Curry College
Milton, Massachusetts

Rudolf Schnackenburg
University of Würzburg
Germany

Bernard Brandon Scott
Phillips Graduate Seminary
Tulsa, Oklahoma

Klyne Snodgrass
North Park Theological Seminary
Chicago, Illinois

Dorothy Jean Weaver
Eastern Mennonite Seminary
Harrisonburg, Virginia

Ronald D. Witherup
St. Patrick's Seminary
Menlo Park, California

We express appreciation to Michael Matlock, graduate student at
Asbury Theological Seminary, for preparing the bibliography and
indexes, and to Melissa C. Powell, Director of Financial Aid at Trinity
Lutheran Seminary, for typing and correcting the manuscript.

Abbreviations

ACNT	Augsburg Commentary on the New Testament
ATANT	Abhandlungen zur Theologie des Alten und Neuen Testaments
ATJ	*Asbury Theological Journal*
ATLA Journal	*American Theological Library Association Journal*
ATR	*Anglican Theological Review*
BDF	F. Blass, A. Debrunner, and R. W. Funk, *A Greek Grammar of the NT*
BETL	Bibliotheca ephemeridum theologicarum lovaniensium
BEvT	Beiträge zur evangelischen Theologie
BFCT	Beiträge zur Förderung christlicher Theologie
BGBE	Beiträge zur Geschichte der biblischen Exegese
BibSac	*Biblica Sacra*
BibLeb	*Bibel und Leben*
BR	*Biblical Research*
BTB	*Biblical Theology Bulletin*
BW	*Biblical World*
BZ	*Biblische Zeitschrift*
CL	*Comparative Literature*
CBQ	*Catholic Biblical Quarterly*
CChrSL	Corpus Christianorum–Series Latina
CNT	Commentaire du Nouveau Testament
CSEL	Corpus scriptorum ecclesiasticorum latinorum
CTM	*Concordia Theological Monthly*
CurTM	*Currents in Theology and Mission*
Ebib	Etudes bibliques
EKKNT	Evangelisch-katholischer Kommentar zum Neuen Testament
ETL	*Ephemerides theologicae lovanienses*
ETS	Erfurter theologische Studien
EvT	*Evangelische Theologie*
ExpTim	*Expository Times*

FRLANT	Forschungen zur Religion und Literatur des Alten und Neuen Testaments
HBT	*Horizons in Biblical Theology*
HeyJ	*Heythrop Journal*
HKNT	Handkommentar zum Neuen Testament
HNT	Handbuch zum Neuen Testament
HTKNT	Herders theologischer Kommentar zum Neuen Testament
HTR	*Harvard Theological Review*
HTSsup	Hervormde Teologiese Studies Supplement
HUCA	*Hebrew Union College Annual*
IBS	*Irish Biblical Studies*
IDB	G. A. Buttrick (ed.), *Interpreter's Dictionary of the Bible*
Int	*Interpretation*
IRT	Issues in Religion and Theology
JAAR	*Journal of the American Academy of Religion*
JBL	*Journal of Biblical Literature*
JJS	*Journal of Jewish Studies*
JQR	*Jewish Quarterly Review*
JR	*Journal of Religion*
JRE	*Journal of Religious Ethics*
JRS	*Journal of Roman Studies*
JSNT	*Journal for the Study of the New Testament*
JSNTSup	Journal for the Study of the New Testament—Supplemental Series
JSOT	*Journal for the Study of the Old Testament*
JSOTSup	Journal for the Study of the Old Testament—Supplemental Series
JSS	*Journal of Semitic Studies*
JThSB	*Jahrbuch der theologischen Schule Bethel*
JTS	*Journal of Theological Studies*
KeK	*Kritisch-exegetischer Kommentar über das N.T.*
LB	*Linguistica Biblica*
LD	Lectio divina
MBTh	Münsterische Beiträge zur Theologie
NCBC	New Century Bible Commentary
NIBC	New International Biblical Commentary
NovT	*Novum Testamentum*
NovTSup	Novum Testamentum, Supplements
NTAbh	Neutestamentliche Abhandlungen

NTD	Das Neue Testament Deutsch
NTL	New Testament Library
NTS	*New Testament Studies*
PEQ	*Palestine Exploration Quarterly*
PG	J. Migne, *Patrologia graeca*
PL	J. Migne, *Patrologia latina*
PTMS	Pittsburgh (Princeton) Theological Monograph Series
QD	Quaestiones disputatae
RevQ	*Revue de Qumran*
RB	*Revue biblique*
RHPR	*Revue d'histoire et de philosophie religieuses*
RNT	Regensburger Neues Testament
SB	Sources bibliques
SBEC	Studies in the Bible and Early Christianity
SBLASP	SBL Abstracts and Seminar Papers
SBLDS	SBL Dissertation Series
SBS	Stuttgarter Bibelstudien
SBT	Studies in Biblical Theology
ScEccl	*Sciences ecclésiastiques*
ScEs	*Science et Esprit*
SJLA	Studies in Judaism in Late Antiquity
SNT	Studien zum Neuen Testament
SNTSMS	Society for New Testament Studies Monograph Series
ST	*Studia theologica*
Str-B	[H. Strack and] P. Billerbeck, *Kommentar zum Neuen Testament*
TBei	*Theologische Beitrage*
TD	*Theology Digest*
TDNT	G. Kittel and G. Friedrich (eds.), *Theological Dictionary of the New Testament*
THKNT	Theoligischer Handkommentar zum Neuen Testament
TNTC	Tyndale New Testament Commentaries
TQ	*Theologische Quartalschrift*
TrinJ	*Trinity Journal*
TS	*Theological Studies*
TU	Texte und Untersuchungen
TynBul	*Tyndale Bulletin*
USQR	*Union Seminary Quarterly Review*
WUNT	Wissenschaftliche Untersuchungen zum Neuen Testament

Introduction

DAVID R. BAUER AND MARK ALLAN POWELL

The most significant collection of essays on Matthean scholarship to have been published in English in this century is probably *The Interpretation of Matthew*,[1] edited by Graham Stanton. The essays in that volume provide an overview of Matthean studies from 1928 through 1974. In his introduction, Stanton describes the field of Matthean studies as "a new storm center"[2] and concludes with a note on methodology:

> In recent years Matthean scholarship has been dominated by redaction criticism. Undoubtedly this method has been very fruitful . . . but unless its assumptions and procedures are reconsidered carefully it may become increasingly barren. And if our understanding of the origin and purpose of the Gospel is to be clarified further, redaction criticism will certainly need to be complemented by a variety of other approaches.[3]

In retrospect, Stanton's words certainly seem prophetic, for the past decade of Matthean studies (and Gospel studies in general) has been characterized primarily by the refinement and supplementation of redaction criticism. Predictions of a paradigm shift[4] have not been fulfilled, but neither has dissatisfaction with exclusively author-centered concerns abated.

---

[1] Graham Stanton, ed. *The Interpretation of Matthew* (Philadelphia and London: Fortress and SPCK, 1983).

[2] Stanton, "Introduction: Matthew's Gospel A New Storm Centre," in Stanton, *Interpretation*, 1–18, esp. p. 1.

[3] Stanton, "Introduction," 17.

[4] In the 1980s many scholars were suggesting that the entire historical-critical approach to biblical interpretation might be supplanted by literary-critical or ideologically oriented schemes. For an example of the anxiety this produced among supporters of historical criticism, see Leander Keck, "Will the Historical-Critical Method Survive?" in *Orientation by Disorientation: Studies in Literary Criticism and Biblical Literary Criticism Presented in Honor of William A. Beardslee*, PTMS 35, ed. Richard Spencer (Pittsburgh: Pickwick, 1980), 115–27.

1

In the United States, the principal forum for scholarly discussion of the First Gospel has been the Matthew Group of the Society of Biblical Literature. Within this group, questions of method have been considered from perspectives that are both conscientious in their regard for hermeneutical integrity and pragmatic in their concern for interpretation of particular texts and themes. The Matthew Group began in 1985 as a two-year Consultation under the leadership of Jack Dean Kingsbury and Charles H. Talbert. Given the enthusiastic response of the many scholars involved, the Matthew Group was then officially constituted in 1987 with Kingsbury and Talbert as co-chairs for five more years of intensive study. Since interest remained high even at the end of this period, the Group was granted an extension for another five years under the joint leadership of David R. Bauer and Mark Allan Powell. Most of the essays contained in this volume were originally presented as papers to the Matthew Group, though all of them have been reworked and updated in accord with their reception there and with subsequent developments in the field. The essays in this volume are organized according to three broad topics: Composition, Narration, Reception.

Composition

"Composition" refers to the process whereby the Gospel of Matthew assumed its present form. As such, it relates primarily to redaction criticism, the method that held sway in Gospel studies from the end of World War II until around 1975. As is well known, redaction criticism examines the evangelist's editorial activity in relation to the gospel tradition as it came to him in order to discern the theology of the evangelist and the situation of his community.[5] Although in the past twenty years New Testament scholarship has seen the emergence of several new methods, especially literary criticism, these new methods have not, in fact, supplanted redaction criticism. Indeed, Norman Petersen, in an early work in New Testament literary

---

[5] The best introduction to New Testament redaction criticism remains Norman Perrin, *What is Redaction Criticism?* GBS (Philadelphia: Fortress, 1969). For a fine example of the way in which redaction criticism has been applied to the synoptic Gospels, see Joachim Rohde, *Rediscovering the Teaching of the Evangelists*, NTL (London: SCM, 1968). The pioneering work in the redaction criticism of Matthew is a collection of essays by Günther Bornkamm, Gerhard Barth, and Heinz Joachim Held, *Tradition and Interpretation in Matthew* NTL (Philadelphia: Westminster, 1963).

criticism, suggested that literary criticism could assist redaction critics in their work.[6]

Thus, redaction criticism continues to account for a large proportion of scholarly work in Matthean studies. It is to be noted, however, that redaction criticism has developed over the years. The early redaction critics, such as Willi Marxsen,[7] Hans Conzelmann,[8] and Günther Bornkamm[9] emphasized the editorial process, focusing primarily on the *changes* the evangelist introduced to his received tradition; they tended to assume that the material an evangelist took over from the tradition that came to him reveals little about the evangelist's theological commitments and claims. By the 1970s, however, many redaction critics came to believe that the traditional material the evangelist incorporated untouched into his Gospel could be (almost) as significant as the editorial changes he introduced. This perspective gave rise to "composition criticism." Composition critics emphasized the total editorial achievement of the evangelist; they focused on the overall "product" of the evangelist's editorial work, rather than the minute "process" according to which the evangelist brought about changes, omissions, and additions to his *Vorlage*.[10] Nevertheless, even composition critics continued to pursue a careful examination of the evangelist's modifications to traditional material.

The essays presented here represent the wide range of contemporary redaction-critical studies in two ways. First, they reflect diversity in scope: two of them deal with the Gospel as a whole, while a third focuses upon a single passage. Second, the three essays address major issues that occupy redaction critics at the present time and, for that matter, have occupied them for the past several decades: the

---

[6] *Literary Criticism for New Testament Critics* GBS (Philadelphia: Fortress, 1978) 9–48.

[7] *Mark the Evangelist: Studies on the Redaction History of the Gospel* (Nashville: Abingdon, 1969). The German original first appeared in 1956.

[8] *The Theology of St. Luke* (Philadelphia: Fortress, 1982). The original German edition, published under the title *Die Mitte der Zeit*, first appeared in 1953.

[9] See *Tradition and Interpretation*.

[10] The three major composition-critical studies on Matthew's Gospel are: William G. Thompson, *Matthew's Advice to a Divided Community: Mt. 17:22–18:35*. Analecta Biblica Investigationes Scientificae in Res Biblicas 44 (Rome: Biblical Institute Press, 1970); Peter F. Ellis, *Matthew: His Mind and His Message* (Collegeville: Liturgical, 1974); and Jack Dean Kingsbury, *Matthew: Structure, Christology, Kingdom* (Philadelphia: Fortress, 1975), now available in a paperback edition with a new introduction (Minneapolis: Fortress, 1989).

community of Matthew, and the relationship of that community to the law and the synagogue.

In his essay, "The *Sitz im Leben* of the Gospel of Matthew," Donald A. Hagner, a prominent scholar who has written the Matthew volumes in the Word Biblical Commentary series,[11] addresses the most central and perduring issue facing Matthean scholars: the situation of Matthew's church in relation to Judaism on the one hand and Gentile Christianity on the other. Hagner employs an approach that takes into account Matthew's redactional alterations, Matthew's "special" source material, and the totality of the final form of the Gospel. In the process, Hagner emphasizes that any solution to the problem of Matthew's community must take seriously the tension that exists within the Gospel between particularism (i.e., indications that the kingdom of God is limited to Israel, with concomitant negative portrayal of Gentiles) and universalism (i.e., indications pointing to the inclusion of Gentiles and the Gentile mission, with concomitant negative portrayal of Israel and especially Israel's leaders).

Hagner avers that this tension must not be relieved by relegating either the particularism or the universalism to inconsequential status in determining the situation of Matthew's community. On the contrary, the very presence of this tension, and the specific ways Matthew has developed it, points to a Jewish-Christian author and readership, and to a community that

> partook of two worlds, the Jewish and the Christian. Although they saw their Christianity as the true fulfillment of Judaism, they also were very conscious that they had broken with their unbelieving brothers and sisters. They were struggling to define and defend a Jewish Christianity to the Jews on the one hand and to realize their unity with Gentile Christians on the other.

Hagner notes how this thesis is supported by, and in turn illumines, certain major themes in Matthew's Gospel: the law, the religious leaders, Israel, fulfillment, the kingdom of heaven, Christology, ecclesiology, eschatology, and salvation history.

Hagner concludes that this situation requires neither a post-Yavneh (i.e., post-85) date nor the determination of a specific geographical provenance: Matthew was probably written sometime after 70 CE, and although it originated in a particular historical

---

[11] *Matthew 1–13*. Word Biblical Commentary (Waco: Word, 1993). The second volume, comprising Matt 14–28, is scheduled to appear soon.

situation, that situation can no longer be identified. But, in the end, this lack of precise geographical identification is no problem, since "there is . . . a magisterial and universal character to Matthew that transcends every time and place."

In his essay, "The Temple Tax in Matthew 17:24–27 and the Principle of Not Causing Offense," David Garland pursues the background and meaning of that much debated pericope. As Garland points out, scholars have typically interpreted the passage according to their individual assumptions regarding the situation of Matthew's community. Thus, this passage can be made to fit into, and lend support for, a variety of reconstructions of Matthew's situation. All of these construals assume that the passage was intended to address a specific problem in Matthew's church.

But Garland argues that these various proposals do not enjoy the support of historical or redactional evidence. The passage reflects neither a debate within Jewish Christianity regarding its obligation to the temple, nor the requirement that Jews (including Jewish Christians and perhaps even Gentile Christians) pay the *Fiscus Iudaicus*, the Roman tax imposed upon Jews as reparation for the Jewish War of 68–70 CE, nor the controversy involving the appropriateness of paying civil taxes, nor the (putative) contributions urged by the Pharisees of Yavneh to support their religious and scribal activity. Rather, consideration of Matthean redaction, theology, and literary arrangement indicate that Matthew has adopted a story that came to him, probably representing an actual event in the ministry of the historical Jesus, in order to make a general theological (and pastoral) point: that Christians should surrender any claim to their own rights in order to live peaceably with others and not to harm others by causing unnecessary offense. In this way, Garland is able to show how his construal of the passage is confirmed by, and contributes to, broad Matthean emphases, such as Jesus' divine Sonship, the superior status of Christians over against Israel, the freedom Christians experience in relation to the Jewish cult, and the role of Peter as one who represents the church in its role as learners who are effectively instructed by Christ. Garland arrives at this conclusion by the kind of close attention to Matthean redaction and the history of the Matthean community he pursued in his influential study of Matthew 23,[12] and by careful

---

[12] *The Intention of Matthew 23*, NovTSup (Leiden: Brill, 1979).

analysis of the coherence of Matthew's narrative as reflected in his recent commentary on Matthew.[13]

One of the most vexing problems associated with Matthew's presentation of Jesus and Judaism surrounds the function of the law. As in the case of particularism and universalism, the issue of the law in Matthew is characterized by tension; indeed, this tension exists even within individual passages, such as 5:17–20. Matthew seems to put forward different, and even contradictory, views regarding the law. In his essay, "Matthew and the Law," Klyne Snodgrass charts a course through this maze of seeming contradictions with a view toward arriving at an understanding of Matthew's theology of the law that does justice to all the data within the Gospel. More than is the case with either Hagner or Garland, Snodgrass eschews appeal to Matthew's editorial alterations of received tradition in favor of a "vertical" reading of Matthew, which involves ascertaining the function of the various statements in the final form of the document, the composition that Matthew has created.

In a way reminiscent of his treatment of New Testament ethics in general (as represented in his book, *Between Two Truths: Living with Biblical Tensions*[14]), Snodgrass is able to demonstrate the deep, inner consistency of all the Matthean passages concerning the law by arguing that Matthew has placed the law within the larger framework of the whole of Old Testament revelation, with the result that Matthew has shifted the emphasis from the holiness code (which was the focus in Palestinian Judaism) with its stress on separation and exclusion, to love and mercy. Thus, the law continues in force, but all its commands are now understood as expressions of love toward God and neighbor.

Narration

In redaction criticism, Matthew's Gospel has been read variously as a catechism, a lectionary, an administrative manual, or an apologetic or polemical treatise, but not primarily as the one thing that it most obviously is: a story about Jesus. In recognition of this, many Matthean scholars have sought new paradigms that would take the narrative character of the book seriously. Several have turned to the eclectic

---

[13] *Reading Matthew: A Literary and Theological Commentary on the First Gospel* (New York: Crossroad, 1993).

[14] *Between Two Truths: Living with Biblical Tensions* (Grand Rapids: Zondervan, 1990).

literary-critical methodology called "narrative criticism," which in New Testament studies was first applied to the Gospel of Mark.[15] While not antithetical to historical criticism, narrative criticism does differ from traditional historical-critical approaches in significant ways:

> Narrative criticism views the text of Matthew's Gospel as a unified and coherent document, rather than as a compilation of loosely related pericopes. Narrative criticism focuses on the finished form of the Gospel, rather than on the compositional processes through which the text came into being. Narrative criticism deals with the "poetic function" of the text to create meaning and affect readers, rather than with its "referential function" to serve as a resource for historical reconstruction.[16]

Whereas redaction criticism tries to reconstruct what the evangelist who edited this Gospel intended to communicate to his original readers, narrative criticism tries to elucidate the communication event that transpires between the implied author of Matthew's Gospel and its implied readers. By "implied author," narrative critics mean the perspective from which the work appears to have been written, a perspective that must be reconstructed by readers on the basis of what they find in the narrative. As it now stands, the Gospel of Matthew probably contains ideas that originated from a variety of sources, including the historical Jesus, Mark, Q, and the evangelist himself. But rather than trying to separate these strands so as to interpret the various perspectives on their own terms, narrative critics seek to discern the overall perspective of the final composition. An analogy may be presented from the interpretation of modern films. By the time a motion picture is shown in theaters, it usually has undergone a process that allows for influence at many levels, and film critics do sometimes focus on the individual contributions of writers, editors, directors, actors, or producers. The bottom line, however, is usually an interest in describing the impact of *the film*, that is, the effect of the finished product when all levels of influence are considered together. Indeed, critics may speak of the film itself as espousing a particular viewpoint.[17] In the same way, narrative critics hold that the Gospel of

---

[15] On the development of narrative criticism, see Stephen D. Moore, *Literary Criticism and the Gospels: The Theoretical Challenge* (New Haven: Yale University Press, 1989) 1–68. For a description of narrative-critical method, see Mark Allan Powell, *What is Narrative Criticism?* (Philadelphia: Fortress, 1990).

[16] Mark Allan Powell, "Toward a Narrative-Critical Understanding of Matthew," *Int* 46 (1992) 341.

[17] Seymour Chatman observes that a narrative will have a single implied author

Matthew evinces a set of values, beliefs, and perceptions that, in spite of multiple sources, are now representative of a single (albeit complex) perspective, which they designate as the viewpoint of Matthew's "implied author."

Implied readers are imaginary persons who would actualize the potential for meaning in Matthew's text by responding to it in ways consistent with the expectations ascribed to its implied author. The concept of implied readers is a heuristic construct that allows narrative critics to limit the subjectivity of their analysis by distinguishing between actual responses to a narrative and those that the text appears to invite. People make such distinctions in daily life when, for example, they read a story and say, "It's supposed to be funny, but it isn't." In such instances, people are able to determine that they are expected to respond to a text differently than they actually do. In narrative-critical terms, they are able to identify how the implied reader would respond even though the actual responses of many real readers (including themselves) may be different. Such determinations are not usually made on the basis of an explicit statement of intent from the author, but on the basis of literary cues that indicate the effects the story is expected to have. Similarly, narrative critics believe that reading Matthew's Gospel in accord with certain widely-accepted canons of literary criticism allows them to discern the effects that this Gospel is expected to have on its implied readers.

Shifting the focus of exegesis to a concern for communication between the implied author and implied readers rather than that between the evangelist and the original readers has significant hermeneutical implications. The connection between meaning and historical context is weakened, for narrative critics seek to define not the message conveyed to a particular community at a particular place and time but the message conveyed to anyone who reads the text in the way that it is expected to be read. The expected manner of reading includes matters that are historically determined,[18] but in general the goal of narrative criticism is to determine the meaning of the text in a

---

even though it "may have been composed by a committee (Hollywood films) or by a disparate group of people over a long period of time (many folk ballads)." See *Story and Discourse: Narrative Structure in Fiction and Film* (Ithaca, NY: Cornell University Press, 1978) 140.

[18] Implied readers are expected, for instance, to know and to believe certain things appropriate for the historical context in which the narrative was written. See Mark Allan Powell, "Expected and Unexpected Readings of Matthew: What the Reader Knows," *ATJ* 48/2 (1993) 31–52.

more timeless sense than that attempted by redaction critics. If redaction critics seek to uncover what Matthew (the evangelist) meant, narrative critics seek to discover what Matthew (the narrative) means.

Significant contributions to narrative criticism of Matthew have been made by many scholars in the past decade, including Janice Capel Anderson,[19] Warren Carter,[20] John Paul Heil,[21] David B. Howell,[22] Frank J. Matera,[23] and Augustine Stock.[24] The most prominent figure, however, has certainly been Jack Dean Kingsbury, whose book *Matthew as Story*[25] and numerous journal articles[26] have set the standard for the field. Kingsbury comes to narrative criticism as one whose work as a redaction critic had already emphasized the importance of composition analysis.[27] The move is logical in that the latter approach also seeks to understand the Gospel in light of its literary structure and overarching themes rather than simply in terms of emendation of sources. Still, composition criticism calls for readers to identify themselves with first-century Christians whose lives were

---

[19] See especially Janice Capel Anderson, *Matthew's Narrative Web: Over, and Over, and Over Again*, JSNTSS 91 (Sheffield: JSOT, 1994), a revision of her 1985 dissertation.

[20] See especially Warren Carter, "Kernels and Narrative Blocks: The Structure of Matthew's Gospel," *CBQ* 54 (1992) 463–81; idem, "The Crowds in Matthew's Gospel," *CBQ* 55 (1993) 54–67; idem, *Households and Discipleship: A Study of Matthew 19–20*, JSNTSS 103 (Sheffield: JSOT, 1994; idem, "Challenging by Confirming, Renewing by Repeating: The Parables of 'The Reign of the Heavens' in Matthew 13 as Embedded Narratives," in *Society of Biblical Literature 1995 Seminar Papers*, forthcoming.

[21] See especially John Paul Heil, *The Death and Resurrection of Jesus: A Narrative-Critical Reading of Matthew 26–28* (Minneapolis: Fortress, 1991).

[22] See David B. Howell, *Matthew's Inclusive Story: A Study in the Narrative Rhetoric of the First Gospel*, JSNTSS 42 (Sheffield: JSOT, 1990).

[23] See Frank J. Matera, "The Plot of Matthew's Gospel," *CBQ* 49 (1987) 233–53.

[24] See especially Augustine Stock, *The Method and Message of Matthew* (Collegeville, MN: Liturgical, 1994).

[25] Jack Dean Kingsbury, *Matthew as Story*, 2nd ed. (Philadelphia: Fortress, 1988).

[26] See especially "The Figure of Jesus in Matthew's Story: A Literary-Critical Probe," *JSNT* 21 (1984) 3–36; "The Developing Conflict Between Jesus and the Jewish Leaders in Matthew's Gospel: A Literary-Critical Study," *CBQ* 49 (1987) 57–73; "Reflections on 'the Reader' of Matthew's Gospel," *NTS* 34 (1988) 442–60; "The Plot of Matthew's Story," *Int* 46 (1992) 347–56; "The Rhetoric of Composition in the Gospel of Matthew," *NTS* 41 (1995) forthcoming. These and others will soon be published in a single volume, *The Art of Matthew* (Minneapolis: Fortress, forthcoming).

[27] Cf. *Matthew: Structure, Christology, Kingdom*. On composition criticism, see the discussion above.

affected by the social, political and religious circumstances that
prevailed at the time when Matthew wrote. Narrative criticism seeks to
interpret the text from the perspective of a person who visits the
autonomous world created by Matthew's narrative and, by so doing,
gains a new perspective on the real world in which he or she actually
lives. Thus, these methods are distinct but compatible.[28] Narrative
criticism also employs categories of analysis not found in composition
criticism, including characterization, plot, and point of view.

The type of narrative criticism set forth by Kingsbury also finds
expression in the work of his many students, three of whom have
offered the selections that make up the entire second portion of this
volume.[29] In his monograph *The Structure of Matthew's Gospel*,[30] David
Bauer developed a system for analyzing compositional relationships
that help to define literary structure and then determined how these
function in the Gospel of Matthew. These concerns continue in this
volume in his article, "The Literary and Theological Function of the
Genealogy in Matthew's Gospel." In his analysis of Matthew 1:1–17,
Bauer emphasizes the significance of rhetorical movements such as
chiasm, climax, particularization, and substantiation. These lead him
to decisions concerning the literary structure of the passage, which
have implications for its theological interpretation. The claim that
Matthew presents Jesus as the one who is the Son of David and the Son
of Abraham by virtue of the fact that he is the Son of God is supported
by at least two observations: 1) Matthew 1:1 serves not only as the
introduction to the genealogy proper (1:1–17) but also to the first
major block of Matthew's narrative (1:1–4:16) in which Jesus is
presented pre-eminently as Son of God; and, 2) the climactic character
of 1:16, which through a divine passive presents Jesus as one whose
origin is in God, introduces a dialectic with the preceding chiastic
identification of Jesus as "Christ," "Son of David," and "Son of
Abraham" in a way that presents Jesus as one who fulfills but also

---

[28] Jack Dean Kingsbury, *Matthew*, 2nd ed., Proclamation Commentaries (Philadelphia: Fortress, 1986), 16–18.

[29] Other significant narrative-critical studies of Matthew by students of Jack
Kingsbury include Keith Howard Reeves, *The Resurrection Narrative in Matthew: A
Literary-Critical Examination* (Lewiston, NY: Mellen, 1993); Ronald D. Witherup,
"The Cross of Jesus: A Literary-Critical Study of Matthew 27" (diss., Union Theolo-
gical Seminary in Virginia, 1985).

[30] David R. Bauer, *The Structure of Matthew's Gospel: A Study in Literary Design*,
JSNTSS 31 (Sheffield: Almond, 1988).

transcends identifications associated with the history of Israel. A similar point is made with regard to Mary, whose mention in 1:16 has a separate purpose that underscores but also surpasses the point of mentioning four other women in 1:3, 5, 6.

As such, Bauer's arguments may seem to be in line with traditional concerns. But if, as he notes, most studies of the Matthean genealogy have employed historical methods to achieve historical goals, Bauer does not wish simply to develop new literary methods to achieve those same goals. Herein lies an essential difference between redaction criticism and narrative criticism. The former would employ some of Bauer's techniques in order to gain insight into the concerns of the evangelist's community. Bauer's purpose, ultimately, is to discern the *literary* function of the genealogy and to use this literary function as an index to the theology of the text. The genealogy introduces Matthew's implied readers to the narrative by establishing the implied author's point of view concerning Jesus in a way that provides a basis for testing the reliability of viewpoints concerning Jesus expressed by characters in the ensuing drama. The theme of Davidic sonship, for instance, is picked up in the account of the Magi, as is that of Abrahamic sonship in the story of John the Baptist. In addition, the genealogy facilitates the implied readers' entry into the narrative world of Matthew's Gospel by providing the temporal setting according to which the story of Jesus is to be understood.

Mark Allan Powell, the author of *What Is Narrative Criticism?*, investigates "Characterization on the Phraseological Plane in the Gospel of Matthew" in his article. The general topic is "Characters," one of the major components of most literary constructs of plot; more precisely, the topic is "characterization," or the process through which the implied author reveals characters to the implied readers; more precisely still, the topic is characterization through speech (the phraseological plane). Powell thus investigates the extent to which the implied author of Matthew's Gospel uses the speech of characters to reveal those characters to the implied readers.

Powell finds that the speech of Jesus typically serves to correlate and confirm what has been said of him by others. The speech of the disciples usually serves to reveal their failings, whereas Jesus' speech concerning the disciples is more likely to highlight their potential. And, in what is probably the article's most significant insight, Powell discovers that the speech of the religious leaders reveals their true character only when it is "indirect." That is, the religious leaders in

Matthew's Gospel only say what they really think of others when they are talking about them "behind their backs." The latter observation has exegetical implications for interpretation of such passages as 12:33–37 and 23:2–3. Beyond these details, however, one of the most interesting aspects of Powell's research is the simple recognition that he can find such a high degree of consistency in the role speech plays for characterization. This would never have been suspected before the advent of narrative-critical study, for the passages examined derive from diverse sources (Mark, Q, M) and establishing consistency of speech patterns has never been attributed to this evangelist's redactional agenda. Powell's observations argue that the Gospel is intentionally organized to work *as a story* and that this organization has theological—indeed pastoral—significance. As Powell notes, Matthew might have simply told us outright that religious leaders are often duplicitous and that their true character is more likely to be revealed by what they say *about* people than by what they say *to* people. But, by presenting this point through story rather than explicit commentary, Matthew offers his readers practice at learning to detect such duplicity on their own.

Dorothy Jean Weaver also chooses a topical approach to one facet of Matthew's rhetoric of characterization in her essay, "Power and Powerlessness: Matthew's Use of Irony in the Portrayal of Political Leaders." She demonstrates that with regard to the three major political figures in Matthew's narrative—Herod the king, Herod the tetrarch, and Pontius Pilate—the implied readers are presented with two conflicting portraits. On the one hand, all three of these characters are portrayed as persons with enormous power, notably power over life and death. On the other hand, all three are portrayed as persons whose apparent power proves to be illusory, especially with regard to power of life and death. Thus, Herod the king is able to slaughter infants, but in the final analysis his signal aim to destroy Jesus is foiled and he himself lies dead (2:15, 19, 20). Or again, Herod the tetrarch appears to have power of life and death over John the Baptist, but this power is mitigated by his own fears (14:5) and, ultimately, he is left to fear the one he regards as "John the Baptist raised from the dead" (14:2). Pontius Pilate, finally, accorded all the trappings of power in Matthew's story, is able to order the execution of Jesus, but he is unable to make the crowds accede to his wishes much less to prevent the resurrection to ensure that Jesus stays dead. All these characters are presented in contrast to Jesus and to John the

Baptist who, in these portions of the narrative, generally remain passive and silent, completely vulnerable to the initiatives of those about them. When it becomes apparent that they, not the political rulers, are bearers of genuine potency, Matthew's implied readers are expected to realize that kingship and power are realities that become manifest in unlikely forms and places.

Two observations concerning Weaver's essay are pertinent for understanding the hermeneutics of narrative criticism. First, her approach assumes a unified rhetoric for the narrative even with regard to passages that appear contradictory. Rather than explaining the discrepant portraits of Pilate and the Herods as the products of divergent source traditions that Matthew has failed to reconcile, she assumes that the story can be meaningful with the discrepancies intact. Indeed, by describing the portrait of power as a level of apparent reality that is subverted for the reader by the portrait of powerlessness on the level of true reality, she discovers that discrepancy is essential to meaning. In this regard, Weaver's essay here recalls her helpful monograph, *Matthew's Missionary Discourse*,[31] in which she tackled a text that appears to be a mess of patchwork editing and showed that it could be read as a coherent communication between Matthew's implied author and implied readers. Second, by drawing upon irony as the conceptual principle through which the implied readers are to make sense of the discrepant portraits of political rulers, Weaver inevitably moves narrative criticism into a consideration of reception. By definition, irony is a rhetorical device that tends toward subtlety and that derives its power from the recognition that it will not always be grasped.[32] Because irony is often missed, recognition of ironic meaning offers readers a shared experience and bonds them to the implied author through persuasion that "rests on implicit flattery."[33]

Reception

Concern for reception often begins with the question of polyvalence. Competent readers can and do decide that texts mean different things. Who is to adjudicate which reading is correct?

---

[31] Dorothy Jean Weaver, *Matthew's Missionary Discourse: A Literary-Critical Analysis*, JSNTSS 38 (Sheffield: JSOT, 1990).

[32] Wayne C. Booth, *The Rhetoric of Fiction*, 2nd ed. (Chicago: University of Chicago Press, 1983) 3–4.

[33] Chatman, *Story and Discourse*, 229.

Redaction critics seek to describe meaning from the perspective of original readers and narrative critics seek to describe meaning from the perspective of implied readers, but in either case, the meaning so-described is not universal. Redaction critics readily acknowledge a hermeneutical differentiation between "the meaning then" and "the meaning now."[34] Narrative critics recognize that the interpretations they attribute to a text's implied readers are dependent upon a particular reading strategy and will seldom correspond exactly to interpretations arrived at by real readers.[35] Or, as Powell has said, narrative criticism attempts to bridge the chasm between "then" and "now" but in so doing opens "a gulf between the story world of the narrative and the real world of the reader."[36] Since, ultimately, all critics must concern themselves with interpretation now, in the real world, attention to reception is inevitable.[37]

The first article representing reception theory is by Russell Pregeant, "The Wisdom Passages in Matthew's Story." Pregeant's interest in Matthean Christology dates at least to 1978, when he published an innovative monograph that addressed the topic through a new methodological approach called "process hermeneutic."[38] The

---

[34] Krister Stendahl, "Biblical Theology, Contemporary," *IDB* 1.418–31.

[35] A common misunderstanding of narrative criticism holds that the discipline somehow privileges the perspective of the implied reader such that, once defined, this interpretation can be used to evaluate the legitimacy of other views. The assignment of authoritative status to the implied readers' hermeneutical viewpoint would be a confessional issue that transcends methodology. While it is possible that individual narrative critics might make such a move, it is by no means intrinsic to the discipline that they do so. In practice, most narrative critics seem to regard the implied readers' understanding of the text in a sense analogous to a control group in a scientific experiment. The implied readers' understanding is not definitive of how a text should be read, but it is instructive as a basis for comparison with ways in which the text actually is read. Real readers may contrast their own responses to the text with those that seem to be expected of the implied readers and then seek to explain the divergences.

[36] Powell, *Narrative Criticism*, 100.

[37] Aside from those who have essays in this volume, scholars who have taken a reception-oriented approach to Matthew include Fred W. Burnett, Richard A. Edwards, and Robert M. Fowler. For a sampling, see Burnett, "The Undecideability of the Proper Name 'Jesus' in Matthew," *Semeia* 54: 123–44; idem., 'Prolegomenon to Reading Matthew's Eschatological Discourse," *Semeia* 31: 91–109; Edwards, *Matthew's Story of Jesus* (Philadelphia: Fortress, 1985); Fowler, "Reading Matthew Reading Mark: Observing the First Steps Toward Meaning-as-Reference in the Synoptic Gospels," in *Society of Biblical Literature 1986 Seminar Papers*, ed. Kent Harold Richards (Atlanta: Scholars Press, 1986) 1–16.

[38] Russell Pregeant, *Christology Beyond Dogma: Matthew's Christ in Process*

essay that appears in this volume provides a sample of the sort of work Pregeant encourages in his textbook, *Engaging the New Testament*,[39] for it provides a reader-oriented interdisciplinary study of Matthew's Christology. To be precise, Pregeant addresses the issue of a Wisdom Christology in the Gospel that was first propounded by M. Jack Suggs in 1970,[40] and subsequently adopted by many scholars. The work of Suggs represented a thoroughgoing redaction criticism; he argued that Matthew consistently modified the Q passages at 11:19, 25–27, and 23:34–38 in such a way as to point to Jesus as Wisdom incarnate. Other scholars, such as R. G. Hammerton-Kelly,[41] took this thesis further, claiming that Matthew presents a developed notion of pre-existence.

Pregeant notes that even redaction critics have raised questions regarding such a Wisdom Christology, and posits that the issue turns on what the "implied reader," i.e., the ideal reader guided by the prompting of the text itself, knows. To this end, Pregeant employs a type of "reader-response criticism" normally associated with the work of Wolfgang Iser.[42] He moves in a painstaking fashion through the text of the Gospel in order to discern how the reader comes to think of Jesus, and concomitantly, how the flow of the narrative prompts the reader to construe the meaning of those passages that Suggs identified as pointing to a Wisdom Christology.

Pregeant concludes that although such a process allows for a reading according to which Jesus is understood to be Wisdom incarnate, it does not necessarily lead to such a reading; and, indeed, it actually points to a "preferred reading" in which Jesus is understood to be not Wisdom incarnate, but rather the Messiah/Son of God, whose origin is the virgin conception, whose divine Sonship is contingent upon his constant obedience to the will of his Father, and who manifests his divine Sonship ultimately through suffering and death. According to Pregeant, when interpreted from the perspective of

---

Hermeneutic. Semeia Supplements 7 (Philadelphia: Fortress, 1978).

[39] Russell Pregeant, *Engaging the New Testament: An Interdisciplinary Introduction.* (Minneapolis: Fortress, 1995).

[40] *Wisdom, Christology, and Law in Matthew's Gospel* (Cambridge, MA: Harvard University Press, 1970).

[41] *Pre-Existence, Wisdom, and the Son of Man: A Study of the Idea of Pre-Existence in the New Testament* (Cambridge: Cambridge University Press, 1973).

[42] See, e.g., *The Act of Reading: A Theory of Aesthetic Response* (Baltimore: Johns Hopkins University, 1978); and *The Implied Reader: Patterns of Communication in Prose Fiction from Bunyan to Beckett* (Baltimore: Johns Hopkins University, 1974).

literary clues intended to guide the reader, the passages Suggs cites as support for a Wisdom Christology actually underscore the plot of Matthew's story of Jesus the Son of God, who is rejected by Israel and in turn withdraws from Israel, but who will exercise his rule in the post-Easter age of the church as transcendent, exalted Lord.

The value of Pregeant's study is not only his discussion of Wisdom in Matthew's Christology, but also his presentation of a hermeneutical model according to which reader-response criticism can engage and test conclusions from redaction-critical study. The term "engage" is significant, for Pregeant is concerned to do more than indicate how a reader-response approach can correct certain conclusions from redaction criticism; he also points to ways in which reader-response criticism can illumine issues of redaction and contribute to the redaction-critical enterprise.

In her monograph, *Narrative Web,* Janice Capel Anderson emphasizes that "the 'implied reader', pretending to be a neutral concept, masks a real reader: the Gospel critic herself (or more often himself) with a very particular social location."[43] Thus, Anderson presents her work with the belief that "narrative and reader-response criticisms provide a set of reading conventions that continue to reveal/create new and exciting interpretations" while at the same time qualifying it with the admission that "narrative/reader criticism constitutes one code through which the Gospels can be read along with historical, social-scientific, theological, and gender codes."[44]

A similar perspective informs Anderson's essay in this volume, "Matthew: Sermon and Story." On one level, the paper examines connections between the Sermon on the Mount and the overall narrative of Matthew's Gospel. This analysis goes beyond traditional observations regarding key words and themes to focus on how passages within the sermon contribute to the development of character and plot in the ensuing narrative. At another level, however, Anderson asks that her own reading of the Gospel be compared and contrasted with other interpretations as a test case for reflection on the reading process. In doing so, she appeals to Iser's concept of implied readers as one that preserves the tension between the role the text plays and

---

[43] Anderson, *Narrative Web,* 7.

[44] Anderson, *Narrative Web,* 8–9. On the concept of multiple disciplinary codes, see Mieke Bal, *Murder and Difference: Gender, Genre, and Scholarship on Sisera's Death* (Bloomington: Indiana University Press, 1988).

the role that real readers play in creating meaning as individuals.[45] She raises questions about how biblical scholars can allow for multiple readings in a way that avoids naive relativism and about what the criteria should be for determining which readings are better than others. Anderson insists that biblical scholars engage such issues intentionally and that they at least acknowledge that "each approach follows conventions," that is, commitments related to gender, culture, theology, and ideology that may pre-determine the outcome.

The essays by Rudolf Schnackenburg ("Matthew's Gospel as a Test Case for Hermeneutical Reflections") and Ulrich Luz ("The Final Judgment [Matt 25:31–46]: An Exercise in 'History of Influence' Exegesis") appear here for the first time in English translation. They belong together, in that they both deal with the reception theory known as "Wirkungsgeschichte," "the history of influence." This approach derives from the hermeneutical reflections of Hans-Georg Gadamer,[46] and in biblical studies emerged in Europe and finds expression especially in the major commentary series "Evangelisch-Katholischer Kommentar zum Neuen Testament." But no one has done more to advance this approach than Ulrich Luz, both in his commentary on Matthew,[47] as well as his monograph, *Matthew in History*.[48] Luz himself describes this method in the following way:

> The history of influence of biblical texts is much more than the history of interpretation. The history of influence includes not only the study of written commentaries on the biblical texts but also study of the influences of these texts on piety, prayer and songs, dogma, Christian action and politics, literature and art, not only within Christian churches but beyond them as well.

The history of influence approach serves a heuristic function; it allows the various ways in which a biblical passage has been appropriated to

---

[45] Whereas Chatman explicates the implied reader as a construct of the implied author that lies within the text itself (*Story and Discourse*, 149–50), Iser defines the implied reader as a construct of the real reader's interaction with the text (*Implied Reader*, xii). Thus, for Iser, individual readers may construct different implied readers against which they measure their personal responses. Booth now speaks of the implied reader in both senses (*Rhetoric of Fiction*, 421–31; "Interview with Wolfgang Iser," *Diacritics* 10 [1980] 57–74).

[46] *Truth and Method* (New York: Seabury, 1975).

[47] *Matthew 1–7: A Commentary* (Minneapolis: Augsburg, 1989). Prof. Luz is just now completing the German edition of his commentary, and the English translation is awaited.

[48] *Matthew in History* (Minneapolis: Fortress, 1994).

point to dimensions of meaning and significance of the text that otherwise would remain outside the consideration of the interpreter. As such, it does not replace traditional exegesis that has as its goal the capturing of the "original meaning," but dialogues with traditional exegesis in such a way as to clarify and expand the meaning of the text and its significance for present-day readers. The history-of-influence approach relates also to reader-response criticism by providing a historical review of the ways in which readers have construed the meaning of texts, thereby complementing and clarifying the work of reader-response critics, who are concerned with how the literary clues in the text guide "ideal readers" toward meaning.

Rudolf Schnackenburg, a New Testament scholar known especially for his magisterial commentaries on the Gospel of John[49] and the Epistles of John,[50] but also for his commentary on Matthew,[51] presents here a brief, yet provocative, theoretical introduction to the history-of-influence approach, using Matthew's Gospel as a testing-grounds.

Schnackenburg notes that the process of actualizing, adapting, and re-interpreting the words and acts of Jesus began already in the formation of the gospel tradition; indeed, the Gospel of Matthew itself participated in this process, in that Matthew so construed and presented the Jesus tradition that came to him as to make it relevant for his community. At some points Matthew's treatment of the Jesus tradition stood in continuity with the original meaning of Jesus' words and actions, at other points it contradicted the original meaning, and at still other points it expanded upon a dimension of the original significance. In this way, Matthew's own activity encourages us to enlarge the notion of hermeneutics to include the "present horizon," i.e., to explore the process of actualization of the tradition that began with Matthew's redactional activity and continues on throughout the history of influence, even into our own time, the contemporary or present horizon.

Schnackenburg examines the history of influence of three Matthean passages in order to identify some of the challenges involved in this approach. His examination of the Sermon on the Mount indicates that at points our present horizon, influenced as it is by issues that may have been quite foreign to the evangelist, can blur

---

[49] *The Gospel according to St. John*, 3 vols. (New York: Crossroad, 1987).

[50] *The Johannine Epistles: A Commentary* (New York: Crossroad, 1992).

[51] *Matthäusevangelium*, 2 vols. (Wurzberg: Echter, 1985–87).

rather than clarify the original meaning of a text; the "primacy word" to Peter in 16:18 indicates how the history of influence can present a wide diversity of construals; and Matthew's presentation of Jesus' attitude toward the Jews points to ways in which the history of influence can illumine unfortunate and dangerous interpretations that must now be countered by a serious re-examination of the text.

Whereas the essay by Schnackenburg deals with some of the hermeneutical issues involved in the history-of-influence approach, the article by Luz applies the approach to a specific passage: Matt 25:31–46. Luz begins by identifying the three primary ways readers have understood this passage, examining not only commentaries and scholarly discussions, but also art, literature, legends, and appropriation of the imagery of the passage by various leaders and movements. He discusses (1) the "universal interpretive model," according to which the passage points to Christ's participation in the suffering of all persons, not simply Christians; (2) the "classical interpretive model," according to which this passage refers to the judgment of persons within the church; and (3) the "exclusive interpretive model," according to which the passage describes not the judgment of the church, but of pagans, on the basis of how they have responded to Christians or to Christian missionaries. Luz then moves to a process of traditional exegesis of the passage, concluding that exegetical considerations argue that the "classical interpretive model" is closest to Matthew's intention. Luz finally pursues the ultimate question: Is it possible to make use of interpretations represented in the history of influence that stand in tension with the original, intended meaning of the passage? To this question, at least as it pertains to this particular passage, Luz gives a qualified "yes." He notes that the interpretation provided by the universal interpretive model stands in continuity with the history of Jesus we know otherwise, including the history of Jesus presented elsewhere in Matthew's Gospel, and that this interpretation also stands in continuity with certain dimensions of the original meaning of this very passage. He argues also from a pragmatic basis, insisting that any new interpretation must produce love; and he finds that the universal interpretive model does, in fact, prompt love. In the end, the ultimate concern is to allow Christ, who stands behind and speaks through all Scripture, to encounter us in and transform us by the biblical text.

Bernard Brandon Scott and Margaret E. Dean address the subject of reception from a completely different angle in their essay, "A Sound

Map of the Sermon on the Mount." For some time now, Gospel scholars such as Werner Kelber[52] and Thomas Boomershine[53] have been calling attention to the importance of orality for biblical exegesis. Simply put, the problem is that all discussions of "original readers," "implied readers," and the like overlook the fact that the Gospel narratives were almost certainly intended to be received aurally rather than visually. Should we not speak of *hearers* rather than *readers?* While most members of the guild have offered tacit acknowledgment that this seems right, few have known what to do about it. The general mood seems to have been puzzlement as to the possibility and necessity of developing an oral hermeneutic for exegesis. Typical questions include 1) How can we consider the oral reception of the Gospels with any integrity when all we have are written documents? and, 2) What practical differences for interpretation does the mode of presumed reception make? The "Sound Map" offered by Scott and Dean provides a partial answer to both of these questions. Granted the inherent contradiction of providing a *graphic* diagram of what is intended to be *heard*, their map nevertheless shows how combinations of phonetic, syntactical, and semantic devices present in the written text offer clues to the aural rhythm of the intended recitation. When this rhythm is accepted as providing the primary receptive clue to the text's organization, aspects of the text are highlighted that may be overlooked when organization is understood in terms of rhetorical, literary, or ideological analysis alone.

In at least one respect, the paper moves in a direction counter to the general tendency of recent scholarship. Concern for reception has usually led scholars to be more open to multiple interpretations and to acknowledge (if not celebrate) the degree of subjectivity with which readers derive meaning from texts. Scott and Dean seek to demonstrate the possibility of a more empirical approach. In fact, by attempting to define how the text was originally meant to be understood, they are in some sense revisiting the hermeneutical domain of redaction criticism. Still, of all the papers in this volume, theirs is the most adventuresome, offering what they call "a first step." It is a

---

[52] See especially Werner H. Kelber, *The Oral and the Written Gospel: The Hermeneutics of Speaking and Writing in the Synoptic Tradition, Mark, Paul, and Q* (Philadelphia: Fortress, 1983).

[53] See, for example, Thomas E. Boomershine, "Mark 16:8 and the Apostolic Commission," *JBL* 100 (1981) 225–39.

promising experiment with a new approach that appears to have enormous potential for future study.

In the final essay of this volume, "Discharging Responsibility: Matthean Jesus, Biblical Law, and Hemorrhaging Woman," Amy-Jill Levine offers a provocative discussion of Matthew 9:18–26 and of the treatment this text has received in traditional exegesis. This article exemplifies the significance of social location for reception of texts. Attention to the social location of both Matthew's original readers and contemporary readers has been a distinguishing mark of Levine's work on the Gospel. The former is apparent in her published dissertation, *The Social and Ethnic Dimensions of Matthean Salvation History,* in which she argues that the distinction between Jew and Gentile has been transcended in Matthew's community by a more fundamental and enduring distinction between privileged and marginalized.[54] The latter comes to the fore in her article on Matthew in *The Women's Bible Commentary,* where she discusses several passages in which women may find their contributions recognized.[55]

Both concerns are evident here in the study of Matthew 9:18–26. Levine challenges construals of Matthean context that suppose purity laws were viewed as a source of ostracism in general or as a basis for marginalization of women in particular. Furthermore, she connects these construals of the social context for Matthew's original readers to those of modern interpreters, suggesting that the modern Christian critic worries much more about Levitical purity legislation than did any Jewish woman in the first century. Such construals, she suggests, are not only wrong, but dangerously so, for they lead to the "potentially anti-Jewish supposition" that Jesus must abrogate the Levitical Law and overcome the barriers that it inevitably creates in order to establish a truly egalitarian community.

Levine's approach is shaped by her own identity as a Jewish woman interpreter. As she notes, the traditional (i.e., Christian) understanding of this passage builds upon numerous assumptions regarding Jewish context that have no direct support within the text—purity laws are not even mentioned in this passage! Levine's own understanding

---

[54] Amy-Jill Levine, *The Social and Ethnic Dimensions of Matthean Salvation History: "Go Nowhere Among the Gentiles . . . "(Matt. 10:5b),* Studies in the Bible and Early Christianity 14 (Lewiston: Mellen, 1988).

[55] Amy-Jill Levine, "Matthew," in *The Women's Bible Commentary,* ed. Carol A. Newsom and Sharon H. Ringe (Louisville: Westminster/John Knox, 1992) 252–62. See also her article "Ruth" in the same volume, pp. 78–84.

of Matthew 9:18–26 focuses on what is explicit, the presentation of Jesus as one who overcomes not purity laws but disease and death. In addition, she sees in this story of bleeding, death, and resurrection a number of factors that anticipate the passion.

Conclusion

In a survey of Matthean scholarship from 1983–1993, Janice Capel Anderson notes that this decade was marked by at least three new major currents: literary critical, social scientific, and feminist.[56] If this is so, then the present volume of essays may be viewed as primarily representative of the first of these streams.[57] Developments in the field of modern literary criticism have clearly influenced the approaches to Matthew evident here. The very organization of this volume exemplifies this, in that the categories Composition, Narration, and Reception parallel the orientations expressed in the classic literary-critical paradigm, "Author-Text-Reader." This paradigm, which derives from Roman Jakobsen's model for communication theory,[58] is often cited by literary theorists as providing convenient categories for describing

---

[56] Anderson, "Life on the Mississippi: New Currents in Matthean Scholarship, 1983–1993," in *Currents in Research: Biblical Studies* 3 (1995) forthcoming. For reviews of Matthean scholarship that deal (mostly) with literature before this time, see David R. Bauer, "The Interpretation of Matthew's Gospel in the Twentieth Century," *American Theological Libraries Association Proceedings* 42 (1988) 119–45; Graham N. Stanton, "The Origin and Purpose of Matthew's Gospel: Matthean Scholarship from 1945–1980," in *Aufstieg und Niedergang der Römischen Welt*, ed. H. Temporini and W. Haase (Berlin: Walter de Gruyter, 1889–1951), II. 25. 3.

[57] The article by Levine in our final chapter may represent a confluence of all three. Anderson ("Life on the Mississippi") offers a fine bibliography for those who wish to follow either of the other two streams. In particular, for social-scientific approaches, see David L. Balch, ed., *Social History of the Matthean Community* (Minneapolis: Fortress, 1991); Bruce J. Malina and Jerome H. Neyrey, *Calling Jesus Names: The Social Value of Labels in Matthew* (Sonoma, CA: Polebridge, 1988); J. Andrew Overman, *Matthew's Gospel and Formative Judaism: The Social World of the Matthean Community* (Minneapolis: Fortress, 1990). For a feminist approach, see Elaine M. Wainwright, *Towards a Feminist Critical Reading of the Gospel according to Matthew* (New York: Walter de Gruyter, 1991).

[58] See, for example, Roman Jakobsen, "Closing Statement: Linguistics and Poetics," in *Style in Language*, ed. Thomas Sebeok (Cambridge: Technology Press, 1960), 350–77. In its full form, the model has six components: addresser, message, addressee, context, contact, code. For discussions of how this model may be applied to biblical studies, see Robert M. Fowler, *Let the Reader Understand: Reader-Response Criticism and the Gospel of Mark* (Minneapolis: Fortress, 1991) 52–58; Norman Petersen, *Literary Criticism for New Testament Critics*, GBS (Philadelphia: Fortress, 1978), 23–48.

critical methods as "author-oriented," "text-oriented," or "reader/ audience-oriented."[59] In similar fashion, the authors of the essays in this volume pursue exegetical strategies that reveal primary hermeneutical interest in authorial intention, textual dynamics, or interpretative consequences.[60]

Author-oriented modes of inquiry have fallen out of favor in secular literary studies, but continue to be very influential in Gospel research. On the one hand, the fact that only three of the essays in this volume make thoroughgoing use of redaction criticism may provide evidence that Stanton's concern for redaction criticism to be "complemented by a variety of other approaches"[61] has been met. On the other hand, those three essays are themselves evidence that redaction critics are still contributing significantly to the field of Matthean studies. Stanton's 1983 collection of essays was dominated by redaction-critical studies, even though the editor viewed that method as limited. In the current 1995 collection of essays, the number of redaction-critical studies is limited, but these are presented without apology. Thus, the use of redaction criticism in Matthean studies seems to have moved quite rapidly through three phases: prior to 1980, redaction criticism enjoyed a commanding position among the biblical sciences; during the 80s, redaction criticism seemed more often than not to occupy a defensive posture; and, now, in the 90s, redaction criticism appears to be viewed with almost unqualified acceptance as one of the variety of methods through which the Gospels ought to be studied.[62]

---

[59] This is the system followed in Mark Allan Powell, with the assistance of Cecile G. Gray and Melissa C. Curtis, *The Bible and Modern Literary Criticism: A Critical Assessment and Annotated Bibliography* (Westport, Conn.: Greenwood, 1992).

[60] For an attempt to relate all six components of Jakobsen's model to exegetical method in biblical studies, see Mark Allan Powell, "What is 'Literary' About Literary Aspects?," in *Society of Biblical Literature 1992 Seminar Papers*, ed. Eugene H. Lovering, Jr. (Atlanta: Scholars Press, 1992), 40–48. Powell proposes the following relationships: Addresser—redaction criticism; Message—narrative criticism; Addressee—reader-response criticism; Context—historical and social-historical criticism; Contact—text-criticism; Code—structuralism. In this article, Powell also argues that deconstruction should not be considered just one more approach to be added to the scheme; instead he seeks to preserve its (admittedly uncomfortable) status as a movement that critiques all methods.

[61] Stanton, "Introduction," 17.

[62] The influence of these phases can be seen in Stanton's own work, for in his most recent book he uses redaction criticism and defends its legitimacy, while also drawing upon social scientific method and literary theory. See *A Gospel for a New*

In literary criticism as it is practiced apart from the field of biblical studies, text-oriented approaches now occupy a position similar to that ascribed above to redaction criticism during the 1980s. Having once been dominant, so-called "formalist methods" (including structuralism, New Criticism, and narratology) are often viewed as reactionary or irrelevant by theorists, although they still form the basis for much of what is actually practiced and taught in the field (for example, in undergraduate college literature courses). In addition, some prominent theorists, including Wayne Booth,[63] Seymour Chatman,[64] Wolfgang Iser,[65] and Peter Rabinowitz[66] represent a sort of neo-Formalism that grants a considerable (if limited) role to textual dynamics in the determination of meaning. The latter have had significant influence on contemporary Gospel studies, as is witnessed by the essays in the second part of this volume.

Concern for reception remains dominant in modern literary theory, but this interest is manifest in a plethora of pursuits incorporating interests in such diverse matters as deconstruction, new historicism, psychoanalytical analysis, interpretive communities, ideological criticism, and resistant reading. Reader-response criticism is no longer viewed as a method or even as an approach, but as a general orientation. As we have indicated, this multiplicity of strategies is mirrored by Gospel scholars interested in reception as well. The approaches evident in the third part of this volume, however, do not correspond exactly to ones followed in the secular field. This may be due in part to genre differences between the Gospels and the literary works that occupy critics of, say, modern fiction. It is also no doubt due to the different hermeneutical concerns that come into play when studying literature that is regarded as scripture. The confessional issues and respect for tradition that are discussed explicitly in the papers by Luz and Schnackenburg are exemplary of wide-ranging concerns that may affect Gospel interpretation. Of course, some would claim that such concerns affect all varieties of Gospel criticism, in ways that are often not acknowledged, but the significance of the readers'

People: Studies in Matthew (Edinburgh: T. & T. Clark, 1992).

[63] See especially Booth, *Rhetoric of Fiction*.

[64] See especially Chatma n, *Story and Discourse*.

[65] See especially *Act of Reading* and *Implied Reader*.

[66] See especially Peter J. Rabinowitz, *Before Reading: Narrative Conventions and the Politics of Interpretation* (Ithaca, NY: Cornell University Press, 1987).

(and critics') social orientation becomes more obvious in a hermeneutical paradigm that accentuates reception.

One general conclusion we may draw then is that, although the influence of modern literary theory on Gospel criticism has been great, Matthew scholars are not allowing developments in the secular field to determine their agenda. This is evident, first of all, in the somewhat stubborn retention of redaction criticism and in the insistence upon the necessity of such work even by scholars whose primary interest is not authorial intention. It is also evident in the observation that the new approaches have not been so much adopted as adapted by Gospel scholars, to the extent that the most influential of these (narrative criticism and *Wirkungsgeschichte*) appear to be specifically designed for dealing with biblical material (as does redaction criticism). It is further evident in what may be described as a lack of fragmentation in Matthean studies, that is, in the tendency among Matthew scholars to view various reading strategies as more complementary than they seem to be regarded in the general field of modern literary criticism.[67]

With regard to the latter point, we wish to affirm the overall spirit of cooperation that has characterized the Matthew Group. The diversity of the group is pronounced, yet no member has sought preference in defining its agenda and all members have respected the commitments and concerns of the rest. If such is the tenor of Matthean studies in general, then the metaphor of a storm center seems no longer apt to describe discussions within this field. Debated matters are certainly numerous—consensus is still lacking on such basic issues as structure, sources, community, christology, and salvation history. One might have thought the introduction of new methods would complicate discussion further, but, instead, it seems to have provided ways for scholars to discuss the Gospel without first resolving matters where deliberation has reached an impasse. The image that seems best to fit the current status of Matthean scholarship is that of the treasure described in 13:52 of the Gospel itself. The wise exegete draws out of this treasure what is new and what is old.

---

[67] Admittedly, this tendency is sometimes critiqued as fostering a naive eclecticism that fails to take seriously epistemological and hermeneutical reasons for preferring one reading strategy to another.

Chapter One

The *Sitz im Leben* of the Gospel of Matthew

DONALD A. HAGNER

Reconstructing the life-setting of the evangelists and their communities is among the most challenging tasks that face the New Testament interpreter. The slight evidence external to the Gospels is late and relatively untrustworthy, and therefore one is left with the difficult job of proceeding inductively, inferring the life-situation from the internal evidence, attempting to ascertain which clues in the text actually point to an author's specific situation as opposed to "innocent" elements of the common tradition, and trying to understand what and how much significance to give to these clues. Redaction criticism is the most important aid in discovering the *Sitz im Leben* of an evangelist. By seeing how Matthew and Luke have altered the passages they borrowed from Mark and Q—what is added, omitted, or changed—we may carefully infer some of their special concerns. I say "carefully" because not every such alteration points to a significant difference in perspective. A second important aid in determining the life-situation of an evangelist is to be found in his "special" material, i.e., material drawn from special sources and unique to the particular gospel. The results of these two aids, mutually informing each other, should enable the scholar—albeit tentatively— to come to a knowledge of an evangelist's special interests and concerns, which in turn may be taken to reflect the life-situation in which he and his intended readers found themselves. The unavoidable circularity in discerning the life-setting from text and then reading the text in the light of that life-setting must be faced and taken into account, but need not paralyze us. It should be obvious, however, that the reconstruction of the life-situation of an evangelist is necessarily a speculative enterprise. It is a kind of educated guesswork, and the results of such an undertaking can, in the nature of the matter, seldom be considered as final.[1]

The final test of a reconstructed *Sitz im Leben* is how well it enables us to understand the varied contents of a Gospel as a whole. It is the Gospel as it stands that must finally be explained, for it is this that the author put into the hands of his readers. The better sense we can make of the particular emphases and distinctives of the Gospel, its content and organization, the more satisfactory will be the hypothetical *Sitz im Leben*.[2] It is in this regard—discerning the coherence of the totality—that the Gospel of Matthew presents scholars with a serious challenge. What *Sitz im Leben*, if any, is capable of explaining the divergent emphases and remarkable polarities of this Gospel? Can the apparently disparate elements in Matthew be brought under common denominators?

The purpose of this paper is to focus on the question of particularism and universalism in the Gospel of Matthew, together with the closely related question of Israel and the Church. These are universally regarded as issues of central importance in Matthew and have been given much attention by Matthean scholars. We shall look in turn at the following: (I) Tensions in Matthew; (II) The Relation of Matthew to Contemporary Judaism; (III) The *Sitz im Leben* of

---

[1] Nowadays, when the newer literary critical approaches to the Gospels have become so popular, one almost feels the need to apologize for pursuing historical interests. Studying the Gospels from a purely literary perspective is without doubt a productive enterprise (see the books mentioned in the next note). Given the nature of these documents, however, literary and historical approaches should be regarded as complementary rather than mutually exclusive.

[2] A salutary trend is currently underway wherein attention is increasingly being directed to the study of the Gospels as self-contained entities, each of which must be understood holistically and on its own terms. For Matthew, the following studies may be noted: R. A. Edwards, *Matthew's Story of Jesus* (Philadelphia: Fortress, 1985), who approaches Matthew through narrative analysis; W. G. Thompson, *Matthew's Advice to a Divided Community* (Rome: Biblical Institute Press, 1970), who proposes "vertical analysis"; O. L. Cope, *Matthew. A Scribe Trained for the Kingdom of Heaven* (Washington, D.C.: The Catholic Biblical Association of America, 1976), who advocates "linear reading." See now especially J. D. Kingsbury, *Matthew as Story* (Philadelphia: Fortress, 2nd ed., 1988); D. B. Howell, *Matthew's Inclusive Story. A Study in the Narrative Rhetoric of the First Gospel*, JSNTSS 42 (Sheffield: JSOT, 1990); J. C. Anderson, *Matthew's Narrative Web. Over, and Over, and Over Again*, JSNTSS 91 (Sheffield: JSOT, 1994). New commentaries from this perspective have also begun to appear: M. Davies, *Matthew: Readings, A New Biblical Commentary* (Sheffield: JSOT, 1992); D. E. Garland, *Reading Matthew. A Literary and Theological Commentary on the First Gospel* (New York: Crossroad, 1993).

Matthew's Community; (IV) Distinctive Emphases in Matthew; (V) The Date and Provenance of the Gospel; and (VI) Matthew in the Context of First Century Christianity.

I. Tensions in Matthew

Matthew is the only Gospel that records Jesus' startling words restricting his and his disciples' immediate ministry to Israel. According to 10:5f., when he sends the Twelve out on their mission he begins with a stern prohibition: "Go nowhere among the Gentiles, and enter no town of the Samaritans, but go rather to the lost sheep of the house of Israel" (cf. 10:23, "all the towns of Israel"). Later in the narrative, when Jesus himself is entreated by a Gentile woman, he not only ignores her request (initially), but responds by saying, "I was sent only to the lost sheep of the house of Israel" (15:24). So contradictory is this attitude to that of the evangelist's day, when the Gentile mission was an undeniable and growing reality, that these passages excellently satisfy the criterion of dissimilarity (so far as the early church is concerned, but not of course so far as Judaism is concerned), and hence most scholars accept these sayings as authentic. We may note here simply that this particularist emphasis in Matthew is in harmony with the thoroughly Jewish orientation of this Gospel.

On the other hand, and seemingly against this particularism, there is an implicit universalism (i.e., that the good news of the gospel is for Gentiles too) throughout the Gospel. Thus, e.g., the genealogy of Christ which contains Gentile names (Ruth and Rahab; 1:5); the magi from the East (2:1–12); the Roman centurion ("Truly, I say to you, not even in Israel have I found such faith;" 8:5–13; cf. Luke 7:1–10);[3] "in his name will the Gentiles hope" (12:21; cf. Isa. 42:4); "the field is the world" (13:38); the Canaanite woman (15:21–28; Mark 7:24–30);[4] the parable of the tenants (21:33–43; Mark 12:1–12; Luke 20:9–19);[5] the parable of the marriage feast (22:1–10; Luke 14:15–24);[6] and the Roman soldiers' confession in 27:54.[7] What is implicit earlier becomes

---

[3] Matthew's redaction of Q intensifies this logion by the addition of *amen* at the beginning and the phrase *par' oudeni* after *legō hymin*.

[4] Only Matthew has the emphatic logion "O women, great is your faith."

[5] The verse of key importance, 21:43, is found only in Matthew.

[6] Matthew heightens the implied universalism with *hosous* (22:9) and *pantas* (22:10).

[7] Only Matthew has those on watch with the centurion join in the confession.

explicit in 24:14 (Mark 13:10) where Jesus says, "And this gospel of the kingdom will be preached throughout the whole world,[8] as a testimony to all nations; and then the end will come'; and, of course, most impressively in the commission of 28:19 (Luke 24:47 [cf. Mark 16:15]), "Go therefore and make disciples of all nations, baptizing them in the name of the Father and of the Son and of the Holy Spirit."

It seems clear that this tension between particularism and universalism in Matthew is closely related to another polarity of the Gospel, that involving Israel and the church. In Matthew we encounter an apparent polemic against the Jews that is all the more striking because of the favored position of the Jews already noted and because of the generally Jewish tone of the Gospel. Probably most conspicuous here are the passages referring to a transference of the Kingdom from Israel to those who believe (the church). Thus in 8:11 (Luke 13:28f.), just following the compliment of the Roman centurion for his faith, we read, "I tell you, many will come from east and west and sit at table with Abraham, Isaac, and Jacob in the kingdom of heaven, while the children of the kingdom will be thrown into the outer darkness; there people will weep and gnash their teeth."[9] And in 21:41 (Mark 12:9; Luke 20:16), at the end of the parable of the tenants, the tenants pronounce their own judgment: "He will put those wretches to a miserable death, and let out the vineyard to other tenants who will give him the fruits of their seasons."[10] This is followed by Jesus' words (21:43), "Therefore I tell you, the kingdom of God will be taken away from you and given to a nation (*ethnei*) producing the fruits of it." Agreeing with this emphasis is the parable of the marriage feast, where those invited "would not come" (22:3) and thus the invitation is extended to all: "Go therefore to the thoroughfares, and invite to the marriage feast as many as you find" (22:9).

To these passages may be added others that speak of the judgment of unbelieving Israel. Upbraiding the cities of Galilee where his miracles had been done (11:20–24; Luke 10:12–15), Jesus concludes, "But I tell you, it shall be more tolerable on the day of judgment for Tyre and Sidon . . . [and] for the land of Sodom . . . than for you." In

---

[8] Only Matthew has the phrase "in all the world."

[9] Luke has added "north and south" to emphasize the theme of universality, while Matthew is content with the Old Testament language of "east and west" (Isa 59:19; Mal 1:11). Matthew as usual retains the Jewish terminology "kingdom of heaven," and he alone has the comparable phrase "sons of the kingdom."

[10] Matthew intensifies the judgment motif with *kakous kakos*.

12:45 he refers to "this evil generation."[11] In 13:10–15 (cf. 13:13 with Mark 4:12; Luke 8:10) Matthew alone describes the unbelieving with the full quotation of the judgment oracle of Isa 6:9f.: "With them indeed is fulfilled the prophecy of Isaiah which says: 'You shall indeed hear but never understand, and you shall indeed see but never perceive. For this people's heart has grown dull, and their ears are heavy of hearing, and their eyes they have closed, lest they should perceive with their eyes, and hear with their ears, and understand with their heart, and turn for me to heal them'" (cf. Acts 28:26–27.). In the parable of the marriage feast, it is noted that "those invited were not worthy" (22:8; omitted in Luke 14:21). In 23:38 (Luke 13:35) Jesus, lamenting over Jerusalem, states, "Behold, your house is forsaken and desolate." And finally we may note the bitter and fateful words of 27:25, unique to Matthew: "His blood be upon us and on our children," words that have tragically and unjustifiably been used to promote anti-Semitism.

On the other side of the transference passages are those who believe, a "nation" (*ethnos*) producing the fruit of the kingdom (righteousness), those who repent, those whose eyes are blessed to see and whose ears hear what "many prophets and righteous people longed to see and hear" (13:16–17). In view, of course, is the new community, called in chapters 16 and 18, with deliberate anachronism, the *ekklēsia*, the church.

The church and Israel thus stand in obviously painful tension in Matthew. Reflecting this tension are the references to "their synagogues" (4:23; 9:35; 10:17; 12:9; 13:54),[12] "your synagogues" (23:34), "their scribes" (7:29), and "the Jews to this day" (28:15)—most references unique to Matthew, and the last reminiscent of the use of "the Jews" in the Fourth Gospel. Throughout the book, moreover, it is the Pharisees, those whose viewpoint dominates Judaism especially after the destruction of Jerusalem in 70 CE, that are the main antagonists of Jesus, and who are repeatedly shown to be inferior to Jesus in their understanding of Torah. Thus "when Jesus finished these sayings, the crowds were astonished at his teaching for he taught them as one who had authority, and not as their scribes" (7:28f.). And at the

---

[11] Words added by Matthew to the Q material reflected also in Luke 11:24–26.

[12] This expression may of course be innocuous, as for example in 4:23 (paralleled in Mark 1:39 and Luke 4:15) and 9:35. But this is probably not the case in 10:17. The only other synoptic reference is Mark 1:39.

end of the bitter denunciation of the scribes and Pharisees in chapter 23, Jesus can say, "Fill up, then, the measure of your fathers. You serpents, you brood of vipers, how are you to escape being sentenced to hell?" (23:32–33). Finally, the evangelist speaks explicitly of Jewish persecution of the church: "Beware of others; for they will deliver you up to councils, and flog you in their synagogues" (10:17); and "Therefore I send you prophets and sages and scribes, some of whom you will kill and crucify, and some you will scourge in your synagogues and persecute from town to town" (23:34).

Redaction-critical study of these passages shows that Matthew has given these motifs much greater emphasis than the other synoptic writers. Much of the material is unique to this Gospel; and where Matthew depends upon Mark or Q, Matthew usually intensifies the hostility. Matthew indeed is only second to the Fourth Gospel in apparent animosity against the Jews.

Here, then, we have what is probably the major puzzle in the Gospel of Matthew. On the one hand, we have the particularism that limits Jesus' and his disciples' ministry to Israel. Together with this exclusivism, the normal Jewish viewpoint, is the generally Jewish tone of the Gospel with, among other things, its stress on the abiding validity of the Law, the necessity of righteousness, and the fulfillment of messianic prophecy. On the other hand, standing in rather sharp contrast to the preceding, is the universalism of the Gospel, its striking motif of the transference of the Kingdom and the particularly harsh sayings against the Jews.

II. The Relation to Contemporary Judaism

How is this state of affairs in the Gospel to be explained? Most redactional-critical analysis of Matthew has centered on this problem in one way or another. In my opinion, however, most Matthean scholarship has too quickly opted for dichotomistic solutions that have necessitated regarding certain important threads of the Gospel as being irrelevant to Matthew's readers and their *Sitz im Leben*. In what follows I hope to explain the divergent emphases of the Gospel through the positing of a plausible and realistic life setting for Matthew's community.

1. In his excellent overview of the study of Matthew from 1945 to 1980, Graham Stanton discusses four main views that have been held concerning the relationship between Matthew's Christian community

and contemporary Judaism:[13] (1) the "traditional" view, i.e., that Matthew is the earliest Gospel, written by the apostle in Aramaic for a Jewish Christian community; (2) that the Gospel was written to a Jewish Christian community after 70 CE but prior to 85, a community "closely related to Judaism" (intra-muros); (3) that the Jewish Christian recipients of the Gospel had already experienced a definite break with the synagogue (thus after 85 CE), yet remained in debate with Judaism (extra-muros); and (4) that the evangelist was a Gentile, and perhaps his readers too, and that discussion with Judaism had long since come to an end. It is readily apparent that the first two views put greatest weight on the Jewish character of the Gospel, whereas the third and fourth views find the motifs of hostility toward the Jews and the transference of the Kingdom to the Gentiles to be of determinative importance.[14]

Stanton's analysis shows clearly that a key issue in these discussions is the question whether the phenomena described above reflect a situation in which a clear break between the church and synagogue has taken place. In view here is the decision, which may have been made at Yavneh (Jamnia) around 85 CE, to force Jewish Christians out of the synagogue by an addition to the liturgy of the synagogue cursing the minim or "heretics" (the *Birkhat ha-Minim*, twelfth of the Eighteen Benedictions, the *Shemoneh Esreh*). This event, it is commonly argued,[15]

---

[13] "The Origin and Purpose of Matthew's Gospel: Matthean Scholarship from 1945 to 1980," in *Aufstieg und Niedergang der Römischen Welt*. eds. H. Temporini and W. Haase, II (Principat), 25.3 (Berlin/New York: Walter de Gruyter, 1985), 1910–1921.

[14] A recent, unflinching advocate for a variant of the fourth view, but with a Jewish, and not Gentile, author for the Gospel, is U. Luz: "The fissure between community and synagogue is final. Any attempt to situate the Matthean community within the Jewish synagogue system must be considered a failure." *Matthew 1–7. A Commentary* (Minneapolis: Augsburg, 1989) 88.

[15] E.g., G. Strecker, *Der Weg der Gerechtigkeit. Untersuchung zur Theologie des Matthäus* (Göttingen: Vandenhoeck & Ruprecht, 3rd ed., 1971) who argues that the Gospel is directed toward Gentile Christians and that "die Judenchristen eine ältere Entwicklungsstufe des Gemeindelebens repräsentieren" (35); W. Trilling, *Das wahre Israel. Studien zur Theologie des Matthäus Evangeliums* (München: Kösel, 3rd ed., 1964) 214ff.; R. Walker, *Die Heilsgeschichte im ersten Evangelium* (Göttingen: Vandenhoeck & Ruprecht, 1967) 128; G. Kilpatrick, *The Origins of the Gospel According to St. Matthew* (Oxford: Oxford University Press, 1946) 111; other names that can be mentioned here are Haenchen, Stendahl, Schweizer, Sand, Frankemölle, Hare and Meier. See especially Meier's discussion in *Law and History in Matthew's Gospel* (Rome Biblical Institute Press, 1976) 12–13. Meier agrees about the separation of synagogue and church, but with Schweizer holds that this does

accounts for such distinctive elements in the Gospel as the hostility toward the Jews in Matthew, the transference of the Kingdom sayings, Matthew's interest in *panta ta ethnē*, and the (alleged) cessation of the mission to the Jews. On this hypothesis, accordingly, the pro-Jewish elements in the Gospel, the stress on Law and fulfillment of prophecy, and especially the exclusivistic or particularistic sayings, are understood as remnants of earlier tradition which the evangelist did not assimilate to his own viewpoint. But this is to relegate important emphases in the Gospel to the status of archaisms irrelevant to the life-situation of the readers. With some justification Kümmel describes this as "a completely untenable position."[16]

We may point out here that those who offer this analysis of the data often argue further for Gentile readers and perhaps even a Gentile author.[17] That is, the strongly negative attitude toward Israel, it is said, must be the result of the dominance and bias of a Gentile church. Clark writes, "a Jewish Christian of about 90 would hardly be found writing a gospel whose theme is the definite and final rejection of Israel by her God."[18] Advocates of Gentile authorship can point to some minor difficulties in the view that the author was a Jew (e.g.,

---

not entail an end of discussion between the two.

[16] *Introduction to the New Testament*, trans. H. C. Kee from 17th ed. (Nashville: Abingdon, 1975) 116.

[17] Here we must include not only Strecker (*op cit.*, 15–35) and Trilling (*op. cit.*, 215), but also K. W. Clark, "The Gentile Bias in Matthew," *JBL* 66 (1947) 165–72, now also available in *The Gentile Bias and Other Essays* (Leiden: E. J. Brill, 1980) 1–8; the Danish scholar, P. Nepper-Christensen, *Das Matthäusevangelium. Ein judenchristliches Evangelium?* (Aarhus: Universitetsforlaget, 1958); R. Walker, *op. cit.*; and J. P. Meier, *Law and History in Matthew's Gospel*, 14–21; idem, *The Vision of Matthew* (New York: Ramsey/Toronto: Paulist, 1979) 17–25; S. van Tilborg, *The Jewish Leaders in Matthew* (Leiden: E. J. Brill, 1972) 171; H. Frankemölle, *Jahwebund und Kirche Christi* (Münster: Aschendorff, 1974) 200; and L. Gaston, "The Messiah of Israel As Teacher of the Gentiles. The Setting of Matthew's Christology," *Interp* 21 (1975) 24–40. See, too, S. Sandmel, *A Jewish Understanding of the New Testament* (1956): The Gospel "was composed not by a Jewish Christian, but by a Gentile, out of the awareness that law and regulation are inescapably necessary for religious discipline . . . Matthew has little regard or respect for the Jewish Law; it is a new Christian law which he is introducing" (167); and D. Flusser, "Two Anti-Jewish Montages in Matthew," *Immanuel* 5 (1975) 37–45.

[18] Clark, "Gentile Bias," p. 2. So too in a similar vein, S. van Tilborg, *The Jewish Leaders in Matthew*, 171; the response of D. R. A. Hare (*The Theme of Jewish Persecution of Christians in the Gospel According to St. Matthew*, 170.) to such a conclusion is appropriate: "The bitterness of the persecution and the frustration of a fruitless mission are sufficient, however, to account for so pessimistic a view of Israel on the part of a Jewish Christian author."

putting the Pharisees and Sadducees together; the possible misunderstanding of Zech 9:9 in 21:1–9 to involve two animals rather than one),[19] but their hypothesis flies in the face of the overwhelming Jewish character of the Gospel of Matthew. It does not suffice simply to say that these Jewish elements, so fundamental to Matthew, are simply anachronisms carried over from an earlier period and that they have no special relevance to the identity and circumstances of the evangelist or his readers.

Other influential Matthean scholars are convinced that the Gospel of Matthew reflects the time prior to the separation of church and synagogue (i.e., the putative Yavneh decision of c. 85).[20] They point to the Gospel's argument concerning Jesus as Messiah as evidence that the mission to the Jews has not ceased. They call attention to marks of a Jewish Christianity in such things as the positive note about the Pharisees in 23:2, the avoidance of offense by the payment of the Temple tax (17:24ff.), and especially Matthew's view of the Law (5:17ff.). These data, together with much else that could be mentioned,[21] point to the continuing relationship between Jewish

---

[19] See Meier, *Vision*, 19ff. On this point, however, Stanton's ("Origin and Purpose," 1919) cautionary note seems wise: "There are simply too many gaps in our knowledge of Judaism in the period 70–100 A.D. to enable us to pronounce a confident verdict on the extent and accuracy of the evangelist's knowledge of Judaism."

[20] G. Bornkamm, "End-Expectation and Church in Matthew," in *Tradition and Interpretation in Matthew* (Philadephia: Westminster, 1963 [translation of German article of 1956]) 15–51. Meier, however, calls attention to a shift of emphasis in Bornkamm's later articles. See especially Bornkamm's 1970 article "The Authority to 'Bind' and 'Loose' in the Church in Matthew's Gospel," now available in *The Interpretation of Matthew*, ed. G. Stanton (Philadelphia/London: Fortress/SPCK, 1983) 85–97. On p. 88 Bornkamm argues that the break has already taken place. See Meier, "Law and History," 9ff. and Stanton, "Origin and Purpose," p. 1913–14); G. Barth, "Matthew's Understanding of the Law," in *Tradition and Interpretation* (1963 translation of German original of 1955) 58–164; R. Hummel, *Die Auseinandersetzung zwischen Kirche und Judentum im Matthäusevangelium* (München: Chr. Kaiser, 2nd ed., 1966); W. D. Davies, *The Setting of the Sermon on the Mount* (Cambridge: Cambridge University Press, 1963); M. D. Goulder, *Midrash and Lection in Matthew* (London: SPCK, 1974); S. Brown, "The Matthean Community and the Gentile Mission," *NovT* 23 (1980) 216.

[21] E.g., failure to explain Jewish customs and practices, as in the omission of Mark's detailed explanation of the practices of the Pharisees (cf. Mark 7:1–4 with Matt 15:1–2); retention of untranslated Hebrew vocabulary; the omission of Mark 10:12 about a wife divorcing her husband; the addition of the exception clause (*porneia*) in 5:32 and 19:9; the derogatory references to Gentiles (6:7; 18:17). For details, see A. Wikenhauser and J. Schmid, *Einleitung in das Neue Testament*

Christians and their non-Christian Jewish kinsfolk.[22] But in this perspective, as Rohde has rightly pointed out,[23] insufficient attention has been paid to the other side of the tension, i.e., to the universality of the Gospel and the transference of the Kingdom motif.

Matthean scholarship thus finds itself in the strange circumstance of having been forced into two camps by emphasizing one side of the data in the Gospel to the neglect, if not the exclusion, of data on the other side. In the instance of Strecker and Trilling, certain Jewish motifs are pronounced anachronistic and hence essentially irrelevant to the life-setting of the evangelist. In the case of Bornkamm, Barth, and Hummel, such things as the hostility toward the Jews and the transference of the Kingdom motif find no convincing place in the life-setting of the Jewish Christianity represented by the evangelist and his community.

2. It is not surprising that in recent years a number of scholars have tried to find a mediating position between these two poles, one that would do more justice to the various perspectives contained in the Gospel. Indeed, to some extent, the third view in Stanton's analysis, viz. that "Matthew's [Jewish Christian] community is extra-muros yet

---

(Freiburg: Herder, 6th new ed., 1973) 245.

[22] The intra-muros view, wherein Matthew's community is understood as a sect within Judaism, has recently been defended in essays by A. Segal ("Matthew's Jewish Voice"), A. J. Saldarini ("The Gospel of Matthew and Jewish-Christian Conflict"), and L. M. White, "Crisis Management and Boundary Maintenance: The Social Location of the Matthean Community"), all in *Social History of the Matthean Community. Cross-Disciplinary Approaches*, ed. D. L. Balch (Minneapolis: Fortress, 1991), 3–37, 38–61, and 211–42 respectively. See now too Saldarini's full-length exposition of this viewpoint in *Matthew's Christian-Jewish Community* (Chicago/London: University of Chicago Press, 1994). Saldarini's approach emphasizes only the Jewishness of Matthew's Christianity and its continuity with Judaism, regarding it as essentially a reforming interpretation of Judaism. But Matthew's Christianity also involves a very clear discontinuity with Judaism: a new gospel, fulfillment amounting to a turning point in the aeons, and a new eschatological present in the *ekklēsia*, composed of Gentile brothers and sisters, presided over by the risen Lord. Matthew's Christianity is characterized by a combination of old *and new* (cf.13:52); Saldarini has focussed only on the old. Cf. the criticisms of R. H. Gundry in "A Responsive Evaluation of the Social History of the Matthean Community in Roman Syria," which responds both to Segal and Saldarini (*Social History of the Matthean Community*, 62–67). See too J. D. Kingsbury's demur in his summarizing analysis ("Conclusion: Analysis of a Conversation") in the same volume (259–69), 268.

[23] *Rediscovering the Teaching of the Evangelists* (Philadelphia: Westminster, 1968). Bornkamm "is not really able to explain" the theme of universality (54).

still defining itself over against Judaism,"[24] is exactly such an attempt in that although it affirms the c. 85 break with Judaism, it also finds ongoing significant concern with Judaism.[25]

Obviously what is required is a hypothesis that treats the tensions in the Gospel with all seriousness, as truly reflecting the life-situation of the readers.[26] A number of writers have thus begun to address these tensions very directly. A somewhat older article by K. Tagawa remains one of the most effective statements of the problem.[27] Tagawa rightly emphasizes how important it was for Matthew's Jewish Christian community with its continuing national consciousness to understand itself as the true Israel. Furthermore, and again rightly, in my opinion, the evangelist is not alleging that the Gentiles have replaced Israel, argues Tagawa, or that the mission to Israel is ended. Tagawa nevertheless leaves his readers finally with a confused picture wherein Matthew can speak of both a limited and a universal mission depending on whether he is conceiving the church as a "national

---

[24] Stanton designates this view as "a 'mediating' position" between the second and fourth views in his analysis. "Origin and Purpose," 1915.

[25] In this category Stanton includes K. Stendahl (*The School of St. Matthew and its Use of the Old Testament* [Philadelphia: Fortress, 2nd ed. 1968]); C. F. D. Moule ("St. Matthew's Gospel: Some Neglected Features," in *Studia Evangelica* II, [*TU* 87 (1964)] 91–99, now available in his *Essays in New Testament Interpretation* [Cambridge: Cambridge University Press, 1982] 67–74); E. Schweizer (*Matthäus und seine Gemeinde* [Stuttgart: KBW Verlag, 1974]); and W. G. Kümmel (*Introduction to the New Testament*). Stanton includes himself as holding to this view, referring to his article "5 Ezra and Matthean Christianity in the Second Century," *JTS* 28 (1977) 67–83. See too "The Gospel of Matthew and Judaism," *BJRUL* 66 (1984) 264–84. Both essays are now available in Stanton's *A Gospel for a New People: Studies in Matthew* (Edinburgh: T & T Clark, 1992). Holding to approximately the same view is B. Przybylski, "The Setting of Matthean Anti-Judaism," in *Anti-Judaism in Early Christianity. Vol 1, Paul and the Gospels*, ed. P. Richardson and D. Granskou (Waterloo, Ontario: Wilfrid Laurier University Press, 1986) 181–200.

[26] Mention must be made here of M. J. Cook's view which attempts to obviate the whole discussion. "Interpreting 'Pro-Jewish' Passages in Matthew," *HUCA* 54 (1983) 135–46. Cook, who leans to Gentile authorship, denies that Matthew contains any "pro-Jewish" passages. Hence the various attempts that have been made to solve the dilemma are quite unnecessary. "I find no inconsistency in Matthew between anti-Jewish and pro-Jewish elements because the latter are not really pro-Jewish but only a function of and entirely consistent with Matthew's overall anti-Jewish stance" (140). Pro-Jewish passages thus become "merely a literary device by which Matthew is setting up the Jews for eventual vilification" (142). But the passages in question seem too natural and matter-of-fact to be explained in this way, and Cook underestimates the Jewish tone of the Gospel.

[27] "People and Community in the Gospel of Matthew," *NTS* 16 (1969–70) 149–62.

community" or "a chosen community of faith distinguished from the Jewish nation."[28] Adding further to the confusion, these communities overlapped in Matthew's mind, according to Tagawa, and for Matthew "there can be no Gentile church" since Gentiles become a part of "Israel" when they become Christians.[29]

A very creative and interesting approach to the tensions of the Gospel is to be found in several articles by S. Brown.[30] The evangelist, according to Brown, finds himself in a Jewish Christian community with a strong particularist strain, for whom the limitation of the mission to Israel remains a present reality, and not simply something of the past. The evangelist could not ignore this and yet he espouses and desires to promote the Gentile mission. Although the mission is implied earlier in the Gospel, and in Matthew's central section (10:18), the evangelist's advocacy of the Gentile mission can only be accomplished by a *deus ex machina*, as Brown designates the final scene (28:16–20). The strength of Brown's proposal is that it takes the particularist passages with all seriousness, and does not relegate them to the category of historical relics. Yet is seems to me that when Brown argues that the limitation to Israel is still in effect among Jewish Christians living in the Diaspora (even if, as he speculates, they had moved from Palestine to Syria) he requires too much of us. Further, Brown's hypothesis requires that Matthew's community was seriously divided over an issue of greatest significance. Would not that degree of tension have been unbearable? And would not the evangelist have addressed it more directly? Finally, Brown does not relate his hypothesis directly to much else within the Gospel that demands explanation. Suggestive as this argument is, then, it remains unconvincing.

---

[28] Ibid., 161.

[29] Ibid., 162. Tagawa's entire discussion is carried on without any reference to the date of the Gospel or the location of the readers.

[30] "The Two-fold Representation of the Mission in Matthew's Gospel," *Studia Theologica* 31 (1977) 21–32; "The Mission to Israel in Matthew's Central Section (Matt 9:35–11:1)" *ZNW* 69 (1978) 73–90; and "The Matthean Community and the Gentile Mission," *NovT* 22 (1980) 193–221. Cf. too J. Jervell, "The Mighty Minority," *Studia Theologica* 34 (1980) 13–38, now available also in *The Unknown Paul. Essays on Luke-Acts and Early Christian History* (Minneapolis: Augsburg, 1984), for the argument that the Gentile mission must be defended to Matthew's community (47). So too now, on this last point, see especially U. Luz, *Matthew 1–7*, 84ff.

Also stimulating is the view of B. T. Viviano who accounts for the tension in the Gospel by pointing to the evangelist as a "master of ecumenical healing."[31] Viviano regards Matthew's Jewish Christian community as in a transition caused by a "flood of Gentile converts" at around 85 when the Gospel was written. He rightly indicates on the one hand that "Matthew is locked in an internecine struggle to the death with these nearby [non-Christian rabbinic] opponents and gives them no quarter. They are outside the pale of the messianic community."[32] On the other side of the tension, according to Viviano, Matthew faces Paulinist Christians who for the most part do not follow Torah. Matthew gratefully seizes the tradition about Peter reflected in 16:18ff. as the one who could mediate between the perspectives represented by James on the one hand, and by Paul on the other. These verses, writes Viviano, show "Matthew at his ecumenical best, working out a symbolic figure who could hold the broad center of early Christians together."[33] The particularist traditions in the evangelist's community lose out in the end to the universal perspective reflected at the end of the Gospel.

One way of handling the apparently disparate material of the Gospel is, of course, simply to attribute it to different eras of the Matthean community. S. H. Brooks' relates his analysis of Matthew's *Sondergut* to two distinct stages in the history of Matthew's community: first, a pre-70 group of Jewish Christians who were "relatively at peace within the synagogue," and a later group "constituted apart from, and in ideological opposition to, the Jewish synagogue."[34] Such a hypothesis is necessarily speculative, although it cannot be ruled out

---

[31] "Matthew, Master of Ecumenical Healing," *Currents in Theology and Mission* 10 (1983) 325–32. Along a similar line, see G. W. E. Nickelsburg, "Good News/Bad News: The Messiah and God's Fractured Community," *Currents in Theology and Mission* 4 (1977). Yet he does not attempt to explain the tension, but focuses more on the hostility to the Jews, a theme downplayed by Tagawa and Brown, and thence to the question of the role played by Matthew in later anti-Semitism. For Nickelsburg the tension reflected in the Gospel points to a post 70 date "very close" to the time of the schism between the church and synagogue.

[32] Ibid., 330.

[33] Ibid., 331. Somewhat similar is the view of W. R. Farmer, who describes the Gospel of Matthew as ecumenical, inclusive, and non-sectarian. "The Post-Sectarian Character of Matthew and Its Post-War Setting in Antioch of Syria," *Perspectives in Religious Studies* 3 (1976) 235–47.

[34] *Matthew's Community. The Evidence of His Special Sayings Material,* JSNTSS 16 (Sheffield: JSOT, 1987) 120. Cf. the similar solution of Strecker, quoted above, n. 15.

altogether. Nevertheless, without any hard data to support this hypothesis, it must be regarded as less compelling than one that can make sense of the Gospel as a whole, as it stands, i.e., as addressed to Jewish Christians at a particular point in time.

Therefore the hypotheses considered above that focus on the tension in which the readers of Matthew found themselves are clearly preferable. To my mind, the key to understanding the contents of the Gospel lies in understanding the difficult circumstances of Matthew's community. But before we attempt to reconstruct a *Sitz im Leben* for Matthew that we believe does better justice to the disparate data of the Gospel, we must clear the way by calling attention to two false presuppositions that have often dominated recent discussion and are frequently apparent in the major attempts to explain the Gospel. These grow out of an over-stress on the importance of the date of 85, or thereabouts, and the decisions taken by the rabbis at Yavneh (Jamnia).

3. It is especially important to note how much weight has been put on Yavneh by Matthean scholars in their attempt to understand Matthew and its life-setting. This is all the more remarkable given that knowledge of what took place at Yavneh is tenuous at best.[35]

The view that has been held by the majority of Matthean scholars is that at some time during the course of the ninth decade of the first century the rabbinic leadership took steps to expel Christian Jews from the synagogues as a way of stopping the insidious evangelism that was undoubtedly going on. Thus the *Birkhat ha-Minim*, the "blessing" of the heretics,[36] very probably originated in this decade (probably, however as the modification of previously existing material) and was initially, if

---

[35] Cf. P. Schafer, "Die sogenannte Synode von Jabne. Zur Trennung von Juden und Christen im ersten/zweiten Jh. n. Chr." *Judaica* 31 (1975) 54–64; 116–24; G. Sternberger, "Die sogenannte 'Synode von Jabne' und das frühe Christentum," *Kairos* 19 (1977) 14–21. Along a similar line, D. Flusser, "The Jewish-Christian Schism," *Emmanuel* 17 (1983–84), 32ff.

[36] In the so-called Geniza version (from the Cairo Geniza), it reads: "For the renegades let there be no hope, and may the arrogant kingdom soon be rooted out in our days, and the Nazarenes and the *minim* (heretics) perish as in a moment and be blotted out from the book of life and with the righteous may they not be inscribed. Blessed art thou, O Lord, who humblest the arrogant." The translation is from J. Jocz, *The Jewish People and Jesus Christ* (London: SPCK, 1949) 53, but many scholars have pointed out that the actual wording varies considerably and that explicit reference to *ha nozrim* ("the Nazarenes") could well be a later insertion. See the scholars referred to in footnote 36.

not exclusively, intended against Jewish Christians. It is difficult to doubt, according to this view, that some such formal action against Jewish Christians in the synagogue was taken at this specific time.[37]

Now, however, this conclusion is being increasingly challenged, particularly by Jewish scholars,[38] who find no significance in Yavneh for the relationship between Jews and Jewish Christians. It is at least clear that Matthean scholarship must reconsider the large role that a particular, and possibly incorrect, understanding of Yavneh has played in its analysis of the Gospel. But I want to point out that even if we grant the correctness of the traditional understanding of Yavneh, the conclusions usually drawn are incorrect.

Thus Yavneh has commonly—and mistakenly, in my view—been taken to indicate a fundamental change of attitude and as inaugurating a new climate in Jewish and Christian relationships, quite unlike that which preceded. The *first* false presupposition deriving from this view is that there was no exclusion of Jewish Christians from the synagogue before this date. Indeed, one has the feeling from some writers that before this date there was no hostility between Jewish

---

[37] For the best recent defense of this view, see W. Horbury, "The Benediction of the Minim and Early Jewish-Christian Controversy," *JTS* 33 (1982) 19–61. Horbury rightly notes, however, that the benediction "was not decisive on its own for the separation of church and synagogue, but it gave solemn liturgical expression to a separation effected in the second half of the first century through the larger group of measures to which it belongs" (61).

[38] See especially R. Kimelman, "*Birkat Ha-Minim* and the Lack of Evidence for an Anti-Christian Jewish Prayer in Late Antiquity," in *Jewish and Christian Self-Definition*, vol. 2, eds. E. P. Sanders, A. I. Baumgarten, and A. Mendelson (Philadelphia: Fortress, 1981) 226–44. Kimelman's final two conclusions are worth quoting: "5. Thus *birkat ha-minim* does not reflect a watershed in the history of the relationship between Jews and Christians in the first centuries of our era. 6. Apparently, there never was a single edict which caused the so-called irreparable separation between Judaism and Christianity. The separation was rather the result of a long process dependent upon local situations and ultimately upon the political power of the church" (244). See too, S. T. Katz, "Issues in the Separation of Judaism and Christianity after 70 C.E.: A Reconsideration," *JBL* 103 (1984) 43–76. Katz denies that the *Birkat ha-Minim* was directed specifically against Jewish Christians, concluding that "there was no anti-Christian policy at Yavneh or elsewhere before (if immediately after?) the Bar Kochba revolt" (76). The same conclusion can be found in A. Finkel, "Yavneh's Liturgy and Early Christianity," *JEcSt* 18 (1981) 231–50. "At Yavneh, no act of excommunication was employed against these Jewish Christians" (243). Cf. D. Flusser, "The Jewish-Christian Schism," *Emmanuel* 17 (1983–84) 37–38. But for a Jewish defense of the traditional view, see L. H. Schiffman, "At the Crossroads: Tannaitic Perspectives on the Jewish-Christian Schism," *Jewish and Christian Self-Definition*, vol. 2, 149ff.

Christians and non-Christian Jews at all, and that the former were
universally accepted and made comfortable in the synagogues.[39] In
fact, however, there is sufficient evidence of an early and continuing
hostility between Jews who accepted the Gospel and those who did
not,[40] including forceful exclusion from the synagogue.[41] If any
specific date is to be mentioned as a clear turning for the worsening
relationship between Jews and Jewish Christians, it would have to be
70, but even this date hardly marks the beginning of hostility between
the two groups. Thus the *Birkhat ha-Minim,* even on the traditional
understanding, amounts only to a formalizing and standardizing of
practice, perhaps indeed as the result of mounting hostility, but it
should by no means be thought of as an absolute beginning of hostility
or of the practice of exclusion.[42]

---

[39] The question, of course, cannot be resolved by speaking generally about
"Jewish Christianity" since unquestionably there were several varieties of Jewish
Christians, not to mention variations dependent upon time and place. See below.

[40] According to Acts (apart from 4:1–3, 18, 21) hostility erupts for the first time
with Stephen (6:12ff.; 7:57–8:1), but occurs frequently in Paul's experiences. Cf.
13:45–50; 14:2–6, 19; 17:5–9, 13; 18:6–7, 12–17. Paul's bitter words in 1 Thess 2:14–
15 indicate the intensity of hostility at a relatively early date: "For you brethren,
became imitators of the churches of God which are in Judea; for you suffered the
same things from your own compatriots as they did from the Jews, who killed both
the Lord Jesus and the prophets, and drove us out . . . .." See D. A. Hagner, "Paul's
Quarrel with Judaism," in *Anti-Semitism and Early Christianity. Issues of Polemic and
Faith,* C. A. Evans and D. A. Hagner, eds. (Minneapolis: Fortress, 1993) 128–50. Cf.
A. Harnack, *The Mission and Expansion of Christianity in the First Three Centuries,*
trans. by J. Moffatt from 1908 German original (New York: Harper, 1962): "it
seems untenable to hold with some Jewish scholars that originally, and indeed for
whole decades, peace reigned between the Christians and the Jews" (46).

[41] In addition to the references in the preceding note, consider also the explicit
aposynagogos references in the Fourth Gospel (9:22; 12:42; 16:2). Without
accepting J. A. T. Robinson's dating of the Gospel, I too find no insuperable
reason to deny the use of this term before 70 CE. *Redating the New Testament*
(Philadelphia: Westminster, 1976) 272–73. An important distinction made by D. R.
A. Hare is pertinent. He distinguishes between social ostracism and informal
exclusion on the one hand, and the formal exclusion of the later *Birkhat ha-Minim.
The Theme of Jewish Persecution of Christians In the Gospel According to St. Matthew*
(Cambridge: Cambridge University Press, 1967) 56. Hare finds contemporary
parallels (i.e., pre-70 CE) in the Pharisaic ban, and exclusion practiced at Qumran
(51).

[42] Davies aptly remarks: "Moreover, Paul's letters, like Acts, attest violence on the
part of the Synagogue, and that frequent, so that there is no reason to connect the
passages referred to [Matt 5:11; 23:34; 10:17, 23] in any way specifically with
Jamnian affairs, unless other factors point to this," *Setting,* 297.

The *second* false presupposition drawn from an exaggeration of the significance of Yavneh and the date of 85 is that after this date the mission to the Jews ceased. To be sure, once Christians were more consistently driven out of the synagogues, evangelism of the Jews would have become more difficult and its form necessarily altered. But that it ceased altogether is an unwarranted conclusion. D. R. A. Hare, nevertheless, has argued that the strong judgment passages in Matthew together with the transference of the Kingdom motif point to a situation in which the mission to Israel has been abandoned. Now that Israel has refused the invitation, Hare concludes, "Henceforward the mission is not to Israel and the Gentiles but only to the Gentiles!"[43] More recently, Hare has been joined by D. J. Harrington in this argument that the *panta ta ethnē* of 28:19 excludes the Jews.[44] But because a mission to the Jews within the synagogue must have been abandoned after 85, the end of the Jewish mission itself is hardly necessitated. Christian Jews would have continued to meet their unbelieving kinsfolk in the community where discussions, however tense, undoubtedly continued. It is in the final analysis unthinkable both psychologically and theologically that the Jewish Christian community addressed by the evangelist could have altogether abandoned the mission to their Jewish brothers and sisters. The Apostle Paul can speak in no uncertain terms about the judgment of unbelieving Israel and the new reality of the Church that now stands in the place of national Israel, just as he can wrestle with the actual shift from Jews to Gentiles in the church, without for a moment losing his zeal for the conversion of his people.

---

[43] D. R. A. Hare, *Jewish Persecution*, 148. Hare's insistence that *ta ethnē* in 28:19f. must mean individuals because *baptizontes* is followed by *autous*, is not convincing. The *autous* need only be the members of *panta ta ethnē*, which can clearly include the Jews. See now the same view, but with a little more nuance, in Hare's commentary, *Matthew*, Interpretation Commentary (Louisville: John Knox, 1993), 331–34. Others who argue that the mission to Israel has come to an end are Trilling, Strecker, Walker, and Gaston.

[44] "'Making Disciples of All the Gentiles' (Matt 28:19)," *CBQ* 37 (1975) 359–69. Even if Hare and Harrington were correct about 28:19, their conclusion need not follow. That is, even if the point of 28:19 was the evangelization of the Gentiles, does that in itself exclude a Jewish mission? Does the transference of the Kingdom motif, used in its strongest form, rule out a continuing effort in Jewish evangelism? J. P. Meier, however, has effectively shown that the use of *ethnos/ethnē* in Matthew cannot in every instance be limited to Gentiles, but that in several instances, including 28:19, Israel is to be included. "Nations or Gentiles in Matthew 22:19?" *CBQ* 39 (1977) 94–102.

It seems unlikely, then, that the year 85 (or 90) should be thought of as a watershed providing a radically altered situation that can be used to explain the complex and apparently contradictory data of the Gospel of Matthew. Indeed, there is no solid reason why the phenomena assigned so confidently to the post-85 era by some scholars cannot equally find a place before that time. Thus universalism, the transference of the Kingdom sayings, and the hard sayings against Israel are hardly impossible in the earlier decades. Jesus could have spoken about the future (i.e., post-resurrection period), envisioning a mission to the Gentiles, and thus justifying the transference sayings. All of this would have been quite meaningful in a context where the Gentile mission was thriving, as would the harsh sayings against the Jews, which would have reflected the unbelief of the Jews as well as the continuing and probably growing hostility between the church and synagogue.[45]

Conversely, the items often confidently restricted to a pre-85 setting can have had significance even in the post-85 era. Thus, a Jewish Christian community would naturally find the stress on the fulfillment of prophecy and the messiahship of Jesus meaningful, as well as even the particularist sayings. This we will try to demonstrate in the *Sitz im Leben* we are about to propose.

But the point to be emphasized here is that the measures taken at Yavneh between 85 and 90 serve as no actual and revolutionary turning point in the relation between church and synagogue. They provide no justification for the common allegation that Yavneh constituted a first "break" between synagogue and church. Instead, Yavneh served merely as the formalizing of a hostility that had in fact existed for a long time. Jewish Christian relationships (i.e., between Christian and non-Christian Jews) in the first century, from the time of Stephen onwards, certainly varied according to time and place, but tension, animosity and hatred seem to have been the rule more often than not. In the course of the first century we can see, if we are to generalize, a more-or-less steady crescendo of bitterness and hostility

---

[45] Thus J. A. T. Robinson, who dates Matthew before 70, is correct when he writes:: "These problems reflect a period when the needs of co-existence force a clarification of what is the distinctively Christian line on a number of practical issues which previously could be taken for granted . . . But uneasy co-existence does not necessarily imply an irrevocable break." *Redating the New Testament,* 103.

(and of course especially after 70), rather than a sudden turning for the worse after Yavneh.[46]

III. The Sitz im Leben of Matthew's Community

As we have already said, the merit of a proposed *Sitz im Leben* of any document depends upon the extent to which it can satisfactorily account for the contents of the document, and, we may add, particularly for the elements that appear to be difficult or contradictory. Indeed, the latter may be especially revealing in that they may point to important tensions or commitments in the community which, it was felt, must be preserved. Thus the reconstruction of a *Sitz im Leben* should keep just these disparate elements to the fore, rather than paring away one side or the other, and so making certain data irrelevant to the evangelist's community.

1. We must begin with the strong probability that the readers were Jewish Christians, as was probably the author, too. The data of the Gospel are again and again explained most satisfactorily on the hypothesis that the first readers were Jewish Christians. Among various key items to be mentioned here are the following: the stress throughout the Gospel on fulfillment and especially the distinctive formula quotations ("this happened in order to fulfill what was spoken by the prophet") which point to Jesus as the Messiah and his ministry as the dawning of the messianic age; the importance of Jesus' fidelity to the Law (not only Matt 5:17–20, but cf. Matthew's reductional changes of Mark 7 in chap. 15) and his call to righteousness; Matthew's omission of Mark's explanation of Jewish customs (cf. Mark 7:3–4 with Matt 15:2); and his formulation of several discussions in typical rabbinic patterns (e.g., Matt 19:1ff. on divorce). Also worth noting are the apologetic motifs of the infancy narrative (against Jewish claims of the illegitimacy of Jesus' birth) and the resurrection narrative (explicitly against the Jewish claim that the body was stolen; 28:12–15).

It is, of course, not impossible that Matthew was written to a mixed community or even to Gentiles by a Gentile author. Gentile Christians, after all, were also interested in the fulfillment of the Old Testament and in Jesus as Messiah; they may, furthermore, have been in need of

---

[46] R. T. France comes to the same conclusion. *Matthew. Evangelist and Teacher* (Grand Rapids: Zondervan, 1989) 98–101. I do not agree with him, however, that the extra-muros/intra-muros debate is therefore "an artificial one."

the emphasis on Law to counter antinomian tendencies perhaps stemming from a Pauline enthusiasm. But these explanations seem less natural and, hence, less probable. There is in fact little in the Gospel that is effectively explained as finding its raison d'être in a supposed Gentile readership. Moreover, the hypothesis of a Gentile life-setting leaves other aspects of the Gospel, and especially the particularist sayings, unaccounted for.

A further probability is that both the original readers and the final redactor were Hellenistic Jews, and Jews of the Diaspora rather than Palestinian Jews. This follows not only from the fact that the Gospel was written in Greek, but from the apparent proximity of the readers to a Gentile Christianity. From these data Kümmel concludes, "It is certain that the author of Matthew lived in a Greek-speaking area and wrote for Greek-speaking Christians, most of whom were of Jewish origin."[47]

2. In preparation for what follows, it is worth noting generally the difficult situation in which Jewish Christians have always found themselves, and not least in the later first century. When Jews become Christians they are forced to cope, on the one hand, with their non-Christian Jewish kinsfolk, from whom they have separated themselves, and, on the other hand, with a largely Gentile Christianity among whom they now exist as a minority, but as brothers and sisters nonetheless. To their Jewish kinsfolk, Jewish Christians have always had to answer such charges as disloyalty to the religion of Israel, disloyalty to the Mosaic Law (or at least of association with others who fail to observe it), and of joining an alien, indeed pagan, religion, the large majority of whose adherents are Gentiles. In short, Jews are naturally put on the defensive by their non-Christian kinsfolk, and probably more so if they have insisted on preservation of their Jewishness and have resisted assimilation, thereby making at least the implicit claim of being the true Israel. And it is obvious how such Jewish concerns as these would have been aggravated in the time of crisis that faced Judaism after the destruction of Jerusalem. Christian Jews must have been seen then more than ever as traitors. So far as their Gentile fellow-Christians are concerned, Jewish Christians are always under a subtle pressure to minimize the significance of their Jewishness; their continued observance of Jewish law and customs can

---

[47] *Introduction,* 119.

easily become a theological problem for Gentile Christians and a hindrance to fellowship and a sense of unity. The Gentile Christians in Matthew's day may have rejoiced in (and may have insisted upon) discontinuity between the old and new covenants much more readily than many Jewish Christians would have. Jewish Christians were thus forced to work out their relationships with Gentile Christianity and their understanding of the newness contained in and implied by the reality of Christ.

These Jewish Christians were accordingly in an unenviable position—caught between two loyalties, like people simultaneouly holding passports from two countries at war. They were torn between their Jewish kinsfolk on the one hand and Gentile Christians on the other, wanting to reach back for continuity with the old and at the same time to reach forward to the new work God was doing in the largely Gentile church—answerable at the same time, so to speak, both to Jews and Gentiles. This, as I say, is a situation with which nearly every Jewish Christian has had some acquaintance. But the resultant tensions must have been particularly trying to Jewish Christian communities of the second half of the first century.[48]

3. And so we come to the original readers of the Gospel of Matthew. As Jewish Christians they undoubtedly found themselves in the dilemma we have portrayed. Matthew's community was desperately in need of an account of the story of Jesus that would enable them to relate both to unbelieving Jews and to Gentile Christians. In particular, the increasing success of the Gentile mission and the overall failure of the mission to Israel raised questions not only in the readers' minds, but also among their Jewish opponents. Thus the Gospel was almost certainly written to confirm Jewish believers in the truth of Christianity as the fulfillment of the promises to Israel, which entails the argument that Jesus is the Messiah, that he was loyal to the Law, and that he came to the Jews. Through this material, the readers could gain confidence in the correctness of their faith as something standing in true succession to the scriptures, and at the same time be in a better position to answer their unbelieving kinsfolk in the synagogues.

---

[48] For an illuminating study of the problems from a sociological point of view, with much that supports the present argument, see J. A. Overman, *Matthew's Gospel and Formative Judaism. The Social World of the Matthean Community* (Minneapolis: Fortress, 1990). See too, G. N. Stanton, "Matthew's Gospel and the Damascus Document in Sociological Perspective," in *A Gospel for a New People*, 85–107.

If this is true, we may well also find here the reason for the preservation of the particularist sayings in Matthew. It was important for the author to be able to stress that Jesus came specifically—indeed, exclusively—to the Jews, in order to underline God's faithfulness to His covenant people, i.e., to stress the continuity of God's salvation promises and the actuality of their fulfillment in the first instance to Israel. In the face of an increasingly Gentile church, which must have given its Jewish opponents the embarrassing ability to argue that Christianity was an alien religion, the readers were thus able to realize that they, unlike the Gentiles, had a place in the ministry of Jesus from the beginning. They, as Jewish Christians, were important in the fulfillment of God's plan as a righteous remnant attesting the faithfulness of God to His covenant promise. Matthew thus affirms the rightful place of a Jewish Christianity as the true Israel. Far from renouncing Judaism, as K. W. Clark maintains,[49] Matthew finds in Christianity a perfected or fulfilled Judaism, brought to its goal by the long-awaited Christ.

The particularist sayings, then, are not simply relics of the historical tradition without relevance for the readers of the Gospel, but neither do they indicate a contemporary limitation upon the mission of Matthew's community. They refer historically to what was once the case, during the pre-resurrection ministry of Jesus and his disciples, but have special relevance to the readers as a theological justification of the faithfulness of God to his people Israel,[50] and thus of the propriety of Jewish Christian faith.

If Jesus was sent "only to the lost sheep of the house of Israel," it remains true, however, that Israel largely failed to respond. The Jewish Christian readers of this Gospel would have been painfully aware of the lack of response among their Jewish brothers and sisters. What had happened already in the time of Jesus was happening in their time. Inevitably and by reason of their unbelieving and hostile kinsfolk, Jewish congregations must early have begun to think of themselves as separate from and even as over against, unbelieving Judaism—as a righteous remnant against the proto-rabbinic Judaism represented in the Gospel by the Pharisees. It is not at all unthinkable that Jewish

---

[49] *The Gentile Bias*, 2.

[50] A similar conclusion is drawn by A.-J. Levine, in her study of 10:5b, *The Social and Ethnic Dimensions of Matthean Social History*, Studies in the Bible and Early Christianity 14 (Lewiston, NY/Queenston/Lampeter: Edwin Mellen, 1988).

Christians could have appreciated the harsh sayings in the Gospel against the Jews, the judgment against unbelieving Israel, and could have referred, for example, to "their synagogues" (9:35) or "their scribes" (7:29). The familiar biblical pattern, articulated so frequently by the prophets, would have been seen in Israel's rejection of God, followed by God's rejection of Israel. And from the latter it is only a step to the transference of the Kingdom sayings. In the case of the transference sayings, however, our Jewish Christian readers of course identified themselves as among those nations (*ethnē*, Gentiles, largely but not exclusively), the new people of God to whom the Kingdom was being transferred. Similarly, the record of Jesus' words about the Jewish persecution of Christians (23:34; 10:23) would have been especially relevant to the readers. The considerable polemics against the Jews—and distance from the Jews—in Matthew are thus by no means unimaginable within a Jewish Christian context. The Jewish scholar D. Flusser (although attributing the hostility in Matthew to a Gentile perspective) has correctly called attention to this phenomenon: "Because the majority of Jews did not accept the new message, there is a very high probability that tension with and even hatred of the Synagogue existed among some Jewish Christians."[51] These polemics are thus naturally to be expected under the circumstances, and are quite similar in many ways to the intramural criticism of Israel in the prophetic tradition.[52] The key difference, of course, is that the dispute here is no longer truly intra-muros, but between kinsfolk separated by faith in the risen Christ. Christian Jews had become a part of the new community, the Church, which by the time of the readers was composed mainly of Gentiles, this being no doubt perceived by our readers as the result of the universalism implicit in the messianic prophecies.

This, then, is my hypothesis: the evangelist's community partook of two worlds, the Jewish and the Christian. Although they saw their Christianity as the true fulfillment of Judaism, they also were very

---

[51] "The Jewish-Christian Schism," *Immanuel* 16 (1983) 40. Sandmel makes the following point in a somewhat broader application, but it is also appropriate here: "Early Christianity could conceivably have felt a positive relationship to the ancient Judaism, and yet have an entirely different feeling towards contemporaneous Judaism and Jews." *The First Christian Century in Judaism and Christianity: Certainties and Uncertainties* (New York: Oxford University Press, 1969) 158.

[52] See C. A. Evans and D. A. Hagner (eds.), *Anti-Semitism and Early Christianity. Issues of Polemic and Faith* (Minneapolis: Fortress, 1993).

conscious that they had broken with their unbelieving brothers and
sisters. They were struggling to define and defend a Jewish Christianity
to the Jews on the one hand and to realize their unity with Gentile
Christians on the other. This twofold challenge explains some of the
basic tensions encountered in the Gospel.

It is important at this point to relate this hypothesis to relatively
recent work by R. E. Brown, J. P. Meier, and G. Stanton. In a most
interesting proposal, R. E. Brown has persuasively argued for the need
of much more precision in references to Jewish Christianity and
Gentile Christianity.[53] According to Brown, "during most of the first
century a theological distinction signaled by 'Jewish Christianity' and
'Gentile Christianity' is imprecise and poorly designated."[54] Brown
proceeds to describe four types of Jewish Christianity, each of which
had Gentile converts who shared that perspective. (1) those "who
insisted on *full observance of the Mosaic Law, including circumcision*"; (2)
those who did not require circumcision, but required "converted
Gentiles to keep *some Jewish observances*"; (3) those who insisted neither
on circumcision nor observance of the food laws; and (4) those who
furthermore *"saw no abiding significance in Jewish cult and feasts."*[55]
Although we cannot here enter into a discussion of this proposal, at
least the following must be said. Strictly speaking Brown is correct, and
yet I do not think his argument abolishes the usefulness of a general
distinction between Jewish and Gentile Christianity in the first century.
The great majority of Christians would easily have fallen into groups
two or three, with a preponderance of Jews in group two and of
Gentiles in group three. Group one would have had only a small
minority of Gentile proselytes, and although we must grant the trouble
the Jewish Christian extremists in this group caused for Paul, this
group of Jewish Christians must nevertheless have been small
compared to those in group two. On the other hand, probably only a
very few Jewish Christians belonged to group four.[56] Thus despite the

---

[53] "Not Jewish Christianity and Gentile Christianity but Types of Jewish/Gentile
Christianity," *CBQ* 45 (1983) 74–79; "Introduction," in R. E. Brown and J. P. Meier,
Antioch and Rome: New Testament Cradles of Catholic Christianity (New York/Ramsey:
Paulist, 1983) 1–9.

[54] "Not Jewish Christianity and Gentile Christianity," 75.

[55] *Antioch and Rome*, 2–6; italics are Brown's. Cf. Sandmel, *The First Christians
Century*, 173.

[56] The distinction between groups three and four is difficult to see. Brown puts
Paul in group three, but not in group four (with John and Hebrews) among those

exceptions, at the extremes of Brown's four categories, it does seem possible to speak generally of Gentile and Jewish Christianity in the first century. So far as Jewish Christianity is concerned, it is probably safe to say that Palestinian Jews were mainly to be found in groups one and two, while Hellenistic Jews were mainly in groups two and three.

Can we speculate as to which of Brown's four groups Matthew's community may have belonged? If we are right that this community is a Hellenistic Jewish Christian community, then they are probably to be put either in group two or three. Although the community finds it necessary to sound conservative for the sake of the argument with the synagogue,[57] yet so far as their attitude to the Gentile congregations was concerned, it is not difficult to think of them as belonging to group three.[58]

J. P. Meier, in his stimulating discussion of Antioch, treats Matthew as evidence of the "second Christian generation" in that city. Although he bases much of his argument on a specific date and locale for the Gospel, Meier has presented one of the most satisfactory analyses of the life-setting of Matthew's community. It is a community facing an identity crisis because of the tension between its conservative Jewish Christian members, on the one hand, and its Gentile-Christian members, on the other hand. The former is particularly seen "in a unique plight . . . They were too Christian to go back to the synagogue and too much in the mainstream of Christianity to follow the extreme rightwing [Brown's group one] out of the church."[59] The evangelist, a "liberal conservative," takes the matter into his hands by synthesizing the varied traditions at his disposal into a work of "inclusive synthesis."[60]

---

who "saw no abiding significance in Jewish cult and feasts." But was Paul really as conservative as Brown argues, allowing only freedom from circumcision and food laws? Did he really continue to hold to the abiding significance of the cult and feasts, or does the evidence cited by Brown simply point to Paul's ready expedience (cf. 1 Cor. 9:19–23)?

[57] Thus it is easily possible to think of them as corresponding to group two, as does Viviano, "Master of Ecumenical Healing," 329.

[58] L. Goppelt is probably correct in saying that Jewish Christians of the Diaspora adopted increasingly the freedom from Mosaic ordinances practiced by the growing Gentile Christian communities. *Jesus, Paul and Judaism,* trans. by E. Schroeder from 1954 German original (New York: Nelson, 1964) 124, 129.

[59] *Antioch and Rome,* 50–51.

[60] Ibid., 51, 57.

But what Meier describes as being true of the church of Antioch in the 80's must have been true in many places and much earlier too. Jewish Christians did not have to wait until the 80's, or even until 70, to face the kind of pressures described by Meier. Meier unnecessarily restricts his argument to a later date and a single locale. Among the "external factors" affecting the Antioch situation, Meier mentions the Jewish war, the failure of the Jewish mission, and Yavneh. But the War and Yavneh may only have aggravated circumstances that existed earlier, and the relative failure of the Jewish mission was certainly a reality long before 70.

In an especially insightful essay, G. N. Stanton has focused on Matthew's anti-Jewish polemics, and among recent writers, has come the closest, in my opinion, to a satisfactory explanation of the *Sitz im Leben* of Matthew's community.[61] According to Stanton,

> The evangelist is, as it were, coming to terms with the trauma of separation from Judaism and with the continuing threat of hostility and persecution. Matthew's anti-Jewish polemic should be seen as part of the self-definition of the Christian minority which is acutely aware of the rejection and hostility of its "mother" Judaism.[62]

Thus the anti-Jewish polemic is given a real life-setting in Matthew's community. Stanton refers to four pillars that support his hypothesis: (1) the continuity and serious threat of Jewish opposition to the community; (2) the tension between the community and the Gentile world; (3) the evangelist's increased use of apocalyptic themes; and (4) parallel themes in other early Christian writings.[63]

To my mind, Stanton's description is basically correct. Although he does not refer to Yavneh, nor does he depend upon the widely accepted Antiochene provenance, he does write that "Matthew's community has recently parted company with Judaism after a period of prolonged hostility,"[64] and suggests a date of about 90 for the Gospel. This, as I have already argued, is an unnecessary conclusion.

---

[61] "The Gospel of Matthew and Judaism," *BJRUL* 66 (1984) 264–84. Available also in Stanton's *A Gospel for a New People*, 146–68.

[62] Ibid., 274. Stanton's view is reconfirmed in "Revisiting Matthew's Communities," in *Society of Biblical Literature 1994 Seminar Papers*, ed. E. H. Lovering, Jr. (Atlanta: Scholars Press, 1994) 9–23; see esp. pp.13–18.

[63] Mentioned here are 1 Thessalonians, the Fourth Gospel, the Didache, and 5 Ezra. On the rest, see Stanton's "5 Ezra and Matthean Christianity in the Second Century," *JTS* 28 (1977) 67–83, found also in *A Gospel for a New People*, 256–77.

[64] "The Gospel of Matthew and Judaism," 273.

In addition, Stanton pays too little heed to what must also have been a matter of importance to Matthew's community: its relationship to Gentile Christianity.

IV. Distinctive Emphases in Matthew

We may now note the way in which some of the recognized distinctiveness of the Gospel of Matthew is readily explained by the reconstructed life-setting we have proposed. What is particularly striking, with our hypothesis in mind, is that continuity with the past (i.e., with the concerns of Judaism) is stressed, but always at the same time with the transposing of the elements of the past to a new, undeniably higher level, congruent with the fulfillment into which the readers have entered through Christ. The evangelist thus underlines the faithfulness of Jesus to Moses and the prophets that is so important to the Jewish Christian community, but without sacrificing the inevitable newness brought by Jesus, seen most vividly in the existence of Gentile Christians, with whom Matthew's readers exist as members of the same family of faith. But for the evangelist, this is not a balancing-act in which two irreconcilable perspectives are held in tension; instead, the newness itself is seen by its very nature to capture the true significance of the old.

1. *Matthew's teaching about the Law and righteousness.* Obviously 5:17–18. is in accord with the Jewish view of the Torah: "Think not that I have come to abolish the law and the prophets; I have not come to abolish them but to fulfill them. For truly I say to you, till heaven and earth pass away, not an iota, not a dot, will pass from the law until all is accomplished." The teaching of Jesus is consistently understood throughout Matthew as nothing other than the explication of the true meaning of the Law. Jesus brings this uniquely and finally authoritative interpretation of the Law because of who he is, the Messiah, and what he has brought, the Kingdom. Since Jesus alone is the true interpreter of the Law, to obey his teachings is in effect to obey the totality of the Law, that is, down even to the slightest detail of the Law. This is the meaning of 5:19 which, using rabbinic-like language, refers to the commandments of Torah in their totality. Thus Christian discipleship amounts to the faithful upholding of the Torah to the end of the age.

But always for Matthew the meaning of the commandments of Torah is to be found only in the teaching of Jesus.[65]

The evangelist has thus done his utmost to express the meaning of Jesus in the most effective way possible for his Jewish Christian community, using even the language of Pharisaic Judaism. For the sake of his community, he furthermore portrays Jesus as less radical toward the Law than does Mark.[66] All of this effectively enabled Matthew's community to respond to the charges of the synagogue. It is in the community of Jesus and not in the synagogue that true faithfulness to the Torah is found.[67]

At the same time, Matthew does not forego the newness that comes with the presence of the messianic King. Consonant with Matthew's stress on the messianic authority of Jesus, Jesus can paradoxically transcend the letter of the Law while penetrating to its inner spirit.[68] Newness is also already apparent from 5:20, "For I tell you, unless your righteousness exceeds that of the scribes and Pharisees, you will never enter the kingdom of heaven." This righteousness comes not from a more punctilious observance of the Law than that of the Pharisees, but from participation in the new reality of the Kingdom and faithfulness to the teaching of Jesus.[69]

---

65 Although I differ from J. P. Meier in the exegesis of 5:17–20, I find myself mainly in agreement with his excellent study, *Law and History in Matthew's Gospel.* To my mind, however, the evangelist desires to comprehend discontinuity between Torah and Jesus' interpretation of it within a more basic and larger sense of continuity, i.e., fulfillment.

66 Against Mark 7:1–23, compare Matthew 15:1–20, where Mark's editorial conclusion that Jesus "declared all foods clean," is omitted. Matthew focuses on the less problematic issue of hand-washing. Yet it should be noted that Matthew does not obliterate the difficult material from the tradition (15:11); he simply downplays it for the sake of his Jewish-Christian readers. But he knows well how important this tradition is for Gentile-Christian congregations.

67 For the importance of the Law in the whole matter, see L. H. Schiffman, "At the Crossroads," 117.

68 See 5:32–42 and 19:3–9, denying the possibility of divorce and the application of *lex talionis*; 12:1–14, plucking grain on the Sabbath; and 15:11, denying that what one eats can cause defilement.

69 Jesus' teaching is not to be understood as a "new" Law (building on the possible Moses typology where Jesus in the Sermon on the Mount delivers a new Law comparable to that of Sinai). Jesus instead brings via his teaching the true or intended meaning of the Mosaic Law. It is important to note also that the stress on Law in Matthew occurs in the context of the good news of the presence of the Kingdom. As in the Old Testament, the announcement of grace is antecedent to the call to live out the righteousness of the Law (e.g., the Beatitudes precede the

The emphasis on the Law and the importance of righteousness[70] in Matthew is more probably to be explained as the result of the situation of the Jewish Christian readers vis-à-vis the synagogue than to any direct attempt to counteract a "Pauline" antinomianism, although if such existed in the environs of Matthew's community, this emphasis would have proved to be a handy antidote.[71]

2. *Jesus and the Pharisees.* The infamous material in Matthew concerning the Pharisees is also explainable by our hypothesis. It is the Pharisees who are the great opponents of Jesus in the Gospel, since they also claim to be the faithful interpreters of the Law of Moses. Exactly the same tension existed between Matthew's community and the synagogue. The difficult words of Jesus in 23:2–3 ("The scribes and the Pharisees sit on Moses' seat; so practice and observe whatever they tell you, but not what they do; for they preach, but do not practice") make sense only if they are taken to indicate that Jesus agrees *in principle* with the Pharisees, i.e., insofar as they *truly* expound the meaning of the Mosaic Law. This must be the meaning of "practice and observe whatever they tell you," since in the verses that follow (4, 16, 18) Jesus several times finds fault with their teaching. Elsewhere in the Gospel the teaching of Jesus is of course shown to transcend the tradition of the Pharisees (9:10–17, on fasting; 15:1–20, outer hand-washing/inner defilement). But Jesus has no quarrel with the intent of the Pharisees. In principle they are correct; their goal of attempting to observe the Torah cannot be faulted.

---

exposition of the Law in the Sermon on the Mount). In this case, however, it is the grace of the Kingdom, of eschatological fulfillment, and not simply covenant, that stands in a dynamic tension with the demands of the Law as interpreted by the messianic King.

[70] On the Jewishness of "righteousness" in Matthew, see B. Przybylski, *Righteousness in Matthew and His World of Thought* (Cambridge: Cambridge University Press, 1980). For an argument, however, that Matthew can use the word in other senses than the ethical, see D. A. Hagner, "Righteousness in Matthew's Theology," in *Worship, Theology and Ministry in the Early Church*, FS R. P. Martin, eds. M. J. Wilkins and T. Paige (Sheffield: JSOT, 1992) 101–20.

[71] R. Mohrlang's assessment of Matthew's position regarding the Law is correct: "It is Matthew's dual citizenship in two communities that makes such a combination possible: as a Jew, he cannot conceive of denying either the validity of the law or the basic authority and need of scribal interpretation; but as a Christian, he recognizes that it is Jesus' interpretation of the law that is supremely authoritative, and that sits in judgment upon all others." *Matthew and Paul. A Comparison of Ethical Perspectives* (Cambridge: Cambridge University Press, 1984) 22.

But most characteristic of Matthew is Jesus' intense hostility to the Pharisees, seen especially in Matthew 23, and caused by the fact that the Pharisees claimed to be interpreters of Torah whereas actually they cancelled it (cf. 15:3, 6, 8–9). This would have had special meaning for Matthew's community given their own situation. The wrath of Jesus comes upon the Pharisees for having betrayed what had been entrusted to them, and hence for misleading the people. Throughout the Gospel it is Jesus who truly interprets Torah, and not the Pharisees. The evangelist's Jewish Christian community saw themselves as faithful followers of Torah, as expounded in the teaching of Jesus, and they justified their position from this clash between Jesus and the Pharisees with the argument that they themselves and not the synagogue were in true succession to Moses. And, of course, for these Jewish Christians it was not simply a matter of one rabbinic tradition winning out over another but of the teaching of the Messiah over that of human beings.[72]

3. *Hostility toward the Jews.* We have commented above on how our hypothesis explains the particularly strong anti-Jewish hostility of Matthew. Contrary to the common claim that this shows the un-Jewish character of the evangelist and his community, the strength of this hostility finds a natural explanation in the alienation from the Jews felt by Matthew's Jewish Christian community. Such hostility is readily explainable psychologically. It is a well-known fact that those who leave one religious group to join another[73] are always the severest critics of the group they have left. And in the present instance, where we must deal with very special factors—e.g., the racial and national aspects of Judaism, Christianity as the fulfillment of Jewish hopes (the true Israel), the bitter rivalry concerning the true interpretation of the same scriptures—it is only to be expected that feelings would run strong and lead to the language of alienation and frustration we

---

[72] On the subject in general, see D. E. Garland, *The Intention of Matthew 23*, NovTSup 51 (Leiden: Brill, 1979).

[73] It is not, however, proper to speak of Jews as "converts" to Christianity. Matthew's Jewish-Christians would never have thought of themselves as changing religions. They saw themselves as more faithful to the faith and scriptures of Israel—in short, as "fulfilled" Jews. But the social dynamics would have been similar to what is involved in conversion to a new religion. See especially J. A. Overman, *Matthew's Gospel and Formative Judaism*; G. N. Stanton, "Matthew's Gospel and the Damascus Document in Sociological Perspective," in *A Gospel for a New People*, 85–107.

encounter in the Gospel of Matthew. This hostility, of course, is to be sharply distinguished from anti-semitism, with which it has nothing to do, in spite of the later abuse of these motifs.[74]

4. *Fulfillment of the Old Testament.* Matthew's stress on the fulfillment of the scriptures, as exemplified especially in the unique fulfillment quotations, is especially understandable given the on-going dispute between Matthew's Jewish Christian community and the synagogue. For the evangelist the congruence between the ministry of Jesus and the scriptures is set forth both as a confirmation to his community and a challenge to the synagogue.[75] The inclusion of the Gentiles in the new people of God, undoubtedly a stumbling block to the Jews, is substantiated by the appeal to scripture (e.g., 4:14–16; 12:17–21), as is the failure of Israel (e.g., 13:14–17; 15:7–9). But the main point of the fulfillment quotations is the evidence they afford concerning the continuity of the faith of these Jewish Christians with the past. And if the hermeneutic underlying the understanding of the citations fails to meet modern, grammatico-historical standards, we must remember that it reflected Jewish practices of that era which were both familiar and widespread.[76]

5. *Fulfillment: the Kingdom of Heaven.* It is obvious that this would be important for Jewish Christians, who out of habit would prefer the circumlocution for "the kingdom of God." This kingdom terminology is more frequent in Matthew's teaching than any of the other Gospels, occurring nearly three times as often as in Mark. Although the kingdom has come as a mystery—in an unexpected way—in Jesus it has indeed come: "Blessed are your eyes, for they eyes, and your ears, for they hear. Truly I say to you, many prophets and righteous people longed to see what you see, and to hear what you hear, and did not

---

[74] See S. McKnight, "A Loyal Critic: Matthew's Polemic with Judaism in Theological Perspective," in *Anti-Semitism and Early Christianity. Issues of Polemic and Faith,* C. A. Evans and D. A. Hagner eds. (Minneapolis: Fortress, 1993) 55–79.

[75] O. L. Cope's study of the evangelist's use of the Old Testament (*Matthew. A Scribe Trained for the Kingdom of Heaven*) comes to conclusions consistent with the present hypothesis. Cope argues for a Jewish-Christian redaction and that "Matthew must have been written in a time and for a church which was involved in a severe struggle with Pharisaic Judaism" (126; cf. 130).

[76] See G. N. Stanton, "Matthew's Use of the Old Testament," in *A Gospel for a New People,* 346–63, found also in *It is Written: Scripture Citing Scripture,* FS B. Lindars, ed. D. A. Carson and H. G. M. Williamson (Cambridge: Cambridge University Press, 1988) 205–219.

hear it" (13:16–17). The words and deeds of Jesus point unmistakably to the reality of the present kingdom. It is a Jewish hope that is thus fulfilled, and in Matthew it is set forth in Jewish terms.[77]

6. *The Christology of the Gospel.* As is well known, only in Matthew among the Gospels is Jesus described as the Son of Abraham (1:1), and in Matthew the Jewish titles Son of David and Messiah occur more often than in any other of the Gospels. All of this is especially significant for Matthew's Jewish Christian readers. Other titles of course have obvious significance to Matthew's readership, such as Rabbi, King of the Jews, and Emmanuel, not to mention the wisdom motifs in Matthew's christology. But even the key christological titles in Matthew, Son of God, Son of Man and Kyrios, are full of meaning for Jewish Christians in their debate with the synagogue.[78] Also to be noted is the fact that the confession of Jesus as Son of God is made only by believers (except where it is blasphemy), and only by revelation (16:17; 11:27; cf. 13:11). This distinction would have meant much to Matthew's Jewish Christian readers confronted with the continuing unbelief of the majority of Jews.[79]

7. *The Church.* The concept of the new community would also have had special significance to Matthew's readers. The emphasis that it was upon Kepha that Jesus said he would build his church (16:18) underlined the significance of Jewish Christianity, and the importance of original Jewish believers. To them, in the first instance, fulfillment had come. They constitute the original core of God's new people and as such are of continuing importance. But when the evangelist speaks of the *ekklēsia*, he knows well that it is a new Israel[80] encompassing Gentiles in increasing numbers.[81] Hence, when he addressed certain urgent matters as division, false prophecy, and lawlessness, and stresses

---

[77] See J. D. Kingsbury, *Matthew. Structure, Christology Kingdom*, 128–60; R. T. France, *Matthew. Evangelist and Teacher*, 166–205 .

[78] See R. N. Longenecker, *The Christology of Early Jewish Christianity* (London: SCM, 1970).

[79] See J. D. Kingsbury, *Matthew: Structure, Christology, Kingdom* (Philadelphia: Fortress, 1975), 40–127; *idem, Jesus Christ in Matthew, Mark, and Luke* (Philadelphia: Fortress, 1981) 61–93; R. T. France, *Matthew. Evangelist and Teacher*, 279–317.

[80] On this, see R. E. Menninger, *Israel and the Church in the Gospel of Matthew,* Series VII Theology and Religion 162 (New York: Peter Lang, 1994). Menninger finds the interpretive key in the concept of the Church as the remnant of Israel. See too, R. T. France, *Matthew. Evangelist and Teacher*, 206–41.

[81] See J. D. Kingsbury, *Matthew* (Philadelphia: Fortress, 2nd ed., 1986) 98–100.

that the church is a mixed community of true and false disciples, he may have an eye on the Gentile congregations as well as troubles within his own community or environs.

8. *Eschatology.* The sheer amount of space given to eschatology in the Gospel indicates the importance it has to the evangelist and his readers. These Jewish Christians in particular, given their end-expectations, would have been especially sensitive to the reality of living "between the times," of living in a situation that remained on the way to, rather than having arrived at, the apocalyptic fulfillment described by the prophets. It would have been difficult for them, as it always has been for the church vis-à-vis the synagogue, to make a convincing case for the truth of realized eschatology. Future eschatology was thus vitally important to the evangelist's theology, and especially to his stress on discipleship. It was the crisis of imminent judgment that should motivate the community to proper conduct, the righteousness of the Kingdom.[82]

9. *Heilsgeschichte.* Having touched on some major themes of the Gospel, however inadequately, we may finally point out that Matthew presupposes a *Heilsgeschichte* framework as the transference of the Kingdom motif alone indicates.[83] Whether this framework is thought of as comprising three epochs (Israel, Jesus, and the church) or two, as Kingsbury argues (Israel and Jesus, with the church an extension of the latter),[84] is essentially unimportant. What is significant is that the evangelist sees the work of Jesus the Messiah as constituting a turning point wherein fulfillment has come, involving judgment for unbelieving Israel, but at the same time blessing to a remnant of Israel which has now come together with the Gentiles into a new eschatological reality, a new Israel, the church. It is in the church that Israel finds a true continuity with the past; but this continuity at the same time involves a dramatic newness that is centrally important and

---

[82] See D. A. Hagner, "Apocalyptic Motifs in the Gospel of Matthew: Continuity and Discontinuity," *HBT* 7 (1985) 53–82; *idem*, "Matthew's Eschatology," in *To Tell the Mystery*, FS R. H. Gundry, M. Silva and T. E. Schmidt, eds. (Sheffield: JSOT, 1994) 49–71; *idem*, "Imminence, Delay and Parousia in Matthew," in *Texts and Contexts*, FS L. Hartman, D. Hellholm and T. Fornberg, eds. (Oslo: Scandinavian University Press, 1995) 77–92.

[83] On the importance of *Heilsgeschichte* for Matthew, see esp. R. Walker, *Die Heilsgeschichte im ersten Evangelium.*

[84] J. D. Kingbury, *Matthew: Structure, Christology, Kingdom*, 31–36.

the cause of no small degree of tension for Jewish Christians, who themselves constitute the unique bridge between the promises of God and the realities of the new age.[85]

It is clear then that much of the distinctive content of Matthew is readily explainable on the hypothesis we have set forth. We have looked primarily at theological issues, but the same may be said of many of the formal aspects of the Gospel.[86]

V. The Date and Provenance of the Gospel

It would appear to be very difficult to become much more specific within the general situation we have proposed. The Gospel is capable of a wide variety of specific explanations that concern its character and the *Sitz im Leben* of its readers.[87] Is it possible, however, to narrow down the actual life-setting of the Gospel even so far as date and place are concerned? This I suggest is a much more difficult task than it is often taken to be.

The *Sitz im Leben* portrayed above can easily have existed for a Jewish Christian community before 70. Naturally some degree of hostility existed between Jewish Christians and the unbelieving Jews from the beginning, even before Stephen and the Hellenistic Jewish Christians began to infer elements of discontinuity with the faith of the past. With Stephen, however, there was a dramatic escalation of hostility, directed mainly against the Hellenistic Jewish Christians, with whom *ex hypothesi* Matthew's community had special affinity, albeit from a certainly later time. But not even the so-called Hebraic Jewish Christians, although they probably continued to observe the Law and the temple ritual, were able to exist amicably among the Jews of the

---

[85] A.-J. Levine concludes that Matthew "presents a program of salvation history constructed along two axes: a temporal axis that incorporates ethnic categories and a social axis that transcends the division between Jew and Gentile." *The Social and Ethnic Dimensions of Matthean Social History*, 273.

[86] On which see, P. Gaechter, *Die literarische Kunst im Matthäus-Evangelium*, SBS 7 (Stuttgart: KWB, 1966).

[87] Cf. A. Sand, *Das Gesetz und die Propheten. Untersuchungen zur Theologie des Evangeliums nach Matthäus* (Regensburg: Friedrich Pustet, 1974) 220f. Sand is probably correct when he writes in his review of the possibilities: "Aufgrund der genannten Faktoren ist es wohl kaum möglich, das Matthäusevangelium seinen theologischen Inhalt nach auf einen 'kurzen Nenner' zu bringen" (221). See now the same conclusion in Sand's survey of research, *Das Matthäus-Evangelium*, Erträge der Forschung 275 (Darmstadt: Wissenschaftliche Buchgesellschaft, 1991) 39. Cf. Trilling, *Das wahre Israel*, 220.

synagogue. When James the son of Zebedee was murdered by Herod Agrippa I in 44 CE, "it pleased the Jews" (Acts 12:3) and he turned his hostility to Peter. And although James the Just was admittedly zealous for the Law, he too was nevertheless martyred in 62 (Josephus, *Antiq.* XX.9.1; Hegesippus in Eusebius, *HE* II.23).[88] Although Hare's analysis shows that these events were atypical in pre-war Palestine and that there was no systematic persecution of Christians by the Pharisees, it is nevertheless clear that high levels of tension and hostility existed—and especially in the case of attempted proselytizing.[89] The situation in the Diaspora where Jewish Christians lived alongside and in fellowship with Gentile Christians, and probably in the kind of context Matthew's community was located, was considerably worse prior to the war of 66–70 than that in Palestine according to Hare.[90] It is important to note Hare's conclusion that "although it is probable that the role of the Pharisees and their rabbis in this conflict increased after 70, it cannot be insisted that they played an insignificant role before that time."[91] Further and directly to the point, referring to the floggings of Christians in the synagogue, Hare writes: "There was probably little change in this situation in the period A.D. 50–85."[92]

At the beginning of his study, Hare correctly indicates the "attitude toward the Gentiles" as one of the main challenges to Judaism. The "acceptance of Gentiles as equals without prior naturalization into the Jewish nation undoubtedly aroused a great deal of hostility among those who were diligently seeking full converts to the religion of Torah."[93] From the context of the Gospel it is apparent that this is exactly the situation faced by Matthew's community. But this is a problem that clearly existed long before 70.

One of the pillars of the argument for a late date of Matthew is the possible reference in 22:7 to the destruction of Jerusalem. Yet we can

---

[88] Goppelt refers to this event as "a sign of the first break." *Jesus, Paul and Judaism*, 130.

[89] *Jewish Persecution of Christians*, 78, 126, 168.

[90] Ibid., 78. Hare notes that things turned for the worse for the Judean Jewish Christians after the war.

[91] Ibid., 126–27.

[92] Ibid., 168.

[93] Ibid., 11–12. The "*a priori* case for friction between Jews and Christians" sketched by Hare seems valid for the pre-70 period as well as the post-70 period (18). Hare's dating of the Gospel just prior to Yavneh relegates the reality of persecution to the past and thus renders anachronistic the significant material on this theme in Matthew (127).

hardly be certain about this conclusion concerning the verse, which is hardly a necessary one.[94] Even if one concludes it more likely that 22:7 does refer to the destruction of Jerusalem, that only necessitates a post 70 date, not a post 85 date. There are furthermore a number of references which on a late dating must be treated as archaisms, but which on a pre-70 dating take on new dimensions of meaning (e.g. references to the Temple, 5:23–24; 12:5–7; 21:13; 23:16–22; to the Temple tax, 17:24–27; and to the Sadducees [eight references compared to one each in Mark and Luke]). Other arguments used to favor a late date for the Gospel also fall short of being able to convince beyond any doubt.[95] The traditionally late date assigned the Gospel thus seems to me to be only possible, not necessarily probable.[96]

From our argument about the constant presence of at least some degree of alienation and hostility from the beginning, and its escalation as the synagogue took measure of its dangerous, upstart opponent, it should be apparent how difficult it becomes to speak of any single, clear "break" between the Jewish Christians and the synagogue, especially one so late as 85–90. Jewish Christians had to

---

[94] K. H. Rengstorf argues for the formulaic character of the verse as a common motif in narratives concerning expeditions of punishment. "Die Stadt der Mörder," *Judentum, Urchristentum, Kirche,* FS J. Jeremias, ed. W. Eltester (Berlin: A. Topelmann, 1960). See too, B. Reicke, "Synoptic Prophecies of the Destruction of Jerusalem," in *Studies in New Testament and Early Christian Literature,* ed. D. E. Aune (Leiden E. J. Brill, 1972) 121–34, who traces the content of the verse to Old Testament judgment oracles. One may wonder, if the Gospel was written with a knowledge of the destruction of Jerusalem, why the Olivet Discourse was not edited more helpfully, as it is in Luke 21.

Even if 22:7 refers to the destruction of Jerusalem, it could be a prophecy (cf. Matt 24) unless, of course, such a possibility is ruled out *a priori.*

[95] E.g., the references to the "church" and to "church discipline" need not be post-70, nor the so-called Trinitarian formula of 28:19. For the best, recent defense of an early date for Matthew, see R. H. Gundry, *Matthew. A Commentary on His Literary and Theological Art* (Grand Rapids: Eerdmans, 2nd ed., 1994) 599–609. Although I am not convinced concerning the pre-63 date for the Gospel argued by Gundry, I do think that he has shown how tenuous the evidence is for a date later in the 80's. See too C. F. D. Moule, *The Birth of the New Testament* (San Francisco: Harper & Row, 3rd. ed 1982) 173f.; and R. T. France's discussion, *Matthew. Evangelist and Teacher,* 82–91. If C. P. Thiede is correct in dating P^{64} fragments of Matthew between 70 and the end of the century, this would provide further support for an earlier dating of Matthew than is usually accepted. See his article "Papyrus Magdalen Greek 17 (Gregory-Aland P^{64}): A Reappraisal," *Zeitschrift für Papyrologie und Epigraphik* 105 (1995) 13–20.

[96] See further, D. A. Hagner, *Matthew 1–13,* WBC 33A (Dallas: Word, 1993) lxxiii–lxxv.

some degree broken with the synagogue as soon as they came into existence. And although hostilities were not as overt or disastrous in the earlier years, compared to what they would later become, there was never a time when the two groups found mutual acceptance and friendliness possible. But with the passing of time, the hostility became greater, and of course particularly after the destruction of Jerusalem. It is this post-70 escalation of bitterness more than anything that could possibly favor a post-70 date for the Gospel.[97]

When we turn to the provenance of the Gospel, we find that the evidence for Antioch, the majority opinion, is also surprisingly tenuous. Although nothing argues against Antioch, it seems at best to be only a good guess. What is basically required—a Hellenistic Jewish Christian community (or communities[98]) in close proximity to Jewish synagogues and Gentile-Christian congregations, in an urban setting— can be met by a number of Diaspora cities of the first century.[99]

The all-important tension and consequent existential realities that are so central to my hypothesis concerning the plight of Matthew's Jewish Christian community would unquestionably have been found in any place that the antagonists were both present. Indeed, the problems would have been ubiquitous in the early church. And the issues at stake involved theological questions of the greatest importance, questions such as the meaning of the OT, the person of Christ, the nature of salvation, the identity of the church, the purposes of God. Stanton has also put his finger upon the importance of the issue I am addressing: "for much of early Christianity, and for Matthew in particular, the relationship between Christianity and Judaism was the central problem for Christian theology."[100] The Gospel of

---

[97] "It was the destruction of Jerusalem and the temple which seems to have provoked the final crisis, and led to a complete breach between the two parties." A. Harnack, *Mission and Expansion*, 63.

[98] See now G. N. Stanton, "Revisiting Matthew's Communities," (n. 63 above). Stanton argues for "a loosely linked set of communities over a wide geographical area" (p. 12).

[99] Cf. G. N. Stanton, who after surveying a variety of options, concludes: "there is no shortage of possible cities from which the gospel may have originated" ("Origin and Purpose," 1942). Cf. J. D. Kingsbury's assessment of the state of the question in *Social History of the Matthean Community*, 264.

[100] "The Gospel of Matthew and Judaism," 284. Speaking of "Christianity's understanding of its relationship to ancient Judaism," Sandmel writes "It often seems to me that Christian commentators give far too little attention to this recurrent problem." *The First Christian Century*, 173.

Matthew, it seems to me, is a direct attempt to address this very question. And although initially it undoubtedly did grow out of a quite specific historical situation, knowledge of which is no longer available to us, there is also a magisterial and universal character to Matthew that transcends every specific time and place. The evangelist may well have meant his Gospel to speak authoritatively to a widespread and notorious problem in the important urban churches of the Roman Empire. We may have in Matthew a Gospel to the Jewish Christians, a universal "Gospel according to the Hebrews" of the kind that the early fathers speak, and which some were quite ready to identify with Matthew.[101]

VI. Matthew in the Context of First Century Christianity

The problems faced by the first readers of Matthew were, as we have argued, by no means unique in first century Christianity. Jewish Christians everywhere found themselves in basically the same plight, with perhaps only minor, local variations.[102] Signs of the great importance of the relationships between Christianity and Judaism, and the implied existential dilemma faced by those making the transition from the latter to the former, are found fairly commonly in other New Testament writings.[103] Although the answers or solutions suggested are by no means the same from writer to writer, nevertheless they point to a widely shared complex of problems, familiar to us already from Matthew. Only a few conspicuous examples can be mentioned here.

The initial readers of the Epistle to the Hebrews (perhaps to be dated as early as the late 60's) were very probably in a situation more

---

[101] E.g., Epiphanius who tells us that the Ebionites used the Gospel of Matthew, or a falsified and abridged version thereof, but called it "the Gospel of the Hebrews" (*Haer.* 30.3.7). Irenaeus and Jérome also connect some such document with Matthew. See P. Vielhauer in Hennecke-Schneemelcher, *New Testament Apocrypha* 1:117–165.

[102] "Wherever this new Jewish sect's belief or practice was perceived to be a threat to Jewish institutions and traditions its members would almost certainly come under pressure from their fellow Jews to remain loyal to their unique Jewish heritage." J. D. G. Dunn, "The Incident at Antioch (Gal. 2:11–12)," *JSNT* 12 (1983) 10; cf. 24.

[103] Speaking of Several N.T. writings, Jervell writes: "I can only see the *Sitz im Leben* for this lively discussion in what happened to the Jewish Christians after they had to live in Gentile surroundings, separated and isolated from their own people, still claiming to be Israel." *The Unknown Paul,* 39. Sandmel's study remains valuable: *The First Christian Century,* 143–96.

traumatic than, but similar to, what we have proposed as the life-setting of Matthew. They apparently experienced considerable distress from charges by the Jewish community that they were being disloyal to Judaism in having become Christians. They needed to be assured of the truth that Christianity fulfills the Old Testament and is faithful to the revelation of the past. This the author brilliantly accomplishes. Yet, at the same time, they had to learn that the truth of Christianity involves movement in the process of salvation-history which involves an inevitable degree of newness. Thus, for all the continuity with the past through the fulfillment stressed by the author, there is also in Hebrews an assertion of discontinuity (e.g. 8:6–13) much stronger than anything in Matthew. Without question Hebrews shows a more advanced attitude than Matthew at key points. This may also be seen in the attitude toward the Law reflected in 7:12, 19 and 10:1. These references, however, deal with the sacrificial cult and not with the righteousness that concerns Matthew. On the question of righteousness, Hebrews (cf. 8:10; 10:16) may not be altogether different from Matthew. Moreover even the discontinuity so apparent in Hebrews is to be understood as part of a greater, overarching continuity. The Hellenistic Jewish Christian community addressed by Hebrews faced the same kind of painful questions as did Matthew's community. It is clear that they were put under great pressure from their non-Christian Jewish kinsfolk and hence were sorely tempted to apostatize from their Christianity back into Judaism.

Even earlier than Hebrews, we find Paul, himself a Jewish Christian like the author and community of Matthew's Gospel, struggling with loyalties that reach both ways. But as the apostle to the Gentiles, Paul has clearly worked out a more radical stance on key issues than did Matthew. There is, nevertheless, a similarity not only in the questions faced by the evangelist and Paul in his letters, but also in what may be described as the basic Christian and Jewish loyalties shared by the two writers.[104] Paul too, for all his emphasis on the discontinuity caused by the newness of the gospel, is impelled to argue in his own way for the sense in which the Christian faith is true to the past work of God in Israel. He too is, so to speak, reaching in two directions.[105] Most

---

[104] The important and interesting work of Mohrlang has shown this. *Matthew and Paul*, esp. 42, 67f., 89–90, 106f, 123–24.

[105] Cf. Sandmel. *The First Christian Century*. 187.

interesting in this connection, of course, is his sensitive, accommodating relationship to the Jerusalem church.

Also revealing is Paul's sensitivity to the tension between Jewish and Gentile Christians in the church at Rome. Thus, when Paul writes to the Romans, a mixed church, he cautions the Gentiles not to boast over the Jews, reminding them that Israel is the holy root and they are like wild branches grafted onto the original olive tree by the grace of God (Rom 11:17–24). Undoubtedly the sensitivity Paul asks his Gentile readers to manifest was for the sake of the Jewish Christians in the Roman churches. They needed to hear that Israel continues to have special significance and that God has not only been faithful to his promises in the existence of a remnant (the Jewish believers), but that God in the future would not forget his people "as regards election they are beloved for the sake of their forefathers. For the gifts and the call of God are irrevocable" (Rom 11:28–29). Throughout Romans 9–11 Paul indicates his anguish for his Jewish kinsfolk who have not received the gospel. Paul, or at least a disciple of Paul, reminds the Ephesians that they as Gentiles, once separated from the nation of Israel, have now been made fellow citizens, fellow heirs with the saints and members of the household of God (Eph 2:19).

In a strikingly different way, the Epistle of James addresses Jewish Christians with concerns similar to those of Matthew. Continuity with Jewish tradition is clear both in the form and content of the ethical exhortation that forms the major part of James. In this connection, it is interesting to note the possible dependence upon the teachings of Jesus as found in the tradition underlying Matthew, if not upon the Gospel itself. Perhaps most significant for our consideration, however, is the insistence upon faith and works in obvious opposition to the Pauline extremists (probably Gentiles for the most part), and the author's use of the Pauline prooftext (Gen 15:6) in his own way to counter any antinomian tendencies. The Jewish Christian readers are thus taught the continuing importance of righteousness and the Law, which, however, can now be described paradoxically as the "law of liberty" (1:25). The author writes probably with the synagogue and the Gentile church both in mind.

We have considerable evidence in the New Testament then that, as to be expected, there was an ongoing animosity between Jews and Christian Jews with an ever-present need for the latter to defend their new faith as the legitimate fulfillment of the faith of Abraham, Moses, and the prophets. On the other hand, and perhaps less expected, we have evidence of tension between Jewish and Gentile Christians. Here the Jewish Christians had to learn to balance the specialness of Israel with the universality of the church which was, perhaps alarmingly, becoming increasingly composed of Gentiles.[106]

Thus the New Testament provides sufficient evidence of the difficult and trying social context in which Jewish Christians found themselves. We have furthermore seen that the puzzling data in the Gospel of Matthew can be explained if we assume that the evangelist and his readers were Jewish Christians who faced the kind of circumstances we have described. Reconstruction of a *Sitz im Leben* for any document from the remote past is necessarily speculative. In the present instance, however, we have been able to point to a variety of elements both in the contemporary context and within Matthew itself that support the present hypothesis. These elements not only include theological and historical factors, but social and psychological realities that were also undeniably a part of the total picture.

I would like to note, finally, two oft-cited passages in the Gospel of Matthew that indirectly point to the correctness of my hypothesis. In the first passage (9:16–17), which Matthew takes up from Mark (2:21–22), the evangelist affirms unhesitatingly the newness entailed by the Gospel: "No one puts a piece of unshrunk cloth on an old garment, for the patch tears away from the garment, and a worse tear is made. Neither is new wine put into old wineskins; if it is, the skins burst, and the wine is spilled, and the skins are destroyed; but new wine is put into fresh wineskins and so both are preserved." Matthew's redactional addition of the last words "and so both are preserved," found neither in Mark nor Luke, is congruent with his emphasis in the abiding validity of the Law. For Matthew, what is important is not only the new wine of the gospel, but the wineskins too, by which we are meant to understand forms of conduct leading to righteousness. The difference is that the wineskins are themselves necessarily new, i.e., the Law as definitively interpreted by Jesus the Messiah. So for Matthew is it important that both the new wine of the gospel and the new skins, the correctly understood meaning of Torah (against the mistaken Pharisees), be preserved. Here we see the evangelist reaching in both

---

[106] Much more evidence it seems to me, could be adduced from the New Testament along these lines. Hostility toward the Jews, for example, in many Jewish documents like the Fourth Gospel and the Apocalypse probably finds its explanation in life-situations similar to that faced by Matthew's community.

directions to stress continuity with Moses and Torah and yet at the same time to affirm the radical newness of the gospel.[107]

The second passage is an important one for Matthew's perspective and has been taken by many as having a special applicability to the evangelist himself. After introducing the disciples to the mystery of the Kingdom through a series of parables, Jesus says, "Therefore every scribe who has been trained for the kingdom of heaven is like a householder who brings out of his treasure what is new and what is old" (13:52).

The evangelist and his readers must have rejoiced to have this saying from Jesus. They saw themselves in this reference: *sopherim* (scholars of the Law) having been trained in the Kingdom.[108] But this entailed bridging between the old and the new—precisely what they as Jewish Christians recognized themselves to be doing. If they were caught in the pain of the transition they had a high responsibility both to their unbelieving Jewish kinsfolk and their newly found Gentile Christian brothers and sisters. It was to this sort of community, living at the turning point of the aeons, that the Gospel of Matthew was addressed.

---

[107] We might note that Matthew—even if he had known the saying—would hardly have taken up the words of Luke (found only there) at the end of the same pericope (Luke 5:39): "And no one after drinking old wine desires new; for he says, 'The old is good.'" This is more suitable in a Gentile accounting of Jewish unbelief in the gospel. For Matthew the new is better because it effectively preserves the old within it.

[108] See D. E. Orton, *The Understanding Scribe: Matthew and the Apocalyptic Ideal,* JSNTSS 25 (Sheffield: JSOT, 1989).

Chapter Two

The Temple Tax in Matthew 17:24–25 and the Principle of not Causing Offense

DAVID E. GARLAND

Matthew 17:24–27 presents the interpreter with a conundrum. The passage teaches that one is not to cause offense to "them"; but the problem is, who is in mind? The answer to this question is complicated by how this passage can be made to fit a variety of historical situations envisioned by interpreters.

I. The Historical Jesus

The incident could be a reminiscence from the historical ministry of Jesus. It is not improbable that collectors of the temple dues[1] asked

---

[1] The half-shekel was levied on all males from age twenty; women, slaves, Samaritans, and Gentiles were excluded. According to the *Mishna*, it was due by the beginning of Nisan, announcements went out on the first of Adar, and the money was collected on the fifteenth (*m. Šeqal.* 1:1). The tables of the money changers were set up on the 15th of Adar in the provinces and on the 25th in the temple to change money to ritually acceptable coins (*m. Šeqal.* 1:3). The half-shekel, translated *didramon* in Exod 30:13, Neh 10:32–33 (LXX), no longer existed; and two Roman denars or tetradrachms (Josephus *Ant.* 3.8.2 §§ 194–196) or a Tyrian shekel were substituted (*b. Bek.* 50b; *B. Qam.* 36b). According to *t. Ketub.* 13:3, "all money spoken of in the Torah is Tyrian money." Pledges were collected where a man lives, and it appears that communities had certain persons assigned to make the collections and forward them to Jerusalem (*m. Šeqal.* 2:1). See L. Kadman, "Temple Dues and Currency in Ancient Palestine in the light of Recent Discovered Coin-Hoards," *Israel Numismatic Bulletin* 1 (1962) 9–11, on the hoard of temple dues of approximately 7,800 men, presumably from Galilee, in 67 CE Str-B, 1:761, interpreted *m. Šeqal.* 1:3 to mean that they used distraint in forcing the tardy to pay; but this may have been only wishful thinking read into the past and not actual practice. This does indicate, however, that not everyone was prompt to pay.

The Diaspora communities also collected offerings and sent them to

whether Jesus paid this offering since his orthodoxy and his attitude toward the temple were open to suspicion, although their question, as it is phrased in the Greek, expects a positive answer that Peter readily gives. Because it has been commonly assumed that all Jews faithfully paid the temple tax and that to refuse would be tantamount to withdrawing from Judaism, some have argued that the question would not have been raised during the ministry of Jesus.[2] The evidence, however, belies this assumption. For various reasons, not all Jews did comply; and Jesus could have been suspected of being either indifferent or a conscientious objector.

After citing Deuteronomy 28:47–48, "because you did not serve . . . therefore shall you serve your enemy," the *Mekilta* records the lament of R. Johanan b. Zakkai after the debacle with Rome when he spied a girl picking out barley corns from the excrement of an Arab's horse. He attributed the present plight of Israel to its unwillingness to be subject to God, including, among other things, its unwillingness to pay a head tax to God, a *beka* a head (Exod 38:26), while paying a head tax of fifteen shekels to an enemy government (*Mek. Yithro Bahodesh* on Exod 19:1, Lauterbach, 2:192–193). Freyne took R. Johanan's reproach to mean "that the Galileans did not observe the institution with any great enthusiasm."[3] Whether one can legitimately infer this

---

Jerusalem (Josephus *Ant.* 14.7.2 §§ 110–111, 18.9.1 §§ 312–313; Philo *Spec. Leg.* I.76–78, *Heres.* 38; Cicero *Pro Flacco* 67), but one cannot be sure that all these references refer to the temple dues (see Philo *Gaium* 156).

2 F. W. Beare, *The Gospel According to Matthew* (San Francisco: Harper & Row, 1981) 371, who therefore claimed (372) that the situation envisioned in v. 24 was an artificial construction to set up the saying of Jesus. But see W. Horbury, "The Temple Tax," in *Jesus and the Politics of His Day* (ed. E. Bammel and C. F. D. Moule; Cambridge: Cambridge University Press, 1984) 265–286; and R. Bauckham, "The Coin in the Fish's Mouth," in *Gospel Perspectives. The Miracles of Jesus. Volume 6* (ed. D. Wenham and C. Blomberg; Sheffield: JSOT, 1986) 219–52, who make a case that this incident stemmed from the historical Jesus.

3 S. Freyne, *Galilee From Alexander the Great to Hadrian 323 B.C.E. to 135 C.E.* (Wilmington: Michael Glazier, 1980) 280. According to Freyne, it was not because of the Galileans' ignorance of the law but their conservative resistance to new religious developments that was behind any indifference to the payment of the half-shekel offering (281). The tax was, in his view, a comparatively recent development; and he speculated that, for agriculturalists, the produce of the land rather than money, especially Tyrian money, was a more suitable offering for the temple. See G. Theissen, "Lokal- und Sozialkolorit in der Geschichte von der syrophonikischen Frau (Mark 7:24–30)," *ZNW* 75 (1984) 202–25, on the antipathy of Galileans toward Tyre. See also, Horbury, "The Temple Tax," 281–82; and S. Mandell, "Who Paid the Temple Tax When the Jews Were Under Roman Rule? *HTR* 77 (1984) 223–32, who contended that not all Jews willingly paid the tax.

about Galileans is debatable; but this statement and the provision for an "Old Shekel dues" Shofar-chest in the temple (*m. Šeqal.* 6:5) suggest that, as one might expect when it comes to humans and money, not all were eager (or able) to pay their offering.

Other, more scrupulous Jews also did not pay the tax, but not out of laxity. They claimed special exemption from the tax on the pretext of some loophole found through the exegesis of the Scripture. Schweizer claimed, "even the monastic community at Qumran, which came into being as a protest against the temple at Jerusalem and its priesthood, paid the temple tax without objection."[4] But this misrepresents the case. In his much criticized edition of DJD V, Allegro argued that the half-shekel offering did not become an established institution until the end of the Hasmonean rule, about the time Qumran separated themselves from the temple and the rest of Israel. 4Q159 is an exposition of biblical legislation; and Allegro translated its explanation of the temple dues (2:6–7): "Concerning . . . the money of valuations that a man gives as ransom for his soul: half [a shekel]. Only once shall he give it during his lifetime."[5] On this interpretation, the shekel dues applied to every Israelite upon reaching his twentieth birthday. Liver cogently argued that the relation of the half-shekel in the Pentateuch to an annual tax for the support of the temple was a development after the sect had sequestered itself from the community and that this text was an objection to that institution.[6] However one reconstructs the history of the temple half-shekel, it would seem to be clear that the Dead Sea sectarians interpreted the Scripture so that they did not disobey it but nonetheless relieved themselves from the annual responsibility of temple dues. Vermes contended that this interpretation was a compromise solution to a dilemma:

---

[4] E. Schweizer, *The Gospel According to Matthew* (Atlanta: John Knox, 1975) 356. See also R. H. Mounce, *Matthew* (San Francisco: Harper & Row) 172.

[5] J. M. Allegro, "An Unpublished Fragment of Essene Halakah (4Q Ordinances)," *JSS* 6 (1961) 71–73. See J. M. Allegro and A. A. Anderson, DJD V (1968) 6–9; and corrections by J. Strugnell, "Notes en marge du volume V des 'Discoveries in the Judean Desert'," *RevQ* 7 (1970) 165, nn. 3–5; 175–79.

[6] J. Liver, "The Half-Shekel Offering in Biblical and Post-Biblical Literature," *HTR* 66 (1963) 196–97. See also Horbury, "The Temple Tax," 277–79. Against this reconstruction, see N. J. McEleney, "MT 17:24–27—Who Paid the Temple Tax? A Lesson in Avoiding Scandal," *CBQ* 38 (1976) 180–81.

> Having withdrawn from the sanctuary of Jerusalem because of their
> condemnation of the existing form of Temple worship, and being
> obliged to choose therefore between faithfulness to their convictions and
> obedience to the written law, the sectaries adopted a peculiar exegesis
> and decided to follow the letter of the Bible and pay a single installment
> of ransom money.[7]

This exegesis is not so peculiar, however, when it is realized that
Exodus 30:11–16, which was appealed to as the legal grounds for the
tax, nowhere specifies the frequency of it; and the tendency of 4Q159
is to clear a biblical text of ambiguity but never to contradict it.[8]

Mishna Šeqalim 1:3–5 provides evidence that priests also considered
themselves exempt from the half-shekel on the basis of Leviticus 6:16.
Mishna 4 contains a debate in Yavneh between R. Judah, citing Ben
Buchri, and R. Johanan b. Zakkai over the obligations of priests
concerning the half-shekel. R. Judah is said to have argued that any
priest who did not contribute did not commit any sin. The reasoning
appealed to Leviticus 6:23, "every meal offering of the priest shall be
wholly burnt and not eaten" (the homer, two loaves, and showbread).
These offerings, however, were provided from the shekel
contributions. If the priests contributed to this fund, these offerings
would have to be burnt and not eaten. But Scripture specifically
requires that they be eaten (Lev 6:16); therefore, the priests
apparently maintained they could not contribute to the fund. R.
Johanan countered that the priests interpreted Leviticus 6:16 to their
own benefit. The ruling is that the priests are liable;[9] the conclusion,
however, is, "no pledges may be taken from the priests, for the sake of
peace."[10]

---

[7] G. Vermes, "The Qumran Interpretation of Scripture in Its Historical Setting,"
Post Biblical Jewish Studies (Leiden: Brill, 1975) 42.

F. D. Weinert, "4Q159: Legislation for an Essene Community Outside of
Qumran?" *JJS* 5 (19) 179–207, made a case for 4Q159 originating in a Diaspora
community where Essene values were shared, and that it was later accepted at
Qumran.

[8] See Ibid., 187.

[9] The exemption of the priests is challenged in *y. Šeqal.* 1:46a, 63. R. Leszynsky,
Die Sadduzäer (Berlin: Mayer & Muller, 1912) 287, maintained that certain priests,
probably Sadducees, declined to pay the tax because the half-shekel tax had no
basis in the Torah. See also J. D. M. Derrett, "Peter's Penny: Fresh Light on
Matthew xvii 24–27," *Law in the New Testament* (London: Darton, Longman &
Todd, 1970) 250–51.

[10] The phrase "kings of the earth" is found in the royal Psalms and refers to
earthly rulers who stand in opposition to the king of heaven (Pss 2:2, 76:13 [12],

Jesus could very well have been another conscientious objector; and scholars have come up with various explanations to penetrate his thinking on this issue. The "sons" in the analogy are the king's physical sons,[11] and it argues that kings dun their subjects for taxes, not members of the immediate family.[12] Bauckham contends that the fatherhood of God was central to Jesus' teaching and that he regarded Israel to be God's sons (see 8:12).[13] Jesus objected to the temple tax because it made God into an oppressive despot who exacts a religious tax of his people already encumbered by burdensome civil taxes. The premise of the argument is that God treats his people as sons, not subjects, and does not exact tribute from them. The conclusion is that it is inappropriate—a distortion of God's true character as a loving Father and provider—to raise money for the temple sacrifices by taxation. The miracle confirms this: "Instead of demanding a temple shekel from Peter, God actually provides him with one."[14] If Bauckham

---

89:27 [28], 102:16 [15], 138:4, 148:11; see also Acts 4:26; Rev 1:5, 6:15; 17:2, 18; 18:3, 9; 19:19; 21:24). C. H. Dodd, *Historical Tradition in the Fourth Gospel* (Cambridge: Cambridge University Press, 1963) 381, n. 4, observed: "The 'king of flesh and blood' is a stock character in the rabbinic parables designed to illustrate the dealings of God with men." See also A. Schlatter, *Der Evangelist Matthäus* (Stuttgart: Calwer, 1933) 540. It probably has that same connotation here and does not have some particular system of government in view. It is akin to the phrase, "rulers of the Gentiles" that appears in Matt 20:25. The mention of kings of the earth would immediately bring to mind the heavenly king; and the analogy implies, if this is the case with earthly kings, then how much more so with the heavenly king.

[11] The "sons" would not represent the king's own nation while the "strangers" represent subjugated nations since kings did not exempt their own nation from taxes. See Bauckham, "Coin in the Fish's Mouth," 221–22.

[12] This assumption that kings and their families do not pay taxes to themselves is the basis for R. Johanan's parable in *b. Sukk.* 30a. The human king does what is highly unusual by paying the custom tax which belongs ultimately to him. He does this to set an example for all travelers in hopes that they will not try to evade their tax obligation. The *sugya* concerns invalid offerings; and the parable is intended to show that offerings presented to God that are stolen are invalid even though, technically, everything belongs to God and cannot be considered stolen.

[13] C. Montefiore, *The Synoptic Gospels* (London: Macmillan, 1927) 243, believed that Jesus was thinking of himself and his disciples as the true sons, not all Jews. A. Plummer, *An Exegetical Commentary on the Gospel of Matthew* (London: Robert Scott, 1915) 245, contended that Jesus was aware of his unique relationship with God as his Father and considered himself exempt from any obligation to pay the tax.

[14] Bauckham, "Coin in the Fish's Mouth," 224. A similar conclusion is reached independently by U. Luz, *Das Evangelium nach Matthäus (Mt 8–17)* (EKKNT 1/2; Braunschweig: Benziger; Neukirchen-Vluyn: Neukirchener, 1990) 534. W. D. Davies and D. C. Allison, Jr. *The Gospel According to Saint Matthew* (ICC; Edinburgh:

is correct, then Jesus would have sided with a Sadducean position recorded in the Talmud that the *tamid* should be funded by the free-will offerings of individuals over against the Pharisees' advocacy of the cost coming from the half-shekel fund to which all contributed.[15]

The major weakness of Bauckham's reconstruction is his assumption that the half shekel was a compulsory tax. There is no evidence of a bureaucratic setup in Palestine which kept records of those who did or did not contribute, let alone enforce payment; and Philo presents the so-called temple tax in a quite different light. The contribution, he says, is called "ransom money," and

> The donors bring them cheerfully and gladly, expecting that the payment will give them release from slavery or healing of diseases and the enjoyment of liberty fully secured and also complete preservation from danger (*Spec. Leg.* I.77).

He also argues that what is donated to the temple is given in a spirit quite different from that of cities making payment to their potentates.

> The cities pay under compulsion and reluctantly and groan under the burden. They look askance at tax collectors as general agents of destruction. They trump up different excuses to suit the occasion, and when they discharge the appointed dues and assessments they do so without regard to the time limits allowed. But our people pay gladly and cheerfully. They anticipate the demand, abridge the time limits and think that they are not giving but receiving. And so at each of the yearly seasons they make their contributions with benediction and thankfulness, men and women alike, and with a zeal and readiness which needs no prompting and an ardour which no words can describe (*Spec. Leg.* I.143–144).

While this fervor may be overstated, Philo does not perceive monies contributed to the temple to be some kind of compulsory tax.[16]

In spite of Jesus' declaration of his freedom from the responsibility of contributing the half shekel, he decided to submit to this Jewish custom so as not to offend "them." The "them" could be any number of groups. They could be disciples who had not yet been emancipated

---

T. & T. Clark, 1991) 535, concur with Bauckham's interpretation.

[15] On this debate, see *b. Menah.* 65a. See further, L. Finkelstein, *The Pharisees* (Philadelphia: Jewish Publication Society of America, 1938) 2:683; H. Montefiore, "Jesus and the Temple Tax," *NTS* 11 (1964) 68–71; and S. Légasse, "Jesus et l'impôt de Temple (Matthieu 17, 24–27)" *ScEs* 24 (1972) 376–77. The dominance of the Pharisees' position is reflected by Josephus *Ant.* 3.10.1 § 237.

[16] It is strange if the tax is compulsory that the collectors should ask, "Does he pay?" rather than insist that he pay.

from Jewish legal scruples,[17] or others, who might learn of Jesus' non-compliance without being able to comprehend or accept the reasons behind it. They would be repelled by Jesus' apparent impiety and would then be unable to grasp the truth about Jesus.[18] Or, it may refer to religious rivals, such as the Pharisees, whom Jesus did not want to provide with further evidence to counteract his ministry. If this account is historically accurate, it is interesting that Jesus' response was based on much the same principle that the rabbis endorsed in the reported dispute with the priests over the temple dues. They refrained from demanding payment "for the ways of peace" (*spny drky šlm, m. Šeqal.* 1:3).[19] Jesus refrained from withholding payment, for the ways of peace.

However plausible or implausible these explanations might be, they do not elucidate why Matthew alone chose to preserve the story or why he included it where he did.[20] Therefore, it has been more widely held by scholars that the incident was created or conserved to speak to the special circumstances of the Evangelist and his audience than to

---

[17] See H. B. Green, *The Gospel According to Matthew* (Oxford: Oxford University Press, 1975) 158.

[18] Ibid. G. Stählin, *Skandalon: Untersuchungen zur Geschichte eines biblischen Begriffs* (BFCT 24; Gütersloh: C. Bertelmann, 1930) 249, contended that when the Jews who are true to the law hear of his stance toward the tax they would want to hear nothing more of him and his message. It would prevent them from believing in him. R. Banks, *Jesus and the Law in the Synoptic Tradition* (SNTSMS 28; Cambridge: Cambridge University Press, 1975) 92–94, believed that the issue is "Jesus' willingness or otherwise to observe a custom that is honoured by the majority of his fellow Jews" (94) and argued that since the questioners are not identified as scribes and Pharisees, they are not antagonists. Jesus' response reflects his unwillingness to offend those who were not necessarily antagonistic to his mission as distinguished from his determination to oppose those who, on legalistic grounds, were (see 15:12–14). This, Banks claimed, indicates that for Jesus it is not the practice involved "but the attitude of the people involved" which determines his reaction to them. McEleney, "MT 17:24–27," 186, offered that it could refer to those who would be offended by the messianic pretensions behind Jesus' refusal to pay. Mounce, *Matthew*, 172 thought that Jesus feared setting "a bad example for others." Derrett, "Peter's Penny," 256–58, interpreted *skandalizein* to mean "cause to sin" and argued that Jesus sought to save the collectors from committing a sin by collecting the tax from someone who was exempt as one of God's dependents. To use Derrett's own words, this is an "extraordinary conclusion" (257).

[19] This principle urged rabbis to be lenient in spite of their scruples and appears elsewhere in *m. Git.* 5:8–9; *t. Git.* 3:14; *b. Git.* 59a–61a.

[20] J. P Meier, *A Marginal Jew. Re-thinking the Historical Jesus. Volume Two: Mentor, Message, and Miracles* (New York: Doubleday, 1994) 975, n. 21, criticizes Bauckham for failing to pay enough attention to Matthean redaction and theology.

report an event from the ministry of Jesus.[21] It is then assumed that the issue addressed has to do either with the question of the responsibilities of Jewish Christians regarding the half-shekel for the temple before its destruction, or with the problem presented after 70 CE by Rome's appropriation of the offerings as a war indemnity.[22] Whichever option is chosen, many have argued that Matthew included this account to provide precise moral guidance on the question of the payment of this tax. Davies reasoned that the first possibility best fits the emphasis on avoiding offense (to Jewry); the second best fits the reference to the kings of the earth.[23]

II. The Situation of the Jewish Christian Church

The story could have had its origins in a debate of the Jewish Christian community about its present obligations to the temple.[24] One can imagine conservative Jewish Christians (such as James) having to reconcile their faith that Jesus had offered the atoning sacrifice for the forgiveness of sins (26:28) with their attachment to the temple. They believed themselves to be uniquely related to God through their relationship to Christ. They also may have believed that they were free from cultic restraints because of that relationship. It is possible that this freedom had to be moderated by the consideration that they were surrounded by Jews who are becoming increasingly suspicious and hostile.

The story confirms the freedom of Christians from the half-shekel requirement but urges compliance as a policy to keep from causing offense to unbelieving Jews.[25] On the one hand, failure to pay the dues

---

[21] See W. D. Davies, *The Setting of the Sermon on the Mount* (Cambridge: Cambridge University Press, 1963) 390. E. Lohmeyer, *Das Evangelium des Matthäus* (MeyerK; 3d ed.; Göttingen: Vandenhoeck & Ruprecht, 1962) 275, contended that the passage teaches through the exemplary word and deed of Jesus and answers a practical question of the community.

[22] Davies, *Setting*, 390.

[23] Ibid.

[24] So Allen, *Matthew*, 191; B. W. Bacon, *Studies in Matthew* (New York: Henry Nolt, 1930) 228; R. Bultmann, *The History of the Synoptic Tradition* (New York: Harper & Row, 1968) 34–5; K. F. Nickle, *The Collection* (SBT 48, Naperville: Alec R. Allenson, 1966) 96; W. Grundmann, *Das Evangelium nach Matthäus* (HKNT 1; 5th ed.; Berlin: Evangelische Verlaganstalt, 1981) 409–10; M. D. Goulder, *Midrash and Lection in Matthew* (London: SPCK, 1974) 396; Schweizer, *Matthew* 356; and Beare, *Matthew*, 371.

[25] Schweizer, *Matthew*, 355–357, commented that the point of the incident

would have been the final proof to unsympathetic Jews that the Christians were apostates and had decided to withdraw completely from the community.[26] On the other hand, payment of the tax would have enabled them to remain within the Jewish religious community and would also have helped to avoid conflict and persecution.[27] Grundmann suggested that the account therefore had an example character for how the community of Christ should relate to the Jewish synagogue.[28] And it is possible that this attitude reflects the quietistic community, envisioned by Farmer, that strove to preserve a sense of solidarity within the group over against the world which, though hostile to the group, cannot fault its good works, or, we might add, its Jewishness.[29] The church is then instructed not to cause unnecessary friction over such non-essentials as the temple dues and that it "must deal kindly with the orthodox Jewish world, and have patience with it,"[30] not because of a required loyalty to the temple and the law but because of loyalty to a higher principle of not causing offense to others. This approach may also have been motivated, as Hummel insisted, by a concern that a refusal to pay the tax would finally close the door to any further mission among the Jews.[31]

"combines the fundamental liberty of the community of Jesus with a readiness to follow the prevailing norms of Jewish law in externals like payment of the Temple tax." It emphasizes "the total and fundamental freedom of the Christian community from the Jewish Temple community while maintaining the principle that one must not offend one's Jewish contemporaries in matters that are not central to the faith." He compared this to the prayer that they not have to flee on the Sabbath (24:20; compare Mark 13:18).

[26] A. Schlatter, *Matthäus*, 541, asserted that the renunciation of the temple was for every Jew the final proof of godlessness. Refusal to pay the half-shekel tax would be equivalent to deliberate withdrawal from the religious community of Judaism. See Beare, *Matthew*, 371–72.

[27] G. Barth, "Matthew's Understanding of the Law," in *Tradition and Interpretation in Matthew* (Philadelphia: Westminster, 1963) 92, commented on 24:20 that the concern about flight on the Sabbath has more to do with fear of the dangers from hate-charged Jews than with fear of sin. He cited E. Hirsch, *Die Frühgeschichte des Evangeliums* (Tübingen: J. C. B. Mohr [Paul Siebeck], 1941) 2:313, who, as an ardent Nazi, ironically wrote: "A Christian congregation fleeing on the Sabbath would have been as recognizable in Palestine as a spotted dog." Barth suggested that the desire to pay the temple tax to give no offense may have been attributable to a similar fear of conspicuousness.

[28] Grundmann, *Matthäus*, 409.

[29] W. Farmer, "Matthew and the Sermon on the Mount," *SBLASP* 25 (1986) 66.

[30] Derrett, "Peter's Penny," 261.

[31] R. Hummel, *Die Auseinandersetzung zwischen Kirche und Judentum im*

Some have drawn conclusions about the date and setting of Matthew by assuming that the pericope mirrors the situation of the community. Gundry argued from this incident that Matthew "must be writing before A. D. 70."[32] Bornkamm did not date the gospel this early but did insist in one of his first essays on the gospel that this pericope unmistakably supported Matthew's understanding of the church as clearly conscious of its own special position but as still attached to Judaism because they do not claim any exemption from the temple tax.[33] According to this view, the passage reflects a struggle within its own walls—a struggle of those on the edge of heresy to maintain some semblance of status within Judaism.

If this passage has in view the temple dues, it must have originated sometime before the destruction of Jerusalem. But if one believes that Matthew was composed after that catastrophe, to what would this pericope apply? The rabbis themselves asserted that the laws concerning the shekel dues were valid only while the temple stands (*m. Šeqal.* 8:7). And where would Gentile Christians—assuming that some had become a part of the church—stand in this debate since their contributions would not have been acceptable? Many scholars, while conceding that the story probably evolved while the temple was still functioning, have postulated that it must have been preserved by Matthew to answer a quite different question from that of paying dues to support the temple in Jerusalem.

III. The Tax to the Fiscus Iudaicus

As a token of the subjection of Israel's God to Rome after the failed revolt, payment of the temple half-shekel was diverted by the

---

Matthäusevangelium (BEvT 33: Munich: Chr. Kaiser, 1963) 105; see also D. R. A. Hare, *The Theme of Jewish Persecution of Christians in the Gospel According to Matthew* (SNTSMS 6; Cambridge: Cambridge University Press, 1967) 142; Légasse, "Jésus et l'impôt," 372; and R. H. Gundry, *Matthew: A Commentary on His Literary and Theological Art* (Grand Rapids: Wm. B. Eerdmans, 1982) 356–57, who maintained that Matthew wanted to portray Peter as a paradigm of obedient discipleship in paying the temple tax in order that Jewish Christians might not cause unbelieving Jews to reject the gospel.

[32] Gundry, *Matthew*, 357.

[33] G. Bornkamm, "End-Expectation and Church in Matthew," *Tradition and Interpretation in Matthew* (Philadelphia: Westminster, 1963) 19–20, but his view changes in "Die Binde- und Lösegewalt in der Kirche des Matthäus," *Geschichte und Glaube* (BEvT 53; Munich: Chr. Kaiser, 1971) 2:37–50. In this article, the community is cut off from the Jewish community; and the key passage is 18:19–20 where the community is gathered around Jesus, not the Torah.

Emperor Vespasian to the coffers of the temple of Jupiter on the Capitol.[34] This was an addition to all existing taxes (such as the *tributum capitis* and any duties), and it served to humiliate the Jews further by forcing them to send what was formerly considered sacred money[35] to the principle, idolatrous sanctuary of the enemy, where victorious Roman generals returned in ostentatious triumph. A treasury board, the *fiscus Iudaicus*, was set up to administer collection of the tax.[36] The tax itself was identified as simply the *didrachmon*[37] or as the *timē dēnarion duo Ioudaiōw*[38] or *Ioudaichon telesma*.[39]

Prior to the fall of Jerusalem, those who were considered obligated to pay the temple half-shekel were males, ages 20–50. These contributions were voluntary and were sent out of a sense of piety. Under Vespasian the tax was now compulsory. The age limit appears to have been extended from ages three to sixty-two; and women[40] and slaves were also assessed, the tax for slaves being paid by their

---

[34] Josephus *J. W.* 7.6.6 § 218. Although the tax primarily served to reinforce the subjugation of the Jews, it was also happy timing for the Romans since the proceeds were used to rebuild the temple of Jupiter which had burned during street fighting in December 69 CE. M. S. Ginsberg, "Fiscus Iudaicus," *JQR* 21 (1930–31) 285–86, postulated that after the war Vespasian preferred to conserve the privileges of the Jews than eliminate Judaism and used this tax to increase revenue for a depleted treasury, but S. W. Baron, *A Social and Religious History of the Jews* (New York: Columbia Univ., 1952) II: 106, proposed that it also served to quieten the restless tribes on the Rhine and the Loire who had seen the destruction of the supreme sanctuary as an omen of Rome's impending demise (see Tacitus *Ann.* 4.54). See also S. L. Wallace, *Taxation in Egypt: From Augustus to Diocletian* (Princeton: Princeton Univ., 1938) 172–74.

[35] See Philo *Heres* 186, *to didrachmon to hagion*; and Josephus *Ant.* 16.6.3 § 166, *chrēmata hiera.*

[36] Ginsberg, "Fiscus," 286–287 and E. M. Smallwood, *The Jews Under Roman Rule* (SJLA 20; Leiden: E. J. Brill, 1976) 375, compared it to the *fiscus Asiaticus* and the *fiscus Alexandrinus.* See also Rostowzew, "Fiscus," PW 6/2. 2402–04; and I. A. F. Bruce, "Nerva and the *Fiscus Iudaicus*," *PEQ* 96 (1964) 35. Mandell, "The Temple Tax," 228, however, argued that the *fiscus Iudaicus* simply refers to the bureau that collected the variety of taxes placed on the Jews and should not be identified only with the specific temple tax.

[37] Josephus, *Ant.* 18.9.1 § 312; Suetonius, *Dom.* 12.2; Dio Cassius, *Hist.* 66.7.2; see also Origen, *Epist ad Afric.* 20 (14).

[38] *CPJ* II. nos. 160–168, 170–182, 183a-188.

[39] *CPJ* II. nos. 181, 183, 189–214, 216–230, 421; III. no. 460. See the discussion in Tcherikover, 112–113; and M. Stern, *Greek and Latin Authors on Jews and Judaism* (Jerusalem: Israel Academy of Sciences and Humanities, 1980) 2:129.

[40] On the liability of women, see *CPJ* II, 169, 171, 218, 223, 421.

masters.[41] Smallwood observed that this not only presented an economic burden, particularly for the large family; but, "to Jews of all social and economic levels it will have formed a psychological burden, marking them out as members of a defeated race punished for their nationality."[42] Tcherikover likened it to the "'yellow spot' on Jews' clothes in the Middle ages; it marked the Jews as a dangerous and seditious people."[43] No doubt it also vexed the pious to know that they were contributing to idolatry.

The question that requires our attention is, whom did the Romans consider obligated to pay the tax? Josephus says that it was imposed on "all Jews wherever they resided" (*J. W.* 7.6.6 § 218). This would mean, as most scholars have assumed, that it included all Diaspora Jews even though they were not involved in the revolt.[44] Cassius Dio (*Epit.* 66, 7, 2), however, states that the tax was imposed on the Jews who "continued to observe their ancestral customs" (*ta patria autōn*), that is, practicing Jews. This could be taken to imply that non-practicing Jews were exempt. Smallwood explained the apparent discrepancy between Josephus and Cassius Dio by claiming, "Josephus implicitly excludes apostates by his reference to the former Temple tax, which such people will surely have ceased to pay as a sign of their dissociation from Judaism."[45] She assumed that for Josephus "all Jews everywhere" meant all practicing Jews, not simply those of Jewish stock. The tax was compulsory only for those Jews who wished to continue to practice their religion, and these needed to register with the proper authorities.[46] Mandell argued that the primary data do not support the assumption that all Jews were required to pay the tax because they

---

[41] See Wallace, *Taxation*, 171–72.

[42] Smallwood, *Roman Rule*, 374; see also "Domitian's Attitude Toward the Jews and Judaism," *Classical Philology* 51 (1956) 2–3.

[43] *CPJ* 1:81; see also A. Carlebach, "Rabbinic References to Fiscus Iudaicus," *JQR* 66 (1975–76) 61.

[44] Ginsberg, "Fiscus," 285, maintained that the tax was paid annually by the Jews in all parts of the empire "for the right to practice their religion."

[45] Smallwood, *Roman Rule*, 371. Mandell, "The Temple Tax," 224, n. 6, maintained that *ontes Ioudaioi* in *J. W.* 7.6.6 § 218 means "to live as a Jew."

[46] P. Keresztes, "The Jews, The Christians, and Emperor Domitian," *Vigillae Christianae* 27 (1973) 3. He declared that the privileged *gens Iudaeorum* ceased to exist with the destruction of Jerusalem, and Judaism then became a *religio licita*. It was a small price to pay for the license to continue to be exempt from civic cults and to live by their own rules. It was something denied Christians. Tertullian envied the Jews' privilege calling it "liberty through taxation" (*Apol.* 18.8).

were Jews.[47] No evidence suggests, for example, that Samaritans or Jewish Christians were liable. She believed that it was a religious tax imposed on those "deemed responsible for the revolt," and that it was not a national or race tax. She contended that it was levied only on one sect of Jews, what she called the Pharisaic Rabbinic, who followed the paternal customs and lived a Jewish life.[48] The surviving evidence of tax receipts from Egypt does not tell against this conclusion;[49] those who paid the tax there could be identified as those who wished to continue their practice of Judaism. The ready assumption that Jewish Christians, let alone Christians, were also liable to this tax from its inception because they were Jewish or Jewish-like must therefore be questioned.

Evidence for the reign of Domitian is limited, but it does suggest that he engineered greater severity in the administration of the tax on the Jews. Suetonius recalls the strict enforcement of the tax and an incident of suspected tax evasion:

> Besides other taxes, that on the Jews was levied with the utmost rigour, and those prosecuted who without publicly acknowledging that faith yet lived as Jews as well as those who concealed their origin and did not pay the tribute levied on the people. I recall being present in my youth when the person of a man of ninety was examined to see whether he was circumcised (*Dom.* 12.2).

One can infer from this that Suetonius believed all Jews to be liable to the tax under Domitian and that those suspected of trying to conceal their faith (*inprofessi Iudaicum viverant vitam*) or their Jewishness (*dissimilata origene imposita genti tributa non pependissent*), betokened by their circumcision, were mercilessly interrogated to the point of being strip searched. The latter could include apostate Jews and Jewish Christians. It is probable, then, that Domitian, in the interest of replenishing a depleted treasury (see Suetonius *Dom.* 12.1), extended liability to the tax to all Jews whether they practiced the religion of the fathers or not.[50]

---

[47] S. Mandell, "The Temple Tax," 223–32. See also, Keresztes, "The Jews," 3.

[48] Mandell, "The Temple Tax," 232.

[49] Mandell, "The Temple Tax," 224–25, challenged the identification of the Edfu *Ostraka* and the Arsinoe Papyrus with the *didrachmon* because the amounts on the receipts differ from one another. These discrepancies, however, have been explained by Wallace, *Taxation*, 170–71, whom she did not cite.

[50] See Smallwood, "Domitian's Attitude," 4; and Keresztes, "The Jews," 3–7. C. Hemer, "The Edfu *Ostraka* and the Jewish Tax," *PEQ* 105 (1973) 11, allowed it as a

The coin legend on *sestertii* minted during the reign of Nerva, FISCI IVDAICI CALVMNIA SVBLATA S.C., surrounding a date palm, a symbol of Judea,[51] is another problematic piece of the tax's tangled history; but it sheds more light on the situation under Domitian. The best explanation of the legend is that is proclaims an end to the kind of abuse hinted at by Suetonius that occurred in Domitian's reign. It does not proclaim an end to the tax,[52] nor does it refer to the degrading procedures connected with the collection of the tax. And one would hardly expect the minting of a coin to celebrate the relief of a minority that was widely despised.[53] Cassius Dio reports that when Nerva became emperor he forbade accusations against others of *asebeia* (lack of respect for the gods, including the emperor) and for adopting a Jewish mode of life, and many former informers were condemned to death (*Epit.* 68.1.2). The *calumnia* probably pertains to the terroristic denunciations of people to the office of the *fiscus Iudaicus. Calumnia* means wrongful accusation or perversion of

---

possibility but recognized that the evidence is inconclusive. L. A. Thompson, "Domitian and the Jewish Tax," *Historia* 31 (1982) 329–42, argues that it was a systematic attempt to tax people who previously were not liable, apostates from Judaism and circumcised men who were not Roman citizens. M. Goodman, *Who Was a Jew?* (Oxford: Oxford Centre for Postgraduate Hebrew Studies, 1989) 14–15; and "Nerva, The *Fiscus Judaicus* and Jewish Identity," *JRS* 79 (1989) 40–2, agrees with Thompson. He points out that since Domitian had made conversion to Jewish ways illegal, Gentiles would be accused of neglect of the gods of the state and executed, not required to pay the tax. The strict enforcement would have singled out Jews who have given up their public association with Judaism. M. H. Williams, "Domitian, the Jews and the Judaizers'—A Simple Matter of Cupiditas and Maiestas?" *Historia* 39 (1990) 196–211, argues, however, that the new severity stemmed from Domitian's deep antagonism toward the Jews, their converts and sympathizers.

[51] H. Mattingly and E. A. Sydenham (ed.) *The Roman Imperial Coinage* (London: Spink and Son, 1962) 2:227–28, (Nerva nos. 58, 72, 82).

[52] G. D. Kilpatrick, *The Origins of the Gospel According to St. Matthew* (Oxford: Clarendon, 1946) 42, wrongly claimed (so also Beare, *Matthew,* 373) that the tax was abolished by Nerva and that it must have been obsolete because the rabbis at the beginning of the second century were confused about the details. The tax was still in existence later on as evidenced by the document at Karanis from the reign of Trajan (*CPJ* no. 460). See also Tertullian *Apol,* 18.8; Origen *Epist. ad Afric.* 20 (14); and the assessments of Bruce, "Nerva," 41; Hemer, "Edfu," 10–11; and E. Schürer, *The History of the Jewish People in the Age of Jesus Christ* (rev. and ed. G. Vermes, et. al.; Edinburgh: T. & T. Clark, 1986) 3/1:123 n. 67. Ginsberg, "Fiscus," 290–91, argued for the possibility that the tax was finally abolished by Julian (see *Epist.* 486a), but the evidence does not warrant any conclusion about when the tax ended.

[53] Hemer, "Edfu," 6.

justice.[54] The victims of these denunciations would not be Jews, who would not be wrongfully accused of being Jews and who were quite safe when they had paid the tax, but those who were quite unattached to Judaism and were falsely accused by enemies.[55] Since coins were used for propaganda purposes like stamps are today, Nerva probably minted the coins as part of a public relations campaign to evoke popular applause and to contrast his more enlightened reign with the terrors associated with Domitian.[56] One no longer needed to fear accusations of being a tax evading Jew guilty of *maiestas* or the sycophancy associated with these indictments.

It is difficult to argue convincingly that this pericope was originally composed to meet the situation of Christians now required to pay the tax to Rome. First, as Hummel has pointed out, Jesus' response in 17:25 gives a religious basis for the freedom of the sons from the tax.[57] He understood it to mean that because of the disciples' special relationship to the king as sons they are exempt from the king's taxes.

---

[54] P. G. W. Glare (ed.), *Oxford Latin Dictionary* (Oxford: Clarendon, 1982) 261; and Schürer, *History*, 3/1:123 n. 67.

[55] Hemer, "Edfu," 11, emphasized the literal force of *calumnia* and linked it with the activities of the *delatores* in the later years of Domitian. He wrote:

> When payment of the Jewish tax constituted a *de facto* license to practice Judaism, a religion exempted from the imperial cult, and when also Domitian was enforcing emperor worship as a test of loyalty, an irregular association with Judaism could have been construed as treasonable "atheism."

> Christians and Gentile adherents of Judaism may have been the prime victims. But when the *delatores* were unleashed no man was safe.

He suggested that the coin-legend of Nerva has the emotional connotation of the *delator* in mind and argued that the Jewish tax was convenient grounds for bringing charges against anyone. If one was charged with living a Jewish life *inprofessi*, it would be difficult to disprove. Therefore, Hemer contended that the victims of the *delator* were Gentiles who did not pay the Jewish tax but were accused of Jewish affiliations: "The charge might be unfounded slander, or primarily directed at those whose claims to be regarded as Jews were disputable or legally ambiguous." If this is correct, Christians would have been ready targets for denunciation of treasonable tax evasion. See also Smallwood, "Domitian's Attitude," 4–5; and Kerestzes, "The Jews," 5–7.

For the many other conjectures to explain the legend, see Bruce, "Nerva," 41–5.

[56] See Bruce, "Nerva," 45; Thompson, "Domitian," 341–42; and P. Richardson and M. B. Shukster, "Barnabas, Nerva, and the Yavnean Rabbis," *JTS* 34 (1983) 44. Goodman, *Who Was a Jew?*, 16, and "Nerva," 44, contended that the reform defined a Jew by religion alone and not by race.

[57] Hummel, *Die Auseinandersetzung*, 103–04.

This would only be applicable to the disciples if the king is presumed to be God; and this would only be pertinent to the issue of taxes if it were speaking of some religious tax such as the one intended for the support of the temple. It hardly applies to the later situation of the church when the tax was directed to Rome. In that situation, it is an anachronism.[58] Second, the Romans would be something more than scandalized by a refusal to pay the assessment. It is hard to imagine how Jews would be scandalized by this failure to pay a tax to Rome by those who are probably already judged to be apostates.

Montefiore thought that he could trace the origin of this incident to a controversy in Jesus' life between the Pharisees and Sadducees about the tax but held that Matthew used this inherited tradition to advise Christians to pay the tax to the *fiscus Iudaicus* to avoid creating a scandal with the Roman authorities.[59] Beare, on the other hand, argued that the passage is a vestige of an earlier debate in the church which resolved that Jewish Christians would continue to pay the temple tax; it was now used by Matthew to answer the question whether Jewish Christians would accept the obligation laid upon all other Jews to pay this tax for the Roman cult.[60] Davies suggested that the Romans are in view in 17:24–27, because it follows immediately after the passion prediction in 17:22–23. In the other passion predictions in Matthew, the elders, chief priests, and scribes are

---

[58] Ibid.

[59] Montefiore, "Jesus and the Temple Tax," 60–71. He expressed the opinion that the pericope about the tribute money did not provide sufficient guidance since "it was a secular, not a religious obligation; and it was binding on all non-Romans without exception." According to Montefiore's reconstruction, the Jewish Christians had "the worst of both worlds." They were not regarded as members of the *religio licita* of Judaism and so could not enjoy the privileges that they were afforded. On the other hand, they were not exempted from the tax levied on all Jews (64). Jesus sets the example: They must pay the tax to the Roman authorities not because they were legally bound to pay but to avoid the scandal which might be caused by refusal (65). See also R. Eisler, *Orpheus—The Fisher* (London: J. M. Watkins, 1921) 95–100; McNeile, *Matthew*, 257–58; and Bacon, *Studies*, 228.

[60] Beare, *Matthew*, 373. Beare claimed that this is "undoubtedly" the case, but one cannot say this without providing some evidence. "Undoubtedly" really means here presumably. There is no evidence that his question arose for Jewish Christians except that this text is interpreted to reflect that debate; it is a circular argument.

P. Perkins, "Taxes in the New Testament," *JRE*, 12 (1984) 189, suggested that the question addressed is, how far Christians should become implicated in the plight of the fellow Jews. Payment of the tax by Christians would be a gesture of solidarity with the Jews.

specifically mentioned (16:21, 20:17–19). In 17:22–23, however, Jesus says that he will be betrayed into "the hands of men" who will kill him; and this, Davies believed, refers to the Romans. He then reasoned that this would have led to the question, what attitude should the Christian have toward Rome? This account in 17:24–27 gives the answer that though Christians are not legitimately obligated to pay, they are to comply to prevent scandal with the Romans.[61]

The investigation of the history of the Roman appropriation of the temple dues makes it unwise to conclude that Jewish or Gentile Christians were liable from the beginning since the evidence indicates that those who were considered obligated to pay were those who wished to continue to observe the customs of the fathers—to practice Judaism. This would not have included Christians.[62] The outbreak of violence against Christians in Rome in 64 CE indicates that the Romans were quite able to differentiate Christians from Jews, because the Jews were not targets of the persecution. If this passage were intended to provide guidance to Christians regarding the tax to the *fiscus Iudaicus*, it must be set in the time of Domitian's rigorous administration of the tax when Christians may have been subject to false accusations of tax evasion. But no indications exist elsewhere in Matthew's gospel that the Evangelist is particularly concerned about relations of Christians with the Roman government. Therefore, the Roman appropriation of the temple tax does not appear to be the backdrop for understanding why this pericope was included in the gospel

IV. Taxes in General

Cassidy contended that the tax collectors in the story were taking up a civil tax of two drachma that has been confused with the temple

---

[61] Davies, *Setting*, 391.

[62] D. J. Harrington, *The Gospel of Matthew* (Sacra Pagina; Collegeville: Liturgical, 1991) 262, maintains that this episode allowed Jewish Christians to hold on to their claims about Jesus, to retain their standing as Jews, and to keep out of trouble with the Romans. But the conclusions of E. A. Judge, "Judaism and the Rise of Christianity: A Roman Perspective," *TynBul* 45 (1994) 355–68, brings this conclusion into question. He shows that the Romans clearly distinguished Christians from Jews and did not perceive the two to stand in the same tradition. Because Romans were unaware of the links between Jews and Christians there must have been "a socially clear-cut separation from an early stage" (366).

half-shekel because both were pegged at the same value.[63] According to Cassidy, the question put to Peter raises the volatile issue of civil taxes owed to Rome, which resurfaces in 22: 15–22 (Mark 12:13–17; Luke 20: 20–26). He argued that Jesus' statement about kings of the earth and their subjects delineates a principle concerning civil taxation that has nothing to do with the issue of paying the voluntary religious pledge to the temple. His key argument is that the analogy employs terms for civil taxes. *Kēnsos* is a Latin loan word that refers to Roman taxes based on the provincial census (22:17, 19), and *telos* refers to customs and duties (Rom. 13. 7).[64] Interpreting *skandalizein* to mean "to mislead," Cassidy claimed that the point for Jesus was that he did not wish to mislead the larger community into thinking that he was a Zealot because his view of taxes was similar to these agitators.[65] Therefore, he paid his taxes.

Walker took a similar tack but concluded that the pericope represents the church's concern about paying taxes. Christians asked about their duty to pay taxes to the Roman state, and this story provided one answer. They were free, but they would pay taxes on missionary grounds. They were not to scandalize the powers that be. For Walker, the "them" refers to the kings of the earth and not the tax collectors or Jesus' contemporaries.[66]

While many church fathers understood the passage to contain instruction about the Christian's duty to the state,[67] it is questionable that this was the intent either of Jesus or Matthew. First, the fact that an analogy draws on imagery from the civil world of kings does not mean that the issue revolves around civil taxes. Second, if this did refer to Roman tax collectors, could they be realistically portrayed as politely asking if someone paid an obligatory tax and being satisfied with an affirmative answer rather than payment? This hardly accords with the record of threatening and extortion that is reported about the

---

[63] R. J. Cassidy, "Matthew 17:24–27—A Word on Civil Taxes," *CBQ* 41 (1979) 574.

[64] Ibid., 572–73; see also A. N. Sherwin-White, *Roman Society and Roman Law in the New Testament* (Oxford: Oxford University Press, 1963) 126.

[65] Ibid., 576, n. 19. See also D. Hill, *The Gospel of Matthew* (London: Oliphants, 1972) 272.

[66] R. Walker, *Die Heilsgeschichte im ersten Evangelium* (FRLANT 91; Göttingen: Vandenhoeck & Ruprecht, 1967) 102–03.

[67] See the helpful discussion of the exegesis of this passage by the Greek church fathers in E. Wilhelms, *Die Tempelsteuerperikope Matthäus 17, 24–27 in der Exegese der griechischen Väter der Alten Kirche* (SFEG 34; Helsinki: Finnische Exegetische Gesellschaft, 1980).

collection of taxes.[68] The situation as it is presented best fits the voluntary nature of the temple half-shekel that could not be forced except by moral suasion and fear of shame. Third, the *didrachmon* equals the temple assessment and goes by that name (Exod 30:13, A has *didrachma*; Neh 10:32–33, Josephus *Ant.* 18.9.1 § 312).[69] What civil tax can be so readily identified?[70] Fourth, the tax collectors refer to Jesus as "your teacher" which is the typical designation applied to him by the Jewish leaders in the gospel.[71] Fifth, as Thompson observed, the half-shekel for the temple had rich religious associations for the Jews; and it would seem highly unlikely that this symbolism was suppressed in the service of a purely political question.[72] The issue of tribute to Caesar is addressed later in the gospel and quite unambiguously. Finally, the statement, "the sons are free," would hardly be applicable to the question of civil tribute. Christians did not claim a special bond with the kings of the earth, how could they consider themselves exempt from their taxes? They did understand themselves to be specially related to God, and their accompanying freedom would only be relevant in the case of some religious tax. While one could extract from this story a lesson about civil taxes, as the church fathers regularly did, this was neither its meaning in the ministry of Jesus nor how Matthew understood it in his gospel.

---

[68] See Phil *Spec. Leg.* 2:93–95 and Luke 3:12–15.

[69] One would expect the singular, *didrachmon* in v. 24 rather than the plural, di/draxma. Several explanations have been offered. Some have said that the tax collectors are not asking for the amount but whether or not Jesus pays the taxes. The plural refers to the tax due every year. So McNeile, *Matthew*, 258; and E. Klostermann, *Das Matthäusevangelium* (HKNT 4: Tübingen: J. C. B. Mohr [Paul Siebeck], 1929) 146. M. Black, "*EPHATHA* (Mark 7.34), *TA PASCHA* (Matt 26.18W), *TA SABBATA* (passim), *TA DIDRACHMA* (Mt 17.24 bis)," in *Mélanges bibliques en hommage au R. P. Béda Rigaux.* (ed. A. Descamps and A. de Halleux; Gembloux: Duculot, 1970) 61–62, suggested that the plural is possibly an Aramaised form of *didrachmon* that is a "false plural" in the same way that *sabbata* is an Aramaised form of *sabbaton*.

[70] The examples listed by Cassidy, "Matthew 17:24–27," 578–79, are designed by names and not by the amount assessed. Two drachma may be a plausible amount for a civil tax, but Cassidy cannot identify what that tax might be. The text implies, however, that the tax involved is readily identifiable by its amount.

[71] A. G. van Aarde, "Matthew's Portrayal of the Disciples and the Structure of Matthew 13:53–17:27," *Neotestamentica* 16 (1982) 30; see Matt. 8:19; 12:38; 19:16, 22; 22:16, 23–24, 36.

[72] W. G. Thompson, *Matthew's Advice to a Divided Community* (AnBib) 44; Rome: Biblical Institute, 1970) 67.

V. The Aurum Coronarium

Some scholars have argued that Matthew intended to apply the story to a situation when R. Johanan b. Zakkai established a new central authority for the Jews in Yavneh. Here the study of the law replaced the temple cult. Support for this new enterprise came from voluntary contributions. Later, the so-called *aurum coronarium* was instituted, which was assumed by Thompson to be a legal tax with imperial sanction. Thompson asserted that it was "the true successor to the defunct half-shekel tax."[73] He claimed that Matthew inserted this pericope into his gospel because Jewish members of the community were concerned about their relation to Yavneh:

Such a contribution continued to symbolize solidarity with Judaism and submission to the observances of the law. Therefore, the Jewish Christians wondered whether they should support this new religious institution.[74]

The story advises Jewish Christians to contribute to the High Council to avoid offending their fellow Jews.

The major problem with this hypothesis is that it has no basis whatever in any primary data. Thompson cited only secondary references; and his main source, Juster, appealed to Codex Theodotianus (Theodotius II), which hardly comprises evidence for a practice in the first century.[75] Hagner's comment concerning Yavneh bears repeating: "Our knowledge of what took place at Yavneh is tenuous at best";[76] and Goodman has shown that it took some time before the rabbis became as formidable an institution as imagined by some New Testament interpreters.[77] Also, what evidence we have for contributions to the rabbis shows that the amount was not fixed; and generous donors were given seats of honor.[78] This contrasts with the temple half-shekel which was a set fee for rich and poor alike.

---

[73] Ibid., 68. See also Banks, *Jesus and the Law*, 93.

[74] Ibid.

[75] See J. Juster, *Les Juifs dans l'empire Romain* (Paris: Geuthner, 1914) 1:385–88.

[76] D. A. Hagner, "The *Sitz im Leben* of the Gospel of Matthew," SBLASP (1985) 251.

[77] M. Goodman, *State and Society in Roman Galilee A. D. 132–212* (Totowa, N. J.: Rowman & Allanheid, 1983).

[78] H. Mantel, *Studies in the History of the Sanhedrin* (Cambridge: Harvard Univ., 1961) 197–98.

Therefore, this theory should be discarded as having little or no evidence to support it.

VI. A Theological Object Lesson

Scholars can usually find their presuppositions about the *Sitz im Leben* of Matthew confirmed by what they think this passage is saying about taxes. In my opinion, however, the historical tax issue is a red herring which has caused them to misread Matthew's use of this story. Therefore, I agree with Frankemölle, who argued that the passage no longer has anything to do with the problem of paying the tax but is intent on a *theologische Aussage*.[79] The passage bears all the marks of Matthean redaction,[80] and its similarities with 18:1–20 suggest that the Evangelist has woven together the second prediction of the passion, the tradition about the *didrachmon*, and the issue about greatness and not causing offense.[81] The answer to why this was done is to be found from the context of the passage in the Gospel and not from an imagined historical context in which Matthew wrote.

---

[79] H. Frankemölle, *Jahwebund und Kirche Christi* (NTAbh 10; Münster: Aschendorff, 1974) 176. See also G. Strecker, *Der Weg der Gerechtigkeit* (FRLANT 82; 2d ed.; Göttingen: Vandenhoeck & Ruprecht, 1966) 31 n. 1; S. Schulz, *Die Stunde der Botschaft* (Hamburg: Furche, 1966) 161.

The passage is no more intended to instruct the members of Matthew's church on what to do about the temple tax than Jesus' challenge in 5:23–24 is intended to instruct them on what to do when they are sacrificing in the temple. The latter is an hyperbolic illustration on how to defuse anger as this passage is a whimsical illustration on how to avoid causing others to stumble.

[80] See Plummer, *Matthew*, 248; Kilpatrick, *Matthew*, 41; Strecker, *Der Weg*, 200–01; Goulder, *Midrash and Lection*, 397; and Gundry, *Matthew*, 355–57. More recently, Davies and Allison, *Matthew*, 2:737–38; Luz, *Matthäus*, 532–34; and Meier, *A Marginal Jew*, 883–84, argue convincingly that the Evangelist preserves a tradition which he has retouched. See also B. D. Chilton, "A Coin of Three Realms (Matthew 17.24–27)," in *The Bible in Three Dimensions* (ed. D. J. A. Clines; S. E. Fowl, and S. E. Porter; Sheffield: JSOT, 1990) 269–82. On the textual variants, see J. C. Margot, "Les problèmes posés par la traduction de Matthieu 17.24–27," *Traduire sans trahir: la theorie de la traduction et son application aux textes bibliques* (Lausanne: Age d'homme, 1979) 168–69.

[81] Thompson, *Matthew's Advice*, 85–87, and Meier, *Matthew*, 196, saw it as a bridge to the discourse on church life. T. Brodie, "Fish, Temple Tithe, and Remission: The God-Based Generosity of Deuteronomy 14–15 As One Component of Matt 17:22–18:35," *RB* 99 (1992) 697–718, argues that Matthew has synthesized and adapted Deut 14–15 in constructing this section.

Avoiding Scandal

The primary reason that Matthew included this incident and at this point was to furnish a lesson about relinquishing one's rights to live harmoniously with others and also to avoid offending and perhaps harming them. Jesus decided for payment of the *didrachmon* not because he was bound to do so by the law nor because of fear of recriminations from the authorities but to avoid causing offense. This response then becomes a concrete example of surrendering one's rights out of a loving concern for the interest of others (whoever they may be) and prepares for the emphasis in chap 18 on disinterested concern for the neighbor and the spirit of forgiveness that are to be the hallmarks of the community.[82] The stern warning against causing one of these little ones who believe in me to stumble (18:6) reveals that the principle of not causing offense concerns insiders as well as outsiders, the "them." As "the little ones" who are prone to stumble vary in different settings, so the "them" who are prone to offense may vary in different situations. The principle of how to treat them remains constant.

Patte's structural reading of the passage confirms that the central emphasis of the text revolves around the issue of not causing offense.[83] He pointed out how the reader is constantly misdirected and thrown off guard in the text. Jesus' question, "What do you think?" misleads the reader into thinking that Peter's perception of the matter needed to be corrected (as was the case in 16:22–23; 17:4); and the analogy, which asserts that the sons are free, seems to confirm this impression—they are not obligated to pay. But it turns out that Peter was not wrong; Jesus will pay the tax. This tension, Patte noted, "underscores the reason for paying this tax."[84] Jesus pays, but not because he is obliged to do so or because it is customary to do so, but in order not to scandalize them.

---

[82] J. D. Kingsbury, *Matthew* (Philadelphia: Fortress, 1977) 51–52. See also J. C. Fenton, *Saint Matthew* (London: Penguin, 1963) 284, who believed that the story illustrates the teaching that disciples are not to cause offense which is to developed in the following discourse. G. Barth, "Matthew's Understanding," 85, n. 1, considered it an enactment of the love command.

[83] D. Patte, *The Gospel According to Matthew* (Philadelphia: Fortress, 1987) 246–47. He commented that the text plays with the readers' expectations, misleading them into thinking that there are oppositions only to show that these are not actual oppositions (258, n. 4).

[84] Ibid.

The rationale for paying is also in tension with the reader's expectations. Jesus has consistently ruffled religious feathers. His teaching caused Nazareth to be scandalized, but he responded to this almost indifferently with a pronouncement that a prophet is without honor in his own country (13:57). In 15:1-2, the Pharisees censure the disciples because they violated the traditions of the fathers by eating with unwashed hands. The disciples report that the Pharisees were scandalized by Jesus' parabolic response to their objections (15:12), but Jesus sweeps aside their agitation with a further attack against these Jewish leaders as plants that will eventually be rooted up and as blind guides leading others to destruction (15:13-14). If he did not fret about scandalizing them by his teaching, and if he pronounced blessed those who are not scandalized by his unorthodox ministry (11:6), why does he now shrink from causing offense—to these Jewish tax collectors or any one else who might take umbrage by his stance on this matter?[85] It is possible that this inconsistency requires one to make a distinction between issues that are crucial and those that are not. In this case, the question about the temple half-shekel would not be considered so vital as to allow it to create ill will.[86] Patte proposed, however, that the readers should be puzzled by all this and Jesus' answer "begs for an explanation."[87] The explanation centers on the necessity of denying one's rights and submitting to others and is developed in chap 18. The sons may be free, but they are not free from the claims of love.[88] Chapter 18 will also deal with the question of what are the limits of such an attitude and will show that there are none. The section begins in 17:24-27 with a dialogue between Peter and Jesus and an example from the world of kings and ends with a dialogue between Peter and Jesus and an example from the world of kings (18:21-35). As does 18:21-35, 17:24-27 provides an illustration of how the sons are to conduct their lives. In 18:21-35 they are to be

---

[85] Ibid.

[86] R. A. Edwards, *Matthew's Story of Jesus* (Philadelphia: Fortress, 1985) 64.

[87] Patte, *Matthew*, 247. Schlatter, *Matthäus*, 541, noted this contradiction and explained that 17:26 differs from 15:12 because the latter has to do with a false understanding of purity. Jesus honored the temple, however, along with the requirement of temple dues and never wrangled over money matters.

[88] Meier, *Matthew*, 197. Stählin, "*skandalizō*," *TDNT*, 7:351, commented that one must be able to forego one's own freedom and privileges to guard against causing unbelief in others (see 1 Cor 9:1, 19-20). But this principle applies to more situations than simply forestalling another's unbelief.

those who forgive from the heart; in 17:24–27 they are to be those who make for peace (5:9).[89]

Jesus as the Son

I would argue more tentatively that the tradition was preserved because it also reflects theological suppositions of the Evangelist which emerge elsewhere in the Gospel. The first involves the analogy about the sons. Matthew certainly understood Jesus to be the Son of God. Jesus has been declared by God to be the beloved Son at the baptism (3:17); and this has just been reiterated in the hearing of the disciples at the transfiguration (17:5). He is recognized as God's Son by Satan (4:3, 6) and the demons (8:29). Jesus also knows himself to be God's Son (11:27, 13:37), and frequently refers to God as "my Father."[90] His sonship is confirmed by his acceptance of his Father's will that he must die (17:22–23, 26:39). The fact that Jesus is God's son is beginning to dawn on the disciples as well (14:33, 16:16), although they do not fully understand the implications of this in relation to his death. It will become apparent to the temple hierarchy that Jesus claims to be God's Son with the parable of the wicked tenants (21:33–46);[91] and this, along with his threat against the temple, will be at issue in the trial before the Sanhedrin (26:61–63). It will also resurface in the taunts of the high priests during the crucifixion (27:43). At his death, the centurion confesses that this was truly God's Son (27:54); and the gospel closes with the command to baptize in the name of the Son (28:19).

It is unlikely that Matthew would have understood this incident simply as a lesson about Israel as the sons of a heavenly Father who would not impose burdensome taxes on his children. Jesus, not Israel, is God's faithful Son (4:1–9), and Peter has explicitly identified him as the Son of the living God in the previous section (16:16). The analogy implies that Jesus is claiming a special status over against others who are obligated to pay the tax and whom he does not want to offend. Would they have been scandalized by arguments that all Jews are sons

---

[89] Horbury, "The Temple Tax," 266, observed that this resembles injunctions on secular tax (Rom 13:5, 1 Pet 2:13–15); but it has closer affinities with the fundamental principle, espoused by Paul, of avoiding unnecessary offense to others (see 1 Cor 8:1–13; 10:23–11:1; Rom 14:21; 2 Cor 11:29).

[90] Matt 7:21; 10:32, 33; 11:27; 12:50; 16:17; 18:10, 14, 19, 35; 20:23; 25:34, 41; 26:29, 39, 42, 53.

[91] J. D. Kingsbury, "The Parable of the Wicked Husbandmen and the Secret of Jesus' Divine Sonship in Matthew," *JBL* (1986) 651.

of a loving Father who freely provides voluntary offerings? It is more likely that they would have been offended by anyone who arrogated to himself some special status. In Matthew's theology, Jesus as God's Son is not obligated to pay taxes to his Father. The question about the temple tax therefore provided another opportunity for Matthew to unfold the sonship theme. Through the analogy, Jesus lays claim to a status for which no Israelite qualified. He does not jettison the law concerning the temple half-shekel which affirmed the equality of all Jews in their obligation to pay: "The rich shall not give more and the poor shall not give less than half a shekel" (Exod 30:15). He presumes to be above it. Jesus' claim to exemption from this tax is not based on some exegetical loophole but on the implicit assertion that he is not an equal to the others, the Israelites. Something greater than the temple (12:6), Jonah, and Solomon (12:41–42) is here, someone who is Lord of the Sabbath (12:8), of King David (22:41–45), and of the temple (21:12–27).

This christological interest best explains the fish story attached to this incident. It has prompted all kinds of exegetical *Kunststücke* to solve everything from how a fish could take the bait with a stater in its mouth to why Jesus solved his cash flow problems in such a manner.[92] Other questions arise: What about the payment for the other disciples? Why is the miracle not reported? How could this miraculous expedient possibly give direction to the way Matthew's community should solve whatever dilemma they were facing?

The fact that the miracle is not reported suggests that Matthew was more interested in Jesus' rationale for paying than in the miracle itself, but one should not make too much of this so-called missing ending. Haenchen is correct that neither Matthew nor the reader doubted that it came to pass as Jesus had said.[93] But what would this signify to the

---

[92] J. Weiss, *Die Schriften des neuen Testaments* (2d ed.; Göttingen: Vandenhoeck & Ruprecht, 1907) 1:348, objected that the miracle neither satisfies a human need nor serves a religious goal and appears selfish. See also G. M. Lee, "Matthew 17, 24–27," *Theology* 68 (1965) 380.

[93] E. Haenchen, *Der Weg Jesu: Eine Erklärung des Markus-Evangeliums und der kanonischen Parallelen* (Berlin: Alfred Töpelmann, 1966) 333–34. He maintained that when the interest in the question of the temple tax no longer existed, this account was treasured as a miracle story.

Many have attempted to explain away the miracle. Hirsch, *Frühgeschichte*, 2:236, suggested that it was a dream of Peter's like that in Acts 10 which was later recounted as an actual event. Blass amended the text from "you shall find" to read "it shall find," meaning that the fish will find (sell for) a stater (see C. Jaeger,

believer? Schlatter was on the right track when he compared this to the provision of the donkey in Bethphage and the room in Jerusalem for the last supper; Jesus receives all that he needs from the Father. For Schlatter, this miracle confirms the belief that God will care for their needs.[94] I would suggest, however, that the miracle confirms that Jesus is, as he implied in the analogy, God's Son, because God provides the money for him to pay God's tax. Jesus has a pre-vision of God's provision.[95] Therefore, Chrysostom was not off the mark when he said that the miracle of Jesus reveals who he is, Lord over all, including the sea (Matt. Hom. 58:1 MG, Sp. 567; see 8:23–27; 14:28–33).[96]

The Disciples as Sons and the Jews as Aliens

The analogy contrasts the free sons, Jesus and those who are associated with him, with those who are bound to pay the temple half-shekel, namely, the Jews. Haenchen reasoned that since Christians are to be understood as the sons and the Jews as the aliens, it is a clear sign

---

"Remarques philogiques sur quelques passages des Synoptiques," *RHPR* 16 ([936] 248). Similarly, J. Jeremias, *New Testament Theology* (New York: Chas. Scribners & Sons, 1971) 87, thought that what Jesus originally meant was, "Cast your hook into the sea, sell your catch and pay the tax with the proceeds." The delight in elaborating on stories and the influence of other fish stories resulted in this saying evolving into a miracle. T. H. Robinson, *The Gospel of Matthew* (New York: Harper and Bros., 1927) 150, took it as a joke; the only chance of paying this is to find a fish with a stater in its mouth. See also McNeile, *Matthew*, 259, and R. T. France, *Matthew*, (Grand Rapids: Eerdmans, 1985) 268, "a playful comment on how short the funds are." Goulder, *Midrash and Lection*, 397, believed it to be an instance of Matthean hyperbole; and H. A. Homeau, "On Fishing for Staters: Matthew 17, 27," *ExpT* 85 (1973–74) 340–342, argued for an ironic thrust (originally spoken beside the Dead Sea) that was misunderstood by the literal-minded tradents. If one understood the disciples as fishers of men, one could even argue that Jesus was encouraging Peter to catch a rich convert.

[94] Schlatter, *Matthäus*, 542.

[95] Brodie, "Fish, Temple Tithe, and Remission," 707, claims that the instruction, "take the first fish that comes up," scraps the distinction between clean and unclean (Deut 14:9–10), but similar fish stories in rabbinic literature do not specify that the fish is clean (*b. Šabb.* 119a; *b. B. Bat.* 133b; *b. Giṭ.* 68b; *Gen Rab.* 11:4 / *Pesiq. R.* 23:6; *Qoh. Rab.* 11:1).

[96] The Tyrian silver coins bore the idolatrous images of sea-monsters with riders, either gods or kings, on their backs which would have been understood as a symbol of divine power over the creatures of the sea. A. G. Van Aarde, *God-With-Us The Dominant Perspective in Matthew's Story* (HTSsup5; Pretoria: Hervormde Teologiese Studies, 1994) 226, suggests that the miracle with the fish conveys "the superiority of Jesus as the son of God over the gods of the sea." It is hard to imagine what reader would have made this connection, but what reader would have known that a stater was the equivalent of four drachma?

of later tradition from a time when the two ways of faith have already lived apart from one another.[97] While this need not indicate a later tradition,[98] it would imply that the Evangelist assumes that those related to Jesus belong to the royal family, while unbelieving Jews, who consider themselves obligated to pay the tax, do not. The analogy embraces Matthew's view of the disciples as sons of God through their relationship with Jesus. Frankemölle argued that, for Matthew, Jesus is the mediator between the Father and the disciples: relationship to God depends on relationship to Jesus,[99] not on one's national identity or cultic performance. Jesus also refers to God as "your father,"[100] and recognizes the disciples as his brothers and sisters (12:49–50). The proof that they are indeed sons of the Father will be seen in their behavior as peacemakers (5:9) and in their loving response to those who may persecute them (5:44–45).

Those who reject Jesus, like the "Jews" of 28:15, are the "others" *allotrioi* in the analogy who are not children but aliens and strangers to the Lord of the temple.[101] The truth of this for Matthew is borne out by the increasingly negative statements about the Jewish leaders that appear later in the gospel (21:43, 22:8, 23:38–39, 27:25, 28:15). They are the "sons of those who murdered the prophets" (23:31), and their proselytes "double sons of Gehenna" (23:15). But even these "others" are to be treated with sensitivity so as not to hurt them.[102]

Freedom from the Cultus

The disciples are pronounced free from any obligation to pay the temple half-shekel that went primarily to fund the daily sacrifices in

---

[97] Haenchen, *Der Weg Jesu*, 333–34.

[98] Grundmann, *Matthäus*, 411 n. 10, noted that this conception of freedom can be found as early as Gal 4:21–31 (see also, Gal 3:23–4:7). The concept of Christians as sons can also be found early (see Rom 8:14, 19; 9:26; Gal 3:26; 4:24–26; 2 Cor 6:18).

[99] Frankemölle, *Jahwebund*, 159–77.

[100] See Matt 5:16, 45, 48; 6:1, 4, 6, 8, 9, 14, 15, 18, 26, 32; 7:11; 10:20, 39; 23:9.

[101] E. Lohmeyer, *The Lord of the Temple* (Edinburgh: Oliver and Boyd, 1961) 55. According to Josephus, Eleazar, the son of Ananus, persuaded those in charge of the temple services to refuse any gift or sacrifice from a foreigner (*J. W.* 2.17.2 § 409), which laid the foundation for the war since the sacrifices on behalf of the emperor and paid for by the Roman funds were rejected. The word appears in 1 Clem 7:7 to refer to the Ninevites who were aliens to God.

[102] Brodie, "Fish, Temple Tithe, and Remission," 705–06.

the temple. This autonomy would mean that Matthew viewed the temple cultus as irrelevant to Christians.

Patte argued against extrapolating from this passage any view of the temple, that it is, for example, no longer the center of the community and that its sacrifices are no longer required to reconcile humans to God. It is not that this is necessarily wrong, but he thought that it diverted one's attention from Matthew's primary point about causing offense.[103] I would agree that the sons' freedom from the temple is not the central teaching of the passage, but it should not be ignored.[104] It does reflect a Matthean perception and prepares the reader for further statements about the temple later in the Gospel. The temple in Jesus' estimation has become a den of robbers instead of being a house of prayer (21:13). His violent rejection of it is connected in Matthew as in Mark with the cursing of the fig tree (21:18–22). Jesus is said to abandon it (23:39) and then immediately predicts its imminent destruction (24:1–2). Prior to Jesus' death, the defiling "blood money" for the betrayal of Jesus finds its way back to the *naos* (27:4–7; see 23:35); after Jesus' death, the temple veil is rent in two, from top to bottom (27:51). The temple has become superfluous, because something greater than the temple is here (12:6). For Matthew, Jesus is the rejected stone who will become the head of the corner (21:42); and the temple's predicted obsolescence and the sons' freedom from the temple dues are not unrelated to the issue of atonement.

As mentioned above, the Pharisees insisted that the support for the regular daily sacrifice was to come exclusively from the funds provided by the annual half-shekel offering of the entire community (*m. Šeqal.* 4:1–4, *b. Šeqal.* 29b, *Roš. Haš.* 7a).[105] Lohse noted that since every Jew could not go to Jerusalem to offer sacrifice, the idea of the power of the atonement was widened so that contribution of the half-

---

103 Patte, *Matthew*, 247.

104 D. Daube, "Responsibilities of Master and disciples in the Gospels," *NTS* 19 (1972) 14–15, pointed out that the miracle makes Jesus counsel minimal performance, not compliance. They actually surrender nothing of their own to the temple. Therefore, the principle of avoiding offense when translated into practice is to be "flexible, devious, subtle, clever" (see 10:16). If this is true, the passage reflects some antipathy toward the temple. In a later essay, "Temple Tax," in *Appeasement or Resistance, and Other Essays on New Testament Judaism* (Berkeley/Los Angeles/London: University of California: 1987) 56, Daube calls it "appeasement but no stepping down."

105 See Finkelstein, *The Pharisees*, 282.

shekel itself could atone, since it served to purchase sacrifices for the whole sanctuary.[106] This idea was fostered by the fact that Exodus 30:16 identifies the contribution as "atonement money"; and *Tosepta Šeqalim* 1:6 directly connects the half-shekel to sin atonement: "They exact pledges from the Israelites for their shekels, so that the public offerings might be made of their (funds) . . . . For public offerings appease and effect atonement between Israel and their Father in heaven."[107] If the disciples are free from this obligation, it is because of the atonement which they will receive through the death of Jesus (26:28, 27:42). This incident immediately follows the second of the three predictions of Jesus' passion which will effect atonement, and the remission of sins obtained through Jesus' death is assumed throughout the discourse that follows (18:15, 21, 27, 27, 32, 35). The disciples have been forgiven so much by God, they are expected to be forgiving. Forgiveness from God is related to one's own forgiveness of others and completely bypasses the temple cult. Therefore, Origen was not entirely wrong when he interpreted the freedom of the sons as freedom from sins (Matt. XIII, 10; GCS 40).

The Role of Peter

The freedom extends from Jesus to Peter and through him to the other disciples. Peter has a unique position in this section of Matthew vis-à-vis any other of the disciples. Peter attempts to walk on water like Jesus, but needs to be saved from drowning by Jesus and is rebuked for his little faith (14:22–33).[108] He confesses Jesus to be the Christ, the son of God, and is pronounced blessed by Jesus for the insight given to him by God. He has the keys to the kingdom to loose and to bind (16:13–20). But almost immediately Jesus rebukes him for his satanic misunderstanding of the requirement of suffering (16:21–23). In chap 18, Peter generously offers to forgive the brother who sins against him seven times, but Jesus corrects him by insisting that forgiveness be unlimited (18:21–35). In the temple tax incident, Jesus stands behind Peter's hasty "Yes" (see 5:37), albeit whimsically, but must enlighten him further on the matter. Because just enough money is provided for the payment of the tax for Jesus and Peter ("for me and you,"

---

[106] E. Lohse, *Märtyrer und Gottesknecht* (FRLANT 46, Göttingen: 1955) 22.

[107] It then cites Exod 30:16. See also *b. B. Bat.* 9a, the passages cited in Str-B1:761–62, and 11QTemple 39:7–10. Philo *Spec Leg.* 1:78 identifies the "ransom" (*lytra*) as "the hopes of the pious."

[108] See D. E. Garland, *Reading Matthew* (New York: Crossroad, 1993) 153–54.

singular),[109] Peter is portrayed as the unique leader of the whole church;[110] and "the house" (17:25), which becomes the setting for the discourse in chapter 18, may be intended to evoke the church, a spiritual house (1 Pet 2:5).[111] He is subject to err, however,[112] and must learn to be entirely dependent on the instruction and guidance of Jesus. Jesus is Peter's and the church's teacher (17:25), and his guidance transforms Peter's affirmation from an unthinking conformity to the party line of the Jewish leaders into a clarion call of Christian freedom that remains sensitive and responsible to neighbors.

---

[109] Does this set the stage for the disciples' question that immediately follows, "Who is the greatest?" (18:1)?

[110] R. E. Brown and J. P. Meier, *Antioch and Rome* (Ramsey, N.J.: Paulist, 1982) 69. See also Thompson, *Matthew's Advice*, 58, who saw the freedom extending from Jesus to Peter and through him to the other disciples.

[111] So Brodie, "Fish, Temple Tithe, and Remission," 706.

[112] The fifteen incidents in Matthew which specifically involve him portray him as rash, confused, desirous of reward, overconfident, faltering, and cowardly. He is, nevertheless, the spokesman for the disciples who voices their questions and doubts as well as their faith.

Chapter Three

Matthew and the Law

KLYNE SNODGRASS

Some explanation is required as to why anyone would agree to treat yet once again a subject that makes jugglers of us all.[1] The seeming contradictions in Matthew do provide a challenge for those who like brain-teasers. How should one understand the relation of the statements on the continuing validity of the law in 5:17–20 with the antitheses and other sections of Matthew where the law seems to be challenged or set aside (as 15:11)? How should one understand the contradiction between the warning in 16:11–12 to avoid the teaching of the Pharisees and Sadducees and the instruction in 23:3 to do what the Pharisees say but not what they do? The problem alone is not sufficient reason to treat the subject again, however, for virtually every position possible has been proposed in the abundant material on Matthew.

I would suggest that there are three reasons that justify once again treating this subject. One is the importance of Matthew's statements on law for any society and particularly for the Christian community. Despite our agreements about the necessity of law, most of us have negative feelings about law, including any idea of the law of God. Our statements reveal a necessity to show that the law is inferior and that the law is set aside. Matthew, however, did not share our feelings. He had a revolutionary understanding of the intention of the law which he thought would guide his readers in the will of God. While this is reasonably well-known, our biases against the law need to be addressed once again.

---

[1] Jack Suggs, *Wisdom, Christology, and Law in Matthew's Gospel* (Cambridge, MA.: Harvard University Press, 1970) 112.

99

The second and third reasons for tackling this subject are intertwined. They are the need for sound and relevant methods and the need to hear Matthew. Just as many of us tend to have a bias against the law, there seems to be a bias against Matthew. Because of our theological preferences or our critical conclusions, we rarely actually hear Matthew. We read Matthew reading Mark and changing Q. Should we not be suspicious when Luke's version is nearly always given preference, even though we know of Luke's penchant for streamlining?[2] Does redactional activity always disclose the origin of the material, or can it also show shaping of the material? We have only to read Donald Hagner's *The Jewish Reclamation of Jesus* to realize that Jewish scholars find most acceptable in Matthew the very items with which Christians have the most difficulty and that the very items Christians see as solutions to the problem Jewish scholars see as mistranslations of Semitic originals or later insertions.[3] We interpret Matthew in light of what he should have said if he were Paul.[4] Ought we not allow Matthew to be Matthew?

I am concerned also that our theories about gospel origins prevent us from reading each of the gospels in its own right. I am not prepared to argue against the two source hypothesis, nor am I willing to accept it or any other solution as the template for understanding the gospels. The tendency of New Testament scholarship to create theories on the basis of hypotheses must cause some concern about methodological controls and the viability of our common enterprise.

None of us would want to read Matthew without being aware of the parallel accounts, but if we are to understand Matthew's view of the law, we ought to focus our attention also on a vertical reading of

---

[2] Note, for example, that Matthew is often viewed as adding *iōta hen ē* in 5:18 (cf. Luke 16:17). See Heinz Schürmann, 'Wer daher eines dieser geringsten Gebote auflöst . . .': Wo fand Matthäus das Logion Mt 5,19? *BZ* 4 (1960) 241; and Robert A. Guelich, *The Sermon on the Mount* (Waco: Word Books, 1982) 144. Jan Lambrecht, *The Sermon on the Mount* (Wilmington, DE: Michael Glazier, 1985) 85, suggested that Luke may have dropped the iota because this letter is not particularly small in the Greek alphabet.

[3] (Grand Rapids: Zondervan, 1984), especially pp. 87–132 and 282.

[4] Note, for example, Roger Mohrlang's preference for Paul's thought on the law in his *Matthew and Paul* (Cambridge: Cambridge University Press, 1984) 127–129. It should also be added that in many cases Matthew is being read from the perspective of a misunderstood Paul. See my comments relating to Paul and the law in "Justification by Grace to the Doers: an Analysis of the Place of Romans 2 in the Theology of Paul," *NTS* 32 (1986) 72–93; and in "Spheres of Influence: A Possible Solution to the Problem of Paul and the Law," *JSNT* 32 (1988) 93–113.

Matthew.[5] In addition, we should remind ourselves that we are dealing with popular literature, not a technical theological piece. If so, we possibly can avoid hyper-exegesis and inquire after the function of the various sayings in the overall document.

The Issues Requiring Treatment

The eight occurrences of *nomos* in Matthew[6] seem deceptively simple in comparison with the complexity of the questions about the law that are present in nearly every portion of the book. Before discussing the subject at hand, there is value in isolating the issues so that a comprehensive view of the problems is before us. An adequate treatment of Matthew and the law involves the following:

1) An understanding of the view(s) of the law in Judaism and the diversity of its applications. In particular, did Judaism expect a new torah with the coming of the Messiah?[7]

2) The question whether it is permissible to treat Matthew in light of what is known about other discussions of law in the New Testament. If Matthew was written in Syria, may we assume the author knew of the debates about the law in Antioch years earlier?[8] For many, 5:17–20 reflects debates between factions in

---

[5] The distinction between a vertical reading of Matthew which focuses only on Matthew's tendencies and theology as opposed to a horizontal reading which compares his account to Mark and Luke is derived from William G. Thompson, *Matthew's Advice to a Divided Community* (Rome: Biblical Institute Press, 1970) 6.

[6] 5:17, 18; 7:12; 11:13; 12:5; 22:36, 40; 23:23. The reading *ton nomon* at 15:6 deserves more attention than it usually receives.

[7] W. D. Davies is the person who has focused most on the question of whether Judaism thought the Messiah would bring a new torah. See his *Torah in the Messianic Age and/or the Age to Come* (Philadelphia: Society of Biblical Literature, 1952) and his *The Setting of the Sermon on the Mount* (Cambridge: Cambridge University Press, 1966) 109–190. Despite the admitted lack of support for a theory of a messianic torah, Davies still used the language. See *Torah in the Messianic Age and/or the Age to Come*, 86–90 and *The Setting of the Sermon on the Mount*, 184–190. Some people at Qumran may have viewed the Temple Scroll as torah. See Yigael Yadin, *The Temple Scroll* (Jerusalem: Israel Exploration Society, 1983) 1, 390–392. But this is quite different from the supposed new law brought by the Messiah. Against this idea see especially Peter Schäfer, "Die Torah der messianischen Zeit," *ZNW* 65 (1974) 27–42. I do not think Matthew should be interpreted as a new torah.

[8] See Ernst Käsemann, The Beginnings of Christian Theology, *New Testament Questions of Today* (London: SCM, 1969) 86–89; Eduard Schweizer, *The Good News According to Matthew*, (Atlanta: John Knox, 1975) 105–106; and Ulrich Luz, *Das Evangelium nach Matthäus (Mt 1–7)* Zurich: Benziger, 1985) 238–239.

the Church,[9] and for some Paul is the target of these sayings.[10]

3) A determination of what one may conclude from silence. Are we to conclude that circumcision was still practiced in Matthew's community or that it had been abandoned?[11]

4) A determination of the character of Matthew's community. Had there been a split with the synagogue or not?[12] Were there opponents (charismatics or antinomians) in the community?[13] In particular, should 7:15 and 7:22–23 be read as referring to the same group?[14] Less attention will be given to a description of the Matthean community in this paper. The time and circumstances of the break with the synagogue are not as clear as some have argued.[15] Certainly the attempt by W. D. Davies to see the

---

[9] E.g., Gerhard Barth, "Matthew's Understanding of the Law," *Tradition and Interpretation in Matthew*, ed. Günther Bornkamm, Gerhard Barth, and Heinz Joachim Held (Philadelphia: Westminster Press, 1963) 64–65; and Francis Wright Beare, *The Gospel According to Matthew* (San Francisco: Harper & Row, 1981) 141.

[10] E.g., Hans Dieter Betz, "The Beatitudes of the Sermon on the Mount (Matt. 5:3–12): Observations on Their Literary Form and Theological Significance,"in *Essays on the Sermon on the Mount*, (Philadelphia: Fortress, 1985) 20.

[11] Mohrlang, 44–45, assumed that circumcision was still being practiced by the Matthean community. John P. Meier, *Law and History in Matthew's Gospel: A Redactional Study of Matthew 5:17–48* (Rome: Biblical Institute Press, 1976) 61 and 64, thought that the community had dispensed with circumcision.

[12] Günther Bornkamm, "End-Expectation and Church in Matthew," *Tradition and Interpretation in Matthew*, 22, thought that the community had not yet broken with Judaism, but later changed his mind in "The Authority to 'Bind' and 'Loose' in the Church in Matthew's Gospel," *The Interpretation of Matthew*, ed. Graham Stanton (Philadelphia: Fortress, 1983) 88. See the discussion in Meier, 9–13, who thought the community had already separated.

[13] Käsemann, 83f., argued Spirit enthusiasts are opposed. Numerous others suggest Matthew argues against antinomians; e.g., Lambrecht, p. 90; and Eduardo Arens, *The ELTHON-Sayings in the Synoptic Tradition* (Freiberg: Universittsverlag, 1976) 94. However, James E. Davison, "*Anomia* and the Question of an Antinomian Polemic in Matthew," *JBL* 104 (1985) 617–635, effectively demonstrates that *anomia* is a general word for sin and has no special connotation of antinomianism. From this he concluded there is only one front against which Matthew argues. That front is moral laxity, whether evidenced by charismatics or Pharisees.

[14] See the discussion in David Hill, "False Prophets and Charismatics: Structure and Interpretation in Matthew 7,15–23," *Biblica* 57 (1976) 327–348, who argued that two different groups are intended in 7:15 and 7:22–23.

[15] See Reuven Kimelman, "Birkat Ha-Minim and the Lack of Evidence for an Anti-Christian Jewish Prayer in Late Antiquity," in *Jewish and Christian Self-Definition*, Vol. II, ed. E. P. Sanders with A. I. Baumgarten and Alan Mendelson (Philadelphia: Fortress, 1981) 226–244; and Steven T. Katz, "Issues in the Separation of Judaism and Christianity after 70 C. E.: A Reconsideration," *JBL* 103

Sermon on the Mount as a Christian counterpart to the rabbinic restructuring of Judaism at Jamnia is not convincing.[16] In addition, the more that one takes a literary- critical approach to Matthew and includes a discussion of the implied reader, the more fog factor there is potentially between us and the Matthean community. The implied reader and the actual reader are not necessarily the same.[17] Are we even certain that the gospel was written for the author's community rather than, for example, as a catechetical tool for a larger group?

5) An interpretation of the exegetical mine field in 5:17–20. Why does Matthew have the law or the prophets? What does *plērōma* mean? What is the relation of the four sayings in this section? Does 5:19 interpret 5:18 or 5:17? What is the relation and meaning of the two *heōs* clauses in 5:18? Does 5:18d refer to the death and resurrection of Jesus?[18] Are the "least commands" a reference to Jesus' commands?[19] Does 5:19 mean there is ranking in the kingdom or does it refer to exclusion from and entrance into the kingdom? Do all four of these sayings present a unified thought or are parts of them intended to counter other parts?[20]

6) Does Matthew present Jesus as abrogating the law? In many ways this is the most important question, but unfortunately a variety of answers is given. Arguments have been presented that none or as many as four of the antitheses abrogate the law.[21] In addition

---

(1984) 43–76.

[16] Davies, *The Setting of the Sermon on the Mount*, 256–315.

[17] Daniel Patte, *The Gospel According to Matthew* (Philadelphia: Fortress, 1987) 13. If the gospels are not suitable for discovering the historical Jesus, they are hardly any better suited for discovering the early church. I am indebted to my former colleague John Phelan for pointing this out forcefully. See the critique of the prinicple of transparency given by Jack Dean Kingsbury, "Conclusion: Analysis of a Conversation" in *Social History of the Matthean Community*, ed. David L. Balch (Minneapolis: Fortress, 1991) 259–269.

[18] E.g., Meier, 63–64; Guelich, 168, saw 5:18d as pointing to Jesus' entire ministry.

[19] Robert Banks, *Jesus and the Law in the Synoptic Tradition* (Cambridge: Cambridge University Press, 1975) 222–223; Schweizer, 108; Betz, "The Hermeneutical Principles of the Sermon on the Mount (Matt. 5:17–20)," in *Essays on the Sermon on the Mount*, 48.

[20] Guelich, 168; Meier, 60–64; Arens, 92.

[21] The following views are representative: Suggs, 113, viewed the third, fourth, fifth, and sixth antitheses as abrogating the law; Schweizer, 110, viewed the third, fifth, and sixth as abrogations; Meier, 159, viewed the third, fourth, and fifth as

people have found possible violations of the law in 8:22;[22] 12:1–8; 15:1–20; and 19:3–9.

7) How antithetical are the antitheses? Is *de* in these sayings to be understood as a strong adversative? We usually interpret the antitheses as if *alla* were used. J. Levison, however, argued that they are not antithetical at all.[23] In addition, if they are oppositional in character, what is being opposed, the written torah or the rabbinic tradition?

8) What is the role of Hosea 6:6 in Matthew and, especially, how absolutely did he understand the words "not sacrifice"? Was the cultic law no longer valid for him?

9) What is the role of the love command in Matthew?

10) How should we understand 23:2–3 and other statements such as 23:23 and 24:20 that suggest a concern for detailed observance of the law?

11) What kind of author/editor/theologian was Matthew? Was the person who crafted this document careful and artistic or somewhat sloppy and inconsistent? Did he have a consistent approach to the subject of the law?

Obviously it is not possible to deal with all these issues here, but hopefully enough can be treated to chart a course for understanding Matthew and the Law.

Options for Understanding Matthew with Reference to the Law

Before dealing with the texts, a summary of the attempts to explain Matthew's attitude to the law will be helpful. The following are the most popular ways by which people have explained the phenomena in Matthew:

1) Matthew thought the Old Testament law was no longer valid after the coming of Jesus. Statements stressing the validity of the law are traditions that Matthew has retained, but qualified by his own views. The Old Testament law was either set aside because Jesus

---

abrogations; and Brice Martin, "Matthew on Christ and the Law," *TS* 44 (1983) 54–70, argued that none of the antitheses is an abrogation.

[22] This is the position of E. P. Sanders, *Jesus and Judaism* (Philadelphia: Fortress, 1985) 252–255 and 267. See the discussion of this text in Martin Hengel, *The Charismatic Leader and his Followers*, (New York: Crossroad, 1981), 3–15.

[23] Jack Levison, "A Better Righteousness: The Character and Purpose of Matthew 5:21–48," *Studia Biblica et Theologica* 12 (1982) 171–194.

as Messiah brought a new torah[24] or because he fulfilled the law through his death and resurrection.[25]

2) Jesus thought the Old Testament law was no longer valid, but that Matthew rejudaized or retorahized the message of Jesus.[26] A rejudaizing tendency could be combined with other explanations.

3) The law was partially valid for Matthew. Relatively few people currently would say Matthew distinguished the moral law from the ceremonial and civil laws. But many would argue that he presents Jesus as radicalizing or intensifying the torah so that some laws are set aside.[27]

4) The law was completely valid as far as Matthew presents Jesus' teaching of it.[28]

5) The law was interpreted by a specific hermeneutical key so as to reveal the divine intention of the law.[29]

---

[24] R. G. Hamerton-Kelly, "Attitudes to the Law in Matthew's Gospel: A Discussion of Matthew 5:18," *Biblical Research* 17 (1972) 31–32; Richard S. McConnell, *Law and Prophecy in Matthew's Gospel* (Basel: Friedrich Reinhardt Kommissionsverlag, 1969) 51f. and 93–95; and Terence L. Donaldson, *Jesus on the Mountain* (Sheffield: JSOT Press, 1985) 112–117. While I am not impressed with suggestions that Matthew presents Jesus as a new Moses, one should note Dale C. Allison, Jr., *The New Moses: A Matthean Typology* (Minneapolis: Fortress, 1993).

[25] Meier, 63–64; Hamerton-Kelly, 21 and 28–32; cf. Guelich, 168; and Schweizer, 108.

[26] See Hans Hübner, *Das Gesetz in der synoptischen Tradition*, 2d ed. (Göttingen: Vandenhoeck & Ruprecht, 1973), especially pp. 237f. Hübner argued for a retorahizing instead of a rejudaizing. His book is an assessment of E. Stauffer's argument (in *Die Botschaft Jesu damals und heute*, Bern, 1959) that Jesus argued against the torah and that his message was requmranized and rejudaized. G. D. Kilpatrick, *The Origins of the Gospel According to St. Matthew* (Oxford: Clarendon, 1946) 101f., argued similarly. Cf. T. W. Manson, *The Sayings of Jesus* (London: SCM, 1949) 135, and the views of Davies, *The Setting of the Sermon on the Mount*, 256–315 and 400, and Beare, 31, that Matthew has rabbinized the message of Jesus.

[27] Barth, 102; McConnell, 50; Mohrlang, 12; and W. J. Dumbrell, "The Logic of the Role of the Law in Matthew V.1–20," *NovT* 23 (1981) 20. See also David L. Balch, "The Greek Political Topos *Peri nomōn* and Matthew 5:17, 19, and 16:19," in *Social History of the Matthean Community*, ed. David L. Balch (Minneapolis: Fortress, 1991) 68–84, who argues that, like Josephus and others, Matthew claims the law has not been abolished, but then shows that certain laws are changed or annulled.

[28] Among others, Martin; A. E. Harvey, *Jesus and the Constraints of History* (Philadelphia: Westminster, 1982) 53–54. Bornkamm, "End-Expectation and Church in Matthew," 24; and Allen Verhey, *The Great Reversal* (Grand Rapids: Eerdmans, 1984) 83, argued that Matthew retained even the oral law.

[29] Birger Gerhardsson, "The Hermeneutic Program in Matthew 22:37–40," in *Jews, Greeks, Christians*, ed. R. Hamerton-Kelly and R. Scroggs (Leiden: E. J. Brill,

It is within the framework of the last option that I suggest we investigate Matthew's attitude to the law.

Toward a Solution

Three studies relevant to Matthew and the law have been particularly helpful in constructing a paradigm for interpretation. They are the works of Alexander Sand,[30] Marcus Borg,[31] and Daniel Patte.[32] Others have made similar points, but usually not with the same force. While all Matthew's statements on the law may not cohere easily, what he really believed about the law is clear. In his mind a proper understanding of the law is a prophetic reading of the law in which the love command and the call for mercy demonstrate the true requirements of the law. As M. Borg has argued, Jesus substituted the mercy code for the holiness code.[33] These statements are open to misunderstanding; but the issue is not prophets against law. The law itself is the source of the focus on love and mercy, even in the holiness code of Leviticus 17–21. True holiness is always characterized by love and mercy, and Matthew presents Jesus as buttressing this thinking by his use of the prophets. M. Borg's statement that Jesus substituted the mercy code for the holiness code refers to Jesus' effecting a paradigm shift from what the holiness code had become in first century Judaism to a renewed focus on love and mercy.[34] A defense of this approach is made more easily in Matthew than in any other document.

That Matthew wanted his readers to understand the law prophetically is not a new suggestion.[35] We would do well, however, to

---

1976) 134 and 140f.; Eduard Schweizer, "Observance of the Law and Charismatic Activity in Matthew," *NTS* 16 (1970) 216; and James D. G. Dunn, *The Living Word* (Philadelphia: Fortress, 1987) 53, among others.

[30] Alexander Sand, *Das Gesetz und die Propheten* (Regensburg: Verlag Friedrich Pustet, 1974).

[31] Marcus J. Borg, *Conflict, Holiness and Politics in the Teaching of Jesus* (New York: Edwin Mellen, 1984).

[32] Patte, *The Gospel of Matthew*, see n. 17.

[33] Borg, 123 and 128. See also John Riches, *Jesus and the Transformation of Judaism* (New York: Seabury, 1982) 142–143; and Anthony J. Saldarini, *Matthew's Christian-Jewish Community* (Chicago: University of Chicago Press, 1994) 131, 139, 141, and 162.

[34] Borg, 52, 123, 128, and 134.

[35] Sand, 59, 125, 193, 208, 221. Meier, 86, viewed the prophets as the canon within the canon, but he did not see a prophetic reading as the explanation of the problem.

notice how he presents his discussions of law. Four of the eight occurrences of *nomos* are in the expression *ho nomos ē kai hoi prophētai* (5:17; 7:12; 11:13 in reverse order; and 22:40). Two more are in the contexts where *ho nomos ē kai hoi prophētai* occurs (5:18 and 22:36). One is in a context where Hosea 6:6 is quoted to validate Jesus' comments (12:5), and the last is an allusion to Micah 6:8 (23:23). Also when the issue of eating with unwashed hands (15:1f.) becomes a debate about the command of God, a word from the prophets (Isa 29:13) provides commentary on the hypocrisy of evading responsibility for one's parents. Even the regulation of temple activities is determined by words from the prophets (Isa 56:7 and Jer 7:11 at Matt 21:13). In addition, the point is underscored in 23:29–36 that the Pharisaic application of the law is not in keeping with the prophetic view and is therefore wrong. The Pharisees, who think they are law abiding, are actually lawless (23:28) because they do not understand what the law is really about.

Clearly Matthew does not want his readers to conceive of the law as an entity by itself. One should not think merely of the law, but of the law and the prophets. Scholars have often felt that *ē tous prophētas* in 5:17 was out of place,[36] but it was not for Matthew. Already, even though the rest of 5:17–20 focuses only on questions of the law, Matthew wanted his readers to think of the law and the prophets. The inclusio with 7:12 underscores the point. The title of this paper is, therefore, a misnomer. To discuss only Matthew's understanding of the law is to misunderstand him. For him the law cannot be understood apart from the prophets. Jesus himself is presented as a prophet who gives the authoritative interpretation of the law.[37] A closer analysis of 5:17–20 appears below.

That the love commands encompass for Matthew the intention of the law and the prophets is obvious. In 22:34–40 the great commandment is identified as the requirement to love the Lord your God with all your heart, soul, and mind (Deut 6:5), but a second

---

[36] C. G. Montefiore, *The Synoptic Gospels* (London: Macmillan, 1927) 2, 47; Hübner, 33. Banks, 206, suggested that the insertion is the result of an unconscious association of ideas. Lambrecht, 83, correctly argued that the law or the prophets hardly differs from the law and the prophets.

[37] Sand, 138f.; Harvey, 57. Note that Matthew presents Jesus as the climax of the prophetic tradition: e.g., 21:11; 21:33–46; 23:34–39. See also J. Daryl Charles, "The Greatest or the Least in the Kingdom?: The Disciple's Relationship to the Law (Matt 5:17–20)" *TrinJ*, 13 (1992) 142–143.

command is said to be like this one, the commandment to love one's neighbor as oneself (Leviticus 19:18). Familiarity with this text ought not prevent us from noting that love of fellow humans is put on the same level as love for God. The important point, of course, is 22:40 where all the law and the prophets are said to hang (*krematai*) on these two commands. It is not so much that all the others may be deduced from these two as that these two determine how all the others are to be understood and applied.[38] Similarly, the golden rule is said to encompass the law and the prophets (7:12). Surely the golden rule is to be understood as synonymous with the love command in Leviticus 19:18.[39]

The focus that Matthew places on the love command can be seen in other ways as well. The arrangement of the antitheses suggests that the love command in 5:43–47 is both the climax of the section and the principle underlying all the antitheses.[40] (Note the inclusio between 5:20 and 5:47 with *perisseusē* and *perisson*.) In 19:19, unlike the parallel accounts in Mark and Luke, the love command is listed along with some of the social commands from the decalogue as the commands that should be kept to enter eternal life. In Matthew's mind the love command is the prism through which the others are to be understood and the command that shows clearly that the rich young man had not kept the commandments. It is no accident that in Matthew *teleios* occurs only here and at 5:48, both in close proximity to the love

---

[38] McConnell, 13; Barth, 77–78. Schweizer, *The Good News According to Matthew,* 425, suggested that these two commands were the only ones that need to be obeyed. This can hardly be what Matthew intended. See also the discussion by Terence L. Donaldson, "The Law that 'Hangs' (Mt. 22:40): Rabbinic Formulation and Matthean Social World," in *Society of Biblical Literature 1990 Seminar Papers,* ed. David J. Lull (Atlanta: Scholars Press, 1990), 14–33; and R. F. Collins, "Matthew's *Entolai:* Towards an Understanding of the Commandments in the First Gospel," in *The Four Gospels: 1992,* ed. F. Van Segbroeck, C. M. Tuckett, G. Van Belle, and J. Verheyden 3 vols.; (Leuven: University Press, 1992), 2, 1325–1348.

[39] Note that Didache 1.2 connects the love command and the golden rule. The whole section appears to have been influenced by Matthew. Meier's attempt (p. 42 n. 4) to disparage the golden rule is misguided. See the treatment by Paul Ricoeur, "The Golden Rule: Exegetical and Theological Perplexities," *NTS* 36 (1990) 392–397.

[40] Cf. Patte, 82, who viewed the last antithesis as the logical conclusion of the others, and McConnell, 49–54. On the love command, see Victor Paul Furnish, *The Love Command in the New Testament* (Nashville: Abingdon, 1972), especially 74–84; John Piper, *'Love Your Enemies'* (Cambridge: Cambridge University Press, 1979); and Willard M. Swartley, ed., *The Love of Enemy and Nonretaliation in the New Testament* (Louisville: Westminster/John Knox, 1992).

command.[41] In 19:21 the rich young man is not given a higher level counsel of perfection, but a commentary to understand the intention of the commands and the nature of discipleship.[42] We ought not overlook as well that, while the love command is not explicitly mentioned in 25:31–46, the verdict at end judgment is based on whether one practiced love.[43] Matthew 24:12 is also important, for here *anomia* and *agapē* are viewed as opposites.

Parallel to the emphasis on the love command is the focus in Matthew on mercy. I would not see this focus as something different from the love command, but merely another way to express it.[44] Mercy is clearly an important theme for Matthew, not only because of his double use of Hosea 6:6 as the basis for showing the intention of the law (9:13 and 12:7), but also because of the importance of the theme for him generally. In 23:23 justice, mercy, and faithfulness are identified as the weightier matters of the law. *Dikaiosunē* and *eleēmosunē* seem to be equated in 6:1–2. In 5:7 the merciful are promised mercy and in 18:33 the point of the Parable of the Unforgiving Servant is that the mercy of God requires (*edei*) that people show mercy to each other.

While Hosea 6:6 is paradigmatic for Matthew, it is not clear how strongly he understood the words "not sacrifice". M. Borg argued that

---

[41] On *teleios* see P. J. Du Plessis, *TELEIOS: The Idea of Perfection in the New Testament* (Kampen: Uitgave J. H. Kok, [1959]); Barth, 97–103; and E. Yarnold, "*Teleios* in St. Matthew's Gospel," in *Studia Evangelica*, IV, ed. F. L. Cross (Berlin: Akademie, 1968) 269–273. Beare, 163, pointed out that what is meant in this context is the completeness of love. There is little difference between 5:48 and the parallel in Luke 6:36. Certainly, there is no doctrine of perfectionism here. The verse merely means that God's people take their character from their God. The person who is *teleios* lacks nothing, but expresses unswerving devotion to God. Relationship with God is assumed, but the attempt by Guelich, 234–237, to downplay the moral element and the radical call to obedience is unjustified.

[42] Contra Lamar Cope, *Matthew, A Scribe Trained for the Kingdom of Heaven* (Washington D.C.: Catholic Biblical Association of America, 1976) 116. That 19:21 is not a counsel of perfection is obvious if one compares the call to discipleship here with the call to discipleship in 16:24. I cannot accept that Jesus' recitation of the commands in this context is possibly simply a set-up as suggested by Douglas J. Moo, "Jesus and the Authority of the Mosaic Law," *JSNT* 20 (1984) 13.

[43] Depending, of course, on how one interprets 25:40. Some interpret this verse of the reception of missionaries and thereby lessen the focus on love. See e.g., J. Ramsey Michaels, "Apostolic Hardships and Righteous Gentiles: a Study of Matthew 25:31–46," *JBL* 84 (1965) 27–37.

[44] Cf. Sand, 208.

no objection to the cult is presupposed in Matthew's use of this text.[45] Texts like 5:23–24 and 17:24–27 seem to assume acceptance of the temple and its worship. A. E. Harvey is not far wrong in saying that Jesus (and for our purposes Matthew) had little interest in the cult[46] even with the account of the cleansing of the temple. At least, we can conclude with E. P. Sanders that Jesus (and Matthew) did not consider the temple inviolate.[47] There is one greater than the temple who has appeared (12:6), so if the temple cult has any validity, it is not because the temple is valid in and of itself, but only in so far as the temple practice is subsumed under the teaching of Jesus, or more explicitly, under the demands for both mercy and love.[48] However, I do not think we can exclude the possibility that for Matthew the words "not sacrifice" provide an implicit rejection of the cult. It is surprising that he did not make more of these words, especially if his gospel was penned after 70 CE.

To say that Jesus substituted the mercy code for the holiness code may be too strong, but, at least in Matthew, Jesus disregarded the holiness code in favor of the mercy code. Whereas the holiness code focuses on separation and caused the Pharisees constantly to fear contamination, the mercy code is inclusive, even to the extent of loving one's enemies, and assumes that true holiness, not uncleanness, is contagious.[49] One has only to read Matthew 8–9 in which Matthew underscores that Jesus willingly touched a leper, a hemorrhaging woman, and a girl believed to be dead and was willing to enter the house of a Gentile. His same lack of concern for cleanliness regulations is obvious in 15:1–20. At least we must conclude that the concern of much of the Old Testament law with cultic cleanliness regulations was viewed as peripheral by Jesus in Matthew. That concern is unimportant in light of the demand for love and mercy which is the key to understanding the law and the prophets.

The real issue, as several people have pointed out, is how one reads the scriptures. The issue is thus not one's relation to torah, but

---

[45] Borg, 362 n. 168.

[46] Harvey, 64.

[47] Sanders, 251.

[48] Cf. Sand, 44; and Cope, 67–70. Tikva Frymer-Kensky, "Jesus and the Law," in *Jesus in History and Myth*, ed. R. Joseph Hoffmann and Gerald A. Larue (Buffalo: Prometheus, 1986) 131, commented that *ḥesed* is a dangerous principle of law since it cannot be legislated!

[49] Borg, 123–138; cf. Sand, 210.

how one interprets all the scriptures. There can be little doubt that in Judaism the torah was given greater importance than the prophets and the writings.[50] The Samaritans and Sadducees accepted only the torah, and the other groups took their identity from torah much more than from any other portion of scripture. In Matthew, however, Jesus will not allow reading only torah or sections of torah. One must read all the law and the prophets. With this is the recognition that not all of the law (and the prophets) is of one piece. The law is not a uniform codex.[51] There are parts of it that are more important than other parts. (E.g., Deuteronomy 24:1 is a concession, but Genesis 2:24 points to the divine intention.) What one must seek in reading the scriptures is the pure unconditioned will of God. As J. Suggs pointed out, what we confront in Matthew is law opposed to law.[52] In Matthew, Jesus provides a hermeneutic for reading the scriptures. Everything is to be understood in light of the requirements of love and mercy. To the question "What is the law?" the answer is, "The love command and the demand for mercy." To the question, "When is the law not law?" the answer is, "When it is only law and not in keeping with the tenor of all the law and the prophets." The wry humor in 12:12 (cf. 10:31) that decides in favor of doing good on the sabbath is merely an extension of this hermeneutic of love and mercy.[53]

Matthew 5:17–20

The legitimacy of reading Matthew in this way depends to some degree on showing how specific texts can be interpreted on the basis of finding a hermeneutical center to Matthew's understanding of the law. Matthew 5:17–20 is both the most important text and the most difficult to treat. On the other hand, possibly the text is not as difficult

---

[50] The point was made at least as early as J. A. Bengel that the prophets were valued less than the torah (*Gnomon*, [Edinburgh: T. & T. Clark, 1877] 1, 168). See also Beare, 139; Bennett Harvie Branscomb, *Jesus and the Law of Moses* (New York: Richard R. Smith, 1930) 27–30; Sand, 180; Meier, 71–72; and Donald A. Hagner, *Matthew 1–13*, WBC (Dallas: Word, 1993) 105. Note *Midr. Ps.* 90.4; *Yad* IV.3; *Roš. Haš.* IV.6; *Meg* IV.1–5; *b. Meg.* 14a; *y. Meg.* 70d.

[51] Barth, 78; Sand, 40, 193 and 207; Mohrlang, 21.

[52] Suggs, 107–108.

[53] With reference to a hermeneutical approach to the law in Matthew, see (in addition to the works listed in n. 29) Patte, 74, 167–168, and 315; Borg, 71 and 161; and Sand, 188, 193, and 216. Bengel, 1, 227, had already suggested that Hosea 6:6 was an axiom of interpretation.

as we have made it.[54] Many of the problems seem to be caused by the difficulties modern interpreters have with the law, especially in relation to what they know from Paul. Why else would people conclude that texts like 5:20 and 48 are to drive the reader to despair?[55] Why else would someone conclude that 5:20 is not about the law but about Christian righteousness?[56] Why would T. W. Manson suggest that 5:18 was originally bitter irony which meant, It is easier for heaven and earth to pass away than for the scribes to give up the smallest bit of that tradition by which they make the law of none effect.[57] Why would J. P. Meier conclude that with law Matthew had to grapple with resistant building blocks?[58] Why would K. Berger seek to avoid a reference to the torah with the expression the law and the prophets?[59] And why would 5:17–20 be interpreted partly with reference to Jesus' words so that F. D. Bruner would suggest 5:17 honors both the Old Testament and the New Testament, 5:18 honors especially the Old Testament, and 5:19 honors especially the New Testament.[60] Granted that there are difficult issues in this text, we have made the problems worse. Matthew did not see or intend any difficulty.

Often the solution to this text is found in tradition historical approaches that argue Matthew brought together sayings with which he did not fully agree or that he used one saying to contradict another. The position typical of these approaches is that 5:17–20 reflects debates between the conservative Jewish Christian community and a freer, probably Hellenistic, community. Sayings such as those in vs. 18 and 19 preserve, at least partly, the argument of the conservative

---

[54] Cf. Phillip Sigal, *The Halakah of Jesus of Nazareth According to the Gospel of Matthew* (Lanham, MD: University Press of America, 1986) 19–23.

[55] Which Beare, 152, rightly rejected.

[56] Lambrecht, 89.

[57] Manson, 135.

[58] Meier, 23.

[59] Klaus Berger, *Die Gesetzesauslegung Jesu: Teil I: Markus und Parallelen* (Neukirchen-Vluyn: Neukirchener Verlag, 1972), 208 and 219. See also Kari Syreeni, *The Making of the Sermon on the Mount. Part I: Methodology and Compositional Analysis* (Helsinki: Suomalainen Tiedeakatemia, 1987) 196–202. Note also his negative evaluation of Matthew here and in his "Matthew, Luke, and the Law: A Study in Hermeneutical Exegesis," in *The Law in the Bible and in its Environment*, ed. Timo Veijola (Göttingen: Vandenhoeck & Ruprecht, 1990) 126–155.

[60] Frederick Dale Bruner, *The Christbook: A Historical/Theological Commentary: Matthew 1–12* (Waco: Word, 1987) 168.

group. Matthew 5:18d and 20 are viewed as the evangelist's drastic alteration or negation of these conservative ideas and are the only parts that express what Matthew really thinks. In these reconstructions Matthew ends up holding a Pauline position which is the opposite of what he seems to be saying. R. Guelich's view is illustrative. In his view, 5:17–19 was a misunderstanding and distortion of Jesus' ministry. Matthew added "or the prophets" in 5:17 and "until all things come to pass" in 5:18 to point to Jesus' teaching and ministry. Surprisingly, Matthew included 5:19, but countered it by 5:20 and the antitheses so that the question of keeping the legal demands of the law becomes moot, since a righteousness that comes from keeping the law is inadequate for entering the kingdom.[61]

Almost certainly there were debates about the law which, indeed, made the subject important to Matthew, but I doubt very much whether 5:17–20 reflects the arguments of those debates. Furthermore, one must ask what Matthew thought he was doing on such an approach. Can we believe that Matthew thought his reader would know that he really meant the opposite of the words he was writing?

The placement of these verses in Matthew's overall construction must be given due attention. Clearly Matthew has hurried through the necessary elements in the story of Jesus to get to this point. Note what a brief and rapid summary of Jesus' early ministry is given in 4:12–25. In Matthew's mind the most important part of the ministry of Jesus is his teaching on the proper understanding of God's law. Here W. D. Davies is surely correct: ". . . the penetrating demands of Jesus . . . were part of 'the bright light of the Gospel', that is, they were revelatory".[62] As I understand Matthew, the demands of Jesus are not something different from the law, but an explanation of what the law and prophets really are. Matthew placed the Sermon on the Mount early in his Gospel because he believed the call to such holy living would be a revealing invitation to the kingdom. Therefore, because of its location,

---

[61] Guelich, 134–174. See also Meier, 40f. and especially 64, where Meier suggested that prior to his death and resurrection Jesus confined himself to the land and people of Israel and remained faithful to the law. After the death and resurrection, the new heavens and the new earth have come, and the binding force of the Mosaic law has passed. Hamerton-Kelly, 20f., found three distinct views of the law in Matthew. For this kind of approach, see also Arens, 91–116; Luz, 227–244; McConnell, 6–41 (who on p. 34 suggested that 5:18–19 were included because of a missionary motive); and Banks, 203–226.

[62] Davies, *The Setting of the Sermon on the Mount*, 437.

we must assume that 5:17–20 was of unquestioned importance for Matthew.[63] He thought he was providing a foundation from which to understand the rest of Jesus' teaching and its relation to the Hebrew scriptures.

The work of Daniel Patte is especially important here. He pointed out that authors use oppositions, of which we have three in 5:17–19, as the primary mode of expression of their intentions.[64] Such oppositions remove ambiguity and express the main points of the text. "'Explicit oppositions,'. . . can be viewed as a direct expression of the author's convictions."[65] Usually the oppositions are conveyed with old knowledge (imagery and symbols that make sense for the audience).[66] If this is true, both because of the placement and the form, Matthew did not record material with which he was in disagreement. Rather, these verses express what he really believed. Regardless of the origin of these sayings,[67] for Matthew they provide a coherent statement about Jesus' interpretation of the law.

Instead of providing a detailed account of how the exegetical issues in these verses have been treated, I will only suggest how I think these sayings should be understood. In 5:17 there are two items that require comment: the law and the prophets and *plērōsai*. The expression the law and the prophets is intended to point to the Hebrew scriptures as a whole.[68] The intention with this statement is to place the rest of the scriptures on a par with the law and as the means to a proper understanding of the law.[69] The term *plērōsai* has created frequent debates and is somewhat surprising. One would have expected *stēsai* or something similar (cf. Romans 3:31). I do not think that Matthew used *plērōsai* because of his emphasis on the predictive function of the scriptures.[70] This section prepares one to understand

---

[63] Luz, 230–231. See also his "Die Erfüllung des Gesetzes bei Matthäus (Mt 5,17–20)," *ZTK* 75 (1978) 398–435.

[64] Patte, 6–11.

[65] Ibid., 7. (Italics his.)

[66] Ibid., 10.

[67] Wolfgang Trilling, *Das wahre Israel* (München: Kösel-Verlag, 1964) 167f.; and Suggs, 116, are representative of those who would see 5:17–20 as composed of four unrelated logia.

[68] Jack Dean Kingsbury, *Matthew as Story* (Philadelphia: Fortress, 1986) 66; Georg Strecker, *Die Bergpredigt* (Göttingen: Vandenhoeck & Ruprecht, 1984) 56.

[69] Sand, 180.

[70] Contra Meier, 80.

Jesus' teaching, not his actions, and Matthew does not have another of his formula citations until 8:17. There is no thought of fulfilling and therefore transcending, as Banks suggested.[71] Exactly which translation is preferable is difficult to decide, but the thought of Matthew is clear enough. His intention is to say that Jesus did not come to set aside or nullify the scriptures; rather his purpose was to affirm them and bring them to reality.[72] Possibly the word "accomplish" is a suitable translation and would also serve well in the similar construction at 3:15. Matthew's point is that Jesus came so that people would live according to the scriptures.

There is a parallel to this use of *plērōsai ton nomon* in Romans 8:4; 13:8; and Galatians 5:14. Surprisingly, in the last two texts, the fulfillment of the law is also seen in the love command. We do not need to suggest, as did J. P. Meier, that the pre-Matthean form read *poiein* or some similar word,[73] for the parallels in Paul and the context of Matthew verify a meaning for *plērōsai* that focuses on doing, obeying, or fulfilling in speech and action.[74] In other words, 5:17 expresses that Jesus' purpose was not to destroy the scriptures, but to bring them to actuality in people's lives.

With 5:18 the questions are the meaning of the *heōs* clauses and the reference of one iota and one hook. The latter are merely metaphorical for the least important commands. Whether the first *heōs* clause means "never"[75] or at "the end of the age"[76] is almost irrelevant from the standpoint of Matthew's readers. Even if 24:35 intends a higher valuation of Jesus' words than what is said about the law, the readers do not know that yet. What they do know is that as long as

---

[71] Banks, 210. Nor does *plērōsai* contain an element of discontinuity.

[72] Barth, 68–69; Strecker, 57; Arens, 105–106; Charles, 149–151; see Henrik Ljungman, *Das Gesetz Erfüllen* (Lund: C. W. K. Gleerup, 1954), especially pp. 53f. See also James D. G. Dunn, *The Partings of the Ways* (London: SCM, 1991) 101–102. Ferdinand Hahn, "Mt 5,17 Anmerkungen zum Erfüllungsgedanken bei Matthäus," in *Die Mitte des Neuens Testaments*, ed. Ulrich Luz and Hans Weder (Göttingen: Vandenhoeck & Ruprecht, 1983) 45, argues against this interpretation.

[73] Meier, 85; on p. 80 he had rejected the meaning doing for *plērōsai*, but then had to reconstruct the text to bring back this meaning. He had noted that Paul used *plērōsai* with reference to law, but inexplicably rejected any relevance of this for Matthew (pp. 75–76).

[74] Suggs, 117; Patte, 72; Sand, 185–186; cf. Gustaf Dalman, *JesusJeshua*, (London: SPCK, 1929) 56, who said that *plērousthai* is akin to *teleisthai*, to be accomplished.

[75] Strecker, 58; Arens, 92.

[76] Patte, 71; Meier, 61.

their lives continue on this earth the law has validity. The second *heōs* clause is more difficult, but surely the reference is not to the death and resurrection or to all the ministry of Jesus.[77] The two clauses may be tautologous,[78] or as many suggest, the second possibly should be interpreted ethically to mean until all the law demands is accomplished (i.e., until the will of God is fully realized).[79] In either case the reader knows that the law has not and will not be set aside, at least until God's purposes for this earth are accomplished.

Matthew 5:19 is not a literary fossil[80] or an undigested morsel.[81] This saying functions as further confirmation of the points made in 5:17–18. The primary question here is the intention of the expression, "one of the least of these commands." The attempt to interpret this as a reference to Jesus' teaching is unfounded.[82] Certainly Matthew's readers could not be expected to understand this. Nor is there a reference to Paul[83] or to the ceremonial laws.[84] The reference is to the same items as intended in 5:18 with one iota and one hook. The intention is to underscore the importance of proper teaching about and obedience to the law. There is also a question whether this text teaches only a lesser place in the kingdom for those who teach and obey inappropriately or whether such language is metaphorical for exclusion.[85] I would suggest that the saying is metaphorical, but that it portrays what is valued by God or is displeasing to God (similar to the reward language of chapter 6).

The meaning of 5:20 for Matthew is clear. A righteousness is required that goes beyond what the scribes and Pharisees thought was satisfactory. *Dikaiosynē* is to be understood of ethical behavior rather

---

[77] Hamerton-Kelly, 30f., attempted to verify the death-resurrection as the end of the law by recourse to 28:11.

[78] Hübner, p. 19; and W. D. Davies and Dale C. Allison, Jr., *A Critical and Exegetical Commentary on the Gospel According to Saint Matthew* (Edinburgh: T. & T. Clark, 1988) 1, 495. A. M. Honeyman, "Matthew V.18 and the Validity of the Law," *NTS* 1 (1954) 141–142, argued that the second clause stated positively what the first stated negatively.

[79] Sand, 38; Luz, 237.

[80] As Lambrecht suggested, 88.

[81] As Meier suggested, p. 104.

[82] See n. 19 and note the saner discussion in Collins, 1325–1348.

[83] See n. 10.

[84] Strecker, p. 60.

[85] Schweizer, *The Good News According to Matthew*, 105.

than a gift from God.[86] The greater righteousness is both quantitative and qualitative.[87] The antitheses demonstrate what this greater righteousness entails, and 5:48 is essentially a restatement of 5:20.[88]

No stretch of the imagination is required to accept that Matthew intended 5:17 and 20, but could he have intended 5:18–19? The important question is not whether he intended these verses, however, but how legalistically he intended them. The difficulty emerges when we treat these or any other sayings atomistically; Matthew placed them together in a unit and within a larger work. He has already warned the reader that absolute statements such as the one in 5:18 are not to be read legalistically, but within the framework of the whole of scripture (and/or Jesus' sayings). In 4:4 an absolute statement from scripture is given: "A person will not live from bread alone, but from every word proceeding from the mouth of God." So in 4:6 the devil takes a word from God as the basis of the second temptation, but that word is set aside by another that is more important. One may not merely plug in individual texts. Matthew does not intend for absolute statements to be interpreted legalistically. Matthew 5:18–19 has the function of underscoring the permanency of scripture and the value that God places on proper teaching and obedience.[89]

In effect, 5:18 and 19 both are hyperbole. Some have argued against the suggestion of hyperbole,[90] but here and elsewhere in Matthew, including 23:2–3, there are several examples. R. H. Stein has underscored the use of hyperbole in the teaching of Jesus and provided criteria for recognizing it. Among the criteria relevant to our discussion are logical impossibilities (such as fulfilling iotas and hooks) and conflicts with other sayings. Commissive language which seeks to

---

[86] See Benno Przybylski, *Righteousness in Matthew and his World of Thought* (Cambridge: Cambridge University Press, 1980) 84; and Donald Hagner, "Righteousness in Matthew's Theology," in *Worship, Theology and Ministry in the Early Church*, ed. Michael J. Wilkins and Terence Paige (Sheffield: JSOT, 1992) 111, although he argues that 3:15; 5:6; and possibly 21:32 refer to the righteous saving activity of God. That this article is concerned to deal with the role of grace in Matthew suggests a Pauline grid, as does the explanation that concern for faithfulness to the law must stem from Jewish Christians for whom Matthew writes.

[87] Przybylski, 85; Strecker, 64.

[88] Sanders, 260–262, is wrong to see in 5:17 a strict legalism and in 5:20 a call for Jesus' followers to be more righteous than the Pharisees *by the same standard*. (Emphasis his.)

[89] Cf. Patte, 73–74.

[90] E.g., Meier, 44 n. 15.

cause things to happen tends more toward hyperbole.[91] That is exactly what is happening in Matthew. Strong statements are made to persuade the reader that scripture is of permanent validity and is to be practiced as the will of God. This is popular literature, not a technical, theological writing, and we should expect to find forms like hyperbole.

Did Jesus Abrogate the Law?

The question is not, "Did Jesus break the oral law?" for certainly he did. The question is, "Did he break the written law?" To answer this, we will have to look at individual texts, but the question presupposes some unfounded assumptions. The question wrongly assumes that the law is a monolithic entity in which all of its statements point in one direction. There are numerous statements that pull against each other just like the tension between Psalm 91:11–12 and Deuteronomy 6:16 in Matthew 4:6–7. One of the most obvious areas where there are diverse statements is the question of divorce. Not only do we find the concession of Deuteronomy 24:1 set over against Genesis 2:24, but we find that in certain texts divorce is mandated to protect the wife (Exod 21:11 and Deut 21:14), whereas other texts prohibit divorce to protect the wife (Deut 22:19 and 29). Both sets of texts have the same goal, but they propose opposite actions. Examples like this could be multiplied easily. How does one harmonize the command not to seek peace or good relations with Ammonites and Moabites in Deuteronomy 23:6 with the demand to love the alien in the same book (10:16–19)? The Hebrew scriptures are not monolithic. What Jesus does in Matthew is show one how to read the scriptures and discern the will of God.

Another assumption behind this question is that no other Jew abrogated the law. Is it an abrogation of the law that the death penalty is not carried out in Judaism for breaking the sabbath (Exod 31:15)? Is it an abrogation of the law that financial penalties were substituted for literal obedience to the lex talionis?[92] Is it an abrogation of the law that Yohanan ben Zakkai abolished the trial of the suspected adultress

---

[91] Robert H. Stein, *Difficult Sayings in the Gospels: Jesus Use of Overstatement and Hyperbole* (Grand Rapids: Baker, 1985) 36–37, 89. He listed 5:17–18, 33–37, 39–41, 42, 48, and 23:3 all as hyperbole. To classify texts as hyperbole is not to say that they may be ignored. It merely means the texts are not absolute. See also Hagner, *Matthew 1–13*, 106–108.

[92] See the discussions in David Daube, *The New Testament and Rabbinic Judaism* (London: Athlone, 1956) 255–259; and Branscomb, 31–32.

and presided over the dissolution of the sacrificial system?[93] Certainly there were statements about the law in Judaism that were as absolute as Matthew 5:18,[94] and E. P. Sanders is at least partly right in saying that there is no precedent in Judaism for making distinctions within the law.[95] No one argued for keeping only the moral law; that there was discussion about light and heavy commands, however, shows that there were valuations made among the different commands, even if the assumption was that all commands would be kept.[96]

Unanswered questions still remain about what Jews in Jesus' day really believed about the law. It is one thing to quote general and absolute statements, but it is another thing to note what really is practiced. The law was believed totally, but it was also assumed that the meaning of the law is ambiguous and must be debated.[97] Rabbinic majority opinions were given, but dissenting opinions suggesting entirely different practices were dutifully recorded.[98] Sometimes one passage of scripture is quoted as justification for not obeying another passage.[99] In fact, P. Sigal argued that abrogation of specific precepts of the written torah was not unusual in Jesus' milieu.[100] This kind of activity to justify not doing a written precept seems to be what is going on with oaths (5:33–37) and with gifts to avoid caring for parents (15:4–9). The point in Matthew in these instances is that regardless of what one does scripturally or exegetically to justify his or her action, the word and will of God have been nullified. S. Westerholm's comment that the learned of Israel understood the law as containing statutes, whereas Jesus did not may be appropriate.[101]

---

[93] See the discussion in Frymer-Kensky, p. 130. Cf. Num Rab 19.8.

[94] *Exod. Rab.* 6:1; *Lev. Rab.* 19:2; *Cant. Rab.* 5:11.3; cf. Bar 4:1; Wis 18:4; 4 Ezra 9.37.

[95] Sanders, 248.

[96] ʾAbot II:1; IV.2; *Midr Ps.* 9:3; *Deut. Rab.* 6:2; *Sifre Deut.* 48, 79, 82.

[97] *Ḥag* 1:8; *Pesiq. R.* 21; *Midr Ps.* 12:4. Note the hidden things of the law in 1QS 5:11. How seriously should we understand the rabbinic statements that the oral law is more important than the written so that even God gives heed to the elders (*Sanh.* XI.1; *Pesiq. R.* 3.1–2.)? So much attention is given to the written and oral law that not even miracles or a bath kol can set it aside (*b. B. Meṣ.* 59a).

[98] E.g., *Sanh.* X:3; XI:1; *Gen. Rab.* 7.2.

[99] See the discussions in Sigal, 48–51, 68; Harvey, 60–61; and Sanders, 248–249.

[100] Sigal, p. 23. See also Davies and Allison, I, 492.

[101] Stephen Westerholm, *Jesus and Scribal Authority* (Lund: C. W. K. Gleerup, 1978) 59–60, 112–113.

In other words, one could claim to believe the law totally, but not
do what it says. That was true for people who sought ways to avoid the
intention of the law. It was also true for crisis times such as with the
Maccabeans in regard to sabbath observance during war and for the
Qumranites who would not participate in the temple worship. Some of
the issues with regard to Jesus' observance of the law may similarly
derive from the crisis nature of his ministry.[102] More importantly, the
question is, "What is the law?" Jesus in Matthew provides insight into
the intention of the scriptures and presses people to an obedience that
goes to the core of their being.

Even with this in mind, we still must ask whether Jesus' teaching
sets aside the law. The answer to that question depends on the
treatment of several texts and on how atomistically and legalistically
one wishes to treat the Hebrew scriptures.

The Antitheses

The antitheses are clearly intended to provide an explanation of
the greater righteousness that is demanded in 5:20. The point in every
case is to go beyond a surface level to the intention of the will of God
in expressing the law. What is required is an integrity of being that is
characterized by love, mercy, and truth. The two important questions
in approaching the antitheses are whether there is strong opposition
or continuation between the two halves of the statements and, if there
is opposition, whether it is the word of God or scribal tradition that is
being opposed. The attempt to see in the antitheses a contrast
between the word of God and the word of Jesus[103] is unfounded and
very difficult to reconcile with 5:17–20. The arguments that the
antitheses are not strong oppositions must be given serious
consideration.[104] At the same time, it is not satisfactory to say that the
opposition is merely to the scribal interpretation.[105]

---

[102] Harvey, 60–65; Manson, 189.

[103] As Dalman, 73; Jack Dean Kingsbury, "The Place, Structure, and Meaning of
the Sermon on the Mount Within Matthew," *Int* 41 (1987) 139; Meier, 133.

[104] Daube, 55–62; Levison, 173–176; and Sanders, 260, who said the antitheses
affirm the law, but press beyond it. Matthew more likely would say they affirm the
law and press to its center. See also Davies and Allison, I, 481 and 507.

[105] As Harvey, 55; and Sand, 19. Hagner, *Matthew 1–13*, 110–112, argues the
antitheses oppose a shallow and inadequate understanding of the law and that
Jesus came to bring the law and the prophets to their intended fulfillment. Yet, he
finds it necessary to speak of the antitheses as the surpassing of the Old and of
Jesus' transcending the law.

In each of the antitheses, *de* has to be analyzed in its own right.[106] In the first two antitheses *de* seems to show continuation. The intention in both is to show how far-reaching is the concern of the commands. There is no contrast with either God's word or scribal interpretation. There is only an extension of the command to show what kind of integrity is demanded. With the third, fifth, and sixth antitheses there seems to be a mild adversative tone. One could argue, as J. Levison did, that the scripture is not a point of contrast, but a basis for teaching.[107] Still, the content of the second half shows that the concern of the will of God is not in the first half, but in the concerns for love, mercy, and truth. With the fourth antithesis, the opposition seems even stronger, and at least formally there is a setting aside of texts like Deuteronomy 6:13. But it seems clear that we are dealing with scribal interpretation and the abuse of oaths, as is evidenced by 23:16–22.[108] If the function of oaths was to verify truth, and casuistry led to the avoidance of truth, then Jesus did not abrogate the law by limiting people to the simple truth. As E. P. Sanders argued, it is not against the law to be stricter than the law requires.[109]

---

[106] Many have noticed that not all the antitheses are alike; e.g., Meier, 125–161; Suggs, 113.

[107] Levison, 174.

[108] See the discussions in David E. Garland, *The Intention of Matthew 23* (Leiden: E. J. Brill, 1979) 132–136; Westerholm, 104–113; Guelich, 211–219. Meier, 156, rejected any use of 23:16–22, but the parallels are too strong and seem intentional. Material later in the gospel cannot be ignored in interpreting the Sermon on the Mount unless one accepts the unlikely hypothesis that the Sermon on the Mount was transmitted intact and integrated by Matthew as H. D. Betz suggests in his "The Sermon on the Mount (Matt. 5:3–7:27): Its Literary Genre and Function," in *Essays on the Sermon on the Mount,* 18. A similar suggestion is made by William R. Farmer, "The Sermon on the Mount: A Form-Critical and Redactional Analysis of Matt 5:1–7:29," in *Society of Biblical Literature 1986 Seminar Papers,* ed. Kent Harold Richards (Atlanta: Scholars Press, 1986) 56. Matthew 23:16–22 must be used in interpreting 5:33–37 just as 19:3–9 must be used in interpreting 5:31–32. Matthew treated themes briefly in chapters 5–7 and expanded on those subjects later in the document. For a critique of Betz's position, see Charles E. Carlston, "Betz on the Sermon of the Mount: A Critique," *CBQ,* 50 (1988), 47–57; Graham N. Stanton, "The Origin and Purpose of Matthew's Sermon on the Mount," in *Tradition and Interpretation in the New Testament,* ed. Gerald F. Hawthorne with Otto Betz (Grand Rapids: Eerdmans, 1987) 181–192 (now in his *A Gospel for a New People* [Edinburgh: T. & T. Clark, 1992] 307–325); and my "A Response to H. D. Betz on the Sermon on the Mount," *BR* 36 (1991) 88–94.

[109] Sanders, 260. See also his *Jewish Law from Jesus to the Mishnah* (Philadelphia: Trinity, 1990) 1–96 for further discussion of the Synoptic Jesus and the Law, which includes treatments of the sabbath, purity, and oaths.

There is thus no necessary abrogation of the law in any of the antitheses. The antithesis dealing with divorce is not an abrogation, for Deuteronomy 24:1 is not a legitimation of divorce, but the prohibition of a divorced woman from returning to her first husband after being defiled by a second. Furthermore, an absolute prohibition of divorce seems to be expressed in CD 4.21–5.2 and 11Q Temple Scroll 57.17–19 (if the regulations for the king were a model for the whole community, as J. Fitzmyer has argued).[110] If this is so, Jesus' comments would not be perceived as a violation of the law. Rather, as the discussion in 19:3–9 shows, his concern is for the divine intention in marriage.

The fifth antithesis is an abrogation of the law if one ignores the function of the lex talionis in its context. But the moment that one admits that the purpose of the lex talionis was to limit revenge and to make sure that wrong doing was not ignored (Deut 19:19–21), then the statement of Jesus is not a violation of that function. Without playing with words, however, Jesus' teaching is a redirection, a paradigm shift. It asks that disciples of the kingdom no longer stand on their rights; the concern is not for personal legal satisfaction. Instead, through hyperbole people are asked to implement the mercy code. If it is not a violation to be stricter than the law, it surely is not a violation to be more loving than the law requires. Jesus' concerns are different from those of the lex talionis, but an absolute understanding of Jesus' statements is not possible either.

Similarly the sixth antithesis, the climax of this section, is a redirection. As elsewhere, Jesus will not allow limits to be set on one's responsibility. Integrity in the kingdom requires that the love command control all relationships, including relationships with enemies. There is a different orientation from much of the Old Testament, but the origin of this teaching is the Old Testament itself. The issue again is how the scriptures are to be understood and what in them is to be emphasized.

Other Possible Abrogations of the Law

Matthew 8:22 is not an abrogation of an Old Testament law, although it would have been seen as an abrogation of the oral tradition.[111] Nor would Matthew have concluded that Jesus was

---

[110] Joseph A. Fitzmyer, "The Matthean Divorce Texts and Some New Palestinian Evidence," *TS* 37 (1976) 213–221; Sigal, 112–114; and Yadin, *The Temple Scroll,* 1, 353–357.

[111] Contra Sanders, *Jesus and Judaism,* 252–255. See Harvey, 60. This passage does

violating what the scriptures taught about the sabbath. When I started this paper, I intended to argue that Jesus violated the written law at only one point: the food laws in 15:11. Clearly if this statement is understood in an absolute sense, the legislations about unclean foods are set aside. However, I think now that this is to read Mark 7:19 into Matthew. In Matthew the issue is the tradition of the elders concerning ceremonial washings. Jesus contrasted their tradition with the word of God. He told the people that eating with unclean hands does not defile, but that breaking God's law does. (Note that the sins that defile in Matt 15:19 are mostly violations of the decalogue.) It would be hazardous to conclude from this text that Jesus taught against and violated kosher food laws, particularly since this was still a difficult issue in the early church.[112] Mark drew the conclusion that all foods were clean, but Matthew did not. It is fair to say that Jesus disregards uncleanness issues in Matthew, but how Matthew or his community dealt with the issue of kosher food (or circumcision) is not known. From the evidence we have, Matthew did not think that Jesus abrogated the law.[113]

What of the "Legalistic Elements"?

There are still some texts in Matthew that suggest that Matthew not only did not abrogate the law, but that he was legalistic in observance of the law. Matthew 23:2–3, 23, and 24:20 all express attitudes that are surprising.

I have already indicated that 23:2–3 is hyperbole and must not be taken out of its context.[114] The tension set up by these verses is

---

show that following Jesus supersedes any other religious duty.

[112] Barth, 89–90; Branscomb, 180; Sanders, *Jesus and Judaism*, 266.

[113] See Alan F. Segal, "Matthew's Jewish Voice," in *Social History of the Matthean Community*, ed. David Balch (Minneapolis: Fortress, 1991) 7, 22.

[114] Stein, 38–39; Patte, 321, only says that it is not literal; Beare, 448, that it is a foil; and Garland, 54–55, (following Banks, 176) that it is a rhetorical preparation, a strategem. Christine Heubult, "Mt 5:17–20: Ein Beitrag zur Theologie des Evangelisten Matthäus," *ZNW* 71 (1980) 147–148, suggested that 23:3 does not refer to teaching, but means that the community should comply with what the Pharisees say because of the emergency situation. The emergency is that the Pharisees sit on Moses' seat, and the Christian community is powerless. This is unlikely. In a significant forthcoming article in *JBL* ["Do and keep what Moses Says (Matthew 23:2–7),"] Mark Allan Powell argues that this text is not about accepting Pharisaic preaching, but rejecting Pharisaic practice. Rather, the text assumes that scribes and Pharisees control accessibility to the text. They are the ones who possess copies of the Torah and tell others what Moses said. Disciples are instructed to keep what the Pharisees recite from the Torah, but not to follow

intentional.[115] The validity of the task of the scribes and Pharisees is affirmed, but their practices are rejected as hypocrisy. The qualification of these strong statements in the following verses would have prevented any misunderstanding on the part of Matthew's readers.

The call for focus on the weightier matters of the law in 23:23 is well in keeping with Matthew's whole approach to the law, but the call not to leave aside tithing of spices is unexpected. Jesus did not argue against tithing, and surely the intention here is to provide an emphatic way of saying that less important items ought not be neglected. The law is concerned primarily with issues of justice, mercy, and faithfulness, but it addresses many other parts of life too that ought not be neglected. This statement must be kept within the tenor of all of Matthew's teaching on the law. It is impossible to accept that the intention was to foster practice that would divert attention away from the weightier elements. This is not a call to legalism.[116]

Matthew 24:20 is difficult to treat because it is so cryptic. Possibly Matthew assumes his readers keep the sabbath strictly.[117] However, this is less likely since emergency situations allowed for breaking the sabbath, and it would make Matthew's view stricter than the Pharisaic view. It may be as A. Schlatter and E. Hirsch argued, that Christians would be as conspicuous as spotted dogs fleeing in the middle of a Jewish conflict.[118] However, a more plausible solution is that the difficulty of flight on the sabbath is related to the fact that shops and gates would be closed.[119] In any case, it is difficult to believe that the attitude reflected in 12:1–14 is altered by this text.

---

their interpretation of Torah. They speak Torah, but do not do it. For an investigation of this text in light of rabbinic material, see Han-Jürgen Becker, *Auf der Kathedra des Mose: Rabbinisch-theologisches Denken und antirabbinische Polemik in Matthäus 23,1–12* (Berlin: Institut Kirche und Judentum, 1990).

[115] Patte, 321.

[116] See the discussion in McConnell, 84; and Patte, 325–326. Westerholm, 59, assigned a minor place to tithing, but the text seems instead to assign a minor role to tithing minor things.

[117] Patte, 539.

[118] Quoted in Barth, 92.

[119] Banks, 102. For further discussion of this text, see Graham N. Stanton, "'Pray that your Flight may not be in Winter or on a Sabbath' (Matthew 24.20)," *JSNT* 37 (1989) 17–30 [now in his *A Gospel for a New People*, 192–206]; and the rebuttal by Eric Kun-Chun Wong, "The Matthean Understanding of the Sabbath: A Response to Graham Stanton," *JSNT* 44 (1991) 3–18.

Conclusions

Matthew's view of the law is that it is unquestionably enduring in validity. He does not present a legalistic view of the law, but nor does he leave the suggestion that Christians may be lax in their obedience to the law. Judgment is still an important theme for Matthew, and the law is to be lived.

The law, however, for Matthew was not a monolithic entity. It was diverse with some laws pointing in different directions, thereby creating tension. In Matthew's presentation of Jesus' teaching those diverse laws are organized by and subsumed under the love commands and the mercy code. Whereas his contemporaries had organized the law under ideas of holiness and ritual purity, Jesus reorganized it in keeping with God's love. The law is not to be treated as the focus of the canon. Rather, one must read the law and the prophets and interpret all the scriptures in accordance with the love commands, the golden rule, and God's desire for mercy instead of sacrifice. As a variation on the statement, "People are more important than things," Matthew would say, "People are more important than religion." How he worked out the cultic questions that were debated in the early church is unknown. Such questions are virtually ignored. The weightier matters of the law, justice, mercy, and faithfulness are the items about which Matthew is concerned and that expects to be lived in the faith community. These core concerns of the law direct all else and produce the integrity that is the goal of the proclamation of the kingdom.

This is not to suggest that living the law is some type of works righteousness. Even to say this is to insert Paul's thought into Matthew. There is no thought that one obeys the law by mere human effort; the focus of Matthew from first to last is that God, Jesus, or God in Jesus is with us (1:23; 18:20; 28:20). Nor is there a belief that the law is the center of relation to God. Whereas that was true with Judaism, for Matthew and his readers the center of their relation with God is Jesus.[120] Disciples do not gather around the torah; they gather in the name of Jesus. In his presence they experience the presence of God and live in accordance with his will.

---

[120] See Bornkamm, "The Authority to 'Bind' and 'Loose' in the Church in Matthew's Gospel," 91; and J. M. Gibbs, "The Son of God as the Torah Incarnate in Matthew," in *Studia Evangelica*, ed. F. L. Cross (Berlin: Akademie, 1968) 4, 38–46.

To make such statements raises the question of the relation of law and christology in Matthew. Often the suggestion is made that the hermeneutical key for understanding Matthew on the law is christological. R. Banks repeatedly argued that in contexts treating law, the real issue is christological.[121] E. Fuchs argued that "In the Gospel according to St. Matthew Jesus does not give a new law, but he substitutes himself for the law."[122] Further, Ingo Broer asserted that the authority of the law is derived from the authority of Jesus and that after Jesus the law only has authority from Jesus.[123] But, how have law and scripture become set over against Jesus and christology?[124] Such an antithesis is foreign to Matthew's theology. The law is not removed by christology. Rather, the word of God and the Son of God cohere and function together like hand and glove. The Son of God appeals to the word of God for guidance and validation (4:1–11). Jesus is the authoritative interpreter of the law, but Matthew does not now suggest that we merely follow Rabbi Jesus. The law is no longer the center of gravity; Jesus is. The Son of God is the one to whom the scriptures point and who lives in conformity with God's will and law and who teaches others to do so as well. But he is not merely a teacher. This teacher is Son of God who mediates the presence of the Father to his people. Conformity to the will of God, obedience to the love command, and following Jesus all belong together in Matthew, as 19:16–22 shows.

One further item should be mentioned. The discussion of law in Matthew suggests that Matthew's view of scripture needs to be given more serious attention. Usually Matthew is viewed as having used his scriptures as a prophecy book. Those elements are present, but Matthew seems to have a much more nuanced view of scripture and its interpretation. A reconsideration of that view would be beneficial not

---

[121] Banks, 107, 123, 131, 142, 163–164, 242, and especially 226.

[122] Ernst Fuchs, "The Parable of the Unmerciful Servant (Matt. 18,23–35)," in *Studia Evangelica*, ed. Kurt Aland et al. (Berlin: Akademie, 1959) 492.

[123] Ingo Broer, *Freiheit vom Gesetz und Radikalisierung des Gesetzes: Ein Beitrag zur Theologie des Evangelisten Matthäus* (Stuttgart: Katholisches Bibelwerk, 1980) 71, 127. See also his "Anmerkungen zum Gesetzesverstndnis des Matthäus," in *Das Gesetz im neuen Testament*, ed. Karl Kertelge (Freiburg: Herder, 1986) 128–145.

[124] Mogens Müller, "The Gospel of Matthew and the Mosaic Law," *ST* 46 (1992) 109–120, offers the connection between law and christology as Matthew's way of showing the law is sustained, but is invested with new meaning.

only for understanding Matthew, but also for current discussions about scripture.

Chapter Four

The Literary and Theological Function of the Genealogy in Matthew's Gospel[1]

DAVID R. BAUER

Matthew's genealogy of Jesus (1:1–17) has been the object of intense scrutiny since the earliest centuries of the Christian church. For the greatest part of this period, the passage was examined for the purpose of ascertaining the nature and value of its historical witness to the progenitors of Jesus. Interpreters commonly focused attention upon such issues as the provenance of the list and the relationship of this genealogy to that found in Luke 3, often with a view toward defending the historical worth of the Matthean genealogy.[2] In more recent times, scholars have generally abandoned the attempt to harmonize the two genealogies, insisting that the purpose of the NT genealogies is theological rather than biographical.[3] Attention has

---

[1] An earlier form of this paper appeared under the title, "The Literary Function of the Genealogy in Matthew's Gospel," in *The Society of Biblical Literature 1990 Seminar Papers*, ed. David J. Lull (Atlanta: Scholars Press, 1990) 451–68.

[2] Julius Africanus (160–240 CE) was the first to deal in a thorough and systematic fashion with the historical issues surrounding the progenitors of Jesus and the relationship of Matt 1:1–17 to Luke 3:23–38. His work is presented by Eusebius in *H.E.* I.7. The most complete modern attempt to relate historically the genealogies in Matthew and Luke is from Karl Bornhäuser, *Die Geburts- und Kindheitsgeschichte Jesu: Versuch einer zeitgenossischen Auslegung von Matthäus 1 und 2 und Lukas 1–3* (Gutersloh: Bertelsmann, 1930). For a survey of various proposals for harmonizing the two genealogies, see Marshall D. Johnson, *The Purpose of the Biblical Genealogies: with special reference to the setting of the genealogies of Jesus*, SNTMS 8, 3rd ed. (Cambridge: Cambridge University Press, 1988) 140–45.

[3] This recognition of the religious purposes behind the creation and promulgation of the genealogies does not undermine the importance of the human descent of Jesus for christology; NT christology generally considers it of utmost importance to affirm especially Jesus' Davidic descent. See Christoph

shifted to the religious role the genealogies played in the early Christian communities and to their function in the theology of the evangelists.[4]

Most recent studies of the Matthean genealogy have employed historical methods in order to achieve historical goals. They have employed historical methods in that they give primary consideration to Jewish or Hellenistic parallels, the development of traditions standing behind the extant list, and the evangelist's editorial procedures and redactional aims. They have pursued historical goals in that they examine the genealogy in order to illumine the *Sitz im Leben* of the evangelist's community or to reconstruct the theology of the evangelist.[5] These historical issues, associated with the discipline of redaction criticism, are significant and worthy of serious consideration. But the passage invites us also to consider its literary function within

---

Burger, *Jesus als Davidssohn* (Göttingen: Vandenhoeck & Ruprecht, 1970); Oscar Cullman, *The Christology of the New Testament* (Philadelphia: Westminster Press, 1963) 117–36; Raymond E. Brown, *The Birth of the Messiah* (Garden City, NY: Doubleday, 1979) 505–12.

[4] The intentional and systematic attempt to interpret the genealogies in light of their theological function within the Gospels can be seen already in such works as Paul-Emile Vincent, *Les Généalogies de Jésus: Étude Critique de Matthieu I, 1–17, et de Luc III, 23–38* (Alencon: Guy, 1886); and G. H. Box, "The Gospel narratives of the Nativity and the alleged influence of heathen ideas," *ZNW* 6 (1905) 80–101. But the enterprise was given significant impetus on the one hand by the rise of redaction criticism, and on the other hand by studies into the socio-religious role of genealogies in Near Eastern antiquity. See especially Robert R. Wilson, *Genealogy and History in the Biblical World* (New Haven, CT: Yale University Press, 1977).

[5] This historical orientation of method and goals is represented, e.g., in the four major treatments of the Matthean genealogy which have appeared within the last twenty-five years: Anton Vögtle, "Die Genealogie Mt 1,2–17 und die matthaische Kindheitsgeschichte," *BZ* 8 (1964) 45–58, 239–62; 9 (1965) 32–49; Johnson, *Purpose*; Herman C. Waetjen, "The Genealogy as the Key to the Gospel according to Matthew," *JBL* 95 (1976) 205–30; Brown, *Birth*. This is also the case with the treatment of the genealogy in most of the recent major commentaries, e.g., Robert H. Gundry, *Matthew: A Commentary on his Handbook for a Mixed Church Under Persecution*, 2nd ed. (Grand Rapids: Eerdmans, 1984) 13–19; Leopold Sabourin, *L'Évangile selon Saint Matthieu et ses Principaux Paralleles* (Rome: Biblical Institute Press, 1978) 17–20; W. D. Davies and Dale C. Allison, *A Critical and Exegetical Commentary on the Gospel according to Saint Matthew, Vol. I: Introduction and Commentary on Matthew I-VII*, ICC (Edinburgh: T. & T. Clark, 1988) 149–90. None of these works examines the function of the genealogy within the narrative of Matthew's Gospel in any serious way. There are, however, a few exceptions to this emphasis upon a primarily historical approach; see Charles Thomas Davis, "The Fulfillment of Creation: A Study of Matthew's Genealogy," *JAAR* 41 (1973) 520–35; and (from a structuralist perspective) Daniel Patte, *The Gospel according to Matthew: A Structural Commentary on Matthew's Faith* (Philadelphia: Fortress, 1987) 18–20.

the story world of the Gospel. The method of literary criticism, especially the form of literary criticism known as narrative criticism,[6] is singularly suited for this kind of inquiry, since it seeks to understand the world we encounter within the Gospel itself and to give attention to the major components of this "narrative world." This paper will employ insights from narrative criticism in order to explore the meaning of the genealogy and its role within the Gospel.

Although narrative criticism takes many specific forms, it always involves the following features. First, narrative critics focus upon the final form of the text, without (immediate) concern for sources or traditions that lie behind the final form. Second, narrative critics attempt to derive meaning from the story itself, rather than using the story as a means to reconstruct elements that lie outside the story itself, such as historical events to which the story might point (as does historical criticism), or to the *Sitz im Leben* of the evangelist's community (as does redaction criticism). This attempt to derive meaning from the story itself is precisely what narrative critics mean when they speak of entering the "narrative world" of the story. Indeed, narrative critics are not concerned, in the first instance, with the actual historical author or the original readers; rather, narrative critics speak of the "implied author," which is the image of the author that one construes from the narrative, and of the "implied reader," which is the image of the reader that one construes from the narrative.[7] Third,

---

[6] Presentations of New Testament narrative criticism can be found in the following: David Rhoads and Donald Michie, *Mark as Story: An Introduction to the Narrative of a Gospel* (Philadelphia: Fortress, 1982); Jack Dean Kingsbury, *Matthew as Story*, 2nd ed. (Philadelphia: Fortress, 1988); R. Alan Culpepper, *Anatomy of the Fourth Gospel: A Study in Literary Design*, Foundations and Facets: New Testament (Philadelphia: Fortress, 1983); and Mark Allan Powell, *What is Narrative Criticism?*, GBS (Minneapolis: Fortress), 1990.

[7] One should not conclude, however, that historical criticism and redaction criticism on the one hand, and narrative criticism on the other, are diametrically opposed to one another and have no overlapping concerns or interests. Redaction criticism does give some consideration to the shape of the narrative. And literary criticism can provide insights into a narrative that will assist redaction critics as they go about their work of separating tradition from redaction and identifying the editorial tendencies of the redactor. Narrative criticism can also assist historical critics in relating the world of the narrative to the historical events in the life of Jesus to which the narrative points. For the potential contribution of literary criticism to historical and redaction criticism see Norman R. Petersen, *Literary Criticism for New Testament Critics*, GBS (Philadelphia: Fortress, 1978) 25–48; Jack Dean Kingsbury, "Reflections on 'The Reader' of Matthew's Gospel," *NTS* 34 (1988) 458–60; *Matthew as Story*, 147–60.

narrative critics examine the way in which rhetorical features within the story cause the reader to gain meaning from the text.

Two words of methodological clarification, however, are in order. The first word of clarification involves the role of the OT within the narrative world of the Gospel. When an implied author makes explicit reference to other writings, thus drawing attention to these writings, they become part of the narrative world the implied author creates. As such, the use an implied author makes of these materials is significant for narrative criticism, as are all other elements that make up the world of the text. Thus, narrative criticism is concerned about the use Matthew makes of the OT and will consider his use of the OT while interpreting passages within the narrative. The significance of this point for the genealogy is obvious.

The second point of clarification involves the role of historical background in narrative criticism. Narrative critics make a fundamental distinction between the narrative world and the external world of historical events and flesh-and-blood persons. Narrative critics insist that one must not allow what we know of the external world to determine our understanding of the narrative world. This separation between the external world and the narrative world is appropriate and necessary, but the separation cannot always be maintained absolutely. Although the narrative world of the Gospel is self-consistent and distinct from the external world of historical events and persons, it is not hermetically sealed from the external world. There are points in the Gospel at which it is clear the implied author assumes knowledge that is not found in the text but rather belongs to the external world. When this occurs, we can say that the narrative points beyond itself and requires that we explore the kind of historical knowledge that is assumed by the text.[8]

Matthew 1:21 contains a rather obvious example of historical knowledge shared by the implied author and implied reader but not presented explicitly within the narrative: "you shall call his name Jesus, for he will save his people from their sins." The substantiation of the first statement by the second (note *gar*) suggests a material connection

---

[8] See Powell, *Narrative Criticism*, 20: "The implied reader . . . does know some things that are not stated in the text. For example, the implied reader of the Gospel surely knows that a talent is worth more than a denarius (the text assumes this), although real readers today might not have this knowledge." See also Ellen F. Davis, *Swallowing the Scroll: Textuality and the Dynamics of Discourse in Ezekiel's Prophecy*, JSOTSS 78/BLS 21 (Sheffield: Almond, 1989) 75–109.

between the name Jesus and salvation, but the connection is not made explicit by the narrative. The substantiation indicates that the implied author and implied reader share knowledge external to the narrative itself, viz., (1) that the Greek name *Iēsous* is a translation of the Hebrew *Yehošua'*; and (2) that the meaning of *Yehošua'* is "Yahweh saves." It is thus necessary to draw information from the external world in order to make sense of the narrative world at that point; in fact, the narrative itself invites this consideration of external historical knowledge. This observation points to the demands the text places upon the reader, even when he or she approaches the text as a narrative critic.

There may be certain elements in the genealogy that assume knowledge not explicitly expressed in the narrative; the role of the women and the significance of the number fourteen come to mind. The narrative may give some clues regarding the meaning of these elements, but not provide full understanding. Yet one should not conclude prematurely that the narrative fails to answer certain questions it raises; one should examine the narrative carefully, in order to determine what direction the narrative gives in answering questions raised by the text.

I will now explore the function of the genealogy by examining (1) the structure of the genealogy, including the "breaks," or interruptions in the otherwise consistent pattern of the genealogy; and (2) the ways in which the genealogy introduces the reader to the narrative of the Gospel.

I. The Structure of the Genealogy[9]

A. The Function of 1:1

A significant structural problem confronts the reader with the very first verse. There has been wide disagreement among scholars regarding the function of 1:1.[10] Some contend that 1:1 serves as the heading for only the genealogy, or at most for the genealogy and infancy narratives of chapters 1–2.[11] Those who argue that 1:1 relates

---

[9] For the role structural analysis plays in narrative criticism, see David R. Bauer, *The Structure of Matthew's Gospel: A Study in Literary Design*, JSNTSS 31/BLS 15 (Sheffield: Almond, 1988); and Powell, *Narrative Criticism*, 32–34.

[10] For a critical survey of the various views regarding the function of 1:1, see Jack Dean Kingsbury, *Matthew: Structure, Christology, Kingdom* (Philadelphia: Fortress, 1975) 9–11; and Bauer, *Structure*, 73–77.

[11] Ernst Lohmeyer, *Das Evangelium des Matthäus*, ed. W. Schmauch, Kritisch-exegetischer Kommentar uber das Neue Testament, 4. Aufl. (Göttingen:

only to the genealogy maintain that *genesis* is generally employed in the strictly technical sense of referring to genealogical lists, and that its use in 1:18, where it introduces a birth story, is quite uncommon and essentially different from that of 1:1. These scholars fail to take into account, however, that 1:1 alludes to the LXX of Genesis 2:4, where no genealogical list exists,[12] and to the LXX of Genesis 5:1, where the term introduces a genealogical list *and* a body of narrative.[13] Matthew may therefore be drawing the attention of the "implied reader,"[14] who knows the OT and is directed to the OT repeatedly by Matthew, to a use of the phrase that involves more than a genealogical list.

Other scholars argue that 1:1 is a title to the Gospel as a whole.[15] These scholars contend that (a) in the OT *genesis* was sometimes employed to introduce narratives, not genealogies (Gen 6:9; 37:2); (b) this passage is not analogous to Gen. 5:1 since the latter passage introduces the genealogy of the progenitor, while Matthew 1:1 speaks of *biblos geneseōs Iēsou Christou*, the progeny; (c) Matthew may have intended 1:1 to echo the LXX title to the Book of Genesis; (d) *genesis* can be translated as "history;" (e) in the NT *biblos* means only "book," and never refers to a portion of a book; and (f) it was common for prophetic and apocalyptic books in Judaism to begin with a summary sentence announcing the content of the work.

Vandenhoeck & Ruprecht, 1956) 4; Brown, *Messiah*, 58–59; Floyd V. Filson, *The Gospel according to St. Matthew*, Black's New Testament Commentaries (London: A. & C. Black, 1960) 52; A. H. McNeile, *The Gospel according to Matthew: the Greek Text with Introduction, Notes, and Indices* (London: Macmillan, 1938) 1; Johnson, *Purpose*, 146; Gundry, *Matthew*, 13.

[12] See John Skinner, *A Critical and Exegetical Commentary on Genesis*, ICC (Edinburgh: T. & T. Clark, 1910) 40, where he indicates that *genesis* should be translated "origin."

[13] S. R. Driver, *The Book of Genesis: with Introduction and Notes*, Westminster Commentaries, 6th ed. (London: Methuen, 1907) 75; Edgar Krentz, "The Extent of Matthew's Prologue: Toward the Structure of the First Gospel," *JBL* 83 (1964) 411; Kingsbury, *Structure*, 11. But cf. Claus Westermann, *Genesis 1–11: A Commentary* (Minneapolis: Augsburg, 1984) 355.

[14] I use the name "Matthew" to refer to the implied author of the First Gospel. The use of this name is not meant to suggest that Matthew the Apostle was the author.

[15] Theodor Zahn, *Das Evangelium des Matthäus*, 4. Aufl. (Leipzig: Erlangen, 1922) 39–43; Erich Klostermann, *Das Matthäus-Evangelium*, HNT, 4. Aufl. (Tübingen: J. C. B. Mohr, 1971) 1; Paul Gaechter, *Das Matthäus Evangelium: Ein Kommentar* (Inssbruch: Tyrolia, 1966) 61; W. D. Davies, *The Setting of the Sermon on the Mount* (Cambridge: Cambridge University Press, 1966) 67–70; Davies and Allison, *Matthew*, 149–60.

Each of these arguments has some problems. In the case of (a), the passages cited are not analogous to Matthew 1:1, since they make reference only to *genesis* and do not contain the phrase *biblos geneseōs*, as do Genesis 5:1 and Matthew 1:1; and Genesis 6:9 and 37:2 are unusual, for by far the majority of OT references to *genesis* refer to genealogies or to generations. As far as (b) is concerned, it will be argued below that Matthew had structural and theological reasons for altering the normal procedure by speaking of the *genesis* of progeny rather than that of the progenitor. With regard to (c), the title to the first book of the LXX is *Genesis*, not *biblos geneseōs*; and there is no reason to think that Matthew shaped his Gospel in any significant way along the lines of the Book of Genesis. Although (d) asserts that *genesis* can be translated "history," this is not the usual meaning of the term, and it would require that *genesis* in 1:1 be understood entirely differently than the same term in 1:18. The argument of (e) is not as strong as it may at first appear, since *biblos* occurs only nine times in the NT (never again in Matthew); moreover, the issue is not the meaning of *biblos*, but the meaning of *biblos geneseōs*, which is certainly attested in Genesis 2:4 and 5:1 as referring to a part of a document as opposed to an entire book. With regard to (f), the fact that some Jewish books began with general headings does not mean all of them did, or even that the majority of them did; it simply means that such a practice was not unknown at the time. But there is no known example of a book employing *biblos geneseōs* as a title. Furthermore, it would be confusing for a writer to use *genesis* (in the sense of "history") as a title for the entire document, only to follow this title immediately with a genealogical list.

One of the scholars who have argued most strongly that 1:1 is a superscription to the entire Gospel is W. D. Davies.[16] He maintains that this superscription should be translated, "Book of the Genesis . . ." and serves to introduce the Gospel as the story of the "new creation"

---

[16] Davies first set forth his views in his 1966 work, *The Setting of the Sermon on the Mount*, 67–72; more recently he has presented the same general proposal regarding 1:1 in his commentary on Matthew 1–7 (written in collaboration with Dale C. Allison) in the International Critical Commentary series, 149–60. See n. 5 above for bibliographic data. See also, e.g., X. Leon Dufour, *Études d'Évangile: Parole de Dieu* (Paris: Editions der Seuil, 1965) 40–63; Jean Danielou, *The Infancy Narratives* (New York: Herder and Herder, 1968) 12; F. W. Beare, *The Gospel according to Matthew* (San Francisco: Harper & Row, 1981) 64–65; Waetjen, "Genealogy," 220–25; Andre Paul, *L'Évangile de l'énfance selon saint Matthieu*, nouv. ed., Lire la Bible 17 (Paris: Cerf, 1984) 39–41.

that God has brought about through Christ. Davies points out that Genesis 5:1 reads *biblos geneseōs tōn anthropōn* and is immediately followed by reference to the creation of Adam and Eve, and that Genesis 2:4 is set in the midst of the two creation accounts at the beginning of Genesis. In fact, Davies goes so far as to suggest that the genealogy of Matthew 1:2–17 may correspond to the "catalogic account of the stages of the process of creation which culminates in man" in Genesis 1:1–2:3, while Matthew 1:18–25 may correspond to "the story of the actual creation of man" in Genesis 2:4–25.[17] Matthew 1 would thus be structured in close analogy to Genesis 1–2.

Moreover, Davies observes that Paul and John saw Jesus as "the counterpart of the creation account narrated in Genesis,"[18] for Paul speaks of the "new creation" and the "last Adam," while John introduces his story of Jesus with the prologue describing the role of the *Logos* at creation (1:1–18). Davies also contends that Judaism tended to view the time of eschatological redemption as a new beginning, or new creation, and that such an understanding is found in Matthew's Gospel: (a) 1:1 refers back to the title of the LXX Genesis and indicates that this Gospel is a counterpart to that book of beginnings; (b) Matthew speaks of the "new world" (*palingenesia*) in 19:28; (c) the Spirit descending to the waters of Jordan reminds the reader of Genesis 1:2, where the Spirit "hovered" over the face of the waters; (d) the analogy Matthew draws between Jesus and Moses refers to the new creation that Jesus introduces, for the Exodus was often associated in the Jewish mind with creation; (e) when Jesus calms the sea (8:23–27) he demonstrates he has the power of the king of creation, who in the OT rules the turbulent waves; (f) the conception of Jesus by the Spirit in 1:18–22 corresponds to the role of the Spirit in generating life at the beginning of creation in Genesis.

Davies' proposal fails to persuade. Although it is true that Matthew 1:1 alludes to Genesis 5:1 and 2:4, and that the latter two passages appear in the context of creation themes, it by no means necessarily follows that Matthew wished to draw all of this context from Genesis into the thought of his narrative. Had Matthew wished to emphasize the theme of creation here, he would no doubt have begun his genealogy not with Abraham, but with Adam. As we shall see, the focus of the genealogy is history, and especially the relationship of the Christ

---

[17] Davies, *Setting*, 71–72.
[18] Davies and Allison, *Matthew*, 150.

to the history of Israel; the genealogy is not concerned with matters of creation.

Moreover, the allusions to creation in Matthew which Davies identifies are for the most part highly problematic. The reference to *palingenesia* in 19:28 refers not to the birth and earthly life of Jesus, but to the parousia.[19] There is little connection between the Spirit "hovering" over the water in Genesis 1:2 and the descent of the Spirit upon Jesus in 3:16.[20] The suggestion that Jesus is linked to Moses, and Moses is linked to the Exodus, and the Exodus is in turn linked to creation is hopelessly contorted, and such connections (besides possibly the first in the chain, that between Jesus and Moses) are not found in Matthew's narrative.[21] And it is hard to see how Jesus' conception by the Spirit corresponds to the Spirit's role in the creation of life in the Genesis account. For one thing, the *pneuma theou* is not involved in the creation of life in Genesis.[22] For another thing, Matthew gives no indication that the conception of Jesus in 1:18–20 is a new creation, analogous to the creation of Adam; Matthew nowhere presents Jesus as the "representative human being," or as the essence of the "new creation." Finally, Davies' proposal requires that *geneseōs Iēsou* in Matthew 1:1 be understood as a subjective genitive: "the [new] beginning which Jesus effects." In light of the list of Jesus' progenitors in 1:2–16 and the *tou Iēsou genesis* of 1:18, which introduces the account of Jesus' conception and birth, it is much more natural to take the genitive of 1:1 as objective.[23]

---

[19] And even here the emphasis is upon the relationship of the disciples (the church?) to the people of Israel; cf. 19:28b.

[20] It is true that some of the same terms appear, e.g., *pneuma theou, tou hydatos.* But in Matthew 3 the Spirit does not "hover," but "descends" (*katabainō*); and the focus is not upon the Spirit's relationship to the water, but to Jesus. Moreover, the Spirit in Matthew 3 is not a creative force, but an enabling force; it is in the power of the Spirit that Jesus is able to perform eschatological ministry.

[21] The same criticism applies to Davies' contention that Jesus' stilling of the sea links him with the OT king of creation who rules over the sea.

[22] The term *pneuma* is found in the creation accounts of Genesis only at 1:2. The terms employed in Genesis 2:7 ("and breathed into his nostrils the breath of life") are *emphysaō* and *pnoē.*

[23] Additional problems could be identified with this proposal. For example, the fact that Paul (and possibly John) presents a christology influenced by new creation motifs has little relevance for Matthew. Matthew's christology must be determined by the text of the Gospel itself, not by the ever-present temptation to import theological ideas from other NT witnesses.

If Matthew 1:1 does not refer solely to the genealogy and is not a superscription to the entire Gospel, does it serve as a general heading to 1:1–4:16? I have argued at some length elsewhere that this is precisely the function of 1:1;[24] here I will simply highlight some of the main reasons for understanding the role of 1:1 in this way.

We have already seen that Matthew 1:1 alludes to Genesis 5:1, which introduces both a genealogy and subsequent narrative material. This observation does not necessarily mean, of course, that Matthew 1:1 has the same relationship to the following material as does Genesis 5:1 in its context. But there is evidence within the text of the Gospel itself that 1:1 is a general heading that is expanded, or spelled out, in the whole of 1:2–4:16. Matthew 1:1–4:16 stands as a discrete major unit in Matthew's Gospel, introduced by 1:1, and set off from the material that follows: (a) 1:1–4:16 deals exclusively with events prior to the inauguration of the ministry of Jesus, which begins in 4:17; (b) 1:1–4:16 is concerned to present the person of Jesus as such to the reader as background for understanding the ministry of Jesus in the remainder of the Gospel, whereas in 4:17–16:20 Jesus is presented to the reader principally in terms of his announcement of the kingdom to Israel and in 16:21–28:20 principally in terms of his passion and resurrection; (c) in the process of presenting the person of Jesus as such to the reader in 1:1–4:16, Matthew emphasizes Jesus' role as Christ, Son of David, and Son of Abraham (cf. 1:1), and develops in a careful and systematic way the specific meaning of each of these titles;[25] (d) 1:1–4:16 is tied together by a chain of reliable witnesses to the person of Jesus, beginning with the witness of Matthew himself presented in 1:1 and in the genealogy that follows; (e) 1:1–4:16 is also tied together by a climactic development in the presentation of Jesus as Son of God, a climactic development that begins already in the genealogy (1:16) and culminates in the explicit declaration from God that Jesus is his Son in 3:17.[26]

To say that Matthew 1:1 is a heading to the first major division of the Gospel does not preclude the possibility that this verse also introduces in a more specific way the genealogical list of vv. 2–17.[27] In

---

[24] See Bauer, *Structure*, 73–77; also Kingsbury, *Structure*, 11–16.

[25] See Bauer, *Structure*, 76–77.

[26] Although it would be possible to understand 1:1 as a heading for chapters 1–2, all the considerations listed in this paragraph under (a) to (e) indicate that it is preferable to interpret 1:1 as a superscription to 1:1–4:16.

[27] J. C. Fenton, *Saint Matthew*, Westminster Pelican Commentaries (Philadelphia:

fact, it is unlikely that Matthew would have followed *biblos geneseōs* with a genealogy if he had not meant for it to serve as a title to the genealogy. Moreover, Matthew elsewhere uses the same passage to play two different structural roles. Matthew 16:21 serves as a general heading to the third major division of Matthew's Gospel (and is thus, as a superscription, set off from the narrative that immediately follows), but is also presented as a specific statement made by Jesus at a particular point in time which draws forth a reaction from Peter.[28] Another Matthean example of a passage that serves two distinct structural roles is 5:17–20, which may be a general heading both for Jesus' teaching regarding the "greater righteousness" throughout 5:21–7:12, and (more immediately and specifically) for the antitheses of 5:21–48.[29] If 1:1 is a superscription both to the first major division of the Gospel (1:1–4:16) and to the genealogy proper (1:1–17), the *biblos geneseōs* of 1:1 would be understood in two ways: insofar as 1:1 introduces the whole of 1:1–4:16, it would be understood as "book of the origin;" but insofar as 1:1 introduces the family register of 1:1–17, it would be understood as "book of the genealogy." This discussion regarding the twofold nature of 1:1 leads naturally into an investigation of the structure of 1:1–17 itself.

B. Structural Analysis of 1:1–17

The overall structure of Matthew 1:1–17 is straightforward. It can be divided into three main units, with v. 1 serving as the general heading, vv. 2–16 as the genealogical list itself, and v. 17 as a concluding summary. Matthew divides the genealogical list into three sub-units, although he indicates this breakdown not within the list itself, but in the summary statement of v. 17: (a) vv. 2–6a: From Abraham to David; (b) vv. 6b–11: From David to the Deportation; and (c) vv. 12–16: From the Deportation to Christ.

Westminster, 1963) 36; Davies and Allison, *Matthew*, 153–54.

[28] For 16:21 as a general heading to the remainder of the Gospel, see Kingsbury, *Structure*, 7–11, 22–25; and Bauer, *Structure*, 96–108. Its close narrative connection with 16:22–23 is obvious.

[29] For 5:17 as a heading for 5:17–7:12, see Ulrich Luz, *Matthew 1–7: A Commentary* (Minneapolis: Augsburg, 1989) 255; Sabourin, *Matthieu*, 64–65; and Robert Guelich, *The Sermon on the Mount: A Foundation for Understanding* (Waco. TX: Word, 1982) 38–39. Most commentators link 5:17–20 specifically with 5:21–48; cf. Gundry, *Matthew*, 82, 100. Jack Dean Kingsbury ("The Place, Structure, and Meaning of the Sermon on the Mount," *Int* 41 [1987] 136–42) recognizes that 5:17–20 belongs specifically to 5:21–48, but also that the whole of 5:21–7:12 coheres around the theme of "greater righteousness" from 5:20.

1. *1:1 as General Heading.* Matthew 1:1 relates to the genealogy that follows in two ways. First, v. 1 is a superscription, or a title, to the genealogy; as such, it indicates that the material that follows is to be understood formally as a *biblos geneseōs,* i.e., a genealogy. As a title to the genealogy, 1:1 alludes to genealogical lists and especially headings to genealogical lists in the OT. But in the OT the headings to genealogical lists normally identify the genealogy with the forefather rather than with the final descendant; for example, Genesis 10:1 reads, "These are the descendants (*geneseis*) of Shem," followed by a list of Shem's progeny.[30] It would thus strike the implied reader as remarkable that a genealogy from Abraham to Jesus would be entitled, "Book of the genealogy of Jesus Christ," rather than "Book of the genealogy of Abraham." Some scholars have concluded from this extraordinary circumstance that 1:1 is not a title to the genealogy at all.[31] But it is much better to take this departure from normal practice as indicating the uniqueness of Jesus as the Christ, who stands at the end of salvation history and therefore can have no progeny. It should also be remembered that in typical genealogical lists, the descendants gained meaning and identity from their forefathers. The unusual practice here of entitling a genealogy according to the name of the last descendant serves to subordinate the forefathers to this last descendant and indicates that they gain their meaning and identity from the final progeny, i.e., from Christ.

The second way in which 1:1 serves as a general heading to the genealogical list is that the threefold claim made regarding Jesus in 1:1 is substantiated and particularized in 1:2–16.[32] By this I mean that in

---

[30] A possible exception to this rule may be found in the LXX of Genesis 5:1, which speaks of *hē biblos geneseōs anthropōn* (contra MT, which has *ʾadam*). The LXX translators rendered *ʾadam* as *anthropōn* here probably in order to relate 5:1 to 2:4; even as 2:4 spoke of the *genesis* of the "heavens and the earth," so 5:1 introduces a genealogy that deals with human beings. Thus, even here the heading to the genealogy does not designate the last descendant. In the genealogical tradition of the OT as a whole, including the genealogical lists at the beginning of 1 Chronicles (from which the list in Matthew 1:2–12 is mostly drawn), the genealogies are designated according to forefather rather than descendant.

[31] E.g., Zahn, *Matthäus,* 40–42; Klostermann, *Matthäus,* 1; Walter Grundmann, *Das Evangelium nach Matthäus,* THNT, 5. Aufl. (Berlin: Evangelische Verlagsanstalt, 1981) 34–35, indicates that this consideration points to the relationship between 1:1 and 1:2ff. as secondary.

[32] The designation "Jesus Christ" in 1:1 is both a personal name and a title. Its use as a personal name is obvious. That "Christ" is a title as well is indicated by the structure of the genealogy: (a) the genealogy reaches its climax in Jesus "who is

vv. 2–17 Matthew supports ("substantiates") the claim he has made regarding Jesus in v. 1, viz., that Jesus is the Christ, the Son of David, and the Son of Abraham. In the process of supporting this threefold claim, Matthew spells out ("particularizes") the specific meaning of each of these designations for Jesus; Matthew indicates something of what it means for Jesus to be Christ, Son of David, and Son of Abraham. Furthermore, Matthew reinforces this substantiation and particularization by the use of chiasm:[33]

	Christ	A
General Assertion (1:1)	Son of David	B
	Son of Abraham	C
	Abraham (v. 2)	C'
Particular Substantiation (1:2–17)	David (v. 6)	B'
	Christ (v. 16)	A'

This use of chiasm is significant for three reasons. First, this chiasm supports the claim advanced above that 1:1 is immediately and directly linked to the genealogical list. Second, the chiasm indicates that 1:1 serves as a title for the genealogical list in 1:2–17, and not as a title for the entire chapter. It thus suggests a structural break after v. 17.[34] Third, the chiasm serves to clarify the relationship between the titles "Christ," "Son of David," and "Son of Abraham," as employed in this passage. It does so by linking the order of the titles in the general

---

called Christ," pointing to a confessional title; (b) the chiasm (Christ-David-Abraham-Abraham-David-Christ) links the reference to "Christ" in v. 1 to the confessional title in v. 16; (c) the summary statement of v. 17 employs "Christ" as a title (note that *Christos* is articular, while the other two personal names are anarthrous).

A chiasm that would involve Jesus (Jesus-Christ-David-Abraham-Abraham-David-Christ-Jesus) and run through the naming of Jesus in 1:25 is ruled out by the considerations that (a) "Jesus" is not used as a title, but simply as a personal name (this is true in spite of the theological significance given to the name in 1:18–25; see Kingsbury, *Structure*, 84–85); (b) the genealogical list reaches its climax in "Christ;" and (c) the summary statement (v. 17) provides closure to the genealogy and thus separates 1:1–17 and 1:18–25.

[33] Surprisingly, few scholars have taken note of this chiasm. John C. Fenton, "Inclusio and Chiasmus in Matthew," in *Studia Evangelica* 1, TU 73 (Berlin: Akademie, 1959) 176–77, makes reference to it, but judges that it "may not carry conviction." In fact, it is much clearer than many of the other examples Fenton cites. Subsequent to the initial publication of this paper, Donald Hagner has noted the chiasm in 1:1–17 and its significance for the meaning and structural role of 1:1. See Donald A. Hagner, *Matthew 1–13*, WBC (Waco, TX, 1993) 5.

[34] Verse 17 is clearly included with vv. 2–16 because it summarizes vv. 2–16.

heading to the climactic development in the genealogical list, thereby giving priority to the title "Christ;" this title is the first mentioned in the general heading, and stands in the final, climactic position in the genealogical list.[35]

2. *Climax of 1:16.* That the genealogy reaches its climax with the birth of Jesus "who is called Christ" indicates the significance of the title: Jesus is the Christ in that he has been anointed by God to bring salvation history, which began with Abraham, to its climax. As the high point of culmination toward which all of Israel's history has been moving, Jesus the Christ gives meaning and significance to that history. This implies that the meaning of Israel's history is ultimately incomprehensible outside of Jesus the Christ as he is presented in Matthew's Gospel.

This affirmation, made here in the genealogy, forms the theological and hermeneutical basis for the "fulfillment quotations" that punctuate the narrative of the Gospel. Conversely, the fulfillment quotations illumine the meaning of the genealogy; for they indicate that Jesus as the Christ does not simply bring salvation history in general to fulfillment, but that he brings to full realization all that was implicit in individual events, persons, and declarations within Israel's history. Thus, for example, 2:15 declares that the meaning and significance of the Exodus can be grasped only in light of its fulfillment in Jesus. The climactic character of v. 16 is underscored by the differences in its form over against the previous verses. Climax always involves a dialectic between continuity and discontinuity with the preceding, and such a dialectic is emphasized here by Matthew. There is continuity in that Jesus as Christ brings to fulfillment the

---

[35] The chiasm draws attention to the relationship between these titles and to the order in which they are presented. The notion that the chiasm of 1:1–17 involves a "concentric" or "ring" structure in which the middle element is emphasized is ruled out by the relative lack of prominence given to "Son of Abraham" both in this passage and in the Gospel as a whole. Moreover, Matthew often emphasizes the first and last members (the A element) in chiasm used in individual passages (e.g., 5:45b; 5:45–48; 6:24; 9:13; 11:17–19; 11:21–22/23–24; 13:15; 17:25–26). The prominence of "Christ" in the genealogy is indicated not only by the fact that the list reaches its climax in Jesus *ho legomenos Christos*, but also by the considerations that (a) the summary statement of v. 17 declares that the divinely ordered flow of salvation history comes to its high point of culmination in *ho Christos*; and (b) the title "Christ" refers to Jesus' fulfillment of the entire history of Israel, including the roles played by Abraham and David; therefore, "Christ" is a more comprehensive title and contains "Son of David" and "Son of Abraham" within it.

entire history of Israel, especially the promises regarding sons made to Abraham and David. The titles "Christ," "Son of David," and "Son of Abraham" all have to do with Jesus' relationship to the history of Israel. The discontinuity is indicated by the passive voice which is, as almost everyone recognizes, the "divine passive"; it points to Jesus' role as Son of God. The form of this climactic verse suggests that Jesus cannot ultimately be understood in terms of the history of Israel. In fact, he can function as Christ (which necessarily includes Son of David and Son of Abraham) because he is also Son of God, whose *genesis* is not only in Israel, but also in God (1:18–25). The genealogy thus points to the paradox of Jesus as the Christ: he is both new and not new, of Israel and yet beyond Israel, a product of history and yet also of God's transcendent action. This paradox between the historical (i.e., the human-historical) and the supra-historical continues in 1:18–2:23, where the emphasis is upon the transcendent breaking into, and directing, human history.

The close association of the title "Christ" with the theme of fulfillment, so prominent in the genealogy, is not emphasized in the rest of the Gospel; for the most part, "Christ" is used to refer to Jesus generally as the Messiah. But Matthew does develop the connection, introduced in the genealogy, between "Christ" on the one hand, and "Son of David" and "Son of God" on the other. He links "Christ" with Jesus' Davidic sonship in 2:4, and with "Son of God" in 16:16 and 26:63. Two crucial passages for understanding the relationship between "Christ" and these other titles are 1:18–25 and 22:42, where Matthew indicates that "Christ" is to be understood primarily in terms of Son of God, and in a secondary way in terms of Son of David, a view reflected already in the genealogy.[36]

3. *Interruptions in the Pattern of the Genealogy.* At several points Matthew breaks the otherwise consistent pattern of the genealogy, thus highlighting these interruptions by way of contrast. It is obvious that he wishes to draw attention to these interruptions, and that they serve to introduce the reader to the narrative. The meaning of these interruptions have stood at the center of scholarly debate throughout the history of interpretation. An exhaustive examination of each of these interruptions therefore lies outside the scope of the present

---

[36] See Kingsbury, *Structure*, 96–98.

study. This paper will simply explore how the narrative world of Matthew's Gospel may illumine the meaning of these statements.

(a) The phrase *"and his brothers"* is added in vv. 2 and 11, and in the latter instance linked to another interruption, the single reference to an event: *"the deportation to Babylon."* The fact that Matthew employs "and his brothers" twice, and each time at a crucial point in salvation history, indicates that he wishes the reader to understand these two references in light of one another. In each case the phrase points to the lateral implications of the genealogy over against its otherwise linear emphasis: Jesus is the Christ not only as one who stands at the end of a straight line from Abraham through David, but also as one who has significance for all Israel.

In v. 2 the phrase refers to the whole of Israel at the beginning of its national existence, pointing to the promise and privilege inherent in the covenant made with Abraham, Isaac, and Jacob and granted to the elect children of Jacob (the twelve tribes of Israel), and not only to Judah, whose descendants were to hold the scepter (Gen. 49:10). This reference forms the basis for the presentation, found throughout Matthew's Gospel, of Israel as the son/sons of God, with the privileges and potential that belonged to that role, including the possession of the kingdom of God.[37]

---

[37] Note the emphasis upon the special standing of the whole people of Israel throughout Matthew's Gospel. The whole of Israel is God's "son" (2:15); and it is through their connection with Abraham, Isaac, and Jacob that the people of Israel are "sons of the kingdom" (8:12; cf. 1:2), who possess the kingdom of God (21:43). To Israel God has graciously sent prophets and finally even his own Son (21:33–43); and to Israel God extended the first invitations to participate in the wedding feast of the kingdom (22:1–14). This privilege and promise of the people of Israel is reflected in the ministry of Jesus and the disciples: Jesus has been sent "only to the lost sheep of the house of Israel" (15:24) and commands his disciples to restrict their ministry in the same way (10:5–6).

A.-J. Levine, *The Social and Ethnic Dimensions of Matthean Salvation History: "Go nowhere among the Gentiles" (Matt. 10:5b)*, SBEC 15 (Lewiston, NY: Mellen, 1988) 76, suggests that v. 2 points to the whole people in Egyptian exile, even as v. 11 pictures the whole people in Babylonian exile (cf. ch. 2). But it is not clear that Matthew views Israel's experience in Egypt as an exile, and although chapter 2 necessarily mentions the flight into Egypt, the emphasis there is upon the Exodus (2:15).

Several scholars (e.g., Vögtle, "Genealogie," 41) argue that v. 2 points to the sovereign selection of God in choosing Judah, the fourth-born son, over first-born Reuben to be the channel of the Messianic line. I argue below that divine selectivity stands behind the reference to Zerah; the notion may therefore be present here. But it is difficult to see that emphasis in v. 11, which links this phrase

The phrase "and his brothers" in v. 11 refers to brothers of Jeconiah, i.e., the sons of Josiah.[38] Thus, on the surface, this phrase seems to apply only to a group of kings who reigned at the end of the 7th century BCE. But the observations that this phrase refers back to its counterpart in v. 2, which clearly has the people of Israel in view, and that Matthew links this statement with the Babylonian Exile, which involved the deportation of the whole people, suggest that Matthew wishes the reader to think once again of the entire people. But here the people are pictured, not as recipients of covenant, election, and promise, but as objects of judgment; for the Babylonian Exile is consistently presented in the biblical tradition as just punishment for Israel's rebellion.[39] The promise and privilege granted to the people as a whole in v. 2 had turned sour, because the people of Israel rejected God's will and purpose which were inherent in their election as the people of God. The nation that held such promise at the outset of its national existence was now deported to a strange, heathen land because of its failure to function as the covenant people of God. The only event Matthew mentions in the genealogy is the Deportation to

---

to the Deportation.

[38] The problem of this reference to the brothers of Jeconiah, who according to the OT had only one brother (1 Chr 3:16) need not detain us. It is unnecessary to emend the text to read "Jehoiakim;" see Robert T. Hood, "The Genealogies of Jesus," in *Early Christian Origins*, ed. A. Wikgren (Chicago: Quadrangle, 1961) 10–11; Hugo Schollig, "Die Zählung der Generationen im matthaischen Stammbaum," *ZNW* 59 (3–4, 1968) 261–66; cf. Anton Vögtle, "Josias Zeugte den Jechonias und seine Bruder (Mt 1,11)," in *Lex Tua Veritas*, hrsg. Heinrich Gross and Franz Mussner (Trier: Paulinus, 1961) 307–13. But even if that were the original reading, it would make no substantive difference in our interpretation, for in any case the reference has theological rather than merely historical import.

The question as to whether "Jeconiah" originally read "Jehoiakim" is linked to the problem that there are only thirteen generations in the last section of the genealogy; if "Jehoiakim" appears in v. 11, then there would be fourteen generations in both the second and third sections. But it is most likely that Matthew wished the reader to count Jeconiah twice, since (a) reading "Jehoiakim" in v. 11 would produce a gap in the flow of the genealogy, for Jeconiah would then be mentioned as a father in v. 12 without prior introduction as a son; (b) the fact that there are only thirteen generations in vv. 2–6a (although fourteen names appear) indicates that Matthew is not especially meticulous about the precise number of generations named in each of the three sections; and (c) the reference to the Deportation in v. 11, which is the sole reference to an event, created the possibility of counting Jeconiah on both sides of that event.

[39] See, e.g., Martin Noth, *The Deuteronomistic History*, JSOTSS 15 (Sheffield: JSOT, 1981) 79–99; *The Chronicler's History*, JSOTSS 50 (Sheffield: JSOT, 1987) 97–106; Gerhard von Rad, "The Deuteronomic Theology of History in I and II Kings," in *The Problem of the Hexateuch and other Essays* (London: SCM, 1984) 205–21.

Babylon, for, as far as he is concerned, this event most accurately depicts the essential character of Israel's history.

The connection between "and his brothers" in v. 2 and in v. 11 prepares the reader, then, for Matthew's understanding of the history of Israel: throughout its history, Israel has been characterized by both privilege and rebellion, opportunity and failure, grace and judgment. The climax to this pattern of rejection of the will of God leading to judgment comes in Israel's rejection of Jesus the Messiah, which results in loss of the kingdom (21:33–22:10), destruction of the nation (21:41; 22:1–8; 23:29–24:3) and eschatological judgment (8:10–12; 22:11–14).[40] Already Matthew prepares the reader for the rejection of Jesus by Israel and sets it within the context of Israel's sinful rejection of the will of God throughout its history.

One should note also that the Deportation forms the climax to the second series of the genealogical list, that which involves the period of the monarchy (vv. 6b–11). This series begins with reference to David "the king," which points to the promise and potential inherent in God's election of David and his descendants to sit upon the throne, even as "and his brothers" in v. 2 pointed to the promise and potential inherent in God's election of Israel. But immediately a shadow is cast upon the reign of the Davidic kings, for David was the father of Solomon "by the wife of Uriah," recalling both David's adultery and complicity in murder. By introducing the period of the monarchy in this way, Matthew suggests that this kind of moral and religious failure characterized the entire period and led finally to the destruction of the monarchy with the Deportation. The Deportation thus points both to the failure of the nation to fulfill its role as son of Abraham and to the failure of the Davidic kings to fulfill their role as sons of David. Failure in both of these areas points ahead to Jesus, who as the Christ fills up all that was lacking in Israel's history.

(b) The addition of "*and Zerah*" in v. 3 alludes to the story of the birth of Perez and Zerah in Genesis 38:27–30. This draws attention to the selectivity and overruling sovereignty of God in salvation history. Zerah appeared to be the firstborn, but God's providence was at work in the reversal within the birth process. This reference suggests that

---

[40] Matthew's understanding of the history of Israel in the genealogy, which is necessarily laconic and suggestive, should be interpreted in light of clear statements regarding the essential character of that history found later in the Gospel, esp. 21:33–22:14; 23:29–39.

God is directly, purposefully, and surprisingly involved in the individual events in salvation history, even as the 3x14 scheme in v. 17 suggests that God was carefully moving salvation history as a whole toward its climax in Christ.

(c) At four points Matthew mentions the names of women: Tamar (v. 3); Rahab (v. 5); Ruth (v. 5); and "the wife of Uriah" (v. 6). To this list may be added Mary (v. 16). The role of these women is the most debated issue in the interpretation of the genealogy, and consequently a full investigation lies outside the scope of the present study. I will simply review the major proposals and offer some general remarks.

Three major proposals have been advanced.[41] First, from the days of Jerome many scholars have argued that the four women were sinners (guilty especially of sexual misconduct), and that their inclusion in the genealogy points to Jesus' role as savior of the unrighteous and friend of the moral outcasts (e.g., 9:13). This view is held by few scholars today, since the OT itself does not present all these women as sinners; Jewish piety generally held them in high regard; and it would be impossible to characterize Mary as a sinner.

A second proposal contends that Matthew draws attention to irregularities in the sexual activities of the four women, and that these irregularities reach their climax in the most anomalous event of all: the conception of Jesus by the Holy Spirit. Stated thus, the proposal is quite general, and scholars have therefore offered specific forms of it. Raymond Brown, for example, insists that these women shared two things with Mary: scandalous sexual irregularities in their union with their partners; and a willingness to take the initiative and play a major role in the plan of God, so that "they came to be considered the instrument of God's providence or of His Holy Spirit."[42] The combination of scandalous sexual unions and self-initiative works well in the case of Tamar and, to some extent, Bathsheba, but encounters serious difficulties with the other women. Moreover, it is not clear how Mary took the initiative; and the "scandalous" character of Mary's situation does not seem to be emphasized in 1:18–25. Furthermore,

---

[41] For discussions of the major proposals, see Johnson, *Purpose*, 152–79; Brown, *Birth*, 71–74; and Levine, *Salvation History*, 59–88.

[42] Brown, *Birth*, 73. See also Paul, *Matthieu*, 22–36; and Krister Stendahl, "Quis et Unde? An Analysis of Mt 1–2," in *The Interpretation of Matthew*, ed. Graham Stanton, IRT 3 (Philadelphia: Fortress, 1983) 60–61.

the link between the four women and the Holy Spirit is tenuous, since such a link is entirely absent from the OT, and rabbinic references are spotty and late. Finally, the connection between scandalous union, initiative of the women, and the Holy Spirit is not clear. Brown has presented a complex matrix of features in the attempt to bring all five of the women under a common umbrella, but has been unable to establish that all of the features were present in any one case, or to demonstrate the interconnectedness of these features.

A third proposal contends that the four women were Gentiles, and their inclusion in the genealogy points to the universalism of the Gospel. This view has many proponents, and is supported by the reference to "Son of Abraham" in v. 1 (which may allude to Jesus as one who fulfills the divine promise to Abraham that in Abraham's seed all the nations of the earth would be blessed), by the designation of Bathsheba in v. 6 as "the wife of Uriah" (according to 2 Samuel, "the Hittite"), and by the emphasis throughout Matthew upon the incorporation of the Gentiles into the people of God. Scholars have identified problems with this proposal as well. A.-J. Levine, for example, has recently raised the following difficulties: (a) it is not clear from the OT accounts that Tamar and Bathsheba were Gentiles; (b) in Jewish circles, Ruth and Rahab were regarded as proselytes and would not therefore have been viewed as *bona fide* Gentiles by most Jewish readers of the period; (c) Jewish and rabbinic materials indicate some ambiguity regarding Tamar's Gentile ancestry; (d) Uriah is not explicitly identified as a Hittite in the genealogy, but rather as the husband of Bathsheba, thus pointing to conjugal activity versus Gentile association; (d) had Matthew wished to stress Ruth's Moabite origins, it is strange that he does not mention Naamah the Ammonite, the mother of Rehoboam (1 Kgs 14:31; 2 Chr 12:13), especially since Ruth and Naamah are often mentioned together in rabbinic materials; (e) Matthew does not link "Son of Abraham" or the figure of Abraham himself with the inclusion of Gentiles; and (f) this view would have to exclude Mary, who certainly was not a Gentile.

It seems best to conclude that the women play a dual role in the genealogy. The four women are presented as Gentiles who point to Jesus' role as the Son of Abraham who brings Gentiles to the worship of God and causes them to be incorporated into the community of faith. The arguments against this view are not convincing. Although it cannot be "proved" that Tamar and Bathsheba were presented as Gentiles in the OT accounts, there is good reason to believe that the implied author and implied reader share a body of knowledge according to which these women were Gentiles.[43] That they were viewed as proselytes contributes to the very point Matthew wishes to make: their inclusion in the OT community of faith points ahead to Jesus who brings Gentiles to the worship of God and causes them to be included in the new, eschatological community. In other words, it reminds the reader that God had the inclusion of Gentiles in mind all along, but that this inclusion could be fully accomplished only in Jesus. Matthew did not include Naamah, who was certainly a Gentile, because the implied reader would have been less familiar with her than with the others; all the other women are subjects of OT narrative accounts. Finally, there is every reason to believe that Matthew employs Son of Abraham to refer to Jesus' role as savior of Gentiles: Such a connection is present in the two other Matthean passages which speak of children/sons of Abraham (3:7–10; 8:5–13); and it is most likely that Abraham and David are singled out in the genealogy because they received promises of sons, to which promises Matthew is referring the reader. The mention of the four women thus supports and gives specific content to the claim of v. 1 that Jesus is the Son of Abraham.

The differences between the mention of the four women and that of Mary should be taken seriously into account. Both the passive voice and the reference to Mary in v. 16 point to the extraordinary circumstance that Jesus is the Son of David and Son of Abraham by virtue of the fact that he is Son of God, whose origin is in God. The reference to Mary does not draw attention to her own role as much as it does to the role of God, in that it indicates that Jesus was not the natural son of Joseph, but was the Son of God. In 1:18–25, the emphasis is upon neither the role or character of Mary, nor the anomolous character of the birth, but rather upon the divine origin of Jesus.[44] The mention of Mary and Joseph is therefore to some extent separate from the mention of the four women.

Yet in addition to this discontinuity between the four women and Mary there may also be an element of continuity. Matthew may have wished to provide a (secondary) connection between the four women

---

[43] See review of evidence in Johnson, *Purpose*, 159–79.

[44] The lack of emphasis upon Mary in 1:18–25 has led some scholars to make an essential connection between the four women and *Joseph*. See, e.g., Waetjen, "Genealogy," 215–30; Levine, *Salvation History*, 80–88; Davis, "Fulfillment," 532–33. Moreover, although the birth of Jesus is by the nature of the case anomolous, the narrative of 1:18–25 does not emphasize its anomolous or irregular character.

and Mary in that they were all relatively powerless, marginalized, and in need of help. In spite of their lowly condition they were uniquely used by God in furthering the course of salvation history toward its climax in Christ. The very fact that all were women indicates something of their marginal and powerless state, since in the narrative world of Matthew women are generally subordinate and acted upon, and appear as those in need (5:31–32; 8:14–17; 15:21–28; 19:3–9; 26:6–13).[45] Moreover, the Gentile status of the four indicates marginalization in that it points to the disdain Gentiles experienced in Jewish contexts, a disdain reflected in the negative statements regarding Gentiles found throughout the Gospel (5:47; 6:7, 32; 10:5; 18:17; 20:19, 25).

All four of the women in the genealogy found themselves in a position of danger arising from their powerlessness, and yet were delivered from danger; in spite of their marginal, vulnerable status they became instruments in the divine plan. The same is true of Mary, who was powerless before the danger of the shame and ostracism associated with an illegitimate pregnancy, but was delivered by Joseph's obedient response to the divine revelation and assumed a central role in the birth of the Messiah. All of this points ahead to the concern for the poor, powerless, and marginal in Matthew's Gospel, who are the special recipients of the ministry of Jesus, and who are generally more receptive to the proclamation of the kingdom than are the well-placed and powerful.[46]

4. *Summary of v. 17.* Matthew concludes the genealogy with a summary in which he directs the reader to certain proper inferences from the list (note *oun*), which Matthew wishes to emphasize. Above all, Matthew points out that the genealogy can be divided into three sets of fourteen generations. On the basis of the narrative itself, it is likely that fourteen represents a doubled seven, since Matthew emphasizes the number seven,[47] and in one crucial passage he

---

[45] Janice Capel Anderson, "Matthew: Gender and Reading," *Semeia* 28 (1983) 3–27. I emphasize that this is the way women are *generally* regarded in Matthew's narrative world, for there are a few exceptions, most notably 14:1–12; cf. also 27:19.

[46] Levine, *Salvation History*; J. M. Gibbs, "Purpose and Pattern in Matthew's Use of the Title 'Son of David,'" *NTS* 10 (1963–64) 446–64; Jack Dean Kingsbury, "The Title 'Son of David' in Matthew's Gospel," *JBL* 95 (1976) 591–602.

[47] 12:45; 22:25–28; note the seven fulfillment quotations in 1:1–4:16, the seven parables in chapter 13, and the seven woes in chapter 23, and possibly seven

employs a multiple of seven (18:21–22); if so, the number fourteen would indicate a fullness or completeness brought about by God.[48] The reference to *three* periods may also signify fullness; the number three is used frequently by Matthew, sometimes with the sense of completeness.[49] Thus, the 3x14 indicates that God has carefully and with sovereign purpose directed salvation history toward its fulfillment in Jesus the Christ. This also implies that all of history is under the control of God, especially the history of Jesus that Matthew is about to narrate. The narrative world of the Gospel is therefore above all God's world; and the point of view of God is ultimately normative for the narrative world of Matthew.

It is possible, as well, that the number fourteen here represents a *gematria* on the name "David" (i.e., the Hebrew letters of the name "David" add up to fourteen).[50] It is tempting to think that just as the mention of the (Gentile) women in the genealogy supports the claim of v. 1 that Jesus is the Son of Abraham who brings salvation to Gentiles, so the emphasis upon fourteen in the genealogy supports the claim that Jesus is the Son of David. There is evidence that *gematria* was rather widely practiced in Jewish circles of the period; and the implied reader of Matthew's Gospel seems generally acquainted with Jewish practice. There is, however, a question as to whether the implied reader of the Gospel knew Hebrew. Here the evidence is somewhat mixed: Matthew often provides translations of Hebrew and Aramaic terms (1:23; 27:33, 46); yet one could argue that in these cases there is a theological, rather than a merely informational, reason for the translation. On some occasions Matthew allows Aramaic terms to stand without translation ("mammon:" 6:24; "Gehenna:" 5:22; 29, 30; 10:28; 18:9; 23:15, 33). Moreover, Matthew sometimes makes connections

---

petitions in the Lord's Prayer (6:9–13). See W. C. Allen, *A Critical and Exegetical Commentary on the Gospel according to S. Matthew*, ICC, 3rd ed. (Edinburgh: T. & T. Clark, 1912) lxv; Paul Gaechter, *Die Literarische Kunst im Matthäus-Evangelium*, SB 7 (Stuttgart: Katholisches Bibelwerk, 1955) 12–18.

[48] *TDNT*, s.v., "*Hepta*," by Karl Heinrich Rengstorf, 2:627–35.

[49] Allen, *Matthew*, lxv; Davies and Allison, *Matthew*, 61–70; *TDNT*, s.v. "*Treis*," by Gerhard Delling, 8:216–25.

[50] This interpretation was first put forth by Gfrörer, and is espoused by many commentators, e.g., Joachim Jeremias, *Jerusalem in the Time of Jesus: An Investigation into Economic and Social Conditions during the New Testament Period* (Philadelphia: Fortress, 1975) 292; Box, "Narratives," 85; Pierre Bonnard, *L'Évangile selon Saint Matthieu*, CNT (Geneva: Labor et Fides, 1982) 15; Brown, *Birth*, 74–81; Gundry, *Matthew*, 18; Beare, *Matthew*, 63.

that assume at least a general knowledge of a Hebrew term (e.g., 1:21; see discussion above). Finally, it may be argued that the one clear instance of *gematria* in the NT indicates that this device could be employed with a Gentile audience that did not know Hebrew at all; in all likelihood Revelation 13:8 presents a *gematria* on the Hebrew transliteration of the Greek name "Nero."[51] But this passage in Revelation represents an unusual and highly unexpected situation, and it is doubtful that it can shed much direct light on Matthew's use of *gematria*. I would judge that the evidence allows but does not demand the conclusion that the implied reader of Matthew's Gospel has the kind of knowledge that would cause him (the implied reader is a male; cf. 5:28, 31–32; 19:3–12) to see *gematria* in the number fourteen. *Gematria* on the name of David may be present here, but this is difficult to determine, and lies farther from the narrative itself than does the notion of doubled seven.[52]

II. The Genealogy as Introduction to the Gospel

The genealogy introduces the reader to the Gospel in two ways: (a) it establishes Matthew's point of view regarding Jesus; and (b) it facilitates entry into the narrative world of Matthew's Gospel.

---

[51] See, e.g., G. B. Caird, *The Revelation of St. John the Divine*, HNTC (New York: Harper & Row, 1966) 174–77. It should be noted, however, that the Revelator makes explicit mention of his use of *gematria*, while no such explicit indication is found in Matthew 1:17. *Gematria* also appears in the Sybilline Oracles I. 324ff., but this involves the numerical value of Greek letters.

[52] Some scholars have argued that Matthew is emphasizing here the number forty-two, and in analogy to the Apocalypse of Weeks in 1 Enoch is presenting Jesus as standing at the very end of the old order (the end of the sixth week); according to this interpretation, Matthew wishes to indicate that Jesus signals the end of the old order and the imminent inception of the new. See, e.g., Bornhäuser, *Geburts*, 16–17; Leon-Dufour, *Études*, 56–58; Daneliou, *Infancy Narratives*, 14–15. In my judgment, this interpretation is fundamentally flawed, for (among other considerations) the focus of concern in the Matthean genealogy is clearly upon the number fourteen, not forty-two. Little needs to be said regarding this proposal in the wake of the penetrating and devastating criticism by Anton Vögtle, "Genealogie," 34–36 (II. Teil). Waetjen, "Genealogy," has argued for an analogy between the fourteen generations of the Matthean genealogy and the Baruch Apocalypse, but his proposal involves extremely tenuous interpretations not only of the genealogy but also of the christology of Matthew's Gospel, and there is more discontinuity than continuity between the Baruch Apocalypse and Matthew 1:1–17.

A. *The Genealogy as the Witness of Matthew*

In 1:1–4:16 Matthew introduces the person of Jesus to the reader through the testimonies of several reliable witnesses. In this way, 1:1–4:16 establishes the point of view according to which Jesus is to be understood and prepares the reader for the ministry of Jesus that is narrated throughout the remainder of the Gospel. Matthew begins by giving his own witness to Jesus, and this witness is found in the genealogy. Matthew 1:1–17 thus provides the basic orientation to the person of Jesus, and thereby determines the reliability of all subsequent statements about him. In fact, 1:1–17 is the only passage in the Gospel in which the narrator (who for all intents and purposes is identical to the implied author) bears explicit testimony to the identity of Jesus.[53]

The essential witness of Matthew is found in 1:1: Jesus is the Christ, the Son of David, the Son of Abraham. As indicated above, 1:1 is a superscription to 1:1–4:16, and therefore this threefold claim made by Matthew is intimately linked to the subsequent material in the first major division of the Gospel. But Matthew links it most closely to the genealogical list in 1:2–17, for he does not make this claim on his own authority, but immediately substantiates it by appeal to salvation history as reflected in the genealogy. This appeal to salvation history is actually an appeal to God, who reveals his plan and purposes through the divinely ordered flow of salvation history towards its culmination in Jesus.

The witness of Matthew is followed by the infancy narrative, which contains the witness of the angel and of the wise men (1:18–2:23).[54]

---

[53] With the exception of 1:18, and possibly 11:2.

[54] A number of factors unite 1:18–2:23 and set it off from 1:1–17: (a) repetition of the revelation of divine commands through dreams (often involving angelic visitation), followed by obedient response which protects God's salvation historical purpose in Christ (1:20–25; 2:12, 13–15, 19–21, 22–23); (b) an overarching contrast between negative response to Jesus represented by Herod, all Jerusalem, and the chief priests and scribes, and positive response to Jesus represented by Joseph and the wise men; (c) repetition of five fulfillment quotations (1:23; 2:6, 15, 17, 23); (d) several common elements between 1:18–25 and 2:19–23, which serve to frame the segment, e.g., "fear" on the part of Joseph (1:20; 2:22), and concern about what Jesus will be "called" (*kaleō*); (e) references to the "birth" of Jesus in 2:1, 2, 4, which connect the narrative of ch. 2 with 1:18–25; (f) basic shift from genealogy to narrative dealing with Jesus' life; (g) summary statement of v. 17 providing closure for the genealogy. Although 1:18–25 belongs primarily with ch. 2, the former passage is transitional, since it continues the theme of *genesis* from 1:1–17 and in v. 18 Matthew continues to make some direct statements

The reliability of the angel's testimony is established in part by its agreement with the testimony of Matthew: Jesus has been conceived by the Holy Spirit; Jesus is the Son of David through Joseph, son of David. Moreover, 1:18–25 clarifies and gives specific content to several elements found in the genealogy: (a) how Jesus can be the Son of David, even though he was not the natural son of Joseph; (b) the meaning and significance of v. 16; (c) the relationship between Jesus as Son of David and as Son of God, along with the preeminence of Jesus' divine Sonship over against his Davidic Sonship; and (d) the continuity between the sovereign direction of God in salvation history leading up to the Christ, and the immediate involvement of God in the life of Jesus itself. Since the angel is an emissary from the Lord ("angel *of the Lord*"), his testimony is also linked to divine revelation.

Even as the angel bore witness to Jesus as Son of David and Son of God, so the wise men point to Jesus as Son of Abraham and Son of David. The coming of these Gentiles to the worship of Jesus indicates that Jesus is the Son of Abraham in whom "all the nations of the earth will be blessed" (LXX Gen.12:2; 18:18; 22:18). Their coming both supports the claim in 1:1–17 that Jesus is Son of Abraham, and gives specific content to that claim.

The wise men inquire regarding "the king of the Jews," a title which, according to the genealogy (cf. 1:6), alludes to Jesus' role as Son of David. This reference provides Matthew the opportunity to develop the meaning of the Davidic Sonship of Jesus, which he does by means of the contrast between the kingship of Jesus and the kingship of Herod. Herod's tyrannical kingship is characterized by the selfish desire to maintain his own power at all costs, even to the point of taking the innocent lives of his subjects, while the kingship of Jesus is described in the quotation of 2:6: this Davidic king will "shepherd" his people. As shepherd, he rules over his people by dying for them (27:11, 29, 32–54; cf. 2:16–18), thus saving them from their sins (1:21). The testimony of the wise men is reliable because it agrees with the point of view of Matthew (1:1–17) and the angel (1:18–25). Moreover, like that of Matthew, their testimony also stems from divine revelation: God has revealed the birth of "the king of the Jews" through his created order (2:2; cf. Num. 24:17), and this revelation through creation is confirmed and clarified by OT prophecy (2:6).

---

regarding Jesus' identity. For the relationship between 1:1–17 and 1:18–2:23, see David R. Bauer, "The Kingship of Jesus in the Matthean Infancy Narrative," *CBQ* (forthcoming).

Matthew also presents Jesus in this material as Christ and Son of God. The notion that Jesus is Son of God, first introduced in the genealogy (1:16), is given support and specific content in 2:15, where we learn that the divine Sonship of Jesus is linked to Israel's experience as son of God. Jesus is Christ as the one who fulfills the promises and hopes of the end-time Davidic ruler (2:2–6), thus continuing the connection in the genealogy between "Christ" and the theme of fulfillment. Indeed, throughout chapter 2 Jesus is pictured as bringing to fulfillment the whole history of Israel (including the experience of Moses, the Exodus, the Exile, and the return from Exile).[55]

Matthew 3:1–12 contains the witness of John the Baptist. He declares that Jesus is "the coming one" (*ho erchomenos*). When this designation is used by John, it points to Jesus' role as Christ (cf. 11:2). As the coming one Jesus is the end-time figure who far outstrips John, the greatest of all the prophets (11:7–15), in both majesty and power. Moreover, as the coming one (or the Christ), he not only stands as the culmination of salvation history (1:1–17), but also as the culmination of all history; he is the eschatological judge who will determine the destiny of all persons. The testimony of John, who is both a prophet and comes in fulfillment of prophecy (3:3), also reflects divine revelation.

The theme of Abrahamic Sonship is also picked up in the preaching of John the Baptist; and in this passage, as in the genealogy, it alludes to the inclusion of Gentiles into the people of God. But here the emphasis is not upon the cause (Jesus as Son of Abraham brings salvation to Gentiles), but upon the effect (Gentiles replace unbelieving Jews as sons of Abraham when they give heed to the proclamation of the kingdom). Again, the Abrahamic Sonship of Jesus is supported and explained.

The final witness to Jesus in 1:1–4:16 is God himself, who declares in 3:17 that Jesus is his Son. The circumlocutionary reference to Jesus' divine Sonship in v. 16 of the genealogy thus stands at the beginning of a development that reaches its climax in this explicit testimony from God. The structure of the genealogy therefore reflects (and anticipates) the structure of 1:1–4:16; both the genealogy and the first

---

[55] Brian M. Nolan, *The Royal Son of God: The Christology of Matthew 1–2 in the Setting of the Gospel* (Göttingen: Vandenhoeck & Ruprecht, 1979) 34–46; Patte, *Matthew*, 36–40.

major division of the Gospel come to a climax with the divine Sonship of Jesus. This observation lends support to the claim that "Son of God" is the preeminent christological title in Matthew. It is also to be noted that 3:17 and its immediate context indicate that Son of God involves more than divine conception, as the genealogy and 1:18–25 suggest; Jesus is Son of God as one who, in contrast to Israel God's son, perfectly obeys the will of his Father (3:15; 4:12–16; 4:1–11, cf. 2:15).

The first major division of the Gospel ends with a reference to the significance of the ministry of Jesus for the salvation of the Gentiles (4:15–16), thus again drawing attention to the role of Jesus as Son of Abraham, and forming a bracket with the assertion regarding Jesus' Abrahamic Sonship in 1:1.

In summary, the genealogy (a) establishes Matthew's point of view regarding Jesus; (b) provides a basis upon which to judge the reliability of subsequent statements regarding the person of Jesus; (c) introduces the conviction that all reliable testimony to the person of Jesus stems from divine revelation; (d) sets forth the major categories according to which Jesus is to be understood, and prepares the reader for a fuller development of these categories and their relationship to one another in the remainder of the first major division of the Gospel.

B. The Genealogy as Entry into the Narrative World

The distinction, made by narrative critics, between the external world and the narrative world suggests that an implied author must assist the reader to enter the narrative world at the beginning of the work, as well as aid the reader to re-enter the external world at the end of the work. The beginning of the work thus serves to orient the reader to the world of the narrative, even as the conclusion serves to move the reader back into the real world. Narrative critics, following Boris Uspensky, refer to this process of facilitation as "framing."[56] The frames at either end of Matthew's Gospel are the genealogy and the missionary commissioning (28:16–20).

As indicated above, the genealogy introduces the reader to the narrator, or the implied author, and to the point of view of the implied author regarding the identity and significance of Jesus. Moreover, the genealogy sets forth the person of Jesus in terms of his progenitors and origin, and thus prepares the reader to assume Jesus'

---

[56] Boris Uspensky, *A Poetics of Composition: The Structure of the Artistic Text and Typology of a Compositional Form* (Berkeley, CA: University of California Press, 1973) 137–65.

point of view throughout the remainder of the narrative. But the primary way in which the genealogy serves as an introductory frame is by orienting the reader to Matthew's understanding of time and history. In other words, the genealogy provides a temporal setting which is assumed in the rest of the narrative, and according to which the story of Jesus is to be understood.[57]

The genealogy indicates that the narrative world begins, temporally, with Abraham. The genealogy requires the reader to enter the world of Matthew's Gospel by way of the history of Israel, which began with Abraham. In this way, Matthew indicates that one can understand the story of Jesus only as one comes to it through the flow of salvation history as Matthew presents it in the genealogy. Yet the genealogy also serves to incorporate the history of Israel within the narrative world of the Gospel, thus signifying that the history of Israel can no longer be understood on its own terms, but only as it gains meaning and significance from its function within the narrative of Matthew's Gospel. In the genealogy the past history is taken up and made a part of the history of Christ. The whole of the OT and OT history is thereby subordinated to the story of Jesus in Matthew's Gospel.

The genealogy thus introduces the reader to the time between Abraham and Christ, a temporal period which receives significant attention in the Gospel. This is a period of "the prophets and the law" (11:13), before the law and the prophets found their fulfillment in Christ (5:17; 26:56). It is a time before Christ, and therefore a period in which God does not yet dwell with his people, at least not in the sense of Emmanuel (1:23). It is above all the period of anticipation of Christ and witness to Christ, and therefore finds its chief expression throughout the narrative in the fulfillment quotations, which interpret Christ in light of the OT revelation, and at the same time interpret OT revelation in light of the career of Jesus.

The counterpart to the genealogy is the missionary commissioning. As with the genealogy, the primary concern here is with time and history. But whereas the genealogy looks back as far as Abraham, the missionary commissioning looks ahead as far as "the end of the age," i.e., the parousia. The genealogy and the missionary commission-

---

[57] On the issue of setting, see Seymour Chatman, *Story and Discourse: Narrative Structure in Fiction and Film* (Ithaca, NY: Cornell University Press, 1978) 138–45.

ing together, then, define the temporal boundaries of the narrative world: from Abraham to the parousia.[58]

The time between the resurrection and the parousia also receives significant attention in Matthew's Gospel. It is a time in which post-Easter disciples experience the fulfillment of OT expectations; but above all it is a period characterized by the promise of Christ and the presence of Christ. The emphasis upon the presence of Christ in the experience of the post-Easter church is indicated by the lack of closure in the final passage of the book, 28:16–20. The Gospel remains open-ended, and concludes with Jesus in the midst of his disciples, promising to be *with* them to the end of the age (28:20). Even as the period between Abraham and Christ finds its chief expression in the fulfillment quotations, so the period between the resurrection and the parousia finds its chief expression throughout the narrative in the predictions of Jesus, which function primarily in terms of encouragement and command.

If the period between the resurrection and the parousia is characterized above all by the realization of OT expectations and the presence of Christ in the midst of his people (28:20), it follows that there is essential continuity between this period and the period of the earthly Jesus; for the time of the earthly Jesus was also characterized by fulfillment and the presence of Jesus with his disciples (1:23). Indeed, we encounter much more continuity here than we do between the two periods depicted in the entry frame: the period of anticipation (Abraham to Christ) and the period of fulfillment in the coming of Christ. This consideration supports the claim that Matthew conceives of salvation history in two epochs: the time of preparation, the law and the prophets; and the time of fulfillment, the presence of Christ (earthly and exalted) among his people.

Both the genealogy and the missionary commissioning focus upon Christ, thus pointing to the gospel's primary emphasis on Christology. In the entry frame of the genealogy we encounter the voice of the narrator, which will be the predominant and determining voice as we travel through the narrative world of the Gospel. But in the exit frame

---

58 There are a few passages in Matthew that go beyond these boundaries, referring back before Abraham to creation (19:3–9) or to Noah (24:37–39), and pointing ahead beyond the parousia to the post-parousia experience of eternal torment or reward (8:12; 13:42, 50; 24:51; 25:30, 34, 41, 46). But these references are infrequent, and are not developed at all; they serve as exceptions to prove the rule.

of the missionary commissioning we encounter not the voice of the narrator, but the voice of Jesus; in this way Matthew indicates that the predominant and determining voice in the real world of post-Easter discipleship is that of the exalted and ever-present Christ. Both of these passages relate the person of Jesus to the people of God; the genealogy describes the connection between Jesus and Israel, while the missionary commissioning portrays Jesus' association with his disciples (church). The framing thereby draws attention to the shift in the people of God from Israel to the church (including Gentiles), a shift that occurs because of the ministry, death, and resurrection of Jesus, as narrated in the intervening chapters of Matthew's Gospel.

Finally, one should note the logical correspondence between 1:1 and 28:20: "beginning" (*genesis*), and "end" (*synteleia*). The bracketing of the Gospel with references to beginning and end reinforces the notion, discussed above, that 1:1 and 28:20 serve as temporal narrative boundaries to the world of Matthew's Gospel. But beyond that, this demarcation of the temporal boundaries of the narrative world points to the sovereign control of God over this entire narrative world; for in the biblical tradition in general, and in Matthew's Gospel in particular, the beginning and the end belong solely to God; they are the points at which God exercises the exclusive prerogative of sovereign action.[59] This narrative world is bracketed by implicit references to God's sovereign action, i.e., to God's rule, and this bracketing pointing to God's sovereign rule defines the nature of the narrative world as a whole: it is the sphere where God is manifesting his rule in the person of his Son.

---

[59] In the biblical tradition as a whole see, e.g., Genesis 1:1; Revelation 1:11; in Matthew see, e.g., 19:4; 13:24–30, 36–43; also with special reference to the sole, sovereign, and ultimately determinative action of God at the beginning of salvation history in the patriarchal period, see 22:29–33. Cf. Edward W. Said, *Beginnings: Intention and Method* (New York: Columbia University Press, 1984) xiii.

Chapter Five

Characterization on the Phraseological Plane in the Gospel of Matthew

MARK ALLAN POWELL

Matthew's Gospel is being studied increasingly from perspectives derived from modern literary theory.[1] To date, the greatest amount of attention has been given to formalist approaches such as narrative criticism[2] and structuralism.[3] Formalism is text-centered in orientation. In other words, the primary concern of formalist criticism is to determine how various signals within the text guide the reader in deciding what the text means.[4] This orientation may be compared with other reader-centered approaches that emphasize the ways in which

---

[1] An annotated list of 61 such studies can be found in *The Bible and Modern Literary Criticism: A Critical Assessment and Annotated Bibliography*, by Mark Allan Powell, with the assistance of Cecile G. Gray and Melissa C. Curtis (Westport, CT: Greenwood, 1991).

[2] See Mark Allan Powell, "Toward a Narrative-Critical Understanding of Matthew," *Int* 46 (1992) 341–46; *What Is Narrative Criticism?* GBS (Minneapolis: Fortress, 1990); Jack Dean Kingsbury, *Matthew As Story*, 2d ed. (Philadelphia: Fortress, 1988).

[3] See Daniel Patte, *Structural Exegesis for New Testament Critics*, GBS (Minneapolis: Fortress, 1990); *The Gospel According to Matthew: A Structural Commentary on Matthew's Faith* (Philadelphia: Fortress, 1987).

[4] Introductions to formalist theory include J. Timothy Bagwell, *American Formalism and the Problem of Interpretation* (Houston: Rice University Press, 1986); Cleanth Brooks, "The Formalist Critics," *Kenyon Review* 13 (1951) 72–81; Edgar V. McKnight, *The Bible and the Reader: An Introduction to Literary Criticism* (Philadelphia: Fortress, 1985). For a critical perspective, see Frederic Jameson, *The Prison House of Language: A Critical Account of Structuralism and Russian Formalism* (Princeton, NJ: Princeton University Press, 1972); Lynn M. Poland, *Literary Criticism and Biblical Hermeneutics*, AARAS 48 (Chico, CA: Scholars Press, 1985).

interpretation of a text may be shaped to fit the reader's own interests or circumstances.[5]

This paper is a study in one particular aspect of formalist literary theory (characterization) as applied to one particular literary work (the Gospel of Matthew).[6] Specifically, this study concerns what is usually called the *discourse* component of characterization in Matthew's Gospel. Literary critics distinguish between the elements of *story* (what a narrative is about) and *discourse* (how the story is told).[7] This study is concerned not so much with what the characters in Matthew's Gospel are like, but with *how* the reader comes to know that this is what they are like. What signals in the text guide the reader's interpretation of the characters?

This paper is limited in that it does not attempt to look at all of the characters in Matthew's narrative, but focuses only on the three major characters: Jesus, the disciples, and the religious leaders.[8] In addition, this paper examines only one aspect of characterization, that which is related to speech or phraseology. A more complete or detailed study would have to take other aspects into account as well.

Characterization in Formalist Literary Theory

Narrative criticism emphasizes two components of characterization: "evaluative point of view" and "character traits."[9] Evaluative point of view refers to the norms, values, and general worldview that govern the way a character looks at things and renders judgments upon

---

[5] Text-centered and reader-centered approaches need not be in conflict. Only the most extreme reader-oriented critic would say the text offers no guidance for interpretation, and only the most extreme formalist would deny that individual readers make any contribution to the interpretative process. The distinction is primarily one of degree and focus.

[6] More studies have been done on characterization in Luke than in Matthew. See especially John A. Darr, *On Character Building: The Reader and the Rhetoric of Characterization in Luke-Acts* (Louisville: Westminister/John Knox, 1992); William S. Kurz, *Reading Luke-Acts: Dynamics of Biblical Narrative* (Louisville: Westminster/John Knox, 1993).

[7] See Seymour Chatman, *Story and Discourse: Narrative Structure in Fiction and Film* (Ithaca, NY: Cornell University Press, 1978).

[8] It has become customary to treat both "the disciples" and "the religious leaders" as single characters in Matthew's narrative. Although technically both are what literary critics call "character groups," they function in the story as single characters. See Kingsbury, *Matthew As Story*, 13, 18; Powell, *What Is Narrative Criticism?*, 51, 58.

[9] Powell, *What Is Narrative Criticism?*, 53–55.

them.[10] Traits are persistent personal qualities that describe the character involved.[11] The process of characterization consists of an author (or implied author[12]) ascribing an evaluative point of view and a particular set of traits to the characters in a narrative.

In order for the narrative to work, what has been ascribed to the characters must be communicated to the reader. The Russian formalist Boris Uspensky has proposed a typology for analyzing the planes of expression on which such information is communicated between author and reader: (1) the ideological plane concerns values and beliefs; (2) the phraseological plane concerns speech, or thoughts if these are articulated as speech ("he said to himself . . ."); (3) the spatial and temporal planes concern actions; (4) the psychological plane concerns motives.[13] The evaluative point of view and the set of traits that an author ascribes to a character in his or her narrative are communicated to the reader by what is presented on any or all of these planes. In other words, judgments that readers make regarding characters in narrative literature are typically based on such factors as values, speech, actions, and motives.

Studies in the *discourse* of narrative literature are interested in which of these planes, if any, is dominant. It is one thing to recognize that Sherlock Holmes is "perceptive"; it is quite another thing to inquire as to *how* Sir Arthur Conan Doyle leads us to recognize this. Do we regard Holmes as perceptive primarily on the basis of what he says or on the basis of what he does? Do Holmes' motives or values have any significance in this regard, or would we view him as perceptive even if they were quite different? Formalist literary studies have found that one or another of Uspensky's four planes is frequently more significant for characterization within a given narrative than the others.

Sometimes what is communicated on one plane may conflict with what is communicated on another plane. Speech may be inconsistent with actions, actions may be incompatible with motives, motives may

---

[10] Boris Uspensky, *A Poetics of Composition: The Structure of the Artistic Text and Typology of a Compositional Form*, trans. by Valentina Zavarin and Susan Wittig (Berkeley and Los Angeles: University of California Press, 1973) 8.

[11] Chatman, *Story and Discourse*, 121.

[12] On the concept of "implied author," see Wayne Booth, *The Rhetoric of Fiction*, 2d ed. (Chicago: University of Chicago Press, 1983) 66–77; Chatman, *Story and Discourse*, 147–51; Powell, *What Is Narrative Criticism?*, 5–6.

[13] Uspensky, *Poetics of Composition*, 8–100.

contradict values, and so on. Uspensky refers to such discrepancies as instances of "nonconcurrence." When the reader encounters nonconcurrence, he or she must struggle to discern which of the planes presents the more accurate characterization. Typically, the reader will decide on the basis of various clues within the text that what is communicated on one or more of the planes is unreliable and must be discounted in light of what is communicated elsewhere. In Matthew's Gospel, the character of Herod as revealed on the psychological plane (he is frightened by news of Jesus' birth, 2:3) is nonconcurrent with his character as revealed on the phraseological plane (he wants to worship Jesus, 2:8). The tension thus created for the reader is partially resolved in verse 12 and in verse 13 when God and an angel issue warnings about Herod—warnings that would not be necessary if Herod truly wished only to worship Jesus. Herod's subsequent actions on the spatial-temporal plane (he tries to kill Jesus, 2:16) confirm the reader's suspicion that Herod's statement in 2:8 was a lie. Thus, Matthew overrides the unreliable information concerning Herod presented on the phraseological plane with more reliable information offered either on other planes (psychological, spatial-temporal) or through the phraseology of others (God, angels).

Direct and Indirect Phraseology

Our immediate concern is with point of view on the phraseological plane. This study will investigate the extent to which the speech of various characters in Matthew's Gospel reveals those characters to the reader. At this point I must depart somewhat from Uspensky, whose categories for classifying phraseology are drawn from modern literature and are sometimes inapplicable to the Gospels. Instead, I have focused on one basic distinction, namely that between what I call "direct phraseology" and "indirect phraseology."

Every evaluative speech act contains at least three elements: a *sender* who offers an evaluation of something; a *subject* that is evaluated; and a *recipient* who hears or receives this evaluation. In direct phraseology, the subject and the recipient are identical. For example, when John the Baptist addresses the Pharisees and Sadducees with the words, "You brood of vipers . . ." (3:7), he offers his evaluation of the Pharisees and Sadducees directly to the Pharisees and Sadducees themselves. In this instance, John the Baptist may be identified as sender, and the Pharisees and Sadducees may be identified as both subject and recipient.

Indirect phraseology assumes a distinction between subject and recipient. If, for example, John the Baptist were depicted as saying to the crowds, "The Pharisees and Sadducees are a brood of vipers," that would be an instance of indirect phraseology. John the Baptist would be identified as sender, the Pharisees and Sadducees as subject, and the crowds as recipient.

Two further points need to be made. First, although there may be some instances in which this distinction does not apply, most speech acts are at least implicitly evaluative. When Jesus says to the crowds, "Repent, for the kingdom of heaven is at hand" (4:17), the implied evaluation of the crowds is that they are in need of repentance. When he says to his (future) disciples, "Follow me and I will make you fish for people" (4:19), his words carry an implicit evaluation regarding their acceptability to him and potential for ministry. Similarly, interrogative speech may qualify as direct phraseology if the speaker asks for the opinion of the party who is being addressed, or as indirect phraseology if the speaker asks for the opinion of someone else (cf. the indirect phraseology of Jesus in 6:13 with his direct phraseology in 6:15).

Second, the distinction between direct and indirect phraseology is not the same as the distinction that Uspensky and others make between direct and indirect discourse. The latter distinction identifies the manner in which the speech is reported. The following four examples should illustrate the possible ways in which these two distinctions can overlap:

1. John said, "You are a brood of vipers."
    (direct discourse/direct phraseology)
2. John said, "They are a brood of vipers."
    (direct discourse/indirect phraseology)
3. John told them that they were a brood of vipers.
    (indirect discourse/direct phraseology)
4. John told us that they were a brood of vipers.
    (indirect discourse/indirect phraseology)

With these theoretical and methodological points in mind, we may turn now to observations concerning what is communicated on the phraseological plane with regard to the characterization of the three major characters in Matthew's narrative.

The Phraseology of Jesus

Literary-critical studies have described Jesus in Matthew's narrative as a "round character,"[14] that is, as a character who exhibits a great number and variety of traits.[15] Jesus is "obedient" toward God, "compassionate" toward the crowds, "confrontational" toward his enemies, "faithful" and "enabling" toward his disciples, and so on. Despite this variety of traits, Jesus is consistently portrayed in a positive light, as a character who always evinces an evaluative point of view aligned with that of God. God calls Jesus "Son" and is pleased with Jesus (3:17; 17:5).

Our present concern is with the role that the phraseology of Jesus plays in communicating this portrait to the reader. Although space does not permit us to consider every instance of Jesus' speech in the Gospel, my own analysis of that speech has allowed me to draw the following conclusions:

(1) The phraseology of Jesus is not the primary means by which Matthew communicates his characterization of Jesus to his readers. Jesus hardly speaks at all before the beginning of his ministry in 4:17;[16] instead, his characterization is established in the initial portion of the narrative through other means: comments by the narrator (1:1, 16–18), intercessions of angels (1:20–21; 2:13, 19–20), recollections of prophecy (1:22–23; 2:4–6, 15, 17, 23), reactions of other characters (1:24–25; 2:1–2, 3, 11, 16), and testimony from God (3:17). Thus, Matthew's reader comes to know that Jesus is born of a virgin (1:25); that he is the unique Son of God (3:17); that God is present with him (1:23); that he is to be worshiped (2:11); and that he will both save his people from sins (1:21) and execute judgment by baptizing people with the Holy Spirit and with fire (3:11–12). By establishing Jesus' characterization early in the narrative in ways that do not depend upon Jesus' own phraseology, Matthew avoids giving any impression of Jesus as one who testifies on his own behalf. Rather, the basic and initial testimony to Jesus is that of the narrator, the prophets, the

---

[14] On "round" and "flat" characters, see E. M. Forster, *Aspects of the Novel* (New York: Harcourt, Brace, Jovanovich, 1927).

[15] See, e.g. Jack Dean Kingsbury, "The Figure of Jesus in Matthew's Story: A Literary-Critical Probe," *JSNT* 21 (1984) 3–36; *Matthew As Story*, 11–13.

[16] See, only, 3:17; 4:4, 7, 10. Significantly, Jesus does not speak about himself in any of these instances, but simply quotes scripture and speaks of what is necessary to fulfill all righteousness.

angels, and God. In this way, Matthew also indicates that the phraseology of Jesus alone may not be sufficient for a full apprehension of who Jesus is. Indeed, as the Gospel progresses, it becomes apparent that people who regard Jesus simply as "teacher" or as "prophet" have not fully grasped who he is.[17]

(2) The phraseology of Jesus serves to confirm, illustrate, and amplify the characterization of Jesus that is established through other means. Jesus' own phraseology testifies to the unique and intimate relationship that he has with God (11:25–27), as well as to his role as both savior from sins (9:3,6, 13; 20:28; 26:28) and eschatological judge (5:20; 21:32, 43; 23:33–36; 24:30–31; 25:31–46; 24:64). Further examples of this confirming role for the phraseology of Jesus abound: Jesus' comment that he has compassion on the crowds (15:32) confirms a trait that has been twice ascribed to him by the narrator (9:36; 14:14); Jesus' claim to have authority (9:6; 28:18) confirms what the narrator says has caused others to be astonished by him (7:28–29; cf. 9:8). In this way, Matthew indicates that, even though Jesus is not primarily a character who testifies on his own behalf, what he does have to say about himself is completely consistent with what is reported through reliable sources elsewhere.

(3) The phraseology of Jesus is absolutely reliable in what it communicates concerning the characterization of Jesus in Matthew's narrative. There is not a single instance of nonconcurrence between what is revealed through Jesus' speech and what is revealed through his actions, motives, or values. Congruence of the phraseological and spatial-temporal planes is especially pronounced, as examination of any of the themes highlighted above will indicate. Jesus not only says he has compassion (15:32), but also acts compassionately (15:35–38); he not only claims to have authority (9:6), but also acts authoritatively (9:5–8). In this way, Matthew presents Jesus as a character of integrity, who stands up to examination under his own principle that those who speak the truth are to be recognized "by their fruits" (7:16, 20;

---

[17] In Matthew, the terms "Teacher" and "Prophet" are never used for Jesus by persons with faith. On "Teacher," see Günther Bornkamm, "End Expectation and Church in Matthew," in Günther Bornkamm, Gerhard Barth, and Heinz Joachim Held, *Tradition and Interpretation in Matthew* (Philadelphia: Westminster, 1963) 41–42. On "Prophet," see Kingsbury, "Figure of Jesus," 14.

12:33).[18] Unlike the scribes and the Pharisees (23:2–3), Jesus not only speaks the will of God, but also does it.[19]

(4) The distinction between direct and indirect phraseology proves to be irrelevant with regard to the characterization of Jesus. What Jesus says *to* other characters does not portray him in any different light than what he says *about* other characters. To illustrate, let us consider the evaluative phraseology of Jesus concerning the religious leaders in Matthew's narrative. What follows is a comprehensive summary of Jesus' *indirect* phraseology concerning the leaders:

A   They will not enter the kingdom of heaven (5:20).

B   They will persecute Jesus' followers (10:17).

C   They will be condemned in the final judgment (15:13; cf. 13:24–30, 36–43).

D   They are blind guides (15:14).

E   People should beware of their teaching (16:6, 11–12).

F   They will be responsible for Jesus' death (16:21; 20:18).

G   Although they sit on Moses' seat, they do not practice what Moses intends (23:2–3).

H   They make burdensome demands and show no concern for helping people (23:4).

I   Their outward display of piety is hypocritical (23:5–7; cf. 6:5).

Every one of these statements may be compared with instances of Jesus' *direct* phraseology, with statements that Jesus makes directly to the religious leaders:

A'   The kingdom on God will be taken away from them (21:43; see also 23:13).

B'   They will persecute Jesus' followers (23:34).

C'   They will be condemned in the final judgment (12:41–42; 23:35).

D'   They are blind guides (23:16, 24; cf. 23:17, 19, 26).

E'   They turn their proselytes into children of hell (23:15).

F'   They will be responsible for Jesus' death (21:33–39, 45).

G'   Their practices nullify the true intent of Moses' teaching (15:3–9).

---

[18] Kingsbury describes Jesus as a "man of integrity" in *Matthew As Story*, 12.

[19] On the congruence of word and deed in Matthew 23:2–3, see Mark Allan Powell, "'Do and Keep What Moses Said' (Matt. 23:2–3)," *JBL* 114 (1995): 419–35; *God With Us: A Pastoral Theology of Matthew's Gospel* (Minneapolis: Fortress, 1995) 75–81.

H' They demand sacrifices from people without regard for showing mercy (12:7).

I' Their outward appearance of righteousness is hypocritical (23:27–28).

Although the correspondences are not always exact, we may conclude that, in Matthew's Gospel, Jesus says nothing significant *about* the religious leaders that he does not also say *to* them. In this way, Matthew underscores his presentation of Jesus as a person of integrity. Not only are his words consistent with his deeds, motives, and actions, but what he says directly to characters is consistent with what he says indirectly about them.

The Phraseology of Jesus' Disciples

Literary studies of Jesus' disciples in Matthew's Gospel have cast them, too, as round characters who exhibit traits that are not only varied but actually in conflict with each other.[20] They can, for instance, be described as "enlightened" in one scene (13:11, 16–17) and as "unperceptive" in another (16:5–12). They seem "loyal" and "sacrificial" when they leave all to follow Jesus (4:20, 22; 9:1; cf. 19:27), but "disloyal" and "self-concerned" when they desert him in the fact of danger (26:56, 69–74). Their evaluative point of view is sometimes aligned with that of God (16:16–17) and at other times with that of Satan (16:22–23).

This complexity of characterization is evident in the disciples' phraseology. An analysis of this phraseology allows the following conclusions:

(1) The great majority of the phraseology attributed to the disciples in Matthew's narrative serves to expose their flaws. Their speech presents them as characters who lack faith (8:25; 14:30) and understanding (8:27; 16:7), who harbor false assumptions (18:21; 17:25; 19:25) and superstitious fears (14:26), who are slow to realize what God is able to accomplish (14:15–17; 15:33–34; 21:20), and who are reluctant to accept the costs of discipleship (8:21; 16:22; 26:70, 72, 74). The disciples sometimes appear to sympathize with Jesus' enemies (15:12) and to criticize his friends (26:8–9). Statements in which they offer evaluations of themselves are unrealistically positive (14:28; 19:27; 20:22; 26:33–35). Sometimes, the disciples' speech presents them in a more neutral light, as when they ask seemingly innocent

---

[20] See, e.g., Kingsbury, *Matthew As Story*, 13–17.

questions (13:10, 36; 15:15; 17:10; 18:1; 24:3; 26:17) but, even then, Jesus' response may indicate that the question implies a lack of understanding (15:16) or improper attitude (18:2). Only rarely does the phraseology of the disciples reveal them to be characters of faith and insight (14:33; 16:16).

(2) The characterization of the disciples presented through their own phraseology is consistent with that presented through Matthew's description of their actions. Although their actions may sometimes offer the reader a favorable picture of them as responsive (4:20, 22; 9:9) or obedient (21:7; 26:19) to Jesus, these actions also expose the kinds of flaws evident in their phraseology. To cite but a few examples: The failed exorcism in 17:14–17 reveals their lack of faith (17:19–20); the rebuke of people with children in 19:13 shows a failure to understand what Jesus said earlier in 18:5; and the flight at Jesus' arrest (26:56) demonstrates their reluctance to accept the costs of discipleship. By establishing this consistency of characterization, Matthew indicates that, although the disciples may be flawed characters, the nature of their flaw does not involve a discrepancy between speech and actions. In this regard, they, too, are unlike the scribes and Pharisees (23:2–3).

(3) The distinction between direct phraseology and indirect phraseology seems to be irrelevant with regard to Matthew's characterization of Jesus' disciples. Statements offered directly to Jesus (e.g., 8:21, 25; 14:15–17, 30; 15:33–34; 16:22; 17:19; 18:21; 19:10, 25; 21:20) are no more or less likely to expose their flaws than statements made about Jesus to others (8:27; 14:26; 16:7; 17:25; 26:70, 72, 74). For example, in dealing with people who they don't think should see Jesus, they are just as likely to rebuke those people directly (19:13) as they are to ask Jesus to do so for them (15:23). Significantly, the same consistency holds with regard to their virtues. Matthew contains only two instances in which the disciples' phraseology presents them as characters of faith and insight and, of these, one is an instance of direct phraseology (16:16) and the other is an instance of indirect phraseology (14:33). In this way, Matthew presents the disciples as characters who are at least sincere and genuine in what they say. They do not try to cover up their faults or to put on false fronts. They may be flawed characters with little faith, but they are not hypocrites.

The one obvious exception to what has just been said is the character of Judas. The direct phraseology of Judas presents him as a character who feigns innocence and pretends to be friendly to Jesus

(26:25,49), while the indirect phraseology of Judas presents him as a character who is a traitor (26:14, 48; 27:4). The unreliable direct phraseology serves to highlight the duplicitous character of Judas' treachery.

(4) The characterization of the disciples presented through their own phraseology in Matthew's narrative needs to be supplemented by information that is communicated to the reader through another source, namely the phraseology of Jesus. What Jesus says to and about his disciples usually presents them in a much more positive light than does their own speech. Jesus refers to them as his family (12:49) and as part of the church that he will build (16:18–19; 18:15–18). He describes them as "guiltless" (12:7) and as privileged to know the secrets of the kingdom of heaven (13:11, 16–17). He promises them protection (10:30–31) and assures them of his continuing presence with them (18:20; 28:20). He says that in the future they will "fish for people" (4:19), minister in the face of rejection and persecution (10:5–23), make disciples of all nations (28:19), and judge the twelve tribes of Israel (19:28). In short, Matthew supplements the mostly negative portrait of the disciples offered through their own speech with a much more positive portrait offered through the speech of Jesus. By doing this, he indicates that the positive aspects of the disciples' characterization derive from Jesus and can only be realized through him. Jesus is the one who chooses the disciples (4:19, 21; 9:9) and Jesus is the one who can provide them with the authority (10:1; 28:18) and understanding (13:51; 16:12) they need. The reader ultimately views these disciples as characters with tremendous potential. The reader realizes, however, that this potential does not derive from any qualities the disciples evince on their own, but from what Jesus sees in them and is able to impart to them.

The Phraseology of the Religious Leaders

Literary studies of the religious leaders in Matthew's narrative have observed that they are flat characters who function as the antagonists of Jesus in the story.[21] Their root character trait is "evil," and other qualities such as "hypocrisy" and "blindness" may be subsumed under

---

[21] See, e.g., Kingsbury, "The Developing Conflict Between Jesus and the Jewish Leaders in Matthew's Gospel: A Literary-Critical Study," *CBQ* 49 (1987) 57–73; *Matthew As Story*, 17–24.

this basic characteristic. Their evaluative point of view is consistently opposed to that of God.

Once again, we are primarily interested in the extent to which the leaders' own phraseology conveys this characterization to the reader. Our conclusions are as follows:

(1) The characterization of the religious leaders presented through their own phraseology offers two inconsistent portraits of them. Sometimes, their speech presents them as characters who regard Jesus as a blasphemer (9:3; 26:65), as an imposter (27:63), as one who wrongly eats with tax collectors and sinners (9:11), as a colleague of Beelzebul (9:34; 12:24), as one who deserves death (26:66), and as one whose inability to save himself proves that he is not the Son of God (27:42–43). At other times, however, their speech seems to present them as would-be disciples (8:19), as sincere questioners (12:10; 19:3; 22:16–17, 24–28, 36), or, at least, as polite skeptics (12:38; 21:21). The issue for the reader, then, is whether the religious leaders should be regarded as implacable opponents of Jesus who wish to bring about his demise or as possible converts who are not sure what to make of him.

(2) In every instance in which the leaders' phraseology allows the more positive portrait, Matthew overrides this image by offering the reader compelling information through some other means. He does this is a variety of ways that utilize all four planes of expression:

(a) *ideological plane*—in 22:25, Matthew tells the reader that the Sadducees do not really believe in the resurrection, so that the reader will know their question in 22:24–28 is actually insincere.

(b) *phraseological plane*—in 12:39–42; 19:4; 21:16, 27; 22:18, 19, Matthew uses the always reliable phraseology of Jesus to reveal opposition that is not apparent in the leaders' own words. Jesus responds to their seemingly innocuous speech with words of harsh condemnation, denouncing them for things their own speech did not reveal. Also, in 8:19, 12:38; 22:16, 24, 36, Matthew has the leaders address Jesus as "Teacher." Although this word does not express opposition in and of itself, it is never used in Matthew's Gospel as an address by persons of faith (cf. 19:16, 22; 26:18, 25, 49).

(c) *spatial-temporal plane*—in 12:14; 22:15, Matthew reports actions of the religious leaders that reveal a hostility not evident in their words. This correlates with Jesus' warning elsewhere to the effect that their deeds and words are inconsistent (23:2–3).

(d) *psychological plane*—in 12:10; 19:3; 21:15; 22:18, 35, Matthew reveals motives that present the religious leaders in a much more negative light than what is apparent from their speech alone. They ask Jesus innocent sounding questions in order to accuse him, put him to the test, or entangle him in his talk.

Thus, the reader of Matthew's Gospel is led to realize that only the phraseological statements that present the more negative picture of the religious leaders are reliable. Statements that might present them in a neutral or positive light are nonconcurrent with more reliable information presented in other ways.

(3) The distinction between direct and indirect phraseology becomes quite significant in an examination of the religious leaders' speech. Almost without exception, the reliable statements that offer the reader a negative picture of the leaders are instances of indirect phraseology. The unreliable statements that offer the reader a more neutral or positive picture of the leaders are all instances of direct phraseology. To illustrate this point, let us compare a list of statements that the religious leaders make *about* Jesus in Matthew's narrative with a list of statements that they make *to* Jesus.

The text of all of the indirect phraseological statements that the religious leaders make about Jesus is given below.[22]

A "This man is blaspheming" (9:3).

B "Why does your teacher eat with tax collectors and sinners?" (9:11).

C "By the ruler of demons, he casts out the demons" (9:34).

D "It is only by Beelzebul, the prince of demons, that this fellow casts out the demons" (12:24).

E "He has blasphemed! Why do we still need witnesses? You have heard his blasphemy. What is your verdict?" (26:65–66).

F "He deserves death" (26:66).

G "He saved others; he cannot save himself. He is the King of Israel; let him come down from the cross now, and we will believe in him. He trusts in God; let God deliver him now, if he wants to; for he said, 'I am God's Son'" (27:42–43).

H "Sir, we remember what that imposter said while he was still alive, 'After three days I will rise again.' Therefore command the tomb to be made secure until the third day; otherwise his disciples may go and steal him away, and tell the people, 'He

---

[22] English text is from the New Revised Standard Version. I am not aware of any instances where variations of text or translation would affect the basic point that is here illustrated.

has been raised from the dead,' and the last fraud will be worse than the first" (27:63–64).

In all of these statements, opposition to Jesus is clearly and consistently expressed. The indirect phraseology of the religious leaders presents them, without exception, as implacable opponents of Jesus.

The text of all of the direct phraseological statements that the religious leaders make to Jesus is now given below.[23]

I   "Teacher, I will follow you wherever you go" (8:19).

J   "Is it lawful to cure on the sabbath?" (12:10).

K   "Teacher, we wish to see a sign from you" (12:38).

L   "Is it lawful for a man to divorce his wife for any cause?" (19:3).

M   "Do you hear what these are saying?" (21:16).

N   "By what authority are you doing these things, and who gave you this authority?" (21:33).

O   "Teacher, we know that you are sincere and teach the way of God in accordance with truth, and show deference to no one; for you do not regard people with partiality. Tell us, then, what you think. Is it lawful to pay taxes to the emperor, or not?" (22:16–17).

P   "Teacher, Moses said, 'If a man dies childless, his brother shall marry the widow and raise up children for his brother. Now there were seven brothers among us; the first died childless, leaving the widow to his brother. The second did the same, so also the third, down to the seventh. Last of all, the woman herself died. In the resurrection, then, whose wife of the seven will she be? For all of them had married her" (22:24–28).

Q   "Teacher, which commandment in the law is the greatest?" (22:36).

R   "Have you no answer? What is it that they testify against you?" (26:62).

S   "I put you under oath before the living God, tell us if you are the Messiah, the Son of God" (26:63).

T   "Prophesy to us, you Messiah! Who is it that struck you?" (26:68).

In Matthew's narrative, every one of these statements occurs in a context of opposition between the religious leaders and Jesus.[24]

---

[23] The religious leaders also speak to Jesus in 12:2; 15:2; 21:27, 41; 22:42, but their speech does not offer an evaluation of Jesus in any of these instances.

Divorced from their context, however, the statements do not all express this opposition. In most cases, the leaders' speech appears to be simply innocuous or even friendly to Jesus. Only in the last three instances, which occur in the climactic trial before the Council, is the hostility between the leaders and Jesus apparent in the leaders' own direct phraseology. Otherwise, these instances of direct phraseology are identical with the instances cited above in which Matthew must override an unreliable characterization with additional information.

Unlike the phraseology of Jesus and the disciples, then, the phraseology of the religious leaders is a reliable indicator of their point of view only when it is indirect. Their real opinion of Jesus is expressed only when they speak about him to other characters, not when they speak to him directly. This observation, furthermore, extends also to the religious leaders' phraseology concerning the disciples. They criticize Jesus to the disciples (9:11) and they criticize the disciples to Jesus (12:2; 15:2), but they are reluctant to criticize either face to face.

At times, Matthew actually portrays Jesus as responding directly to criticisms that the leaders have made indirectly (9:3–4; 12:2–8, 24–37). Even at the crucifixion, the leaders mock Jesus with indirect phraseology that contrasts with the more direct attacks of the passers-by (27:39–40). These rather unnatural extremes, by which Matthew almost strains the logic of his narrative, indicate how important it is for him to establish this contrast between the religious leaders' direct and indirect phraseology.

What effect does such a contrast have on the reader? Matthew uses this contrast to present the religious leaders as duplicitous.[25] The duplicity evident in their phraseology is but one part of their overall

---

[24] I assume that this opposition is obvious in every instance except perhaps 8:19. Kingsbury believes that opposition is evident even here. See Jack Dean Kingsbury, "On Following Jesus: The 'Eager' Scribe and the 'Reluctant' Disciple (Matt. 8:18–22)," *NTS* 34 (1988) 45–59.

[25] Patte is correct in his observation that the leaders' indirect negative comments constitute "the kind of judgment that is against God's will," but he misses the point in contrasting these with the judgments of Jesus which, because they are more direct, he regards as not "a judgment/condemnation but a call to repentance" (*Gospel According to Matthew*, 126, 129, 227 n.1). Actually, Jesus does not offer the religious leaders any opportunity for repentance but judges and condemns them in the harshest of terms. But he does this with phraseology that is both direct and indirect. What is distinctive about the indirect phraseology of the leaders is not that it is more judgmental than that of Jesus, but that it is inconsistent with their direct speech, and so highlights the duplicity of the latter.

characterization as hypocrites (15:7; 22:18; 23:13, 15, 23, 25, 27, 28, 29; cf. 6:1–6, 16–18; 23:1–7).[26] In 12:36, Jesus tells the religious leaders that, on the day of judgment, they will have to give account for every *careless* word they utter. Careless words, apparently, are virtually synonymous here with indirect phraseology. When the leaders are careful, they are able to "speak good" even though they are evil, but when their guard is down, their careless words reveal what is truly in their hearts (12:34). The duplicity that Matthew ascribes to the religious leaders, then, goes beyond a simple disparity between words and deeds (cf. 23:2–3) to extend also to a disparity between careful words (direct phraeology) and careless ones (indirect phraseology).

Jesus, whose point of view is always expressed consistently and reliably regardless of whether his phraseology is direct or indirect, seems to be particularly perturbed by this aspect of the religious leaders' duplicity. "Either make the tree good and its fruit good,' he says, 'or make the tree bad, and its fruit bad" (12:33). In context, his assertion in 12:33 that "a tree is known by its fruits" refers not so much to deeds as to "careless words." The fruit by which religious leaders may be known is the quality of their unguarded speech, that is, the content of what they say when they are not making an effort to deceive or to impress. It is by such speech that religious leaders are justified or condemned (12:37).

Matthew could, of course, simply tell his readers outright that the religious leaders are duplicitous and often speak in ways that do not reveal their actual point of view. By taking the more subtle route and incorporating this aspect of their characterization into the discourse of his narrative, he scores an additional point. The reader is left to discover for him or her self that the guarded, direct phraseology of these characters is unreliable, while their careless, indirect statements are more revealing. Thus, by the very act of reading this narrative,

---

[26] On Matthew's notion of hypocrisy, see Sjef Van Tilborg, *The Jewish Leaders in Matthew* (Leiden: E. J. Brill, 1972) 8–26. Cf. Dan O. Via, *Self-Deception and Wholeness in Paul and in Matthew* (Minneapolis: Fortress, 1990) 77–98. Via's conception of hypocrisy in Matthew as "self-deception" fails to account for the type of data presented in this study, where the leaders appear to deceive others intentionally. I believe that the leaders *are* self-deceived in Matthew, but Matthew's word for self-decption is not "hypocrisy" but "blindness." The irony is that the leaders, who as hypocrites intentionally deceive others, are also blind characters who have somehow deceived themselves. They have become, as it were, victims of their own hypocrisy.

Matthew's reader gains practice in the art of learning to recognize a tree by its fruits.

General Conclusions

The phraseology of Jesus in Matthew's narrative provides the reader with reliable information for his characterization. This information serves primarily to confirm, illustrate, and amplify the characterization of Jesus presented through other sources, including the words of God, prophets, angels, other reliable characters, and the narrator. In this way, Matthew guides the reader to see that one might not be able to appreciate fully who Jesus is on the basis of Jesus' words alone, although those words are certainly consistent with what is revealed elsewhere. Jesus' phraseology also depicts him as a character of integrity, whose words are consistent with his deeds, and who does not speak any differently about other characters than he does to them.

The phraseology of Jesus' disciples in Matthew's narrative provides the reader with reliable information for their characterization. Still, the mostly negative portrait conveyed by the disciples' own speech must be supplemented by the more positive information regarding the disciples found in the phraseology of Jesus. In this way, Matthew emphasizes that the disciples' best attributes derive from Jesus, that is, from what he sees in them and is able to impart to them. The disciples' phraseology also depicts them as characters of integrity, who do not present false fronts or attempt to hide their flaws. Their speech, even when it reveals their flaws, is at least genuine and sincere.

The phraseoogy of the religious leaders in Matthew's narrative provides the reader with reliable information for their characterization only when it is indirect. When the leaders use direct phraseology, their speech is usually not expressive of their actual point of view, which must be discerned through other means. In this way, Matthew highlights the duplicity of the religious leaders and guides the reader to recognize the deceptive way in which hypocrites may try to hide their real nature.

Chapter Six

Power and Powerlessness: Matthew's Use of Irony in the Portrayal of Political Leaders

DOROTHY JEAN WEAVER

In his discussion of irony in the Gospel of John[1] Paul D. Duke cites Haakon Chevalier's statement that "the basic feature of every Irony is a contrast between a reality and an appearance."[2] Duke goes on to observe that "in each case the irony emerges when the appearance is corrected or exploded by the contrasting reality perceived by the ironist and perceptive audience. *Irony, then, is a leap from what seems to be to what is.*"[3] And, as Duke demonstrates throughout the remainder of his book, this ironic "leap from what seems to be to what is" is an act of mental gymnastics fundamental to the reading of the Gospel of John.

What proves true for the Gospel of John is true as well for the Gospel of Matthew. While no comparable attention has as yet been devoted to the use of irony within Matthew's narrative,[4] the evidence provided by the text of Matthew's Gospel would nevertheless appear to warrant such attention. Nowhere is this more evident than in the characterizations of the three political leaders who figure within Matthew's narrative: "Herod the king" (2:1–23), "Herod the tetrarch" (14:1–12), and "Pilate the governor" (27:1–2, 11–38, 54, 62–66; 28:1–

---

[1] Paul D. Duke, *Irony in the Fourth Gospel* (Atlanta: John Knox, 1985).

[2] Ibid., 15. Cited from Haakon Chevalier, *The Ironic Temper: Anatole France and His Time* (New York: Oxford University Press, 1932) 42.

[3] Ibid., 15. Emphasis mine.

[4] I have not succeeded in locating any major studies, whether essays or monographs, which deal with Matthew's use of irony as a literary technique. Note, by contrast, the bibliographical citations on irony in the Gospel of John as listed by Duke (157, nn. 3, 4) in his own monograph on that topic.

15). On the one hand, Matthew invests each of these characters with both the title and the attributes of power. Yet on the other hand, Matthew works in unmistakable fashion to subvert the very portraits of power which he himself has painted. In this way Matthew invites the perceptive reader to make the ironic "leap" from "the power that seems to be" to "the powerlessness that is."

In the following paper I will analyze the character portrayals of Herod the king, Herod the tetrarch, and Pilate the governor in order to determine Matthew's ironic methodology and to assess the impact of Matthean irony on the reader of Matthew's Gospel. I will work at this task in three stages: (1) I will identify the basic shape and qualifying characteristics of irony as a literary strategy; (2) I will work text by text with the Matthean character portrayals of the three political leaders in question; and (3) I will offer concluding observations with reference to Matthew's use of irony.

Towards a Definition of Irony

In his book *The Compass of Irony* D. C. Muecke identifies irony in terms of three basic elements.[5] The first of these is what he describes as a "double-layered or two-storey phenomenon" in which "the lower level is the situation either as it appears to the victim of irony . . . or as it is deceptively presented by the ironist" and "the upper level is the situation as it appears to the observer or the ironist."[6] Between the lower and the upper levels there is, secondly, an "opposition" consisting of "contradiction, incongruity, or incompatibility," such that "what is said may be contradicted by what is meant" or "what the victim thinks may be contradicted by what the observer knows."[7] The third basic element of irony is that of "innocence," the situation in which "a victim is confidently unaware of the very possibility of there being an upper level or point of view that invalidates his own, or an ironist pretends not to be aware of it."[8]

Typologies of irony distinguish, in the broadest of terms, between verbal ironies, dramatic ironies, and situational ironies. Verbal ironies are those in which the ironist communicates the irony in his/her own

---

[5] D. C. Muecke, *The Compass of Irony* (London: Methuen, 1969) 19–20. Cf. Duke, 13, 17.

[6] Ibid., 19. Cf. Duke, 14.

[7] Ibid., 19–20. Cf. Duke, 14–16.

[8] Ibid., 20. Cf. Duke, 16–18.

voice or in the voice of an "innocent" character within the narrative itself.[9] In such a case the ironist is "someone consciously and intentionally employing a technique."[10] Such ironies are by definition ones in which the speaker knows more than he/she appears to know.[11]

Dramatic ironies,[12] by contrast, are those in which the ironist communicates in oblique fashion, through the actions and events of the narrative itself. In this case the ironist "arranges that the characters . . . expose themselves in their ironic predicament directly to the audience or reader."[13] In such instances the irony hinges on the fact that the audience or reader has information of which the character in question is not yet aware.[14]

Situational ironies emerge, as do dramatic ironies, from the actions or events of the narrative. They distinguish themselves from dramatic ironies, however, in that their effectiveness does not depend on the foreknowledge of the audience or reader.[15] A categorization of ironic situations includes such types as irony of simple incongruity, irony of events, irony of self betrayal, irony of dilemma, and irony of characterization.[16]

Clues to the ironic intent of a literary work can come to the audience or reader in a variety of ways. Wayne Booth, in his book *A Rhetoric of Irony*, identifies five means which an author has for communicating irony within any given literary work: (1) "straightforward warnings in the author's own voice"; (2) "known error proclaimed" within the work; (3) "conflicts of facts within the work"; (4) "clashes of style"; and (5) "conflicts of belief."[17]

There is likewise a diversity of objects which an author can target within any given literary work. As Muecke observes, "The object of irony may be a person . . . , an attitude, a belief, a social custom or

---

[9] Thus the first three of Muecke's four "modes" of irony (61–63; cf. Duke, 30–31): "impersonal irony," "self-disparaging irony," "ingenu irony."

[10] Muecke, 42.

[11] Thus Duke, 23.

[12] This constitutes the fourth of Muecke's four modes of irony (61–63).

[13] Ibid., 92.

[14] Thus Muecke, 104; M. H. Abrams, *A Glossary of Literary Terms*, 3rd ed. (New York: Holt, Rinehart and Winston, 1971) 82; Duke, 24.

[15] Thus Duke, 26.

[16] See Muecke, 99–115; Duke, 26–27.

[17] Wayne Booth, *A Rhetoric of Irony* (Chicago: University of Chicago Press, 1974) 53–76.

institution, a philosophical system, a religion, even a whole civilization, even life itself."[18]

Matthew's Portrayals of Political Leaders

Herod the king (2:1–23). The first political figure to appear on the scene in Matthew's narrative is Herod the king (2:1–23), who is introduced to the reader in connection with the mention of Jesus' birth: "Now when Jesus was born in Bethlehem of Judea *in the days of Herod the King . . .*" (2:1).[19] This designation at first appears to be merely a historical signpost by which to date the birth of Jesus.[20] But the immediately following text makes it clear that what is at stake here is not historical dating but rather ironic portrayal: "Now when Jesus was born in Bethlehem of Judea *in the days of Herod the king,* astrologers from the East arrived in Jerusalem, saying, 'Where is *the one who has been born King of the Jews?*'" (2:1–2a).[21]

No sooner has Matthew's narrator handed the title of "king" to Herod and made Herod's "kingship" over Judea a "fact" in his narrative than he challenges that very "kingship" by characterizing the newborn Jesus as "the one who has been born *king of the Jews.*" With this abrupt and pointed juxtaposition of "Herod the king [over Judea]" and "Jesus . . . the king of the Jews" the narrator puts the reader formally on notice that the "fact" of Herod's "kingship" cannot be trusted as ultimate truth. Rather, it is merely an "apparent fact" which will be undercut by the "true fact" of Jesus' "kingship."[22] Accordingly, the reader is immediately alerted to the presence of two opposing levels of reality within the narrative: the lower level of apparent reality, in which Herod is "king [over Judea]"; and the upper level of true reality, in which Jesus is "the king of the Jews."

The lower level of the narrative, for its part, yields a comprehensible and consistent portrait of "Herod the king" as a

---

[18] Muecke, 34.

[19] All biblical citations within this essay represent my own translations of the texts in question.

[20] As, for example, Luke 1:5; 3:1–2; cf. 2:1–2.

[21] Cf. the comments of Francis Wright Beare, *The Gospel According to Matthew* (San Francisco: Harper & Row, 1981) 77: "If [Matthew] mentions Herod, it is not for the sake of a dating, but that he may serve as the false king who trembles at the thought of the coming of the true king, and resorts to desperate measures to eliminate him as a threat to his power."

[22] Cf. n. 21 above.

character of enormous power. Matthew draws this portrait in both explicit and implicit fashion. While Herod is most frequently identified simply in terms of his given name (2:7, 12, 13, 15, 16, 19, 22), he is first and most prominently introduced to the reader in his role as "Herod *the king*" (2:1). This title then reappears in the corresponding designations "*King* Herod" (2:3), and "*the king*" (2:9).[23] With these references to Herod's "kingship," the narrator attributes power to Herod explicitly.

Implicit attributions of Herod's power are no less prominent throughout the narrative. Herod's reign ("the days of Herod the King," 2:1) is the political reality in relation to which other events are dated. Herod himself is depicted as a man of enormous political clout, whose actions have immediate impact on the lives of those around him. His personal moods affect "all Jerusalem" (2:3). People both Jewish and Gentile come into Herod's presence when he calls them (2:4, 7). They answer Herod's questions when he asks them (2:5–6 cf. 2:4; 2:7). They leave when Herod sends them (2:9b cf. 2:9a), and they carry out the commands that Herod issues to them (2:9–11 cf. 2:8; 2:16–18).

In addition to his political clout Herod possesses a range of personal characteristics which taken together represent power put to work for evil purposes. He is astute: When he hears of the existence of "the one born King of the Jews," he recognizes immediately the political implications for himself and his own kingship (2:3 cf. 2:1–2).[24] He is decisive: When challenges arise, he takes immediate action (2:4–5; 2:7–8; 2:13 cf. 2:20; 2:16). He is cunning: He works "secretly" and deceptively to carry out his evil intentions (2:7–8, 13, 16–18, 20), all the while convincing others that his intentions are nothing but the very best (2:8). He is cynical and ruthless: It does not matter to Herod

---

[23] Cf. 2:22, where Archelaus is said to be "*ruling (basileuei)* Judea in place of his father *Herod*."

[24] Cf. the comments of Daniel Patte (*The Gospel According to Matthew: A Structural Commentary on Matthew's Faith* [Philadelphia: Fortress, 1987] 33): "Herod's negative reaction to the announcement of the birth of the Christ is clarified by the contrast that the text sets up between the newborn king (2:2), a phrase that means 'one who is king by right of birth,' and Herod, who is 'king' (2:1, 3), but not by right of birth. Matthew assumes, therefore, that readers would identify Herod as the Idumean usurper, indeed as a conniving and ruthless tyrant (see 2:7–8, 16). Thus one could expect that Herod would be troubled by the news of the birth of the king of the Jews. From his perspective, the Christ threatens his political authority." In a similar vein see Beare, 77.

whom he deceives (2:7–8) or how many people he has to destroy (2:16–18) enroute to achieving his personal goals.

Most significant, however, with respect to the characterization of Herod, is the fact that he both possesses and wields the power of life and death over his subjects.[25] On the one hand Herod "[seeks] the child in order to destroy him" (2:13; cf. 2:20), a threat so real and so deadly that it causes Joseph to take his family and flee the country altogether (2:14–15). And on the other hand Herod proves his power over life and death in an especially vicious move, when he "[does] away with all the children in Bethlehem and the surrounding regions who [are] two years old and under (2:16)." By means both explicit and implicit the narrator leaves the reader in no doubt that Herod is a man of enormous political clout and personal power.

The character portrayal of Jesus, "the one who has been born king of the Jews" (2:2), presents a striking contrast to that of Herod. On the one hand, Jesus is clearly identified in "kingly" terms: "the one who has been born king of the Jews" (2:2); "the Messiah" (2:4); the "leader who will shepherd my [= God's] people Israel" (2:6); and "my [= God's] Son" (2:15).[26] On the other hand, the single most prominent term used to designate Jesus throughout this narrative is the term "child" (paidion; 2:8, 9, 11, 13—twice, 14, 20—twice, 21), a term which implies "weakness" and "dependence" in contrast to "political clout" and "personal power."

That the narrator's explicit designation "child" implies the "weakness" and "dependence" of Jesus as a character in the narrative finds further support in the narrator's implicit characterization of Jesus through the events of the story. In seven instances Jesus is the subject of a verbal form, but in four of these instances the verbal form is passive in voice: "Jesus *[is] born (gennēthentos)* in Bethlehem of Judea" (2:1); the astrologers inquire about the location of "the one *who has been born (techtheis)* king of the Jews" (2:2); Herod inquires of the Jewish authorities "where the Messiah *[is] to be born*" *(gennatai;* 2:4); and the apparent biblical citation in 2:23 states that "he *will be called (klēthēsetai)* a Nazarene." In one case the verb is merely a copulative: "the place

---

[25] As Patte indicates (36–37), "The political and human authority of Herod is based on fear, indeed terror, that his use of the power of life and death inspire in people (see 2:16). Herod's authority is exerted through the use of disruptive and destructive power or force."

[26] In 2:23 Jesus is likewise identified as the "Nazarene," a term not directly associated with his "kingly" identity.

where the child *was*" (*ēn*; 2:9). Only the prophecy cited by the Jewish authorities depicts Jesus as an actor in the narrative in his own right: "For out of [Bethlehem] *will come forth (exeleusetai)* a leader *who will shepherd (poimanei)* my [= God's] people Israel" (2:6; cf. Mic. 5:2).

By contrast there are sixteen instances in which Jesus is the effective object of the actions of other people. The astrologers "see his star" (2:2), "make a diligent search" for him (2:8), "find" him (2:8), "see" him (2:11), "worship" him (2:2, 11), and "present him with gifts" (2:11). Herod announces his intentions to "worship" Jesus (2:8), while in reality he intends to "seek" him (2:13; cf. 2:20) in order to "destroy" him (2:13). Joseph, for his part, "takes" Jesus first to Egypt (2:13, 14) and then back to Israel (2:20, 21) at the command of the angel of the Lord. And finally, God "calls" Jesus ("my son") out of Egypt (2:15).

As the narrator portrays him on the lower level of the narrative, then, Jesus is a character who appears as powerless as Herod appears powerful. He has no voice of his own, nor does he initiate any actions. He is depicted rather as a helpless, dependent "child" who is acted upon, whether for good or evil, by all the other characters of the story. There appears to be no question as to where "power" lies, and where it does not lie, in this narrative. But appearances are deceiving. In reality the narrator has established the "facts" of a "powerful Herod" and a "powerless Jesus" only to undermine the reliability of these "facts" within the world of the narrative. As noted above, he begins the process of undermining the "apparent facts" of his narrative already in 2:1–2 with the juxtaposition of "Herod the king" and "the one who has been born king of the Jews." The progress of this undermining process can then be traced through the respective character portrayals of Herod and Jesus from this beginning point all the way to the conclusion of the narrative.

The next clue that the narrator provides to the true character of Herod is the revelation that "King Herod" is "terrified" at the news of "one who has been born king of the Jews" (2:3 cf. 2:2). The revelation that "the king is terrified of the child" signals to the reader not only that Herod's position as "king over Judea" is being challenged but also that Herod's power is itself more appearance than reality. This impression finds further support in Herod's discovery that he has been "tricked by the astrologers" (2:16 cf. 2:8). The irony is especially biting here, since it is Herod himself who has been attempting to trick the astrologers with his "secret" activities (2:7) and his smooth doubletalk about "worship" (2:8). Now it becomes apparent that not only is

Herod powerless to accomplish his own purposes through deceiving others, but in addition he is powerless to prevent himself from being "tricked" in turn by those same people.

Nor is this the end of the matter. What Herod does not know—but what the narrator repeatedly makes clear to the reader—is the reason for Herod's continuing failure to accomplish his primary goal. As the reader discovers, it is the prior initiatives of the angel of the Lord that consistently foil Herod's best efforts to destroy the child.[27] Before Herod can get word of the whereabouts of the child (2:8), the angel of the Lord instructs the astrologers not to return to Herod with such information (2:12). Before Herod is able to send his henchmen out to find and destroy the child (2:13b), the angel of the Lord instructs Joseph to flee to Egypt together with his family (2:13a, 14). As long as Herod is alive and capable of pursuing the child (2:20b), Joseph keeps his family safe in Egypt as the angel of the Lord has commanded (2:13b). Only when Herod is no longer a threat to the child (2:19, 20b) does the angel of the Lord instruct Joseph to return to Israel (2:20a). And before Herod's son Archelaus has any opportunity to carry out what his father failed to do (2:22a), the angel of the Lord warns Joseph to settle his family in Galilee rather than Judea (2:22b-23).

The unfolding events of the narrative thus successively unmask Herod's apparent "power" as "king over Judea" as virtual powerlessness vis-à-vis the genuine power of divine initiative. The most prominent confirmation of this fact, however, lies in the threefold mention of the death of Herod (2:15, 19, 20). Here lies the ultimate irony of the narrative. In the end it is Herod "the king" (2:1, 3, 9; cf. 2:22), whose signal aim throughout the narrative has been to "destroy the child" (2:13; cf. 2:20), who himself lies dead; while his intended victim is alive and well in Nazareth of Galilee (2:22–23). Nor can there be any doubt that it is divine initiative which has once again foiled Herod's plans.[28]

With this turn of events the true shape of reality is now clearly visible: All outward evidence to the contrary, Herod is not in fact the genuine "king over Judea" nor is his "power" genuine power. Instead, true kingship belongs to Jesus "the one who has been born king of the

---

[27] While there is no specific mention of the angel of the Lord in the dreams of 2:12 and 2:22, the parallels between these dreams and those of 1:20, 2:13, and 2:19 appear to establish the angel of the Lord as the speaker here as well.

[28] As Patte observes (36), "For the readers of the Gospel, there is no doubt about who has the power of life and death over Herod: it is God."

Jews"; and true power belongs to Jesus "the child" (2:8, 9, 11, 13, 14, 20, 21), who says nothing, takes no actions, and is by contrast totally vulnerable to the initiatives of those around him. With this fundamental redefinition of terms, the narrator signals to the reader that from here on and throughout the narrative both "kingship" and "power" are to be understood in a paradoxical light and to be identified in the unlikeliest of forms and places.[29]

Herod the tetrarch (14:1–12). The second political figure to appear on the the scene in Matthew's narrative is Herod the tetrarch (14:1–12), introduced into the story just as word about Jesus' ministry of "power" spreads throughout Galilee: "At that time Herod the tetrarch got word of Jesus. And he said to his servants, 'This is John the Baptist. He has been raised from the dead. And it is on this account that [these] powers are at work in him'" (14:1–2). But while it is the ministry of Jesus that occasions the initial mention of Herod (14:1–2), it is the prior ministry of John the Baptist that figures in the events of the flashback recounted in the following verses (14:3–12). It is John the Baptist who serves as the primary counterpart to Herod the tetrarch within this narrative; and it is the character of John the Baptist against which Herod's character is highlighted.

Here, as with the character portrayal of "Herod the king" (2:1–23), Matthew's narrator paints a "lower-level" portrait of Herod the tetrarch as a man of significant power. To begin with, Herod's power becomes clear from the explicitly "powerful" titles attributed to him. While he is most frequently identified simply as "Herod" (14:3, 6—twice), he is initially introduced as "Herod *the tetrarch*" (14:1) and later identified as "*the king*" (14:9). Beyond these explicit designations, Herod's power becomes clear from a variety of implicit indicators. Herod has "servants" (14:2) who carry out the actions he "commands" (14:9b; cf. 14:10–11). He exercises the authority to "seize" people, "bind" them, and "put [them] in prison" (14:3). At the same time he exercises the contrasting authority to "promise [others] . . . whatever [they] might request" (14:7). Most important, however, Herod the tetrarch, just as

---

[29] Cf. Patte's observation (37) that "true authority, divine authority, is not based on the use (or the threat of use) of power. Consequently, the recognition that Jesus has divine authority also demands abandoning one's commonly held views about authority: the views concerning political authority and also the views concerning religious authority."

Herod the king before him, wields the ultimate power of life and death over his subjects (14:9b-11; cf. 14:5a).

Beyond these indications of power the narrator attributes to Herod the tetrarch the same fundamental character traits previously visible in Herod the king. Herod the tetrarch is astute: He knows what actions are politically expedient at any given moment and responds accordingly (14:3a cf. 14:3b-4; 14:5a cf. 14:5b; 14:9b-11 cf. 14:9a). Nor is he any less brutal than Herod the king before him: It does not matter whom he has to destroy (14:5) nor how gruesome the actions he has to initiate (14:8, 11) as long as he accomplishes that which is politically expedient. The character of Herod the tetrarch, just as Herod the king before him, exhibits power put to work for evil purposes.

By contrast, the narrator's "lower-level" portrait of John the Baptist shows John to be fundamentally powerless. Within the flashback itself (14:3–12) John serves as the subject of only one active verb: ". . . because John *kept on saying (elegen)* to him, 'It is not proper for you to have her'" (14:4). Beyond this single action attributed to him, John does nothing. By contrast he functions 13 times as the effective object of the actions of others, actions sometimes good and sometimes evil.[30] The crowd "considers [John] to be a prophet" (14:5). Herod "seizes" John (14:3), "binds" him (14:3), "puts [him] in prison" (14:3), "wants to kill" him (14:5), "commands that [John's head] be given" (14: 9), and finally "sends and has [John] beheaded" (14:10). At the prompting of her mother the daughter of Herodias demands that Herod "give" her the head of John the Baptist (14:8). And after John's head has been "brought" (14:11) and "given" to her (14:11), she then "brings" the head to her mother (14:11). Finally, John's disciples "take" his corpse (14:12) and "bury" it (14:12). The contrast in power between Herod the tetrarch and John the Baptist could scarcely be more pronounced at the lower level of the narrative.

But once again appearances are deceiving. Here, as with Herod the king, the narrator creates a portrait of political power on the one hand only to subvert it on the other. This process of subversion begins in 14:1–2 with the introduction of Herod the tetrarch: "At that time Herod the tetrarch got word of Jesus. And he said to his servants, 'This

---

[30] In some instances John functions as the object of an active verb and in other instances as the subject of a passive verb.

is John the Baptist. He has been raised from the dead. And it is on this account that [these] powers are at work in him.'"

No sooner has the narrator introduced the reader to Herod, the powerful "tetrarch" who has "servants" to do his bidding, than he subverts his own portrait by showing Herod to be deeply superstitious and fearful. Here the reader learns what Herod does not know, namely that Herod is hearing reports about Jesus, not John the Baptist. To the reader, therefore, Herod's mistaken conclusion that this figure is "John the Baptist raised from the dead" signals, even in advance of the flashback itself, that Herod fears John and his "powers" as a man "raised from the dead" precisely because it is Herod himself who has put John to death.

The irony here is not to be overlooked. In spite of his apparently ultimate power over the life and death of his subjects, Herod's comments reveal the true state of affairs: Herod fears the man he himself has killed and in so doing implicitly acknowledges the futility of his own power. Herod has taken the ultimate action which he can take against John the Baptist; and his action has been in vain. As Herod sees it, his sentence of death has been overturned by an act of God and the one he has executed has now been invested with "powers" even greater than before. That this is not in fact the case merely heightens the irony of the situation. Not only does Herod himself implicitly acknowledge that he is powerless to achieve his own goals. But in addition the reader recognizes what Herod cannot see, namely that the object of Herod's fear ("John the Baptist . . . raised from the dead . . . in whom [extraordinary] powers are at work") is not reality but rather a figment of his own imagination and the product of his own bad conscience.

This portrait of Herod as a man powerless to accomplish his own aims and frightened of his own imagination finds further support throughout the flashback account of 14:3–12. Here the narrator portrays Herod as a man who fears everyone with whom he comes in contact and whose actions are consistently motivated by those whom he fears: John the Baptist (14:3 cf. 14:4), the crowd (14:5a-b cf. 14:5c), his wife Herodias (14:9–11 cf. 14:3–4, 8), the daughter of Herodias (14:9–11 cf. 14:6–8), the guests at the party (14:9c-11 cf. 14:9a-b). As a result the reader encounters Herod the tetrarch as a man fundamentally powerless to carry out his own desires. When he wishes to kill John (14:5a), his fear of the crowds prevents him from doing so

(14:5b-c). When he wishes to keep John alive (14:9a),[31] his fear of the guests at his party prevents him from sparing John's life (14:9b-10).[32] Even more ironic, however, is that Herod's own apparent power is by the same token his most obvious weakness. It is precisely because Herod has promised the daughter of Herodias "whatever she might request" (14:7) that he finds himself compelled to act against his wishes and have John executed (14:9–10). Accordingly, in spite of his apparent power, Herod is effectively a puppet on a string, operated now by this outside force and now by that one. His fears render him incapable of taking independent initiatives and leave him the single option of reacting to the actions of others.

By the same token John the Baptist, who at first glance appears powerless, in fact exhibits the real power that Herod lacks. John has been carrying out among the people a ministry of such effectiveness that they have recognized him as a "prophet" (14:5). John has exercised his prophetic role with a power of which Herod can only dream. In a face to face encounter John has thrown expediency to the winds and bluntly condemned Herod's marital relationship with Herodias, the wife of his brother Philip: "It is not proper for you to have her" (14:4b cf. 14:3b).

The power of this act is manifest in its contrast to the actions of Herod. While Herod will shortly demonstrate his powerlessness to achieve his political aims or carry out his personal desires, John exhibits the power to disregard the constraints of expediency and to act instead on personal conviction. The power of John's act is likewise manifest in its impact on the tetrarch. Herod fears John's condemnation to such an extent that he takes the penultimate initiative of seizing John, binding him, and putting him in prison in order to silence his voice (14:3a cf. 14:4). John the Baptist is the "powerful" figure who "makes things happen" within this account; Herod the tetrarch for his part is reduced to the "powerlessness" of a "reactive" role.

The ultimate irony lies in the outcome of this series of events. Herod, who thinks he has rid himself of his nemesis by executing John the Baptist (14:10), finds instead that he now faces a "John the Baptist

---

[31] Cf. Patte, 214.

[32] As Patte notes (208), "the social relationship of Herod with his guests when he does not want to retract his oath in front of them is valued more than John's life and more than his relationship with the people he governs."

raised from the dead" (14:2) who has even greater "powers" than the John he has executed. And since this outcome (14:1–2) is narrated prior to the events themselves (14:3–12), the reader knows all along what Herod finds out only when it is too late: Herod's actions, even when he takes them, are futile in their impact, and Herod's power, even when he exerts it, is impotence vis-à-vis the power of God.

Pilate the governor (27:1–2, 11–38, 54, 62–66; 28:1–15).[33] The final political figure to appear on the scene in Matthew's narrative is "Pilate the governor" (27:1–28:15), to whom Jesus is "handed over" by the Jewish authorities: "And when it was morning all the chief priests and elders of the people conferred against Jesus, in order to put him to death. And they bound him and led him away and handed him over to Pilate the governor" (27:1–2). Here, as was the case with Herod the king and Herod the tetrarch, the narrator paints a "lower-level" portrait of Pilate as a man of significant power. This power is visible on the one hand in the titles attributed to him. The narrator first introduces him to the reader as "Pilate *the governor*" (27:2). And in the following accounts the narrator alternates between the designations "Pilate" (27:13, 17, 22, 24, 62, 65) and "*the governor*" (27:11—twice, 14, 15, 21; 28:14). When the Jewish authorities themselves address Pilate, they do so with the respectful term "*Sir*" (*kyrie,* 27:63).

Pilate's power as governor is likewise visible in implicit fashion in the words of those around him. Virtually all of the other characters who come on stage within this section of the narrative make pointed appeals to Pilate as the person with the real power to grant their requests. The chief priests and elders of the people first "bring charges" to Pilate against Jesus (27:12–13) and later urge him to "secure" the tomb where Jesus' body has been buried (27:62–64). Pilate's wife implores him to "have nothing to do with that righteous man" (27: 19); while the crowds demand that Pilate carry out their wishes concerning Jesus (27:20, 22, 23) and Barabbas (27:20, 21). Even when Pilate is not on the scene, other characters attribute power to him. The chief priests and Pharisees assure the Roman soldiers who have been delinquent in their task of guarding the tomb that "if this comes to the attention of the governor, we will . . . keep you out of trouble" (28:14).

---

[33] I have intentionally limited the designated text to those segments of the broader narrative which make specific reference to Pilate and those acting at his behest.

Nor is there any question as to the nature of Pilate's authority. As Roman governor he is, above all, the person who wields the power of life and death over his subjects, whether they be Jewish or Roman. When the chief priests and elders of the people want to "put [Jesus] to death" (27:1), they "hand him over to Pilate the governor" (27:2). Having done so, they then incite the crowds "to ask [Pilate] for Barabbas and to have Jesus destroyed" (27:20). The crowds for their part oblige the religious leaders by demanding that Pilate "release" Barabbas (27:21; cf. 27:15, 17) and "crucify" Jesus (27:22, 23).

Pilate confirms by his actions that power which others attribute to him. He questions Jesus, the prisoner handed over to him (27:11, 13–14); takes his seat on the "*bēma*" in order to pass judgment (27:19); and finally "releases" Barabbas to the crowds (27:26) and "hands [Jesus] over to be crucified" (27:26). But Pilate's power is ultimately evident in the actions that others take at his command. At his word the soldiers of the governor take Jesus to Golgotha and crucify him along with several other criminals (27:31b-38). Pilate's power over the life and death of his subjects is no matter for debate.

By contrast the narrator's lower-level portrait of Jesus is again a portrait of powerlessness. By way of titles the narrator offers the single designation "Jesus" (27:1, 11–twice, 20, 26, 27). Other characters within the narrative make use of titles that serve to evaluate Jesus but do not connote power per se ("that righteous man," 27:19 cf. 27:24; "that deceiver," 27:63). Even when Pilate and his soldiers designate Jesus with "powerful" titles ("Jesus who is called Messiah," 27:17, 22; "king of the Jews," 27:29; "Jesus the king of the Jews," 27:37), they do so precisely in contexts that highlight Jesus' powerlessness. "Jesus who is called Messiah" is a prisoner whom Pilate has authority to "release" (27:17) or "crucify" (27:22). The "king of the Jews" is a condemned man being tortured and mocked prior to his execution (27:27–31). "Jesus the king of the Jews" is an executed criminal hanging on a Roman cross (27:37).

Nor does the portrait of Jesus' powerlessness change when viewed from the perspective of actions taken or received. Three references are made to what Jesus has previously done or said: Pilate inquires "what evil [Jesus] has done" (27:23); and the religious authorities recount to Pilate what "that deceiver said" (27:63) "while he was still living" (27:63). Twice the narrator indicates that Jesus "does not reply" to words directed to him (27:12, 13). But only twice within this account does the narrator portray Jesus as an actor or speaker on stage in his own right: Jesus "stands" before the governor (27:11a) and "says" something in response to the governor's question (27:11b).

By contrast Jesus functions consistently throughout this account as the effective object of the actions of others. Jesus' opponents "confer against him" (27:1) in order to "put him to death" (27:1), "bind" him (27:2), "lead him away" (27:2, 31), "hand him over" (27:2, 18, 26), "ask" him questions (27:11), "say" things to him (27:13), "bring charges/witness against" him (27:12, 13), seek to "have him destroyed" (27:20), "scourge" him (27:26), "take him along" (27:27), "strip" him (27:28, 31), "put [clothing] around him" (27:28), "put [things] on/over his head" (27:29, 37), "put [something] into his right hand" (27:29), "kneel down before" him (27:29), "mock" him (27:29, 31), "spit" on him (27:30), "strike him on the head" (27:30), "dress" him (27:31), "crucify" him (27:35; cf. 27:22, 23, 26, 31), and "guard" him (27:54). Pilate's wife, for her part, urges Pilate to "have nothing to do with" Jesus (27:19). There appears to be no question that Jesus is as powerless in this setting as Pilate is powerful.

But once again appearances are deceiving. Just as he did with Herod the king and Herod the tetrarch, the narrator subverts his own portrait of "Pilate the powerful governor" and unmasks him by stages as "Pilate the powerless puppet." This process of unmasking begins early in the narrative, continues to the end, and is one in which Pilate plays a decisive role through his own actions. The first signal of Pilate's powerlessness comes in the repeated indications that Pilate intentionally places himself at the mercy of the crowds and their wishes: "And at each feast the governor had a custom of releasing one prisoner to the crowd, *whomever they wished*" (27:15); "So when they had gathered together, Pilate said to them, '*Whom do you want me to release to you?*'" (27:17); "And the governor replied and said to them, '*Which of the two do you want me to release to you?*'" (27:21).

Pilate's vulnerability to the wishes of the crowds then progresses from the level of inquiry to the level of shouting match, a public debate in which Pilate and the crowds hurl questions and answers back and forth (27:17/20, 21a/21b, 22a/22b, 23a/23b) with ever increasing "vehemence" (27:23b) until a full-scale "riot" is underway (27:24). As the reader discovers, Pilate is manifestly powerless either to influence the views or to control the actions of the crowds. Importantly, not only does the narrator reveal Pilate's powerlessness to the reader; but Pilate himself acknowledges his impotence vis-à-vis the crowds: "And when Pilate saw *that he was accomplishing nothing . . . .*" (27:24). With this acknowledgement Pilate's powerlessness is open to full view, his humiliation is complete, and the narrator's irony has reached its peak. "Pilate the powerful governor" has been fully unmasked as "Pilate the powerless puppet."

All that Pilate can do now is to act against his own better wisdom and capitulate to the demands of the crowds. Pilate knows that the religious authorities have handed Jesus over to him out of jealousy (27:18). He has heard the counsel of his wife to "have nothing to do with that righteous man" (27:19). He knows in his own heart that Jesus "has done no evil thing" (27:23). Yet in spite of all this knowledge, Pilate is powerless to act on his own convictions. Instead he "washes his hands" of the matter and, in an act of obvious expediency, grants the crowds their demand: "I am innocent of the blood of this man. See to it yourselves!" (27:24). With this declaration he releases the "notorious prisoner" (27:16) whom the crowds want freed (27:26a) and hands over for crucifixion the "righteous man" (27:19) whom they want dead (27:26b).

Pilate, the most powerful man in Palestine, is ultimately powerless to do the one thing he knows is the right thing to do. Rather, the "governor" reveals himself as the puppet of those whom he purports to "govern," namely, the Jewish crowds and the religious authorities who stand behind them.[34] There has been no question all along that it is the religious authorities who have masterminded the death of Jesus and manipulated Pilate into executing their scheme (27:1–2, 12, 20; cf. 27:62–64). In 28:12–14 the narrator offers one final confirmation of this fact; Pilate, who has been manipulated once to bring about the death of Jesus, will be manipulated once again to ensure that Jesus forever "stays dead" in the public perception. "Pilate the powerful governor" is indeed "Pilate the powerless puppet."

---

[34] Cf. the comments of Michael Goldberg, *Jews and Christians, Getting Our Stories Straight: The Exodus and the Passion-Resurrection* (Nashville: Abingdon, 1985) 190: "Jesus' last hope would seem to be Pilate. Surely, if anyone has the power to save him, it ought to be the governor who is backed up by the might of imperial Rome. But up to now, other sources of human strength . . . have consistently failed to save . . . . So too, the kind of dominion manifested by human government now proves equally powerless to rescue him from death. Pilate, though he has all of Rome behind him and though he knows Jesus to be guiltless, nevertheless fears a riot brewing and thus, to keep the peace, determines that Jesus' life is expendable." Contra Patte's apparent conclusions (380), however, the narrator does not paint a portrait of Pilate's powerlessness in order to absolve him of guilt.

The ultimate irony here, however, is one which reveals the powerlessness not only of Pilate but of the crowds and the religious authorities as well. Jesus, the one whose execution has been masterminded by the religious authorities, demanded by the crowds, and carried out by Pilate, does not "stay dead." Instead, just as he has predicted (cf. 27:63) and the angel of the Lord has announced (28:5–7), Jesus "is raised from the dead" in an act of God which gives the lie to all human claims of ultimate power. Pilate the governor, just as Herod the king and Herod the tetrarch before him, does indeed have the power to take life away. But this power itself is revealed as impotence in the face of a God whose infinitely greater power "raises [people] from the dead." In the light of Jesus' resurrection human power is robbed of its potency and human powerlessness transformed by the power of God. And this, as Matthew sees it, is the ultimate irony of power.

Concluding Observations

In speaking about the function of irony as a literary strategy Duke offers the following observations:

> In using irony an author invites the reader to reject an ostensible structure of meaning. The meaning to be rejected is often far more than the literal meaning of a particular sentence or expression, but rather a whole structured "world" of meanings or values which the author spurns. . . . On one level the reader's search is a literary one. . . . If ultimate meaning or values are at stake in the irony, however, then when the literary search is over and the higher structure has been discovered, the excitement of that interpretive leap is easily transferred to the possibility of a more ultimate leap. Particularly when irony is artfully done, the choice to share the author's perspective on a narrative world may become a decisive step toward dwelling with that author in a deeper sense and embracing a new perspective on the real world.[35]

It is this "new perspective on the real world" to which Matthew invites his readers as he paints conventional portraits of political power on the one hand only to subvert them on the other. To be specific, Matthew invites his readers to join him on the high ground from which he and they together can view the impotence of all human power in the political arena vis-à-vis the genuine potency of divine initiative. In Matthew's view, this perspective on the real world is what will empower the believers of the Matthean church for their inevitable

---

[35] Duke, 34, 37.

encounters with the "Herod's" and "Pilate's" of their own day, the "governors and kings" before whom they will be called to bear witness to their faith (cf. 10:18).

Chapter Seven

The Wisdom Passages in Matthew's Story

RUSSELL PREGEANT

Introduction

In 1970 M. Jack Suggs and Felix Christ published independent studies concluding that in the gospel of Matthew, Jesus appears as the incarnation of personified Wisdom.[1] Christ's study of the entire synoptic tradition found a Wisdom christology also in Luke and already in Q, but Suggs argued that it was Matthew's redaction of Q that effected the identification. While several earlier scholars had observed a Wisdom component in Matthew's christological thought, Suggs argued the point in a systematic way and claimed a much more prominent place for that component than his predecessors had suggested. In general, his treatment has received a warmer reception than that of Christ; for it is precisely his claims regarding Matthew's modifications of Q in terms of the relationship between Jesus and Wisdom that many find convincing. Not only have a number of scholars embraced his thesis almost *in toto*, but his work has formed the basis for further investigations that have provided important insight into the theology of the first gospel.[2]

---

[1] Felix Christ, *Jesus Sophia: Die Sophia-Christologie bei den Synoptikern*, ATANT 57 (Zürich: Zwingli-Verlag, 1970); M. Jack Suggs, *Wisdom, Christology, and Law in Matthew's Gospel* (Cambridge: Harvard University Press, 1970).

[2] See, for example, Fred W. Burnett, *The Testament of Jesus-Sophia: A Redaction-Critical Study of the Eschatological Discourse in Matthew* (Washington, D.C.: University Press of America, 1981); Celia Deutsch, *Hidden Wisdom and the Easy Yoke: Wisdom, Torah and Discipleship in Matthew 11.25–30* (Sheffield: JSOT Press, 1987); R. G. Hamerton-Kelly, *Pre-Existence, Wisdom, and the Son of Man: A Study of the Idea of Pre-Existence in the New Testament* (Cambridge: Cambridge University Press, 1973), ch. 2; John P. Meier, *The Vision of Matthew: Christ, Church, and Morality in the First Gospel,* Theological Inquiries: Studies in Contemporary Biblical and Theological Problems (New York: Paulist, 1978) 70, 76ff., 165; Eduard Schweizer, *The Good*

Dissenters, however, have raised some important objections that have not, to my mind, been fully answered. One crucial question stems from the fact that Suggs bases his case on redactional activity. Can we reasonably imagine that readers not privy to the author's sources would in fact make the identification of Jesus with Wisdom that the redaction seems to intend? It would thus seem worthwhile to approach the passages upon which Suggs bases his argument from the perspective of reader-response criticism in order to determine just how they function in the Matthean story-line and how they relate to the more generally acknowledged aspects of Matthew's christology.[3]

The following, then, is my method of procedure. In section I, I will review the case for Matthean Wisdom christology made on the basis of redaction criticism, as well as some of the more important objections to it, and offer a preliminary evaluation. Section II will be devoted to a reader-response analysis with an emphasis upon the ways in which the narrator elicits explicit christological confessions from the reader. Finally, in section III, I will evaluate the results of the reader-response analysis and discuss their relevance to the questions raised by the redactional approach.

I. The Case for a Redactional Emphasis: Pro and Con

Suggs finds the most forthright identification of Jesus with Wisdom at 11:19. In the Q version (Luke 7:35), it is said that Wisdom is justified by *pantōn tōn teknōn autēs*—a reference, presumably, to Jesus and John the Baptist as envoys of Wisdom.[4] By substituting *ergōn* for *teknōn*, Matthew accommodates the saying to the phrase *ta erga tou Christou* at 11:2 and thus presents the messianic deeds of Jesus recounted in 11:2–24 as Wisdom's own deeds. The purpose of the redaction, Suggs concludes, is "*to identify Jesus with Wisdom*"; thus "it would not greatly

---

News According to Matthew. (Atlanta: John Knox, 1973) 264ff., 434ff., 528ff., and *Matthäus und Seine Gemeinde* (Stuttgart: Verlag Katholisches Bibelwerk, 1974) 54ff.

[3] I do not propose that a reader-oriented approach to the text can in itself answer the questions posed by redaction criticism. The critic is asking in the one case about the author's intentions, but in the other about the interaction between the text itself and the reader. It is quite possible that different meanings—perhaps even contrary meanings—will arise from readings from the two different perspectives. But this does not mean there can be no creative interaction between the two modes of criticism.

[4] Suggs, 55, citing Rudolf Bultmann, "Der religionsgeschichtliche Hintergrund des Prologs zum Johannes-Evangelium," in *EUCARISTHRION: Studien zur Religion und Literatur des Alten und Neuen Testaments, Hermann Gunkel zum 60. Geburtstage,* ed. Hans Schmidt, FRLANT 36 (Göttingen: Vandenhoeck und Ruprecht, 1923) 15.

overstate the case to say that *for Matthew* Wisdom has 'become flesh and dwelled among us' (John 1:14)."[5]

The identification of Jesus with Wisdom is reinforced by the revision of another Q passage resulting in the transfer of a saying of Wisdom into the mouth of Jesus. At 23:34 the shift from *hē sophia tou theou eipen; apostelō* (Luke 11:49) to *idou egō apostellō* clearly assigns to Jesus the role of commissioning prophets—"a function," Suggs notes, "which belongs to no figure in pre-Christian Judaism except Wisdom and God . . . ."[6] When, a few verses later (37–39), Jesus pronounces his lament over Jerusalem, it is easy for Suggs to hear once again the voice of incarnate Wisdom: "It is in Wisdom's person that Jesus can speak of 'how often' in relation to Jerusalem, for the call of Wisdom has been heard again and again in 'the prophets and those sent' . . . ." Jesus here speaks, in other words, not as a merely historical person but as a trans-historical figure who has appealed to humanity "in every generation."[7]

The final link in Suggs's argument has to do with the redaction of 11:25–27. The placing of the passage, to begin with, ensures that the term *tauta*—i.e., the things hidden from "the wise and the intelligent"[8] and given to "infants"—refers specifically to the messianic deeds of Jesus. The addition of vv. 28–30 once again creates an identification of Jesus and Wisdom. Whereas parallel passages in Jewish wisdom literature speak of the yoke of Wisdom, this yoke is never that of the teacher; in this passage, however, Jesus invites submission to *his* yoke and thereby assumes Wisdom's traditional role.[9] Moreover, given the Rabbis' identification of Wisdom and Torah, as well as their language about the "yoke of the law," 11:28–30 must mean that the Jesus who speaks as Wisdom also speaks as "the embodiment of Torah."[10]

R. G. Hamerton-Kelly endorses Suggs's thesis and goes on to claim a rather well-developed notion of the pre-existence of Christ in Matthew. Arguing largely from the parallels between the Matthean image of the Son of Man on the throne (25:31) and passages in 1 Enoch, he contends that "for Matthew, as in Enoch, the term 'Son of

---

[5] Ibid., 57, emphasis original.

[6] Ibid., 59.

[7] Ibid., 71.

[8] Biblical quotations in English follow the NRSV.

[9] Ibid., 95–96.

[10] Ibid., 99–106, 127.

Man' signifies a pre-existent heavenly being."[11] He also finds a correlation between Son of Man and Wisdom/Torah with respect to the pattern of humiliation of the exalted one. And, picking up on a point made by Gerhard Barth, he interprets Jesus's presence with the disciples at 28:20 and 18:15–20 to mean that "he is the locus of the Shekinah."[12] "We have, therefore," Hamerton-Kelly concludes,

> a complex of Christological ideas which begins with the presence of the exalted Lord in the congregation and goes on to identify him as Wisdom, Torah and Shekinah. The time of his earthly life is viewed as a time of humiliation for the pre-existent one.[13]

Another scholar who has made important use of Suggs's thesis is Fred W. Burnett, who interprets Matthew's eschatological discourse as a kind of farewell testament of the rejected Jesus-Sophia. Burnett is indebted also to Felix Christ's work for the systematic attestation of a complex of motifs in pre-Christian Jewish literature that involves Wisdom's fruitless attempts to gain acceptance in Israel and her subsequent withdrawal. As Burnett notes, one need not accept—as do Suggs and Christ—Bultmann's hypothesis regarding an actual Wisdom *myth* to acknowledge the availability to Matthew of an ongoing mythological *speculation* involving Wisdom's tragic relationship to Israel. It is enough to acknowledge "that a generalized picture of Wisdom's rejection and withdrawal existed and could have been used by Matthew . . . ."[14] Reading Matthew 23 in light of this rejection-pattern, Burnett argues that 23:38 (*aphietai hymin ho oikos hymōn erēmos*) identifies Jesus, who is at this point speaking as Wisdom, with the Shekinah dwelling in the Temple.[15] Thus, Jesus' departure from the Temple at 24:1 actually constitutes the final withdrawal of Wisdom/the Shekinah from Israel, a point attested both by the Matthean redactions of 24:1 and by the fact that Jesus never enters the Temple again.[16]

---

[11] Hamerton-Kelly, 81–82.

[12] Ibid., 69–70, citing Gerhard Barth, "Matthew's Understanding of the Law," in Günther Bornkamm, Gerhard Barth, and H. J. Held, *Tradition and Interpretation in Matthew*, (Philadelphia: Westminster, 1963) 135; cf. also Suggs, 66.

[13] Ibid., 70–71.

[14] Burnett, 94, citing Christ, 158–63; also Burnett, 43–45, and Elisabeth Schüssler Fiorenza, "Wisdom Mythology and the Christological Hymns of the New Testament," in Robert L. Wilkens, ed., *Aspects of Wisdom in Judaism and Early Christianity* (South Bend, IN: University of Notre Dame Press, 1975).

[15] Ibid., 68–81.

[16] Ibid., 112ff., 166f.

Burnett claims that the question is no longer whether Matthew has a Wisdom christology but how important it is in the gospel as a whole.[17] Given Burnett's own work (and assuming the two-document hypothesis), it would indeed seem that we may now be relatively confident on three important points: 1) Matthew edited the wisdom passages in Q in a systematic way, with specific intentions in mind; 2) as a result of Matthew's editorial activity, sayings once attributed to personified Wisdom are now assigned to Jesus; 3) in the Gospel of Matthew the dual themes of Jesus's rejection by Israel and God's subsequent judgment upon Israel are informed by the motif of Wisdom's rejection and withdrawal in pre-Christian Wisdom speculation.

Matthew's redaction of the wisdom passages was something central, and not tangential, to the main thrust of the gospel. It seems to me, however, that the precise sense in which one may speak of a Wisdom christology remains a debatable matter. To begin with, it is not beyond dispute that the redaction of 11:19 (a crucial passage in Suggs's argument) results in the actual identification of Jesus with Wisdom. Marshall D. Johnson suggests that Matthew intended 11:19b as an analogy, not a statement of the literal equation of the deeds of Wisdom with those of Jesus. Positing a Jewish proverb that refers to Wisdom's justification through her works at creation, he speculates that

> the meaning of 11:19b for [Matthew] would be that the response to Jesus' deeds is parallel to the response to Wisdom; just as at the creation Wisdom "was justified" (aorist) by her works, so Jesus (and John) will be vindicated by their deeds.[18]

It should also be said that even if we grant that for Matthew Jesus' *deeds* are in fact to be identified with those of Wisdom, this does not necessitate the view that Jesus *is* Wisdom—certainly not in the specific sense of an incarnation. Such an interpretation is possible, but is

---

[17] Ibid., 46.

[18] Marshall D. Johnson, "Reflections on a Wisdom Approach to Matthew's Christology," *CBQ* 36 (1974) 57–58. The speculation is not without basis. Noting "the frequency with which the terms *erga* and *dikaioun* (and variant forms) occur in the wisdom literature," Johnson goes on to document a link between *ta erga tou theou* on the one hand and the *dikaiosynō kyriou* on the other (cf. Prov. 8:22; 16:9, 11[LXX], Sir. 1:19; 18:1–4). "These passages," Johnson argues, "reflect what was perhaps a common view that Wisdom was shown to be righteous by her work in creation."

hardly required; so the question is whether other aspects of the gospel lend it sufficient support.

Suggs finds such support at 11:25–30; it is supposedly Matthew's addition of vss. 28–30—the logion of the easy yoke—that makes the identification of Jesus and Wisdom. Matthew's readers might indeed know that Jesus here issues an invitation that traditionally could have been offered only by Wisdom or God, but this is not necessarily to say they would conclude that Jesus is Wisdom incarnate. Graham Stanton concurs with Johnson in deeming such a conclusion difficult in light of Jesus' self-presentation in vss. 25–27 as the *Son*. Both these scholars too readily assume that readers in the Matthean community would have rejected the notion of the incarnation of the female Wisdom in a male, overlooking the elements of a proto-feminism in the early tradition. The real problem is not that Jesus is male but that his self-definition in this passage is based upon his relationship to the *Father*. Stanton raises a valid question when he asks whether the readers would identify Jesus as the incarnation of female Wisdom immediately after a dramatic verse in which he presents himself as Son of the Father.

Evidence that Matthew has transferred a saying of Wisdom to Jesus at 23:34–36 is admittedly a strong point in Suggs's case. But here again it is difficult to identify the specific import of such a redactional move. Johnson's claim that Matthew "deliberately avoids an identification of Jesus with Wisdom"[19] makes some sense in light of the fact that in the course of the transfer the reference to Wisdom has dropped out entirely. The question, then, is whether we have sufficient reason to think that Matthew's intended readers would make the identification of Jesus and Wisdom at 23:34. Johnson clearly does not think so: "Mt's readers would in all probability not have the occasion to check his source, and would therefore not derive from this passage any association of Jesus with Wisdom."[20] The identification of Jesus with Wisdom is one way of interpreting the redaction of the passage, but unless we assume some factor outside the text that would provide the needed hint we can hardly be certain that a first-century reader would draw such a conclusion.

---

[19] Johnson, 55; also R. Pregeant, *Christology Beyond Dogma: Matthew's Christ in Process Hermeneutic*, SS 7 (Philadelphia: Fortress; Missoula, MT: Scholars Press, 1978), 93.

[20] Johnson, 55.

The reality of such a factor is admittedly quite possible. If, as Burnett surmises, "Matthew is the product of a school rather than of an individual as Stendahl believes, then it is very probable that the community knew the sources used in the gospel."[21] Both Stendahl and Hamerton-Kelly in fact presume that Matthew's community had already made the identification of Jesus with Wisdom.[22] The problem is that both the existence of the Matthean school and its specific interest in Wisdom are hypothetical. While the wisdom passages in Matthew may be admitted as evidence in this direction, it is a circular argument to point to the presumed school as a way of justifying a particular reading of those passages. We are left with the rather impotent claim that if we assume the readers had already made the equation of Jesus with Wisdom, then it makes sense to envision them finding it in the passages under discussion.

A redactional analysis of 23:34–39 nevertheless tends to confirm the view that Matthew intended to present Jesus as a trans-historical figure at least on the model of Wisdom. At the very least, Jesus' *ego apostellō* at vs. 34 establishes him as a sovereign being who commissions emissaries. James D. G. Dunn is probably right in arguing that the readers will most readily identify the "prophets, sages, and scribes" with those commissioned by the exalted lord of the Church;[23] for it is clear from the reference to crucifixion that the post-resurrection situation is the focus of Matthew's attention. It is odd, however, that Dunn makes his case on the basis of the redactor's shift from future to present tense. It is the future tense that, in the mouth of Jesus, would logically have pointed ahead from Jesus' own time to that of emissaries sent to the church and thereby discouraged the reader from identifying the "prophets, sages, and scribes" with those sent to Israel in the past. The present, however, is ambiguous. The reader can understand it in a continuing sense that includes both the future situation of the church and Israel's past.

The shift from future to present at vs. 34 would thus seem to constitute a very strong argument in Suggs's favor. And when the phrase "[h]ow often have I desired" at vs. 37 is read against such a background it indeed seems to express the frustration of a trans-

---

[21] Burnett, 42.

[22] Hamerton-Kelly, 70–71; Krister Stendahl, *The School of St. Matthew and Its Use of the Old Testament* (Philadelphia: Fortress, 1968) 142.

[23] James D. G. Dunn, *Christology in the Making: A New Testament Inquiry into the Origins of the Doctrine of the Incarnation* (Philadelphia: Westminster, 1980) 202.

historical, heavenly figure who has vainly sought Israel's love throughout the generations—a figure clearly reminiscent of personified Wisdom.

At this point, however, some broader questions must be raised. It is relevant, in the first place, to ask why an emphasis that seems so central should in some ways be submerged. Why are there actually so few passages that even so much as imply Jesus' status as Wisdom incarnate, and why is the point never made directly? And why are these passages confined to two chapters in the gospel? One may also ask whether the notion of the incarnation of a pre-existent being is compatible with the virgin birth motif.[24] Does not the reference to the conception by the Holy Spirit (1:18) naturally suggest itself as an indication of the *origin* of the Messiah whose lineage has just been recounted? It would seem so, especially if (along with Krentz, Kingsbury, Bauer, and others) we understand the phrase *biblos geneseōs* at 1:1 as applying to the whole section extending through 4:16.[25] On such a reading this introductory section functions precisely as an account of Jesus' origin. Of course *genesis* might be intended in a penultimate sense, as referring to the beginning of the earthly career of a pre-existent being, but some specific warrant would seem required to import such a reference.

Hamerton-Kelly supports a case for the notion of pre-existence in the birth narrative by claiming that the phrase *biblos geneseōs* links the story with the book of Genesis and that the spirit-motif at 1:18 reinforces the connection. Since the Spirit is mentioned in the creation story, "the conception of Jesus by the Spirit . . . indicates that a new creation is coming into being."[26] The general point here is well taken, but I do not see that it constitutes evidence for pre-existence. One could as easily argue that if the birth of Jesus is seen as a new creation it is also a real beginning and not simply the transition of an already existing being into another state.[27]

---

[24] See Raymond E. Brown, *The Birth of the Messiah: A Commentary on the Infancy Narratives in Matthew and Luke* (Garden City, NY: Doubleday, 1977), 31, 69, 137ff.; Dunn, 49, 202.

[25] See Edgar Krentz, "The Extent of Matthew's Prologue," JBL 83 (1964) 409–14; Jack Dean Kingsbury, *Matthew: Structure, Christology, Kingdom* (Philadelphia: Fortress, 1975) 1–37. Bauer's arguments are presented in his essay in this volume.

[26] Hamerton-Kelly, 77–78.

[27] There is of course a parallel between John 1:1 and the Genesis creation story, so that one might legitimately point out that the notion of a "new creation" is

Turning now to the question of the paucity of relevant passages, one may of course appeal to the limited number of such passages in the sources employed in the Gospel's composition. But there was after all an extensive body of pre-Christian Wisdom speculation upon which Matthew could easily have drawn—not to mention the fact that many redaction critics believe this author engaged in rather free composition at various points.

As to why Matthew never states explicitly that Jesus appeared as the incarnation of a pre-existent being, it is fair of Hamerton-Kelly to ask whether the synoptic tradition "develops any idea explicitly or non-symbolically."[28] But one may grant the implied point without denying that all three synoptic gospels have ways of encouraging theological reflection as well as feeling, value judgment, personal commitment, and the like. It will thus be important in the reader-response analysis to give close attention to the question of how the text leads the reader to make specific confessions regarding the identity of Jesus and also to ask whether and in what ways the wisdom passages participate in the process.

It should be noted that the whole issue is complicated by the division of opinion among the proponents of a Wisdom christology in Matthew on the issue of pre-existence. In contrast to Hamerton-Kelly, Dunn suggests that Matthew identified only the exalted Jesus with Wisdom, intentionally avoiding the notion of pre-existence.[29] Eduard Schweizer also finds Matthew uninterested in pre-existence, but he differs from Dunn in understanding Matthew as primarily concerned to link Wisdom to the earthly Jesus as interpreter of the law:

> Bei Matthäus . . . ist die Weisheit nicht im Blick auf ihre Existenz vor und ihr Mitwerken bei der Schöpfung, sondern im Blick auf ihre Offen-barungstätigkeit als Repräsentantin des Willens Gottes gesehen. Ihre Gleichsetzung mit Jesus beschreibt also nicht dessen Präexistenz, sondern dessen Tätigkeit als des vollmächtigen und abschließenden Interpreten des Willens Gottes, wie dieser im Gesetz schon ausgedrückt ist.[30]

---

quite compatible with the notion of incarnation. John's *archē*, however, refers only to the creation and is not used in relation to the incarnation. The incarnation makes present in the world what was also present at creation but is not presented as a new creation.

[28] Hamerton-Kelly, 102.

[29] Dunn, 202–206.

[30] Schweizer, *Matthäus und Seine Gemeinde* (Stuttgart: Verlag Katholisches

"If God's Wisdom, Word, and Law have, so to speak, become flesh in
Jesus, there can be no question of tossing the Law overboard . . ."[31]

Dunn's view is the more difficult to defend, since it tends to
undercut the very reasons Matthew might have had in editing the
Wisdom passages. If it is only the exalted Jesus who is identified with
Wisdom, then neither Wisdom nor Torah has in fact "become flesh in
Jesus"! One is left to wonder about the intended force of a merely
post-resurrection identification. Schweizer, on the other hand, would
seem to be on the right track in arguing that Matthew's real interest
was in applying the Wisdom motif to the specifics of Jesus' earthly
existence. That assumption goes a long way toward explaining the
absence of an explicit development of pre-existence. The fact remains,
however, that 23:34–39, at least when read in light of redaction
criticism, seems clearly to present Jesus as a trans-historical being. A
fully adequate reading of Matthew's use of the Wisdom materials will
have to address the issue of the precise meaning and function of this
passage more directly than Schweizer has done. One must also ask
whether Schweizer's insistence upon the term "incarnation" is really
appropriate, given his view on the pre-existence motif.

II. *A Reader-Response Analysis*

A. *Preliminary Considerations*

It would be helpful at this point to make four clarifications
regarding my understanding of a reader-response approach. First, by
"the reader" I mean the "implied" or "ideal" reader that the critic must
discern from an encounter with the text itself, not a reader defined
primarily in historical/sociological terms. Second, however, it is
impossible to locate the implied reader in total abstraction from
historical considerations. The critic's delineation of the reader's
reaction to wisdom materials, for example, is necessarily dependent
upon a decision as to whether that reader is familiar with Jewish
Wisdom speculation. Third, I understand the reader specifically as a
first-time reader. The critic's role is to imagine the reactions of
someone who remembers all that has gone before and can project
toward the future, but who remains naive and expectant as to what will

---

Bibelwerk, 1974) 56–57.

[31] Schweizer, *Good News*, 447. Schweizer even suggests that the absence of a
notion of pre-existence in Matthew might reflect the evangelist's "reaction against
such doctrines [as those of Paul and John] as too much for a Jew to accept . . .."

happen next and as to the ultimate outcome of the plot. Fourth, I am intentionally employing a reader-response analysis in the present case with the limited goal of discerning how the narrator leads the reader to make specific christological confessions. This does not mean that I think that the richness of a narrative can be reduced to ideational terms; it does mean that I believe, as I stated earlier, that narrative can, along with its many other functions, lead the reader to engage in theological reflection.[32]

While a genuine reader-response analysis must respect the implied reader's ignorance of the future, in addressing the *critic's* reader it necessarily presupposes a particular grasp of the scope of the entire narrative. In the present case, I will make use of the three-fold division of Matthew's gospel proposed by Edgar Krentz, Jack Kingsbury, and David Bauer, among others. I do not think the main points in the following analysis are absolutely dependent upon this scheme, and I use it primarily as a means of organizing the material for the readers of this paper. I nonetheless find this structure complementary to what I have uncovered about the development of christological affirmation in the gospel.

According to Bauer, "in 1.1–4.16 Matthew is concerned to establish a picture of Jesus for the reader which is presupposed throughout the narrative concerning Jesus' work and passion."[33] It will therefore be important, even though none of our wisdom passages occur in this section, to begin in sub-section B by tracing the narrator's presentation of Jesus in 1:1–4:16. Then, in sub-sections C and D I will treat each of the clusters of wisdom passages in context, trying to establish just how the reader will receive each passage and subsequently reflect upon it, given all that has gone before. Because we will be attending to the entire plot in some detail, it should be helpful at various "check-points" to summarize the results of the analysis in progress and to ask explicitly whether the narrator has as yet given the reader sufficient clues to identify Jesus with Wisdom incarnate.

---

[32] See C. Clifton Black II, "Depth of Characterization and Degrees of Faith in Matthew" in David J. Lull, ed., *Society of Biblical Literature: Seminar Papers, 1989* (Atlanta: Scholars Press, 1989) 202, for a statement on the relevance of literary criticism to an understanding of the evangelists' theological concerns.

[33] David R. Bauer, *The Structure of Matthew's Gospel: A Study in Literary Design* JSNTSup 31 (Sheffield: Almond, 1988) 78.

B. *The Identity of Jesus in 1:1–4:16*

1. *The Reader's Actions in Progress.* With the opening sentence the narrator informs the reader that the story about to be told is the story of Jesus, who is given the three-fold designation of Christ, son of David, and son of Abraham. The reader will thus know that the story concerns the Jewish Messiah and will understand the ensuing genealogy as attestation of that claim through proof of Davidic lineage through adoption. Moreover, the repetition of the term *Christos* at 1:16, 17, together with the narrator's comments upon the schematic history of generations leading up to Jesus' birth, will reinforce the point. The reference to the schematic history will also prepare the reader to accept the view that what is happening now is under God's supervision, a point reinforced in 1:18–25 by the motif of the virgin birth, the references to the Holy Spirit, and the narrator's claim regarding the fulfillment of prophecy. Reference to the action of the Spirit will also lead the reader to conclude that this Jesus-Messiah is himself of divine origin: not only his lineage, but his very generation is an act of God.

The explanation of Jesus' name at 1:21 also encourages reflection upon his role as Messiah: he is to save his people from their sins. The narrator's translation of "Emmanuel" (1:23) pushes the matter one step further and points to the conclusion that in Jesus God is somehow made present. The ambiguity of the phrase *meth' hēmōn ho theos* ("God [is?] with us")[34], however, may lead the reader to desire a fuller definition of how and in what sense God is present in this Messiah.

The reader may be surprised at 2:1 to discover that Gentiles enter the story but may also recall that the genealogy was populated with references to foreign women. The Jewish Messiah, who will save his people, apparently has relevance in the Gentile world as well. The magi themselves, however, refer to the child as *ho techtheis basileus tōn Ioudaiōn* (2:2), and the scriptural quotation at 2:6 concludes with an emphasis upon the promised ruler's role in "shepherding" Israel. Jesus' Jewish, and specifically Davidic, roots and function thus remain prominent in the reader's mind.

Since the magi's journey is apparently under divine guidance, the reader will pay attention to their evaluation of Jesus, noting not only their designation of his status but their attitude toward him: they have come specifically to worship him (2:2) and in fact do so (2:11). Such

---

[34] Note NRSV: "God is with us."

an attitude will seem commensurate with the title Emmanuel and the translation *meth' hēmōn ho theos*. The reader will thus conclude that Jesus is worthy of worship, a point underscored by the fulfillment-quotation at 2:15 implicitly naming him Son of God: "Out of Egypt I have called my son."

The lengthy account of Jesus' origins will have prepared the reader to identify him as the subject of John the Baptist's announcement of the coming one in 3:3 and thus to associate him explicitly with the *basileia* (3:2). The conversation between John and Jesus in the baptism scene establishes Jesus' superiority to John, and the voice of God at 3:17 not only provides reliable confirmation of Jesus' identify but establishes the designation Son of God as God's own evaluation of Jesus. The descent of the Spirit at 3:16 reminds the reader of Jesus' miraculous conception and signifies that Jesus is empowered by that same Spirit in his ensuing ministry.

In considering the qualifier the voice adds to Jesus's designation as Son—"with whom I am well pleased" (3:17)—the reader will realize that the only action Jesus has as yet performed is his insistence upon baptism, which he justified as necessary for the fulfillment of "all righteousness" (3:15). It is therefore specifically Jesus's obedience that is pleasing to God,[35] a judgment immediately confirmed in the temptation story: Jesus withstands Satan's temptations and cites a scriptural passage regarding obedience to God's word (4:4). Although the early introduction of the term Son of God is a reminder of the divine origin of the hero of the story, Jesus' replies place his own steadfastness squarely in the category of *human* obedience. Not only does he support all three refusals with God's commandments to human beings, but in the first instance the quotation explicitly names *ho anthropos* as the one who does not live by bread alone. Most importantly, in the third and climactic refusal Jesus clearly acknowledges that he, together with all humanity, owes worship to God alone: "for it is written, 'Worship the Lord your God, and serve only him.'" The reader thus notes that even the Son of God is subordinate to God but will also remember that the magi—with the

---

[35] Contra Richard A. Edwards, *Matthew's Story of Jesus* (Philadelphia: Fortress, 1985) 17, who assumes that since the reader has observed only one incident in Jesus' activity, God's pleasure "must be based on who Jesus is rather than on what he has done or said." Not only does this view undervalue Jesus' submission to "all righteousness" in the baptism story but it seriously undercuts the the the theme of his obedience that pervades the gospel.

apparent approval of the narrator—worshipped Jesus. Forced at this point to hold the commandment to worship God alone together with the image of the legitimate worship of Jesus, the reader will read on in search of clarification.

Such clarification is not immediately forthcoming, however. At 4:12–16 the reader's attention is directed to other matters. The notations regarding John's imprisonment and Jesus' return to Galilee invite questions as to what Jesus will do next. The fulfillment-quotation at 4:15–16, for its part, places Jesus' geographical location in the context of God's unfolding plan. The mention of Gentiles, moreover, reminds the reader that Jesus' significance is apparently universal, and the reference to the light shining on those in darkness reemphasizes the theme of fulfillment.

2. *Check-Point 1: The Reader at 4:17.* At the close of the first major section of the Gospel, the reader already knows a great deal about Jesus. He is the Messiah/Son of David/Son of Abraham who will bring salvation to God's people Israel and apparently extend it to Gentiles as well. Conceived by the Holy Spirit and born of a virgin, he has also been empowered by the Spirit for his ministry; and he is Son of God by God's own declaration. In fact, in him God is present in the world. His status is such that the proper response to him is actual worship. Yet his sonship also involves his own obedience to God; clearly subordinate to God, he seeks only to do God's righteousness in all things and indeed has so far shown himself faithful.

Insofar as the reader will reflect at all on Jesus' ultimate origins, there is nothing as yet to suggest that the narrator is interested in encouraging speculation about pre-existence or incarnation. The magi's phrase *ho techtheis basileus tōn Ioudaiōn* would in fact seem to reinforce the natural reading of the virgin birth motif: it is precisely in this miraculous act that God brings the Messiah/Son of God into being. The emphasis upon Jesus' human obedience, moreover, tends to work against the notion of pre-existence to the extent that it suggests that Jesus's status is contingent, subject to loss; the temptation story in particular loses its dramatic weight if the reader is not allowed to imagine the possibility that he will succumb.[36]

---

36 Jack Dean Kingsbury, "The Form and Message of Matthew," in James Luther Mays, ed., *Interpreting the Gospels* (Philadelphia: Fortress, 1981) 73, implies the contingency of Jesus' status when he says that Jesus "resists the calculated temptations of Satan to effect the loss of his sonship, rendering perfect obedience

The reader has a long way to go before finishing the story but has nevertheless formed a rather clear understanding of the identity of Jesus. If it is to be altered substantially, it will be incumbent upon the narrator to provide directives.

C. Matthew 11:16–19, 25–30 in Context

1. *4:17–11:15. The Reader's Actions in Progress.* At 4:17 the narrator alerts the reader to a turn in the plot: Jesus is now entering his public ministry, proclaiming the *basileia*. The reader also learns (4:23) that his messianic work includes not only preaching but healing as well. As Jesus proceeds to teach, the reader will be struck by his authority. Although declaring that he has come not to abolish but to fulfill the law and the prophets (5:17–20), he issues at 5:21–48 a series of sayings, each of which, prefaced with the emphatic *egō de legō*, either intensifies or overturns (5:31) a component of the received tradition. Apparently, then, the law remains in effect as an agent of salvation; Jesus, after all, quoted it in relation to his own obedience in the temptation story. Nevertheless, Jesus is clearly the definitive interpreter of the law; he is, in fact, in some sense sovereign over it. Both aspects of this conclusion are confirmed as the discourse progresses. At 7:12 Jesus refers again to the "the law and the prophets" as authoritative, but at 7:24–27 obedience to Jesus' own words appears as the criterion for salvation. Thus when the narrator comments on the authoritativeness of Jesus's teaching at 7:28, the reader must conclude that this teaching *is* God's will, which is to say it *is* Torah.

Following a series of healing-stories, the fulfillment-quotation at 8:17—"He took our infirmities and bore our diseases"—reminds the reader that at 4:23 the narrator had included healing among Jesus' activities. At 8:18–22 Jesus provides an image of discipleship based upon his own wandering lifestyle. It will be self-evident to the reader that at 8:20 Jesus applies the title Son of Man to himself, but neither Jesus' words nor the narrator's comments call attention to the term, invite reflection upon it, or in any way provide it with specific

---

to his Father (4:1–11)." Black, 616, makes the point more explicitly in relation to later passages: "the crises at Gethsemane (26:36–46) and Golgotha (27:33–50) should be taken at their suspenseful face value: despite prior indications of his resolve (4:1–11; 16:21; 17:22; 20:17–19), Jesus' own will is sorely challenged by his Father's (note the anguish suggested by 26:37–38); Jesus *could* have aborted the mission to which he was called (26:39, 42; cf. 20:28) and, on the cross, expressed abandonment by God when he chose not to do so (27:46)."

content.[37] The reader will accept it as a simple self-designation and associate it with Jesus' humility.

At the beginning of the story of the storm-stilling at 8:23, the reader will have a dual image of Jesus fresh in mind: possessed of enormous divine power, he wanders homeless on the earth, bearing the infirmities of the weak. When Jesus actually calms the storm, however, the disciples can only ask, "What sort of man is this . . . ?" Since Jesus rebukes the disciples for their "little faith," the reader will perceive the question as emanating from an inadequate understanding. Already having heard the testimony of God's voice at 3:17 and the acknowledgement of the supernatural opponent in the temptation story, the reader is also reminded at 8:29 of the proper answer to that question as the Gadarene demoniacs address him as Son of God just before he casts the demons out.

The development of the story of the paralytic in 9:1–8 will come as something of a surprise to the reader, who will expect another tale of a miraculous messianic deed. Instead of healing the paralytic immediately, Jesus pronounces this person's sins forgiven and thus incurs the charge of blasphemy from some scribes. The question of identity thus re-emerges, and Jesus claims authority specifically as Son of Man as he effects the healing. The reader will take note of this correlation but will also be struck by the narrator's startling comment to the effect that the authority Jesus exercises is given by God *tois anthropois*. Having earlier associated the term Son of Man with Jesus' homelessness, the reader now links it to his authority, but in a paradoxical way: it is an authority exercised specifically *on earth*, and it seems to be shared by other human beings; yet precisely as the power to forgive sins it is clearly a divine function.

Proceeding through chapter 9, the reader encounters various reactions to Jesus. Pharisees object to his association with tax collectors, eventually attributing his exorcisms to the prince of demons, and John's followers question his disciples' failure to fast. The crowds, however, marvel at his miraculous deeds and spread his fame;

---

[37] See Jack Dean Kingsbury, "The Figure Jesus in Matthew's Story: A Literary-Critical Probe," *JSNT* 21 (1984) 3–36, who argues on the basis of a narrative-critical study that Son of Man is distinct from all other christological titles in that "it does not function 'confessionally' to inform the reader of Jesus' identity, i.e., of 'who Jesus is.'" (p. 22) For opposing views, see David Hill, "The Figure Jesus in Matthew's Story: A Response to Professor Kingsbury's Literary-Critical Probe," *JSNT* 21 (1984) 37–52 and Meier, 217–19.

and the two blind men who come for healing address him as Son of David.

When in chapter 10 Jesus formally invests his disciples with authority as he sends them out in mission, the reader will make an association with the earlier reference to authority given *tois anthropois.* The reference in vs. 23 to the coming of the Son of Man invites the reader to broaden the scope of this title. Already linked with Jesus, the term now takes on an eschatological dimension, since it follows upon a reference to "the end" in vs. 22. It is precisely as Son of Man that Jesus will exercise eschatological authority, presumably that of judgment. In all of this, however, the reader's understanding of Jesus' role remains unchanged in substance; and certainly there is no hint of an invitation to reflect specifically upon the categories of incarnation or pre-existence.

The question of identity appears peripherally in 10:24–25 as Jesus, instructing the apostles as he commissions them for missionary work, alludes back to the Pharisees' charges at 9:32–34 in order to link the persecution of his followers to his own rejection. Then at 9:32 it becomes explicit: Jesus' acknowledgement of his followers before God depends upon their acknowledgement of him in the world. The reader will conclude that an essential part of discipleship is explicit acknowledgement of Jesus and will naturally look back to the ways in which the narrative has already defined his identity and characterized his mission—to the titles Messiah, Son of David, Son of Abraham, Son of God, Son of Man; and to his obedience and his wonderful deeds.

The reader is thus prepared to entertain the question John's disciples bring from prison at 11:2: "Are you the one who is to come, or are we to wait for another?" The phrase *ta erga tou Christou* combines with Jesus' own summary of his deeds in vs. 5 and his pronouncement in vs. 6 to alert the reader to a crucial point: Jesus' deeds cry out for response; one is either offended by them, as were the Pharisees in the earlier stories, or one receives them as signs of his identity—i.e., as performances of the *basileia* the Messiah/Son of God initiates.

With vs. 7 the narrator shifts attention to the identity of John. The reader will have noted with some surprise John's doubt expressed at 11:2 and will be interested to know how Jesus will evaluate him. What the reader learns is essentially positive: more than a prophet, John is actually Elijah himself. When Jesus notes, however, that the person least in the *basileia* is greater than John, the reader will have to conclude that it is only with Jesus that the *basileia* actually begins.

2. *Check-Point 2: The Reader at 11:16.* The reader's view of Jesus will not have changed substantially since 4:16. Having come at that point to understand Jesus essentially as Messiah/Son of God, the reader will now have observed him at work, engaged in messianic teaching and deeds. Unless we assume that the term Son of Man is in itself suggestive of pre-existence, there is no reason to imagine that the reader will be any closer to an understanding of Jesus as Wisdom incarnate at this point than at 4:16.

There has, however, been some specification of the messianic role: Jesus' teaching is so authoritative as somehow to constitute Torah itself, and it is specifically with Jesus that the *basileia* begins. A new title has also been added to the reader's repertoire: Jesus speaks of himself as the Son of Man, who wanders homeless on earth but also exercises an authority of divine origin that is somehow shared by other human beings, but which Jesus himself will display in an eschatological context.

3. *The first cluster—11:16–30: The Reader's Actions in Progress.* The adversative *de* at 11:16 alerts the reader to a contrast: "this generation" obviously does not grasp the point Jesus has just made: that John is Elijah and the *basileia* is beginning in Jesus' ministry. In fact, the reader learns quickly that this generation has acted like petulant children by rejecting both John and Jesus, the former for one reason and the latter for its opposite. Having defended himself to John's disciples by reference to his messianic deeds at 11:4–6, Jesus now defends himself (and perhaps John also) before the whole generation on the same grounds: "Yet [W]isdom is vindicated by her deeds."

The reader will hear in the reference to Wisdom's deeds an echo of *ta erga tou Christou* in 11:2 and will know that it is Jesus' mighty works that testify to his identity: it is by these that the people of this generation should have recognized the Messiah. But what will the reader make of the reference to Wisdom? A reader who recognizes the saying as an existing aphorism will understand it as an analogy, and a reader who already thinks of Jesus as Wisdom incarnate will understand it as Jesus' direct self-reference. A reader with neither of these specific bits of knowledge might conclude that the deeds of Jesus, Messiah/Son of God, are deeds commissioned by Wisdom, whether the latter is understood in a fully mythological sense or as a metaphor for God's self-expression at creation.

In any case, the reader immediately finds Jesus issuing a judgment against the Galilean cities for failing to receive his works as messianic deeds—and thus beginning to manifest the judgmental function indicated in John's original statement about the coming one. The judgment-theme recedes somewhat, however, as Jesus gives thanks to God for hiding "these things" from the "the wise and the intelligent" and revealing them to "infants." The reader will understand that Jesus speaks here of the significance of his messianic deeds and will hear the ironical reference to the "the wise and the intelligent" as signifying those who have failed to respond to Jesus, namely, the Pharisees and scribes. The "infants," by contrast, will mean those who have received what Jesus has offered: the disciples themselves, who have taken no offense in him (11:5).

Jesus' words on revelation emphasize his unique relationship to God and teach the reader that just as God reveals to Jesus, so Jesus reveals to human beings. These words also indicate that both knowledge and lack of knowledge regarding Jesus' identity and the meaning of his deeds are rooted in God's will. The invitation Jesus offers at 11:30 will thus appear as potential revelation,[38] which will apply both to Jesus' hearers in the story and to readers of the story. Since Jesus calls God Father and himself Son, the reader will be reminded of the crucial junctures at which Jesus has been directly and indirectly designated Son of God and will now associate that title with Jesus' revelatory function.

The invitation Jesus issues will add to the transcendent quality of his person in the reader's mind; as a word of overwhelming grace, it will carry an emotional appeal. Jesus' self-description as "gentle and humble in heart" will remind the reader of the compassion and mercy he has shown so far in his ministry, just as the reference to "rest" and the description of his yoke as "easy" and his "burden" as "light" will enhance the gracious quality of the invitation. Familiar with the phrase "yoke of the law," the reader will also understand that in inviting hearers to "his" yoke Jesus points back to his teaching, which the reader already knows is to be understood as Torah.

4. *Check-Point 3: The Reader at 12:1.* Nothing in the reader-response analysis up to this point has dispelled the ambiguity that attended the earlier redactional treatment of the first cluster of wisdom passages.

---

[38] Deutsch, 32, identifies those oppressed by burdens in 11:28 as persons who have not *yet* received the revelation Jesus offers.

Given the reader's understanding at 4:16, which apparently involved the view that Jesus' conception by the Spirit and birth from the womb of a virgin was his origin, the reference to Wisdom's deeds at 11:19 seems insufficient as an invitation to identify Jesus with Wisdom herself. The use of Son of Man is an unexceptional self-reference of Jesus that adds nothing specific to the reader's understanding of the term.

Matthew 12:25–30 clearly present Jesus as a transcendent figure, but in somewhat undefined terms. It is of course possible that the reader will hear in the phrase "Come to me . . ." echoes of the voice of personified Wisdom and/or will conclude that for Jesus to speak of his own yoke is in fact to identify himself with Wisdom and Torah. If so, then the reader can also look back to 1:19 and find reinforcement for the point. What we have not seen as yet, however, is any evidence that the narrator has prepared the reader to render such specific judgments or has, outside 11:25–30 itself, given any reason to revise the view of Jesus formed in 1:1–4:16.

The reader will, however, have observed an important turn in the plot of the story. Jesus' words and deeds have on the one hand gained him a following but on the other sparked opposition. The people of "this generation" are behaving like perpetually dissatisfied children; unable to receive the revelation from God that Jesus brings, they refuse to repent, and are thus subject to judgment.

5. *12:1–16:20: The Reader's Actions in Progress.* The narrator now takes the reader through a series of controversy stories in which the Pharisees appear as unmerciful (12:7, 11–12) in contrast to the humble, unassuming Jesus (12:17–21). The reader will understand the stories as illustrating Jesus' "easy yoke" of 11:30 and will now know that those who "are weary and are carrying heavy burdens" (11:28) are those who suffer under the Pharisees' application of the Torah. The reader will also note an escalation in the controversy theme: the Pharisees now actually begin to plot Jesus' death (12:14).

The issue of identity is never far from the surface. At 12:6, 8 Jesus asserts that "something greater than the temple is here" and claims authority as Son of Man over the Sabbath. The question, "Can this be the Son of David?" at 12:23 leads to the Beelzebul controversy, which Jesus rounds off with a series of sayings that draw the lines of demarcation more sharply. Jesus' opponents are bad trees bearing bad fruit and will be condemned (12:33, 37). Rejecting their request for a sign, Jesus nevertheless offers one they cannot grasp—the cryptic "sign of Jonah," which remains unexplained for the reader also.

Proceeding through chapter 13, the reader hears Jesus relate and interpret parables of the *basileia.* Jesus' words at 13:10–17 link the use of parables to the revelation-theme at 11:25–27, explaining people's ability/inability to comprehend God's sovereign will. When Jesus interprets the sower of 13:24 as the Son of Man in the explanation at 13:36–43, the reader will know on the basis of prior passages that Jesus is referring to himself and will make the same identification in 13:41 where this term now refers explicitly to the eschatological judge. Matthew thus reinforces the notion that the Jesus who now performs works among the people will appear in glory and power at the close of the age.

The return of Jesus to his home area in 13:53–58 becomes the occasion for questions about the source of his power that lead into Herod's explicit speculation on Jesus' identity in 14:1–2. The identity issue is thus prominent as the reader proceeds through the feeding story (14:13–21) into the mysterious scene on the lake where Jesus demonstrates an awesome power over nature. When Peter has failed to follow Jesus on the water and is pronounced a person of "little faith," the reader learns that the disciples worship him and proclaim him Son of God. The linking of these two motifs directs attention back to the early chapters of the gospel in which the magi worshipped Jesus and the voice of God pronounced him Son.

Thus given a dramatic demonstration of the proper response to Jesus, the reader immediately encounters the scribes and Pharisees asking him a question obviously designed to discredit him (15:1–2). The response of Jesus (15:3–20) reinforces the reader's negative impression of the attitude of the religious leaders, just as the story of the persistent faith of the Canaanite woman (15:21–28) provides a positive contrast. A second feeding story (15:32–39) precedes a second request for a sign from Jesus' opponents (16:1–4), which Jesus once again, as at 12:38–40, answers with a reference to the sign of Jonah. The reader will remember the earlier statement and accept the repetition as indicating significance; yet the meaning will remain elusive.

As a result, after Jesus' condemnation of the "yeast" of the Pharisees and Sadducees at 16:5–11, the reader comes to the scene at Caesarea Philippi at 16:13 with some clear conceptions bracketed by some puzzling questions. Jesus, Messiah/Son of David and Son of God, now works on earth as Son of Man but will also appear under that rubric as the powerful, eschatological judge at the close of the age. The Jewish leadership fails to understand his words and deeds or grasp who he is, although the disciples, blessed by God's revelation, do. The reader understands even more clearly than the disciples, but like them, remains uncertain as to how Jesus' messiahship is to work itself out. The opposition seems ominous, and betrayal has already been indicated; Jesus speaks strangely of a sojourn in the earth and a period of mourning.

It is no real surprise for the reader to find Jesus at 16:13–20 eliciting from Peter the confession, "You are the Messiah, the Son of the living God" in response to the question, "Who do people say the Son of Man is?" But there are three new elements: 1) Jesus himself now pronounces explicit blessing upon the one making this identification; 2) he links the confession to the later life of the Church; and 3) he implicitly pronounces certain designations false: "John the Baptist" (revived) and "Jeremiah or one of the prophets." The reader will conclude that confession of Jesus as Messiah/Son of God is constitutive of discipleship in the church, just as response to Jesus during his lifetime expressed one's response to the *basileia*. But the reader will also ponder the fact that Jesus now commands secrecy about his identity as Messiah (16:20).

6. *Check-Point 4: The Reader at 16:21*. Between 12:1 and 16:20 the reader has observed a heightening of Jesus' controversy with his opponents, a controversy in which the question of his identity has been central. Whereas the plot has "thickened," however, the reader's understanding of Jesus still remains largely unchanged since 4:16. To be sure, the "correct" evaluation of Jesus has been made more explicit and Jesus' transcendent status has been reinforced. But in no way has the narrator indicated that the reference to Wisdom at 11:19 constitutes a key to Jesus' identity. Nor has the reader been given any explicit indication that the Jesus whose words do indeed constitute the "yoke" of Torah is to be identified *as* that Torah or as the incarnation of Wisdom herself. As to the term Son of Man, Kingsbury has made the telling point that the question at 16:13 shows clearly that far from clarifying Jesus' identity in Matthew, the term itself appears as in need of clarification.[39]

---

[39] Kingsbury, "The Figure of Jesus in Matthew's Story," p. 23.

D. *Matthew 23:34–39 in Context*

1. *16:21–23:33*: With 16:21 the narrator begins to clarify Jesus' earlier cryptic statements. The passion prediction makes Jesus' coming death and resurrection explicit, and 16:24–28 explains the reference to taking up the cross at 10:38–39. The latter passage also completes the reader's knowledge of coming events by referring to the eschatological appearance of the Son of Man. It can now be inferred that it is only after dying and rising from the dead that Jesus will appear as eschatological judge.

The transfiguration scene at 17:1–8 provides confirmation of Jesus' acceptance of Peter's confession and redoubles the narrator's emphasis upon Jesus' transcendent status. The voice from heaven for a second time pronounces Jesus God's Son with whom God is "well pleased." This not only reminds the reader of the baptismal scene and implicitly ties together all the christological confessions so far made; it also indicates that God remains pleased with Jesus, i.e., that all that he has so far done is in accord with the divine will. The additional command, "listen to him," then directs attention forward; the reader understands that it will be important to listen to Jesus' further teaching.

The first thing the disciples and the reader now hear from Jesus is his injunction not to be afraid (17:8). The second is another command to secrecy (17:9), this time followed by a qualification: "until after the Son of Man has been raised from the dead." Already informed that Jesus' death and resurrection are central to his mission, the reader will now understand that secrecy must prevail until these climactic events have taken place.[40]

The repetition of the full passion prediction at 17:22–23 reinforces the significance of Jesus' death, so that the reader is well prepared to understand chapter 18 as Jesus' way of preparing his disciples for life in the post-resurrection church. His promise at 18:10 to be present with those who gather in his name reminds the reader of the Emmanuel passage at 1:23 and gives it a more explicit meaning. Jesus will make God present to his later followers by himself being present in their midst. The promise of Jesus' presence also gives substance to Jesus' injunction against fear at 17:7. When at 20:17–19 Jesus yet again predicts his death and resurrection the reader will know not only that these events are inevitable but that they are imminent.

---

[40] See Jack Dean Kingsbury, *Matthew as Story* (Philadelphia: Fortress, 1986) 80.

As Jesus departs from Jericho (20:29–34), two blind men hail him
as Son of David. This scene combines with the quotation at 21:5 to put
Jesus' specifically messianic role in the forefront of the reader's mind
as Jesus enters Jerusalem. The cries of the crowds on the road (21:9)
and the children in the temple (21:15) intensify the focus upon the
messianic category, and the objections of the chief priests and scribes
prepare the reader for renewed controversy over Jesus' identity.

When Jesus enters the temple, controversy in fact ensues over his
authority (21:23), and he responds with a series of parables that once
again draw a sharp contrast between those who accept him and those
who reject him (21:28–22:14). The reader will not only recognize the
son of the householder at 21:37 as Jesus but will decode from the
parables the whole history of God's dealings with Israel—down
through the transfer of the *basileia* from Israel to "a people that
produces . . . fruits" (21:43), the destruction of Jerusalem (22:7), and
the end of the age (22:13). At this point it is clear not only who Jesus is
but how his ministry and his rejection by Israel fit into God's plan.

The identity question is kept alive as the disciples of the Pharisees
address Jesus as "teacher" in an attempt to trip him up (22:16) and as
Jesus himself confronts the Pharisees with the question as to "whose
son" the Messiah is (22:41–42). When Jesus rejects their subordination
of the Messiah to David, the reader will think back to passages in which
Jesus' divine, transcendent status is made clear and will understand it
is because the Messiah is Son of God that he is greater than even
David. The point is reinforced a few verses later (23:10) when Jesus,
now pronouncing his invective against the scribes and Pharisees,
proclaims that the Messiah is in fact the "one instructor" (*kathēgētēs*) of
those who follow him.

Jesus' condemnation of his opponents nevertheless focuses upon
issues of true obedience to God rather than upon their rejection of
him. It is their neglect of "justice and mercy and faith" (23:23) in favor
of trivialities that constitutes their blindness. Even at 23:29, where Jesus
pronounces that the scribes and Pharisees share in their predecessors'
guilt for murdering the prophets, the reader will most naturally think
of their moral failure and hypocrisy as justifying this judgment. At
23:32, however, Matthew directs the attention of the reader forward:
"fill up, then, the measure of your ancestors." What Jesus' opponents
are going to do in the future will bring Israel's past apostasy to its
logical conclusion.

2. *Check-Point 5: The Reader at 23:34.* It is apparent, once again, that although the plot has developed, the reader's view of Jesus has changed very little. Jesus' messianic function has received further and important definition; his death and resurrection are now explicitly in view, and his presence in the later church has been promised; but the narrator has added virtually nothing to the christological confession expected of the reader since the dramatic scene at Caesarea Philippi. The term Son of Man has appeared at several junctures (16:13, 27, 28; 17:9, 12, 22; 19:28; 20:18, 28) but has taken on no additional nuances other than an association with Jesus' coming death and (20:28) a passing link with the ransoming effect of that death.

The reader's immediate interest at 23:34 is in the guilt of the scribes and Pharisees. At the forefront of concern will be their continuity with those who murdered the prophets, which places the religious leaders in the long history of Israel's apostasy. The reader will also be aware, however, of the immediate progress of the plot of the story of Jesus' career: Jesus, in conflict with bitter opponents who reject him, is on his way to death. And, having just heard of the fundamental hypocrisy of the scribes and Pharisees, the reader will link their failure to respond to Jesus to a failure of the heart: inside they are "full of greed and self-indulgence" (23:25).

3. *The Second Cluster: 23:34–39.* Jesus' *egō apostellō*, in conjunction with the ensuing words, will create in the reader's mind the image of Jesus as a heavenly figure who commissions agents. Against the background of 23:29–32, the phrase "prophets, sages, and scribes" will remind the reader of figures of the past, but the reference to crucifixion and persecution from town to town will clearly direct attention to the tribulations of the church. The reader will thus place the emissaries to be sent to the church in continuity with those sent to Israel. So when Jesus once again pronounces judgment upon this generation as the culmination of apostasy at 23:36, the reader will include the treatment of the church after Jesus' time as partial reason for that judgment.

The reader will also know that Jesus' death is imminent and will think of it in light of Israel's continual rejection of God's emissaries. Matthew 23:39, however, refocuses attention on the present and future. The reader, now completely filled in on the details of God's plan, will know that Jesus is referring to his coming death and eventual return as eschatological judge.

4. *Check-Point 6: The Reader at 24:1.* If the reader has made an identification of Jesus with Wisdom in chapter 11, the second wisdom-cluster will reinforce it. On the other hand, the reader who has not made the identification may well do so now on the basis of 23:34, for by this point Jesus' transcendent character has been made amply clear. In either case, it will then be natural to understand the prophets, sages, and scribes as including those sent earlier to Israel, so that Jesus appears explicitly as the trans-historical Wisdom sending emissaries to every generation. The phrase "how often" at 23:37—especially since it follows a reference to the rejection of Israel's prophets—will reinforce the point.

One might, however, read 23:34 without identifying Jesus as incarnate Wisdom or as trans-historical in any sense that extends into the past. By this point it is clear not only that Jesus must die but that he will be raised from the dead, will subsequently be present with the church, and will return at the end of the age. It will therefore be possible for the reader who knows nothing of the redactor's shift from the future tense to the present to hear *apostellō* as referring exclusively to Jesus' intention to commission emissaries to the later church. The reader who does so can also understand "how often" in 23:37 as referring only to Jesus' earthly career, although the prophets, sages, and scribes of 23:34 will clearly appear as standing in continuity with those sent earlier to Israel.

5. *24:1–28:20: The Reader's Actions in Progress.* The narrator's indication at 24:1 that Jesus leaves the temple draws the reader momentarily into the present and immediate future. Knowing that Jesus is soon to die, the reader will undoubtedly sense that his departure from the temple (after an extended stint of teaching ending in a dramatic pronouncement of judgment against Israel) constitutes a significant step toward the climax of the plot. The reader will sense finality in the encounter Jesus has with the Jewish leadership. The comment from the disciples and Jesus' reply, however, quickly refocus attention upon the more distant future and, more specifically, upon the eventual fate of the temple. The reader will easily connect the prediction of destruction with 23:38–39 and understand that destruction as God's judgment upon Israel's apostasy, which is about to be filled up to full measure (23:32).

Thinking now about the destruction of the temple in light of the eschatological future, the reader hears the disciples voice the pertinent question (24:3): "when will this be, and what will be the sign of your coming and of the end of the age?" One effect of Jesus' reply, however, is to disconnect the coming destruction of Jerusalem from the actual end of the age (24:6): "for this must take place, but the end is not yet." From that point Jesus proceeds to outline the eschatological events in such a way as to prepare his followers for the turbulent times to come and encourage faithfulness in the interim period. Continually referring to his return, he issues both explicit (24:44–51; 25:13) and implicit (25:30, 41–46) warnings regarding readiness.

At 26:1–3 the narrator alerts the reader to yet another turn toward the culmination of the plot. Jesus now connects his death to the Passover, only two days away, and the Jewish leaders explicitly plot his arrest. At the Passover meal, Jesus then interprets his death as effecting forgiveness of sins (26:28) and predicts the disciples' apostasy.

Prepared now to have the story culminate in Jesus' death and resurrection—indeed, having heard from Jesus' own mouth about the necessity of these events—the reader will experience a degree of suspense[41] during the scene in Gethsemane. Jesus' agony at 26:38 and his plea at 26:39 encourage the reader to imagine two alternatives to the expected outcome: perhaps, on the one hand, God can accomplish the divine plan in another way; perhaps, on the other hand, Jesus will lose courage and the plan will actually fail. Of course the reader, having witnessed Jesus' victory over temptation at 4:1–11, will expect him to remain obedient to God. But the note of contingency is real and will presumably carry over into the trial scenes. The reader will be aware, as Jesus is questioned, of the possibility that he might after all renounce his claims.

When Jesus is eventually arrested and brought before Caiaphas, the latter raises once again the question of identity. That he explicitly asks whether Jesus considers himself "the Messiah, the Son of God" (26:63) both reminds the reader of all previous confessions of Jesus' status and also forges a connection between Jesus' death and the titles Messiah and Son of God. It is specifically in relation to Jesus' claim to the status these titles imply that he is crucified; the reader must therefore conclude that Israel's final failure lay precisely in its refusal to accept him according to the implications of these titles.

---

[41] See above, n. 36.

Jesus' answer, however, employs the term Son of Man as a self-designation and thus brings this title into relationship with that of Messiah and Son of God. As Son of Man, Jesus has exercised authority on earth, yet he now faces humiliation and death. At the close of the age, however, he will return in the role of Son of Man as the powerful eschatological judge. In all this—his earthly exercise of power, his humiliation and rejection, and his reappearance at the close of the age—he is Messiah/Son of God.

As Jesus appears before Pilate, it is appropriately the narrowly Messianic titles that are at issue. Pilate asks whether he is "King of the Jews" (27:11) and refers to him as *ton legomenon Christon* (27:17, 22). "Son of God," however, reappears when the Jewish leaders mock him on the cross (27:43) and in the confession of the centurion and other observers (27:55). That Jesus does not renounce his claims but goes to his death in accordance with God's will, refusing even to respond to taunts of the Jewish leaders as he hangs on the cross, completes the reader's image of Jesus as God's obedient servant. The cry of despair at 27:46 contributes to this image in a paradoxical way, just as did Jesus' agony in Gethsemane. That Jesus was in fact subject to despair only underscores the radical nature of his obedience precisely as *human* obedience.

The final scene (28:16–20), that of Jesus' commissioning the disciples on a mountain, draws together numerous themes from the story. The reader is reminded of the status of Jesus as one worthy of worship, of the authority Jesus receives from God and passes on to his followers, of the crucial importance of the teaching of Jesus, and of the abiding presence of Jesus with his followers as they go about their mission in the world.

6. *Check-Point 7: The Reader at the Close of the Gospel.* Jesus' employment of the trinitarian formula at 28:20 reminds the reader that the one who will be present with the later Christian followers, and in whose name they baptize and teach, is the Son of God. The close association of Jesus with the Father and the Holy Spirit, together with the sovereign command issued from a mountain top, reinforces the reader's sense of Jesus as a transcendent being that was encouraged not only at 23:34, 37 but also at the transfiguration scene and at 11:25–30. If at some point the reader has already interpreted Jesus' transcendence in light of the categories of pre-existence or incarnation, then this passage can be read in light of that

interpretation. In itself, however, it in no way either demands such a reading or encourages the reader to think back to the passages in chapters 11 and 23 with these categories in mind. Nor has there been any indication in the material since 23:39 that the reader should revise earlier understandings of Jesus. If the identification has not been made prior to that point, it certainly will not be made afterward.

Nor has the usage of the term Son of Man in the concluding section taken on any additional nuances. It has been brought into connection with the titles Son of God and Messiah but has functioned only in ways already familiar to the reader: in reference to Jesus's coming death (26:2, 24, 45) and in reference to his eschatological return (24:27, 30, 37, 39, 44; 25:31; 26:64).

The Jesus who issues his sovereign command from the mountain, moreover, is still for the reader the Jesus who went obediently to his death despite the real, agonizing temptation to abandon the mission. The reader will think at this point not of the ascent of a savior who once descended from glory but of the Messiah/Son of God, who, being obedient to God in the face of temptation, rejection, humiliation, and death, is now, as the resurrected one, present to the church as it undergoes its own sufferings, struggles, and temptations in the world.

III. *Conclusion: Three Readers Reading*

Does a reader-response analysis of the gospel of Matthew reveal a Wisdom christology, an explicit identification of Jesus as Wisdom incarnate? We have seen that given specific interpretive moves at one point or another, the reader could in fact make the needed identification; most importantly, 23:34–39 is particularly suggestive of Jesus' trans-historical character. The other wisdom passages, moreover, are amenable to interpretation along such lines and, if read in light of that interpretation, could be counted as narrator's support. It would appear, then, that it is possible for a reader to interpret Matthew in such a way as to hear the text calling for an identification of Jesus with personified Wisdom. To put the matter differently, we can conclude that the narrator has not foreclosed such an interpretation.

To fail to foreclose such a reading, however, is not to endorse it. We have in fact seen nothing to indicate a specific interest in eliciting a confession regarding Jesus' status as Wisdom or his pre-existence. It is possible, moreover, to read the wisdom passages in context without identifying Jesus as Wisdom incarnate or understanding him as a trans-historical being. Although the redactor's moves at 23:34 can be interpreted as an attempt to make the identification, our reader-response analysis reveals that a reader might well understand Jesus' commissioning of prophets, sages, and scribes in an exclusively future sense. And, finally, the fact remains that the identification of Jesus as the incarnation of pre-existent Wisdom stands in tension with the natural sense of the story of the virgin birth.

A reader-response analysis thus discloses that alternative readings are possible: the reader may respond to Matthew's wisdom passages in more than one way without violating the text. To say this, however, is not to say that all readings are equal in the eyes of the implied author. What I would like to offer now is what might be called a "preferred" reading, the reading I believe is most commensurate with the narrator's promptings. I will also argue that this reading offers a fuller explanation of the redactor's intentions than has as yet been proposed. This "preferred" reading constitutes a middle position between an outright identification of Jesus with Wisdom and an interpretation of 23:34 in a purely future sense that avoids an understanding of Jesus as a trans-historical being altogether.

When the reader comes upon the reference to Wisdom's deeds at 11:19, it is in the specific context of a turn in the plot. At 11:12 Jesus notes that the *basileia* "has suffered violence," and the ensuing pericope on the children in the market places records the irrational rejection of both John and Jesus. While the reader will understand the deeds of Jesus (and perhaps John) as at least paralleling, and very likely constituting, Wisdom's own deeds, the reader's task is to recognize that these deeds are in some sense the work of Wisdom, but not necessarily to reflect any further upon the precise nature of the relationship between Jesus and Wisdom. The point is neither that Jesus is Wisdom's envoy nor that he is Wisdom incarnate, but that his deeds, in which Wisdom herself is active, vindicate him in the face of his opposition. To say that they are Wisdom's deeds, or at least analogous to Wisdom's deeds, is to say that they issue from the same source as the creation of the world, that they are ultimately grounded in the plan and will of God. The reader is thus encouraged to note that Jesus is in fact being rejected, but that his deeds show his rejection to be ill-founded: they are proof positive that his mission is Wisdom's own, which is to say, God's own.

At 11:25, however, there is a slight shift in focus. At this point the narrator wants the reader to reflect more explicitly upon the details of

Jesus' status, and to that end the Son-Father terminology is introduced. Jesus' authority is that of Son of God so that precisely in his role as Son Jesus can offer the yoke of Torah as his own. "All things," after all, have been delivered to him by the Father! When, in the ensuing chapters, the reader observes Jesus' opponents openly attacking him, the impact is heightened by the memory of 11:25–30. The Jesus who is suffering rejection is God's own Son, who in mercy offers the "easy yoke." He is the Messiah of Israel, who as such performs the very deeds of Wisdom.

The reader will not, on this reading, make an explicit identification of Jesus and Wisdom at either 11:25–30 or 23:34–40, but something very close to this will happen. Jesus' words at 11:28–30 encourage a sense of Jesus' transcendent status that is variously reinforced in the ensuing material. The disciples see Jesus in his glorified state on a mountaintop, confess him as Son of God and Messiah, and even worship him. They also learn of his eventual return in glory as the Son of Man and hear him promise (18:20) to be with them in the post-resurrection church. The reader will thus be well prepared by 23:34 to hear Jesus speak as a transcendent being: "Therefore I send . . . ." Although the focus is primarily on the future at this point—the prophets, sages, and scribes to be sent to the church—the reader will hear both the "I send" of 23:34 and the "how often" of 23:37 as reaching back into Israel's long history. The reader will, in other words, hear Jesus speaking in a trans-historical capacity.

This is not to say that Jesus speaks as Wisdom incarnate. It is only to say that as Son of God/Messiah, to whom "all things" have been delivered and who can speak of the yoke of the Torah as his own, he occupies a vantage point that is as close as possible to God's own. He can speak *for* God, who has sent emissaries to intransigent Israel throughout the years. If strict logic demands that Jesus's words in 23:34 refer only to future emissaries, the narrator is unconcerned. What the reader must grasp is that the rejection of these later emissaries is of a piece not only with the rejection of Jesus but with the earlier rejection of those God sent to Israel. The point is that the Jesus who speaks in chapter 23 is the middle term in this tragic history; his rejection is the turning point, Israel's definitive rejection of God. His sovereign "I send" and "how often" are important indicators of his unique, transcendent, and divine status; and by placing them in Jesus' mouth the narrator has him assume for the moment a trans-historical *posture.* The narrator does not, however, invite the reader to speculate on Jesus' pre-existence or his precise relationship to Wisdom.

The figure of Wisdom thus remains in one sense tangential to the *reader's* concerns. If, however, this particular understanding of the reader's task in the Matthean story is used as the basis for assessing the *redactor's* intentions, it appears that the Wisdom motif played a very important role in the shaping of this story. The "preferred reading" I am suggesting coalesces not only with many of Schweizer's observations but with a central element in Burnett's argument. It is above all the pattern of Wisdom's rejection and withdrawal that attracted Matthew, who apparently found in it a way of articulating the dual theme of Israel's rejection of Jesus and God's subsequent abandonment of Israel.

Burnett notes that although the rejection of Jesus is foreshadowed at 2:3 and is articulated in the accusations of the scribes at 9:3, 34, it "is not clarified for the reader until the parable of the children in the market place."[42] That is to say, the first cluster of wisdom passages appears in precise conjunction with the first explicit articulation of the rejection theme. In comparing "this generation" to dissatisfied children, Jesus indicates their rejection of both John and himself. And the rejection of Jesus leads logically to his rejection of Israel: the parable is followed immediately by Jesus' pronouncement of woes upon the Galilean cities, which in turn leads into 11:25–30 with its contrast between those to whom God has revealed "these things" and those from whom God has "hidden" them.

The second cluster of wisdom passages also occurs at a crucial juncture in the development of the rejection-motif: at the end of Jesus' extended condemnation of the scribes and Pharisees in chapter 23. Coming after the "parables against Israel" in 21:33–22:14, this speech must be interpreted as a rejection of Israel itself and not just its leadership.[43] The "formal" acts of rejection are of course still to come: Jesus departs from the Temple at 24:1[44] and is rejected not only by the Jewish leadership but by the people as a whole in the trial scene. But the ominous words in 23:38–39 show that at this point the die is irrevocably cast. As the first cluster signals the inception of the rejection-theme, the second brings it to a climax.

---

42 Burnett, 100–101.

43 Ibid., 109.

44 Ibid., 112ff.

It would thus appear that the redactor was indeed expressing a central concern in using and reshaping the wisdom passages. This concern, however, had everything to do with the earthly career of Jesus as the rejected Messiah who in turn carried out God's rejection of Israel, but apparently had nothing to do with a desire to encourage the reader to speculate about Jesus' pre-existence or identify him with Wisdom incarnate. The pattern of Wisdom's rejection and subsequent withdrawal must have seemed the perfect "model" for grasping the paradox of a crucified Messiah, but it was apparently not to the figure of personified Wisdom herself that Matthew turned in order to articulate who Jesus was.

Confirmation of the redactor's specific interest in the notion of withdrawal can be found in an article by Deirdre Good on the use of the verb *anachōreō* in Matthew.[45] What Good uncovers is a pattern of "hostility/withdrawal/prophetic fulfillment" that is (somewhat imperfectly) expressed in the seven theologically significant occurrences of the verb in Matthew, all but one of which are found in special Matthean material. Thus the magi (2:12), Joseph (2:14, 22), and Jesus himself (4:12; 12:15; 4:13) all withdraw in the face of hostility. In all but two of these instances there follows an explicit reference to the fulfillment of prophecy, and in the remaining cases one can argue that the theme is in fact implied.[46] In the seventh instance, which Good terms ironic, it is Judas who "withdraws into a place of death."[47]

Through an examination of the theme of withdrawal in the LXX and other Jewish literature, Good concludes that the redactor derived the first two elements of the pattern specifically from apocalyptic wisdom materials and then supplied the third. The net effect of Matthew's use of *anachōreō*, on her view, is that "the reader understands the withdrawal of Jesus as Wisdom to be part of the larger pattern of God's design . . . . So it is not *retreat from* hostility but rather

---

[45] "The Verb *ANACHŌREŌ* in Matthew's Gospel," *NovT* 32 (1990) 1–12.

[46] Good, 4. The two exceptions are 14:12–14 and 15:21–28. Regarding the first, Good notes "it would not be hard to understand the following feeding of the five thousand as a fulfillment of prophecy by implication." And regarding the second, she comments, "To be sure, the specifically Matthean formula of fulfillment is absent. Perhaps that is because the passage makes articulate the previous promise of the location of Jesus' ministry in 'Galilee of the Gentiles'" (4:15).

[47] Ibid., 5.

withdrawal for the fulfillment of prophecy that demonstrates Matthew's intention in his creation of this pattern."[48]

To be sure, Good does accept the identification of Jesus with Wisdom. It is not a point she presses, however, but one she qualifies in a significant way: "the inclusion of Joseph and Judas in the pattern means that the pattern is not intended to emphasize a specific christology so much as to present a repeated theme."[49] That point complements my own argument with respect to the role of the wisdom passages in Matthew. Although the verb *anachōreō* is not used in these passages, they clearly serve the theme of rejection. If we combine this point with the insight from Good, we see that the specific function of the Wisdom motif for Matthew is that it provides the means for articulating the *meaning* of Jesus' rejection: it must be understood as the fulfillment of prophecy and thus as a component of God's plan.

In summary, then, Matthew employs the story of Wisdom primarily to interpret the plot of the story of Jesus. To that extent, it serves the theological purpose of articulating the cause and meaning of Jesus' death. It does not serve directly to elaborate on the identity of Jesus.

Whether Matthew intentionally avoided the categories of pre-existence and incarnation, or was merely uninterested in them, is in my estimation anybody's guess. But, assuming the validity of my "preferred reading," it might be instructive to note the consequences of the redactor's limited use of the wisdom materials. We have in Johannine Logos christology some indication of what a christology based upon the incarnation of Wisdom might look like, and one way of understanding the significance of the presumed Wisdom christology in Matthew is to locate it in a developmental scheme, i.e., to place it on a trajectory leading through John to Chalcedon. Thus, Dunn not only speaks of the "development" constituted by Matthew's redaction of Q but also argues that it

> opens up . . . all the possibilities of moving from a christology which thinks of Jesus as (quantitatively) *different in degree* from earlier prophets to one which thinks of Jesus as (qualitatively) *different in kind* from earlier prophets, of moving from a christology which speaks of Jesus' divinely given *function* to one which speaks of Jesus' metaphysical *status* . . . .[50]

---

[48] Ibid., 12.

[49] Ibid., 11.

[50] Dunn, 205.

If, however, Matthew employed the Wisdom materials not in order to identify Jesus with Wisdom incarnate but primarily to articulate the dual theme of rejection, then a movement from function to status was not in fact at work. Dunn himself acknowledges that this distinction was probably foreign to the thought of the biblical writers themselves and that Matthew betrays no actual consciousness of having taken such a monumental step.[51] This latter observation is consistent with an important result of my reader-response analysis. On the one hand, Matthew's story presents Jesus as a divine being carrying out a pre-ordained plan of God; but, on the other, it presents Jesus' obedience as *human* obedience that takes place in a drama that is in some sense open and contingent. If we were to remove this note of contingency, the story would lose much in depth and intensity.

But what a contrast we find in the gospel of John: a virtually "passionless" Jesus who strides through the story with an almost alien form of sovereignty! It should hardly surprise us (if something like Raymond Brown's reconstruction of the history of the Johannine community be accepted)[52] that it could quickly foster a thoroughgoing docetism. Precisely by foregoing the category of pre-existence, Matthew preserved the texture of a story that is, for all its mythic qualities, still a profoundly human one.

It should be emphasized that the Wisdom materials in Matthew enhance the human and concrete dimensions of the story. My judgment that the first gospel does not in fact contain a genuine Wisdom christology will appear in some respects disappointing from a feminist perspective. But one should not forget that it is precisely the figure of Wisdom that stands as Matthew's model for the career of the Messiah/Son of God who passionately sought to win the allegiance of human beings only to suffer tragic rejection.[53]

Although I have identified Matthew's redactional motive primarily in terms of applying the pattern of Wisdom's rejection and withdrawal to Jesus' life, I can agree partially with Schweizer that the link between Jesus and Wisdom has to do with his relationship to the Law. The point is not, however, that Jesus *is* Wisdom and therefore *is* Torah. As Messiah, he can interpret and even *issue* Torah. But as one who is

---

[51] Ibid.

[52] Raymond E. Brown, *The Community of the Beloved Disciple: The Life, Loves, and Hates of an Individual Church in New Testament Times* (New York: Paulist, 1979).

[53] Cf. esp. Prov 1:20–33.

himself obedient to God, he remains in some sense subject to it. In this limited and "weak" sense one can say, with Suggs, that he "embodies" Torah. It is not, however, because the Law (supposedly) becomes flesh in Jesus that it cannot (in Schweizer's phrase) be "tossed overboard"; the point is rather that a major part of the role of Jesus as God's Messiah is precisely to interpret the Law, which by God's own will must abide "till heaven and earth pass away" (5:18).

If Jesus in a "weak" sense "embodies" Torah, it is in a stronger sense that he plays the role of the Shekinah. That his continuing presence with the community is formally parallel to the presence of the Shekinah with Israel can scarcely be denied. Jesus' assumption of this role is not a function of his identification with Wisdom, however, but of his status as Messiah/Son of God. Because Matthew obviously wished to assign Jesus the highest possible standing in relation to God, it was virtually necessary that Jesus *supplant* the figure of the Shekinah, that he actually assume the status of God's very presence in the world. But Matthew encourages speculation neither upon the "mechanics" of Jesus' presence nor upon the intricacies of his relation to God as Messiah/Son.[54] The ambiguity of *meth' hēmōn ho theos* remains; the reader who wants to know its meaning must read the story again.

---

[54] Proponents of a Wisdom christology in Matthew generally acknowledge that it remains implicit and undeveloped. Note, for example, Burnett's statement (p. 171): "The problem . . . is that [Matthew] does not explicitly state the myth(s) of pre-existence which he assumes, nor does he elaborate upon the 'nature' of the pre-existent Christ. Matthew's main interest seems to be in the incarnation of Christ and the soteriological function which he performs in the history of salvation. Even in the infancy narratives, a place where he could explicitly depict a clear understanding of Christ's pre-existence, Matthew only seems to imply that Jesus was pre-existent in the mind of God when God planned the soteriological function of Christ as the fulfillment of the scriptures (cf. 1:8–25)." On the "preferred" reading I have proposed, Matthew is indeed interested in Jesus' soteriological function in the history of salvation and in the unique status of Jesus as Son of God/Messiah, but not in his pre-existence. The reason we find nothing beyond the implication that "Jesus was pre-existent *in the mind of God*" is that Matthew in fact intended nothing more than *that God always planned to send the Messiah*. It is important to distinguish among the various senses of "pre-existence" so as not to pre-judge the case on the basis of an over-simplified definition of the term (see Fred B. Craddock, *The Pre-Existence of Christ in the New Testament* [New York: Abingdon, 1968] 18–19; and Hamerton-Kelly, 21, 77–79). But I do not see that it contributes very much to an understanding of Matthew's christology to claim for it this very limited sense of pre-existence. It seems almost self-evident that Matthew believed that the appearance of Jesus was in accordance with God's preconceived plan. But I do not see that this warrants talk of *Jesus'* pre-existence or of *incarnation*.

Chapter Eight

Matthew: Sermon and Story

Janice Capel Anderson

Die Zweideutigkeit des Geistes scheint ein Problem jeder charisma-tischen Bewegung vor allem in der zweiten und in späteren Gene-rationen zu sein. Das macht die konkrete Bestimmung unserer Falschpropheten schwierig. Entsprechend vielfältig ist die Palette der Vorschläge: Zeloten, Pharisäer, Essener, strenge Judenchristen, Pauliner. Am meisten Zustimmung findet heute der Vorschlag von G. Barth, in den Falschpropheten hellenistische Antinomisten zu sehen. Der text gibt keine genaueren Informationen. – Ulrich Luz, *Das Evangelium nach Matthäus* (1. Teilband; EKK; Zurich: Benziger Verlag und Neukirchen-Vluyn: Neukirchener Verlag, 1985) 402–403.

To read is to play the role of a reader and to interpret is to posit an experience of reading. - Jonathan D. Culler, *On Deconstruction* (Ithaca: Cornell University Press, 1982) 67.

Introduction

This essay is an exercise in reader-response criticism. It has two purposes. The first is to demonstrate that the Sermon on the Mount plays an integral role in the Gospel as narrative—to show several inseparable connections between sermon and story. [1] The second is to raise the question of the criteria modern biblical scholars use to

---

[1] In a 1987 essay Edgar Krentz noted that narrative analysis must take the lengthy Matthean discourses seriously ("Community and Character," in *Society of Biblical Literature 1987 Seminar Papers*, ed. Kent Harold Richards [Atlanta: Scholars Press, 1987] 567 and n. 17). He praised Richard Edwards *(Matthew's Story of Jesus* [Philadelphia: Fortress, 1986]) for doing so and criticized (unfairly, I think) Jack D. Kingsbury *(Matthew As Story* [Philadelphia: Fortress, 1986]) for not doing so. That narrative criticism of the gospels arose primarily in conjunction with Mark perhaps explains why scholars have not emphasized the role of discourses more frequently.

measure the adequacy of various readings of the Gospel and the set of values and interests those criteria embody.[2]

Many interpreters have drawn attention to connections between the Sermon on the Mount (SM) and the rest of the Gospel. Key words and themes have been traced. Some have argued that the SM (5–7) and the miracle chapters (8–9) are the meat in a sandwich formed by two summary passages concerning Jesus' teaching, preaching, and healing (4:23–25=9:35).[3] The SM and the miracle chapters offer a scenic depiction of the activities described in the summaries. Other interpreters have noted the similarities between the warnings against unspecified hypocrites in 6:1–18 and the condemnations of the scribes and Pharisees in Chapter 23.[4] I will show how two passages, 5:31–32 and 7:15–20, contribute to the development of character and plot as the Gospel unfolds. I will focus on the part these passages play in the temporal process of reading the narrative. Thus, my essay involves in a certain sense a re-telling of the Gospel.[5] It also follows the convention of treating the Gospel as a coherent whole.[6]

In order to encourage conversation between the practitioners of various scholarly methods, I will limit my use of literary jargon. I will bracket the complex issues of defining plot and character, simply assuming standard English dictionary conceptions.[7] Given the

---

[2] After all, as Robert Scholes ("Deconstruction and Communication," *Critical Inquiry* 14 [1988] 294) points out, even Derrida holds that there are "protocols of reading." Many of the concerns I have are illuminated by Elisabeth Schüssler Fiorenza's SBL presidential address, "The Ethics of Interpretation: De-centering Biblical Scholarship," *JBL* 107 (1988) 3–17, Werner Kelber's presentation at the 1987 SBL annual meeting, "Gospel Narrative and Critical Theory" (*BTB* 18 [1988] 130–136) and Rudolf Bultmann's classic, "Is Exegesis without Presuppositions Possible?" in *Existence and Faith* (New York: World, 1961) 287–296.

[3] H. J. Held, "Matthew as Interpreter of the Miracle Stories," *Tradition and Interpretation in Matthew*, ed. G. Bornkamm, G. Barth, and H. J. Held (Philadelphia: Westminster, 1963) 249f., Jack D. Kingsbury, "The 'Miracle Chapters' of Matthew 8–9," *CBQ* 40 (1978) 566ff., and William G. Thompson, "Reflections on the Composition of Matthew 8:1–9:34," *CBQ* 33 (1971) 366ff.

[4] For example, W. D. Davies, *The Setting of the Sermon on the Mount* (Cambridge: Cambridge University Press, 1966) 291–292, who asks us to compare 7:15–21 with 23:2–3; 7:1ff. and 23:4; 5:14–16 and 23:16; 6:16–18 and 23:25–28; 5:12 and 23:34–36.

[5] This procedure should be familiar from Edwards, especially 9–10.

[6] For a discussion of this convention, see Stephen D. Moore, "Are the Gospels Unified Narratives," in *Society of Biblical Literature 1987 Seminar Papers*, 443–458 and the response by Mary Ann Tolbert (Private Circulation).

[7] As in M. H. Abrams, *A Glossary of Literary Terms* (4th ed.; New York: Holt,

concerns and content of this essay, however, the question "Who is the *reader*?" must be answered. Recent theoretical discussion has multiplied *readers* beyond number.[8] Shlomith Rimmon-Kenan notes that the list yields two extremes:

At one extreme the concept is of a real reader, whether a specific individual or the collective readership of a period. At the other, it is a theoretical construct implied or encoded in the text, representing the integration of data and the interpretive process "invited" by the text.[9]

When I speak of the reader I want to allude to both extremes because I want to hold in tension the role the text plays and the role real readers play in creating meaning as individuals and as possessors of shared conventions and codes. I wish to privilege neither text nor reader.[10] It is for this reason that I am partial to Wolfgang Iser's

---

Rinehart, Winston, 1981).

[8] For helpful surveys of reader-response criticism see Jane P. Tompkins, "An Introduction to Reader-Response Criticism," in *Reader-Response Criticism: From Formalism to Post-Structuralism,* ed. Jane P. Tompkins (Baltimore: Johns Hopkins University Press, 1980) ix-xxvi; and Robert M. Fowler, "Who is the Reader in Reader Response Criticism?" *Semeia* 31 (1985) 5–26. To these in 1995 I would add Stephen D. Moore's discussion in Chapter 6 of *Literary Criticism and the Gospels* (New Haven: Yale University Press, 1989) and Fowler's "Reader-response Criticism: Figuring Mark's Reader," in *Mark and Method: New Approaches in Biblical Interpretation,* ed. Janice Capel Anderson and Stephen D. Moore (Minneapolis: Fortress, 1992) 50–83.

[9] *Narrative Fiction: Contemporary Poetics* (London and New York: Methuen, 1983) 119. For Rimmon-Kenan the implied reader is an intratextual concept, an it, not a he or she.

[10] Feminist criticism helps to illumine many hermeneutic issues. If one simply thinks of a woman reading a patriarchal text—of the double movement of identifying with and resisting—one can see both the power of the text and the power of the reader and a third power—literary, social, and political codes and conventions. See Judith Fetterly, *The Resisting Reader* (Bloomington: Indiana University Press, 1978); Annette Kolodny, "A Map for Reading: On Gender and the Interpretation of Literary Texts," *NLH* 11 (1980) 451–67; Elizabeth. A. Flynn and Patricinio P. Schweickart, eds., *Gender and Reading* (Baltimore: Johns Hopkins University Press, 1986); Jonathan Culler, *On Deconstruction* (Ithaca: Cornell University Press, 1982) 43–64; Wayne C. Booth, "Freedom of Interpretation: Bakhtin and the Challenge of Feminist Criticism," *Critical Inquiry* 9 (1982) 45–76; Robin R. Warhol and Diane Price Herndl, eds., *Feminisms: An Anthology of Literary Theory and Criticism* (New Brunswick: Rutgers University Press, 1991. For Matthean criticism see Jane Schaberg, *The Illegitimacy of Jesus* (San Francisco: Harper and Row, 1987) 14–19 and my "Matthew: Gender and Reading," *Semeia* 28 (1983) 3–27; Antoinette Clark Wire, "Gender Roles in a Scribal Community " in *Social History of the Matthean Community,* ed. David L. Balch (Minneapolis: Fortress, 1991) 87–121; Elaine M. Wainright, *Towards a Feminist Critical Reading of the Gospel According to Matthew* (New York: de Gruyter, 1991) and Amy-Jill Levine, "Matthew" in *The*

definition of the implied reader. He defines the implied reader as a concept which "incorporates both the prestructuring of the potential meaning by the text, and the reader's actualization of this potential through the reading process."[11] His definition focuses on the interplay between internal textual structures and the standing point outside. It leaves room for the roles of text, reader, and context (including interpretive communities) in reading.[12]

Finally, although strong verbal repetition links both 5:31–32 and 7:15–20 to other portions of the Gospel, I am not concerned here with saying something about repetition *per se*. Rather, I am concerned with saying something about the reading process and interpretation. My treatment of the passages assumes the important functions of verbal repetition as it engages the memory, reduces noise in the communication channel, creates expectations, increases predictability, persuades, and reduces alternative interpretations. It also assumes the importance of variation (including the creation of contrasts and the creation of uncertainty requiring decision) and narrative context (including the building of associations and drawing of similarities and contrasts) in conjunction with repetition.[13]

Women's Bible Commentary, ed. Carol Newsome and Sharon H. Ringe (Louisville: Westminster/John Knox, 1992); Kathleen E. Corley, *Private Women/Public Meals: Social Conflict in the Synoptic Tradition* (Peabody, MA: Hendrickson, 1993).

[11] *The Implied Reader* (Baltimore: Johns Hopkins University Press, 1974; German orig. 1972) xii.

[12] Some will consider me retrograde and overly text-oriented for choosing Iser. Also, distinctions could be multiplied. For example, we could also distinguish the narratee and/or the encoded reader/narratee—all as intratextual functions. See Kingsbury, *Story*, 36–38, relying on Seymour Chatman, *Story and Discourse* (Ithaca: Cornell University Press, 1978) and Norman R. Petersen, "The Reader in the Gospel," *Neotestamentica* 18 (1984) 39–43, influenced by Peter J. Rabinowitz's distinction between actual audience, authorial audience (the intratextual hypothetical audience the author has in mind when he or she writes), narrative audience (the intratextual narratee who naively accepts the narrator's tale), and the ideal narrative audience ("Truth in Fiction: A Reexamination of Audiences," *Critical Inquiry* 4 [1977] 121–41 and "'What's Hecuba to Us?': The Audience's Experience of Literary Borrowing," in *The Reader in the Text*, ed. Susan Rubin Suleiman and Inge Crosman [Princeton: Princeton University, 1980] 241–263). In Matthew, since the narratee is not highly characterized, the distinction between the narratee and implied reader is blurred.

[13] For a discussion of verbal repetition in Matthew, see Janice Capel Anderson, "Double and Triple Stories, the Implied Reader and Redundancy in Matthew," *Semeia* 31 (1985) 71–90; Fred W. Burnett, "Prolegomenon to Reading Matthew's Eschatological Discourse: Redundancy and the Education of the Reader in Matthew," *Semeia* 31 (1985) 91–110; and my dissertation "Over and Over and Over

5:31–32

In the Sermon on the Mount Jesus offers an authoritative legal interpretation to the disciples and crowds forbidding divorce except on the grounds of unchastity. Later, as Jesus enters Judea on his way to Jerusalem and the passion, the Jewish leaders question him about divorce. The questioning occurs in the context of a series of controversies (19:3–9; 21:15–16, 23–46; 22:1–45) and passion predictions (20:17–19, 28) that leads up to the harsh condemnations of the Jewish leaders in Chapter 23. Jesus' authoritative interpretation in the Sermon on the Mount prepares the reader to view the Jewish leaders and their actions in a negative light in the later context. This contributes to the building tensions between Jesus and the Jewish leaders which lead to the passion. Below I will trace the reading process involved in more detail.

The implied reader finds 5:31–32 in a series of antitheses that contrast Jesus' stricter interpretation of the law with what was said by the men of old.[14] The effect of the antitheses is to establish Jesus as the authoritative interpreter of the law. In 5:31–32 he recalls the requirement of a bill of divorce, an allusion to Deuteronomy 24:1–4.[15] In contrast, he forbids divorce except on the grounds of unchastity (*porneias*). This authoritative teaching sets the stage for what is to come in 19:3–9.

The implied reader comes to 19:3–9 fresh from the community discourse and a summary passage indicating Jesus' entry into Judea beyond the Jordan. The reader knows the significance of this geographical shift from 16:21, 17:9–13, and 17:22–23. Jesus is moving closer to Jerusalem and the passion. The Pharisees approach Jesus, tempting him with a legal question about the grounds for divorce. The implied reader already knows from 5:31–32 that there is only one proper ground for divorce. The reader has knowledge superior to that of the tempters. Jesus cites Genesis 1:27 and 2:24 as evidence that God

---

Again: Studies in Matthean Repetition," University of Chicago, March 1985 (revised edition *Matthew's Narrative Web: Over and Over and Over Again* [JSNTSS 91; Sheffield: Sheffield Academic Press, 1994].

[14] See G. Barth, "Matthew's Understanding of the Law," *Tradition and Interpretation in Matthew*, 93ff.

[15] See Alan H. McNeile, *The Gospel According to St. Matthew* (Grand Rapids: Baker, 1980; reprint Macmillan, 1915) 66; W. C. Allen, *St. Matthew*, (3rd ed.; ICC; Edinburgh: T. and T. Clark, 1977) 51–52; and Robert Guelich, *The Sermon on the Mount* (Waco: Word, 1982) 198–199.

does not will divorce. Here the reader is given new information—the basis for Jesus' injunction in 5:31–32. The Jewish leaders refer to Moses' command to give a bill of divorce and to dismiss, i.e., what was said (5:31=19:7), what has already been rejected. Jesus responds that Moses allowed this because of their hardness of heart, "but from the beginning it was not so." What the Pharisees view as God's will was only a concession to hardheartedness. Jesus then repeats the authoritative interpretation of 5:32 with slight variation (5:32=19:9, twelve words in common).[16] Jesus confirms his earlier teaching in a new context. In the process the implied reader judges the Jewish leaders negatively.

The negative characterization of the Jewish leaders is accomplished not only through the implied reader's prior knowledge of Jesus' authoritative interpretation of the law, but also through (1) the narrator's characterization of them as "tempting him" (*peirazontes auton*) and (2) through the arrangement of subsequent episodes and passion predictions. The description of the Pharisees *approaching* and *tempting* Jesus in 19:3 echoes 16:1 where the narrator says Pharisees and Sadducees *approached* Jesus *tempting* him by asking for a sign.[17] It anticipates 22:18 and 22:35. In 22:18 Jesus calls the Pharisees and Herodians hypocrites, echoing 6:2, 5, 16 and 15:7 and anticipating 23:13, 15, 23, 25, 27. He asks why they *tempt* him. They have tried to ensnare him with another legal question, tribute to Caesar. In 22:35 a Pharisee *tempts* Jesus with yet another legal question, the greatest commandment. The Jewish leaders are not only false interpreters of the law, they are aligned with the devil, the *"tempting one"* (4:3). As the narrative continues after 19:3–9 the reader learns that the question about divorce is simply one in a series of incidents in which the Jewish leaders seek to tempt and entrap Jesus. Along with the passion predictions and the Bethany-Temple scenes, these scenes are part of a pattern that prepares the reader for Jesus' condemnations of the Jewish leaders in Chapter 23 and for the passion in Jerusalem.

Previous scholars have noted the verbal similarities between 5:31–32 and 19:3–9. The existence of two similar passages has provoked interpretation. However, most scholars have simply explained away their existence by assigning them to different sources. Thus, they have missed their role in the characterization and plot and the important

---

[16] The variations seem associated with making the connection to 19:10–12.

[17] Tempting was not something the Jewish leaders had done in the initial sign of Jonah episode (12:38–42=16:1–4).

effects their existence has on the reader as the Gospel unfolds through time.[18] They have not seen the important link between sermon and story, or rather that the sermon is an inseparable part of the story.

Matthew 7:15–20

In the latter portions of the Sermon on the Mount, Jesus warns the disciples and crowds, and thus the implied reader, against false prophets who are wolves in sheep's clothing. These false prophets are to be known by their evil fruits. This nonspecific warning echoes the words of John the Baptist in 3:7–10 which warn the scribes and Pharisees that they must produce fruit and not count on their Abrahamic ancestry to save them from the coming wrath. It, along with 3:7–10, prepares the implied reader for Jesus' outright condemnations of the Jewish leaders as those who produce evil fruit or no fruit at all in 12:33–37 and in Chapter 21. Like 6:1–18, 7:15–20 warns about characters indirectly in order to prepare the reader to take a certain view of them and to prepare for the subsequent role they play in the plot. These passages plant suspicions that narrative events and verbal repetition reinforce when very similar words are specifically applied later in the narrative. The reader has the sense, "Aha, I suspected as much. I knew it all along." This is at least one reading of the role that the actual reader is invited to play.[19]

However, many real readers have actualized the "reconstruction—inviting structures"[20] of the text rather differently. The identity of the false prophets particularly is an interpretive crux. The existence of readings of the false prophets as diverse as Hellenistic antinomian charismatics, Pharisees, Jewish-Christians, Essenes, gnostics, Zealots, Paulinists, etc. indicates both something about the role of the reader in the text and the actual readers outside the text.[21] After examining

---

[18] The exceptions are Edwards (69) who notes that "Jesus affirms what had been said earlier about the reasons for divorce" (5:31) and Daniel Patte (*The Gospel According to Matthew: A Structural Commentary on Matthew's Faith* [Philadelphia: Fortress, 1987] 266), who notes about 19:9: "Jesus' concluding statement is thematic . . . and thus expresses the preceding points in terms of the knowledge of readers who should recall the saying in 5:32."

[19] This is, in fact, the reading I gave in "Over and Over and Over Again," 132–37 (in *Matthew's Narrative Web*, 105–08).

[20] Rimmon-Kenan, 119.

[21] For bibliographies and summaries of various readings of the passages see Guelich, 390–403; David Hill, "False Prophets and Charismatics: Structure and Interpretation in Matthew 7:15–23," *Biblica* 57 (1976) 327–348; and Ulrich Luz,

the interpretations of a number of modern scholars, certain points of departure in the text can be recognized.[22] These include the following:

1. The term beware (*prosechete*, 7:15; 6:1; 10:17; 16:6, 11, 12).
2. The term false prophets (*pseudoprophētōn*, 7:15; 24:11, 24)
3. The term lawlessness (*anomian*, 7:23, 13:41, 23:28, 24:12).
4. The wolf in sheep's clothing motif and the terms wolf (7:15 and 10:16) and sheep (7:15; 9:36; 10:6; 10:16; 12:11, 12; 15:24; 18:12; 25:32–33).
5. Prospective and retrospective associations with producing fruit (3:7–10=7:15–20=12:33–37 and Chapter 21).
6. The inclusio of 7:16–20 (Does this enclose a comment on 7:15 or is it a parenthesis after which the discussion of false prophets continues in 7:21–23. Does 7:21 introduce a new topic?).
7. Relationships between this passage and other passages not specified above (variously identified and construed).
8. The verbal and social codes and general knowledge the text presupposes (Again, variously identified and construed).

The implied reader must form various hypotheses in response to these points. He or she may form several hypotheses over time, the first not being quite effaced by the last.[23] The fact that almost all of the points mentioned involve references forward and backward over the course of the Gospel indicates the importance of the temporal ordering of reading (or hearing). Thus, in interpreting 7:15–20 and its role in the Gospel as a whole, it is important to ask what information the reader has been given prior to reading the passage? What

---

Das Evangelium nach Matthäus (1. Teilband, Mt. 1–7; *EKK;* Zurich: Benziger Verlag and Neukirchen-Vluyn: Neukirchener Verlag, 1985) 400–411.

[22] Stanley E. Fish ("Interpreting the Variorum," in Tompkins, 164–184) first taught me to look to interpretative cruxes as indications of the reading experience. The points of departure I have noted are indications of where the text elicits a reader's activity. As points uncovered by looking at scholarly practice, they could be considered evidence of Michael Riffaterre's superreader ("Describing Poetic Structures: Two Approaches to Baudelaire's 'Les Chats,'" in Tompkins, 37–38). Menakhem Perry ("Literary Dynamics: How the Order of a Text Creates its Meaning," *Poetics Today* 1:1–2 (1979) 35–64 and 311–361) also analyzes various scholarly responses. In his case they are to Faulkner's "A Rose for Emily." He also emphasizes the character of the reading experience along what he calls the text-continuum.

[23] Real readers base their readings on one or more of these points of departure. Often they give more weight to some points than others in constructing their interpretations.

expectations, what kind of "set" has been created? How has the reader been trained to read the passage? Then we must ask whether the reader's provisional interpretation is confirmed or confounded as the narrative continues.

Prior to the SM the birth story introduces Jesus as Messiah, Son of David, Son of Abraham, savior of his people, Emmanuel-God with Us, King of the Jews, and Shepherd of God's people Israel. Jesus is established as the central character and as a reliable character aligned with the values of the implied author. The story of Herod and the Magi foreshadows indirectly the conflict with the Jewish leaders and the expansion of mission to the Gentiles later in the Gospel. Immediately following the birth story, John the Baptist is introduced as a reliable character. John confronts the Pharisees and Sadducees. He calls them a brood of vipers. He warns them about bearing good fruit and the coming eschatological Judge. The description of the Judge forms the introduction to Jesus as an adult. Jesus is baptized and blessed by the reliable supernatural voice as God's son. Following the baptism, there is the temptation of Jesus as God's son. After John is delivered up, Jesus departs to Galilee of the Gentiles. Jesus, then, begins his ministry with the exact proclamation that John earlier made (3:2=4:17). He calls four disciples (4:18–22). A summary passage describes Jesus' teaching, preaching, and healing activities and the crowds which surround him as a result. This sets the stage for the SM delivered to the disciples and crowds.

The beginning of the SM establishes Jesus as the authoritative interpreter of the law, calls for a righteousness to exceed that of the scribes and Pharisees, warns against hypocrisy, teaches where one's proper loyalty belongs, etc. Chapter 7:15–20 comes toward the end of the sermon. It belongs to a series of exhortations preceding the parable of the two builders. The first word in 7:15, *prosechete*, echoes the warning in 6:1 not to be like the hypocrites. The most striking echo of previous material, however, is the parallel between John's warning to the Pharisees and Sadducees to bear good fruit in 3:7–10 and Jesus' warning about the false prophets. Extensive verbal repetition engages the reader's memory (3:10b=7:19, eleven words in common). Since John has been established as a reliable character and since he and Jesus preach the same message, verbal repetition leads the implied reader to suspect, at least provisionally, that the false prophets are the Jewish leaders. There have been no prior references to false prophets, wolves or sheep—except to Jesus as one who will shepherd my [God's] people Israel (2:6). No "bad guys" have been introduced save for Herod, the devil-tempter, the potentially bad Pharisees and Sadducees, and the unspecified hypocrites in 6:1–18.

If 7:20 forms the end of the passage and 7:21 introduces a new topic, then the reader must simply continue reading passages subsequent to the SM to see if the hypothesis is correct. If the reader views 7:16 and 7:20 as a parenthesis, however, then the hypothesis must be enlarged or modified by verses 21–23. The reader learns that what counts is doing the will of the Father. Simply calling Jesus "Lord" or even *prophesying* (supplying a possible link to the pseudo-*prophets* of 7:15), exorcizing or doing mighty works in Jesus' name is not sufficient. People who call Jesus "Lord" but who do not do the will of the Father work lawlessness (*anomian*). Perhaps, then, the Jewish leaders will call Jesus "Lord," but will not do the will of the Father, but lawlessness. Perhaps the false prophets are not the Jewish leaders but, like them, need to produce fruit, do the will of the Father, rather than lawlessness. Perhaps the Jewish leaders are a subgroup of a larger group that could be labeled false prophets.

The SM ends with the parable of the two builders emphasizing hearing and doing Jesus' words found in the sermon. The narrator notes the crowd's (to whom the Sermon was addressed along with the disciples) reaction of astonishment: "For he was teaching them as one having authority, and not as their scribes (7:29)." This brief indication along with the rest of the Gospel through Chapter 21 confirms the implied reader's initial hypothesis that the false prophets are the Jewish leaders, a group that produces evil fruit or no fruit at all.

In Chapters 8 and 9 Jesus' miraculous healings and exorcisms demonstrate to the implied reader his power from God. They also provoke various reactions from different character groups that will be developed as the narrative continues. The implied reader begins to judge characters by their contrasting reactions to Jesus. In 9:1–7 the first confrontation between Jesus and the Jewish leaders occurs. Some of the scribes inwardly accuse Jesus of blasphemy. Jesus reads their thoughts, knowing that they think *ponēra* in their hearts (bearing *charpous ponōrous*). The conflict gradually builds in 9:10–13 and 9:32–34. In 9:35 the summary passage which forms an inclusio around chapters 5–9 appears. In 9:36–10:42 Jesus exhibits concern for the crowds and sends the twelve on a mission with a lengthy charge. The narrator reports that Jesus viewed the crowds as "*sheep* without a shepherd" (9:36). Jesus commissions the twelve to go to "the lost *sheep* of the house of Israel" (10:6=15:24). In 10:16–18 he sends the disciples forth as *sheep* in the midst of wolves, the only other reference to wolves in the Gospel. The sheep metaphor indicates to the implied reader at this point members or potential members of God's flock; so far it has only been used to refer to the Jewish crowds and disciples. The wolves are "men" of whom the disciples are to beware (*prosechete*, 10:17=6:1=7:15=16:6, 11, 12).[24] They will deliver the disciples to councils, scourge them in *their* synagogues, and bring them before leaders and kings for Jesus' sake for a testimony to *them* and to the Gentiles. The wolves are not explicitly identified as the Jewish leaders, but the reader perceives a very thin veil. If *they* called the housemaster Beelzebul, how much more the members of his house (10:25=9:34=12:24).

As in the SM there are general references in the Missionary Discourse which are developed and attached explicitly to the Jewish leaders later in the Gospel. The words of 10:17, 23 are applied to them in 23:34, 36.[25] Verse 25 alludes to the Jewish leaders' earlier claim that Jesus exorcizes by the power of the ruler of demons (9:34). It foreshadows 12:24 when they will say that he exorcizes by Beelzebul, the ruler of demons.

In chapters 11 and 12 Jesus' conflict with the Jewish leaders blossoms. In 12:9–15 Jesus compares the man with the withered hand to a *sheep* who should be pulled out of a ditch on the Sabbath. Again, Jesus cares for members of the flock. The Jewish leaders use the man's predicament to accuse Jesus—of violating the law (12:10). Following the healing, the Jewish leaders begin the process that leads to Jesus' death—they "take counsel" to destroy him (12:14).[26] This is followed by the exorcism (mentioned above) after which the Jewish leaders declare that Jesus exorcizes by the power of Beelzebul (9:32–34=10:25=12:22–24). Jesus responds with a lengthy condemnation in which he applies the same words that John had used to warn the Jewish leaders in 3:7–10 and Jesus had used against the unspecified false prophets in sheep's clothing in 7:15–20. In the first instance the Jewish leaders were warned that they needed to repent and could not rely on being children of Abraham. In the second the crowds and

---

[24] Matthew always uses *prosechete* to warn against the Jewish leaders, explicitly in 16:6, 11, 12 and implicitly in 6:1, 7:15, 10:17. See Guelich, 390.

[25] Complicating factors are the verbal parallels between 10:17–22 and 24:9–14.

[26] The words *symboulion elabon* play an important role in the Jewish leaders' plot against Jesus (12:14=22:15=27:1=28:12, see also 26:3–4).

disciples were warned of false prophets who looked like members of God's flock, [27] but were wolves who produced evil fruit. Here the Jewish leaders are specifically condemned as those bad trees producing bad fruit, as evil men who must put forth out of their evil treasure. The Jewish leaders have blasphemed against the Holy Spirit, a sin that cannot be forgiven. As the Gospel unfolds, the Jewish leaders are increasingly portrayed as evil and incapable of the repentance for which John called. The fruit imagery and their reactions to Jesus in the first twelve chapters reinforce the characterization of the Jewish leaders as bad trees producing evil fruit. The reader gradually sees them in a worse and worse light, more and more opposed to Jesus.

A great deal more might be said about passages which confirm the proposed initial reading of 7:15–20; I will discuss only two more. The first is Chapter 21. There the reader finds the final references to the Jewish leaders as those who produce evil fruit or no fruit at all.[28] In chapter 21 Jesus triumphantly enters Jerusalem, cleanses the temple, and heals the blind and lame. The chief priests and scribes are incensed at the marvels he has done and the cries of the children, "Hosanna to the Son of David" (21:15). After they confront him, he leaves the city for Bethany. On his return the fruit imagery becomes concrete. He curses a barren fig tree which withers instantly. Reentering the temple, he again confronts the Jewish leaders. The chief priests and elders of the people question the source of his authority. He responds with a question concerning the authority of John. They dare not answer because they fear the crowd, who "have John as a prophet" (21:26). Jesus proceeds to tell them two parables, the parable of the Two Sons (21:28–32) and the parable of the Wicked Tenants (21:33–41). He concludes by saying, "Therefore, I tell you, that the kingdom of God will be taken from you and will be given to a nation producing the fruits of it" (21:43). Although the phrase is very short, the reader hears the echoes of 3:7–10, 7:15–20, and 12:33–34 where the Jewish leaders and the production (*poieō*) of fruit are linked. Like the fig tree, the Jewish leaders are barren. They do not do the will of the Father (21:31=12:50, five words in common). They have not responded properly to Jesus. They do not render the fruits of God's vineyard to God. They will be judged and wither as the cursed fig tree.

---

[27] Or who were dressed in prophetic garb. See Guelich, 392 and McNeile, 95.

[28] This section on Chapter 21 comes essentially from my "Over and Over and Over Again," 136–137 (*Matthew's Narrative Web*, 108–109).

The chief priests and Pharisees know that Jesus tells the two parables concerning them and seek to seize him. However, they fear the crowds who have Jesus, like John, as a prophet (21:46=21:26, five words in common). The Jewish leaders are portrayed as the enemies of John and Jesus, who warn the reader that the character of the leaders can be known by their fruits.

A final passage that both confirms and raises questions about the reader's hypothesis that 7:15–20 is to be read as a distinct unit and refers to the Jewish leaders is 23:25–28. Jesus labels the scribes and Pharisees as hypocrites (=6:1–18 where the hypocrites are not specifically identified) who are outwardly beautiful and righteous but within (*hesōthen de*) are full of robbery, intemperance, hypocrisy, and lawlessness (*anomias*). This accords well with the description of the false prophets of 7:15–20 as sheep without and wolves within (*hesōthen de*). However, the term lawlessness provides a retrospective connection with 7:23 and 13:41 as well as a prospective connection with 24:12. These passages all speak of lawlessness in an eschatological context. In 13:36ff. Jesus explains to the disciples the parable of the tares. The ones doing lawlessness are tares who will be burnt in the fiery furnace. In Chapter 24 again addressing the disciples—in response to the disciples showing him the temple—Jesus offers the eschatological discourse.[29] In 24:12 Jesus says that "because of the increase of lawlessness, the love of the many will grow cold." This reference to lawlessness comes in close contiguity with the only other Matthean references outside of 7:15 to false prophets, 24:11, 24. False prophets *will* arise to lead many astray before the end (24:11). The end will not occur until the kingdom has been preached to all nations. False Christs and false prophets *will* arise showing great signs and wonders to lead astray, if possible, even the elect (24:24).

If the false prophets of 7:15, 24:11, and 24:24 are construed as part of the same group, then the reader may retrospectively abandon the original hypothesis that the false prophets were the Jewish leaders and include 7:21–23 as part of the warning beginning with 7:15. The false prophets who produce lawlessness are people who call Jesus "Lord," who produce mighty works and prophesy in his name. The elect must be wary of them and identify them by their fruits. *Or*, the reader, given 12:22–37; 3:7–10; 23:25–28; etc., may read the references to false prophets in 24:11, 24 as Jewish leaders who may lead the disciples and

---

[29] Cf. Burnett, 98–101.

the "many" astray.[30] The possible flies in the soup for this reading are the references to *anomian* in 7:23=24:12. *Or,* the reader may decide that the false prophets in 24:11, 24 are not related to 7:15. *Or,* the reader given all the alternative hypotheses constituted reading processually—7:15–20 read as a single unit, 7:15–23 as one unit, and reading both prospectively and retrospectively in the light of all the other passages mentioned above—may see all those who do not do the will of the Father, who are workers of lawlessness, who bear evil fruit, who will lead astray—all those present and future—as false prophets and enemies whether they claim to be members of God's flock, as members of the character group the Jewish leaders or as those who claim allegiance to Jesus.[31]

What do we make of the reading process as I have constructed it? Do we choose between alternative final hypotheses or interpretations achieved after the whole text has been actualized? Do we concentrate on the experience of reading and the effect of various hypotheses formulated as the reader reads, each one not quite effaced by the previous one? How do we decide? What are our criteria? What is at stake? The very least one can say, given my reconstruction and the various scholarly interpretations, is that in the course of reading the Gospel the identity of the false prophets is very much in question.

---

[30] The immediate context of 24:11 may suggest, but does not require, that the false prophets arise from among the disciples—the "you." Jesus expands his comments beyond the twelve with his references to the "many" and the "elect." There is no immediate context surrounding 24:24 which determines the origin of the false prophets and false Christs.

[31] This both/and suggestion is different from Guelich's both/and alternative: "Rather than *either* a Jewish or a Christian group . . . , the *false prophets* represented *both* elements as vigorous Jewish Christians who sought to implement the strict adherence to the Mosaic Law (Käsemann, "Beginnings," 86–87) and may have sought to impede the Gentile mission of Matthew's church as well (*Sermon,* 393)." It differs in that it does not go outside the story world to posit a "real" group represented and in emphasizing the reading experience along the text continuum. It also differs from Paul S. Minear's ("False Prophecy and Hypocrisy in the Gospel of Matthew" in *Neues Testament und Kirche. Für Rudolf Schnackenburg,* ed. Joachim Gnilka [Freiburg: Herder, 1974] 76–93) suggestion that 7:15–23 (read as about Christian false prophets) and passages about hypocrisy (including Chapter 23 directed in the narrative to the scribes and Pharisees) are both warnings to prophet-leaders in Matthew's community.

Conclusion

The two purposes of this essay were to demonstrate links between the Sermon on the Mount and the rest of the Matthean narrative and to raise questions about the criteria biblical scholars use to judge readings of the Gospel. With regard to the first purpose, my analysis makes a case that the sermons in Matthew are an integral part of the Gospel as narrative—and of the experience of reading it. They are not simply plunked-down repositories of teaching in the midst of an independent story. My analysis indicates how elements of the SM lead the reader to view characters and events in a certain light. It points to the effect of the arrangement of elements along the text continuum. In traditional categories, it shows how certain elements contribute to the development of character and plot.[32] It shows that if one reads the Gospel as a narrative whole there are important links between sermon and story.

With regard to the second purpose, my analysis begins to point to conventions governing the creation of various sorts of readings, and implicitly, the criteria by which they are judged. For example, the central goal of historical critics is to reconstruct the meaning of the Gospel in its original historical context not to create a reading of the Gospel as a coherent narrative. Imagining the experience of a first-time reader reading the Gospel from beginning to end may seem beside the point to historical critics. Indeed, both form and redaction critics treat the Gospel as full of seams and inconsistencies rather than as a coherent narrative. These seams and inconsistencies reflect the historical circumstances which shaped the Gospel. In the same way that Pauline scholars imaginatively reconstruct Paul's conversation partners, historical critics treat elements of the Gospel as transparent keys to an original historical situation. Narrative or reader-response critics, however, challenge historical critics on this very point. They argue that historical critics tend to jump to their hypothetical historical contexts at least one step too quickly. They do not take seriously the entire reading process. Possible external referents are more important than the relationships of elements within the Gospel.

---

[32] An important side comment I would like to make is that I am not sure we have gotten all the gold out of the mine of a formalist approach to the gospels yet. After the fragmentation of previous years, there is still much to be learned by analyzing the gospels as wholes apart from historical or other objectives. Traditional narrative categories still can teach us a lot.

Historical critics treat the Gospel as an allegory. For narrative critics, characters and character groups are not merely ciphers for individuals or groups in the evangelist's historical context or that of the historical Jesus. The interpreter should not assume, for example, that the disciples directly represent the members (or leaders) of Matthew's church or that the Jewish leaders directly represent opponents. Further, since the Matthean implied reader judges *all* the characters— referred to and depicted—from the perspective of the implied author, actual readers do not necessarily identify with one group or another.

Different goals and methods govern how historical and literary critics read and judge readings of Matthew. Nevertheless, for some critics historical and literary approaches complement one another. With regard to 7:15–20, for example, my analysis reveals aspects of the reading process that led Barth to label the false prophets Hellenistic antinomians or Hill to label them the Pharisees across the street.[33] From my "points of departure," one can see how each actualized the text's potentialities, the particular interpretive assumptions and moves they made. This foregrounds the presuppositions underlying each historical reconstruction. Similarly, one can ask what the reading experience might reveal about the authorial audience, the audience the author posited when composing. What prior knowledge is presumed on the part of the audience? Where are they located in space and time? What moves seem designed to educate them? Petersen, Culpepper, and Kingsbury have treated the implied reader as an index to the authorial audience in Mark, John, and Matthew respectively.[34] In reconstructing an authorial audience, we would still not have a description of the original audience. However, we would at least have an interpretation of the actual author's view of them.

Given this angle of inquiry, my analysis raises the question of why the actual author might have created the reading experience described. Why is the reader given knowledge superior to that of the Jewish leaders? Why are they not pictured as members of the audience

---

[33] Even using traditional methods Barth's argument could be questioned because he does not explain 23:25–28.

[34] See Petersen, "The Reader in the Gospel," Culpepper, *Anatomy of the Fourth Gospel* (Philadelphia: Fortress, 1983) 203–24 and Kingsbury, *Story*, 120–33. Many interpreters find direct commentary from narrator to narratee especially helpful in reconstructing an authorial audience. There are problems, however. How are implied reader, narratee, and authorial audience defined, distinguished (if they are distinguished) and related to one another?

for the SM? Why are they progressively tarred? Why, in the case of 7:15–20, create certain hypotheses and cause their reconsideration, if not effacement? In asking such questions, we must keep in mind (1) that the answers might simply have to do with narrative logic and (2) that the resultant picture is an interpretation. Historical critics reconstruct an historical context out of the Gospel and limited additional data and proceed to use that context to interpret the Gospel.

My analysis suggests that the reception history of Matthew could supply additional extra-gospel data for building such interpretations. Early commentaries, manuscript versions, and quotations from the Gospel would provide a record of some of the earliest responses. This would help to describe the role of the implied reader as well as how some actual readers construed the gospel. It also *might* bring us closer to reconstructing the kind of responses the Gospel elicited from the original audience—if that is our goal.

A reader-response analysis highlights the importance of goals, assumptions, and conventions. The interaction of text, individual interpreters, and interpretive communities is complex. The notion of "points of departure" and the undeniable existence of multiple interpretations raises difficult questions about the nature of a text and the way we "know" texts. Who decides which readings are better than others, for what purposes, according to what criteria? I have created one sort of reading of Matthew, a powerful text which is both sermon and story. I hope that I have also stimulated discussion about the roles and powers of its readers.

Epilogue 1995

I originally wrote "Matthew: Sermon and Story" for the 1988 Annual Meeting of the Society of Biblical Literature's Group on Matthew. Today I doubt that many narrative critics would challenge my first thesis, the integration of the Matthean sermons with the rest of the gospel. The extensive network of verbal repetition throughout the Gospel constitutes strong evidence. When this is combined with the central presupposition of Gospel narrative criticism—reading the Gospel as a narrative whole—integration is almost a foregone conclusion. It is hard to imagine discussing characterization or plot while ignoring a significant portion of the Gospel. Yet the integration of sermon and story may remain a question for scholars who focus on the Gospel as a collection of redacted traditions. They are predisposed to see the sermons as alien tracts plopped down into a preexisting Markan outline or collections of teachings that Mark could easily eliminate when he created an epitome of Matthew. Some reader-response critics would emphasize that my reconstruction involved constructs of an implied reader and a first-time reading process that mask my own role as a critic who interprets from a very specific social location. These observations, however, lead me to believe that questions about interpretive criteria and conventions are just as relevant today as they were seven years ago. How does a particular method shape a reading? How do gender, culture, theology, and ideological commitments do so? Should biblical scholars insist on a single reading or allow for multiple readings? If they allow for multiple readings, what are the criteria for judging those readings?

Examining scholarly and other readings of a text, particularly readings of those textual elements we label interpretive cruxes, highlights the dance of interpretation between text and interpreters through time and across cultures. Over the past seven years the differences among scholarly dance partners have become even more apparent as narrative, reader-response, social-scientific, historical-critical, and post-structuralist approaches have increasingly established themselves as distinct alternatives. There have also been increasingly different sorts of partners on the dance floor as Feminist, Womanist, Mujerista, African-American male, and various Two-Thirds World critics have come to the fore. The more partners on the floor, the more the dances look different even when each is dancing with Matthew. The second goal of my essay, encouraging discussion of criteria biblical scholars use to judge readings of the Gospel, seems even more important today. I am not arguing for a kind of naive relativism in which one interpretation is as good as another. I do hope that discussants will acknowledge that each approach follows conventions. Each reveals and conceals, includes and excludes. Polkas, minuets, and the twist are all dances, even if they are not identical.

Chapter Nine

Matthew's Gospel as A Test Case for Hermeneutical Reflections[*]

RUDOLF SCHNACKENBURG
TRANSLATED BY RONALD D. WITHERUP, S.S.

Joachim Gnilka dedicated a contribution to me, in the Festchrift published on the occasion of my 60th birthday, entitled, "Methodology and Hermeneutics: Reflections on the Situation of Exegesis."[1] Now fifteen years later, in this Festchrift on the occasion of his own 60th birthday, I would like to take up his question again and continue with some hermeneutical reflections in the contemporary situation which has changed again. The methodological instruments of our discipline in the intervening years have developed further and been refined, without making the hermeneutical question less difficult. Since we exegetes like to work on concrete material, I choose Matthew's Gospel with which I have dealt more intensively in the recent past, not as a test case for methodology, the evolution of which I presume, but for hermeneutics, the discipline of understanding. Even if I cannot discuss its philosophical, linguistic, and practical theological meaning, I hope to clarify somewhat its importance by means of concrete material from the Gospel. Concerning the reception of the biblical text in the contemporary horizon, when it comes to a melding of interpretational horizons (H. Gadamer), the altered contemporary situation must be taken into account. I do not go into the question of the general crisis of faith of our times, since others might want to elaborate the reasons

---

[*] *Editor's Note.* This article first appeared in German in *Vom Urchristentum zu Jesus: Für Joachim Gnilka,* ed. H. Frankemölle and K. Kertelge (Freiburg: Herder, 1989) 136–53.

[1] In *Neues Testament und Kirche: Für Rudolf Schnackenburg,* ed. J. Gnilka (Freiburg/Basel/Vienna: Herder, 1974) 458–75.

and influences of this issue. Rather, I restrict myself to the contemporary situation which, by means of the development of New Testament studies, imparts knowledge to believers and raises questions of the consequences of their understanding of faith. At the end of the parable discourse, according to Matt 13:51, Jesus asks the disciples, "Have you understood everything?" And the disciples answer—as if it were self-evident—"yes." In view of the Jesus tradition, would we so easily answer in the same way? The process of understanding, precisely through exegesis, has become much more complicated for us. Indeed each of us should become a "learned scribe" who "became a disciple of heaven's reign."[2] In accord with the brevity allotted to me, I have much to gather together.

1. *Observations on the Transformation of the Jesus Traditions in Matthew*

Scholars generally accept the transformation of the Jesus traditions in the post-Easter view of the early church and its special formulation by the evangelists.[3] Several layers of understanding were formed as a consequence. The original meaning from the mouth of Jesus is covered by the post-Easter community, but this is only accessible to us by means of the tradition of the evangelists who did not merely pick up the tradition but at the same time wanted to explain it and tailor it according to the interests of the listeners and readers of their time. In this way linguistically ever-new texts were "generated," and exegetes of the Gospels generate their own text according to their own methodologically advanced knowledge. However, what we can test (by means of redaction criticism) is the adoption and transformation of the primitive Christian Jesus tradition of the different evangelists. Let us now, for instance, illuminate the method of Matthew by means of some examples in order to draw out some hermeneutical ramifications. We have chosen such cases that let us discover reliable

---

[2] See my contribution, "Jeder Schriftgelehrte, der ein Jünger des Himmelreiches geworden ist (Mt 13,52)," in *Wissenschaft und Kirche: Festschrift für Eduard Lohse*, eds. K. Aland and S. Meurer (Bielefeld: Luther, 1989) 57–69.

[3] Compare recent commentaries: W. Grundmann, *Das Evangelium nach Matthäus* (THKNT 1; Berlin: Evangelischeverlagsanstalt, 1968); E. Schweizer, *The Good News according to Matthew* (Atlanta: John Knox, 1975); F. W. Beare, *The Gospel according to Matthew* (San Francisco: Harper and Row, 1981); R. H. Gundry, *Matthew: A Commentary on His Literary and Theological Art* (Grand Rapids: Eerdmans, 1982); U. Luz, *Matthew 1–7: A Commentary* (Minneapolis: Augsburg, 1989); R. Schnackenburg, *Matthäusevangelium*, 2 vols. (Würzburg: Echter, 1985–87); J. Gnilka, *Das Matthäusevangelium*, 2 vols. (Freiburg: Herder, 1986–88); A. Sand, *Das Evangelium nach Matthäus* (Regensburg: Friedrich Pustet, 1986).

Jesus tradition and/or that let us visualize a firm tradition of the early Christian church.

1.1 *The Prohibition of Divorce*

There can be no doubt that Jesus spoke such a command. But it is tangible in the form of traditions that diverge from one another in Matthew 5:32 and Luke 16:18, as well as in the controversy stories of Mark 10:2–12 and Matthew 19:3–9. Every form of the tradition implies an explanation or application toward the circle of listeners and readers of the respective evangelists. This is most clearly observed in Mark 10:11–12 because here the Hellenistic-Roman marriage law is presumed, which gives the right of divorce to women as well as to men. It is debated whether the Matthean formulation (Matt 5:32), disregarding the *porneia* clause, or the Lukan form (Luke 16:18) stands closer to the original saying of Jesus. It seems to me that Matthew 5:32 conforms more to the Jewish way of thinking. But this is not what I want to elaborate; rather, I want to pose the question whether the form and context (in the Sermon on the Mount!) brings us closer to the understanding of Jesus' judgment? To ask the question more acutely: What relation does the Matthean text have to the presupposed judgment of Jesus? Usually Jesus' prohibition of divorce is regarded in its contemporary context and according to the otherwise expressed stand of Jesus (the criterion of coherence). This leads us to the explanation that Jesus wanted to support women who were handled in an unjust and unfavorable way. U. Luz rightly criticized this, observing that for a divorced woman the prohibition against remarriage must have been devastating. Rather this would only be understandable if we accept the fact that Jesus proclaimed God's will from the authority of the kingdom of God. The controversy story in Mark 10:2–12 has understood this correctly.[4] This is equally confirmed by the Matthean context of the antitheses, especially through the "radical" expression about sexual desire (Matt 5:28–31). Even the controversy with the Pharisees (Matt 19:3–9) is arranged in this perspective, in that what Jesus wants to proclaim forcefully goes back to the original will of God, the Creator.[5] Note that this is Matthew's perspective. Jesus' intention

---

[4] Luz, *Matthew 1–7* 302–303.

[5] One can scarcely use the criterion of discontinuity for the saying of Jesus in view of Qumran texts. Compare CD 4:21 (a man is not permitted to take two wives during his lifetime); 11QTemple 57:17–19 (for the king). Notable is the reference to Gen 1:27 in CD 4:21. The saying of Jesus is distinguished by its announcement

with regard to the prohibition of divorce, which was transmitted in the
early church without knowledge of the concrete situation, is thereby
not directly decided. But in comparison with the other view (the
protection of women) the understanding of Matthew in the framework
of Jesus' proclamation of the kingdom of God is weighty. That is his
retrospective on the preaching of Jesus.

Now, through the fornication clause, we encounter also a
perspective on the situation of the Matthean community, a Jewish-
Christian one which sees the will of God in the obligation of an
adulterous wife to be separated from her husband. In this case, doesn't
Matthew get into conflict with the absolute indissolubility of marriage?
J. Gnilka is correct in stating that with the theological evaluation of the
fornication clause we must notice a distancing from Jesus' instruction.
"The possibility or duty of the husband to dismiss the wife has to be
regarded as a time-conditioned demand."[6] But Matthew regards it as
just, even as commanded, to adjust this way of Jewish thinking with his
understanding of God's will. For us today the force of this style of
Jewish thought no longer exists. Rather, we are compelled to follow an
opposite, prior understanding, above all that of Jesus, which demands
repeated pardon to the male or female sinner, which means that even
after adultery the woman is not to be rejected. The fornication
exception clause (Matt 5:32; 19:9) that originated from a Jewish-
Christian view is obsolete. However, do we not still have to reconsider
anew the consequences of the prohibition of divorce in today's
sociological context? The practice of different churches is
questionable.[7] Only conformity to the entire preaching and behavior
of Jesus, based upon God's will, will convince us. On account of the
ambiguity of the Jesus tradition that hardly remains a completely
resolvable task. The Matthean interpretation always forces us to
examine the will of God which has been revealed in Jesus and which
cannot be altered by any sociological considerations.

1.2 *The Place of Children*

This is not such a pressing and explosive question but is still
instructive for hermeneutics. Again there can be no doubt that Jesus
once spoke a word, whether in the context of blessing children or

---

of the inbreaking reign of God.

   6 Gnilka, *Matthäusevangelium* 1.170.

   7 See Luz, *Matthew 1–7* 307–10; R. Schnackenburg, *Die sittliche Botschaft des Neuen
Testaments* 1 (Neubearbeitung; Freiburg/Basel/Vienna: Herder, 1986) 152–53.

some other occasion, such as in Mark 10:14c (and par), "to such ones (i.e., children) belongs the kingdom of God." More difficult is the foundation for the tradition of the connected saying in Matthew and Luke about "the acceptance" of the reign of God "like a child," which in Matthew is in another location and another wording (Matt 18:3) in connection with the question of being great in the kingdom of God. Without attempting a reconstruction of the original saying of Jesus, we still have to say that a similar saying was extant in the early church.[8] For our question the relocation of Mark 10:15 according to Matthew 18:3, as well as the different formulation, is relevant. Matthew wanted to keep the pericope of the blessing of the children free for actual children. More important for him was the metaphorical understanding of child-like existence (*Kindsein*), which is already evident in Mark 10:15 ("like a child"). Matthew, however, wanted to give more prestige to this sense in another context ("Who is the greatest in the kingdom of heaven?"). The minor unity of Matthew 18:1–5[9] is redactionally and purposefully formed: the actual symbol of the child is explained by verse 3 and referenced to the community. The members of the community should "turn around" and become like little children. In the following editorially shaped verse 4 everyone is addressed in connection with a specified behavior. According to another logion of Jesus expressed by Matthew in 23:12, everyone is supposed to "humble oneself" in order to be made greater by God. In the framework of the teaching to the community and in view of 23:11, the logion which immediately precedes 23:12, the meaning becomes clearer: he must become a servant of the community as is once more emphasized in Matthew 20:26–27 (out of the Markan tradition). The closely connected verse 5 appears to mean: those who accept such

---

[8] Compare R. Pesch, *Das Markusevangelium* (Freiburg/Basel/Vienna: Herder, 1984) 1.133: "The statement certainly goes back to Jesus." J. Gnilka, *Das Evangelium nach Markus* (Zurich/Neukirchen: Neukirchener Verlag, 1979) 2.82, "From an historical aspect, the logion in verse 15 can no longer be regarded as a direct word of Jesus." I suppose he makes this judgment on account of the doubtful formulation of the saying. R. Bultmann, *History of the Synoptic Tradition* (rev. ed.; New York: Harper & Row, 1963) 105 includes Mark 10:15 among the logia which one can ascribe with confidence to Jesus. Critically, see E. Haenchen, *Der Weg Jesu* (Berlin: Töpelmann, 1966) 344–47 (346: "v. 15 does not belong to the ancient traditions").

[9] See my contribution to the Festschrift for W. Pesch, "Großsein im Gottesreich. Zu Mt 18,1–5," *Studien zum Matthäusevangelium: Festschrift für Wilhelm Pesch*, ed. L. Schenke (Stuttgart: Katholisches Bibelwerk, 1988) 269–82.

"children," that is, disciples who know themselves to be small and ready for selfless service, accept Jesus himself. There is no question in this verse (as perhaps in Mark 9:37) of talk of loving acceptance of needy children, as is still widely accepted,[10] but about the high esteem of the community for those members who, in the spirit of Jesus, want to be regarded as small in it.

Matthew has not created something entirely new with a new portrait of the scene as Jesus makes a child stand in the midst of the disciples. However, Matthew has tailored the symbolic act of Jesus and his word more forcefully to his community and made it a teaching. Mark had difficulties with his catchword composition in Mark 9:33–50 to combine and smooth out the traditional words about "children" and "little ones" (cf. v. 37 with v. 41).[11] Matthew, in his orientation toward his community, finds a way to divide both scenes with children (the child as a model and the blessing of the children) and to position Jesus' words in a matching framework. This yields a clearer picture to the later church.

1.3 *The Meaning of Parables*

The transformation of the parables of Jesus in the post-Easter horizon is well known and has been thoroughly investigated, even if instances of divergent interpretations of single passages are prevalent. Matthew was a diligent collector of such traditions of parables which he in part created from sources unknown to us (described in a simplified way as *Sondergut*). In his discourse composition in chapter 13 he has connected seven parables, designating them together as parables of the kingdom of heaven. The way he proceeds in his elucidation is visible in connection with the interpretation of the parable of the sower, taken over from the Markan tradition (Matt 13:18–23, but with some variations, cf. v. 23), and especially from the "clarification" retained by him in the parable of the weeds (13:36–43). This has been thoroughly investigated and evaluated for Matthean

---

[10] Compare W. Vischer, *Die evangelische Gemeindeordnung. Matthäus 16,13–20,28* (Zollikon/Zurich: Evangelischer Verlag, 1946) 59–61; W. Trilling, *Hausordnung Gottes. Eine Auslegung von Mt 18* (Düsseldorf: Patmos, 1960) 27–28; W. Grundmann, *Matthäus* 414 (he also mentions, however, the other meaning); A. Sand *Matthäus* 366–67.

[11] See Gnilka, *Markus* 2.55 regarding Mark 9:37: "Thus we have before us in v. 37 an already well stated logion about children which comparably underlies another saying in Matt 10:40. The coordination of the little ones in the community with children is a post-Easter perspective (cf. 9:42)."

theology.[12] Two peculiarities, however, have not been examined sufficiently: the insistence on the understanding of the parables (vv. 13–15 [red.],19,23,51[red.]), and the clear division between the parables offered to the people and those reserved for the disciples after the dismissal of the crowds (from v. 36).

According to Matthew the listeners to Jesus' message are divided into those who understand and those who do not understand. This acute division of the listeners is certainly connected with the polemic of this evangelist against the unbelieving and stubborn group of Jews from his own time. This is mirrored in the changing of the Markan presentation from, "*so that* they look and still do not see, etc." (Mark 4:12) to, "*because* they look and still do not see" (Matt 13:13). This is no weakening but an intensification of the sense of the text: being blind and deaf has already happened. This understanding is verified by the Matthean insert of the saying in v. 12: whoever "does not have" will be deprived of what little he does have (which occurs in Mark 4:25 in another context and with a different sense). This provides a window into the situation in which Matthew lived and made his judgments. The turning toward the disciples indicated by the verse, "blessed are *your* eyes, etc." (v. 16), which comes after the fulfillment citation in vv. 14–15, indicates a similar line of thought. Besides this polemical tendency of Matthew another aspect which comes to the fore is his intention to call the Christian community toward the mercy and demands of God's reign. When the eyes and ears of the disciples are declared blessed in Matthew 13:16, the good fortune, happiness, and the grace of their calling is supposed to be acknowledged by them (and later communities). And following this immediately (v. 18 with the same address *hymeis oun*) the heirs of God's kingdom are to draw out the consequences for their lives. The early Christian meaning of the parable of the sower, essentially taken over from Mark 4:14–20, is placed under the call to hear and *to understand*, as the call resounds negatively at the beginning (v. 19) and positively at the end (v. 23). The intermediate warnings of apostasy (v. 19b-c), of lacking perseverance in distress and persecution (vv. 23–24), and of the temptations of a worldly life (v. 22) belong in this framework. But

---

12 Compare the commentaries above in note 3. In addition, J. D. Kingsbury, *The Parables of Jesus in Matthew 13* (Richmond: John Knox, 1969); A. Kretzer, *Die Herrschaft der Himmel und die Söhne des Reiches* (Stuttgart/Würzburg: Echter, 1971) 93–149. Individual parables from Matthew 13 are discussed in well known works about parable interpretation but not in connection with the entire chap. 13.

whoever hears and understands will produce much fruit, even if not always a hundredfold, nonetheless sixty- or thirtyfold (v. 23). This is the word of the admonisher and instructor of his community.

The parable of the weeds among the wheat (13:24–30) is inserted by Matthew into the first part when the crowd of people is still listening (cf. v. 34a). This first section of the parable discourse is addressed simultaneously to those who do not and those who do understand; polemical and encouraging tones are intermingled. But the meaning of the parable of the weeds (13:36–43) is already bestowed in its entirety upon the community in the address to the disciples. In *their* rows the devil plants his poisonous seed (v. 37), and the threat of judgment remains valid for those of the community who scandalously give up, as the comparison of v. 41b with 7:23 shows. The threat, however, ends in v. 43 with the promise that the "righteous" will shine like the sun in the kingdom of their father. The following parables of the treasure in the field and of the priceless pearl (vv. 44–46) have a reinforcing effect. Naturally, Matthew cannot resist bringing in the threat of judgment (according to 13:41–42) once more in the parable of the dragnet (13:47–48, selecting the good!), which originally was oriented in a different fashion. Generally, however, he is satisfied in this second section of the parable discourse to lead the community to "understanding" by warning and admonition (cf. v. 51).

But what does this "understanding" mean? According to what we have said it certainly does not mean simply a spiritual comprehension of the "teaching" of the parables. Rather, it means an existential comprehension and being moved by the compelling power of the reign of God! Because God's reign is brought into the parable discourse in word and in reality, the "parables of growth" clarify and make comprehensible the process directed by God of collecting those who accept it and rejecting those who decline it.[13] In spite of all the weakness and discordance, the believing community—the church—is the preeminent "location" for Matthew of God's reign. Therefore the

---

[13] See E. Jüngel, *Paulus und Jesus. Eine Untersuchung zur Präzisierung der Frage nach dem Ursprung der Christologie*, 2d ed. (Tübingen: Mohr/Siebeck, 1964) 139–74. For more recent interpretations of the parables which more readily utilize the research literature, see H. Weder *Die Gleichnisse Jesu als Metaphern*, 2d ed. (Göttingen: Vandenhoeck & Ruprecht, 1980) 11–57; W. Harnisch (ed.), *Die neutestamentliche Gleichnisforschung im Horizont von Hermeneutik und Literaturwissenschaft*, Wege der Forschung 575 (Darmstadt: Wissenschaftliche Buchgesellschaft, 1982). Further literature is found in H.-J. Klauck, *Allegorie und Allegorese in den synoptischen Gleichnissen*, 2d ed. (Münster: Aschendorff, 1986) 362–64.

disciples, representing the community, answer without hesitation, "yes," to the question of whether they have understood Jesus.

There would be much more to say about this matter, but I only wanted here to elucidate the acceptance and transformation of the Jesus tradition through Matthew with regard to his community and the "truly existent" church of Jesus Christ in his time. Before we draw hermeneutical deductions, we have to ponder one more aspect, one which came into clearer view in recent years through the series, "Evangelisch-Katholischer Kommentar zum Neuen Testament" (EKKNT): the question of the "history of influence" (*Wirkungsgeschichte*).

(*Translator's Note*: The word *Wirkungsgeschichte* is difficult to translate accurately into English. The expression can mean the "history of influence" of a text, which is the translation used here. Yet it means much more than this English expression conveys. Ulrich Luz, in his commentary on Matthew referred to in this article, provides an adequate description of all that is meant by the expression. *Wirkungsgeschichte* is the "history, reception, and actualizing of a text in media other than commentary, e.g., in sermons, canonical law, hymnody, art, and in the actions and suffering of the church." See *Matthew 1–7: A Commentary* [Minneapolis: Augsburg, 1989] 95.)

2. The Influence of Wirkungsgeschichte on the Process of Understanding

It is a fact that the Gospel of Matthew had a broad and deeply felt influence in the early church at least until the time of Irenaeus.[14] If we as exegetes search for the redaction-critical understanding of Matthew and learn from it about the process of interpretation in the early church, then it may seem superfluous and rather disturbing to question the understanding of his Gospel in later times. But if we incorporate the present horizon under the aspect of hermeneutics and ask how contemporary Christians are able to accept the biblical text and make the Jesus tradition their own, then the later history of influence of the text cannot be overlooked.[15] According to today's

---

[14] See E. Massaux, *The Influence of the Gospel of Saint Matthew on Christian Literature before Saint Irenaeus* (Leuven: Peeters, 1990); W.-D. Köhler, *Die Rezeption des Matthäusevangeliums in der Zeit vor Irenäus*, WUNT 2.24 (Tübingen: Mohr, 1987).

[15] Cf. Luz, *Matthew 1–7* 9, in the forward to his commentary: "First, I am convinced that a commentary which not only explains biblical texts but aids in their understanding must not remain simply in the past but must draw lines into the present. Second, I am convinced that the history of interpretation of a book can contribute greatly to this understanding."

communication theory, which is derived from linguistics, it is very important in the transmission of the content of faith in talks, sermons, and instruction that the speakers reflect on the efficacy of their communication, the transfer of their thoughts, and the possible reception of them among their hearers. The levels of the text and reader of the past must be raised to the level of the speaker and listener of the present. A commentary, in contrast to the previously described text, is already a meta-text, which must be aimed at the users' capability to comprehend if it is not to leave them entirely empty. Therefore, one cannot turn away from the interpretational limitations of long-lasting, frequently changing, and contradictory tradition.

Naturally, Matthew could not know or scarcely assess the effectiveness of his Gospel in later times. But if he did not write his Gospel for an actual occasion and for a limited territory, but strove for a universalism (cf. Matt 24:14; 28:19), one could still not deny the intention to achieve with his work an influence on the growing and expanding great church.[16] With our knowledge of the history of influence, even if it is still not sufficiently researched, we are able to determine whether and to what extent he was successful. The effects which reach from distant centuries to our own time influence, whether expeditiously or with hindrance, our contemporaries' capability of understanding.

Can the history of influence be an aid for exegetical endeavors to the exegete of our day who works with the tools of science? One often gets the impression from U. Luz, who in his commentary on Matt 1—7 has accumulated a large amount of material relating to the history of influence, that he has used the divergent interpretations, the specific confessional views, and the inspirations of specific eras to come closer to the meaning of the texts themselves. Of course, he remains faithful to a methodologically strict analysis and explanation of the text, but with a view toward the history of influence he sensitizes the reader to ponder questions that are connected to the text. We constantly question the text, and these questions are posed and delivered to us

---

16 By itself the universalistic understanding of *ekklēsia* in Matt 16:18, the church of Jesus Christ, points in this direction. Another question is whether this intention of the evangelist writing in Antioch penetrated other provinces of the church. See the interesting perspective John P. Meier sketches in R. E. Brown and J. P. Meier, *Antioch and Rome* (New York/Ramsey: Paulist, 1983) 11–86.

more strikingly through the history of influence. They are a help in asking correct and relevant questions which we cannot forego.

I shall point to three locations as examples which can demonstrate the impact of the history of influence on texts.

2.1 *The Sermon on the Mount and its Extreme Demands*

In order to feel the dynamite of the Sermon on the Mount, one needs only to remember the discussion among Christians about peace and renunciation of violence. We can surely recognize the love of enemies, the pinnacle of the Matthean antitheses, certainly in the context of that time as in no way restricted to Jesus alone and an exceptionally extreme demand, but it can be "clarified," on the other hand, as a consciously provocative "new" instruction of Jesus within the framework of his preaching. But we have not decided what consequences this bears in our time, how to realize here and now love of enemies in the sense that Jesus meant it—the most urgent interest of our contemporaries. The answers supplied throughout the centuries cannot be equally valid for us. Rather, they should challenge us to find better solutions, perhaps even in contrast to earlier responses, for the urgent problems of preventing wars, disarmament, peace among peoples, and freedom for oppressed groups. The same extends to other problems presented in the biblical text, such as sexuality and marriage, protection of human life, dealing with money and goods, and so on. Exegetes cannot avoid these questions. Many an answer will be acquired through their prior knowledge, perhaps unconsciously, so that their interpretations will not remain free from subjective bias. Some burning questions that are not defined by clear contours they will seek to answer by the general attitude given to them by education and development rather than by the texts themselves. The hermeneutical question catches exegetes before the explanation of the text and does not let them loose during the process of interpretation. The extreme demands of Jesus acquire again and again through history a new appearance and constantly enter into new historical horizons.[17]

---

[17] D. Lührmann maintains at the end of his tradition-historical study of the command to love one's enemies: "In this history of the tradition . . . it is clear that Jesus' command receives new meanings with each new situation into which it is transmitted. Yet exactly as a word of *Jesus* the achieved actualizing of the text in each case is evaded; it remains free and does not give up its own interpretation, so much has its history of tradition contributed to its understanding." "Liebet eure Feinde (Lk 6,27–36/Mt 5,37–48)," *ZTK* 69 (1972) 412–38, citation from p. 438.

2.2. *The Transfer of Power to Peter and his Role in the Church*

While with the Sermon on the Mount we dealt with a provocative question for all Christians, in the question of Peter we deal with a volatile topic for ecumenical dialogue between churches. If we can disregard the Roman Catholic view that the papacy started with the legitimate succession of the service or office of Peter—a question that supersedes the domain of the New Testament—we must see that the evidence from the Gospel of Matthew forces us into a special position. The message about binding and loosing, which is spoken to the first disciple in Matthew 16:19, appears in Matthew 18:18 in the plural and is understood there in context as legitimation for the community in its expulsion of stubborn sinners. The different attempts to reconcile this tension are well known and cannot be discussed here. Remaining on the redactional level of Matthew yields many riddles for the image of Peter in Matthew's Gospel.[18] We cannot entirely discount an increased interest by the evangelist and his community in this leading figure, although the view of W. Schenk, according to which the Gospel of Matthew was originally intended as a "Gospel of Peter," has hardly been substantiated.[19] This problem is much more complicated under the aspect of the history of influence and hermeneutics. The early history of the exegesis of Matthew 16:18 shows a diversified view.[20] But the later discussion stands under the aspect of controversial theological positions on account of the disputed question of the papacy during the period of the Reformation.[21] Although scientific

---

[18] See R. E. Brown, et al, *Peter in the New Testament* (Minneapolis: Augsburg; New York: Paulist, 1973) 75–107; P. Hoffmann, "Die Bedeutung des Petrus für die Kirche des Matthäus. Redaktionsgeschichtliche Beobachtungen zu Mt 16,17–19," in *Dienst an der Einheit. Zum Wesen und Auftrag des Petrusamtes*, ed. J. Ratzinger (Düsseldorf: Patmos, 1978) 9–26; F. Mußner, "Petrusgestalt und Petrusdienst in der Sicht der späten Urkirche" in Ratzinger, *Dienst an der Einheit* 27–45, esp. 28–34; J. D. Kingsbury, "The Figure of Peter in Matthew's Gospel as a Theological Problem," *JBL* 98 (1979) 67–83; R. Pesch, *Simon-Petrus. Geschichte und geschichtliche Bedeutung des ersten Jüngers Christi* (Stuttgart: A. Hiersemann, 1980) 140–44; R. Schnackenburg, "Petrus im Matthäusevangelium," in *A cause de l'Evangile. Mélanges offerts à Dom J. Dupont*, LD 123 (Paris: Cerf, 1985) 107–25.

[19] W. Schenk, "Das 'Matthäusevangelium' als Petrusevangelium," *BZ* NF 27 (1983) 58–80.

[20] J. Ludwig, *Die Primatsworte Mt 16,18–19 in der altkirchlichen Exegese*, NTAbh 19.4 (Münster: Aschendorff, 1952).

[21] Compare J. Burgess, *A History of the Exegesis of Matthew 16,17–19 from 1781 to 1965* (Diss.; Basel, 1965); F. Obrist, *Echtheitsfragen und Deutung der Primatstelle Mt 16,18f in der deutschen protestantischen Theologie der letzten dreißig Jahre*, NTAbh 21.3–4

exegesis could add something to the mellowing of this dispute, we cannot deny that judgments conditioned by confession still cloud and darken the horizon of our understanding. This makes homogeneous answers difficult and prevents a uniform reception of the text in the Roman Catholic and Evangelisch-Lutheran churches, and even in the Orthodox churches. The hermeneutical question appears rather blatantly here.

2.3 *The Attitude toward the Jews*

It is evident that Matthew is prejudiced and polemically narrow in his view toward Judaism (not ancient Israel) because of the post-70 CE historical situation. One only has to read the anti-Pharisaic discourse in chapter 23 to verify this observation. The section is far from containing a just judgment and indeed contradicts the commandment of love of enemy which Matthew so well defined.[22] One should also reflect on the dangerous historical-theological explanations and the accusations against the Jewish people that are connected with Matthew 27:25 and that led to terrible persecutions of the Jews.[23] This history of influence extends to our own day, and we will be able to undo its influence only gradually. The warding off of Jewish accusations (the theft of the body of Jesus, Matt 28:13) also belongs to this topic. An additional difficulty is the tendency of faithful readers of the Bible today to historicize their understanding, which itself has a long pre-history.

From these examples, which could easily be multiplied, we can recognize the incriminating consequences of the history of influence which inhibits a proper understanding of the Jesus tradition and the evangelist's explanation of it in Matthew's Gospel.

(Münster: Aschendorff, 1961).

[22] See E. Haenchen, "Matthäus 23," *ZTK* 48 (1951) 38–63; H. Frankemölle, "'Pharisäismus' in Judentum und Kirche. Zur Tradition und Redaktion in Matthäus 23," in *Gottesverächter und Menschenfeinde? Juden zwischen Jesus und frühchristlicher Kirche*, ed. H. Goldstein (Düsseldorf: Patmos, 1979) 123–89.

[23] See R. Kampling, *Das Blut Christi und die Juden. Mt 27,25 bei den lateinischsprachigen christlichen Autoren bis zu Leo dem Großen*, NTAbh NF 16 (Münster: Aschendorff, 1984). This history of influence admittedly must have been pursued further in the following centuries.

3. Hermeneutical Deductions: Retrospective and Prospective

3.1 A Further Inquiry about Jesus

Since the Gospel of Matthew does not offer a direct reflection of Jesus' words nor a firsthand account of his actions, we cannot reach reliably the primitive foundation of the Jesus tradition. We stand on ground which covers several layers: early oral tradition, first collections of Jesus' words and deeds which in their selection and editing already represent a post-Easter layer of understanding, predecessors of written sources (Q, Mark, other hypothetical sources which undergird the special sources [Sondergut]) and orally transmitted stories, and finally the redactional composition and formation of the evangelists themselves. The methodological workings of this entire process of tradition,[24] which presents sufficient problems, need not concern us here. Rather, the hermeneutical question does: whether and to what extent can we successfully grasp the message of Jesus that concerns us and binds us? Matthew himself lays this obligation upon us when the resurrected Lord commands his disciples, "Teach them to keep all that I have commanded you." (28:20). Both Matthew and the early church were convinced that the words and sign-like actions of Jesus include a heritage for the Christian faith that is never to be given up and is an abiding duty for Christian life. The expression, "From Early Christianity to Jesus," in the title of this Festschrift assents to this position.

The endeavor, then, to advance toward the "genuine" words of Jesus and his rules of conduct based upon certain criteria is methodologically justified and necessary according to our present knowledge. Such a standard of criteria has already been worked out and, in my opinion, can be employed successfully, if only the weight and restrictions of individual criteria are sufficiently respected.[25] Not all questions have been clarified or solved, for example, the relationship between the sayings traditions and those of the actions of Jesus, the cooperation between the criteria of discontinuity and of coherence, and the danger of methodological narrowness.

---

[24] See F. Mußner, "Methodologie der Frage nach dem historischen Jesus," in *Rückfrage nach Jesus. Zur Methodik und Bedeutung der Frage nach dem historischen Jesus,* ed. K. Kertelge QD 63 (Freiburg/Basel/Vienna: Herder, 1974) 118–47.

[25] See F. Lentzen-Deis, "Kriterien für die historische Beurteilung der Jesusüberlieferung in den Evangelien," in Kertelge, *Rückfrage* 78–117.

If one determines a relatively secure range of "genuine" Jesus traditions, it would be a mistake to regard it as the "entire" Jesus. The available Jesus tradition consists of a selection which goes back to the needs of the early communities. F. Hahn identified in the selection of Jesus traditions a multifaceted procedure of reducing the collection of original traditions.[26] But what appears to us as a loss can also be reckoned as a gain for establishing the true contours of the image of Jesus. The post-Easter perspective intensified the view of what remained most important for that which determined the life of the communities in connection with their Lord. The "earthly," historical Jesus is encompassed by the risen Christ through faith, perhaps not adhered to in all details, yet recognized in his substantial form. We cannot erect another Jesus from the Gospels, but this image is sufficient for faith and it imposes an obligation on faith. An image of the "historical" Jesus detached from this faith remains an illusion.

Joachim Jeremias' attempt to reproduce the *ipsissima verba* of Jesus, and to establish from this a general understanding of the preaching and person of Jesus, is well known. Certainly he was correct in finally arriving at the message and basic substance of Jesus and observing that many perspectives, such as the meaning of the parables, were altered in the early church. But this process of transformation was necessary if the early church wanted to carry forth the substance of Jesus in its post-Easter setting. For J. Jeremias, the history of Jesus abruptly ends with his resurrection. According to his view, the disciples had to have experienced the apparitions of the risen one as "the inbreaking of the turn of the ages"; "they were witnesses of the beginning of his rule; in other words, *they experienced the parousia.*"[27] From this perspective not only is our view of the further history of the early church blocked, but also the retrospective view of Jesus loses its sphere of influence, its ability to be taken up in our own time. Matthew's method reveals another understanding of the Jesus tradition: the resurrected one, who lives in and with his church, speaks the same words to it as the earthly Jesus, but in such a way that they need a new explanation and application to penetrate into the life of the community in order to feed and shape it.

---

[26] F. Hahn, "Methodologische Überlegungen zur Rückfrage nach Jesus," in Kertelge, *Rückfrage* 11–77, esp. 14–18.

[27] J. Jeremias, *New Testament Theology: The Proclamation of Jesus.* (New York: Charles Scribner's Sons, 1971) 310. (A second volume on the theology of the early church has not appeared.)

3.2 *Preview and Crossectional View of the Community*

From the beginning Matthew has his community in view in the transmission of the Jesus tradition, not in a way that everything is a "model" and ideal, but in such a way that precisely through the words, behavior, and will of Jesus the "reign of heaven" unfolds its power. In this fashion Matthew gives the Jesus tradition a prospective dimension and a creative power which can be effective in a new way even in later times. At the same time, the history of influence warns us from no few of its texts that Matthew's Gospel cannot be used as a totally adequate foundation for our understanding of Jesus. The "substance of Jesus" appears in Matthew, is contained and preserved in it, but not grasped exhaustively nor completely filled out by the Gospel. The image of Jesus must be filled out and pondered by other New Testament witnesses. But the Gospel of Matthew is an indicator of how one ought to deal with the Jesus tradition, and it becomes a bridge for inserting this tradition into our own horizon of understanding.

In connection with this we also have to examine the limitations of the historical-critical methods. We achieve a better understanding of the texts in their historical context with these methods, but not yet an adequate understanding in new historical contexts. The reduction to an "existential" understanding, such as with R. Bultmann and his students, as valuable as this was in comparison with a historicizing interpretation,[28] has nonetheless been recognized as having its drawbacks above all in relation to the "social" message of Jesus. The text not only demands a new existential understanding on the part of the believer, but also a social engagement that Jesus called for in the movement toward faith. This especially stands out in the Matthean presentation of the Jesus tradition. The disciples, in spite of having been given individual commands, are understood as representatives of the community who are supposed to bring the message of Jesus into action and spread it to the world.[29] Thus, historical-critical exegesis,

---

[28] See the "Epilegomena" in R. Bultmann, *Theologie des Neuen Testaments*, 9th ed. completed and enlarged by O. Merk (Tübingen: Mohr, 1984) 585–600. Bultmann maintains that the work on the NT documents can be conducted from a twofold interest, either from reconstruction or from interpretation. Although there cannot be one without the other, he wants to make the historical work of interpretation serviceable under the presumption that the NT writings "have something to say to the present" (600).

[29] On the function of the "disciples" in Matthew's Gospel, see U. Luz, "Die Jünger im Matthäusevangelium," *ZNW* 62 (1971) 141–71. On the meaning of the Sermon on the Mount, see G. Lohfink, "Wem gilt die Bergpredigt?," *TQ* 163

also by incorporating aspects of sociology, can elaborate the picture. But we have not yet resolved how the church which emerged from the Jesus movement is supposed to put into action the tasks of our day. Other recently applied methods of exegesis (materialistic, depth-psychological, spiritual interpretation) can hardly solve the problem. The hermeneutical question remains potent and gives us no rest.

Retrospective and prospective aspects are related and depend on one another. As Matthew shows us in his view of the community, remembrance of Jesus' words and actions demands an application to the present and a view oriented to the future. If one wanted to concentrate solely on questions and needs of the present, one could easily lose sight of the intentions of Jesus and betray the substance of Jesus for the sake of accommodating social conventions and values. We must always turn back to Jesus from the worldwide situation of the present-day church as the source of faith who has never been and can never be surpassed. Yet the early church, in its acceptance and application of the Jesus tradition in its own situation, is an indispensable connecting link. We cannot omit their interpretations of the logia of Jesus because they stand close to their source and bring this closer to us than later interpretations. Therefore we can say: from the church of the present to Jesus, but through the early church, and again: from Jesus through the early church to the present one. The "church of the beginning," which had its origins in the word and work of Jesus, has "its own form which must remain the authentic form."[30]

3.3 "New and Old"—Continuity and Discontinuity

Matthew gives us an important hermeneutical hint in one notable place. At the end of the parable discourse, which is an example of contemporizing interpretation, he presents the Christian "learned scribe," who, like a good master of the household, brings forth from his storehouse "new and old" (13:52). By means of this comparison, which perhaps uses a commonly available image, we ask what sense is meant by the words "new and old." The scholarly opinions of the

---

(1983) 264–84; and more basic, G. Lohfink, *Wie hat Jesus Gemeinde gewollt? Zur gesellschaftlichen Dimension des christlichen Glaubens*, 7th ed. (Freiburg/Basel/Vienna: Herder, 1987).

[30] H. Schürmann, *Ursprung und Gestalt. Erörterungen und Besinnungen zum Neuen Testament* (Düsseldorf: Patmos, 1970) 9 (preface). Compare the Festschrift dedicated to him, *Die Kirche des Anfangs: Festschrift für Heinz Schürmann zum 65. Geburtstag*, ed. R. Schnackenburg, et al. (Freiburg/Basel/Vienna: Herder, 1978).

meaning are varied and should not be discussed here.[31] The prevalent view is that the evangelist meant by "new" the preaching of Jesus, and by "old" meant the previous and still valid revelation and instruction of God seen in the expression "the law and the prophets" (cf. 5:17; 7:12; 22:20). A contrary view, which arose with Adolf Schlatter and is repeatedly noted,[32] is that for Matthew the "old" is the sermon of Jesus which occurred once and is already in the past and which the scribe must enrich and connect with new insights. Both interpretations appear to me to be worth scrutinizing. If one glances at the entire Gospel of Matthew, the understanding becomes clearer that Matthew wanted to emphasize the "newness" of the message of Jesus, but without it becoming detached from the old covenant and the prior history of the Gospel. The following above all speak in favor of this understanding: the "fulfillment citations," the continual reference to scripture, and the view of salvation history that is already alluded to in the genealogy (1:1–17) and that remains throughout the Gospel. But in the *narrower context* of the parable discourse the other interpretation has its validity also. The parables of Jesus have obtained a new aspect in the Matthean interpretation; they are conveyed to the community in a new, transposed, and actualized way while remaining enticing and demanding.

In any case, by means of the expression "new and old," Matthew draws attention to a problem which remains for all historical transmission of the message: continuity and discontinuity. A principle answer to this question is that Matthew affirms both the "new and old" and connects them together in their "understanding." The "new" may not displace the "old," and the "old" must be incorporated into the "new." In today's context the retrospective binding to the old covenant and to the history of the people of God, so emphasized by Matthew, is important. It makes it our duty to keep in mind even more than in the past the roots of Jesus in his people and their traditions. At the same time we must expose what has blossomed "anew" in the person and

---

[31] On this refer to my contribution mentioned in note 2 above.

[32] A. Schlatter, *Der Evangelist Matthäus. Seine Sprache, sein Ziel, seine Selbständigkeit,* 7th ed. (Stuttgart: Calwer, 1982) 450–51; cf. W. Pesch, *Matthäus der Seelsorger,* SBS 2 (Stuttgart: Katholisches Bibelwerk, 1966) 76; W. Trilling, "Amt und Amtsverständnis bei Matthäus," in *Mélanges Bibliques en hommage au R. P. Béda Rigaux* (Gembloux: Duculot, 1970) 29–44, on this issue, esp. 32–34. R. H. Gundry, *Matthew* 281 thinks that "old" refers to what the disciples had already understood prior to Jesus' parable discourse and that "new" refers to what they have learned subsequently through it.

preaching of Jesus. Yet the other view still has an important function in our day. In all the turmoil we encounter in the church and in society it is important to adhere to the "old" in the message of Jesus. At the same time, we have to interpret it anew and to translate it into the interpretational horizon of our own times, just as Matthew did for his community.

How can we succeed? Matthew also gives us invaluable advice for this issue: whoever wants to become a real Christian interpreter of scripture must first become a "disciple of the kingdom of heaven." This does not, however, mean only to be instructed into the "mysteries of the reign of God," but rather to submit oneself entirely to them and to witness to them in one's own way of life. Only this constitutes true "understanding" of the inbreaking reign of God as Jesus preached it.

Chapter Ten

The Final Judgment (Matt 25:31–46): An Exercise in "History of Influence" Exegesis

ULRICH LUZ
TRANSLATED BY DOROTHY JEAN WEAVER

The philosopher H. G. Gadamer has introduced the concept of "history of influence" [*Wirkungsgeschichte*] as a dimension of the hermeneutical task.[1] As Gadamer sees it, we do not assume the position of neutral observers or critics vis-à-vis the texts which shape our history; rather, we ourselves are indebted to the history which they have brought about. Accordingly, to become aware of the history of influence of a text means to become aware of how we ourselves have been shaped by the text. This means at the same time that we must become aware of our own position vis-à-vis the text, a position which is never simply a neutral one. Only the person who becomes aware of his/her personal, ecclesiastical, and societal position vis-à-vis the text and learns to assess what he/she owes to the text can adequately appropriate historical or literary critical interpretation for a present day understanding of the text. Awareness of the history of influence of a text leads to a present day understanding of the text which moves beyond the distancing and neutralizing effects of scientific exegesis. In the working group of the German-language "Evangelisch-Katholischer Kommentar zum Neuen Testament" the confessional aspect of the task was especially important. To be aware of the history of influence

---

[1] H. G. Gadamer, *Truth and Method* (New York: Seabury, 1975). For my own work in this area, see especially U. Luz, *Matthew in History* (Minneapolis: Fortress, 1994).

meant at the same time to explain how we, through reading the very same biblical texts, became Catholics or Protestants.

As a result, it is already evident that the history of influence is not merely oriented toward the study of the tradition. Rather, applying the history of influence to biblical texts always has an ecumenical dimension. Those who engage in this task are made aware not only of what they themselves but of what others as well have owed and continue to owe to the very same texts. In this way the study of the history of influence widens our own horizons, leads us into ecumenical discussion, and makes us aware not only of what the texts have given us but also of what they might have given us. The enlarging of our own horizons means at the same time the sharpening of our critical capacities. The history of influence opens our eyes to discover where and how texts have functioned in one-sided and problematic fashion. Every critical interpretation of a biblical text which is not simply historically blind or dogmatically rigid must take into consideration the historical influences created by this text up to the present time, just as it takes into consideration the other critical criteria which guide present-day biblical scholarship. On this point as well the history of influence offers a contribution to contemporary biblical interpretation by moving beyond that exposition of the biblical texts which merely establishes historical evidence.

As a result it is also evident that an interpretive model which includes the history of interpretation takes as its premise that every interpretation of a biblical text will take place in a new historical situation and with new readers and will lead, accordingly, to a new understanding of the text. To understand a biblical text does not, as a result, mean to carry forward the old established historical-critical sense of the text into the present. Every genuine understanding of biblical texts is determined by two factors: The texts themselves, which seek to define and to move their readers, and the readers, who out of the matrix of the given texts fashion new and self-specific interpretations. Viewed from this standpoint, the history of interpretation belongs together with reader-response exegesis. While reader-response exegesis which is oriented toward literary criticism asks the aesthetic-interpretive question of how the interaction between text and reader takes place, the history of influence asks the reception-historical question of how these interactions take place throughout the course of centuries and in various cultures and churches. Accordingly, the history of influence provides both the illustrative material for reader-response exegesis and at the same time prevents this exegesis from becoming an unhistorical effort in which the literary critic uses his/her reception-aesthetic theory to make him/herself master over the texts.[2]

Naturally the use of the history of influence to interpret biblical texts means a virtually endless task. The history of influence of biblical texts is much more than the history of interpretation. The history of influence includes not only study of written commentaries on the biblical texts but also study of the influences of these texts on piety, prayers and songs, dogma, Christian action and politics, literature and art, not only within the Christian churches but beyond them as well. No person can research all of this in exhaustive fashion. If I myself attempt to write a "history of influence" commentary of the entire Gospel of Matthew,[3] I am nevertheless aware that I am forced to remain a dilettante, able only to make more or less random discoveries within a gigantic field of study. Or am I, in an age of highly specialized exegetical professionalism, freed by the history of influence so that I may remain a dilettante? I would rather think of it in this light! In the following essay I wish to present a "history of influence" exegesis of the Final Judgment (Matt 25:31–46), which today has become one of the most central biblical texts. This study emerges from my work on the third volume of my commentary on Matthew.[4] My readers can easily identify not only the potential but also the limits of this attempt.[5]

1. History of Interpretation and History of Influence of Matt 25:31–46

Over the course of history there have been three major approaches to this text. I begin with the one which today has the strongest impact not, to be sure, on exegesis *per se* but rather on theology overall. This is the interpretation which has turned Matt 25:31–46 into a biblical *crux interpretum.*

---

[2] Especially important for the literary critical reception of the history of influence is H. R. Jauss, *Literaturgeschichte als Provokation,* 4th ed. (Frankfurt: Suhrkamp, 1974) 144–207.

[3] Vol. 1: *Matthew 1–7: A Commentary* (Minneapolis: Augsburg Fortress, 1989); Vol. 2: *Das Evangelium nach Matthaus (Mt 8–17)* EKK 1/2 (Neukirchen-Vluyn: Benziger/Neukirchener, 1990). Volume 2 of the American edition will appear in the Hermeneia commentary series.

[4] Volume 3 (Matt 18–25) will appear in 1996.

[5] One of the most obvious limits of this attempt is that I concentrate again and again on the relatively easily accessible history of interpretation and deal with the subsequent history of influence only in piecemeal fashion.

1. The Universal Interpretive Model. "When the Son of Man comes, he will judge all the nations. The judgment will be determined by the deeds of love and mercy shown to the marginal, the poor, and the suffering persons of the world, the least among Jesus' brothers and sisters."6 *Accordingly, the brothers and sisters of the Son of Man are all the suffering persons of the earth, both non-Christians as well as Christians.* It is for this reason that I designate this approach to the text the *universal interpretive model.* Here it is frequently the motif of "unawareness" which is determinative. Prior to the final judgment these persons do not know that it is Christ himself to whom they have done good deeds. In these persons the heavenly judge is present in the world. According to this interpretive model the text is understood as "the masterpiece of Gospel literature."7 Only very few Gospel texts hold so great a fascination today as this *crux interpretum.* There are many dimensions of meaning which contribute to this fascination. I will attempt to give an overview of these:

a) Matt 25:31–46 is an exemplary basis for an *nondogmatic and practical Christianity.* It has to do only with love of neighbor, not with confession or with faith. "The love of God" (or of Christ) is, according to some, "interpreted as the love of neighbor."8 This concentration of love of God on love of the neighbor has found its most beautiful expression in Tolstoy's well-known story, "Where Love Is, There Is God."9 The shoemaker Martin Avdeitch grieves the death of his only child. Then he hears the voice of Christ, who promises that he will come to him the next day. On the next day Martin sits at the window the entire day and waits. Different people come past. First comes an old man who is exhausted from shoveling snow. Then comes the wife of a soldier with her tiny child, both of them on the point of freezing to death. The third visit comes from an old woman who is arguing with a street urchin over a stolen apple. Martin speaks with them and gives them

---

6 J. R. Donahue, "The 'Parable' of the Sheep and the Goats: A Challenge to Christian Ethics," *TS* 47 (1986) 3.

7 S. Légasse, "Jésus et l'enfant," Ebib (1969) 85.

8 H. Braun, "Die Problematik einer Theologie des Neuen Testaments," *Gesammelte Studien zum Neuen Testament und seiner Umwelt,* 2nd ed., ed. H. Braun (Tübingen: Mohr, 1967) 337; similarly U. Luz, "Einige Erwägungen zur Auslegung Gottes in der ethischen Verkündigung Jesu," EKK Vorarbeiten 2 (1970) 127: "The needy person is the 'where; of God in the world."

9 L. N. Tolstoj, *Sämtliche Erzählungen in fünf Bänden, III,* ed. G. Drohla (Frankfurt: Insel, 1990) 327–341.

something to eat and drink. These three people were Christ; but Martin does not know it. Only as he reads Matt 25:35, 40 that evening does he discover this. For Tolstoy God is that love which lives in all humans and binds together everything which has been separated. 1 John 4:7–8 is for him one of the most central biblical texts.

b) It is not surprising that throughout all the eras of church history Matt 25:31–46 has become one of the *foundational texts of the diaconate*. The classical list of seven "works of compassion" is based on this text. Lactantius drew on Tob 1:17 and expanded the list from Matt 25:35–36 to include the burial of the dead. Since the High Middle Ages this list has remained unchanged.[10] "For medieval *caritas* the saying concerning the least of the brothers was precisely the central focus."[11] "The one saying . . . Matt 25:40 has become far more important for the care of the sick than entire systems of worldly wisdom."[12] In all the important texts up to the new Catholic catechism[13] Matthew 25 is always cited when there is concern to encourage people for the diaconate or to ground the diaconate theologically.

c) Matt 25:31–46 appears to express in exemplary fashion that *that which is good, above all, love, can be done strictly for its own sake*. The people in our text do not know that they have shown love to Christ (vv. 37–39). This is especially important for the interpretation of Immanuel Kant. The heavenly judge has declared that precisely those who "have offered help to the suffering, without so much as considering that such an action is worthy of reward, . . . are the true elect within his kingdom." When reward becomes the driving force behind action, then human action is no longer moral and no longer corresponds to the true natural religion.[14] This idea of Kant's defined the liberal

---

[10] Lactantius, *Epit* 65 = *CSEL* 19, 746; Thomas Aquinas, *Summa Theologica* 2/II, qu 32, art 2; in the commentaries cited in Dionysius Carthusius, *Ennarationes piae ac eruditae in quattuor Evangelistas, Opera XI* (repr. Tournai, 1900) p. 277; Thomas Aquinas, *Super Evangelium S. Matthaei Lectura*, ed. R. Cai (Torino: Marietti, 1951), no. 2098; frequently in iconographic representations, and since the 12th century also in representations of the final judgment (*LCI* I, 245–251).

[11] See W. Brandt ("Die geringsten Brüder: Aus dem Gespräch der Kirche mit Mt 25,31– 46," *JThSB* 8 [1937] 7) for the citations of inscriptions from the founding of hospitals.

[12] W. Liese, *Geschichte der Caritas, I* (Freiburg: Caritas, 1922) 33.

[13] *Katechismus der Katholischen Kirche* (Munich, Oldenbourg, 1993), nos. 1503, 1932, 2447.

[14] I. Kant, *Die Religion innerhalb der Grenzen der blossen Vernunft*, Werke VI, ed. E. Cassirer (Berlin: B. Cassirer, 1923) 310–311, citation 311 (= IV 1/1).

exegesis of the 19th century.[15] But this idea is older than Kant. In his day Pascal formulated it as follows: "The elect ones ignore their virtues and those who are damned ignore the extent of their crime."[16]

d) Matt 25:31–46 plays a major role in *liberation theology.* G. Gutiérrez discusses this text in connection with the "conversion to the neighbor." *There is no way to God which bypasses the "sacrament of the neighbor,"* "since the love of God can do nothing else but express itself in the love of neighbor."[17] To believe thus means to side with the poor. "To place oneself on the side of the poor means to see the likeness of Christ in the tortured and the slum-dwellers, the degraded and the insulted, the afflicted and the humiliated. This is the way which Martin Luther King and Camillo Torres went."[18] Accordingly, for liberation theologians Matt 25:31–46 is not primarily a foundational text for ethics but rather for ecclesiology and christology. J. Moltmann formulates the following basic ecclesiological principle: "The little ones determine *where* the church belongs."[19] The christological dimension of the text comes to expression impressively in a drama by the Korean author Chi-Ha Kim entitled *The Gold-Crowned Christ.* In front of a Korean church stands a gold-crowned statue of Jesus made of cement. Beggars sit in front of it. A fat priest and a business man pass by without paying attention. A policeman even attempts to drive the beggars away. One of the beggars begins to revile the cement statue: "What sort of relationship can there be between this lump of cement and me?" He wants to steal the (genuine!) gold crown of the cement statue. Then the statue begins to weep. It says to the beggar, "You have freed me from my prison! Take the gold crown! For me a crown of thorns is good enough! Take the gold and divide it!" The drama ends as the priest, the business man, and the policeman return, tear the crown away from the beggar, and arrest him. Jesus once again becomes expressionless

---

[15] Thus, e.g., F. C. Baur, *Vorlesungen über neutestamentliche Theologie* (1864; repr. Hildesheim: Olms, 1973) 110–111: "The highest moral deed can . . . only be that which takes place for the sake of the pure idea of the good"); H. J. Holtzmann, *Lehrbuch der neutestamentlichen Theologie, I,* 2nd ed. (Tübingen: Mohr, 1911) 394: "If they had done it with awareness, then the motive of their actions would have been egotistical"; J. Weiss, *Das Matthäus-Evangelium,* SNT I, 2nd ed. (1907) 389.

[16] B. Pascal, *Pensées,* ed. L. Brunschwieg (Paris: Hachette, 1914) no. 515.

[17] G. Gutiérrez, *Theologie der Befreiung* (Munich, Mainz: Kaiser, Grnewald, 1973) 179, 188, 186. Cf. L. Boff, *Jesus Christus der Befreier* (Freiburg: Herder, 1986) 72–73.

[18] W. Jens, "Traktat vom Frieden, von der Gewalt und der Revolution," H. J. Schultz, *Politik ohne Gewalt?,* 2nd ed. (Frankfurt: Suhrkamp, 1980) 149.

[19] J. Moltmann, *Kirche in der Kraft des Geistes* (Munich: Kaiser, 1975) 148.

stone.[20] Accordingly, it is in the poor that Christ becomes a human being. His incarnation continues. Here lies the center of the liberation theology enterprise.[21]

e) Matt 25:31–46 is also important in the *Jewish-Christian dialogue*. The exegetical starting point here is the possibility that the "least of the brothers"—at the level of the Jesus tradition—perhaps refers to all the poor of Israel.[22] *The brothers and sisters of Jesus Christ are therefore the Jews.*[23] Viewed in this light Matt 25:31–46 portrays the bankruptcy of Christianity, which shares in the guilt of Auschwitz. "A world which portrays itself as Christian looked on idly, while the people of the covenant were systematically wiped out, not mindful of what Christ the Judge will say: 'What you have done to one of the least of these my brothers and sisters, you have done to me!'"[24] G. van Norden recounts an impressive story which a journalist published in Silesia in 1933. After the so-called "Brown Synod" of September 1933 a German Christian pastor in Silesia cited the "non-Aryan" clause in challenging the Jews of his congregation three times to leave his church. As he did so, something moved; and the movement was on the cross standing on the altar. The Crucified One came down from the cross and left the church, with the words of Matt 25:45.[25]

f) Matt 25:31–46 also plays a significant role in Christian attempts to define *the relationship of Christianity to other religions*. Again and again there is fascination with the convergence between the Matthean catalog of deeds of love (vv. 35–39, 42–44) and statements from other religions. There is nothing specifically Christian about this list of deeds

---

[20] Thus Byung Mu Ahn, "Jesus and People (Minjung)," *Asian Faces of Jesus*, ed. R. S. Sugirtharajah (London: SCM, 1993) 163–165. For the English translation of the drama see Chi-Ha Kim, *The Gold-Crowned Jesus and Other Writings*, ed. S. K. Chong and S. Killen (Ann Arbor: UMI, 1978).

[21] It is not new. See below [p. 8, par. 2a].

[22] B. Klappert, *Zu richten die Lebenden und die Toten*, RKZ 1994, no. 1, Theologische Beilage, 5–6. In the case that the text goes back to Jesus, this meaning is plausible.

[23] E. L. Ehrlich, *Umkehr und Erneuerung*, ed. B. Klappert and H. Stark (Neukirchen: Neukirchener, 1980) 25.

[24] Schalom Ben Chorin, "Freundesbrief an Ferdinand Hahn," *Anfänge der Christologie: Festschrift für Ferdinand Hahn*, ed. C. Breytenbach and H. Paulsen (Göttingen: Vandenhoeck, 1991) 11.

[25] G. van Norden, G. Schönborn, V. Wittmutz, eds., *Wir verwerfen die falsche Lehre: Arbeits- und Lesebuch zur Barmer Theologischen Erklärung und zum Kirchenkampf* (Wuppertal, 1994) 174.

of love. To the contrary, it resembles material found in other religious texts.[26] Here it is to be noted that the people of Matt 25:31–46 do not know that they are dealing with Christ. The norm according to which the Son of Man of Matt 25:31–46 judges the people appears to have nothing to do with any specific religious faith; rather, it is universal. In this respect our text is comparable to the Pauline text of Rom 2:12–16, according to which the Gentiles are justified in terms of the law which has been written on their hearts. It has also been influential for Protestant theology that already in his day Luther emphasized in a sermon that the deeds of Matt 25:35–44 were carried out sooner by Turks and heathen than by the Germans of his day.[27] Since the Enlightenment there has been the idea of natural reason and a religion of love which stands as the ultimate criterion for judging all historically developed religions and which has found outstanding verbal expression in Matt 25:31–46. Can Matt 25:31–46, accordingly, serve as the foundational text of a Christian theology of religions? P. Tillich, to whom we are indebted for our most important thoughts concerning the "latent church," to which even persons from non-Christian religions belong,[28] sees in Matt 25:31–46 an important witness for a Christianity which is bounded by righteousness and is therefore only "conditionally exclusive." For Tillich Matt 25:31–46 is a text which "*frees the picture of Jesus from a particularism* which would make him the possession of any specific religion."[29] The Japanese theologian and philosopher of religion Takizawa distinguishes the divine "foundational word" [Urwort], a word which is universally valid and operative in all religions and which he calls "Immanuel," from its historical incarnation, thus, e.g., from Jesus. Accordingly, for Takizawa

---

[26] The Egyptian *Book of the Dead* is frequently cited (see n. 123 below); see also GinzaR 1:105 = Lidzbarski 18:5ff. (compassion to the hungry, thirsty, naked, imprisoned); 2:42 = 36:13ff. (similarly); Ovid, *Metamorphoses* 8:607–715 (Philemon and Baucis show hospitality to the gods, disguised as poor wanderers). The closest parallel is an early Buddhist Tripitaka text, where Buddha says to the monks: "Whoever, O monks, would serve me, should serve the sick!" (Vinayo Mahavaggo 8:26, cited by A. J. Edmunds and M. Anesaki, *Buddhist and Christian Gospels* [Tokyo: Yuhokwan, 1905] 105).

[27] M. Luther, *D. Martin Luthers Evangelien – Auslegung II,* 4th ed., ed. E. Mühlhaupt (Göttingen: Vandenhoeck, 1973) 853–854, 857.

[28] P. Tillich, *Systematische Theologie, III* (Stuttgart: Evangelisches Verlagswerk, 1966) 179–182, esp. 181.

[29] P. Tillich, *Die Frage nach dem Unbedingten, Werke V* (Stuttgart: Evangelisches Verlagswerk, 1964) 66–67.

Matt 25:31–46 points to this "Immanuel" and thus relativizes the confession of faith in Jesus, the founder of the religion.[30]

g) Matt 25:31–46 acquires *fundamental theological significance in a post-Christian, atheistic, modern society*. Already in his day Bultmann designated this text "the most impressive sermon on the transformations of God" in the New Testament. God enters into history. He is encountered in the "this worldly" and the immanent. This text can assist modern humanity, for whom the word "God" has become a meaningless requirement of the tradition, not toward a new *concept* of God but rather toward a new *encounter* with God.[31] D. Sölle has expanded this idea in a dialogue with Marxism; and she understands the incarnation of God as that "progressive process of divine self-realization within history" which makes God recognizable and knowable in the poor.[32] "That God was and is insulted and tortured, burned and gassed in this world, that is the bedrock of Christian faith, whose hope is that God might find his identity."[33] In different and yet related fashion, Matt 25:31–46 is a key text for the Japanese theologian of the "pain of God," Kazoh Kitamori: "God hides himself behind the reality of the world [*Weltwirklichkeit*]." God wants "to be loved through our love for the reality of the world." The reality of the world is "painful reality, hunger, thirst, the plight of the refugees, nakedness, sickness, and imprisonment." God suffers the pain of the world; and this pain, because it is the pain of God, becomes the place where humans experience transcendence and grace.[34]

This interpretation of Matt 25:31–46, which has as its central point the identification of "the least of the brothers" with *all* of suffering humanity, is today the most widely circulated[35] and has become virtually the common property of interpreters. But this interpretation

---

[30] K. Takizawa, *Buddhismus und Christentum*, typescript from 1950, 117–118.

[31] R. Bultmann, "Der Gottesgedanke und der moderne Mensch," *Glauben und Verstehen, IV* (Tübingen: Mohr, 1965) 127.

[32] D. Sölle, *Das Fenster der Verwundbarkeit* (Stuttgart: Kreuz, 1987) 50.

[33] D. Sölle, *Stellvertretung* (Stuttgart: Kreuz, 1965) 204.

[34] Kazoh Kitamori, "Theologie des Schmerzes Gottes," *Thö* 11 (1972) 98–103, citation 98.

[35] S. W. Gray (*The Least of My Brothers: Matthew 25:31–46, A History of Interpretation* SBLDS 114 [1989]), the industrious chronicler of the history of interpretation of our text, has listed (225–227) ca. 550 exegetical studies of this text within the 20th century. Of these 550 studies, 440 represent the thesis that *panta ta ethnē* is to be interpreted universally, while approximately 326 maintain a universal meaning for "the least of the brothers."

is not old. It became important only in the early 19th century.[36] In the early church, in the Middle Ages, and at the time of the Reformation—in spite of opinions to the contrary[37]—this viewpoint was represented only infrequently.[38] On the "tree" of the history of interpretation of Matt 25:31–46 this viewpoint is, accordingly, a recent, and, in my perspective, a typically modern "branch."

2. *The classical interpretive model.* Until ca. 1800, however, the generally circulated ecclesiastical interpretation of Matt 25:31–46 viewed *"the least of my brothers" as the members of the Christian church.* Most often this meant all the members of the church. Now and then there was explicit reference to baptism as the distinguishing characteristic.[39]

---

[36] It is presented as a possibility by H. E. G. Paulus (*Kommentar über die drei ersten Evangelien, III* [Lübeck: J. F. Bohn] 488) and later, among others, in the commentaries by C. F. A. Fritzsche, W. M. L. de Wette, and H. Ewald. It appears frequently in the second half of the 19th century.

[37] Gray, for whom this is very nearly the only question he deals with in discussing the history of interpretation, offers, to be sure, a somewhat different picture. According to him numerous interpreters, above all between 325 and 750 CE, represent the "universal" interpretation of "the least of the brothers." The analysis of Gray is in part misleading: (1) he pays too little attention to the fact that his question itself is a modern one which would hardly have interested the early writers; (2) he pays too little attention to the fact that since the Constantinian turning-point the existence of the pagans became less and less of a reality for the interpreters; and, accordingly, it became self-evident within the *corpus Christianum* that to speak of "people" meant to speak of "Christians"; (3) he does not indicate clearly enough that writers who emphasized, most often secondarily, that deeds of compassion must also be carried out *vis-à-vis* non-Christians, could, nevertheless, for this reason see Christians in "the least of my brothers."

[38] Unambiguous references to a universal interpretation of the "least of the brothers" are, for example, the following: Caesarius of Arles, *Sermo* 199:3 = CChrSL 104, 804–805 and *Sermo* 29:3–4 = CChrSL 103, 127–129; from the Middle Ages, Theophylact (*Ennaratio in Evangelium Matthaei,* PG 123 [1883] 432) as a possibility; Tostatus, qu 393 (according to Gray 193; it is the lineage from Adam which is decisive). John Chrysostom also tends in the direction of a universal interpretation, e.g., when he refuses every previous test of the guests who are knocking (R. Brändle, *Matth 25,31–46 im Werk des Johannes Chrysostomus,* BGBE 22 [1979] 248–250). Jerome (*Commentariorum in Matthaeum, libri IV* CChrSL 77 [1959] 244) knows of a universal interpretation but rejects it.

[39] From the early church, e.g., Clement of Alexandria, *Quis dives salvetur* 30:1 = BKV II/8, 261; Tertullian (see Gray 25); John Chrysostom, *Commentarius in sanctum Matthaeum Evangelistam* 79:1 = PG 58 (1862) 718 (baptism); Jerome, 244 ("*non . . . generaliter*"); Augustine (frequently; references in Gray 69–70); Ambrosius, *De Officiis* 2:28 = BKV I/32, 197 (the Christian poor are the treasures of the church); Basil (references in Gray 42–43); from the Middle Ages, e.g., Paschasius Radbertus, *Expositio in Evangelium Matthaei,* PL 120, 866 (not all the poor but the "*pauperes Christi*"); Christian of Stavelot, *Expositio in Matthaeum Evangelistam,* PL

By contrast there were relatively few interpretations which narrowed down the meaning of "brothers" still more, for example to the apostles or to the "perfected Christians."[40] For the most part the interpreters understood "all nations" in a universal sense, such that the role of the non-Christians in the final judgment often remained unclear. But they also often restricted *panta ta ethnē* to "all Christians."[41] This provided a clear sense: For Christians the criterion used in the final judgment is the deeds of compassion which they have done or failed to do for their poor and suffering Christian brothers and sisters. The thrust of the interpretation is for the most part parenetic: The text intends to motivate the church to carry out deeds of compassion. The fact that the people do not recognize Christ has no real place in this interpretive model. This lack of awareness was readily interpreted as

---

106, XX, 1470; Thomas Aquinas, *Super Evangelium S. Matthaei Lectura,* no. 2103; from the Reformation time, e.g., J. Calvin, *Evangelien-Harmonie,II,* ed. H. Stadtland-Neumann *et al* (Neukirchen: Neukirchener, 1974) 297; J. L. Wolzogen, *Commentarius in Evangelium Matthaei* (Irenopolis, 1656) 399; W. Musculus, *In Evangelistam Matthaeum commentarii . . .* (Basel: Heruagius, 1561) 539; H. Grotius, *Annotationes in Novum Testamentum, II* (Groningen: Zuidema, 1827) 273; C. a Lapide, *Commentarius in IV Evangelia: Argumentum in S. Matthaeum* (Antwerp: Meurstum, 1660) 465 ("*proprie*" the text refers to the apostles or the religious; "*consequenter*" it refers to all baptized Christians). Christ does not speak here about giving alms to non-Christians and heretics; but it would not be forbidden to do this). On the early church, see further M. Puzicha (*Christus Peregrinus: Die Fremdenaufnahme [Mt 25,35] als Werk der privaten Wohltatigkeit im Urteil der alten Kirche,* MBTh 47 (1980) 17– 22.

[40] Thus Origen, *Matthäuserklärung,* ed. E. Klostermann, ser 73 = GCS Orig. XI (1933) 174. This corresponds to the Gnostic-Manichaean interpretation. See M. Hutter, "Mt 25,31–46 in der Deutung Manis," *NovT* 33 (1991):276–282. Conversely, *Ps Clem Virg* 1:12 (= ANFa VIII, 59–60) challenges the wandering charismatics to visit those within the established Christian communities who are suffering. In the monastic rules this text is naturally applied above all to one's own monastic community. Thus, e.g., Basil, *Reg. brev.,* no. 284; *Regula Benedicti,* no. 36, but not in exclusive fashion. In his homiletical application Luther (854–855) thinks above all of pastors and teachers, not because they formed an elite group, but rather because things went especially badly for them at that time.

[41] Already in his time Origen (ser 70 = GCS Orig. XI, 164) found it difficult to decide between these alternatives. The following interpreters speak of the judgment of Christians: Lactantius, *Inst* 7:20 = CSEL 19, 647–650; Caesarius of Arles (in Gray 103–104); Venerable Bede, *In Matthaei Evangelium expositio,* PL 92, 109; J. de Valdes, *Commentary upon the Gospel of St. Matthew,* tr. J. B. Betts (London: Trbner, 1882) 447; Grotius 271. For the most part there are no clear alternatives here. The judgment of Christians is often merely the result of the homiletic or parenetic climax of the text. Where the world view of the text is made precise, as in the post-medieval Catholic exegesis, the final judgment is always universal and includes, for example, the infants as well (J. Maldonatus, *Commentarii in Iv Evangelistas, I* (Moguntiae: F. Kirchheim, 1874) 500–501; Lapide 462).

an expression of the humility of the righteous ones or, alternatively, of the lack of discernment of the unrighteous ones.[42]

Splendid examples of parenetic interpretation emerge above all from the sermons of John Chrysostom, who cites this text some 170 times.[43] In homily 79 he emphasizes that the commands of compassion are easy to fulfill and bring with them a surpassing promise, because God himself receives the alms in the person of a beggar. As a result all those who are baptized are brothers of Christ, not only the monks and hermits in the mountains.[44] Over and over John lays on the hearts of his church members in Antioch and Constantinople the plight of the poor, of which there were masses in these cities.[45] Often the lapdog of the wealthy woman is better off than her homeless brothers and sisters.[46] It does not suffice that the congregations have *xenodocheia* (guest-houses); rather, all Christian homeowners should make a room in their house available as a *kellion Christou* for the homeless, where Christ can be present.[47] John belongs to those writers who expressly desire that both Jews and pagans should enjoy hospitality, and even, when in doubt, heretics as well.[48] The 14th address of Gregory of Nazianzus is also an impressive document concerning love for the poor, a love which reaches its climax in Matt 25:31–46.[49] But it was more than sermons and expositions which gave rise during the Middle Ages in the West to the legend passed on by Sulpicius Severus concerning the catechumen Martin of Tours. Martin, a soldier, gave half of his soldier's cloak, his last possession, to a poor man at the city gate of Amiens. In the following night Christ appeared to him, clothed in this half of Martin's cloak; and Christ explained to him in the words

---

[42] See *Opus Imperfectum: Diatriba ad Opus Imperfectum in Matthaeum, PL* 56, 944: "*O humilitas!* . . . *Vir* . . . *bonus etiam debitam sibi laudem fugit.*" Conversely, the question of the damned in v. 44 is an expression of their continuing sinfulness: They do not *want* to perceive (*Opus* 946).

[43] See the summary in Brändle 16–42.

[44] Chrysostom, 79:1 = PG 58, 718.

[45] On the social history see Brandle 75–121.

[46] Chrysostom, *Ad Rom*, hom 11:6 = PG 60, 492.

[47] Thus Chrysostom, *Act Apost*, hom 45:4 = PG 60, 319. Likewise Musculus (542) takes aim at the common custom in the West, current in his time, of sending travelers to the guest houses, thus avoiding the task of extending hospitality.

[48] Brändle 248–249.

[49] Gregory of Nazianzus, *Or* 14 = BKV I/59, 273–308. On the connection with Matthew 25 see *Or* 14, 307–308.

of Matt 25:40 that it was he himself whom Martin had met in the guise of the poor man.[50]

A few isolated reflections, which belong in the framework of this "classical" interpretation, are important and deserve special mention:

a) *Christologically* our text was reflected on deeply in the light of the doctrine of the two natures: as God Christ is incapable of suffering (*apathēs*), but he suffers in his body, the church.[51] He is true God and true human, rich with regard to that which is his, but poor with regard to that which he has from humankind.[52] When the Lord identifies himself with his poor people, his suffering lasts until the end of the world.[53] The humanity of Christ and his suffering are therefore not a temporary episode. The Antiochene John Chrysostom also knows this thought of a continual passion: "I suffered great distress for you formerly, I suffer great distress even now for you, in order . . . to move you to compassion. . . . On the cross I suffered thirst for you; even now I thirst in the person of the poor, in order . . . to move you to love for the sake of your own salvation."[54]

b) *Which deeds* are meant in vv. 35–44? In general the literal interpretation was dominant. That is, one knew that the text had to do with actual deeds of compassion for actual poor people. But already in his day Origen interpreted the deeds of compassion spiritually and referred to them as being nourished with spiritual food, clothed with the clothing of wisdom, and visited with spiritual correction or comfort by the family of faith.[55] In the following time social and spiritual deeds were often placed side by side; even prayer or the offering of right teaching can be an act of compassion.[56]

c) In the Reformation time the *meritorious character of the deeds of compassion* became a point of contention. Calvin emphasized in v. 34

---

[50] Sulpicius Severus, *Vita Martini* 3 = BKV I/20, 22–23.

[51] Origen, ser 73 = GCS Orig XI, 172–173.

[52] Leo the Great, *Sermo* 91:3 = BKV I/55, 281.

[53] Leo the Great, *Sermo* 70:5 = BKV I/55, 187.

[54] Chrysostom, *Ad Rom*, hom 15:6 = PG 60, 547–548; cf. Brändle 56, 326–327, 344.

[55] Origen, ser 72 = GCS Orig XI, 168–172. A beautiful spiritual interpretation lies in Makarius (hom 30:9 = BKV I/10, 260–261): Hospitality refers to the lodging of Christ in the human soul. Jerome (*In Jes* 16 [to 58:6–7] = CChrSL 73A, 667) thinks about the warmth of the church, the clothing of baptism, and the food of right teaching.

[56] Thus, e.g., Calvin 295; Musculus 536, 538; Even professors can also be saved!

that the salvation of the blessed consisted of the free grace of God, which God had destined for the redeemed prior to all human deeds. The reward is a reward of grace; *gar* (v. 35) does not mean that the deeds were the real basis for the redemption.[57] For those who followed Calvin's thought the acts of compassion were not viewed as the basis for redemption, but rather were designated as the "signa" of election.[58] The Catholic exegetes opposed Calvin's interpretation. *Gar* (v. 35) is to be understood as causal and not consecutive; salvation is given "non solum post laborem, sed etiam propter laborem," thus is actual merit.[59] The younger Jansen, the founder of the Catholic Jansenism, formulated the synthesis: "You should now in reality take possession of the kingdom which has been predestined for you from eternity, . . . in order that you might respond to divine predestination with good morals and good deeds."[60]

3. *The exclusive interpretive model.* Since the 18th century[61] a new interpretive model has emerged, which was represented occasionally in the 19th century[62] and since ca. 1960 has been represented more and more frequently.[63] *This interpretation understands panta ta ethnē not*

---

[57] Calvin 294–295; cf. J. Calvin, *Institutes, III* 18, 1–3.

[58] Cocceius, *Commentarius sive notae breves in Matthaei Evangelii, Opera IV* (Frankfurt, 1702) 40. Similarly the Catholic Valdes (449): The deeds attest to our righteousness.

[59] Maldonatus 503; Lapide 464; further proponents of this viewpoint cited in Gray 210–216.

[60] C. Jansen, *Tetrateuchus sive Commentarius in sancta Jesu Christi Evangelia* (Brussels, 1737) 250.

[61] According to Gray (241–242) the first proponent of this viewpoint is the Englishman John Heylin in his *Theological Lectures at Westminster Abbey, I* (1749).

[62] Thus, e.g., by H. Olshausen, *Biblischer Kommentar über sämtliche Schriften des Neuen Testaments . . . , I,* 2nd ed. (Königsberg: Unzer, 1833) 931–932; O Pfleiderer, *Das Urchristentum, I,* 2nd ed.(Berlin: Reimer, 1902) 596; B. Weiss, *Das Matthaus Evangelium,* KEK I/1, 9th ed. (Göttingen: Vandenhoeck, 1898) 440; Th. Zahn, *Das Evangelium nach Matthäus,* KNT 1 (1903) 673–674 (comfort to the disciples); E. Klostermann, *Das Matthäusevangelium,* HNT 4, 2nd ed. (1927) 207; further proponents of this viewpoint cited in Gray (251–252).

[63] Thus, e.g., J. Winandy, "La scène du jugement dernier (Mt 25,31–46)" *ScEccl* 18 (1966) 178–186 (184: "the dramatic staging of" Matt 10:40–42); G. Haufe, "'Soviel ihr getan habt einem dieser meiner geringsten Brüder . . .'", *Ruf und Antwort: Festschrift für E. Fuchs* (Leipzig: Koehler & Amelang, 1964) 484–493; L. Cope, "Matthew 25:31–46: 'The Sheep and the Goats' Reinterpreted," *NovT* 11 (1969) 32–44; J. C. Ingelaere, "La 'parabole' du jugement dernier (Mt 25,31–46)," *RHPhR* 50 (1970) 32–56; I. Broer, "Das Gericht des Menschensohnes über die Völker," *BibLeb* 11 (1970) 292–295 (for Matthew); D. Gewalt, "Matthäus 25,31–46

as "*all the nations*" *but rather as all the pagans.*[64] Thus it is only the non-Christians who stand before the heavenly judge; the Christians, to whom the heavenly judge makes special reference ("these" brothers!), stand to one side and are not judged. Here the "least of the brothers" are for the most part Christians, occasionally also only the Christian apostles and missionaries. The non-Christians are judged according to the way in which they have treated the Christians. Understood in this fashion the text does not have above all a parenetic function, but is rather a word of comfort to the oppressed and persecuted Christian missionaries: They are so important, that the treatment they receive decides the salvation or the damnation of the pagans. What characterizes this interpretation is not the wide open breadth of the universal interpretive model, which does away with all dogma, but rather a narrow, almost sectarian spirit.[65] Matt 25:31–46 is no longer a witness to the relativizing of all dogmas and confessions, but rather a witness to the absolutistic claims of Christianity. Understood in this fashion Matt 25:31–46 is also no longer the goal toward which the entire parenesis of Matt 24:32–25:30 drives forward. To a much greater extent the proponents of this interpretation must accept a final judgment that happens in two stages: After the judgment of the church, an event which is indicated already in 24:25–25:30, an additional text is appended which describes the judgment of the non-Christians.[66]

In the 19th century, as people were actively engaged in mission to the pagans and at the same time were aware that the world could hardly be fully Christianized, a new word about the fate of non-Christians in the final judgment was of significance. Non-Christians are not simply lost; but rather they also have a chance. God will judge

im Erwartungshorizont heutiger Exegese," *LB* no. 25/26 (1973) 9–21; J. Friedrich, *Gott im Bruder, CThM* A.7 (1977) 259–270 (for Matthew); G. Stanton, *A Gospel for a New People* (Edinburgh: Clark, 1992) 207–231; D. Hare, *Matthew,* Interpretation (Louisville: J. Knox, 1993) 288–291; F. Watson, "Liberating the Reader: A Theological-Exegetical Study of the Parable of the Sheep and the Goats (Matt 25:31–46)," *The Open Text,* ed. F. Watson (London: SCM, 1993) 64–66.

64 Viewpoints differ on the question of whether only the pagans are meant or whether the Jews are included with them.

65 Cope 44: "The ethic is a churchly, sectarian one; it does not represent a significant advance in the ethical thinking over the ethics of Judaism of its day."

66 This corresponds to *TestB* 10:8–9 (first judgment of Israel, then judgment of the nations). S. Grossmann (*Das Ende der Welt* [Wuppertal/ Kassel: Oncken, 1991]) senses well the secondary character which 25:31–46 has in this case, when he (101) describes the text as a sort of "refugee camp" for non-Christians.

them not on the basis of their faith but rather on the basis of their deeds of love, that is, according to a criterion which is valid in all cultural circles and which can be expected of pagans as well.[67] This thought could function as a positive impulse in the 19th century. In the present day-world in which the final judgment is foreign to most people and the salvation of non-Christians has become more self-evident, this impulse is no longer so necessary. Nevertheless, ever since ca. 1960 this interpretation has become more popular. As I see it, the reason for this does not lie in the fact that this interpretation corresponds to any specific needs of the present day, but simply in the fact that it is exegetically strong. It has on its side the text of Matt 10:11–15, 40–42 and the normal Judeo-Greek linguistic usage of *ethnē* = *gôyim*. In contrast to the "universal" exegesis which has dominated the scene in our century, this interpretation signifies a radical shift. The text of Matt 25:31–46, which according to the "universal" interpretation was very familiar and "politically correct," has suddenly become foreign. Many exegetes have registered strong theological criticism of this interpretation,[68] even while it appears exegetically unavoidable to them. To make theological and exegetical application in our age of a text understood in this fashion is difficult for most exegetes. This interpretive model appears more and more prominently today, even though hardly anyone welcomes it.

Today the major exegetical alternatives are the "universal" and the "exclusive" interpretive models. The "classical" interpretive model leads a shadowy existence in the current debate. But it is precisely this interpretive model which I would like to support in the following exegesis.

2. *Analysis*

2.1 *Synchronic Analysis*

Matt 25:31–46 is the last text before the Passion Narrative begins; and it is at the same time Jesus' last extensive instruction of his disciples. Accordingly, this text is of great significance. Working backwards, this text is linked, by way of the textual "bridge" of 24:32–

---

[67] In classical fashion the interpretation of J. Jeremias (*Die Gleichnisse Jesu*, 9th ed. [Göttingen: Vandenhoeck, 1977] 205, 207) corresponds to this need.

[68] J. Weiss (388) speaks of "intolerable Christian arrogance." J. Gnilka (*Das Matthäus-Evangelium, II*, HThK I/2 [1988] 375) holds that this interpretation has little to do with Christian or Matthean thought.

25:30, to 24:30–31: Now will be narrated what happens when the Son of Man comes in glory with the angels.

Vv. 31–33 create the introduction, which describes the scenery of the final judgment. This introduction is relatively extensive, because in vv. 32b-33 it is expanded by a comparison of the heavenly judge with a shepherd. As a conclusion v. 46 reports in very brief fashion the ultimate fate of the righteous and the hardhearted. In between, in vv. 34–40 and vv. 41–45, there are two dialogues between the accused and the heavenly judge, who is not called "king." These dialogues are intended to make the sentence of the heavenly judge comprehensible. Such dialogues, which contain on the one hand the charges or the basis for judgment and on the other hand the self-defense of those who are charged, are often found in the depictions of judgment scenes in the Jewish world.[69] The two dialogues of our text correspond with each other in very nearly verbatim fashion. Following the introductory judgment saying (vv. 34 and 41, respectively) there is the basis for the judgment: The heavenly judge lists three sets each composed of two deeds of love[70] which the one group has carried out and the other group has not (vv. 35–39 and 42–44, respectively). There is then the counter-question asked of the heavenly judge, or alternatively, the self-defense of those who have been judged. Both groups take up the list of deeds of love and repeat them as questions introduced by *pote* (vv. 37–39 and 44, respectively). Accordingly, the list of the deeds of love is repeated a total of four times. The farther the text advances, the more distinct becomes the tendency towards conciseness and brevity. Individual substantives are very skillfully omitted and verbal clauses are combined, so that some details of vv. 34–39 no longer find any correspondence in vv. 41–44. At the end of each dialogue, in vv. 40 and 45, respectively, the heavenly judge dismisses the counter-question with a solemn *amēn* saying which reveals his identity with the least of the brothers.

---

[69] References in Hermann L. Strack and Paul Billerbeck, *Exkurse zu einzelnen Stellen des Neuen Testaments: Abhandlungen zur neutestamentlicher Theologie und Archologie*, 2 Pts., Vol. 4 of *Kommentar zum Neuen Testament aus Talmud und Midrasch* (Munich: C. H. Beck, 1956), Pt. 2. 1200, 1202, 1204, 1206, 1209–1210.

[70] *Peinaō* and *dipsaō, xenos* and *gymnos*, as well as *asthenein* and *en phylakē einai* are word pairs which belong together materially. The connections between the words in these word pairs is made clear in vv. 37–39 through the threefold repetition of *pote*.

The text is still entitled "the parable of the final judgment"; but it is no parable in the normal sense of the word.[71] Only vv. 32b-33 are a short parable. The major portion of the text consists of the two large "judgment dialogues" (vv. 34–40 and 41–45). Only with difficulty can one describe Matt 25:31–46 as a "judgment scene":[72] There is neither an apocalypse,[73] since there is no vision; nor is it "judgment parenesis"[74] since it contains no single direct address to the readers.

2.2 Diachronic Analysis

A few exegetes consider the entire text to be Matthean material.[75] Most exegetes, however, hold that this text was taken over by the Evangelist from his special source and was reworked with varying degrees of intensity. *Vv. 31 and 32a* contain very many Matthean expressions[76] and otherwise bring biblical language to mind.[77] In addition this introduction is not only linked to 24:30–31,[78] but also brings to mind 13:40–43, 49–50,[79] 16:27, and above all 19:28.[80] The

---

[71] It is a parable at best only in the sense of the "metaphorical speeches" of Ethiopic *Enoch*.

[72] K. Berger, *Formgeschichte des Neuen Testaments* (Heidelberg: Quelle-Meyer, 1984) 303–304.

[73] Thus D. O. Via, "Ethical Responsibility and Human Wholeness in Mt 25:31–46," *HTR* 80 (1987) 80–82.

[74] Thus E. Brandenburger, *Das Recht des Weltenrichters*, SBS 99 (1980) 110.

[75] Thus Cope 42–44; Haufe 486 ("largely" redactional); W. J. C. Weren, *De broeders van de Mensenzoon: Mt 25,31–46 als toegang tot de eschatologie van Mattes* (Amsterdam: T. Bolland, 1979) 29–73, 240–241; R. H. Gundry, *Matthew: A Commentary on His Literary and Theological Art* (Grand Rapids: Eerdmans, 1982) 511–516; Gnilka 367–370. Quite apart from the results of the linguistic analysis, this hypothesis is difficult; since nowhere else has Matthew freely created such a long text.

[76] The following terms are Matthean: *pas, angelos, tote, synagō, emprosthen, ethnos*; on *panta ta ethnē* see 24:9, 14; 28:19; on *aphorizō* see 13:49. Matthew occasionally creates redactional sayings about the coming Son of Man. See Luz II, 498.

[77] Most important are the connections of vv. 31, 34, 41, 46 with the conclusion of Deuteronomy; cf. Deut 30:16 (*eulogeō, klēronomeō*), 30:19 (*zōē, eulogia katara*), and 33:1–2 (*eulogeō, angeloi met autou*), which Matthew has perhaps strengthened redactionally. A further text for comparison is Joel 3:2, 11. In the case of Zech 14:5 (LXX) there are hardly any verbal connections. Likewise 25:31–32 is hardly dependent on the metaphorical speeches of Ethiopic *Enoch*; the correspondences are limited to the common biblical phrase "sitting on the throne of glory" (contra J. Theisohn, *Der auserwählte Richter*, StUNT 12, [1975] 152–182).

[78] Common catchwords: *ho huios tou anthrōpou, erchesthai, doxa, angeloi.*

[79] Common catchwords: *ho huios tou anthrōpou, kosmos, basileia/basileus, diabolos, angeloi, pyr, dikaios, patēr.*

correspondence between 19:28 and 25:31 is perhaps easiest to explain by suggesting that Matthew here draws once again on his own prior saying (19:28), which has been strongly edited. It is no longer possible to say how the pre-Matthean introduction to this text would have sounded. We know neither who it was who originally stood before the judgment, nor whether the text originally spoke about the "Son of Man."[81] In *vv. 32b-46* the Matthean expressions are much more sparse.[82] Above all the syntactical structure appears to be shaped by Matthew, while the vocabulary is in part traditional.[83] Accordingly, it is most reasonable to assume that Matthew adopted an oral tradition about the final judgment, a tradition whose basic elements are well preserved in vv. 32b-46. Perhaps he assimilated this tradition to the conclusion of Deuteronomy.

The tradition-historical reflections are very difficult as they relate to this text. In the original text is it God[84] or Jesus who is identified

---

[80] *Hotan kathisē ho huios tou anthrōpou epi thronou doxēs autou.*

[81] But neither can one prove that *ho huios tou anthrōpou* was merely a redactional addition. For tradition historical reasons, however, the expression as it is used here appears to be relatively new. *Ho huios tou anthrōpou* shows up elsewhere in old Synoptic texts only in individual sayings and words of commentary, but not, as for example in the metaphorical speeches of Ethiopic *Enoch*, as a statement in a longer composition. The exceptions to this rule (Mark 9:9, 12 parr.; 13:26 parr.; Matt 13:37; 16:13; Luke 21:36; 22:48; 24:7) are secondary, often redactional texts.

[82] The following terms are Matthean: *tote, erō, deute, patēr mou* (v. 34); *gar* (v. 35); *tote, apokrinomai, dikaios, legōn, kyrie, ē* (v. 37); *de, ē* (vv. 38–39); *apokrinomai, erō, amēn legō hymin, heis toutōn* (v. 40); *tote, erō, pyr, aiōnion, diabolos* (v. 41); *gar* (v. 42); *tote, apokrinomai, legōn, kyrie, ē, diakoneō*—on this word, cf. 20:26, 28; 23:11 (v. 44); *tote, apokrinomai, legōn, amēn legō hymin, heis toutōn, oude* (v. 45); *aperchomai, de, dikaioi* (v. 46). The above-listed vocabulary points in widely differing degrees to Matthean redaction.

[83] This applies in particular to the *hapaxlegomena kataraomai* (v. 41), *episkeptomai* (vv. 36, 43), *kolasis* (v. 46). In an altogether non-Matthean fashion *synago* is used in the sense of "welcoming a guest" (vv. 35, 38, 43). The concept of "angels of the devil" (v. 41) is likewise unique. Even *elachistos* is not redactional; the concept of the brothers of Jesus also shows up in the tradition (Mark 3:35). Sometimes the use of *basileus* in v. 34a is considered to be redactional (thus, for example, J. A. T. Robinson, "The 'Parable' of the Sheep and the Goats," *NTS* 2 [1955/56] 230). But for Matthew *basileus* plays no major role as a designation for Christ. Rather, it appears only in 2:2, 21:5, and 27:11–42, in settings which are very different from each other and never eschatological. The Matthean preference for *basileus*-parables (18:23; 22:2, 7, 11, 13) points away from redactional use, since these parables refer to God and not to Christ. On the other hand Matthew knows the *basileia* of the Son of Man (13:41; 16:28; 20:21), but otherwise never designates the Son of Man as "king."

[84] Thus, for example, R. Bultmann, *Die Geschichte der synoptischen Tradition,*

with the "least of the brothers"? Only attention to the substance of the text can help to decide this question. The argument for *Jesus* lies in the fact that v. 34 distinguishes the "father" from the "king." In addition there are Christian parallels for an identification of Jesus with humans (Mark 9:37; Q 10:16; Matt 10:42//Mark 9:41). The argument for *God* lies in the fact that in the Jewish world "king" is a wide-spread designation for God, while a transferral of the kingly title to Christ the heavenly judge remains very difficult.[85] In Jewish texts God himself is almost always the heavenly judge. Another argument for God is the content parallels, both biblical and Jewish, which view deeds of love vis-à-vis the poor as decisive in the final judgment of God or which view these deeds as done to God himself.[86] Nevertheless the first hypothesis remains the simpler of the two, because it does not have to deal with a fundamental reinterpretation or reformulation of the text. This

---

FRLANT 29, 4th ed. (1971) 131; Robinson 230; Broer 287–288; E. Schweizer, *Das Evangelium nach Matthäus*, NTD 2 (1973) 311; U. Wilckens, "Gottes geringste Brüder: zu Mt 25,31–46," *Jesus und Paulus: Festschrift für W. G. Kümmel*, ed. E. E. Ellis, E. Grässer (*Göttingen:* Vandenhoeck, 1975) 376–382, etc.

[85] The designation of the Davidic messiah as "king" is relatively widespread (thus Friedrich 180–182). The Davidic messiah is hardly ever identified as heavenly judge. Paul Volz names only *Tg Isa* 53:9 and a late interpretation of Dan 7:9 on the messiah in *Hag* 14a and *Sanh* 38b. See Volz, *Die Eschatologie der Jüdischer Gemeinde im Neutestamentlichen*, 2d ed. (Tübingen: Mohr, 1934) 275. Besides God only the Son of Man appears as heavenly judge, and this in the metaphorical speeches of Ethiopic *Enoch*. But even while individual attributes of God are transferred to the Son of Man in the metaphorical speeches (above all, sitting on the "throne of glory," i.e., on the throne of God), this does not mean that the Son of Man is "king" in those places. A mixture of Son of Man and messianic expectations becomes visible in Judaism only with 4 Ezra 13 (ca. 100 CE). A transferral of kingly attributes to the "messianic" heavenly judge by Jesus or in the early Jesus tradition would thus be an anachronism, entirely apart from the fact that Jesus himself probably understood himself as Son of Man but not as Davidic messiah.

[86] Prov 14:31 ("Those who oppress the poor insult their Maker, but those who are kind to the needy honor him" [NRSV]); 19:17 ("Whoever is kind to the poor lends to the LORD, and will be repaid in full" [NRSV]); *2 Enoch* 44:2–3 ("The one who insults the face of a human, insults the face of a king . . ."). Closely related to this is the *St. Midr Tann* on Deut 15:9, which is cited by Jeremias (205): "When you have given the poor something to eat, I consider it as though you had given me something to eat." In somewhat different fashion there are Jewish parallels which understand God as the model for carrying out deeds of love and which challenge people to imitate him. Thus, e.g., *Sota* 14a = Strack-Billerbeck I, 561 (God has clothed the naked [Gen 3:21!], visited the sick [Gen 18:1], comforted the sorrowing, and buried the dead [Deut 34:6]). On the significance of the deeds of love in the final judgment see n. 123 below.

question is closely connected with that of the origin of the text, a question which is equally difficult to resolve.

The earlier viewpoint, occasionally represented, that the text was originally Jewish,[87] has today been largely abandoned. In my perspective it is also unlikely that the text emerges from Hellenistic Christianity.[88] This text goes back either to Jesus himself[89] or to an editor in an early Jewish-Christian congregation.[90] Pointing in this direction are the (sparse!) Semitisms,[91] the apocalyptic horizon, and the numerous Jewish parallels.[92] The attempts to trace the text back to Jesus stand on shaky ground. Did Jesus originally speak of "King" God as the heavenly judge? But everywhere else in the sayings of Jesus God is "always the father, never the brother of humans."[93] Accordingly, the criterion of coherence works against this hypothesis. Or, did Jesus speak of himself as the coming Son of Man/heavenly judge?[94] But then the parallels Q 10:16, Mark 9:37, and Matt 10:42 would also have to go back to him, something that to me seems very unlikely. A further difficulty with this interpretation is the designation "king." Did Jesus use a title for the Davidic messiah, or perhaps even a divine title, to refer to himself?[95] Even in a formal sense this extensive Son of Man

---

[87] Following Bultmann, 131.

[88] Thus Brandenburger 76–86. He would like to root the text in a Hellenistic-Jewish congregation, because the identification of Jesus with the little ones has its closest parallels in Rom 8:29 and Heb 2:11–18. However, I can find in Matt 25:31–46 neither a christology of pre-existence nor a christology of incarnation.

[89] Thus, Jeremias 206; T. W. Manson, *The Sayings of Jesus*, 2nd ed. (London: SCM, 1949) 249; Broer 288; Friedrich 283–297; Wilckens 379–382.

[90] Thus, e.g., F. Hahn (*Christologische Hoheitstitel* FRLANT 83 [1963] 187), who stands on the side of a Palestinian Jewish-Christian origin.

[91] The use of juxtaposed main clauses with conditional meaning in vv. 35–39 and 41–44 is probably semitizing ("for I was hungry, and you gave me food" [NRSV], etc.); *synagō* = show hospitality (= Heb. *ʾsp, kns*). The use of *heis* for *tis* is not necessarily semitizing (for Greek illustrations see W. Bauer, W. F. Arndt, F. W. Gingrich *A Greek-English Lexicon of the New Testament and Other Early Christian Literature* 15th ed. [Chicago: University of Chicago Press, 1974]), s.v. *heis*, no. 3. What is certainly not to be understood as a Semitism is the (only apparently redundant) *toutōn* in vv. 40 and 45; the heavenly judge might well be indicating his brothers, who are perhaps standing next to him.

[92] See n. 26 above. On the deeds of love see nn. 119–120, 122–123.

[93] Thus Wilckens 379. To be sure, I am using the argument differently than Wilckens, who concludes from this that a piece of Jesus' originality becomes visible here. But for Jesus God is the father, not only of Jesus, but also of humankind.

[94] Thus C. Riniker, *Die Gerichtsverkündigung Jesu*, diss. Bern (1991) 512–522.

[95] See n. 85 above.

text does not fit well with the remaining Son of Man sayings of Jesus, which are very brief. Is it therefore more prudent to trace this highly exceptional text to some early Jewish-Christian disciple of Jesus otherwise unknown to us. I am perplexed and must in all honesty remain with a *non liquet.* The many interpreters who trace this text back to Jesus, often with no hesitation, must ask themselves whether they do so because Jesus has become so important to us children of the 20th century that we only unwillingly deprive him of this text.

3. *Interpretation*

Vv. 31–32a. The introductory verses, 31–32a, shaped by the Evangelist, reveal a portrait of the coming of the Son of Man, Jesus, which is already familiar to the readers from many indications in previous texts.[96] The majesty of the Son of Man is clearly emphasized. As in 13:39, 41, 49, 16:27, 24:31, and elsewhere as well in the early Christian tradition,[97] angels accompany him. As in 16:27 and 24:30, he comes in divine glory; as in 19:28, he sits on the "throne of glory," i.e., in solemn biblical language, on the throne of God. As it is throughout the New Testament, the Son of Man, Jesus, is himself the heavenly judge, not, as in the Danielic tradition, merely the clerk of the court or a trial witness.[98]

Before his throne are gathered *panta ta ethnē.* The narrative focuses on them alone. The third group which is apparently involved with the final judgment, "these" brothers, never appears in the judgment scene. Only in v. 40 are they first mentioned in the direct address of the judge. This is fundamental for the understanding of the text. The readers, as they have done with all the previous texts, will seek here as well to find themselves in the text. They understand only as they identify themselves. With whom will they identify themselves here? That they would, in line with the "exclusive interpretive model," identify themselves with "the least of these my brothers" is, so to speak,

---

[96] 10:23; 13:40–43, 49–50; 16:27–28; 19:28; 24:30–31. Cf. U. Luck, *Das Evangelium nach Matthäus*, ZBKNT 1 (1993) 275: "In Matthew this event throws its shadow far ahead of itself."

[97] Mark 8:38; 13:27; John 1:51 cf. 2 Thess 1:7; Luke 12:8–9.

[98] Herein lies the most important material parallel between the metaphorical speeches of Ethiopic *Enoch* and the *entire* New Testament Son of Man tradition. But at the same time this is a parallel in which the New Testament goes beyond the metaphorical speeches. In the *Enoch* text the "Lord of the spirits" remains present and active as the highest ruler; it is he who has set the "Chosen One" on his throne (cf. 38–40; 46:3; 48:2; 49:2; 51:3; 61:8; 62:2, 14).

narratively impossible. The "brothers" emerge quite incidentally only in v. 40 and are not actors in this final judgment scene; rather, they come only indirectly into the speech of the heavenly judge. If the narrator had wanted the readers to make this identification, he would have had to introduce the "brothers" already at the beginning of the scene, together with the heavenly judge. This would have been easy to do, but it doesn't happen. Do the readers therefore identify themselves with *panta ta ethnē*? This would fit well with the preceding texts about the two slaves, the young women, and the slaves of the traveling capitalist (24:45–25:30), since here as well as there the narrator offers the readers their choice of one of two roles. The readers must decide, not only in the act of interpreting the text but also in the course of life, whether they belong on the side of the wise or the foolish young women, the one slave or the other, those who stand on the right or those who stand on the left. But semantically this identification is difficult to make. Could Jewish-Christian readers identify themselves with *panta ta ethnē*? In the Judeo-Greek world of the Septuagint and in the Gospel of Matthew as well the term *ethnē* for the most part designates the non-Israelite (and non-Christian) pagans.

To begin with, the readers will interpret this expression on the basis of their previous reading in the Gospel of Matthew. On the one hand they will remember 24:30–31. There it is *pasai hai phylai tēs gēs* who become witnesses of the coming of the Son of Man: They lament; and directly afterward the Son of Man sends out his angels, in order to gather together "his elect" from all over the earth. If one understands 25:31–46 as the continuation of 24:29–31, then this suggests a universal meaning for *panta ta ethnē*. But it still leaves open the question of whether the "elect" who are gathered from the four corners of the earth also belong to this group. The readers will likewise remember 24:9, 14, where the expression *panta ta ethnē* was used even earlier. There the *ethnē* were the non-Christian nations; but the context itself was a missionary context. "And this good news of the kingdom will be proclaimed throughout the world, as a testimony to all the nations; and then the end will come" (24:14, NRSV). Now the end which was announced there has come. Does this mean that since then all nations have heard the "good news of the kingdom" and have either received it or refused it? This possibility is highly likely.[99]

---

[99] The Pauline analogy shows that the claim to have "fully proclaimed" (Rom 15:19, NRSV) the good news throughout the whole world from Jerusalem to

Therefore on the basis of 24:9, 14 one cannot say that our text speaks only of those "pagans" who have not come into contact with Christ. In line with Matthew's missions perspective *panta ta ethnē* is most likely a reference to "all nations," including the church.

Four additional considerations confirm this interpretive proposal:

1. Since 24:3 Jesus is speaking to his disciples alone. Since 24:32 he is warning them with continuously new pictures of the judgment which stands before them as well. But Matthew has not yet portrayed the judgment of the church. The entire parenesis of 24:32–25:30 has no purpose at all, if it does not end with a judgment scene which includes the church.[100]

2. Only with this interpretation does our text correspond to the Matthean understanding of judgment: In 16:27 the Evangelist makes clear that the Son of Man will "repay each one (!) for what he/she has done." In 13:38, 41 the kingdom of the Son of Man was the field consisting of the world. And out of the world the angels will gather wheat and darnel, i.e., the righteous and the unrighteous. According to 13:37–43 there is no distinction between church and world so far as the final judgment is concerned. The church itself is a *corpus permixtum*. A special judgment of the non-Christians by the Son of Man would utterly contradict the Matthean view of the church.

3. Matthew concluded three of his previous discourses with texts which spoke of the final judgment, a judgment which also included the church (7:21–27; 13:37–43, 47–50; 18:23–35). Should this text— which is precisely the conclusion of Jesus' final discourse and, by the same token, the conclusion to Jesus' entire instruction of his disciples—now be left off the list, because it is an appendix speaking of something which does not directly affect the church, namely, the judgment of the "others," the non-Christians? That is scarcely conceivable.

4. Both groups address the heavenly judge as *kyrie,* a term which is unambiguously church language and reminds the readers of 7:21–22

Illyricum could readily be linked to the expectation of the Parousia.

[100] If *panta ta ethnē* were limited to non-Christians, then Matt 25:31–46 would create a sort of appendix which provides information to resolve the special problem of the fate of non-Christians in the final judgment. Mattill (107–114), who understands the text in this way, boldly relocates it at the conclusion of the Missionary Discourse, after 10:42. See A. J. Matill, "Matthew 25:13–46 Relocated," *Restoration Quarterly* 17 (1974) 107–114.

and 25:11, 20–24.[101] This form of address will strengthen the readers in their "hypothetical" identification with the two groups to the right and to the left of the Son of Man.

Whether *Israel* is or is not included in "all the nations"[102] is a question which the text does not answer. Just as in 24:9–14, there is no special focus here on Israel. To be sure, Matthew has indicated how the special election of Israel has been taken away and how the guilt for the persecution of the prophets and of Jesus' messengers has come "on this generation" (21:43; 23:34–24:2; cf. 24:15–20) in the destruction of Jerusalem. But up till now Matthew has said nothing about a final judgment of Israel by the Son of Man.

Vv. 32b-33. The judgment by the Son of Man begins with a comparison which explains the actual judgment procedure, the separation (*aphorizō*). To begin with, the heavenly judge separates the righteous and the unrighteous, placing the former on the right ("good") side and the latter on the left ("bad") side.[103] Already at the beginning he has passed his sentence and does not need, as do worldly judges, to establish the truth through a trial of those to be judged. This preliminary separation underlines the sovereignty of the heavenly judge. The subsequent dialogue with the two groups merely provides the basis for the sentence already passed. The comparison with the shepherd[104] explains this decisive act of separation. Presumably this has to do with the act of separating young he-goats destined for slaughter from the rest of the herd of small livestock.

The picture half of the parable is less clear than it appears to most exegetes. The term *eriphos* is translated neither by "buck," "she-goat,"

---

[101] Observation by M. Mayordomo-Marin.

[102] R. Walker (*Die Heilsgeschichte im ersten Evangelium*, FRLANT 91 [1967] 108–109) represents the exclusion of Israel most pointedly. As he sees it, according to 21:33–22:10 and 23:1–24:2 Israel "has been excluded from God's election history"; and the intra-historical judgment of Israel, the destruction of Jerusalem, has for him eschatological character.

[103] In Judaism and the ancient world "left" was the bad side and "right" the good and lucky side. See Billerbeck I, 980–981; Ingelaere 41; W. Grundmann, art. *dexios*, *ThWNT* II, 37:21ff.; 38:14ff. The word *euōnymos* (= "with a good name," "honored") is a euphemism for *aristeros*.

[104] The comparison with the shepherd could remind the readers of 9:36, 14:14, and 18:12–14, where the "shepherd" motif is, to be sure, used in a different fashion. There is no consistent Matthean narrative strategy within this Gospel with regard to the motif of "shepherd," as J. P. Heil ("Ezekiel 34 and the Narrative Strategy of the Shepherd and Sheep Metaphor in Matthew," *CBQ* 55 [1993] 698–708) illustrates.

nor "he-goat."[105] If it had to do with "bucks," i.e., male animals, this might suggest that the shepherd must separate the female animals from the male animals for milking. The bucks would then be placed on the left side, because they give no milk.[106] The scholars who settle on the translation "she-goat," to the contrary, point to the fact that in the mixed herds of Palestine the she-goats were separated from the sheep in the evenings, because they needed more warmth than the less sensitive sheep. However, this lovely Palestinian shepherd's custom exists only on paper and originated through imprecise copying from Dalman's large work on the "Work and Customs in Palestine."[107] Accordingly, why a shepherd separates the she-goats from the sheep remains a puzzle.

But all these considerations are unnecessary, since *eriphos* means neither "buck" nor "she- goat." This is, to be sure, what stands in Bauer's lexicon.[108] But the ancient lexicographers and scholastics provide other very clear information: *Hoi* or *hai eriphoi* are very young kids, in distinction to full-grown he-goats (*tragoi*) and to slightly older "youthful" he-goats (*chimarroi*).[109] Accordingly, *eriphos* has a precise

---

105 In German, where the expression "to separate the sheep from the bucks" has become proverbial, the translations usually follow Luther and the Zurich Bible of 1531 and use the term "*Böcke*" (cf. Vg: *haedus* = buck, he-goat). In English the term "goat" predominates, in French the term "*bouc*" (he-goat), in Spanish the term "*cabras*" (she-goat) next to "*cabritos*" (kid).

106 Thus, e.g., Gnilka 372. Otherwise one reads many amusing things by the older and the more recent theologians about the nature of bucks. A buck is *foetens* (it stinks), *asper, immundus, petulcus* (it butts), *fervens semper ad coitum, lascivus, per praecipitia incedens, rixosus* (it is quarrelsome) (thus, e.g., Jerome 243; Lapide 462); bucks have horns like the devil (thus Friedrich 144, n. 70), etc.

107 G. Dalman (*Arbeit und Sitte in Palästina, VI*, BFCT II/41 [1939] 276) cites a report, according to which this takes place in autumn on the coastal plain. K. Wengst ("Wie aus Böcken Ziegen wurden [Mt 25,32f]," *EvT* 54 [1994] 493–497) illustrates in delightful fashion how a general custom of Palestinian shepherds has grown out of this report of a local and temporally confined procedure from around 1900 through the use of scholarly citations.

108 Bauer, s.v., holds that *eriphos*, whose meaning he falsely identifies as "buck" or "he-goat," refers "when compared with *probata*, merely to goats as such." Wengst (497–498) has checked out the references which presumably illustrate this and has proved them to be incorrect.

109 Eusthatius (*Commentary in Homer's Odyssey*, ed. G. Stallbaum [1825] 1:33, 42ff. and Julius Pollux. *Polluci's Onomasticon*, 3 vols. [Stutgardiae: Teubner, 1967] 1:250) provides lists of the different designations. Maurice Schmidt (ed., *Hesychii Alexandrini Lexicon*, 4 vols. [Tanae, 1860] 2:191) defines *eriphos* as a *mikros aix*, which was born in the spring (of the same year). Further references are found in Johann T. Wettstein, ed., *Novum Testamentum graecum* (1751–52), vol. 1, 511. In the

meaning and can be used neither as a general designation for "she-goats" nor as a general designation for male animals of various species ("buck"). So why does a shepherd separate the kids from the sheep? Perhaps the LXX puts us on the right trail: In almost all places where *eriphoi* appear, they are slaughtered, consumed, or sacrificed.[110] Presumably this is the reason for the selection of the young kids: They were destined for slaughter.[111] The only difficult question remaining is why this herd consists precisely of sheep and kids. Might one suppose that in the Judeo-Greek world of the day the old use of *probata* for "small livestock"[112] was still current? In the LXX this word is almost always the translation of *ṣōʾn*, which generally means "small livestock," thus sheep or she-goats.[113] The picture half of the parable would then be compelling: The shepherd separates certain kids which have been designated for slaughter from the remainder of the herd of small livestock, i.e., from the remaining sheep and she-goats. To be sure, this hypothesis is impossible to prove.[114]

V. 34. The metaphorical language is finished. Jesus continues in ordinary language. With regard to the unusual designation of "king" for the coming Son of Man, it must remain an open question whether the readers remember the "kingdom" of the Son of Man, which was

---

LXX *eriphos* is normally used to translate *gᵉdî* (kid); only once is it used for *ʿattud* (buck). In ten cases out of 27 *eriphoi* is further clarified by the addition of *aigōn*. There is no single example of the use of *eriphoi* for "young sheep"; but the not infrequent juxtaposition of *arnes* and *eriphoi* in biblical and Greek texts indicates that the latter could not be a reference to lambs. Accordingly, *ho/hē eriphos* does not mean "young animal," as Wengst supposes (498); rather it refers more precisely to "young she-goat."

[110] Gen 27:9, 16; 37:31; Exod 12:5; Lev 1:10; Judg 6:19; 13:15, 19; 2 Chr 35:7–8; Tob 2:12–13; Amos 6:4; Jer 28:40; Ezek 43:22, 25; 45:23; cf. Gen 38:17, 20, 23; 1 Sam 16:20; 1 Esdr 1:7.

[111] Similarly Wengst (499–500), who presumes a suppression of the concept of judgment in the euphemistic style of the most recent interpretive history of this picture.

[112] Even in Greek the word *probata* meant "livestock" in general in the eastern Greek, Ionic dialect. It was first in the Attic dialect that this word took on the special meaning of "sheep" (Henry G. Liddell and Robert Scott, eds. *A Greek-English Lexicon*, 2 vols. [Oxford: Oxford University Press, 1843], 2:1471; Preisker and S. Schulz, art. *probaton ktl.*, *ThWNT*, VI, 689:6–13).

[113] This usage appears more than 200 times. To the contrary *probaton* appears only nine times as the translation of *kibesah/kebes* (= ram/lamb).

[114] In Matthew itself the meaning "sheep" is, to be sure, unambiguous in 7:15, 10:6, and 15:24.

mentioned earlier (16:28; 20:21, cf. 13:41);[115] or whether they, on account of the "throne of glory" on which Jesus sits, rather associate Jesus with the "king," God, who according to biblical tradition sits on this throne. In all events the majesty of the heavenly judge, Jesus, is emphasized by means of this expression. At the same time this effectively paves the way for the contrast with the epiphany of the "king" in the "least ones." The heavenly judge calls those who are blessed by God his father into the "kingdom" prepared for them through God's eternal plan. According to Jewish conception the "salvific blessing" [*Heilsgut*], e.g., the Garden of Eden, belongs among the pre-existent things.[116] "You blessed of my father" implies, without spelling it out, the concept of predestination which was self-evident in the Jewish world of that day.[117] That Matthew shows a certain reticence vis-à-vis the concept of a double predestination will be made clear in the parallel verse, 41. Perhaps, with v. 34 (and with vv. 41 and 46), Matthew wants to remind the readers of the conclusion of Deuteronomy, where Moses lays in front of the people both blessing and curse.[118]

Vv. 35–39. Now the actual judgment dialogue begins. Its statements and questions are formulated in the aorist tense, as a reflection back on the present day life of the readers. Accordingly, from this judgment scene which is held in the future, the readers discover something about their own present-day existence. The text has indirect parenetic character, which is strengthened still more by the repeated and urgent "when" (vv. 37–39, cf. v. 44). The list of good deeds which the king enumerates as the basis for his invitation to those on the right sounds familiar to Jewish ears. Similar lists are often found in biblical and early Jewish texts.[119] The later rabbinic theory

---

[115] Working against the viewpoint that the text intends to suggest this association is the observation that *basileia* is used in a different sense here than in 13:41, 16:28, and 20:21, namely in the sense of "salvific blessing" [*Heilsgut*], as in 21:43, *basileia tou theou.*

[116] See Billerbeck I, 974f, 983 (the Garden of Eden and Gehenna are pre-existent.)

[117] See Billerbeck III, 266–272.

[118] See n. 77 above. This literary allusion fits with 2:1–23, 5:1–2, and 7:28–29, where Jesus appears as a new Moses. On the Moses typology of Matthew D. Allison (*The New Moses: A Matthean Typology* [Minneapolis: Fortress, 1993] 267) notes correctly, as I see it: "The New Moses theme remains one of many things, and not the most important."

[119] Isa 58:7 (hungry, homeless, naked); Ezek 18:7, 16 (debtors, hungry, naked);

identified these lists as "deeds of love" ($g^e m \hat{\imath} l \hat{u} t\ has \bar{a} d \hat{\imath} m$) and distinguished them from alms ($s^e d \bar{a} k \bar{a} h$). Actions counted as "deeds of love" if they required not only an outlay of money but also the involvement of the entire person. In the rabbinical literature both money and involvement together belonged among the "good deeds" ($ma^c as \hat{\imath} m\ t \hat{o} b \hat{\imath} m$) which could not, as could the commandments, be defined in precise fashion on the basis of the Torah.[120] The combination of "those who hunger" and "the naked" is especially frequent in such Jewish enumerations, while "visiting the imprisoned" is mentioned only infrequently. Does this reveal an important situation-related characteristic of early Christianity?[121] The deeds of love were very important for Jews, after the destruction of the temple as well as before.[122] According to Jewish texts the doing or neglecting of deeds of love could be decisive in the final judgment.[123] As a result

---

Job 22:6–7 (naked, thirsty, hungry); 31:17, 19, 21, 31–32 (orphans, naked, poor, innocent, strangers); Tob 1:16–17 (hungry, naked, dead); 4:16 (hungry, naked); Sir 7:34–35 (sorrowing, sick); 2 Enoch 9:1 (hungering, naked, fallen, injured, orphans); 42:8; 63:1 (naked, hungry). A. Wikenhauser ("Die Liebeswerke in dem Gerichtsgemälde Mt 25,31–46," BZ 20 [1932] 366–369) and W. Kornfeld ("Die Liebeswerke Mt 25,35f.42f in alttestamentlicher Überlieferung," Theologia scientia eminens practica: Festschrift für F. Zerbst, ed. H. C. Schmidt-Lauber [Vienna: Herder, 1979] 255–265) provide a survey of the biblical and early Jewish material. Of the rabbinic references it is AbotRN 7 (= Billerbeck IV, 567–568), Derek erez rabba 99 (= Wikenhauser 370), and Derek erez zuta 2 (= Wikenhauser 370–371: hungering, thirsty, naked) which come closest to Matthew 25.

[120] Billerbeck IV, 559–560.

[121] Christian missionaries in particular had to deal with the possibility of going to prison; but not only they had to do so. See Q 12:4–12; Mark 13:9–13; 2 Cor 6:5; 11:23. The visiting of prisoners was important, because they were not cared for in the prisons. Only wealthy prisoners could have themselves cared for privately. In the case of the poor T. Mommsen (Römisches Strafrecht, Systematisches Handbuch der Deutschen Rechtswissenschaft I/4 [Leipzig: Duncker & Humblot, 1899] 304) speaks of "atrocious misery." For wandering Christian missionaries, who had no family members in a given area, help from the congregation was especially necessary. Only from the time of Constantine onward was there a fund for rations for all the poor (comment by H. Herzig). Lucian De morte Peregrini, ch.12) describes how one could live well in prison: "The Christian (!) Peregrinus was visited in prison and spoiled by all the members of the congregation, from children to widows to church elders ad infinitum."

[122] According to ʾAbot 1:2 the world rests on the Torah, worship, and the deeds of love. There are further rabbinical references in Billerbeck IV, 562–565 and Friedrich 170–171.

[123] Midr Ps 118 & 17 (= Billerbeck IV, 1212): The deeds of love are the gate of eternity; Sanh 103b (= Billerbeck IV, 567): Hospitality gives one a share in the coming world; Ned 40a (= Billerbeck IV, 577): To visit the sick rescues one from

the dialogue sounds familiar to the Jews and to the non-Jews.[124] The only surprising thing is that the heavenly Son of Man/king says: "You have given *me* something to eat," etc. This formulation is clearly puzzling; and the following counter-question is understandable. The awkward repetition of all the deeds of love in question form (vv. 37–39) has a retarding effect and heightens the tension: How will the heavenly judge/king resolve the puzzle which he has placed before the redeemed?

Those who are judged do not know that they have in fact done their deeds of love to Christ himself. This motif of "unawareness" is of importance in the history of interpretation. Does this have to do, in the sense of Kant and liberal theology, with the good which is done for its own sake? Must one, accordingly, with regard to *panta ta ethnē*, nevertheless think in terms of non- Christians, in line with the "exclusive" and in part the "universal" interpretive models?[125] But here the difficulties immediately become evident. Have the wandering missionaries of Jesus—with whom this text has to do above all (see below)—not said in their proclamation who it is that they are representing? Have they allowed their reception to be separated from the reception of their message? In reality it is first and foremost those people who have received their message who will have supported them with deeds of love. If one wishes to interpret the motif of "unawareness" from the real world, by asking who in reality the people were who did not know Christ, then one might sooner think of Christians in the post-Easter era, who were amazed that they had done a service of love to Jesus himself; because he had died, and they no longer expected to be able to meet him.

But one can probably not transport the motif of "unawareness" out of the world of the text and into the real world. Rather, one must interpret this as a literary motif[126] which serves to enable the christological point of the narrative in v. 40. The heavenly judge of the

---

Gehenna. From the non-Jewish world the text from the Egyptian *Book of the Dead* 125 belongs on this list: The dead gave food to the hungry, water to the thirsty, and clothing to the naked.

[124] See the texts in n. 26 above.

[125] Thus, e.g., Jeremias 207; Haufe 490; Friedrich 276 (for the post-Easter tradition).

[126] Already in his day Calvin (I, 296) thought that through the motif of "unawareness" it is clearly stated for us (!) that Christ himself is affected by what humans do to each other.

text would no longer have to say to those who are judged—and, by the same token, to the hearers and readers—that he identifies himself with the least of the brothers, if the people on the right and the left had already known this during their earthly life. The motif of "unawareness" enables the formulation of the point of the narrative *literarily*. It makes this point emphatic and easy to remember, because the hearers and readers experience the surprise of those who are judged along with them. Beyond this, it illustrates the concept of reward reflected in the text: The righteous have not "calculated," nor have they intended to earn their reward through their love. It is, therefore, in my perception misleading to seek for those people in the world beyond the text who know nothing of Christ, as though the text was concerned only with them. Accordingly, Matt 25:31–46 does not speak of a special route to God without awareness or confession of Christ.[127]

V. 40. In a solemn *amēn*-saying the heavenly judge gives the answer which is the decisive statement of the entire text: Everything which the blessed of his father have done to "one of the least[128] of his brothers" they have done to him himself. How do the readers understand this expression? All likelihood points to the fact that in a Christian congregation one would think first of all about the members of the church, who call each other "sister" and "brother." The few references in the church tradition to "brothers of Jesus"[129] point in this same direction. In the Gospel of Matthew the "brothers of Jesus" are those who do the will of the father, a characterization by which Matthew himself makes clear that he means the disciples (12:49–50). Also in the Easter story he will once again use the expression "my brothers" and relate that term to the disciples (28:10). This fits well with the Christian conception that one day the members of the congregation

---

[127] The following consideration supports this viewpoint: Whoever has read or heard this story knows, once for all, that the heavenly judge is present in the least of his brothers. Therefore the story itself shatters the innocence of its hearers and readers (cf. Via 99). But while it intends to open the eyes of its hearers and readers about the least of the brothers, it does not intend to destroy the possibility of salvation about which it speaks! If that were the case, then everyone should be forbidden to read this text!

[128] *Elachistos* is presumably to be interpreted as a frozen superlative with an elative sense (= quite small, very small). See F. Blass, A. Debrunner, F. Rehkopf, *Grammatik des neutestamentlichen Griechisch* & 60:2.

[129] Mark 3:34f; John 20:17. See also Rom 8:29 and Heb 2:11–18.

will judge the world at the side of the heavenly judge (thus 1 Cor 6:2; Matt 19:28).

Are the "least of the brothers"[130] a special group within the Christian church? In the text the term "least" stands in contrast to the "great" heavenly king and heavenly judge. This expression emphasizes in rhetorical fashion the enormous distance between those who are suffering and the heavenly judge; and it effectively highlights the surprising marvel of his identification with them.[131] Accordingly, one should not construct a meaning for *elachistos* from beyond the text, e.g., from the Christian designation *mikroi*, whoever that may have identified.[132] Only from the content of vv. 35–39 can it be determined who it is about whom the readers will have thought above all.

It can be concluded on the basis of numerous pre-Matthean early Christian texts that the early Christian wandering charismatics, i.e., the missionaries of Jesus, come into special focus with regard to this question. From the Missionary Discourse of Q 10 we know that the messengers of Jesus were poor (Q 10:4). While they were on the road, and therefore *xenoi*, they were dependent on others for their food and drink (Q 10:7–8; cf. Matt 10:42). They possessed only one piece of clothing (Mark 6:9); if it tore, then they were *gymnoi*.[133] They risked their lives (Q 12:4–7) and had to answer to the officials (Q 12:8–9, 11–12; cf. Mark 13:9–13), who could also put them in prison (cf. Q 12:11–12). The Pauline adversity-catalogs (1 Cor 4:11–13; 2 Cor 6:4–10.; 11:23–27) also speak of hunger and thirst, prisons, cold and nakedness. Paul also knows of sickness (2 Cor 12:7–9).[134] The deeds of

---

[130] That this text does not speak of "sisters" is a painful circumstance. The Evangelist, who thought in a thoroughly patriarchal fashion, naturally meant Christian men and Christian women with his use of "brothers"; but in his cultural context he never thought of specifically emphasizing this fact.

[131] *NumR* 14:4 (= Henry Freedman, trans. and ed., and Mauirce Simon, ed., *Midrash Rabbah*, 10 vols. [England: Steven Austire, 1939] 6:581–582): If one hears an interpretation of Torah from the "least in Israel," it should be viewed as if it came from the wisest in Israel, yes ultimately from God himself.

[132] The proponents of a "universal" interpretation point, as I see it, correctly, to the fact that *mikros* may not simply be exchanged with *elachistos* (e.g., Schweizer 313). Matthew clearly could have said *ton adelphon mou ton mikron*, if he had wanted to. The term *elachistos* was chosen to set up a contrast with the heavenly "king" and not because of its proximity to the term *mikroi*.

[133] The term *gymnos* can also mean "inadequately clothed" (Liddell-Scott, s.v. no. 5).

[134] See also the self-description of the Apostle Thomas with the words from Matt 25:35–36 in *Acts Thom.* 145.

love enumerated in Matt 25:35–44 fit perfectly with the situation of the wandering Christian missionaries.

At the same time we know that the Risen Lord identified himself precisely with these wandering messengers and their message. They knew as well that those who rejected them awaited a judgment worse than that of Sodom and Gomorrah (Q 10:12, cf. 6). It is also of them that Jesus says: "Whoever hears you, hears me; whoever rejects you, rejects me" (Q 10:16). This axiom of the early Christian apostolate corresponds to the Jewish "law of the messenger" and lies behind the identification statements of vv. 40 and 45. This axiom is widespread. Paul intensifies it through his theology of the cross (2 Cor 4:10). Luke has the Risen Lord say to Paul, the persecutor of the Christians: "Why do you persecute me?" (Acts 9:4; 22:7; 26:14). And it still was a rule in the congregation of the *Didache* that one should receive a sojourning teacher—if he were a genuine teacher—"as the Lord" (*Did.* 11:2; cf. 4:1).

Accordingly, the readers of the Gospel of Matthew have a rich experiential background and a rich knowledge of the tradition that leads them to associate the "least of the brothers" of Jesus first of all with the wandering charismatics. The relationship between the established communities and the wandering charismatics might, on the pre-Matthean level of the text, have been the experiential background of this text. To be sure, even in the pre-Matthean tradition the first concern was probably not that of offering comfort to the oppressed wandering charismatics.[135] I do not think that our text ever functioned in such a way that the "least of the brothers," who do not appear directly in the text at all, could become a figure with whom the addressees would identify. Rather, the text functioned only in such a way that the members of the established congregation were addressed and questioned concerning their conduct vis-à-vis the wandering charismatics. As I see it, the text worked even then as parenesis and not as self-confirmation for the oppressed Christian missionaries. Only indirectly is there something in this text of an absolutistic claim which was already characteristic of the proclamation of Jesus (cf., e.g., Q 11:31–32; 12:8–9) and which also characterized the

---

[135] Thus, e.g., Zahn 674; Ingelaere 60; Stanton 222. See also the exclusive interpretive model above [pp. 8–9].

proclamation of his messengers after Easter (cf., e.g., Q 10:10–12; 12:10).[136]

But it is not only their knowledge of the tradition and their own experiences but also their reading of the Gospel of Matthew that will have led the readers to think first of all of the wandering charismatics. They will remember the Missionary Discourse of chapter 10, where the talk was of the travels of the disciples and their life as strangers (10:5–15; cf. 28:19), of their poverty (10:9–10), their dependence on hospitality (10:11–15), and the dangers they face from a hostile environment, court trials, and perilous circumstances (10:17–23, 28–31; cf. 24:9). Above all the conclusion of the Missionary Discourse will come to mind, in which they are challenged to offer hospitality to the wandering brothers and sisters (10:40–42). There Matthew, under the influence of Mark 9:37, had formulated the old *logion*, Q 10:16, in such a fashion that it corresponds exactly to our text: "Whoever welcomes you welcomes me" (Matt 10:40, NRSV).

Accordingly, Matt 10:40–42 is the closest parallel to v. 40. This verse has to do above all with the identification of Jesus with the wandering charismatics. Beyond that one might think of Jesus' identification with other "lowly" and "little" ones among the Christians (cf. 18:5).[137] The text does not deal—in the sense of the "universal" interpretive model—with the identification of Jesus with the poorest human beings in general, nor with the general concept of the "likeness of God,"[138] nor even with "the humiliation of the Pre-existent One and his presence as 'brother' in the sphere of typical human misery."[139] The text also does not deal with the Pauline conception of

---

[136] As I see it, one cannot say that Matt 25:31–46 exhibits an "intolerable Christian arrogance" and "fanaticism" (J. Weiss 388), since the text does not serve the purpose of self-legitimation. To be sure, that does nothing to alter the fact that the claim which Jesus and the early Christian wandering charismatics make for themselves seems singularly strange in today's pluralistic society.

[137] Even according to the Missionary Discourse of chapter 10 the wandering charismatics were not simply a clearly delimited group; rather, those disciples whose commission and fate the discourse depicts themselves stood under the judgment and were sharply questioned about their conduct vis-à-vis the messengers. See esp. 10:32–33, 34–39, 40–42 and Luz II, n. 3, esp. 78–79, 154–156.

[138] Thus P. Christian, *Jesus und seine geringsten Brüder*, ETS 12 (1975) 40–41. On the connection between Gen 1:26–27 and Matt 25:35–40 in the early church see Puzicha 109–113.

[139] Brandenburger 83. Brandenburger works outward from the Pauline conception of incarnation; and in this way he legitimates his universal understanding of "brothers."

the "body of Christ,"[140] nor even with the collective concept of the Son of Man[141] (which never existed!). What stands in the background, even in Matthew, is much more the Jewish-Christian "law of the messenger," i.e., the Jewish/early-Christian concept of the *shāliach* or *apostolos*, in whom the heavenly Son of Man becomes manifest.[142]

The location of the readers is the same as in 10:40–42: They are the ones who are being questioned, not those whose claims are now finally being confirmed. They will remember that in their own congregation love has grown cold, lawlessness has gained the upper hand (24:12; cf. 18:6–9), and there is in their midst hatred (24:10) and those "incidents" of power-grabbing for which reason Jesus continually needs to sharpen his message to them concerning humility (18:1–5) and service (20:20–28; 23:8–11). Accordingly, when they read v. 40, they will not afterwards identify themselves with the "least of the brothers," as though they themselves suddenly no longer stood under the judgment of the Son of Man. Rather, they know that they themselves have been challenged just as much by Jesus' proclamation as all other humans and that their own congregation can be just as much the field of the devil as the rest of the world (cf. 13:38–39). They too belong to *panta ta ethnē* and will be judged by the same criterion as all other humans. The very special claim of the disciples of Jesus in the Gospel of Matthew, a claim which actually exists, can therefore not be transformed into triumphalism and self-absolutizing. The disciples of Jesus are, to be sure—not through themselves but through Christ—the most important persons in world history; but whether they themselves are sufficient to the claim which is hidden in this truth is an open question. They are the "light of the world"; but whether this light actually shines, such that people praise the Father on account of their works (5:14–16), is not at all certain. Accordingly, there is in Matthew's thinking no special group of "least brothers," who stand at a special place beside the Son of Man and do not come under judgment.

---

[140] The ecclesiastical interpretation very often reads like this. Thus, e.g., John Chrysostom (see Brändle 286–288) and Augustine (see Puzicha 128–136). Luther (sermon from 1537 = Mühlhaupt 857) has Christ say: "The poor are my feet and limbs."

[141] Thus Manson 249–250.

[142] To that extent it is not simply wrong, when certain interpreters think of the apostles. See, e.g., J. R. Michaels ("Apostolic Hardships and Righteous Gentiles," *JBL* 34 [1965] 30–37).

Metaphorically stated: For Matthew the "least ones" stand in the midst of the others.[143]

Vv. 41–45. The second half of the text, the dialogue of the heavenly judge with those on the left, contains no further great surprises. In v. 41 the symmetry with v. 34 is broken in two places: Matthew sensitively avoids the formulation *katēramenoi tou patros mou*;[144] and he also does not say that the eternal fire has been prepared for the cursed ones from the beginning of creation, since God "has not created humankind for destruction."[145] Matthew has shortened the following part of the dialogue somewhat; but he cannot leave it out altogether, since damnation in the judgment remains a real and threatening possibility for him. In impressive fashion the dialogue makes clear that one's relationship to Jesus cannot be disconnected from one's relationship to real persons, in this case the members of the congregation, who represent Jesus. To honor Jesus means nothing other than to do what he has commanded, above all, to take the "love command" seriously. In v. 44 those who are condemned summarize the deeds of love, in good Matthean style, with the term *diakoneō*. They should have conducted themselves just as the Son of Man conducted himself (cf. 20:26, 28; 23:11). But this part of the text must also not be "universalized," even though the term *adelphoi* no longer appears in v. 45. This word has fallen prey to Matthew's tendency to shorten the text in the second half of the dialogue. But the readers will read v. 45 in the light of v. 40 and assume the presence of this word. That Matthew has left out precisely the word *adelphoi*, whose interpretation today has become so controversial, indicates only that the meaning of this word is clearly unambiguous for him and needs no further explanation.

V. 46. The text concludes very abruptly. The concluding verse, 46, indicates that the main focus of the text does not lie in the announcement concerning the eternal future of those who are saved and those who are lost. The point of the text lies rather in the two

---

[143] This corresponds to the fact that in the Matthean congregation the wandering charismatics are no special group, clearly distinguished from the remaining disciples. Rather, the disciples are all called to the perfection of the wandering charismatic and, to that extent, "potential wandering charismatics." Whether this was already so in the pre-Matthean tradition must, to be sure, remain open.

[144] John Chrysostom 79:2 = PG 58, 719–720: It is not the Father who curses them, but rather their own deeds.

[145] Origen, ser 72 = GCS Orig XI, 172; cf. Thomas Aquinas, no. 2094.

amēn-sayings of vv. 40 and 45. Eternal life and eternal punishment are the result of the verdict of the heavenly judge. Here it is once again clear that Matthew conceives of a twofold conclusion to world history: There is no talk here of universal reconciliation. Here he can forego a special depiction of the terrors of hell (cf. 24:51; 25:30). The time of warnings is now past. The final judgment is now here. The heavenly judge has spoken. Nothing can be changed at this point.

Summary. This concluding text of the Eschatological Discourse fits into Matthean theology. After the lengthy parenesis of 24:32–25:30 Matthew once again takes up the description of the judgment of the Son of Man. His judgment is universal and is carried out over all humankind. But Matthew has in mind above all the church, which now, along with all other humans, must also answer for itself before the heavenly judge. This corresponds to 13:37–43, 49–50. There as well the heavenly judge made no distinction between church and world— the *kosmos* is his *basileia*—but rather asked only whether the fruits were good. This also corresponds to 16:27: The Son of Man will judge *each* person for what he/she has done. According to Matthew, therefore, there will be only *one* judgment, the cosmic judgment of the Son of Man/king before which *all people* must appear. The text offers a minimum of ideological information. It points to the actual judgment scene only in one picture; and after the judgment has taken place, it provides no descriptive details about the ultimate fate of those who are saved or those who are lost or about the new age. The entire focus lies rather on the judgment dialogues, which set forth in fourfold repetition the criterion on which the judgment is based. In this respect Matt 25:31–46 reminds the readers of the small judgment dialogue in 7:21–23. There as well it all has to do with deeds. Zealously saying "Lord, Lord" is of as little use to the faithful there as their miracles and prophecies. It is the deeds that count, not the confession or the charismatic gifts. The criterion in the judgment will be love. Accordingly, this corresponds to the proclamation of Jesus, for whom love is the greatest command (5:21–48; 22:34–40; 23:23). In this criterion, which the heavenly judge sets forth for the nations and for the church, the readers recognize what their Teacher and Lord, Jesus, lived out before them and taught them during his earthly life. Whether as a result in their own self-estimate they identify themselves with those on the right or with those on the left makes no difference; since the judgment consists precisely in the fact that the Son of Man points out the places and not the people. In this way the Matthean version of our text forbids every attempt at Christian self-absolutizing.[146]

Christologically this last extensive teaching text of the Gospel of Matthew is something akin to a collection of Matthean christological motifs. In the background stands the traditional Jewish concept of the "one who is sent" (cf. 10:40–42). This concept is intensified through the promise of Immanuel: The Risen Jesus is with his church as "Immanuel" until the end of the world (1:23; 28:20), even to the extent that he identifies himself with the poverty and the suffering of his disciples. The readers of the Gospel of Matthew also know that Jesus himself during his earthly life was a homeless stranger (8:20) and that he suffered hunger (21:18; cf. 12:1). They will learn in the immediately following Passion Narrative that much worse things happened to him than being thrown into prison. If the Son of Man, in his divine glory at the final judgment, identifies himself with his poor brothers, they will also think back to his earthly life. Accordingly, this text illuminates something of the *entire* road which the Son of Man has traveled,[147] of the identity of the earthly and exalted Jesus, and of the presence of *God* "with us" which is so foundational in the Matthean Immanuel. To that extent the text also lets the church sense something of the foundation which undergirds them, even in the final judgment, but which does not spare them that judgment.

4. *Towards the sense of the text for today*

We have spoken of the fascination of the "universal" interpretation of our text,[148] which is a central evangelical interpretation for many people—and for myself as well—because it opens up fundamental areas of life to Jesus' gospel of unrestricted love. This interpretation is not tenable on the basis of the Matthean text. The Evangelist has seen in Jesus' suffering brothers most likely not every suffering human being but rather suffering disciples. But attention to a text according to the history of influence seeks to take seriously that the sense of an old text can become new for new readers in a new situation. The question is therefore: Is it theologically permissible to interpret a text against its original sense, if the sense which emerges is centrally gospel

---

[146] Accordingly, Matthew has not narrowed the focus of the traditional text, as Friedrich, e.g., maintains (302–303).

[147] Cf. U. Luz, "The Son of Man in Matthew: Heavenly Judge or Human Christ?" *JSNT* 48 (1992) 3–21.

[148] See above, [3–6].

for today's recipients and at the same time helpful to them in their own situation? I would like to answer this question in this instance—not always!—with a "yes" and to point out, on the basis of the biblical text, the reasons and the limits of this "yes."

1. A fundamental point of orientation for every current reading of a text is the history of Jesus, with which new interpretations of biblical texts must correspond.[149] In our case there are different positive points of connection. Jesus himself spoke of unrestricted love, not only to friends but also to enemies (5:43–48). Matthew has handed on this explosive text; even though for himself, as for the entire early church, it is love for the members of the congregation which stands in the foreground (cf. Gal. 6:10). Matthew will further narrate how Jesus in his Passion traveled the road of radical love all the way to the end and how this process broke down the barriers to the Gentiles for Jesus' disciples. If one takes the "crucified interpreter," Jesus,[150] in this fashion as the guideline for working with this individual text, it becomes evident that the "universal" interpretation is able today to break through the boundaries of love in a way which corresponds to that history of Jesus to which the entire New Testament bears witness.[151]

2. On at least one point the sense of direction of the Matthean text corresponds to the universal interpretive model. Matthew was concerned to show that the Christian church has no special privilege in the final judgment, but rather will be asked by her Lord, the Son of Man, only about her deeds of love, no different from all other humans. To this extent this Matthean text carries with it a warning against every attempt at Christian or ecclesiastical self-absolutizing. The modern proponents of the "universal" interpretation have sought

---

[149] See Luz, *Matthew in History*, 82–91.

[150] Thus the happy formulation of Watson (72). Watson encourages the readers (72–80) to a "new disclosure" of the text, which corresponds to the direction of the text and is christologically grounded.

[151] One should not, however, appeal to an original "Jesuanic" sense of this particular text. Naturally one can consider whether Jesus—in the event that this text actually does go back to him—could have understood "the least of the brothers" as a reference to all the poor and oppressed of *Israel* (but not: all humans!). In the early Christian tradition, then, the focus of this text would have been narrowed, as happened with reference to the "poor," "hungry," and "weeping" ones of the Beatitudes (Q 6:20–21). But this consideration remains as vague and uncertain as the possibility of tracing the text back to Jesus in the first place. It is no viable exegetical justification for a desired interpretation.

to take further steps in this same direction of "de-absolutizing" the Christian church. Accordingly, they do not work with the sense of the biblical text itself, but rather with the direction in which it points.

3. Fundamental—and precisely from the point of Jesus—is the question of whether a new interpretation of the biblical text produces love.[152] Today the truth of new theological interpretations of biblical traditions is determined on this basis. Does the "universal" interpretation meet this test? Yes! It provides eyes to rediscover the poor of the world, the non-Christians, yes, even God himself in such a way that the love of which the text speaks becomes a reality.

At the same time it is also true that a new interpretation does not make the text itself unnecessary. I mean this not only in the formal sense that every new interpretation must have a textual starting point on which it builds. I mean this also in a material sense: That in "the least of the brothers" of Jesus—whether this is now a church member or not—the exalted Lord, or for that matter God, hides himself and allows himself to be experienced is no self-evident statement which one can simply make at will. Rather, this has to do with a paradoxical truth which is unrecognizable to human eyes, a truth which is surprising in such a fundamental sense that it can only be imparted to humans from beyond themselves.[153] To this extent the text which does this, or alternatively the Christ who speaks through this text, is far more than a point of departure for new interpretations or the teacher of a universal ethic which ultimately makes the teacher, in turn, unnecessary. Jesus is rather that one who provides new eyes which allow one to see and experience poor human fellow humans and God in new ways; and the text is the source of a power which allows one to stand fast in the final judgment.[154]

---

[152] See Luz (*Matthew in History*, 91–97) for the truth criterion of love.

[153] P. Althaus (*Die letzten Dinge*, 4th ed. [Gtersloh: Bertelsmann, 1933] 193) says that "the judgment will reveal before God the importance of that which is invisible and self-evident." For the disclosure of this truth the judgment of *God* is necessary, or alternatively, a text which speaks of it.

[154] Similarly Watson (79): "The crucified Jesus does not offer a mere *explanation* of the world . . ., for he is the source of liberating grace."

Chapter Eleven

A Sound Map of the Sermon on the Mount

BERNARD BRANDON SCOTT AND MARGARET E. DEAN

This paper is an experiment in understanding the construction of the Sermon on the Mount from the standpoint of hearing. As such its first concern is the text as signifer, the sign's physical aspect. Semantics operates at the level of the sign, the unity of signifier and signified. Yet most often biblical studies neglect the signifier. Because this paper is an experiment, not all the rules are well known or known in advance, but must be discovered by trial and error. Likewise, the payoff (meaning) may turn out to be different from that in which traditional scholarship has invested.

I. *Reading Is Recitatio*

The Sermon on the Mount is contextualized in the Gospel of Matthew as a speech, a common sense observation. Yet the implications of this observation are important. As George Kennedy remarks, "It was the intent of the evanglists to present speeches, and early Christian audiences listening to the Gospels read, heard these chapters as speeches."[1] Two aspects of Kennedy's quote need attention. First, the Sermon the Mount is a speech, and second, the gospels were read aloud, meant to be heard. Both demand that we pay attention to the sound of the text and the implications of that sound.

---

[1] George A. Kennedy, *New Testament Interpretation through Rhetorical Criticism,* Studies in Religion (Chapel Hill, NC: The University of North Carolina Press, 1984) 39.

Reading creates its own characteristic social,[2] conceptual space for its reception.[3] After the invention of the printing press, that space has increasingly become interior and reading a silent process. Discourse was replaced by silent scanning.[4] This points to an essential difference between modern and ancient story-telling. Modern fiction explores a character's interior life and psychological development, while ancient fiction holds up the character as exemplar. The model is dyadic,[5] exterior, and character remains fixed.[6]

Historical criticism builds on the historical difference between the Hellenistic world and our own, and increasingly, social science theory is drawing even stronger differences. Literary criticism, by contrast, has tended to miminize the difference, almost seeing the techniques of narrativity as universals.[7] Rhetorical criticism is challenging this assumption by positing and analyzing a specifically Hellenistic rhetoric.

Since ancient texts were meant to be read aloud,[8] they must employ sound to create public space. Furthermore since sound is the

---

[2] M. A. K. Halladay, *Language as Social Semiotic: The Social Interpretation of Language and Meaning* (Baltimore: University Park Press, 1978).

[3] "Every written text occupies physical space and at the same time generates a conceptual space in the minds of writers and readers. The organization of writing, the style of writing, the expectations of the reader—all these are effected by the physical space the text occupies. Jay David Bolter, *Writing Space. The Computer, Hpyertext, and the History of Writing* (Hillsdale, NJ: Lawrence Erlbaum Associates, 1991) 85.

[4] Elizabeth L. Eisenstein (*The Printing Press as an Agent of Change: Communications and Cultural Transformations in Early Modern Europe* [2 vols. New York: Cambridge University Press, 1979] 1.129–136) deals with some specific outcomes of this shift "From a hearing public to a reading public."

[5] Bruce J. Malina, *The New Testament World, Insights from Cultural Anthropology* (Atlanta: John Knox, 1981) 53–60.

[6] Robert Scholes and Robert Kellogg, *The Nature of Narrative* (New York: Oxford University Press, 1966) 164–7. Theodore J. Weeden (*Mark, Traditions in Conflict*, [Philadelphia: Fortress Press, 1971]) was among the first to draw out the implications of this understanding of character for a study of the gospels.

[7] R. Alan Culpepper, *Anatomy of the Fourth Gospel, A Study in Literary Design, Foundations and Facets* (Philadelphia: Fortress Press, 1983) is a good example. His title plays on the title of Northope Frye's famous book, *The Anatomy of Criticism*. Robert W. Funk, *The Poetics of Biblical Narrative, Foundations and Facets* (Sonoma, CA: Polebridge Press, 1988) attempts to develop a literary criticism based on the texts themselves.

[8] For evidence see especially Paul J. Achtemeier, "Omne Verbum Sonat," *JBL* 109 (1990): 3–27 and sources cited there, and William V. Harris, *Ancient Literacy* (Cambridge: Harvard University Press, 1989) 36. Lentz in dealing with poetry and

first encounter point for audience and text, we would expect sound to have a strongly conventional aspect. Modern readers (i.e., printing press readers) press towards the meaning, the semantics, of a text. As Eisentein notes, they read to learn.[9] The ancients recited to learn; reading was a public, out loud activity. As Harris says about book publication at Rome, "it is assumed to be the *recitatio*, not the book, which will make a man celebrated."[10] This has important implications for our project. A written text was written to be spoken aloud (*recitatio*), not read silently, pointing out the primary importance of sound. Modern silent readers depend on typographic conventions to guide and organize the printed word for semantic digestion.[11] An ancient reader had few such clues beyond the alphabet itself. Ancient manuscripts have few conventions and need preparation to be read.[12]

---

drama maintains, "The Greeks continue, by ancient tradition and contemporary [i.e., Hellenistic] choice, to think of literature as an oral form." (Tony Lentz, *Orality and Literacy in Hellenic Greece*, [Carbondale, IL: Southern Illinois University Press, 1989] 147), and in regard to philosophical writings, "Reading aloud is therefore more widespread than silent reading of philosophical discourse....The simplest practical explanation for this absence [of silent reading] is the high cost of papyrus and the expense of having copies written upon it. Making multiple copies of discouses—for each member of a group, for example—would be prohibitively expensive" (102). Evidence in the ancient literature abounds. For example, Aristotle prescribed in his *Rhetoric*, "that which is written should be easy to read or easy to utter, which is the same thing" (III.v.6). Acts 8:30 and Augustine, *Confessions*, iv. 96, are both examples of private reading out loud. For an extensive recent discussion of the reference from Augustine, see Mary Carruthers, *The Book of Memory: A Study of Memory in Medieval Culture*, (Cambridge: Cambridge University Press, 1990) 170–72. We are not contesting that private reading could be silent, but reading was normally out loud in the ancient world. Str-B 2:687 quotes a number of later references forbidding reading Torah silently. This indicates that the earlier tradition was reading aloud, not silently.

9 Eisenstein, *The Printing Press as an Agent of Change* 1.65.

10 Harris, *Ancient Literacy* 226.

11 Eisenstein, *The Printing Press as an Agent of Change* 1.52: "The highly competitive commercial character of the new mode of book production encouraged the relatively rapid adoption of any innovation that commended a given edition to purchasers." She gives an extensive list with references to the typographical conventions early printers developed.

12 Henri-I. Marrou, *A History of Education in Antiquity*, Wisconsin Studies in Classics. (Madison, WI: University of Wisconsin Press, [1982], 1956) 150–57, provides a detailed analysis of the teaching of reading and writing, indicating that it was not pupil friendly. "Expressive Reading" was not taught until secondary school because of the difficulty in reading a text presented by *scriptio continua* (165–66). Stanely F. Bonner in *Education in Ancient Rome: From the Elder Cato to the Younger Pliny* ([Berkeley and Los Angeles: University of California Press, 1977] 220–22) shows how the lack of punctuation created real problems in reading. On

Ancient reciters and audiences must first concern themselves with a text's sound because it provided their initial and primary clues as to its organization and meaning. As Michael Stubbs has pointed out, "listeners have to understand in real time."[13] They do not have the luxury of re-reading.

This issue of silent reading and sound is frequently dealt with under the categories of oral culture, scribal culture, and print culture. Werner Kelber pioneered this distinction in New Testament studies, drawing upon the work of Ong, Havelock, and Eisenstein.[14] In Kelber's categories, the Hellenistic Mediterranean world is a scribal culture. This term is problematic in two ways, however. First, it sets up a contrast, almost contradiction, between oral culture and scribal culture. As Vernon Robbins has trenchantly shown, this was not the situation in the Hellenistic period, which was characterized by an interaction between oral and scribal environments. Robbins terms this a rhetorical culture, one that "is aware of written documents, uses written and oral language interactively, and composes both orally and scribally in a rhetorical manner."[15] By "rhetorical manner" Robbins means "writing traditional materials clearly and persuasively" and for recitation.[16] Scribal culture is concerned with copying and is part of the elementary writing processes in the Hellenistic world. In a rhetorical culture, one wrote in order to persuade others by reciting; in a scribal culture one copies in order to preserve. As Robbins summarizes:

---

the other hand, Bruce M. Metzger, *The Text of the New Testament*, (3rd ed. [Oxford: Oxford University Press, 1991] 13) seems to think this presents no real difficulty, even though he quotes no evidence to this point.

[13] "[B]ut readers can refer backward and forwards in the text." *Language and Literacy: The Sociolinguistics of Reading and Writing*, Routledge Education Books (London: Routledge & Kegan Paul, 1980) 13.

[14] Werner H. Kelber, *The Oral and the Written Gospel, The Hemeneutics of Speaking and Writing in the Synoptic Tradition, Mark, Paul and Q* (Philadelphia: Fortress Press, 1983).

[15] Vernon K. Robbins, "Progymnastic Rhetorical Composition and Pre-Gospel Traditions: A New Approach," ed. Camille Focant. (BETL. Leuven: Leuven University Press, 1993) 110

[16] Vernon K. Robbins, "Writing as a Rhetorical Act in Plutarch and the Gospels," *Persuasive Artistry: Studies in New Testament Rhetoric in Honor of George A. Kennedy*, ed. Duane F. Watson. Journal of the Study of the New Testament Supplement Series 50, (Sheffield: JSOT Press, 1991) 145–6.

Performing oral and scribal activity in this way creates a rhetorical culture—one in which speech is influenced by writing and writing is influenced by speaking. Recitation, then, is the base of a rhetorical culture. People know that certain traditions exist in writing. They also know that all traditions, whether oral or written, need to be composed anew to meet the needs of the day. Each day as they spoke, they were interacting with written traditions: whenever they wrote, they were interacting with oral traditions. This interaction characterized their thinking, their speaking, and their writing."[17]

Again we are thrown back on the primacy of sound as the access to a composition, even for compositions preserved only as texts.

A second problem in the term scribal concerns the effects of the technology of writing on composition. The space of a scroll is less bounded than that of a codex. It more closely mimics the indeterminancy of oral space. The codex marks a decisive break in this regard with the conventions of orality.[18] Unlike the oral saga, the scroll has a strong beginning, but shares with the oral song a tendency towards a weak ending.[19] The codex has both a strong beginning and end. It imposes a more self-contained structure. Mark seems to exhibit more of the characteristics of scroll space, while Matthew and Luke cohere more with the codex space. The clear segmentations of Matthew cohere with the shaping of space into codex pages.[20]

In a rhetorical culture, the Sermon on the Mount would be heard as a speech. The author, then, faces a problem of verisimilitude. How is the Sermon to be cast and what should it sound like? A Jesus speaking like a Pericles in Galilee would be unbelieveable.[21] Matthew provides a number of clues as to the genre of the Sermon. Since genre is part of the conventions of language, genre would indicate to the

---

[17] Robbins, "Progymnastic Rhetorical Composition" 110.

[18] Bolter, *Writing Space* 85–86.

[19] Even the book divisions in Homer seem to be dictated by later copyists conforming the poem to the length of a scoll (G. S. Kirk, *The Iliad: A Commentary* [5. vols. Cambridge: Cambridge University Press, 1985] 1.45).

[20] If in composing 5 sermons Matthew is thinking of the Pentateuch, then he probably is thinking of five books, not scrolls, regardless of their physical characteristics.

[21] The anonymous rhetorical treatise *Ad Herennium* counsels the following concerning the writing of dialogue: "Dialogue...consists in putting in the mouth of some person language in keeping with his character" (IV. xliii. 55). These matters are probably determined by context as the speeches in Acts would indicate. Paul's tone shifts to fit the context. This would cohere with the dyadic understanding of personality.

audience how the Sermon was to be heard. The Sermon on the Mount is οἱ λόγοι τῆς διδαχῆς as the close parallelism between the Sermon's introduction (5:1–2) and its conclusion (7:28–29) attests. Both speak of words and teaching: ἀνοίξας τὸ στόμα, λέγων, and ἐδίδασκεν (5:2); τοὺς λόγους and ἐπι τῆ διδαχῆ (7:28), διδάσκων (7:29). Likewise the Sermon's final parable begins each example with a reference to μου τοὺς λόγους (7:24, 26). Both λόγοι and διδαχή are important. Διδαχή refers to "one of the most prominent functions of Jesus"[22] and is strongly emphasized in the triad of teaching, preaching and healing in 4:23, the summary statement that precedes the Sermon. οἱ λόγοι indicates that he is imitating what he takes to be the sayings of Jesus. [23] Thus generically the Sermon is teaching (διδαχή) in the form of sayings (λόγοι).[24]

Even though the Sermon is intended to be οἱ λόγοι (oral tradition), it is not a transcription of oral tradition but an imitation by a literate scribe of oral tradition (Matt 13:52). The quest for verisimilitude leads the rhetorical composer to imitate the teaching of a specific oral tradition, the Jesus tradition. Even though this tradition was in Greek from a very early period, it was not organized along Greek lines. Christian oral singers did not employ versification with the resultant use of formulae to sing their tales. Rather, the explicit use of Greek literary forms to preserve or develop the oral tradition occurs when the oral tradition interacts with and becomes absorbed into the rhetorical culture with the use of the chreia to frame sayings. This introduction appears to be typical of the rehearsal of the tradition in writing.[25] Yet the earliest forms of the oral tradition appear to have developed along what we may designate as Hebrew lines. This does not designate the language in which the oral tradition originated or developed, but the cultural constraint on its development. This can be observed in two ways. 1) The forms that typify the oral tradition as it appears in Q-the synoptic Sayings source, the Gospel of Thomas, as

---

[22] Karl Heinrich Rengstorf, "διδάσκω," TDNT 2:139.

[23] Helmut Koester (*Ancient Christian Gospels*, [Philadelphia: Trinity Press International, 1990] 31–33) shows the primacy of this term as a reference to the oral tradition prior to Marcion.

[24] Hans Dieter Betz (*Essays on the Sermon on the Mount*, [Philadelphia: Fortress Press, 1985] 1–16) describes the Sermon as an epitome which coheres with this argument, while his argument about its pre-Matthean character does not.

[25] Burton L. Mack, and Vernon K. Robbins, *Patterns of Persuasion in the Gospels*, *Foundations and Facets* (Sonoma, CA: Polebridge Press, 1989).

well as Mark, are forms primarily associated with Hebrew popular wisdom, parables, aphorisms, etc.[26] 2) Instead of versification,[27] parallelism and chiasm are the more prominent mnemonic devices.[28]

As Matthew constructed Jesus' Sermon, he faced a number of problems resulting from its aural character, from the fact that the text in which the speech is embedded must be recited (*recitatio*).

1) The initial organization of the Sermon cannot be abstract (literate) but aural. Even if the author had in mind an abstract model on which to build the Sermon, à la Bornkamm's elaborate chiasm,[29] such an abstract model must be implemented by means of an aural organization, and thus can be tested by whether it corresponds to an aural organization. In order to understand it, the audience will first have to hear it.[30] To recall the remark of Stubbs, listeners, unlike readers, "have to understand in real time."[31] We have already seen that the careful repetition of phrases between the introduction and

[26] Rudolf Bultmann (*The History of the Synoptic Tradition* [New York: Harper & Row, 1963] 106) appears to be correct in his argument that the province of the Synoptic logia and proverbs is Jewish wisdom.

[27] C. F. D. Moule, *An Idiom-Book of New Testament Greek* (Cambridge: Cambridge University Press, 1963) 199, notes the infrequency and apparently accidental nature of Greek poetic meters in the New Testament.

[28] While there are some similarities between the distinctive parallelism of Hebrew poetry and parallelism in the New Testament, the basic organizational pattern is different. R. C. Tannehill, (*The Sword of His Mouth.* [Philadelphia, Missoula: Fortress Press, Scholars Press, 1975] 41–42) describes some of these differences, including "parallelism of more complex structures" (eg., Matt 6:2–6, 16–18)...[and]...less use of traditional word pairs...." For detailed treatments of parallelism in Hebrew poetry, see J. L. Kugel, *The Idea of Biblical Poetry, Parallelism and its History.* (New Haven: Yale University Press, 1981) 1–58, and L. A. Schökel, *A Manual of Hebrew Poetics.* (Rome: Pontifical Biblical Institute, 1988) 48–63.

[29] Günther Bornkamm, "Der Aufbau der Bergpredigt," *NTS* 24 (1978): 419–432.

[30] This is true of the entire gospel narrative. The author must structure the narrative in such a way that a hearer can hear the divisions, units, and motion in a text. The so-called threefold formula in Matthew or the formula endings of the five sermons are such aural markers. They bear a striking similarity to the formulaic markers of oral versification but in fact are somewhat different. The function of the formulae in oral versification enable the singer to rapidly and automatically complete the metric cycle (Albert B. Lord, *The Singer of Tales,* Harvard Studies in Comparative Literature 24 [Cambridge: Harvard University Press, 1960] 54. See the careful analysis of John Miles Foley, *The Theory of Oral Composition, History and Methodology, Folkloristics* [Bloomington: Indiana University Press, 1988] 41–44).

[31] This observation alone is enough to call into question the highly abstract pattern of Bornkamm.

conclusion provides the hearer with multiple clues as to beginning and ending as well as genre.

Within the Sermon itself, aural clues employing repeated words, phrases and grammatical patterns help the hearer group οἱ λόγοι. The Macro Outline (Appendix 1) indicates the initial aural formulae that allow the construction of a visual-graphic outline of an aural performance. The repetition of μακάριοι as the initial phrase clearly sets up the first group. As the Sermon develops, these initial formulae become more complex. The ἠκούσατε section 4 shows considerable variation in the basic initial aural formula, but the pattern of the whole is clearly implied. Section 6 is by far the most complex in its arrangment and yet a series of patterns recurs to help the hearer sort out its arrangement.

2) Since the author is not an oral singer, but a literate rhetorian, he must imitate οἱ λόγοι. He probably exaggerates the characteristics of that orality. As an example of this exaggeration, a comparison with the Q parallels will show that Matthew normally increases the exactness of the parallelism in positive-negative contrasts. The final parable of Builders (Q 6:47–9) clearly indicates this tendency.[32]

There are other examples of what might be judged imitations of orality. The paratactic structure of the sentences in individual units with little subordination or the infrequent use of participles might indicate oral tradition, but may just as likely indicate the imitation of orality. At other times, in comparison with Q, the Sermon on the Mount appears more concrete. In 4.4 the Sermon reads "right cheek" and the Lucan parallel has the more general "on the cheek" (Luke 6:29).[33] In the Lord's prayer the Sermon has σήμερον while Luke has τὸ καθ᾽ ἡμέραν. In the same prayer, the better parallel structure in the Sermon may well be an imitation of orality.

3) Because the Sermon is an imitation of οἱ λόγοι and since the controlling mindset is literate, even if rhetorical, there are many examples of literacy intruding on the imitation. As an example, one

---

[32] John S. Kloppenborg (*The Formation of Q, Trajectories in Ancient Wisdom Collections, Studies in Antiquity and Christianity* [Philadelphia: Fortress Press, 1987] 172) argues that "there is little in [Q/Luke] 6:20b-49 which does not appear to be a Q text."

[33] In "Jesus as Sage: An Innovating Voice in Common Wisdom," (*The Sage in Israel and the Ancient Near East*, ed. John G. Gammie, and Leo Perdue. [Winona Lake, IN: Eisenbrauns, 1990] 404) Bernard B. Scott argued that such specificity in the Matthean text pointed to oral tradition and to Jesus. In light of the above arguments, I now have to change my mind.

could point to the peculiar lack of paratactic connectives between sections and units.[34] The paratactic connectives *within* units is very strong. This makes the units themselves stand out. The block of material in 6:25–34 has a strong construction based on aural patterns, but it is subordinated both logically and by means of shift in markers (διὰ τοῦτο) to the heading in 6:19. It appears to have a paratactic structure (a linear organization), yet it is clearly subordinated.

Other examples abound. In the μακάριοι section, the beatitude for those who hunger and thirst (Matt 5:6) breaks the beatitude's simple pattern with a double participle and the specification τὴν δικαιοσύνην. While parallel to τῷ πνεύματι (1.1) and τῇ καρδία (1.6), τὴν δικαιοσύνην is an abstract term while the other two are concrete.[35]

We have tried to indicate why the primary organizing character of the Sermon must be aural. Now we turn to an analysis of the Sermon itself to show in detail how that organization operates.

II. *Hearing Is Sound*

The Micro Analysis that follows exhibits in diagram the aural features of the Sermon on the Mount that provide the hearer/reader with the aural clues for its organization. We are aware of the contradiction of exhibiting, i.e., showing, what is meant to be heard.[36] But in a printing press culture that is rapidly becoming graphically orientated, convention will not allow otherwise. The following definitions of terms are employed in the Micro Diagram.

Sections are designated by an *initial aural organizing formula* and usually have a series of *units* that share both an initial formula and a *common organizational pattern*. There is a total of eight sections in the Sermon. The first cardinal number is always the Section Number.

A *unit's* beginning is denoted by an initial aural formula. A unit is a single iteration of the initial formula and organizing pattern. It has a completeness not only formally but thematically as well. The second cardinal number is always the Unit Number.

---

[34] By way of comparison, in the birth narrative the separate units are paratactically connected; eg., 1:18 or 2:1 or even 3:1.

[35] Leander E. Keck, "The Poor Among the Saints in the New Testament," *ZNW* 56 (1965): 100–37 argues that τῷ πνεύματι is not an abstract term, but conjures up a concrete reality.

[36] Even the repertoire of words available to explain our observations tilts in the direction of graphic, visual metaphors for analysis.

The definition of a *line* derives from the poetic Greek hexameter line. It exhibits a complete grammatical function which can be standardized and recurring. The line is analogous to the rhetorical period.

A *lexie* often consists of a single grammatical clause and is exhibited in a single row of printed text. When a lexie is too long to fit on a single row, the second row of text is right-justified and exhibited with a right square bracket ( ]) at the right edge. The lexie is analogous to the rhetorical colon or comma. The status of the line and lexie is derived from their usefulness for analysis. A line may consist of more than one lexie. For example in 4.2.3 the line is recognized by the formula ἐγὼ δὲ λέγω ὑμῖν ὅτι πᾶς ὁ + participle. In section 4, this line has a recurring formula and plays a recurring function in each unit. We have divided the line into three lexies (rows of print) for analysis. A lexie is not denoted by a cardinal number but their number can always calculated from the first lexie in a line.

The initial aural formula is a recurring phrase that denotes the beginning of a unit and its recurrence denotes a section. For example, section 4 employs the phrase ἠκούσατε ὅτι ἐρρέθη τοῖς ἀρχαίοις to introduce each unit. This initial aural formula need not be repeated verbatim at the beginning of each unit, but performancial variations are normal, typical of the compositional technique of rhetorical culture.[37] The full initial formula occurs in 4.1 but is abbreviated in a variety of ways in the other units of section 4.

Each section has a common *organizing pattern* that gives shape to the section's units. The initial aural formula is the first element in the organizing pattern. This pattern is discussed at the beginning of our analysis for each section.

The beatitudes of section 1 provide a ready example. The section is denoted by its common initial aural formula, μακάριοι οἱ. As a result there are nine units in this first section. The common organizing pattern consists of the initial aural formula + plural nominal and ὅτι

---

[37] Greek and Latin literary critics alike encouraged all forms of variation. See for example Dionysius of Halicarnassus (*On Demosthenes* 50) who praises Demosthenes for "his use of all forms of clause and period and of figures of speech to give them variety," and Demetrius (*On Style* II.60–61) who requires repetition with variation as a feature of grand style. Thus Quintilian prescribes, "the structure of prose must be varied if it is to avoid giving offence by its monotony" (*Institutio Oratoria*, IX.iv.60). See also John Dominic Crossan, *In Fragments: The Aphorisms of Jesus* (San Francisco: Harper & Row, 1983) 40–1, who distinguishes between performancial and hermeneutical variations. Hermeneutical variations involve a reinterpretation.

αὐτοί. Because of the pithiness of the μακάριοι formula we have not divided the units into lines although technically according to our definitions each unit consists of two lines and each line has one lexie (except unit 1.9).

Epithets are stock phrases. While we have borrowed this term from Homeric studies the correpondence is not exact since metrical needs are prominent in the classic definition of epithet and that factor is irrelevant here.[38] The epithet's very conventionality encourages variation to fit context. As Foley has recently emphasized of the Homeric epithet, it evokes a whole reference of meaning and memory connected with the stock phrase.[39]

We used the Nestle Aland[26] text but have paid attention to significant textual variations in the footnotes; often our observations bring important evidence to bear on scribal changes. These at times confirm our observations about sound. We have not employed the standard versification and chapter numbers because these frequently are misleading. They lead to a fragmentation of the text and do not represent a scientific analysis, but a convenience dictated by the printing press, even though they allow easy reference. We have employed a hierachial numbering system to indicate how each unit fits into the Sermon's overall design. In our diagram we have striven to follow a consistent set of graphic conventions to indicate relations. This has proved difficult at times, since we would have liked to illustrate more relationships than available graphic clues allow. Deviations from our own conventions are obvious or we have noted them.

bold	initial aural formula
single underline	organzing pattern markers
double underline	same sound or word.
dotted underline	same sound or word.
CAPITAL LETTERS	epithets

1.0–1.8. Μακάριοι (*5:3–10*)

---

[38] Milman Parry defined the epithet formula as "a group of words which is regularly employed under the same metrical conditions to express a given essential idea." Quoted in Albert B. Lord, *The Singer of Tales*, Harvard Studies in Comparative Literature 24 (Cambridge: Harvard University Press, 1960) 30.

[39] John Miles Foley, *Immanent Art: From Structure to Meaning in Traditional Oral Epic.* (Bloomington: Indiana University Press, 1991) 1–60.

1.1 Μακάριοι οἱ πτωχοὶ τῷ πνεύματι,
   ὅτι αὐτῶν ἐστιν Η ΒΑΣΙΛΕΙΑ ΤΩΝ ΟΥΡΑΝΩΝ.

1.2 μακάριοι οἱ πενθοῦντες,
   ὅτι αὐτοὶ   παρακληθήσονται.

1.3 μακάριοι οἱ πραεῖς,
   ὅτι αὐτοὶ κληρονομήσουσιν   τὴν   γῆν.[40]

1.4 μακάριοι οἱ πεινῶντες καὶ διψῶντες τὴν δικαιοσύνην,
   ὅτι αὐτοὶ   χορτασθήσονται.

1.5 μακάριοι οἱ   ἐλεήμονες,
   ὅτι αὐτοὶ   ἐλεηθήσονται.

1.6 μακάριοι οἱ καθαροὶ τῇ καρδίᾳ,
   ὅτι αὐτοὶ τὸν θεὸν ὄψονται.

1.7 μακάριοι οἱ εἰρηνοποιοί,
   ὅτι αὐτοὶ υἱοὶ θεοῦ κληθήσονται.

1.8 μακάριοι οἱ δεδιωγμένοι ἕνεκεν   δικαιοσύνης,
   ὅτι αὐτῶν ἐστιν Η ΒΑΣΙΛΕΙΑ ΤΩΝ ΟΥΡΑΝΩΝ.

While proposals for structuring the beatitudes have proliferated, two approaches predominate. One divides eight beatitudes into two groups of four (1.1–1.4 and 1.5–1.8), contending that the initial π sound and the common passive condition of the blessed unify the first four, while the active ethical condition of the blessed unifies the second group.[41] The other posits a chiastic arrangement between the two groups of beatitudes on the basis of the inclusio established by the epithet in 1.1 and 1.8 and the use of the "divine passive" in 1.2, 1.4, 1.5, and 1.7.[42]

Both proposals ignore several important clues to the section's organization. The first does not explain why the initial π sound was abandoned with the doubling of the verb in the fifth beatitude, nor does it indicate why no distinctive sound occurs in the last four

[40] Some manuscripts reverse 1.2 and 1.3. Although the textual evidence is very weak, the rhetorical effect is strong. πραεῖς and πτωχοὶ are nicely balanced and Matthew frequently employs the contrast between ὁ οὐρανός and ἡ γῆ.

[41] See, for example, Eduard Schweizer, *The Good News According to Matthew* (Atlanta: John Knox Press, 1975) 82; Robert H. Gundry, *Matthew, A Commentary on His Literary and Theological Art*, (Grand Rapids: Eerdmans, 1982) 73; R. Guelich, "The Matthean Beatitudes: 'Entrance Requirements' or Eschatological Blessings?," *JBL* 95 (1976): 431–2; John P. Meier, *Matthew, New Testament Message 3*, ed. Wilfrid Harrington and Donald Senior (Wilmington, DE: Michael Glazier, Inc., 1980) 39.

[42] N. J. McEleney, "The Beatitudes of the Sermon on the Mount/Plain," *CBQ* 43 (1981) 10–13.

beatitudes. The second proposal fails to explain the occurrence of τὴν δικαιοσύνην at the end of the fourth and eighth beatitudes.[43] The repetition of δικαιοσύνην at the end of each group of four beatitudes suggests parallel arrangement, not a chiasm as these theorists propose.

Since our analysis focuses primarily on the Sermon's sound, aural clues govern the following outline. The eightfold repetition of μακάριοι οἱ gives the section its distinctive initial sound and each iteration of the full formula consists of μακάριοι and a nominative phrase with the subsequent ὅτι plus the third person pronoun. This pattern typifies the beatitude form.[44] Three interlocking inclusios unite 1.1 and 1.8. The first overarches 1.1 to 1.8 with the repetition of ὅτι αὐτῶν ἐστιν ἡ βασιλεία τῶν οὐρανῶν. A second inclusio of τῶν οὐρανῶν and τὴν γῆν unites 1.1–1.3. This apparent contrast is a frequent one employed by Matthew in the Sermon (see below, 5.3.7).

A third inclusio unites 1.4–1.8 with the repetition of τὴν δικαιοσύνην at the beginning and the end. Unit 1.4 claims special prominence. It initiates the longer of the two subsidiary inclusios and both the abstract character of the noun δικαιοσύνη and the doubling of the nominative element in the main clause of 1.4 signal a departure from the aural unity of the previous material.

Several phonetic features connect the two groups of units, 1.1–1.3 and 1.4–1.8. The alliterative π crosses over from the first group to the second with its occurrence in the first nominative participle of 1.4, while providing a simple phonetic unity to the first four beatitudes. The -ονται ending of the future passive verb in 1.2 anticipates this repeated feature in the second group. Within the second group the distinctive -ονται ending of the future and future passive verb remains consistent in each ὅτι clause. This group also exhibits three doublets: the repeated ἐλεη- sound in 1.5, the repeated initial κα- in the main clause of 1.6, and the occurrence of θεός in the ὅτι clauses of both 1.6 and 1.7.[45] The beatitudes in this second group stand out as more abstract and less concrete than those in the first group.

1.9. μακάριοί ἐστε (*5:11–12*)

---

[43] W. D. Davies, and D. C. Allison, *A Critical and Exegetical Commentary on the Gospel According to Matthew*, ICC (Edinburgh: T & T Clark, 1988) 1: 429–30.

[44] Jacques Dupont, *Les Beatitudes* (Louvain: E. Nauwelaerts, 1958) 1: 279.

[45] Betz, *Essays on the Sermon on the Mount* 4–5, draws attention to the importance of "seeing" in 1.7 and especially Matt 6:22–23 (Chapter 5).

1.9.1 1 μακάριοί ἐστε[46]
    2 ὅταν ὀνειδίσωσιν   ὑμᾶς
    3 καὶ   διώξωσιν
    4 καὶ   εἴπωσιν
      πᾶν πονηρὸν καθ'   ὑμῶν[47] ἕνεκεν ἐμοῦ.
1.9.2 1 χαίρετε καὶ ἀγαλλιᾶσθε,
    2 ὅτι ὁ μισθὸς   ὑμῶν πολὺς ΕΝ ΤΟΙΣ ΟΥΡΑΝΟΙΣ·
    3 οὕτως γὰρ ἐδίωξαν
    4 τοὺς προφήτας τοὺς πρὸ ὑμῶν.

A performancial variation shifts the initial aural formula in 1.9 and an expressed verb (implied in 1.1–1.8) signals a change in person. Likewise the organizing pattern shifts with a temporal clause and a pair of imperatives followed by a ὅτι clause. Its initial μακάριοι and the recurrence of οὐρανοῖς invokes the epithet ἡ βασιλεία τῶν οὐρανῶν in the inclusio of 1.1 and 1.8 and also connects 1.9 with the preceding eight beatitudes. Yet the altered form of the ninth beatitude effects a transition to section 2 and highlights important structural features. First, ἐστε refocuses the initial structuring formula to the dominant addressee in the Sermon. In Greek oratory apostophe, the shift from a nominal addressee to the real addressee, is a common rhetorical figure.[48] The section unfolds two sets of four lexies. The first set (1.9.1) begins with μακάριοι ἐστε and the second (1.9.2) with the doubled imperative, χαίρετε καὶ ἀγαλλιᾶσθε. The second person pronoun occurs in the second and fourth lexie of each set, employing first ὑμᾶς and then a threefold repetition of ὑμῶν. The first and fourth occurrences of the pronoun appear at the end of the phrase and the middle two occurrences appear in the middle of the phrase. The balanced repetition of the second person pronoun accents the shift to the second person after the μακάριοι in 1.9 and establishes a link to the initial aural formula of section 2, ὑμεῖς ἐστε.

The first set (1.9.1) is erected on a triplet of verbs paratactically arranged, ending in -ωσιν. The center verb of this triplet, διώκω, receives emphasis because it repeats the verb of the initial clause in the

---

[46] ἐστε is bolded to show that it anticipates the initial marker of section 2.

[47] Not only does ψευδόμενοι have a weak attestation (D and a few others), but it can be set aside on stylistic grounds because it breaks up the paratactic organization of the first set. The subordinating use of the participle is infrequent in the Sermon.

[48] Kennedy, *New Testament Interpretation through Rhetorical Criticism* 41.

preceding eighth beatitude (1.8) and anticipates the verb in the center of 1.9.2. This second set also introduces the words μισθός and προφήτας which will become prominent in subsequent sections.

2. Ὑμεῖς ἐστε *(5:13–16)*

2.1   Ὑμεῖς ἐστε <u>τὸ ἅλας τῆς γῆς·</u>

    ἐὰν δὲ τὸ   <u>ἅλας</u> μωρανθῇ,

    ἐν τίνι   <u>ἁλισθήσεται;</u>

    εἰς οὐδὲν ἰσχύει ἔτι

    εἰ μὴ βληθὲν[49] ἔξω

    <u>κ</u>ατα<u>π</u>ατεῖσθαι <u>ὑπὸ τῶν ἀνθρώπων</u>.

2.2 Ὑμεῖς ἐστε <u>τὸ φῶς τοῦ   κόσμου.</u>

    οὐ δύναται πόλις   <u>κ</u>ρυβῆναι

    ἐπάνω <u>ὄρους</u>   <u>κ</u>ειμένη·

    <u>οὐδὲ</u>   <u>κ</u>α<u>ίουσιν λύχνον</u>

      καὶ τιθέασιν   <u>αὐτὸν</u>

                  <u>ὑπὸ τὸν μόδιον</u>

                  ἀλλ᾽ ἐπὶ τὴν <u>λυχνίαν</u>,

    καὶ <u>λάμπει</u> πᾶσιν τοῖς ἐν τῇ οἰκίᾳ.

    <u>οὕτως λαμψάτω τὸ φῶς</u> ὑμῶν

          <u>ἔμπροσθεν τῶν ἀνθρώπων,</u>

    <u>ὅπως</u>   <u>ἴδωσιν</u> ὑμῶν τὰ καλὰ ἔργα

    καὶ   <u>δοξάσωσιν</u> ΤΟΝ ΠΑΤΕΡΑ ΥΜΩΝ ΤΟ ΕΝ ΤΟΙΣ ΟΥΡΑΝΟΙΣ.

The initial aural formula changes to ὑμεῖς ἐστε, echoing the ἐστε of the initial formula in section 1.9.1. The new formula occurs twice, creating two units. Each unit repeats the key vowel sound of its title and ends with a variation of the same recurring formula, ὑπὸ τῶν ἀνθρώπων and ἔμπροσθεν τῶν ἀνθρώπων. Further, each unit contains internal organizing features based on aural clues.

2.1 employs a triple repetition of ἅλας. 2.2, like 1.1–1.4, uses alliteration, this time based on κ from the title word κόσμου in the initial formula. Λύχνον and λυχνίαν form an inclusio that groups a series of four phrases ending with an -ον or -αν sound. A doubling of λάμπω follows the inclusio. Unit 2 ends with the epithet τὸν πατέρα ὑμῶν τὸν ἐν τοῖς οὐρανοῖς. This is the first occurrence of the epithet in the gospel of Matthew. In this transitional section of the Sermon,

---

[49] Other manuscripts read βλήθηναι ἔξω καί (see Nestle-Aland[26]). While the paratactic infinitives are attractive in a Sermon imitating oral style, Matthew does not favor paratactic infinitives, but finite verbs as in 1.9.1.

the epithet serves as a bridge by echoing[50] the three previous formulaic references to ὁ οὐρανός in section 1 and anticipating subsequent occurrences of the epithet ὁ πατήρ ὑμῶν in each successive section of the Sermon.[51] As in section 1, the last unit evidences greater elaboration of the structural pattern.

3. Μὴ νομίσητε *(5:17–20)*

3.0.1 **Μὴ νομίσητε** ὅτι ἦλθον καταλῦσαι ΤΟΝ ΝΟΜΟΝ Η ΤΟΥΣ ΠΡΟΦΗΤΑΣ·
　　　　　οὐκ ἦλθον καταλῦσαι ἀλλὰ πληρῶσαι.

3.0.2 ἀμὴν γὰρ λέγω ὑμῖν·
　　　　　　　ἕως ἂν παρέλθῃ ὁ οὐρανὸς καὶ ἡ γῆ,
　　ἰῶτα ἓν ἢ μία κεραία οὐ μὴ παρέλθῃ ἀπὸ ΤΟΥ ΝΟΜΟΥ,
　　　　　　ἕως ἂν πάντα γένηται.

ὃς ἐὰν οὖν λύσῃ μίαν τῶν ἐντολῶν τούτων τῶν ἐλαχίστων	ὃς δ' ἂν ποιήσῃ
καὶ διδάξῃ	καὶ διδάξῃ,
οὕτως τοὺς ἀνθρώπους, ἐλάχιστος κληθήσεται ΕΝ ΤΗΙ ΒΑΣΙΛΕΙΑΙ ΤΩΝ ΟΥΡΑΝΩΝ·]	οὗτος μέγας κληθήσεται ΕΝ ΤΗΙ ΒΑΣΙΛΕΙΑΙ ΤΩΝ ΟΥΡΑΝΩΝ.]

3.0.3 λέγω γὰρ ὑμῖν ὅτι
　　ἐὰν μὴ περισσεύσῃ ὑμῶν ἡ δικαιοσύνη πλεῖον τῶν γραμματέων
　　　　　　　　　　　　　　　　καὶ Φαρισαίων,
　　οὐ μὴ εἰσέλθητε　ΕΙΣ ΤΗΝ ΒΑΣΙΛΕΙΑ ΤΩΝ ΟΥΡΑΝΩΝ.

Significant phonemes from section 2 are rearranged in section 3 to form new patterns. The phonemes that constitute the key words ὑμεῖς and οὐ/ἀλλά form an aural bridge from section 2 to section 3. The leading phoneme of 3.0.1, μή, echoes ὑμεῖς, while the paired negative and adversive connector, οὐ/ἀλλά, set up in section 2 the antithetical relation that is repeated and elaborated in section 3. The initial phrase is not repeated but the internal repetition of the ἀμὴν

---

[50] Foley has referred to the use of such stereotypical epithets in oral compositions as "value added meaning," or "immanent art" in which the phrase stands for a much larger signified, a part for the whole which is conjured up by the phrase. Foley, *Immanent Art,* chapters 3–5.

[51] The epithet occurs in units 4.5.3 and 4.5.5, 5.0, 5.2, 5.3, 5.4, 6.1.4.1, 6.1.4.4, 7.1, and 8.1.

λέγω γὰρ ὑμῖν formula delineates two lines, both of which are punctuated by the concluding epithet ἐν (εἰς τὴν βασιλείαν) τῇ βασιλείᾳ τῶν οὐρανῶν. An inflection of ἦλθον figures prominently in each line of section 3: ἦλθον is doubled in the introduction, παρέλθη is doubled in the next line (3.0.2), and εἰσέλθητε expresses the goal in the closing statement. The introductory sentence begins with a negative imperative and contains a doublet with the repetition of ἦλθον καταλῦσαι. The phrase τὸν νόμον ἢ τοὺς προφήτας functions as an epithet.

Line 3.0.2 replicates the pattern. The formula ἀμὴν γὰρ λέγω ὑμῖν introduces the line which itself subdivides into two parallel parts. The introduction, like the initial formula, contains a doublet with the repeated verb, παρέλθη. τοῦ νόμου abbreviates the epithet in 3.0.1.[52] The ἕως ἄν phrase is followed by the same phoneme πα, and the double negative οὐ μή before the second παρέλθη nicely balances the phrase.

The two sublines within 3.0.2 exhibit parallel organizational patterns, although the second one abbreviates by means of elipsis. This pattern anticipates the constructions in the ἠκούσατε section wherein the specific case law examples come in parallel units (4.1.4, 4.2.4, 4.3.4, 4.4.4, and 4.5.4.). Both 3.0.2a and b begin with a conditional clause and doubled verb, with διδάσκω as second verb and κληθήσεται in both apodoses. The sublines set up a contrast, foreshadowing the elaboration of contrasts in section 4. Both end with the epithet ἐν τῇ βασιλείᾳ τῶν οὐρανῶν. The concluding double negative echoes the initial μή. The οὕτως/οὗτος phonetic connection links the two sublines and marks the elipsis. A reference to the number one in 3.0.2a establishes a connection to 3.0.1 which mentions one iota and one serif.

3.0.3 likewise begins with λέγω γὰρ ὑμῖν and ends with the epithet εἰς τὴν βασιλείαν τῶν οὐρανῶν. The unit's unpatterned phraseology uses terms important and typical of Matthew, δικαιοσύνη and τῶν γραμματέων καὶ Φαρισαίων.[53] The line's abstract character emphasizes the phrase's semantic value. The lack of patterning breaks form and signals that the previous pattern has been completed,

---

[52] Some scribes even spelled out the epithet; cf., Nestle-Aland[26].

[53] See Gundry, *Matthew* 81–82 and Ulrich Luz, *Matthew 1–7: A Commentary*, Evangelisch-Katholischer Kommentar zum Neuen Testament (Minneapolis: Augsburg, 1989) 56–57.

leading the hearer to expect a new aural formula in the upcoming section.

4. Ἠκούσατε (5:21–48)

The organizing pattern in section 4 consists of five lines.

1. Introductory formula:
   ἠκούσατε ὅτι ἐρρέθη [τοῖς ἀρχαίοις]

2. Statement of Torah:
   (prohibition in 4.1.2, 4.2.2, 4.3.2, implied negative in 4.4.2; positive in 4.5.2.)

3. Counter-statement (negative in 4.4.2; positive in 4.5.2):
   ἐγὼ δὲ λέγω ὑμῖν plus:
   a.) ὅτι πᾶς ὁ (participle),
   b.) μή with the aorist infinitive, or
   c.) present imperative

4. Specific examples from case law, set in parallel.
   Usually includes a conditional or relative clause and an imperative verb or series of verbs.

5. Conclusion.
   Occurs in each unit except 4.4. The conclusion employs rhetorical devices for emphasis. 4.1.5 uses an ἀμήν phrase and double negative. 4.2.5 substitutes an abbreviated form of the ἠκούσατε pattern. 4.3.5 and 4.5.5 use the verb εἰμί as a bracket with a phonetic emphasis in the center, ναὶ ναί and οὔ οὔ in 4.3.5 and chiasm plus epithet in 4.5.5. While 4.4 has no conclusion proper, the last line breaks rhythm (see below at 4.4).

4.1 (*5:21–26*)

4.1.1 Introduction

   Ἠκούσατε ὅτι ἐρρέθη τοῖς ἀρχαίοις,

4.1.2 Law

   Οὐ φονεύσεις·
   ὃς δ' ἂν φονεύσῃ,   ἔνοχος ἔσται τῇ κρίσει.

4.1.3 Counter-Statement

4.1.3a ἐγὼ δὲ λέγω ὑμῖν ὅτι πᾶς ὁ ὀργιζόμενος τῷ ἀδελφῷ αὐτοῦ
                         ἔνοχος ἔσται τῇ κρίσει·
4.1.3b ὃς δ' ἂν εἴπῃ   τῷ ἀδελφῷ αὐτοῦ,
         Ῥακά,   ἔνοχος ἔσται τῷ συνεδρίῳ·
4.1.3c ὃς δ' ἂν εἴπῃ,
         Μωρέ,   ἔνοχος ἔσται ΕΙΣ ΤΗΝ ΓΕΕΝΝΑΝ
                         ΤΟΥ ΠΥΡΟΣ.

Case Law

4.1.4a ἐὰν οὖν προσφέρῃς   τὸ δῶρόν σου ἐπὶ τὸ
                                θυσιαστήριον

        κἀκεῖ μνησθῇς ὅτι   ὁ ἀδελφός σου ἔχει τι
                                κατὰ σοῦ,

        ἄφες ἐκεῖ   τὸ δῶρόν σου ἔμπροσθεν τοῦ
                                θυσιαστηρίου

        καὶ ὕπαγε πρῶτον διαλλάγηθι τῷ ἀδελφῷ σου,
        καὶ τότε ἐλθὼν πρόσφερε   τὸ δῶρόν σου.
4.1.4b ἴσθι εὐνοῶν   τῷ ἀντιδίκῳ σου ταχὺ,
        ἕως ὅτου εἶ μετ' αὐτοῦ ἐν τῇ ὁδῷ,
        μήποτέ σε παραδῷ   ὁ ἀντίδικος τῷ κριτῇ
                                καὶ ὁ κριτὴς[54] τῷ ὑπηρέτῃ
                                καὶ εἰς φυλακὴν βληθήσῃ·

4.1.5 Conclusion

        ἀμὴν λέγω σοι,
        οὐ μὴ ἐξέλθῃς ἐκεῖθεν,
        ἕως ἂν ἀποδῷς τὸν ἔσχατον κοδράντην.

The Sermon's fourth section establishes an elaborate system of parallels labelled with the initial structuring formula Ἠκούσατε ὅτι ἐρρέθη τοῖς ἀρχαίοις. The first unit exhibits the full pattern. In 4.1.1 the introductory aural formula occurs in its complete form. In 4.1.2 the verb φονεύω is doubled[55] and the marker for a relative clause, ὃς δ' ἄν, and the phrase ἔνοχος ἔσται establish a link with the counter statement. The counter-statement section labelled by the formula ἐγὼ δὲ λέγω ὑμῖν ὅτι πᾶς ὁ and introduces the phrase τῷ ἀδελφῷ αὐτου which helps unify this unit.

Lines b and c follow a formulaic pattern: the phrase ὃς δ' ἂν εἴπῃ + τῷ ἀδελφῷ αὐτου as an indirect object (implied in the third elaboration) + a pejorative label in the vocative case + ἔνοχος ἔσται + an indirect object or prepositional phrase. 4.1.3.c ends with an epithet, εἰς τὴν γέενναν τοῦ πυρός, in a construction similar to that of the internal parallel in 3.1.1. Like the insults, the three dative phrases are

---

[54] A number of texts fill in the elipsis with σε παραδῷ. Not only do the earliest witnesses not support this (Nestle-Aland[26]), but we have seen that Matthew frequently employs elipsis.

[55] Lexie 2 in 4.1.2 is unattested in the Hebrew Bible or Jewish literature. Thus it was deliberately doubled probably for phonetic reasons. Repetition allows a hearer to pick up on the theme.

set in escalating order, building on the ἔνοχος ἔσται τῇ κρίσει which concludes 4.1.2 and is repeated in 4.1.3.a. Furthermore, συνεδρίῳ and γέενναν τοῦ πυρός form a correlative binary in reverse order with the epithet ὁ οὐρανὸς καί ἡ γῆ (3.0.2).

The case law example (4.1.4.a) begins with a third class condition marked by ἐὰν οὖν. The example exhibits a series of imperatives, with three imperative verbs in the apodosis (ἄφες, ὕπαγε, πρόσφερε). A threefold repetition of τὸ δῶρόν σου (A) is interspersed with a triple reference to τὸ θυσιαστήριον (B) and ὁ ἀδελφός σου/τῷ ἀδελφῷ σου (C). This sets up the parallel pattern ABC/ABC/A, creating the expectation that B and C will follow. B (τὸ θυσιαστήριον) does follow in elipsis and ἀντιδίκος, the antithesis of ἀδελφός, begins the next subline 4.1.4.b. The verb ἔχει phonetically reinforces the repetition of κἀκεῖ/ἐκεῖ. Πρῶτον occurs with the imperative here, the first of three such uses of πρῶτον in the Sermon.[56]

The second subline (4.1.4b) begins with the imperative ἴσθι and the double reference to the accuser (τῷ ἀντιδίκῳ σου, ὁ ἀντίδικος). In 4.1.4.a the protasis was elaborated into two lines before the first imperative. In 4.1.4.b the imperative comes first and the action (apodosis) is elaborated. Furthermore, the threefold motion from judge to prison parallels the threefold motion of 4.1.3, the counter-statement.

κριτής   κρίσει
ὑπηρέτης   συνεδρίος
φυλακῆς   γέενναν τοῦ πυρός

This last parallel evokes the Matthean epithet about being cast into outer darkness where there will be weeping and gnashing of teeth.[57] A terminal η sound unifies the last series of phrases.

The unit's conclusion begins with the formula ἀμὴν λέγω σοι and employs the definitive form of negation οὐ μή for the future.[58] While on the surface 4.1.5 concludes the subunit 4.1.4.b, the double negative and ἔσχατον confirm the parallel of the series κριτής to φυλακῆς with κρίσει to γέεναν. Thus there is a semantic shift from prison to Gehenna. The concluding section employs ἐκεῖθεν, echoing the repetition of ἐκει earlier in the example.

---

[56] 5:24. The others are 6:33 and 7:5.

[57] Matt 8:12; 22:13; 25:30. See also the last lexie in 4.2.4 which conjures up the whole phrase exactly as Foley describes the functioning of an epithet.

[58] This form of negation is emphatic and "virtually limited to quotations from the LXX and sayings of Jesus" in the New Testament (BDF §365).

4.2 (5:27–32)

4.2.1 Ἠκούσατε ὅτι ἐρρέθη,

4.2.2 Οὐ μοιχεύσεις.

4.2.3 ἐγὼ δὲ λέγω ὑμῖν ὅτι πᾶς ὁ βλέπων γυναῖκα

πρὸς τὸ ἐπιθυμῆσαι αὐτὴν

ἤδη ἐμοίχευσεν   αὐτὴν ἐν τῇ καρδίᾳ αὐτοῦ.

4.2.4[59]

εἰ δὲ ὁ ὀφθαλμός σου ὁ δεξιὸς	καὶ εἰ ἡ δεξιά σου χεὶρ
σκανδαλίζει σε,	σκανδαλίζει σε,
ἔξελε αὐτὸν	ἔκκοψον αὐτὴν
καὶ βάλε ἀπὸ σοῦ·	καὶ βάλε ἀπὸ σοῦ·
συμφέρει γάρ σοι ἵνα ἀπόληται	συμφέρει γάρ σοι ἵνα ἀπόληται
ἓν τῶν μελῶν σου	ἓν τῶν μελῶν σου
καὶ μὴ ὅλον τὸ σῶμά σου	καὶ μὴ ὅλον τὸ σῶμά σου
βληθῇ ΕΙΣ ΓΕΕΝΝΑΝ.	ΕΙΣ ΓΕΕΝΝΑΝ ἀπέλθῃ.

4.2.5.1 Ἐρρέθη δέ,

4.2.5.2 Ὃς ἂν   ἀπολύσῃ τὴν γυναῖκα αὐτοῦ,

δότω αὐτῇ ἀποστάσιον.

4.2.5.3 ἐγὼ δὲ λέγω ὑμῖν ὅτι πᾶς ὁ ἀπολύων τὴν γυναῖκα αὐτοῦ

παρεκτὸς λόγου πορνείας

ποιεῖ αὐτὴν μοιχευθῆναι,

4.2.5.4 καὶ ὃς ἐὰν   ἀπολελυμένην γαμήσῃ[60]

μοιχᾶται.

The introduction to unit 4.2 abbreviates the initial formula, eliminating the indirect object. The statement of the law is similarly brief, quoting the LXX with no elaboration. The third line, the counter-statement, repeats the formula of 4.1, ἐγὼ δὲ λέγω ὑμῖν ὅτι πᾶς ὁ, and the verb μοιχεύω introduced in the legal prohibition. According to the established pattern, the elaboration of case law (4.2.4) presents two parallel examples, the first dealing with the right eye and the second with the right hand. The parallel is nearly perfect with few variations. The two examples use different verbs in the apodosis and the first and last lexies of the two examples show chiastic arrangements. In the first lexie of each example, the noun and adjective δεχιός are reversed, while in the last lines the same is true of

---

[59] In this parallel arrangement words that are *not* paralleled are underlined.

[60] B reads καὶ ὁ ἀπολελυμένην γαμήσας thus making the phrase parallel to the preceeding ὁ ἀπολύων. But the majority reading fits the pattern of the case law example which begins a new line and does not conclude the counter-statement.

the verb and the prepositional phrase εἰς γέενναν. The chiastic arrangement provides closure for the complex parallels of the case law line.

In place of a conclusion, this unit uses a block of material that duplicates in abbreviated form elements 1–4 of the ἠκούσατε section's organizational pattern. The introductory aural formula is reduced to ἐρρέθη δε. A conditional statement introduces the verb ἀπολύω and delivers the statement of law in the apodosis. The formula for the counter-statement remains intact and repeats both the phrase ἀπολύων τὴν γυναῖκα αὐτου from the statement of law and the verb μοιχεύω from the law and counter-statement of 4.2.2 and 4.2.3. This verb as well as ἀπολύω are repeated in the case law example which is reduced to a relative clause joined to the previous main clause by the connective καί.

Several structural features argue for the subordination of 4.2.5 to the main unit 4.2: (1) The transitional character of the connective particle δέ;[61] (2) the abbreviation of the form of the initial aural formula and other lines; (3) the doubled verb μοιχεύω which, when matched with its twofold repetition at the beginning of 4.2.1.2 and .3, forms an inclusio that delineates the beginning and end of the unit; and (4) the lack of a conclusion for 4.2.[62]

4.3 (5:33–37)

4.3.1 Πάλιν ἠκούσατε ὅτι ἐρρέθη τοῖς ἀρχαίοις,

4.3.2 Οὐκ ἐπιορκήσεις, ἀποδώσεις δὲ τῷ κυρίῳ τοὺς ὅρκους σου.

4.3.3   ἐγὼ δὲ λέγω ὑμῖν μὴ ὀμόσαι ὅλως·

4.3.4 μήτε ἐν τῷ οὐρανῷ,   ὅτι θρόνος   ἐστὶν τοῦ θεοῦ,

    μήτε ἐν τῇ γῇ,   ὅτι ὑποπόδιόν ἐστιν τῶν ποδῶν αὐτοῦ,

    μήτε εἰς Ἰεροσόλυμα, ὅτι πόλις   ἐστὶν τοῦ μεγάλου

                                βασιλέως,]

    μήτε ἐν τῇ κεφαλῇ σου ὀμόσῃς,   ὅτι οὐ δύνασαι μίαν τρίχα

                                λευκὴν ποιῆσαι ἢ μέλαιναν.

---

[61] Until unit 5.1, no unit begins with a connective. See below for 5.1.

[62] Gundry, *Matthew* 89, agrees this material is subordinate to 5:27–30, serving as an "appendix" On the other hand, Davies, *Matthew* 504, views it as an independent unit, supplying the third element in a triad with the previous ἠκούσατε units and followed by another triad (4.3, 4.4, and 4.5). See the footnote on πάλιν in 4.3, below. Lacking criteria for the delineation of units, many consider ἐρρέθη δέ as a separate antithesis while stressing its supplementary, subordinate character. So Francis W. Beare, *The Gospel According to Matthew* (San Francisco: Harper & Row, 1981) 153; and Luz, *Matthew 1–7* 299.

4.3.5 <u>ἔστω</u>[63] δὲ ὁ λόγος ὑμῶν   ναὶ ναί,

οὔ οὔ·

τὸ δὲ περισσὸν τούτων ἐκ τοῦ πονηροῦ <u>ἐστιν</u>.

The third unit repeats the the initial aural formula's full form, introduced by πάλιν.[64] The statement of the law includes two verbs in the future, consistent with the expected pattern. The lack of attestation for the quotation reinforces its composition to fit the form. The formulaic introduction to the counter-statement omits ὅτι πᾶς and the participle, which does not occur again in section 4. Ὅλως replaces πᾶς. Both this counter-statement and the next employ μή and the infinitive. Four case law examples follow in parallel, organized by the repetition of μήτε ἐν … ὅτι, and, in all but the the last example, ἐστιν. Forms of the verb εἰμι bracket the subunit's conclusion (4.3.5), with the double ναί/οὔ in the center. In the first three case law examples the verbs in the claim clauses are implied, while expressed (ὀμόσῃς) in the final example. This leads to a shift from impersonal (ὅτι + noun + ἐστιν + genitive) to implied personal. The final ὅτι clause is nicely balanced with the final infinitive ποιῆσαι bracketed by λευκήν and ἢ μέλαιναν, forming a chiasm in the final two lexies of the line. The reference to white and black is part of the Sermon's concreteness, like δεξιός, ἀδελφός, and ἀντίδικος in the the previous case law examples.

4.4(*5:38–42*)

4.4.1 Ἠκούσατε ὅτι ἐρρέθη,

4.4.2 Ὀφθαλμὸν   <u>ἀντὶ</u> ὀφθαλμοῦ

καὶ ὀδόντα   <u>ἀντὶ</u> ὀδόντος.

4.4.3 <u>ἐγὼ δὲ λέγω ὑμῖν μὴ</u> <u>ἀντιστῆναι</u> τῷ πονηρῷ·

4.4.4 a <u>ἀλλ' ὅστις σε</u> ῥαπίζει εἰς τὴν δεξιὰν σιαγόνα [σου],

<u>στρέψον</u> αὐτῷ καὶ τὴν ἄλλην·

b <u>καὶ τῷ θέλοντί σοι</u> κριθῆναι καὶ τὸν χιτῶνά σου λαβεῖν,

<u>ἄφες</u> αὐτῷ καὶ τὸ ἱμάτιον·

a <u>καὶ ὅστις σε</u> ἀγγαρεύσει μίλιον ἕν,

---

[63] B has ἔσται, an interesting reading which more closely parallels the final ἐστιν and parallels 4.5.5.

[64] Davies, *Matthew* 504 interprets the πάλιν variation as a signal of the beginning of a second set of triads in the ἠκούσατε section (triad 1, 5:21–32; triad 2, 5:33–48). Counting the ἐρρέθη δέ section (4.2.5.1) as an independent unit, he observes that the first triad of each set begins with the full form of the initial formula and the first triad uses ὅτι in each instance of the counter-statement.

ὕπαγε μετ᾽ αὐτοῦ δύο.

c τῷ αἰτοῦντί σε
    δός,

b καὶ τὸν θέλοντα ἀπὸ σοῦ δανίσασθαι
    μὴ ἀποστραφῇς

The fourth unit follows the established pattern except that it contains no element five, conclusion. The initial aural formula occurs in abbreviated form. The second line, the law, is set off in parallel phrases around the preposition ἀντί. Unlike other statements of law there is no verb or negative, although the ἀντί implies a negative.

The counterstatement (4.4.3) repeats the same variation of the formula as in 4.3.3, ἐγὼ δὲ λέγω ὑμῖν plus a negative and aorist infinitive. The verbal prefix ἀντι- picks up on its doubled use in 4.4.2, playing on a semantic shift in the preposition's meaning. The substantive adjective πονηρός echoes the previous unit's conclusion (4.3.5), creating an ambiguous referent.[65]

The case law portion of the fourth unit follows the expected parallel pattern. The adversive conjunction ἀλλά introduces the line, indicating a contrast with the law. The organizing pattern is: conjunction + ὅστις σε + specific action + imperative. In the second, fourth, and fifth examples a participle phrase substitutes for ὅστις, with 2 and 5 based on verbs of wishing and 2 and 4 on dative participles. This creates a strong interlocking patern, ABACB. Καί provides a regular rhythmic pattern. The series of clauses show an expansion and then a contraction: the first clause establishes the pattern, the second expands it with a double infinitive bracketing the noun, and the fourth contracts to the essential elements of the pattern, the participle and imperative without modifiers. Since this is the C element in the pattern, it is appropriate that it is the shortest thus drawing attention to itself. The simple, emphatic δός stands out as the positive of μὴ ἀντιστῆναι. The final subjunctive, the only negative, echoes μὴ ἀντιστῆναι in the counter-statement (4.4.3). While not in the form of a conclusion, the break in pattern, the subjunctive of prohibition instead of an imperative verb, and the double reference to the counter-statement, may indicate that these last two lexies function as a conclusion.

---

[65] The exact signified is difficult to specify: the evil one? the evil person? the evil? The case law examples would suggest "evil person," while the conclusion of the previous unit suggests "the evil one."

4.5 (5:43–48)

4.5.1 Ἠκούσατε ὅτι ἐρρέθη,

4.5.2 Ἀγαπήσεις τὸν πλησίον σου
  καὶ μισήσεις τὸν ἐχθρόν σου.

4.5.3 ἐγὼ δὲ λέγω ὑμῖν,
  ἀγαπᾶτε τοὺς ἐχθροὺς ὑμῶν
  καὶ προσεύχεσθε ὑπὲρ τῶν διωκόντων ὑμᾶς,
  ὅπως γένησθε υἱοὶ ΤΟΥ ΠΑΤΡΟΣ ΥΜΩΝ ΤΟΥ ΕΝ ΟΥΡΑΝΟΙΣ,
  ὅτι τὸν ἥλιον αὐτοῦ ἀνατέλλει ἐπὶ πονηροὺς καὶ ἀγαθοὺς
  καὶ   βρέχει   ἐπὶ δικαίους καὶ ἀδίκους.

4.5.4

ἐὰν γὰρ ἀγαπήσητε	καὶ ἐὰν ἀσπάσησθε
τοὺς ἀγαπῶντας ὑμᾶς,	τοὺς ἀδελφοὺς ὑμῶν μόνον,
τίνα μισθὸν ἔχετε;	τί περισσὸν ποιεῖτε;
οὐχὶ καὶ οἱ τελῶναι	οὐχὶ καὶ οἱ ἐθνικοι[66]
τὸ αὐτὸ ποιοῦσιν;	τὸ αὐτὸ ποιοῦσιν;

4.5.5 Ἔσεσθε οὖν ὑμεῖς   τέλειοι
  ὡς Ο ΠΑΤΗΡ ΥΜΩΝ Ο ΟΥΡΑΝΙΟΣ τέλειός ἐστιν.

The fifth unit again follows the formal pattern. It employs an abbreviated form of the initial aural formula, ἠκούσατε ὅτι ἐρρέθη. Only here is the statement of the law expressed in a positive. The law is again expressed in a doublet and the second element is unattested.[67]

The counter-statement occurs in expanded form. The epithet τοῦ πατρὸς ὑμῶν τοῦ ἐν οὐρανοῖς is elaborated into a ὅτι compound clause which includes a chiasm of opposing terms, πονηροὺς/ἀγαθοὺς and δικαίους/ἀδίκους. The case law line again sets specific examples in parallel, first οἱ τελῶναι and then οἱ ἐθνικοὶ as negative examples. The first example emphasizes the verb ἀγαπάω by doubling the sound, expressing it first as an aorist imperative and then an aorist participle as direct object. The direct object of the second example (τοὺς ἀδελφούς) echoes back to the first unit of this section where ἀδελφός was a prominent organizing sound. There ἀντίδικος opposed it, here οἱ ἐχθροί. The parallel pattern of the two examples is obvious: ἐάν +

---

66 Later manuscripts read τελῶναι thus increasing the parallel. Parallels are not expected to be perfect and the difference points to the semantic or ideological level.

67 Given the strong doublet form of the law statement, it seems likely that the second member is the creation of the author on the basis of the Q text. The search for an extra gospel parallel is in vain.

connective + aorist subjunctive + direct object + interrogative phrase + negative intensive + noun + τὸ αὐτὸ ποιοῦσιν.

The conclusion (4.5.5) forms a chiasm which, like 4.3.5, is bracketed by morphemes of εἰμι. It repeats the adjective τέλειος, and places the epithet ὁ πατὴρ ὑμῶν ὁ οὐράνιος in the prominent center position. The epithet forms an inclusio with its previous occurrence in the expanded counter-statement 4.5.3. The inclusio and chaism emphasize the limit (τέλειος) to which the father and ὑμεῖς should go.[68]

5. Ὅταν...μή (*6:1–18*)
5.0 (*6:1*)
5.0 Προσέχετε[69] τὴν δικαιοσύνην ὑμῶν
      μὴ ποιεῖν   ἔμπροσθεν τῶν ἀνθρώπων
            πρὸς τὸ θεαθῆναι αὐτοῖς·
        εἰ δὲ μή γε, μισθὸν οὐκ ἔχετε
    παρὰ ΤΩΙ ΠΑΤΡΙ ΥΜΩΝ ΤΩΙ ΕΝ ΤΟΙΣ ΟΥΡΑΝΟΙΣ.

Like the previous section, the fifth section of the Sermon organizes a large body of material with a repeating phonetic/syntactical pattern. (See Appendix 2 for a schematic display of parallel organization in section 5.) Unlike the ἠκούσατε section, however, the fifth section opens with an introductory statement which stands alone as a thematic reprise.[70] It begins with προσέχετε τὴν δικαιοσύνην ὑμῶν and employs several of the Sermon's primary words and themes: δικαικοσύνη, μισθός, being seen, acting in public, and Matthew's full epithet for God, πάτερ ἡμῶν ὁ ἐν τοῖς οὐρανοῖς. The introductory section also establishes several organizing elements that recur in the subsequent subsections: a prohibitive statement, a result clause pertaining to public behavior, and ὁ μισθός. 5.0 has few internal phonetic markers and a high concentration of abstract terms.

---

68 Margaret E. Dean, "Reading Matthew's Treasure Map: Territoriality in Matthew's Five Sermons" (M.Div. thesis, Phillips Graduate Seminary, 1993) 54–56, proposes the translation of 5:48, "You must be one [who goes to] the limit, as your heavenly father is [one who goes to] the limit," arguing that τέλειος typically denotes the attainment of an end or a termination. In the Sermon it refers to the law's extension to cover a broader category of circumstance.

69 The textual evidence for δὲ probably leans towards excluding it (cf., Nestle-Aland[26]). Supporting this exclusion is that the beginnings of units do not normally employ connectives in the Sermon.

70 Kennedy, *New Testament Interpretation Through Rhetorical Criticism* 57, shows this unit functions rhetorically as a retatement of the theme, our section 3.

As such it sands out and would break a reciter's and hearer's rhythm, calling attention to itself.

Four units with an initial aural formula begin with ὅταν. Tannehill observes this "repetitive pattern [which] can release words from their literal limits" and amplify their meaning.[71] It also makes it possible to hear. One of these units, the unit containing the πάτερ ἡμῶν ὁ ἐν τοῖς οὐρανοῖς, abbreviates, elaborates, and deviates from the organizing pattern while retaining several of the repetitive formal features. The phonetic/syntactical pattern includes the following elements.

1. A temporal clause, usually with ὅταν but once with a participle (5.3.1), which states the unit's topic phonetically (almsgiving 5.1, prayer 5.2, fasting 5.3).
2. A negative imperative clause or a subjunctive of prohibition.
3. A negative comparison with οἱ ὑποκριταί.
4. A causal clause with with a doublet, frequently introduced by ὅτι or γάρ.
5. A purpose clause introduced by ὅπως which refers to public activity.
6. A pronouncement introduced by the formula ἀμὴν λέγω ὑμῖν which refers to ὁ μισθός.
7. A temporal clause with συ, the connective δέ, and a present participle or a subjunctive verb (as in 5.2). The clause contains a doublet and reiterates the unit's topic.
8. A purpose clause [ὅπως] making reference usually to the father ἐν τῷ κρυπτῷ (κρυφαίῳ).
9. A formulaic ending that functions as a refrain, connected to the preceding material with καί and concluding ὁ πατήρ σου ὁ βλέπων ἐν τῷ κρυπτῷ [κρυφαίῳ] ἀποδώσει σοι.[72]

5.1 (6:2–4)
5.1.1 Ὅταν οὖν ποιῇς ἐλεημοσύνην,
5.1.2 μὴ σαλπίσῃς   ἔμπροσθέν σου,
5.1.3 ὥσπερ οἱ ὑποκριταὶ ποιοῦσιν

      ἐν ταῖς συναγωγαῖς
      καὶ ἐν ταῖς ῥύμαις,
5.1.5 ὅπως δοξασθῶσιν   ὑπὸ τῶν ἀνθρώπων·

---

[71] Tannehill, *The Sword of His Mouth* 79–85.

[72] Later manuscripts including *textus receptus* show at the end of this phrase in all three of its occurences ἐν τῷ φανερῷ to balance ἐν τῷ κρυπτῷ.

5.1.6 <u>ἀμὴν λέγω ὑμῖν, ἀπέχουσιν τὸν μισθὸν αὐτῶν.</u>
5.1.7 <u>σοῦ δὲ ποιοῦντος ἐλεημοσύνην</u> μὴ γνώτω ἡ ἀριστερά σου
τί ποιεῖ ἡ δεξιά σου,
5.1.8. <u>ὅπως</u> ᾖ σου ἡ <u>ἐλεημοσύνη ἐν τῷ κρυπτῷ·</u>
5.1.9 <u>καὶ ὁ πατήρ σου ὁ βλέπων ἐν τῷ κρυπτῷ ἀποδώσει σοι.</u>

There is some doubt whether 5.1–5.4 are four units or should be seen as four sections of the single unit 5.0. The opening temporal clause is not as strong an initial aural formula as in other units (although it occurs in every unit) and these are the only units in which a connective occurs in the first lexie. On the basis of our evidence a case could be made for four sequential units or 4 subordinate units. To the ear the difference is not critical and this may well represent a case of the Sermon's mixed nature. These are meant to sound like paratactic units in sequence but semantically they are subordinated to the introduction 5.0.

The first unit (5.1) follows the pattern closely. Its introductory temporal clause states its topic, almsgiving, which is repeated in the second temporal clause (5.1.7) following the ἀμὴν formula (5.1.6). The unit lacks the causal clause (5.1.4) following the negative imperative but the comparative clause (5.1.3) contains a doublet referring to two locations, συναγωγαῖς and ῥύμαις. The second temporal clause (5.1.7) following the ἀμὴν formula employs a second doublet based on the left and right hands. The purpose clause (5.1.8) and conclusion (5.1.9) conform to the formal pattern. The constantly repeated phrases so characteristic of section 5 (see Appendix 2) and the two doublets give this unit a strong rhythmic pattern.

5.2 (*6:5–6*)
5.2.1 Καὶ **ὅταν** <u>προσεύχησθε,</u>
5.2.2 <u>οὐκ</u> ἔσεσθε
5.2.3 <u>ὡς</u> οἱ ὑποκριταί,
5.2.4 <u>ὅτι</u> φιλοῦσιν ἐν ταῖς συναγωγαῖς
καὶ ἐν ταῖς γωνίαις τῶν πλατειῶν
ἑστῶτες <u>προσεύχεσθαι,</u>
5.2.5 <u>ὅπως</u> φανῶσιν τοῖς ἀνθρώποις·
5.2.6 <u>ἀμὴν λέγω ὑμῖν, ἀπέχουσιν τὸν μισθὸν αὐτῶν.</u>
5.2.7 σὺ δὲ <u>ὅταν</u> <u>προσεύχῃ</u>
εἴσελθε εἰς τὸ ταμεῖόν σου
καὶ κλείσας τὴν θύραν σου
5.2.8 <u>πρόσευξαι τῷ πατρί σου τῷ ἐν τῷ κρυπτῷ·</u>

5.2.9 καὶ <u>ὁ πατήρ σου ὁ βλέπων</u> <u>ἐν τῷ κρυπτῷ</u> ἀποδώσει σοι.

The second unit concerning prayer follows the formal pattern exactly, except that the second purpose clause (5.2.8) preceding the formulaic ending (5.2.9) employs the aorist infinitive πρόσευξαι, a performancial variation of ὅπως. Its doublets refer to contrasting locations. The first, συναγωγαῖς and γωνίαις τῶν πλατειῶν, echoes the first doublet in 5.1.3. The second refers to the contrasting location, εἰς τὸ ταμεῖόν σου καὶ κλείσας τὴν θύραν σου, establishing a strong private vs. public contrast with the first doublet. The reference to praying occurs four times, versus three for fasting, foreshadowing the subject's elaboration in the next unit.

5.3 (*6:7–15*)

5.3.1   <u>Προσευχόμενοι</u> δε

5.3.2.1 μὴ βατταλογήσητε

5.3.3.1 <u>ὥσπερ</u> οἱ ἐθνικοί,

5.3.4.1 δοκοῦσιν <u>γὰρ</u> ὅτι ἐν τῇ πολυλογίᾳ αὐτῶν εἰσακουσθήσονται.

5.3.2.2 <u>μὴ</u> <u>οὖν</u>

5.3.3.2   <u>ὁμοιωθῆτε</u> αὐτοῖς·

5.3.4.2 οἶδεν <u>γὰρ</u> Ο ΠΑΤΗΡ ΥΜΩΝ ὧν χρείαν ἔχετε πρὸ τοῦ
                                            ὑμᾶς αἰτῆσαι αὐτόν.]

5.3.7   Οὕτως οὖν <u>προσεύχεσθε</u> ὑμεῖς·

a   <u>ΠΑΤΕΡ</u> <u>ΗΜΩΝ</u> Ο ΕΝ ΤΟΙΣ ΟΥΡΑΝΟΙΣ,

      ἁγιασθήτω τὸ ὄνομά <u>σου</u>·
      ἐλθέτω   ἡ βασιλεία <u>σου</u>·
      γενηθήτω   τὸ θέλημά <u>σου</u>,
      <u>ὡς</u> ἐν οὐρανῷ καὶ ἐπὶ γῆς·

b   τὸν ἄρτον <u>ἡμῶν</u>   τὸν ἐπιούσιον δὸς <u>ἡμῖν</u> σήμερον·
   καὶ **ἄφες** <u>ἡμῖν</u>   τὰ ὀφειλήματα <u>ἡμῶν</u>,
   <u>ὡς</u> καὶ   <u>ἡμεῖς</u> **ἀφήκαμεν** τοῖς ὀφειλέταις <u>ἡμῶν</u>·
   καὶ μὴ εἰσενέγκῃς <u>ἡμᾶς</u> εἰς πειρασμόν,
   ἀλλὰ   ῥῦσαι <u>ἡμᾶς</u> ἀπὸ τοῦ πονηροῦ.

5.3.8.1 Ἐὰν <u>γὰρ</u> **ἀφῆτε** <u>τοῖς ἀνθρώποις</u> <u>τὰ παραπτώματα αὐτῶν</u>,

5.3.9.1 **ἀφήσει** καὶ ὑμῖν
              Ο ΠΑΤΗΡ ΥΜΩΝ Ο ΟΥΡΑΝΙΟΣ]·

5.3.8.2 <u>ἐὰν</u> δὲ μὴ **ἀφῆτε** <u>τοῖς ἀνθρώποις,</u>

5.3.9.2 οὐδὲ   Ο ΠΑΤΗΡ ΥΜΩΝ   **ἀφήσει**
                    <u>τὰ παραπτώματα ὑμῶν.</u>]

Two units on prayer (5.2, 5.3), the length and variation of the second unit, and its central placement in this section indicate its importance. Unit 5.3 presents an elaborate performancial variation of the organizing pattern.[73]

The unit opens with a present participle, a performancial variation of the regular initial aural marker for section 5, ὅταν. The participle expresses the unit's topic, prayer, and the morpheme is repeated after οὕτως οὖν in 5.3.7 where the organization of the unit shifts for the prayer πάτερ ὑμων. The repetition of the προσευχ- morpheme echoes its fourfold repetition in the previous unit. The negative imperative (5.3.2.1 and .2), the comparative clause (5.3.3.1 and .2), and the causal clause (5.3.4.1 and .2) are doubled in this unit and οἱ ἐθνικοί rather than οἱ ὑποκριταί appears as the negative nominal in the comparative clauses (5.3.3.1 and .2). This substitution echoes the parallel in 4.5.4 of οἱ τελῶναι / οἱ ἐθνικοί and contributes to the gospel's narrative objective by building up a system of synonyms for οἱ ἐθνικοί.[74]

The doubling of the negative comparison and its accompanying elements is characteristic of the performancial variation in the first part of this unit. The second μή and comparison lines abbreviate and combine the formula into a verb of comparison (ὁμοιωθῆτε) and pronoun (αὐτοῖς). Instead of the normal doublet in the causal clause (line 4, cf. 5.2.4) there are two lines in two complete doublets of lines 5.3.2.1., .3.1, and .4.1 and 5.3.2.2, .3.2, and .4.2. The doubling signals an upcoming shift which begins with the abbreviated epithet ὁ πατήρ ὑμῶν. This abbreviated epithet is repeated in the unit's last line (5.3.9.2), forming an inclusio. Both the full epithet, πάτερ ἡμῶν ὁ ἐν τοῖς οὐρανοῖς, and a slightly abbreviated version, occur twice inside the inclusio and reinforce it. The two interior epithets are chiastically arranged and bracket the Lord's prayer.

The prayer (5.3.7) functions as a temporal clause (line 7) in the organizing pattern of this unit with οὖν and the present tense

---

[73] Others have noticed the parallel pattern of 5.1, 5.2, and 5.4 and have observed many of its organizing elements in 5.3 but analyses of the pattern typically rest primarily on conceptual, thematic grounds. See, for example, Davies, *Matthew* 572–73, 592–3, and Betz, *Essays on the Sermon on the Mount* 56–64. Luz, *Matthew 1–7* 369, observes some phonetic/syntactical differences between the "you" and "we" petitions but does not indicate the effect or importance of these features.

[74] By identifying οἱ ὑποκριταί and οἱ ἐθνκικοί the author is preparing for the bridge that leads to the command to preach the gospel to τὰ ἔθνη.

providing the temporal sense. The prayer itself reiterates the unit's theme and is also divided into two parts, thus fulfilling all the conditions of line 7. The two parts (α and β) of the Lord's prayer are organized by triplets. The repetition of the morpheme οὐραν- in the first and last lexies of the α part encloses a triplet of imperative verbs + direct object + σου. The β group triplet consists of three clauses joined by καί. The first person plural pronoun punctuates and unifies the prayer's second triplet, creating a distinct difference in voice and person between the two parts. Likewise the first triad is short and staccato in sound; the second longer and more fluid.

As we have arranged it, the second triplet (group β) consists of five lexies. The first lexie stands alone and the remaining four lexies are arranged in two doublets. In the first three lexies a form of ἡμεῖς punctuates the middle and end of each lexie. The first lexie forms a chaism with the second: direct object + ἡμῶν + imperative + ἡμῖν //imperative + ἡμῖν + direct object + ἡμῶν. The second lexie introduces the verb ἀφίημι which repeats in the third lexie in a prominent central position. In lexies 4 and 5, the first person plural pronoun serves as the direct object and precedes a prepositional phrase that completes the parallel between the two lexies. This careful organization by sound and rhythm of the prayer's two parts give each part a distinctive sound and explains its mnemonic ease.[75]

The unit ends with a pair of third class conditions in which ἀφίημι serves as the only verb. The protasis of both conditions (5.3.8.1 and .2) employs an expected element of line 5, the reference to ἀνθρώποι, while the apodosis implies the μισθός (here forgiveness) of line 6. A specific line 5 is missing in this unit. The doubling of the final lines serves to round out the organization of the unit and the doublet patterning also returns to the organizing pattern of the unit's beginning (5.3.2.1–.4.2). The conditions function as purpose clauses (line 8)[76] and the apodoses as conclusions (line 9). The doublet combines parallelism, chiasm, and inclusio. The protasis in both conditions includes ἐάν + a postpositive particle + ἀφῆτε τοῖς

---

[75] Outlines of 6:7–15 offered by Davies, *Matthew* 592, and Betz, *Essays on the Sermon on the Mount* 56–64 do not account for the significance they ascribe to the Lord's prayer. Gundry, *Matthew* 104, remarks on the prayer's "liturgical style" but does not furnish a basis for so classifying the prayer. Our analysis analyzes empirically the prayer's distinctive sound and advances phonetic/syntactical evidence for its semantic importance.

[76] Paraphrased: the purpose of forgiving is that God will forgive.

ἀνθρώποις, while the apodosis includes a reference to ὁ πατὴρ ὑμῶν (A) and the verb ἀφήσει (B). The word order of the two apodoses forms a chiasm: BA/AB. The phrase τὰ παραπτώματα αὐτῶν at the end of the protasis of the first condition and at the end of the apodosis of the second condition marks an inclusio that delineates the lines 5.3.8.1–5.3.9.2.[77]

5.4 (*6:16–18*)

5.4.1 Ὅταν δὲ νηστεύητε,

5.4.2 μὴ γίνεσθε

5.4.3 ὡς οἱ ὑποκριταὶ σκυθρωποί,

5.4.4 ἀφανίζουσιν γὰρ τὰ πρόσωπα αὐτῶν

5.4.5 ὅπως φανῶσιν τοῖς ἀνθρώποις νηστεύοντες·

5.4.6 ἀμὴν λέγω ὑμῖν, ἀπέχουσιν τὸν μισθὸν αὐτῶν.

5.4.7 σὺ δὲ νηστεύων ἄλειψαί σου τὴν κεφαλὴν
   καὶ τὸ πρόσωπόν σου νίψαι,

5.4.8 ὅπως μὴ φανῇς τοῖς ἀνθρώποις νηστεύων
   ἀλλὰ τῷ πατρί σου   τῷ ἐν τῷ κρυφαίῳ·

5.4.9 καὶ ὁ πατήρ σου ὁ βλέπων ἐν τῷ κρυφαίῳ ἀποδώσει σοι.

Unit 5.4 presents in skeletal form the previously established phonetic/syntactical pattern for section 5. There is no doublet in 5.4.4 but 5.4.8 is doubled. The doublet referring to the father's seeing in secret employs κρυφαίῳ rather than ἐν τῷ κρυπτῷ as elsewhere.

6. Μὴ θησαυρίζετε (*6:19–7:6*)

The units of section 6 employ an initial aural formula denoted by three prohibitions, μὴ θησαυρίζετε, μὴ κρίνετε, and μὴ δῶτε. The units are of unequal length. The first, under the heading μὴ θησαυρίζετε, consists of four subunits, each of which contains internal parallelism and a concluding proverb. The first three subunits show stronger organizational similarities to each other than does the fourth subunit. Subunits 6.1.1, 6.1.2, and 6.1.3 resemble each other in their use of summary statements at the beginning and the end of the subunit and antithetical parallels which illustrate these proverbs, as in the μὴ νομίσητε section (3) and ἠκούσατε section (4). Section 6.1.4

---

[77] Following τοῖς ἀνθρώποις of 5.3.8.2 many excellent manuscripts (see Nestle-Aland[26]) fill in the elipsis with τὰ παραπτώματα ὑμῶν. This breaks up the chiasm between the lines (so also Bruce M. Metzger, *A Textual Commentary on the Greek New Testament*, [New York: United Bible Societies, 1971] 17) and the inclusio. Furthermore, throughout the Sermon, Matthew has frequently employed elipsis.

subordinates a fivefold prohibition against anxiety to the major prohibition of 6.1, μὴ θησαυρίζετε.

6.1 *(6:19–34)*

1–Μὴ **θησαυρίζετε** ὑμῖν
θησαυροὺς
ἐπὶ τῆς γῆς,

1–θησαυρίζετε δὲ ὑμῖν
θησαυροὺς
ἐν οὐρανῷ,

2–ὅπου σὴς καὶ βρῶσις
ἀφανίζει

2–ὅπου οὔτε σὴς οὔτε βρῶσις
ἀφανίζει

3–καὶ ὅπου κλέπται
διορύσσουσιν
καὶ κλέπτουσιν·

3–καὶ ὅπου κλέπται οὐ
διορύσσουσιν οὐδὲ κλέπτουσιν·

> ὅπου γάρ ἐστιν ὁ θησαυρός σου,
> ἐκεῖ ἔσται καὶ ἡ καρδία σου.

6.1.1. *(6:19–21)*

μὴ θαυρίζετε, a new initial aural marker, signals a new section. It begins with a set of antithetical parallels contrasting treasure on earth and in heaven. The parallel phrases use identical words and syntax except in the negation. The first parallel lexies combine references to γῆ and οὐρανός, a frequent binary in the Sermon. The second and third sets of lines differ only in the addition of negatives: οὔτε/οὔτε in the second line and οὐ/οὐδέ in the third. The concluding proverb also appears in parallel rather than chiasm. It pairs the treasure with the heart and repeats both the second person singular pronoun and the verb εἰμί, which also appeared in doubled form in the concluding proverbs of units 4.3 and 4.5. It also repeats the adverb ὅπου from lines 2 and 3. The strong rhythmic repetition of the morpheme θησαυρ- singles it out as the subunit's primary theme.

6.1.2. *(6:22)*

6.1.2.1 Ο λύχνος τοῦ σώματός ἐστιν ὁ ὀφθαλμός.
2 ἐὰν οὖν ᾖ ὁ ὀφθαλμός σου ἁπλοῦς,
3   ὅλον τὸ σῶμά σου φωτεινὸν ἔσται·
4 ἐὰν δὲ ὁ ὀφθαλμός σου πονηρὸς ᾖ,
5   ὅλον τὸ σῶμά σου σκοτεινὸν ἔσται.
6 εἰ οὖν τὸ φῶς τὸ ἐν σοὶ σκότος ἐστίν,
7   τὸ σκότος πόσον.

Subunit 6.1.2 contains both an introductory proverb and a concluding one, indicating its subordinate character. The pattern of this subunit is very similar to that of the case law line in section 4 (ἠκούσατε). The opening statement introduces the subunit's key words: σῶμα and ὀφθαλμός. Two parallel third class conditions follow which contrast the sound and evil eye. The verb occurs at the beginning of the protasis of the first conditional statement (lexie 2) and at the end of the protasis in the second (lexie 4). As in the previous subunit, vocabulary and syntax are identical except where the contrast is established: the second phrase substitutes πονηρός for ἁπλοῦς and σκοτεινόν for φωτεινόν. In the protasis of the second condition, the verb occurs at the end of the lexie (4), creating a phonetic rhythm, πονηρὸς ἦ. The concluding statement employs a first class condition and both doubles σκότος and contrasts φῶς and σκότος. Furthermore it contains monosyllabic words until the quick repetition of σκότος at the end creates a strong paratactic ending.

6.1.3 (6:24)

6.1.3. Οὐδεὶς δύναται δυσὶ κυρίοις δουλεύειν·

ἢ γὰρ τὸν ἕνα μισήσει καὶ τὸν ἕτερον ἀγαπήσει,

ἢ ἑνὸς ἀνθέξεται καὶ τοῦ ἑτέρου καταφρονήσει.

οὐ δύνασθε θεῷ δουλεύειν καὶ μαμωνᾷ.

Subunit 6.1.3 exhibits an even tighter parallelism with short phrases. Its opening and concluding proverbs are synonymous but unfold an interesting substitution and elaboration. They parallel each other and employ a wordplay with κυρίος and θεός. The proverbs differ only in that the opening statement places δυσὶ κυρίοις before the infinitive δουλεύειν whereas the closing proverb brackets the infinitive with the names of the two lords, θεῷ and μαμωνᾷ. Their recurring verbs have the same initial sound, δυ-/δου- which also occurs in the word δυσί in the opening proverb. The intervening parallel statements that apply the opening and closing proverbs contrast "the one" and "the other" lord, repeating the number one which first occurs in the opening proverb in οὐδείς. Within the parallel pattern the terms for hate/love and devoted/despise are chiastically arranged.

6.1.4 (6:25–34)

Section 6.1.4 contains five subparts[78] with the prohibition μὴ μεριμνᾶτε as the initial aural marker. It concludes, as do the previous three subunits, with a summarizing proverb. The μὴ μεριμνᾶτε subpart begins with διὰ τοῦτο, which clearly indicates its subordinate character with respect to the larger μὴ θησαυρίζετε unit.[79] This is an example of the Sermon's mixed character. The subpart has many of the characteristics of a section, but the variation and subordinating phrases clearly indicate that both phonetically and semantically it is to be subordinated. The section achieves a logical subordination by means of a sequential arrangement.

Although the subparts do not exhibit the parallelism that is evident in 6.1.1, 6.1.2, and 6.1.3 or in the major sections 4 and 5, it does have a strong organizational pattern. At or near the beginning of each subpart is a morpheme of μεριμνάω. 6.1.4.4–.5[80] exhibit identical phonetic/syntactical markers, μὴ οὖν μεριμνήσατε. Subpart 2 begins with a question, while subparts 1, 3 and 4 have questions beginning in the second lexie. Subpart 1 ends with the question, οὐχ ὑμεῖς μᾶλλον διαφέρετε αὐτῶν (1.6), and the third ends similarly to the first, with the question οὐ πολλῷ μᾶλλον ὑμᾶς, ὀλιγόπιστοι (3.5). Subpart 1 contains two initial questions τὶ φάγητε, τὶ ἐνδύσησθε, while the fourth subpart balances it with 3, adding ἤ τὶ πίωμεν. Subparts 4 and 5 both conclude with a proverb.

Although the subparts do not closely parallel each other, their phonetic/syntactical organizational features lend a formal unity to the

---

[78] Technically they are sub-sub-units, but we will refer to them as subparts to avoid confusion and give them a distinctive marker.

[79] Even though this subunit is quite long, it is not a separate unit or section. This is indicated by the placement of the initial aural marker in second position and the subordinating character of the phrase διὰ τοῦτο in Matthew (see also 12:31 and 21:43 for other occurrences of διὰ τοῦτο with λέγω ὑμῖν; διὰ τοῦτο also occurs in 12:27, 13:13, 13:52, 14:2, 18:23, 23:34, and 24:44). If the intial aural marker occurred in primary position or without the διὰ τοῦτο phrase, this subunit would be classified as a separate section. This decision is based upon the observation of Matthew's style in this Sermon, not on the need to produce a semantics and thus demonstrates the superiority of our method of *listening* to the text before *interpreting* it.

[80] In order to avoid number fatigue, since all the μεριμνᾶτε subparts will begin with the prefix number 6.1.4, that number will be left out in the commentary, except where it might result in confusion. That is, the first number will indicate which of the four subparts is referenced and the second number which line of the subpart.

topically unified μὴ μεριμνᾶτε subunit. The first three all open with interrogative clauses marked by the interrogative pronoun and end with a favorable comparison between the hearers and the subpart's example as grounds for the Father's care. In addition, the first subpart contains a λέγω formula, the formula μὴ μεριμνᾶτε, a negative question, and an imperative, some of which are repeated in the second subpart and the remaining ones are repeated in the third.

6.1.4.1 (*6:25–26*)
6.1.4.1.1b Διὰ τοῦτο λέγω ὑμῖν,
6.1.4.1.1a **μὴ μεριμνᾶτε** τῇ ψυχῇ ὑμῶν
6.1.4.1.2 τί φάγητε
    μηδὲ   τῷ σώματι ὑμῶν
    τί ἐνδύσησθε.
6.1.4.1.3 οὐχὶ   ἡ ψυχὴ πλεῖόν ἐστιν τῆς **τροφῆς**
    καὶ   τὸ σῶμα   τοῦ ἐνδύματος;
6.1.4.1.4a ἐμβλέψατε εἰς τὰ πετεινὰ τοῦ οὐρανοῦ
6.1.4.1.4b ὅτι οὐ σπείρουσιν
    οὐδὲ θερίζουσιν
    οὐδὲ συνάγουσιν εἰς ἀποθήκας,
6.1.4.1.5 καὶ Ο ΠΑΤΗΡ ΥΜΩΝ   Ο ΟΥΡΑΝΙΟΣ **τρέφει** αὐτά·
6.1.6.1.6 οὐχ ὑμεῖς μᾶλλον διαφέρετε αὐτῶν;

Subpart 6.1.4.1 introduces a full complement of features much like the initial unit of a section (i.e., sections 1.1; 4.1; 5.1). λέγω ὑμῖν from the first lexie is repeated in 4.3.1b. The prohibition μὴ μεριμνᾶτε (1.1a) reappears in subparts 4.4.1a and .5. All but the last subpart employ the interrogative pronoun τίς, usually in series. Then the sequence repeats. After the interrogative τίς comes a negative question, here introduced by οὐχὶ (1.3), a feature repeated in 3.3; then an imperative (1.4a), an element that recurs in 4.4a; and finally the favorable comparison (1.6) with the hearer, marked by μᾶλλον.

Within this first subpart several aural features stand out. Following the διὰ τοῦτο introductory phrase, the next six lexies are interlocked by alternating and repeating morphemes and elipses. The prohibition in lexie 2 parallels lexie 4 which is introduced with μηδὲ and the prohibition is supplied by elipsis. The final phrases of these two lexies are set in parallel, τῇ ψυχῇ and τῷ σώματι. This binary organizes the entire μὴ μεριμνᾶτε subunit. Both lexies end with ὑμῶν and are interlaced with parallel interrogatives in lexies 3 and 5 which pick up on their respective prohibitions. ψυχή asks about eating (what goes in) and σῶμα about clothing (what is on the outside). The prohibitions and questions are tied together in 1.3 where the negative question repeats the contrasting pair in the same order, introducing another parallel, τροφή and ἐνδύμα. Thus the parallel equivalences are set up:[81]

ψυχή	φάγητε	τροφή
σῶμα	ἐνδύσησε	ἐνδύμα

The forms of the first parallel are feminine and the second are neuter, producing similar sounds[82] at the beginning and end of the lexies. The whole coheres by means of an oscillating phonetic, syntactic, and semantic pattern for these six lexies.

The imperative clause of line 4 contains a triplet, οὐ σπείρουσιν, οὐδὲ θερίζουσιν, οὐδὲ συνάγουσιν (4b). The negative question and the ὅτι clause of the imperative statement set concrete examples in parallel in a style consistent with sections 4 and 5. 1.5 introduces τρέφει, parallel to τρόφη, creating the expectation that the next lexie will play on ἐνδύμα, which it does not. Unfulfilled expectation is part of the normal elaboration of parallelism.[83] Both phonetically and semantically it plays on the οὐχὶ ἡ ψυχή lexie. The epithet ὁ πατὴρ ὑμῶν ὁ οὐράνιος draws the subpart to a close.

6.1.4.2 (6:27)

6.1.4.2 τίς δὲ ἐξ ὑμῶν **μεριμνῶν**
         δύναται προσθεῖναι
            ἐπὶ τὴν ἡλικίαν αὐτοῦ
               πῆχυν ἕνα;

Subpart 2 radically abbreviates the elements set up in subpart 1 to a question and the initial aural marker, the morpheme μεριμνάω. More importantly it picks up semantically on the expected but missing final parallel of σῶμα /ἐνδύμα. Ἡ ἡλικία is a measurement of σῶμα. Thus subpart 2 finishes out the parallel.

6.1.4.3 (6:28–30)

---

[81] Following τί φάγητε many manuscripts insert ἤ (καὶ) τί πίητε. Besides the textual evidence problems with such an insertion, the careful structuring of lexies 2–7 speak against it. It was most likely picked up from 4.2 below.

[82] The phonic similarity that results from morphemes of conjugation, person, or number in "the logical articulation of the language" is sometimes referred to as poor rhyme. See Schökel, *Manual of Hebrew Poetics* 21.

[83] Kugel, *Idea of Biblical Poetry* 7.

6.1.4.3   καὶ περὶ ἐνδύματος

6.1.4.3.1a/2 τί **μεριμνᾶτε**;

6.1.4.3.4a   καταμάθετε τὰ κρίνα τοῦ ἀγροῦ

6.1.4.3.4b   πῶς αὐξάνουσιν·[84]

           οὐ κοπιῶσιν

           οὐδὲ νήθουσιν·

6.1.4.3.1b   λέγω δὲ ὑμῖν ὅτι

6.1.4.3.3   οὐδὲ Σολομὼν

           ἐν πάσῃ τῇ δόξῃ αὐτοῦ

           περιεβάλετο ὡς ἓν τούτων.

           εἰ δὲ τὸν χόρτον τοῦ ἀγροῦ

           σήμερον ὄντα

           καὶ αὔριον εἰς κλίβανον βαλλόμενον

6.1.4.3.5   Ο ΘΕΟΣ οὕτως ἀμφιέννυσιν,

           οὐ πολλῷ μᾶλλον ὑμᾶς, ὀλιγόπιστοι

The initial lexie of subpart 3 picks up ἐνδύμα explicitly, thus tying 2 and 3 closely together, completing the parallelism initiated by subpart 1. The first two lexies of this subpart form a phonetic chiasm with subpart 2 in which the order of the interrogative and the paralleled element are reversed, tying the two subparts even more closely together. The second lexie of subpart 1 and the first lexie of subpart 2 share a large number of sounds.

                   δύναται προσθεῖναι

                   καὶ περὶ ἐνδύματος

If subpart 2 abbreviates the pattern, subpart 3 repeats it fulsomely. The μὴ μεριμνᾶτε becomes a question as in 2, combining in this subpart the functions of lines 1a and 2. The imperative with three paratactic verbs (3.4b) comes forward to set up the elongated negative comparison (3.3). In subpart 1 the ψυχή/σῶμα comparison had consisted of two lexies. While it still has two parts here, they are elaborated. A new signifier (περιβάλλω in place of ἐνδύομαι) is introduced for the signified, "to clothe" in order to make a word play on βαλλόμενον at the comparison's end. It forms an inclusio for the example of the grass. The epithet (3.5) is abbreviated to the simple ὁ θεός and sets up an ironic contrast between Solomon and God.

---

[84] The unique reading of codex Sinaiticus, οὐ ξένουσιν οὐδὲ νήθουσιν οὐδὲ κοπιῶσιν (they do not card neither do they spin nor toil) is very attractive. See Metzger, *A Textual Commentary* 18.

Solomon, presented in this subpart in glorious raiment, is compared to ordinary grass, whereas God, whose clothing of the grass makes it beautiful, is himself clothed in this subpart in an epithet radically reduced to its one essential feature. Σολομών and θεός form another inclusio for the example (3.3). Δόξης, here ironically ascribed to Solomon, is properly ascribed to θεός. A third signifier, ἀμφιέννυσιν, associated with God, draws an even stronger contrast with Solomon. This sets off the implicit comparison if grass, clothed by God, has greater glory than Solomon, how much more you ὀλιγόπιστοι, who are cared for by God. This accounts for the rearrangement and the placement of the subpart in the center. It likewise explains the reduction of the epithet to ὁ θεός, creating an ironic contrast between God and Solomon and his glory.

6.1.4.4 (*6:31–33*)
6.1.4.4.1a μὴ οὖν μεριμνήσητε λέγοντες
6.1.4.4.2   Τί φάγωμεν;
          ἤ, Τί πίωμεν;
          ἤ, Τί περιβαλώμεθα;
6.1.4.4.3   πάντα γὰρ ταῦτα τὰ ἔθνη ἐπιζητοῦσιν·
6.1.4.4.5   οἶδεν γὰρ Ο ΠΑΤΗΡ ΥΜΩΝ Ο ΟΥΡΑΝΙΟΣ
          ὅτι χρῄζετε τούτων ἁπάντων.
6.1.4.4.4a ζητεῖτε δὲ πρῶτον
6.1.4.4.4b   ΤΗΝ ΒΑΣΙΛΕΙΑΝ ΤΟΥ ΘΕΟΥ[85]
          καὶ   τὴν δικαιοσύνην αὐτοῦ,
          καὶ ταῦτα πάντα προστεθήσεται ὑμῖν.

Subpart 4. turns the interrogative clause (4.2) into a triplet by setting up the doublet φάγωμεν/πίωμεν. The subpart opens with the prohibition μὴ οὖν μεριμνᾶτε and ends with an imperative. In the comparison (4.3) the negative is not expressed but implied in that the activity of τὰ ἔθνη is to be avoided. The repetition of a πάντα ταῦτα-like phrase at the beginning of the line both in 4.3 and the final lexie in 4.4b, and at the end of the final lexie in 4.5 creates a threefold pattern to match the three interrogatives. The middle phrase is surounded on either side by an epithet, ὁ πατὴρ and ἡ βασιλεία. The

----

[85] The textual confusion in the first two lexies of this line is considerable. Both Vaticanus and Sinaticus omit τοῦ θεοῦ, which is very strong evidence. Vaticanus likewise reverses δικαιοσύνην and βασιλείαν. Matthew seldom uses βασιλεία without modifier (normally the modifier is τῶν βασιλείων) and more importantly the simple θεοῦ picks up on the reduced epithet in the previous subpart.

epithet in 4.5 again emphasizes the activity of God (knows what you need). The imperative clause introduces the triplet βασιλεία, δικαιοσύνη, and ταῦτα πάντα, matching the other triplets in subparts 1 and 3. Line 4a presents the second occurrence in the Sermon of πρῶτον with an imperative verb. A chiastic pattern draws the subpart to a close. After the interrogatives, πάντα occurs before ταῦτα, followed by a form of the verb ζητέω. The verb then recurs in imperative form, with ταῦτα πάντα in reversed order. Just as two different signifiers were employed to distinguish Solomon and God, so a compound form of ζητέω distinguishes τὰ ἔθνη from a simple form for ὑμεῖς. Within this chiastic arrangement also occur two epithets, ὁ πατὴρ ὑμῶν ὁ οὐράνιος and τὴν βασιλείαν, and a key word for Matthew, τὴν δικαιοσύνην. The chiastic form, the epithets, and the repetition of key words signals the semantic significance of the unit.

6.1.4.5 (*6:34*)

6.1.4.5. **μὴ οὖν** μεριμνήσητε εἰς τὴν <u>αὔριον</u>,
ἡ γὰρ <u>αὔριον</u> μεριμνήσει <u>ἑαυτῆς</u>·
ἀρκετὸν τῇ ἡμέρᾳ ἡ κακία <u>αὐτῆς</u>.

The abbreviation of the pattern, repetition of morpheme μεριμνάω, the noun ἡ αὔριον in a chiasm, and the end rhyme tightly link the three lexies. The middle lexie participates in both the chiasm and the rhyme, interlocking the two features and phonetically unifying the concluding subpart drawing the whole subpart to a conclusion.

6.2 (*7:1–5*)

6.2 <u>Μὴ</u> <u>κρίνετε</u>, ἵνα <u>μὴ</u> <u>κριθῆτε</u>·
<u>ἐν ᾧ</u> γὰρ <u>κρίματι</u> <u>κρίνετε</u> <u>κριθήσεσθε</u>,
καὶ <u>ἐν ᾧ</u> μέτρῳ <u>μετρεῖτε</u> μετρηθήσεται ὑμῖν.
<u>τί</u> δὲ <u>βλέπεις</u> <u>τὸ κάρφος</u> τὸ <u>ἐν</u> <u>τῷ</u> <u>ὀφθαλμῷ</u> <u>τοῦ</u> <u>ἀδελφοῦ</u> <u>σου</u>,
τὴν δὲ <u>ἐν</u> <u>τῷ</u> σῷ <u>ὀφθαλμῷ</u> <u>δοκὸν</u> οὐ κατανοεῖς;
ἢ πῶς ἐρεῖς <u>τῷ</u> <u>ἀδελφῷ</u> <u>σου</u>,
"Ἄφες <u>ἐκβάλω</u> <u>τὸ κάρφος</u> <u>ἐκ</u> <u>τοῦ</u> <u>ὀφθαλμοῦ</u> <u>σου</u>,
καὶ ἰδοὺ ἡ <u>δοκὸς</u> <u>ἐν</u> <u>τῷ</u> <u>ὀφθαλμῷ</u> <u>σοῦ</u>;
ὑποκριτά, <u>ἔκβαλε</u> <u>πρῶτον</u> <u>ἐκ</u> <u>τοῦ</u> <u>ὀφθαλμοῦ</u> <u>σου</u> τὴν <u>δοκόν</u>
καὶ τότε <u>διαβλέψεις</u>
<u>ἐκβάλειν</u> <u>τὸ κάρφος</u> <u>ἐκ</u> <u>τοῦ</u> <u>ὀφθαλμοῦ</u> <u>τοῦ</u> <u>ἀδελφοῦ</u>
<u>σου</u>.]

Unit 6.2 opens with μὴ κρίνετε, a performancial variation on the initial aural formula for section 6 which phonetically indicates the

unit's theme. Its organization evokes the formal parallelism of 6.1.1 and .2. Following the initial aural formula, the unit opens with a proverb, followed by a double question and then an imperative introducing the final two sets of doublets. In the ninth lexie πρῶτον with an imperative verb occurs for the third time.

The initial aural formula employs the repeated phoneme κρι. The double proverbs introduced by ἐν ᾧ build the phoneme into a triple repetition and then does the same thing with the phoneme μετρ. These two proverbs are set in parallel. Following the proverb, repeated words reverberate throughout the subunit. The phoneme βλέπ- occurs at the beginning in the first τί lexie and at the beginning of the concluding lexie (διαβλέψεις). The verb ἐκβάλλω occurs three times, once in the ἄφες lexie and twice in the ὑποκριταί lexie. The contrasting terms ὁ κάρφος and ἡ δοκός recur in three pairs of lexies. Their order is reversed in the final pair. Three references to ὁ ἀδελφός σου occur, as well as six references to ὁ ὀφθαλμός, two in each sentence. The τί sentence is arranged chiastically: verb, object, eye, modifier//modifer, eye, object verb. After the complicated patterns and rhythms of μὴ μεριμνᾶτε subparts the relative simplicity and repetition of this unit relaxes the demand on the listener and directs attention to the previous subparts.

6.3 (7:6)
6.3 Μὴ δῶτε τὸ ἅγιον τοῖς κυσίν
        μηδὲ βάλητε
            τοὺς μαργαρίτας ὑμῶν
            ἔμπροσθεν τῶν χοίρων,
        μήποτε   καταπατήσουσιν
            αὐτοὺς ἐν τοῖς ποσὶν αὐτῶν
        καὶ στραφέντες ῥήξωσιν ὑμᾶς.

An extended proverb with two parallel parts concludes section 6. The first part begins with a third performancial variation on the initial aural formula for section 6, μὴ δῶτε, and initiates a strong pattern of internal rhyming as did the previous unit. Μὴ δῶτε rhymes with μηδὲ βάλητε. The sentence ends with ἔμπροσθεν τῶν χοίρων which rhymes with ὑμῶν at the end of the previous lexie. The opening lexie of the second parallel part begins with μήποτε which repeats the phonemes of the initial aural formula and then picks up for an internal rhyme the terminal phoneme of the proverb's first line, -υσιν/-ουσιν, which repeats the phonemes with ποσίν and ῥήξωσιν. At the end of the middle lexie of the second parallel part, αὐτῶν echoes the end rhyme ὑμῶν and χοίρων in the first part. Ποσίν and ῥήξωσιν in the last two lexies of the unit repeat the ending sounds of the first and fifth lexies.

7. Αἰτεῖτε (7:7–20)

Section 7 has three units denoted by the occurrence of three imperative verbs: αἰτεῖτε, εἰσέλθατε, and προσέχετε. These serve as the initial aural markers and in 7.1 the pattern is announced by three consecutive imperatives. Thus each unit will be marked by an initial imperative. But the three imperatives of 7.1 also announce the organizing pattern of this section because each imperative is balanced by a verb in the future tense. Each unit carefully balances a series of binaries and this balancing of binaries announces the organizing pattern.

7.1 (7:7–12)

7.1.1α **Αἰτεῖτε** καὶ   δοθήσεται ὑμῖν,

   β **ζητεῖτε** καὶ   εὑρήσετε,

   γ **κρούετε** καὶ   ἀνοιγήσεται ὑμῖν·

   α πᾶς γὰρ   ὁ αἰτῶν   λαμβάνει

   β καὶ   ὁ ζητῶν   εὑρίσκει

   γ καὶ   τῷ κρούοντι ἀνοιγήσεται.

7.1.2 ἢ τίς ἐστιν ἐξ ὑμῶν ἄνθρωπος,

   ὃν αἰτήσει ὁ υἱὸς αὐτοῦ   ἄρτον,

       μὴ λίθον ἐπιδώσει αὐτῷ;

   ἢ καὶ ἰχθὺν   αἰτήσει,

       μὴ ὄφιν ἐπιδώσει αὐτῷ;

7.1.3 εἰ οὖν ὑμεῖς πονηροὶ ὄντες

   οἴδατε δόματα   ἀγαθὰ διδόναι

                  τοῖς τέκνοις ὑμῶν,]

   πόσῳ μᾶλλον Ο ΠΑΤΗΡ ΥΜΩΝ Ο ΕΝ ΤΟΙΣ ΟΥΡΑΝΟΙΣ

       δώσει ἀγαθὰ

                  τοῖς αἰτοῦσιν αὐτόν.]

7.1.4 Πάντα οὖν ὅσα ἐὰν θέλητε

   ἵνα ποιῶσιν ὑμῖν   οἱ ἄνθρωποι,

   οὕτως καὶ ὑμεῖς   ποιεῖτε   αὐτοῖς·

   οὗτος γὰρ ἐστιν Ο ΝΟΜΟΣ ΚΑΙ ΟΙ ΠΡΟΦΗΤΑΙ.

The first unit (7.1) opens with a triplet of imperative verbs joined by καί to complementary verbs in the future (passive) tense, laid out in three parallel clauses. This triplet is repeated in the following πᾶς γὰρ clause where the imperative verbs become participial nouns as subjects of their corresponding verbs in the future tense. The corresponding verb for αἰτέω changes in its parallel clause, from δοθήσεται in the first occurrence to λαμβάνει in the second, differentiating between the giver and the receiver. Ζητέω in the second lexie echoes its previous highlighted occurrence in 6.1.4.4. In the first triplet ὑμῖν occurs at the end of the first and third lexies, bracketing the group.

The remainder of the unit exhibits patterned elements similar to those in the μὴ μεριμνᾶτε subpart while maintaining the doublet organization. 7.1.2 picks up phonetically and thematically on the first imperative αἰτεῖτε. A double question (7.1.2) employing only one interrogative pronoun sets two specific illustrations in parallel. A first class condition (7.1.3) follows, establishing a comparison using μᾶλλον, and finally a conclusion (7.1.4) is drawn. Each of these lines is organized in a doublet, either by way of negative or positive comparison, with a proverb as the unit's conclusion. In the two parallel examples (7.1.2) the relative clauses are chiastically arranged, reversing the order in the second one of the verb αἰτέω and the object of one's asking (fish). The main clause is identical except for the object.

The conditional statement (7.1.3) opens by addressing ὑμεῖς as πονηροί, which continues the negative name calling of the addressee that has been a feature of this part of the Sermon (cf. ὀλιγόπιστοι [6.1.4.3], ὑποκριταί [6.2]). The apodosis repeats the thematic morpheme αἰτέω and includes the epithet that opens the Lord's prayer. The verb δίδωμι and the substantive adjective ἀγαθά occur in both the protasis and the apodosis (lexies 2 and 4) and are set in chiasm with concluding dative phrases set in parallel. τοῖς τέκνοις ὑμῶν parallels τοῖς αἰτοῦσιν αὐτόν. These bracket the epithet ὁ πατήρ, creating a nice semantic bridge effect: children/Father/re-questers.

This density of phonetic/syntactical, rhetorical and semantic clues signals the upcoming conclusion, the proverb beginning πάντα οὖν.[86] As in the μὴ μερίμνατε subunit (subpart 4), the οὖν signals both the conclusion and its connection with what goes before. This line, too, contains a chiasm with the repetition and reversed order of the second

---

[86] While 7:12 concludes unit 7.1, it functions neither as the Sermon's thematic summary nor the conclusion of the Sermon's main body, as most commentators maintain. See the extended discussion below in Section IV, "From Sound to Outline."

person pronoun and the verb ποιέω with subject and indirect object at the ends of their respective lexies. Their endings (οι/οις) create a weak rhyme. The proverb ends with another epithet, ὁ νόμος καὶ οἱ προφῆται. The epithet harkens back to its usage in section 3 and it also parallels the ὁ πατήρ epithet used in the prayer in 5.3. Thus 7.1.3 and .4 implement the common division and correlation in Matthew of ἐν τοῖς οὐρανοῖς and ἐπὶ τῆς γῆς and demonstrate the correspondence between the two.

7.2 (*7:13–14*)

7.2 Εἰσέλθατε διὰ τῆς <u>στενῆς</u> <u>πύλης·</u>
α   ὅτι πλατεῖα ἡ <u>πύλη</u>[87]
β <u>καὶ εὐρύχωρος</u> <u>ἡ ὁδὸς</u> ἡ ἀπάγουσα <u>εἰς τὴν</u> ἀπώλειαν
γ   <u>καὶ</u> πολλοί <u>εἰσιν</u> <u>οἱ εἰσερχόμενοι</u> δι' <u>αὐτῆς·</u>
α   τί[88] <u>στενὴ ἡ πύλη</u>
β <u>καὶ τεθλιμμένη ἡ ὁδὸς</u> ἡ ἀπάγουσα <u>εἰς τὴν</u> ζωήν
γ   <u>καὶ</u> ὀλίγοι <u>εἰσὶν οἱ</u> εὑρίσκοντες <u>αὐτήν.</u>

The imperative aural marker εἰσέλθατε begins unit 7.2 which consists of a another proverb arranged in a parallel doublet. After the initial aural formula, the saying contains two sets of nearly identical lines which highlight the distinctive elements. The parallel pattern draws attention to the contrast between στενῆς and πλατεῖα, εὐρύχωρος and τεθλιμμένη, ἀπώλειαν and ζωήν, and between πολλοί and ὀλίγοι. In the case of the participles οἱ εἰσερχόμενοι (lexie 4) and οἱ εὑρίσκοντες (lexie 7), the first repeats the imperative initial aural marker noting the unit's theme, while the second refers back to the second in the series of triple imperatives that began the section: ζητεῖτε καὶ εὑρήσετε. The contrast between narrow and wide set off in a triple pattern likewise echoes the initial doublets arranged in a triple pattern in 7.1.1.

7.3 (7:15–20)

7.3 Προσέχετε ἀπὸ τῶν ψευδοπροφητῶν,
    οἵτινες ἔρχονται πρὸς ὑμᾶς ἐν ἐνδύμασιν προβάτων,
    <u>ἔσωθεν</u> δέ εἰσιν λύκοι ἅρπαγες.

---

[87] Sinaticus and many patristic quotations omit this noun and its article. But the highly repetitive way this unit is constructed indicates that it belongs.

[88] Many manuscripts (including the first hand in Vaticanus and Sinaticus) read ὅτι, but τί has been widely used in the Sermon for just such an organizational marker. The correcting hand of Vaticanus and Sinaticus would seem to be right.

ἀπὸ τῶν καρπῶν αὐτῶν ἐπιγνώσεσθε αὐτούς.
μήτι συλλέγουσιν ἀπὸ ἀκανθῶν σταφυλὰς
        ἢ ἀπὸ τριβόλων σῦκα;

οὕτως πᾶν	δένδρον ἀγαθὸν	καρποὺς	καλοὺς	ποιεῖ,
τὸ δὲ	σαπρὸν δένδρον	καρποὺς	πονηροὺς	ποιεῖ.
οὐ δύναται	δένδρον ἀγαθὸν	καρποὺς	πονηροὺς	ποιεῖν[89]
οὐδὲ	δένδρον σαπρὸν	καρποὺς	καλοὺς	ποιεῖν.
πᾶν	δένδρον μὴ ποιοῦν	καρπὸν	καλὸν	

ἐκκόπτεται καὶ εἰς πῦρ βάλλεται.
ἄρα γε ἀπὸ τῶν καρπῶν αὐτῶν ἐπιγνώσεσθε αὐτούς.

The third unit opens with the imperative προσέχετε and contrasts the outward clothing with the inward nature of οἱ ψευδοπροφῆται. The opening statement echoes the clothing theme from the μὴ μεριμνᾶτε subpart and its subsequent pattern is similar to the μὴ κρίνετε unit with its multiple repetition of a series of words. The repeated proverb ἀπὸ τῶν καρπῶν αὐτῶν ἐπιγνώσεσθε αὐτούς forms an inclusio that encloses five parallel independent clauses. Inside the inclusio on either side of the five parallel cases is a phrase of gathering (συλλέγουσιν) and casting out (εἰς . . . βάλλεται), emphasizing the strong contrast the parallels establish. The words δένδρον, καρποὺς/καρπόν, and a form of ποιέω are each repeated five times, once in each clause. Of these, only καρποὺς always occurs in the same position; in the second clause δένδρον and its adjective change position and in the fifth clause the participle ποιοῦν precedes καρπόν. Ἀγαθὸν and σαπρὸν alternate as modifiers of δένδρον, coupled with καλοὺς and πονηροὺς as modifiers of καρποὺς. This parallel arrangement emphasizes the verb ποιέω at the end of each lexie and the contrast between ἀγαθὸν/καλοὺς and σαπρὸν/πονηροὺς. This unit likewise ties back to the three imperatives that initiated the section. Those who come are those who knock and one must recognize their fruit before one opens the door.

8. Οὐ πᾶς ὁ (*7:21–27*)
8.1 (*7:21–23*)
8.1 **Οὐ πᾶς ὁ** λέγων μοι,   Κύριε κύριε,
            εἰσελεύσεται εἰς ΤΗΝ ΒΑΣΙΛΕΙΑΝ ΤΩΝ ΟΥΡΑΝΩΝ,

---

[89] Vaticanus substitutes ἐνεγκεῖν for ποιεῖν in an effort to improve the style by relieving the boredom of repeating the same morpheme (so Metzger, *A Textual Commentary* 20). The very style of this section with its strong repetition of phrases would support the majority reading.

ἀλλ' ὁ ποιῶν τὸ θέλημα
ΤΟΥ ΠΑΤΡΟΣ ΜΟΥ ΤΟΥ ΕΝ ΤΟΙΣ ΟΥΡΑΝΟΙΣ.
πολλοὶ ἐροῦσίν μοι ἐν ἐκείνῃ τῇ ἡμέρᾳ, Κύριε κύριε,

οὐ	τῷ σῷ ὀνόματι	ἐπροφητεύσαμεν
καὶ	τῷ σῷ ὀνόματι	δαιμόνια ἐξεβάλομεν,
καὶ	τῷ σῷ ὀνόματι	δυνάμεις πολλὰς ἐποιήσαμεν;

καὶ τότε ὁμολογήσω αὐτοῖς ὅτι

Οὐδέποτε ἔγνων ὑμᾶς·
ἀποχωρεῖτε ἀπ' ἐμοῦ οἱ ἐργαζόμενοι τὴν ἀνομίαν.

A different initial aural formula, Οὐ πᾶς ὁ, indicates a new section.[90] Its first unit consists of a set of parallel statements that draw a contrast between confession and action, followed by three paratactic questions that repeat the phrase τῷ σῷ ὀνόματι and end with an -αμεν/-ομεν rhyme. The unit ends with a concluding statement that negatively reprises the unit's opening. In the initial set of parallels each statement ends with an epithet, first τὴν βασιλείαν τῶν οὐρανῶν and then τοῦ πατρός μου ἐν τοῖς οὐρανοῖς. This latter phrase and epithet recall the third petition of the Lord's prayer. The following line introducing the triplet repeats κύριε, κύριε from the unit's opening lexie, forming an inclusio that brackets the pair of epithets and linking the parallel arrangement to the subsequent triplet. The three lexies of the conclusion reprise in opposition the opening. Ὁμολογήσω parallels λέγων, confirming the contrast between confession and action. The second lexie's harsh never knowing both echoes the ἐπιγνώσεσθε of the last unit of the previous section and serves as the opposite of κύριε. Ἀποχωρεῖτε opposes εἰσλεύσεται. Because the concluding statement lacks phonetic elements characteristic of the previous repetitive patterns, its harsh condemnation receives additional emphasis.

8.2 (7:24–27)

8.2.1 Πᾶς οὖν ὅστις ἀκούει μου τοὺς λόγους τούτους καὶ ποιεῖ αὐτούς,	8.2.2 καὶ πᾶς ὁ ἀκούων μου τοὺς λόγους τούτους καὶ μὴ ποιῶν αὐτοὺς

---

[90] Davies, *Matthew* 693, debates whether to recognize a unit division after 7:20 but dismisses this possibility because he judges that 7:15–23 deals with a single subject, false prophets. His criteria for the delineation of units include thematic coherence and conformitiy with a triadic pattern. He ignores the aural clues of the initial aural formula which holds in 7:7, 7:13, 7:15 and changes for the units beginning 7:21 and 7:24.

ὁμοιωθήσεται ἀνδρὶ <u>φρονίμῳ,</u>	ὁμοιωθήσεται ἀνδρὶ <u>μωρῷ,</u>
ὅστις ᾠκοδόμησεν αὐτοῦ τὴν	ὅστις ᾠκοδόμησεν αὐτοῦ τὴν
οἰκίαν	οἰκίαν
ἐπὶ τὴν <u>πέτραν·</u>	ἐπὶ τὴν <u>ἄμμον·</u>
καὶ κατέβη ἡ βροχὴ	καὶ κατέβη ἡ βροχὴ
καὶ ἦλθον οἱ ποταμοὶ	καὶ ἦλθον οἱ ποταμοὶ
καὶ ἔπνευσαν οἱ ἄνεμοι	καὶ ἔπνευσαν οἱ ἄνεμοι
καὶ <u>προσέπεσαν</u> τῇ οἰκίᾳ ἐκείνῃ,	καὶ <u>προσέκοψαν</u> τῇ οἰκίᾳ ἐκείνῃ,
καὶ <u>οὐκ</u> ἔπεσεν,	καὶ ἔπεσεν
<u>τεθεμελίωτο γὰρ ἐπὶ τὴν</u>	<u>καὶ ἦν ἡ πτῶσις αὐτῆς μεγάλη.</u>
<u>πέτραν.</u>	

The initial aural formula reflects the performancial variation πᾶς οὖν ὅστις/πᾶς ὁ. The section presents a parable consisting of two extended parallels in a style similar to the extended parallel examples of the ἠκούσατε section (4) and section 7. The two parts are nearly identical, drawing attention to its contrasting elements: φρονίμῳ/ μωρῷ/, πέτραν/ἄμμον, οὐκ ἔπεσεν/ἔπεσεν and ἐπὶ τὴν πέτραν/ἦν ἡ πτῶσις αὐτῆς μεγάλη. The double introduction sets up as correlative hearing and doing, in contrast to confessing and not doing of the previous unit. Μου τοὺς λόγους is a reference to the Sermon which establishes the will of God. The narrator's formulaic ending of the sermon will pick up on this description of the sermon: ἐτέλεσεν ὁ Ἰησοῦς τοὺς λόγους. The conclusion of the two parallels contrasts building on rock and not as expected building on sand, but "great was the fall," a type of warning about final destruction that has concluded many units.

III. *Composing in Sound*

Our study of the Sermon on the Mount attends to its aural quality, its *recitatio*, and the deliberate imitation of orality implicit in Matthew's construction of Jesus's speech as οἱ λόγοι. As a rhetorical composition the Sermon sustains an aural rhythm achieved through the combination of phonetic, syntactical, and semantic devices. The most basic of these is the repetition of sound and reiteration of organizing patterns.[91] Our analysis has placed strong emphasis on the initial aural

---

91 Tannehill, *Sword of His Mouth* 41–43, argues that repeated sound creates the patterns that organize a text. "Repetition emphasizes, thus allowing a text to disclose its own points of emphasis and so providing a key to the proper interpetation of a text." This coheres with hearing because one hears in real time.

formula that begins a section and repeats throughout to segment it. The sermon opens with such a formula, μακάριοι, which gives the Sermon's first section its distinctive sound. The initial aural formula was Matthew's primary means of delineating units. In view of our discovery of the Sermon's highly anaphoric character, we have derived our Macro Outline (Appendix 1) from the initial aural formulae and have used them to label the sermon's sections and units.

Variations in the initial aural formula can be substantial. In section 8, for example, only a single syllable repeats, πᾶς, accompanied by various o sounds (ὁ, οὖν, οὐ, ὅστις). The formula for section 7 contains no phonetic repetition at all. Instead, a grammatical form, an imperative verb, occurs at the beginning of each unit in a predictable syntactical arrangement. The initial aural formula sometimes varies by abbreviation and elaboration. In section 4 multiple versions of the initial formula occur: a full form, ἠκούσατε ὅτι ἐρρέθη τοῖς ἀρχαίοις (4.1), a full form with a connecting adverb, πάλιν (4.3), a short form, ἠκούσατε ὅτι ἐρρέθη (4.2 and 4.4), and even ἐρρέθη δέ (4.2).

Organizing patterns can also vary by abbreviation and elaboration. Typically, the pattern appears first in full form, expands through elaboration, then abbreviates. Sections 4 and 5 exemplify this arrangement, with the full statement of an organizational pattern in 4.1 and 5.1, elaborations in 4.2 (modified conclusion) and 5.3 (rearrangement of elements and substantial expansion of one element), and abbreviations in 4.4 and 5.4.

An indication of the Sermon's high rhetorical character is its preference for unbalance. Its eight sections, although clearly marked with initial aural formulae, extend for quite different durations. The subordinate μὴ μεριμνᾶτε subpart unbalances the otherwise evenly balanced section 6. Section 3 is a unit that stands as its own section, and 5.0 falls outside the established structure of its section. The vocabulary of these latter two units also shifts to include abstract terms such as δικαιοσύνη. The lack of aural patterning in the conclusion of 8.1 achieves intensity by avoiding phonetic and syntactical repetition. These imbalances call attention to the units that alter organizational patterns.

Our evidence indicates distinctive stylistic features at the micro level of subunit, line, and lexie. Frequent parallels occur, such as that between salt and light (section 2), divine and human forgiveness (5.3.6.1–.7.2), the treasure and the heart (6.1.1), the one and the other (6.1.3), and the houses built on rock and sand (8.2). Parallels can admit of variation. For example, the verb placement changes from the beginning of the lexie to the end in the protases of the parallel conditions of 6.1.2. Similarly, in the triplet which introduces the verb ἀφίημι in the Lord's prayer (5.3.5), the verb occurs in a different place in each of three lexies. These variations break the monotony of exact reduplication of parallels.

Throughout the sermon, doublets, triplets, and combinations of doublets and triplets organize the material within a unit. Doublings can establish contrast, such as heaven and earth (6.1.1), the narrow and wide way (7.2), or houses built on rock and sand (8.2.1), or they can be synthetic, such as loving and greeting another (4.5.4) or treasure and heart (6.1). A triple imperative begins unit 7.1. Three interrogatives characterize what should not produce anxiety: eating, drinking, and clothing (6.1.4.4).

Doublets and triplets often interlock. In section 2, three phonetically similar lexies occur in each of two units. Each of the two units in section 2 include the triple occurrence of a dominant sound. In 6.1.4.1 the paired terms ψυχή and σῶμα give rise to the triple example of the birds who neither sow, reap, nor gather. Triplets figure prominently in 5.3.5, the Lord's prayer, which concludes with a double condition.

Inclusios, another stylistic feature, often bracket a unit or subunit, as does ὅτι αὐτῶν ἐστιν ἡ βασιλεία τῶν ουρανῶν in μακάριοι (section1) and ἀπὸ τῶν καρπῶν αὐτῶν ἐπιγνώσεσθε αὐτούς (section 7). Inclusios can bracket a set of lines for emphasis, as does τὴν δικαιοσύνην in the μακαριοι section and the repeated Father epithet (5.3.5).

Chiasmus occurs in the Sermon neither as prominently as inclusio nor as frequently as the interlocking doublet and triplet. Typically, chiasm combines with other stylistic features and often in conjunction with an epithet or with the rehearsal of a primary theme. The chiasm formed by πάντα ταῦτα/ταῦτα πάντα in 6.1.4.3, for example, encloses the epithet ὁ πατὴρ ὑμῶν ὁ οὐράνιος, the command ζητεῖτε δὲ πρῶτον τὴν βασιλείαν, and the distinctively Matthean τὴν δικαιοσύνην. Similarly, chiasm in 4.5.3 modifies the Father epithet and, in the same unit, the chiastic conclusion places it in the prominent central position. Chiasm combines with parallels to conclude a subunit in 6.1.3 (the love/hate terms are chiastic, δύναμαι and δουλεύω are parallel) and 6.1.4.5 (μεριμνάω and αὔριον are chiastic, ἑαυτῆς and αὐτῆς are parallel).

Various stylistic features combine to produce organizational patterns, connect material, and create closure. Repetition is the primary means of introducing an organizing pattern. Μακάριοι οἱ repeats eight times, for example, before the initial aural formula changes. Repetition with variation (sections 4 and 5) and repetitive forecasting (section 7) can also establish organizational patterns. Units and sections also often begin or end with proverbs, such as in 6.1, 6.2, and 6.3 and section 7.

Repeated key words or organizing elements forge links between sections, units, or shorter blocks of material. For example, the threefold repetition of διώκω in 1.8–1.9 and the occurrence of ἐν τοῖς οὐρανοῖς in 1.9 connects the μακάριοι ἐστε unit with the beatitudes. The repetition in 5.0 of μίσθον, which functioned as a component of an internal organizing formula in section 4, connects section 5 with the ἠκούσατε section. The specific examples set in parallel in 3.1.1 and the λέγω ὑμῖν formula repeated in 3.1 and 3.2 anticipate key organizing elements of the following section.

The Sermon establishes closure through a variety of means. Section 5's units conclude with a repeated refrain. Some units end with a proverb (6.1.1–.3, 4.5, and 7.3). In 6.1.4.4 and 7.1 the appearance of οὖν in the ultimate and penultimate lines highlights the upcoming conclusion. Closure appears to be a primary function of the epithet in the Sermon. Epithets can signal the end of a unit or section, as in sections 2 and 3 and subpart 6.1.4.1. Epithets conclude parallel specific examples in 3.1.1 and 4.2.1. Parallel lines in 8.1 conclude with two different epithets. Epithets frequently occur within an inclusio (1.8), a chiasm (6.1.4.4 and 4.5, concluding both a unit and a section), or other stylistic feature. The closing of the Lord's prayer in 5.3 combines epithet, inclusio, chiasm, and parallelism. Unit 7.1 provides a particularly interesting example because of its double set of clues for closure. An epithet, a chiasm, a proverb, and the closing signal οὖν occur in each of its final two lines. This doubled ending balances the unit's triple beginning. Often a density of aural devices signals the end of a unit or section, with or without an epithet.

We have seen that detailed observations at the micro level of the phonetic/syntactical features of the text can begin to suggest a description of Matthew's distinctive style. The text's aural features also indicate the Sermon's overall design. (See Appendix 1). We now turn to a discussion of the Sermon's arrangement at the macro level, comparing our analysis of its organization with other outlines of the Sermon.

IV. *From Sound to Outline*

Our outline of the Sermon derives from the level of the signifier. As such we hope it has an empirical basis. The Sermon's sound signals the demarcation of units. Because attention to sound highlights aspects of the Sermon that are difficult to see through other methods, our outline differs in significant ways from others. We have chosen for comparison four recent detailed proposals for structuring the Sermon on the Mount. We examine Georg Strecker's scheme[92] because it represents a major monograph. We include the outlines of W. D. Davies-Dale C. Allison[93] and Ulrich Luz[94] because they represent major commentaries from English-American and German scholarship.[95] We give only brief notice to Günther Bornkamm's classic outline because of its similarity to Luz's scheme.[96]

Strecker's outline agrees with ours in most of its major divisions, except for his sectional division at 7:12 instead of 7:20. He recognizes as our outline does the sequential character of the Sermon's units. He claims the Sermon is thematically organized by "the conceptual structure of [Matthew's] theology" and that this structure is "expressed in the organization of the speech,"[97] but actually his outline conforms to his descriptive observations without imposing a fully developed thematic schema. Strecker contends that the demand for greater righteousness in 5:20, the demand for perfection in 5:48 and the golden rule in 7:12 represent the major dividing lines of Matthew's theological system, but his outline does not consistently reflect this scheme. Verse 5:20 comes at the end of the section he designates as the first major section, but 5:48 falls at the end of the section Strecker

---

[92] Georg Strecker, *The Sermon on the Mount. An Exegetical Commentary*, (Nashville: Abingdon, 1988) 14–15.

[93] D. C. Allison, "The Structure of the Sermon on the Mount," *JBL* 106 (1987): 437–38. Davies, *Matthew* 58–65, adopts Allison's outline.

[94] Luz, *Matthew 1–7* 211–13. The outline follows that of Kürzinger and R. Riesner, "Der Aufbau der Redem im Matthäus-Evangelium," *Theologische Beitrage* 9 (1978) 173–76.

[95] See Appendix 3, Comparative Outline, for a schematic display of all five outlines.

[96] Bornkamm, "Der Aufbau Der Bergpredigt," 419–32.

[97] Strecker, *The Sermon on the Mount* 14–15.

designates as the first subdivision of section 2, and 7:12 marks the conclusion of the same major section. Strecker aligns 5:21–48 (the antitheses, our section 4), 6:1–18 (section 5 in our outline), and 6:19–7:12 as the three major sections of the main body of the Sermon, whereas our analysis finds no evidence at the level of the signifier to support the ascription of equivalent importance to these sections. Neither does our outline indicate a sectional break at 7:12.[98] Rather, we recognize 7:7–20 as a section unified by phonetic/syntactical qualities.

The organizational scheme first proposed by Allison and followed by Davies and Allison posits an elaborate thematic arrangement centered around the same three sections Strecker identifies as the Sermon's core.[99] Allison's observation of triads in the Sermon and throughout Matthew's gospel leads him to argue for this threefold emphasis. Allison correlates this with Simeon the Just's three pillars of the Law: Torah, temple service, and deeds of loving-kindness. Allison argues that, just as many rabbis revised the three pillars after the destruction of the Jerusalem temple in 70 CE, the Sermon represents Matthew's revision.[100]

According to Allison, Matthew's three pillars are Jesus and the Torah (5:17–48), the Christian cult (6:1–18), and social issues (6:19–7:12). The first pillar contains and introductory statement (5:17–20; our section 3) and two triads of instruction, the six antitheses (4 in our outline).[101] The second pillar contains one triad of instruction on almsgiving, prayer, and fasting (our section 5), and the third pillar contains two triads of instruction, a triad on the true treasure (6:19–24) and a triad on one's attitude toward others (7:1–6), as well as two units of encouragement, "do not worry" (6:25–34) and "ask" (7:7–11). According to Allisons's analysis, these three pillars are bracketed by an introduction (4:23–5:12) and statement of the task of God's people (5:13–16) and a concluding statement (7:12), eschatological warning (7:13–27), and conclusion (7:28–8:1).

---

[98] On this point our outline differs from most analyses of the Sermon.

[99] Davies, *Matthew* 61–62, admits that "Matthew's architectonic grandeur does not appear to derive from a clear blueprint," but he does find convincing Allison's observation of a tripartite structure and he accepts Allison's outline.

[100] Allison, "Structure of the Sermon on the Mount" 443.

[101] This argument assumes a unit division at 5:31 beginning with ἐρρέθη δέ which our outline finds subordinate to the unit beginning 5:27.

The Davies-Allison three pillars model fits three of the occurrences of an important key word, δικαιοσύνη, which occurs in 5:20 at the introduction to the first pillar, in 6:1 at the introduction of the second, and at 6:33 in the conclusion to the third. But they ignore several crucial observations at the level of the signifier. For example, Allison argues for the formal unity of 6:19–7:12.[102] On semantic grounds, he aligns 7:1–12 with 6:19–34 as its "structural twin."[103] Further, he contends that the section ends at 7:12 because its reference to the law and the prophets forms an inclusio with a similar reference in 5:17. He contends these verses bracket the main body of the sermon, the exposition of the three pillars.

Allison's analysis of the triadic arrangement of 6:19–7:12 remains unconvincing. His proposal for the unity of 6:19–7:12 ignores the significance of the changed initial aural formula in 7:7 and 7:21. Although 7:1 and 7:6 articulate prohibitions as in 6:29–34, the imperatives change to positive form in 7:7. Nor do these two units share significant phonetic/syntactical qualities. Moreover, whereas our evidence emphasizes the density of the Sermon's aural clues to delineate a unit or section, Allison's outline assigns to a single inclusio the improbable burden of bracketing an extraordinarily long block of material (5:17–7:12), the main body of the sermon. He must append an auxillary category, "encouragement," to his triadic organization to acccount for all material in the third pillar section. In fact, our outline with its section 6 division at 7:6 follows a clearer triadic scheme than Allison's in that it presents first a triple prohibition (μὴ θησαυρίζετε

---

[102] Ibid. 434. Allison claims the formal unity of 6:19–7:12 "has seemed evident to most" and is "no less obvious than that of 5:17–48 or 6:1–18." But the the Sermon's organization must be heard, not "evident," "obvious," or seen. The Sermon's aural clues indicate the sectional unity of 6:19–7:6 (section 6), 7:7–20 (section 7), and 7:21–27 (section 8), not 6:19–7:12.

[103] Ibid. 435–37, 440; Davies, *Matthew* 64. Davies admits that the "encouragement" sections of the Sermon are the only two places where Matthew breaks his triadic pattern (625–7). Davies and Allison find the key to the structure of 6:19–34 (μὴ θησαυρίζετε, unit 6.1 in our outline) in what they take to be parallels with chapter 7:

Introduction:
exhortation	6:19–21	7:1–2
parable on the eye	6:22–23	7:3–5
second parable	6:24	7:6

Encouragement:
the Father's care	6:25–34	7:7–11
The golden rule	7:12	

6:19, μὴ κρίνετε 7:1, and μὴ δῶτε 7:6) and then a triple positive command in section 7 (αἰτεῖτε 7:7, εἰσέλθατε 7:13, and προσέχετε 7:15) with a triple introduction at the beginning of section 7, αἰτεῖτε, ζητεῖτε, and κρούετε. Allison even recognizes the sound repetition in the material designated sections 6 and 7 in our outline and recognizes their theological importance as units, but does not allow these observations to influence his delineation of the sermon's sections.

Moreover, Allison's scheme does not take adequate account of the material that lies outside the three pillars inclusio. Allison's outline does not explain why the Sermon's conclusion (7:13–8:1) should be so elaborated, nor how 7:12 functions at the level of the signifier as a conclusion. Neither does Allison's outline adequately account for the importance of the sermon's opening material. His scheme draws attention to 5:13–16 as a prelude to the three pillars and relegates the beatitudes to the function of introduction, along with the framing material in 4:23–5:2. According to this arrangement, the beatitudes all but disappear. The strong aural pattern of the beatitudes and their thematic importance argues convincingly against this result.

Bornkamm's outline of the Sermon posits a thematic progression from the introduction to the law (5:15–20), antitheses (5:21–48), the practice of piety (6:1–18), new instruction on prayer (6:19–7:6), and the conclusion (7:7–12). Luz's outline uses the same sectional divisions and, like Bornkamm, finds a concentric ring arrangement with the Lord's prayer in the center. His scheme recognizes sound repetitions as structural clues at the beginning and end of the sermon. Luz notices the repetition in 7:28–8:1a of ὄχλοι, διδάσκω, and ἀνα(κατα)βαίνω...ὄρος from 5:1–2, the recurrence of the phrase βασιλεία τῶν οὐρανῶν in the beatitudes as an inclusio and in 7:21, and the inclusio with νόμος καὶ προφῆται which, for Allison, marks off the three pillars of the law (5:17–7:12). He also observes the patterned use of the second and third grammatical person in 5:13–16 and 7:13–27. For his organization of the main body of the sermon, however, Luz changes his theoretical base and relies on conceptual abstractions and observations of comparative length.

The main difficulties of Luz's and Bornkamm's schemes are their chiastic arrangement, the ascription of central status to the Lord's prayer, and their designation of 7:12 as the end of the Sermon's main body. Our outline challenges the centrality for the whole Sermon of the Lord's prayer.[104] We find no evidence at the level of the signifier that the prayer organizes the surrounding material.[105] Far more significant for the sermon's organization is the reprise, unit 5.0, that organizes by momentarily suspending the sermon's repetitive patterns.[106] Finally, Luz's outline like the other three used for comparison here offers no convincing reason to place a sectional break at 7:12.[107] The verse is subsumed in 7.1. where it functions as a proverbial conclusion to the unit. Although a unit break occurs after 7:12 the subsequent rehearsal (7:13) of section 7's initial aural formula indicates the sectional unity of 7:7–20. The new initial aural formula introduced in 7:21 and repeated in 7:24 clearly indicates a sectional break, although the unity of this section is seldom recognized.[108]

Our outline follows the Sermon's initial aural formulae which signal its basic organizational patterns. The Sermon is sequentially organized, with no overarching organizing principle at the level of the signifier. This is due to the the Sermon's paratactic quality that imitates οἱ λόγοι, even though Matthew avoids the common paratactic device of connectives (καί, δέ) at the beginnning of units and sections.

---

[104] See the discussion of 5.3 in the Micro Analysis.

[105] Luz, *Matthew 1–7*, admits that "the architectonic symmetry" which he discerns in the Sermon around the Lord's prayer is "apparent only when the Sermon on the Mount is read in context, and even then it does not reveal itself in the first reading but only to repeated perusal and, in a manner of speaking, in an 'optical' view." Luz concludes that "the Gospel of Matthew was intended in the first place for reading and not for hearing." We strongly disagree and contend that Luz's symmetrical scheme is difficult to see because it does not exist at the level of the signifier and would not have been evident to an ancient auditor of the text, nor would the text have been known except by hearing. If the Gospel of Matthew was intended for silent rereading, it was the only such text in the ancient world!

[106] Daniel Patte, *The Gospel According to Matthew, A Structural Commentary on Matthew's Faith*, (Philadelphia: Fortress Press, 1987) 65, acknowledges the organizational function of this unit. He labels it "framing material" and places the unit at the center of his chiastic outline of the Sermon. While we do not endorse his chiastic scheme, Patte's analysis indicates the importance of 5.0.

[107] Kennedy, *New Testament Interpretation* 59–62, supports our alternative proposal. On the basis of his rhetorical analysis of the Sermon on the Mount, he finds the sectional break after 7:20 as in our outline and not after 7:12. Kennedy argues 7:12 is embedded in a third group of rhetorical headings in the sermon (6:19–7:20, our sections 6 and 7).

[108] Daniel Patte, *The Gospel According to Matthew* 65, recognizes as we do the sectional break at 7:21, although he also designates 7:12 as the end of a section. None of the outlines selected for comparison acknowledge the unity of section 8, despite its clear phonetic/syntactical clues.

Nevertheless, other devices link the sermon's sections and indicate its unity.

The Sermon's first section, μακάριοι, exhibits strong aural clues to its unity: short, highly formulaic units and three interlocking inclusios which establish closure for units 1.1–1.8. Unit 1.9 effects the transition to section 2 with the apostrophe, a shift in grammatical person, and its repetition of διώκω and ἐν τοῖς οὐρανοῖς. Having established strong organizational patterns in its first two units, section 3 fails to repeat an initial aural formula, μὴ νομίσατε. Since the hearer has been led to expect repeated, initial aural formulae, this significant structural deviation signals the thematic importance of section 3 and indicates its organizational function. Likewise, the threefold repetition in the section of the epithet βασιλεία τῶν οὐρανῶν evokes the inclusio in section 1 that brackets beatitudes 1.4–1.8. This link as well as the section's concluding emphasis on ἡ δικαιοσύνη, indicates its importance.

The beatitudes (1.4–1.8), identified for emphasis in section 1 and differentiated from units 1.1–1.3 by a separate inclusio and other features,[109] organize the material in sections 3 and 4. In section 3 those who hunger and thirst for righteousness (1.4) are those who fulfill the law. The merciful (1.5) are those who extend the prohibition against killing to outlaw anger (4.1). The clean of heart (1.6) are those who avoid adultery in the heart (4.2). The peacemakers called sons of God (1.7) are those who do not come ἐκ τοῦ πονηροῦ (4.3). Those persecuted for righteousness (1.8) are those slapped in the face and pressed into service (4.4). Those told to rejoice in their persecution (1.9) are told to pray for their persecutors (4.5). Thus the last five beatitudes thematically link the units in the first half of the sermon.[110]

While the initial aural formula does not repeat in section 3, yet the section's well integrated arrangement clearly defines it as a unit and reinforces the links that unify sections 1–4. The triple reference to the

---

[109] See the discussion of these units in the Micro Analysis for evidence.

[110] One could argue that the beatitudes organize the Sermon's entire first half. Unit 1.1 labels and represents 1.1–1.9 which introduces the Sermon's initial aural formula and articulates the epithet inclusio. The mourners of 1.2 are those trodden on in public in 2.2. Those promised to inherit the earth in 1.3 are declared the light of the world in 2.2 and charged with the task of causing others to give glory to the Father in heaven, suggesting a correspondence between heaven and earth which recurs in the Sermon and is petitioned in the Lord's prayer (5.3.5).

heavenly kingdom in section 3, its reference to heaven and earth after the λέγω formula, and its concluding reference to righteousness evoke the three inclusios that unite the beatitudes, (1.4–1.8). Two of its organizational features anticipate those elaborated in section 4, the recurring λέγω formula and the parallel case law examples. Its opening doublet, frequent epithets, abstract terms, and repeated λέγω formula signal its semantic importance. Thus the hearer's attention is drawn to material that deviates from an expected pattern.

The first unit that falls outside the beatitudes' organizational scheme is the unusually unpatterned reprise, 5.0. While introducing a new organizational pattern for the rest of the section,[111] it exhibits strong aural ties with preceding and subsequent units. The reference to τοῖς οὐρανοῖς recalls the inclusio ἡ βασιλεία τῶν οὐρανῶν that brackets the first eight units of the μακάριοι section. The phrase ἔμπροσθεν τῶν ἀνθρώπων echoes its previous occurrence in ὑμεῖς ἐστε (section 2), the prohibition μὴ ποιεῖν recalls the prohibition of section 3, and μισθόν anticipates the λέγω formula in section 5 which echoes section 4's λέγω formula. The closing epithet, τῷ πατρὶ ὑμῶν τῷ ἐν τοῖς οὐρανοῖς, sets the theme for section 5 where references to the Father close each unit and 5.3 elaborates the prayer that begins with the same epithet. Thus the reprise encapsulates the foregoing material while establishing a new organizational pattern for section 5.

The Sermon's remaining sections present more complex organizational patterns with subtler aural clues. This is to be expected in a text written to be heard, because by the midpoint of a speech the speaker and hearer have rehearsed familiar conventions. Krister Stendahl speaks for many when he claims "VI. 19 - VII. 29 offers material which has been brought into the Sermon on the Mount by Matthew in such a manner that we find no clue as to his arrangement."[112] Yet the signifier continues to instruct the hearer with phonetic/syntactical devices that disclose each sections's limits and internal organization. The reprise at 5.0 signals an upcoming shift in organization and links the Sermon's two halves. After the extensive elaboration of the πάτερ epithet and theme in section 5, sections 6–8 suggest a dialectical movement: section 6 presents three prohibitions,

---

[111] Section 5 might properly be considered a single unit. See the discussion of 5.0 in the Micro Analysis.

[112] "Matthew," in *Peake's Commentary on the Bible* (ed. M. Black and H. H. Rowley; Middlesex: Nelson, 1962) 779.

section 7 three positive commands, and section 8 a synthesis encompassing "all."

The initial formulae of sections 6 and 7 correlate: each of the three units in section 6 opens with a negative imperative, while the three units of section 7 begin with a positive command. In the first unit of section 6, the first three subunits rehearse a similar parallel pattern, while the fourth (6.1.4) exhibits its own organizational pattern: it repeats its initial aural formula five times, thus creating five subunits of unequal duration and twice placing the initial aural formulae in the second position.

Section 7 exemplifies the technique of initial reinforcement, with three imperatives at the beginning of its first unit which signal the formulaic character of the section's subsequent imperatives and forecasts the threefold division of the section into units. Section 8 connects with section 7 through its emphasis on saying "Lord, Lord," (8.1) which evokes the knocking at the door in 7.1. The condemnation in 8.1, "I never knew you," recalls the theme of knowing false prophets by their fruits in 7.3. The Sermon's concluding unit (8.2) refers to and enforces the entire sermon with its repetition of τοὺς λόγους τούτους.

V. *If It Ain't Got That Swing*

Since in a rhetorical world, reading is *recitatio* and writing is for the purpose of *recitatio*, then sound is the first clue in a text's reception and organization. This paper represents an experiment in the effort to understand sound as the primary receptive clue. As we become more familiar with the problems of sound, much more can be done, including the importance of prose rhythm, an issue we almost totally avoided. Two areas need to be pursued, the theoretics of sound reception, and the Hellenistic rhetoricians' exposition of sound, for which there is some evidence.

The contributions of this paper are twofold. First, it offers a close analysis of the Greek text as signifier. Second, we have shown the possibility of a more empirical approach to issues of textual organization and division. We have begun to discover those phonographical clues that parallel modern typographical clues.[113] Our

---

[113] Others have begun to seek and find aural structural features in the literature of the Hebrew Bible. See the analysis of Hebrew prose in H. Parunak, "Oral Typesetting: Some Uses of Biblical Structure," *Biblica* 62 (1981): 153–68. For an

analysis, based on the level of signifier, without any investment in the Sermon's semantics or a theological ideology, has definitively undercut the most significant recent proposals for the Sermon's outline by disproving important linchpins in their construction. We need only point to those dependent on a chiastic structure, like Bornkamm's, or Luz's built on the Lord's prayer, or those that make a major section break at 7:12.

If the analysis of sound is the first step, what should be the second? We would suggest that a comprehensive methodology would involve theoretically four steps: sound analysis, rhetorical analysis, literary analysis, and ideological analysis. Very briefly, we would like to indicate how our analysis supports these others.

The only sustained rhetorical analysis of the Sermon is George Kennedy's.[114] His outline, based solely on rhetorical figures and not sound, corresponds very closely to ours.

Proem	5:3–16	Sections 1–2
Thesis	5:17–20	Section 3
Kephalaia	5:21–7:20	Sections 4–7
Principle of the Law	5:21–48	Section 4
Restatement of Thesis	6:1	Section 5.1
dikaiosynē	6:2–6:18	Section 5.2–7
Epilogue	7:21–27	Section 8
Recapitulation	7:21–23	Section 8:1
Stir the audience	24–27	Section 8:2

These two analyses confirm each other and could enrich the observations of each. Our analysis has shown how 5:17–20 and 6:1 are both eccentric and related, a result Kennedy's analysis confirms. These units stand out because they are the thesis of a literate argument. Both our analyses deny a major section break at 7:12, against an almost universal tendency of traditional scholarship. We both mark the beginning of the conclusion at 7:21. We both see 6:25–34 as a subunit of 6:19 and our two analyses intertwine in their explanations. The close fit of our analysis with Kennedy's confirms that the next step is a rhetorical analysis.

The third step would be a literary analysis, the consideration of the text as art. If one concludes with a rhetorical analysis, much of a text's

---

exploration of poetic patterns, see Thomas P. McCreesh, *Biblical Sound and Sense, Poetic Sound Patterns in Proverbs 10–29*, JSOT, Supplement Series 128 (Sheffield: JSOT Press, 1991).

[114] *New Testament Interpretation through Rhetorical Criticism* 37–63.

power is lost. Both the sound and rhetorical analyses have a strong social referent, while a literary method is more concerned with the creative possiblity of the text itself. The various studies of the Sermon's sections as "focal instance" in Robert Tannehill's *The Sword of his Mouth* illustrate a literary method. He builds at times on observations about the text's sound qualities. Repetition "can release words form their literal limits."[115] The extremeness of the commands in section 4 break the literal limits. "The tension which is an essential part of metaphor gives the metaphor its power to point beyond the literal sense of words. In a similar way, the tension which is part of these commands points the hearer beyond the literal sense to the many situations in which" we encounter other people.[116] Such an analysis moves beyond the rhetorical argument about the purpose of the text as persuasive to demonstrate how it creates new meaning.

A final step would involve an ideological (or mythological) analysis of the text. Our analysis surfaced a number of binaries that need investigation. A primary one is Father/Evil One. One might even conclude from our analysis that the epithet Heavenly Father is the Sermon's presiding metaphor. A second binary is Law/Kingdom. These two binaries correspond to Kennedy's argument that the *Kephalaia* deal with two topics, first the Law and then *dikaiosynē*. Law and Kingdom are binaries in Matthew and it sets up the interesting possibility that *dikaiosynē* and Father are binaries. Other binaries that receive prominence at the sound level are treasure/heart, heaven/earth, ψυχή/body. These binaries present interesting possibilites in ambiguity to develop a rich understanding of the Sermon and then its place in the gospel of Matthew.

For too long New Testament studies have ignored the most basic level of textual reception, the sound of language. It is time we began to pay it serious attention. As the old jazz song says, "it don't mean a thing, if it ain't got that swing."[117]

---

[115] *Semeia Supplements* (Philadelphia, Missoula: Fortress Press, Scholars Press, 1975) 81.

[116] Ibid. 72.

[117] Duke Ellington (1929).

Appendix 1
Sermon on the Mount Macro Outline

Introduction

Ἰδὼν δὲ τοὺς ὄχλους

1. Μακάριοι

1.1-.8 Μακάριοι οἱ…

1.9 μακάριοί ἐστε

2 Ὑμεῖς ἐστε

2.1 Ὑμεῖς ἐστε τὸ ἅλας τῆς γῆς·

2.2 Ὑμεῖς ἐστε τὸ φῶς τοῦ κόσμου.

3. Μὴ νομίσητε

3.0.1 Μὴ νομίσητε ὅτι ἦλθον καταλῦσαι

3.0.2 ἀμὴν γὰρ λέγω ὑμῖν· ἕως ἂν παρέλθῃ ὁ οὐρανὸς καὶ ἡ γῆ,

3.0.3 λέγω γὰρ ὑμῖν ὅτι ἐὰν μὴ περισσεύσῃ ὑμῶν ἡ δικαιοσύνη πλεῖον

4. Ἠκούσατε

4.1 Ἠκούσατε ὅτι ἐρρέθη τοῖς ἀρχαίοις, Οὐ φονεύσεις·

4.2.1 Ἠκούσατε ὅτι ἐρρέθη, Οὐ μοιχεύσεις.

4.2.2 Ἐρρέθη δέ, Ὃς ἂν ἀπολύσῃ τὴν γυναῖκα αὐτοῦ,

4.3 Πάλιν ἠκούσατε ὅτι ἐρρέθη τοῖς ἀρχαίοις, Οὐκ ἐπιορκήσεις,

4.4 Ἠκούσατε ὅτι ἐρρέθη, Ὀφθαλμὸν ἀντὶ ὀφθαλμοῦ

4.5 Ἠκούσατε ὅτι ἐρρέθη, Ἀγαπήσεις τὸν πλησίον σου

5.0 Προσέχετε τὴν δικαιοσύνην ὑμῶν

5.1 Ὅταν οὖν ποιῇς ἐλεημοσύνην,

5.2 Καὶ ὅταν προσεύχησθε,

5.3 Προσευχόμενοι δὲ μὴ βατταλογήσητε ὥσπερ οἱ ἐθνικοί,

5.4 Ὅταν δὲ νηστεύητε,

6.1.1 Μὴ θησαυρίζετε

    6.1.2 Ὁ λύχνος τοῦ σώματός

    6.1.3 Οὐδεὶς δύναται δυσὶ κυρίοις δουλεύειν·

    6.1.4 μὴ μεριμνᾶτε

        6.1.4.1 Διὰ τοῦτο λέγω ὑμῖν,

        6.1.4.2 τίς δὲ ἐξ ὑμῶν μεριμνῶν

        6.1.4.3 καὶ περὶ ἐνδύματος

        6.1.4.4 μὴ οὖν μεριμνήσητε λέγοντες

        6.1.4.5 μὴ οὖν μεριμνήσητε εἰς τὴν αὔριον,

6.2 Μὴ κρίνετε, ἵνα μὴ κριθῆτε·

6.3 Μὴ δῶτε τὸ ἅγιον τοῖς κυσίν

7. Αἰτεῖτε

7.1 Αἰτεῖτε καὶ δοθήσεται ὑμῖν,

7.2 Εἰσέλθατε διὰ τῆς στενῆς πύλης·

7.3 Προσέχετε ἀπὸ τῶν ψευδοπροφητῶν,

8. πᾶς ὁ

8.1 Οὐ πᾶς ὁ λέγων μοι, Κύριε κύριε,

8.2 Πᾶς οὖν ὅστις ἀκούει μου τοὺς λόγους τούτους

Conclusion

Καὶ ἐγένετο ὅτε ἐτέλεσεν ὁ Ἰησοῦς τοὺς λόγους τούτους

Appendix 2
Units 5.1, 5.2, 5.4

1 Ὅταν οὖν ποιῇς ἐλεημοσύνην,	Καὶ ὅταν προσεύχησθε,	Ὅταν δὲ νηστεύητε,
2 μὴ σαλπίσῃς ἔμπροσθέν σου,	οὐκ ἔσεσθε	μὴ γίνεσθε
3 ὥσπερ οἱ ὑποκριταὶ	ὡς οἱ ὑποκριταί,	ὡς οἱ ὑποκριταὶ σκυθρωποί,
ποιοῦσιν ἐν ταῖς συναγωγαῖς	ὅτι φιλοῦσιν ἐν ταῖς συναγωγαῖς	ἀφανίζουσιν γὰρ τὰ πρόσωπα αὐτῶν
καὶ ἐν ταῖς ῥύμαις,	καὶ ἐν ταῖς γωνίαις τῶν πλατειῶν	
	ἑστῶτες προσεύχεσθαι,	
4 ὅπως δοξασθῶσιν	ὅπως φανῶσιν	ὅπως φανῶσιν
ὑπὸ τῶν ἀνθρώπων·	τοῖς ἀνθρώποις	τοῖς ἀνθρώποις νηστεύοντες·
5 ἀμὴν λέγω ὑμῖν, ἀπέχουσιν τὸν	ἀμὴν λέγω ὑμῖν, ἀπέχουσιν	ἀμὴν λέγω ὑμῖν, ἀπέχουσιν
μισθὸν αὐτῶν.	τὸν μισθὸν αὐτῶν.	τὸν μισθὸν αὐτῶν.
6 σοῦ δὲ ποιοῦντος ἐλεημοσύνην	σὺ δὲ ὅταν προσεύχῃ	σὺ δὲ νηστεύων
μὴ γνώτω ἡ ἀριστερά σου,	εἴσελθε εἰς τὸ ταμεῖόν σου	ἄλειψαί σου τὴν κεφαλὴν
τί ποιεῖ ἡ δεξιά σου,	καὶ κλείσας τὴν θύραν σου	καὶ τὸ πρόσωπόν σου νίψαι,
		ὅπως μὴ φανῇς τοῖς ἀνθρώποις
		νηστεύων·
ὅπως ᾖ σου ἡ ἐλεημοσύνη	πρόσευξαι τῷ πατρί σου τῷ	ἀλλὰ τῷ πατρί σου
ἐν τῷ κρυπτῷ·	ἐν τῷ κρυπτῷ·	τῷ ἐν τῷ κρυφαίῳ·
7 καὶ ὁ πατήρ σου ὁ βλέπων	καὶ ὁ πατήρ σου ὁ βλέπων	καὶ ὁ πατήρ σου ὁ βλέπων
ἐν τῷ κρυπτῷ ἀποδώσει σοι.	ἐν τῷ κρυπτῷ ἀποδώσει σοι.	ἐν τῷ κρυφαίῳ ἀποδώσει σοι.

Appendix 3

Scott/Dean	Strecker	Davies/Allison	Bornkamm	Luz
5:1 introduction 1. Μακάριοι	5:1 SETTING	4:23-5:2 INTRODUCTION	4:23-5:2 narrative setting	5:1 FRAMEWORK: situation
	5:3 OPENING			5:3-16 INTRODUCTION: LEADING IN
5:3 Μακάριοι οἱ πτωχοί	5:3 beatitudes	5:3-12 beatitudes	5:3 introduction: beatitudes	5:3 beatitudes
5:11 μακάριοί ἐστε 2 Ὑμεῖς ἐστε		5:13-7:12 TASK OF GOD'S PEOPLE IN THE WORLD		
5:13 Ὑμεῖς ἐστε τὸ ἅλας τῆς γῆς 5:14 Ὑμεῖς ἐστε τὸ φῶς τοῦ κόσμου. 3. Μὴ νομίσητε	5:13 the nature of discipleship	5:13-16 summary, salt and light	5:13 mission (relational)	5:13 "You are the salt of the earth"
		5:17-7:12 THE THREE PILLARS 5:17-48 FIRST PILLAR: JESUS AND THE TORAH	INTRODUCTION	5:17-7:12 THE MAIN PART
5:17 Μὴ νομίσητε ὅτι ἦλθον καταλῦσαι 5:18 ἀμὴν γὰρ λέγω ὑμῖν 5:20 λέγω γὰρ ὑμῖν ὅτι	5:17 the new righteousness	5:17 introductory statement 5:17-20 general principles	5:17 the Law	5:17-20 INTROIT OF THE MAIN SECTION
4 Ἠκούσατε	5:21 THE ANTITHESES	5:21-48 TWO TRIADS OF SPECIFIC INSTRUCTION	PIETY IN THE KINGDOM: ANTITHESES	5:21-48 MAIN SECTION: antitheses

Greek text				
		5:21-32 FIRST TRIAD of instruction		5:21: higher righteousness 1; the antitheses
5:21 Ἠκούσατε ὅτι ἐρρέθη τοῖς ἀρχαίοις, Οὐ φονεύσεις	5:21 the first antithesis: on killing	5:21 murder	5:21 anger	5:21 on killing
5:27 Ἠκούσατε ὅτι ἐρρέθη, Οὐ μοιχεύσεις	5:27 the second antithesis: on adultery	5:27 adultery	5:27 adultery	5:27: on adultery
5:31 Ἐρρέθη δέ, Ὃς ἂν ἀπολύσῃ τὴν γυναῖκα αὐτοῦ,	5:31 the third antithesis: on divorce	5:31 divorce	5:31 divorce	5:31 on divorce
5:33 Πάλιν ἠκούσατε ὅτι ἐρρέθη τοῖς ἀρχαίοις, Οὐκ ἐπιορκήσεις	5:33 the fourth antithesis: on oaths	5:33-48 SECOND TRIAD of instruction 5:33 do not swear	5:33 oaths	5:33 : on swearing
5:38 Ἠκούσατε ὅτι ἐρρέθη, Ὀφθαλμὸν ἀντὶ ὀφθαλμοῦ	5:38 the fifth antithesis: on retaliation	5:38 turn the other cheek	5:38 retaliation	5:38 on nonviolence
5:43 Ἠκούσατε ὅτι ἐρρέθη, Ἀγαπήσεις τὸν πλησίον σου 5 Ὅταν...μή	5:43 the sixth antithesis: on love of enemy	5:43 love your enemy	5:43 love for enemies	5:43: on the love of enemies
	6:1 ON ALMSGIVING, PRAYER, FASTING	6:1-18 THE SECOND PILLAR: THE CHRISTIAN CULT	PRACTICE YOUR PIETY	6:1: HIGHER RIGHTEOUSNESS 2: THE ATTITUDE TOWARD GOD
6:1 (Interlude) Προσέχετε τὴν δικαιοσύνην ὑμῶν	6:1 on almsgiving	6:1 general principle	6:1 practice your piety	6:1-6 RIGHTEOUSNESS BEFORE GOD
6:2 Ὅταν οὖν ποιῇς ἐλεημοσύνην		6:2 A TRIAD OF SPECIFIC INSTRUCTION 6:2 Almsgiving	6:2 almsgiving	

Greek text				
6:5 Καὶ ὅταν προσεύχησθε	6:5 on praying	6:5 Prayer	6:5 praying	
6:7 Προσευχόμενοι δὲ μὴ βατταλογήσητε ὥσπερ οἱ ἐθνικοι	6:9 the Lord's prayer			6:7-15 THE LORD'S PRAYER WITH FRAME
6:16 Ὅταν δὲ νηστεύητε	6:16 on fasting	6:16 Fasting	6:16 fasting	6:16-18 RIGHTEOUSNESS BEFORE GOD
6 Μὴ θησαυρίζετε	6:19 INDIVIDUAL DIRECTIVES	6:19-7:12 THE THIRD PILLAR: SOCIAL ISSUES	6:19 PIETY IN THE KINGDOM: PRAYING	6:19-7:11 MAIN SECTION: possessions, judging, and prayer
		6:19 GOD AND MAMMON		
6:19 Μὴ θησαυρίζετε ὑμῖν θησαυροὺς	6:19 on wealth	6:19 triad on true treasure	6:19 treasure in heaven	6:19 do not collect earthly treasures
6:22 Ὁ λύχνος τοῦ σώματός			6:22 light of the body	
6:24 Οὐδεὶς δύναται δυσὶ κυρίοις δουλεύειν			6:24 God and mammon	
6:25 Διὰ τοῦτο λέγω ὑμῖν	6:25 on anxiety	6:25 encouragement: "do not worry"	6:25 anxiety	6:25 seek the kingdom of God
6:27 τίς δὲ ἐξ ὑμῶν μεριμνῶν δύναται 6:28 καὶ περὶ ἐνδύματος τί μεριμνᾶτε; 6:31 μὴ οὖν μεριμνήσητε λέγοντες Τί φάγωμεν; 6:34 μὴ οὖν μεριμνήσητε εἰς τὴν αὔριον				

Greek				
7:1 Μὴ κρίνετε, ἵνα μὴ κριθῆτε	7:1 on judging	7:1 ON ONE'S NEIGHBOR 7:1 a triad on attitude towards others	7:1 judging	7:1 do not judge
7:6 Μὴ δῶτε τὸ ἅγιον τοῖς κυσίν 7. Αἰτεῖτε			7:6 pearls	7:6 do not give what is holy to the dogs
7:7 Αἰτεῖτε καὶ δοθήσεται ὑμῖν	7:7 on the answering of prayer	7:7 encouragement: "ask"	7:7 conclusion: pray	7:7 courage to pray
	7:12 the golden rule	7:12 CONCLUDING STATEMENT: the golden rule	7:12 golden rule (relational)	7:12 CONCLUSION OF THE MAIN SECTION the golden rule 7:13-27 CONCLUSION: LEADING OUT
7:13 Εἰσέλθατε διὰ τῆς στενῆς πύλης	7:13 CLOSING ADMONITIONS AND PARABLES	7:13-27 THREE WARNINGS, THE PROSPECT OF ESCHATOLOGICAL JUDGMENT	7:13 sermon conclusion	7:13 the narrow and the wide door
7:15 Προσέχετε ἀπὸ τῶν ψευδοπροφητῶν 8: Οὐ πᾶς ὁ	7:13 the gate and the way 7:15 the false prophets	7:13 the two ways 7:15 beware of false prophets		7:15 warning against false prophets
7:21 Οὐ πᾶς ὁ λέγων μοι, Κύριε κύριε	7:21 the necessity of deeds			
7:24 Πᾶς οὖν ὅστις ἀκούει μου τοὺς λόγους τούτους	7:24 the closing parables: on the wise and foolish builders	7:24 the two builders		7:24: conclusion: the two housebuilders

Conclusion	EPILOGUE	CONCLUSION	FRAMEWORK
7:28-29 Καὶ ἐγένετο ὅτε ἐτέλεσεν ὁ Ἰησοῦς τοὺς λόγους τούτους	7:28-29 epilogue	7:28-8:1 conclusion	7:28-8:1a framework: reaction of the hearers
		7:28-29 narrative climax	

Chapter Twelve

Discharging Responsibility: Matthean Jesus, Biblical Law, and Hemorrhaging Woman

AMY-JILL LEVINE

Scholarship on the Gospel of Matthew is presently in flux: debates rage over the social setting of Matthew's community (Galilee, Antioch, the Decapolis), its relation to the synagogue (*intra* vs. *extra muros*), and its connection to "Judaism" (a deviant group, the new Israel, the true Israel, the "new people of God", a *corpus mixtum*, a predominantly Gentile association). Nevertheless, at least two constructs have attained the status of consensus. First, Matthew reserves a central role for the Scriptures—the Prophets, the Psalms, and, especially, Mosaic Law. Second, Matthew offers new life for all who follow Jesus. The invitation extends to fishermen like Peter and John and to a rich, politically connected figure like Joseph of Arimathea. It goes as well to all those considered by modern scholarship to be marginal to or disenfranchised from the "Jewish system": tax collectors, prostitutes, sinners, lepers, the diseased, the possessed, and, especially, women. Problems arise, however, when the two constructs are related, since the Gospel is explicit neither on how the Law is (to be) practiced nor on how the Matthean community views women. Consequently, not the evangelist but modern scholarship provides us the details of the Matthean practical Torah; not the evangelist but modern scholarship provides us the Matthean tractate on women.

The two issues—of the Law as practiced in Matthew's social world and of women's representation and role in Matthew's Gospel—come together inexorably in the scholarship on Matthew 9:18–26. The majority of commentators argue that this conjoined story of a bleeding woman and a dead girl depicts two individuals marginalized in Jewish society because of both gender and purity regulations. Each character is first identified as marginal because she is female; further, the woman is categorized as "unclean" because of what is assumed to be chronic uterine bleeding, and the girl is "unclean" because she is dead (i.e., a corpse). In turn Jesus is depicted as overcoming the barriers Jewish society and Law erect between men and women, clean and unclean. By healing both women, he affirms what his Jewish social context denies: their humanity and worth; by touching them, he ignores and thereby dismisses purity codes. And, once the barriers between clean and unclean are abrogated, the way is open for the establishment of an egalitarian community.

This particular conjunction of women and purity relies on two major premises: that women were marginalized in Matthew's Jewish environment because of its interpretation of biblical Law, and that Jesus overcomes or even transgresses such legal concerns. As Marcus Borg puts it, Jesus substitutes a system of purity with a system of compassion.[1]

I think both premises are wrong. Indeed, I think they are dangerously wrong, and for several reasons: they rely on an interpretation of Matthew's Gospel that is not supported by the text itself, and thus they are bad exegeses; they rely on a construction of both early Judaism and of the Matthean community that cannot be well supported from either internal or external evidence, and thus they are bad history. They proclaim a supersessionist rather than a reformist perspective, and thus they are bad theology. Finally, by concentrating on ritual practices and a monolithic view of gender categories based on an artificial good/bad dichotomy, the premises and the readings they generate are in bad faith. Their narrow foci causes interpreters to underemphasize or even to miss major points of the pericope: that all involved in the action are Jews, and that no one "violates" Jewish practice; that Jesus' "following" the dead girl's father has implications for Matthew's view of discipleship; and that the bodies of women serve as figurations for Jesus' own body as it hangs on the cross and rises from the tomb.

---

[1] Marcus Borg, *Jesus in Contemporary Scholarship* (Valley Forge, PA: Trinity International Press, 1994) 26 and elsewhere. Reconstructions of Jesus' own attitude toward the Law translate in the scholarship to Matthew's view. See the discussion of purity legislation in the works of Borg, N. T. Wright, and J. D. Crossan by Paula Fredriksen, "Did Jesus Oppose the Purity Laws?" *Bible Review* (June, 1995): 18–25, 42–47.

Bad Exegesis

Students of Christian origins are obsessed with Levitical purity legislation: it may well be that scholars worry more about such matters, particularly as they concern women, than did many Jewish women in the first century. In the same way that biblical commentators usually assert that Luke's "Woman who was a sinner" must have been a prostitute (as if women could commit no sin other than one involving the body in general and sexuality in particular), so too do they usually insist that if a woman has a medical problem, the problem must have something to do with "female troubles." And in all cases, Levitical concerns provide these diagnoses a cause.

Symptomatic of this approach is Elaine Wainwright's observation that Peter's mother-in-law, described as lying in bed and sick with a fever (Matt 8:2–3, 5–7) "is a possible pollutant especially if this sickness is connected to her time of ritual uncleanness."[2] Thus general sickness bleeds over into menstrual issues. Wainwright continues: by touching the woman Jesus breaks open the boundaries defining 'clean' and 'unclean.' Her analysis of Matt 9:20, where she describes Jesus as being "touched by a menstruating woman,"[3] makes similar claims. Donald Hagner observes that not only did the woman face "the inconvenience [!] and physical danger of such regular loss of blood but also suffered the stigma of ritual uncleanness in that culture and consequent ostracism."[4] Commenting on Matt 8:2–9:35, David Garland asserts that Jesus "discounts the demarcation of society along purity lines. He does not shun the impure and unholy. He touches a leper, a menstruant, and a corpse . . . the Kingdom of Heaven does not respect the boundaries of purity that the Pharisees and others use to categorize persons and places and to isolate them."[5] Janice Capel Anderson invokes Lev 15:25–33 in observing: "The woman with the hemorrhage is ritually unclean."[6] And, alas, in my own contribution to the *Women's*

---

[2] Elaine Wainwright, *Towards a Feminist Critical Reading of the Gospel According to Matthew* (BZNW 60; Berlin/New York: Walter de Gruyter, 1991) 84, repeated in her "The Gospel of Matthew," in E. S. Fiorenza, ed., *Searching the Scriptures Vol. II:A Feminist Commentary* (New York: Crossroad, 1994) 648.

[3] Wainwright, "Gospel of Matthew," 637.

[4] Donald Hagner, *Matthew 1–13* (WBCommentary 33a; Dallas: Word, 1993) 248.

[5] David Garland, *Reading Matthew: A Literary and Theological Commentary on the First Gospel* (New York: Crossroad, 1993) 107. Garland's association of "impure" with "unholy" is not uncommon.

[6] Janice Capel Anderson, "Matthew: Gender and Reading," *Semeia* 28 (1983):

Bible Commentary, I followed Anderson.[7] Wainwright goes farther. Narrowing the intertext of Matt 9:18–26 to Lev 15:25–27, she proclaims: "It is clear that this [hemorrhaging] debars the woman not only from participation in the religious community but from normal human social relations and especially from sexual relations with her husband. Her unavailability for sexual intercourse or fertility could well have produced a divorce and would certainly have prevented her from remarrying."[8]

Such New Testament scholarship almost invariably reinforces the claim that menstruants were ostracized within Jewish society by citing, in their discussion of Matt 9:18–26, select Jewish (usually rabbinic) materials. The detailed New International Critical Commentary on Matthew by Davies and Allison, for example, notes "other Jewish texts which involve restriction of and repugnance for menstruous women include Ezek 36.17; CD 4.12–5.17; 11QTemple 48.15–17; Josephus, *Bell.* 5.227; *C. Ap.* 2.103–4; *m. Nidda*, passim, and *m. Zabim* 4.1."[9] Wainwright evokes the Mishnaic tractate *Nidda* as operative at the time of Matthew and likely within Matthew's Jewish community.[10] Garland adds that the term "*Nidda*" means "banished."[11] And Davies and Allison even include such charming rabbinic suggestions for curing female discharges as fetching barley grain from the dung of a white mule and holding it for three days, or smearing oneself with sixty pieces of sealing clay.[12] Wainwright concludes that the "*inhuman*

11.

[7] Amy-Jill Levine, "The Gospel of Matthew," in C. A. Newsom and S. H. Ringe, eds., *The Women's Bible Commentary* (London: SPCK; Louisville, KY: Westminster-John Knox, 1992) 256–57.

[8] Wainwright, *Feminist Critical Reading,* 199 n. 52.

[9] W. D. Davies and Dale C. Allison, Jr. *A Critical and Exegetical Commentary on the Gospel According to Matthew,* Vol. 2: VIII-XVIII (ICC; Edinburgh: T & T Clark, 1991), 128.

[10] Wainwright, *Feminist Critical Reading,* 199 n. 53.

[11] Garland, *Reading Matthew,* 106. Garland is technically correct, but etymological origin and actual use are not necessarily equivalent. Thus Jacob Milgrom, *Leviticus I-XVI* (AB 3; New York: Doubleday, 1991) 744–45, claims that the scriptural use of *Nidda* is capable of three meanings: "menstrual impurity"; "impurity in general" or "abomination"; and "lustration." Following etymological observations, he concludes that "in the case of the menstruant, the word originally referred to the *discharge* or *elimination* of menstrual blood, which came to denote menstrual impurity and impurity in general." Only later does it come to connect the menstruating woman with certain restrictions.

[12] Davies and Allison, *Critical and Exegetical Commentary,* 128, citing *b. Shabb.*

restrictions and suffering placed upon her by the Law [are] over and above the suffering due to her illness itself."[13] Thus the Law and those who practice it are not human; they are bestial or demonic. No wonder these poor women needed liberation: Leviticus is worse than death, and those who enforce it must be children of the devil.

Opposed to all this are Jesus and the Matthean church. For Davies and Allison, Matt 9:18–26 "seems to offer a contrast. The woman with an issue is presented in a wholly positive light. The subject of her uncleanness is not mentioned or alluded to. Her touch does not effect indignation. Onlookers do not whisper that Jesus has come into contact with an unclean woman. All of this is surprising."[14]

What is surprising is that such interpretations accompanied by such details attach to a pericope in which, as Davies and Allison observe, uncleanness is never mentioned. The commentators transform an absence of reference into a telling silence, and it is upon this silence that their arguments are based. Ironically, had they wished to draw a negative contrast between the church's view of women and that of its Jewish roots, they had the right story but the wrong part. The *Acts of Pilate* 7 records the following interchange at Jesus' trial: "And a woman called Bernice crying out from a distance said, 'I had an issue of blood and I touched the hem of his garment, and the issue

---

110a-b.

[13] Wainwright, *Feminist Critical Reading*, 200; emphasis mine. Analyses of the parallel pericopes of Mark and Luke are similar. Most recent, and expressed with his typically arresting phrasing, is J. D. Crossan's comment on Mark 5:22–43, "Think about the theological implications of that intercalation, of a purity code in which menstruation is impure so that, from Mark's viewpoint, women start to die at twelve and are walking dead thereafter," in *Who Killed Jesus? Exposing the Roots of Anti-Semitism in the Gospel Story of the Death of Jesus* (San Francisco: Harper SanFrancisco, 1995) 101. See also Marla J. Selvidge, *Woman, Cult and Miracle Recital: A Redactional Critical Investigation of Mark 5:24–34* (Lewisburg: Bucknell University Press, 1990) 83, which claims that the woman with the hemorrhage "stands as a symbol for all Hebrew women [whose] biological differences prevented her . . . experiencing initiation rites, from serving in the sanctuary, and even from participating in the feasts," and Idem, "Mark 5:24–34 and Leviticus 15:19–20: A Reaction to Restrictive Purity Regulations," *JBL* 103 (1984): 619–23. Mary Rose D'Angelo, "Gender and Power in the Gospel of Mark: The Daughter of Jairus and the Hemorrhaging Woman," a version of which was delivered in the Woman in the Biblical World section of the annual meetings of the AAR/SBL (November, 1994), corrects Selvidge's "inappropriate generalization, extravagant rhetoric and naive or specious use of language" (p. 3). I thank Professor D'Angelo for permission to cite from her manuscript.

[14] Davies and Allison, *Critical and Exegetical Commentary*, 128.

of blood, which had lasted twelve years, ceased.' The Jews said, 'We have a law not to permit a woman to give testimony.'"[15]

Surprising also are the pronouncements about the bleeding that the secondary sources make. For example, Jesus is not touched by a menstruant *per se*, so already the scholarship has muddied analytical categories.[16] Nor is it clear that the woman's bleeding is vaginal, since Matthew says nothing about the location of the hemorrhage.[17] Matthew's expression, a participle derived from the compound verb *haimorroeō*, is otherwise unattested in the gospels. It is not the same term used in Mark's parallel pericope; there the expression is *housa en rusei haimatos*, Mark 5:25, cf. LXX to Lev 15:19, 25; 20:18). Nor is it clear that Mark had Levitical legislation in mind. The Matthean term does appear in the LXX to Lev 15:33, where it apparently translates *davah* which means "sickness" or "infirmity" in the expression *ha-davah b'niddatah*: "the infirmity of her menstrual impurity." There are other types of infirmity, which is why Leviticus modifies the expression with *b'niddatah* "of her menstrual flow." Thus neither the Hebrew nor the Greek provides firm or even necessary indication that the flow is uterine or vaginal. If the woman had a sore on her leg, her breast, her nose, etc.—and all these places are possible given the semantic range of "hemorrhage"—then while she would still be ill, she would not be impure.

What then comes first in Matthean scholarship: does one begin with the potentially anti-Jewish supposition that Jesus overcomes exceptionally restrictive Levitical purity legislation and therefore conclude that the bleeding is vaginal? Or does one begin with the potentially sexist presupposition that women's bodies are necessarily

---

[15] Citation from Ron Cameron, *The Other Gospels. Non-Canonical Gospel Texts* (Philadelphia: Westminster, 1982) 171.

[16] The connection of any sort of discharge to menstruation is not uncommon; it already appears in the Talmud, cf. *b. Nidda* 66a, and the comments in S. J. D. Cohen, "Menstruants and the Sacred in Judaism and Christianity," in Sarah B. Pomeroy, ed., *Women's History and Ancient History* (Chapel Hill and London: University of North Carolina Press, 1991) 277–78. This innovative homologizing dates to the third century CE.

[17] Davies and Allison, *Critical and Exegetical Commentary*, 128 are quite sanguine: "A uterine hemorrhage is undoubtedly meant." Ben Witherington, III, *Women in the Ministry of Jesus: A Study of Jesus' Attitudes to Women and Their Roles as Reflected in His Earthly Life*, (SNTSMS 51; Cambridge: Cambridge University Press, 1984) 175 n. 104, has "probably a uterine hemorrhage, making the woman religiously unclean for the whole period"; cf. Hagner, *Matthew 1–13*, 248, on the hemorrhage as "probably (though not necessarily) from the womb."

represented as sexual bodies and so that the bleeding must be vaginal—granting that there is Markan support for this—and therefore conclude that Jesus must be abrogating Levitical Law?

To this connection between impurity and sexuality, perhaps the intercalated story of the ruler's daughter can shed some light. The hemorrhaging woman may not have been bleeding vaginally, but it is certain that the ruler's daughter is dead. Matthew's *arti eteleutēsen* is much starker than Mark's "close to death." Wainwright represents the consensus on the intercalation: "Both are female, both can be considered dead (one socially and religiously, the other physically), and both therefore have the capacity to contaminate life and hence need to be carefully controlled."[18] The girl's father, who states, "My daughter has just died; but come and lay your hand on her, and she will live" (9:18), consequently asks that Jesus place himself in a state of impurity.

The text, of course, says nothing about corpse uncleanness. To invoke Leviticus here would be as much of an overreading as to invoke it in an analysis of Matthew 8:21–22 (cf. Mark 4:35; Luke 9:57–60). To the disciple who asked "Lord, first let me go and bury my father," Jesus responds, "Follow me, and let the dead bury their own dead" (Matt 8:21–22). This is not an attempt to preserve the man from corpse contamination. Nor is touching a corpse "wrong" or "unholy" (although there are certain restrictions placed upon priests) as the Book of Tobit in particular demonstrates; to bury a dead body is a commendable and important form of practical piety.

Some scholars even suggest that the father's request is anomalous in Jewish society not simply because it involves corpse uncleanness, but also because it is concerned with a mere daughter. Once again, Wainwright: "The request is even more extraordinary when one realizes that the child is not a son, an heir needed for the continuation of the patriarchal family line, but rather a daughter, a young unmarried girl as the latter part of the story indicates (v. 25, *korasion*)."[19]

---

[18] Wainwright, *Feminist Critical Reading*, 199, citing Num 19:11–13 on corpse uncleanness and Lev 15:31, which she claims in n. 53 "links uncleanness to death." The text actually states: "Thus you shall keep the people of Israel separate from their uncleanness, so that they do not die in their uncleanness by defiling my tabernacle that is in their midst."

[19] Ibid., 87.

The suggestion that the Jewish father would not care about his daughter is at best uncharitable. By analogy, one might similarly cite Matt 10:35–36 and conclude that Jesus is against parent-child relationships since his message establishes enmity between son and father, daughter and mother, "members of one's own household." But as with the above reference to Matt 8:21–22, such a citation in such a context would be inappropriate and inaccurate. Rather, Matthew directly suggests that the audience of the Gospel would expect parents to care for their children, of both genders. Otherwise, the comment in 10:37b, "Whoever loves son *or daughter* more than me is not worthy of me," would have no impact.

The various contextualizations of Matthew 9:18–26 in terms of purity and patriarchy are possible, but they are by no means necessary. They are supported by no internal textual clues; they are premised on overdrawn stereotypes of Judaism and women. They also fail to engage Matthew's own apparent preservation of the Law from which "not one jot or tittle" will pass away (5:18). Matthew does not abrogate the laws of physical purity any more than the dietary regulations. The woman is healed of her sickness; the girl is raised from the dead. The point is that those who were sick and dead are now alive and healthy, not that Jewish practices have been transgressed or overcome.

Actually, the best intertexts for the raising of the dead girl are other cases where corpses are resuscitated. For example, the raising of the girl evokes the actions of Elijah (1 Kgs 17:17–24) and Elisha (2 Kgs 4:32–37), and so continues Matthew's interest in appropriating scriptural models. Thus the pericope locates Jesus within Jewish tradition without undermining the Law in any way or, indeed, even here evoking it. More, the raising fulfills the response to John's disciples, "the dead are raised" (11:5), and thus it points to Jesus' messianic identity.

Bad History

Even if the hemorrhage were uterine, the readings of social ostracism occasioned by Levitical legislation and cultural codes are themselves overstated. Lev 15:19–33 states:

> When a woman has a discharge, her discharge being blood from her body, she remains in her menstrual impurity seven days; every one who touches her shall be (ritually) unclean until the evening . . . . If a man lies with her, her menstrual impurity will be on him, and he shall be (ritually) unclean seven days, and any bed on which he lies shall be

(ritually) unclean. If a woman has a discharge of blood for many days, not at the time of her menstrual impurity, or if she has a discharge beyond the time of her menstrual impurity, all the days of the discharge she shall be (ritually) unclean; as in the days of her menstrual impurity, she shall be (ritually) unclean. Any bed on which she lies during all the days of her discharge shall be for her as the bed of her menstrual impurity, and anything on which she sits shall be (ritually) unclean, as in the (ritual) uncleanness of her menstrual impurity. And anyone who touches them shall be (ritually) unclean and shall wash his clothes, and bathe in water, and be (ritually) unclean until the evening. . . .

There is nothing here to prevent this woman from participating in "normal human social relations." She is not inhumanly restricted or socially ostracized. There is no prohibition against her touching anyone. Indeed, the concern in the Law for her bedding and anything on which she sits "can only mean that in fact her hands do not transmit impurity . . . . The consequence is that she is not banished but remains at home. Neither is she isolated from her family."[20] Even the Talmud states that a menstruating woman may attend to all of her family's needs, with the exceptions of filling her husband's cup of wine, making his bed, and washing him (b. Ketub. 61a).[21] Neither is it clear that she is unavailable for sexual intercourse, as the phrase "If any man lies with her" indicates, although Lev 18:19 and 20:18 do suggest that there is divine punishment for both partners if they have intercourse while the woman is in a state of impurity. Here one might cite, albeit tentatively, b. Baba Metsia 83b-85a, especially on Rabbi Eliazar's giving permission for marital intercourse to sixty women who have had a flux that may or may not be menstrual.[22]

Uncleanness is not a disease, and it implies no moral censure; it is a ritual state which both men and women likely found themselves most of the time.[23] There are no laws obliging those who come into contact

---

[20] Milgrom, Leviticus I-XVI, 936. The principal text on which such a conclusion concerning complete isolation could be connected is Num 5:1–14, in which the leper, the zabah or zab (one experiencing a discharge from, respectively, vagina or penis), and anyone who has come in contact with a corpse are to be removed from the camp. Nevertheless, as Cohen observes, "If this law were enforced, the number of Israelites outside the camp would rival the number of those within." See his "Menstruants and the Sacred," 276.

[21] For discussion, cf. Milgrom, Leviticus I-XVI, 949.

[22] See discussion, and well-taken warnings concerning rabbinic control over female sexuality, in Daniel Boyarin, Carnal Israel: Reading Sex in Talmudic Culture (Berkeley: University of California Press, 1993) 204–5.

[23] Paula Fredriksen, From Jesus to Christ (New Haven: Yale University Press, 1988)

with a *Nidda,* or a corpse, etc., to appear before a court. Indeed, like the man who has a genital discharge, the woman is responsible for her own activities. As Jacob Milgrom observes, "The absence of the priest from the diagnosis and his confinement to the sanctuary to officiate at the sacrifices (vv 13–15, 28–30) confirm the fact that the diagnosis of genital discharges is left entirely to the skill and honesty of the affected person."[24]

The consequence of such cultic uncleanness primarily involves restriction from the Temple precincts. But there was little if any reason for most people to go to the Temple. Moreover, Matthew—like Mark—locates the woman not in Jerusalem but in the Galilee. The immediate geographical reference is 9:1: "He crossed the sea and came to his own town." Any concern for the purity required by the Temple's holiness is therefore mitigated.[25] Finally, Matthew is apparently writing after the Temple's destruction.

More difficult to evaluate is the practice of such ritual concerns among the Jews in Matthew's own community. The Pharisees may well have been engaged in directing the practices of Temple purity to the home, such that the household table mirrors the Temple altar, and those at the Table eat with the same status as the priests serving in Jerusalem. Thus the Pharisees would be particularly concerned that their food be properly tithed, and that they not be in states of ritual impurity. Particularly in the land of Israel, after the destruction of the Temple, there may well have been increasing attention paid to matters of cultic impurity as they related to daily life. Yet even for Matthew, the Pharisees do not concern themselves with the woman's so-called impurity (as Davies and Allison note). Nor would Pharisaic men always be in ritually pure states. Leviticus 15:18 states that "If a man lies with a

---

106 n. 14. See also E. P. Sanders, *Jesus and Judaism* (Philadelphia: Fortress, 1985) 182–83.

[24] Milgrom, *Leviticus I-XVI,* 905–6. Then again, self-policing can also be a form of social oppression, here fully internalized. This observation applies also to the *bet hatum'ot* discussed below, n. 27.

[25] See also D'Angelo, "Gender and Power," 11. S. J. D. Cohen observes that from the mid-second century BCE until the destruction of the Second Temple, various Jewish groups extended the scarcity of the Temple to their daily lives. However, he also avers that this practice "had only a minimal impact on the Jews at large, who continued to regard the Temple as the single locus of sanctity and the sole place that demanded ritual purity of its entrants." See his "Purity and Piety: the Separation of Menstruants from the Sancta," in S. Groomsman and R. Haute, eds., *Daughters of the King/Woman and the Synagogue. A Survey of History and Contemporary Realities* (Philadelphia: Jewish Publication Society, 1992) 106.

woman and he has an emission of semen, both of them shall bathe in water, and be unclean until the evening" (Lev 15:18). Yet "Be fruitful and multiply"—a command also in the Pharisaic purview—requires precisely that a man lie with a woman and have an emission of semen. Pharisaic men, like all men, were subject to their genital discharges, and these would have put them in a state of impurity.

Although the majority of the biblical laws concerning the exclusion of women because of menstruation and vaginal discharges are directly related to the Temple and the system of purity which surrounds it, one—Leviticus 18:19 and 20:18, the prohibition against "drawing near" to a menstruant for sexual intercourse—does not. Therefore, "Even when the purity system would lapse after the destruction of the second temple in 70 CE., the prohibition of union with a menstruant would remain."[26] Consequently, these laws might be seen as relevant to the interpretation of Matthew's hemorrhaging woman, if she is seen as having a vaginal discharge in the first place.

Yet even here we cannot conclude that the social implications of the laws concerning such a woman were enforced. There is no unambiguous evidence from the Mishna, Josephus, the Gospels, etc. that Jewish groups in Hellenistic and Early Roman times removed the menstruant or one suffering from abnormal vaginal or uterine bleeding from social contact.[27] Such a person was not even barred from religious activities, according to the early Rabbinic view. While the Mishnah prohibits an ejaculant from reciting aloud various benedictions, no parallel restrictions accrue to the lepers, those who

---

[26] See Cohen, "Menstruants and the Sacred," 276.

[27] Ibid., 278. Cohen observes, 278–79, that "Possible evidence for the social isolation of the menstruant in the real world comes from a stray phrase in the Mishna [*bet hatum'ot* or *bet hateme'ot* in *Nidda* 7:4] and from the later practices of the Samaritans and the black Jews of Ethiopia, but this evidence is ambiguous and uncertain." Citing the same Mishnaic passage, Milgrom, *Leviticus I-XVI*, 949, is unhesitant in asserting that the menstruant in the land of Israel was "quarantined in a special house." Cohen appears to be correct: it is unclear whether the Mishnah concerns actual quarantine or simply a place menstruating women frequent. Even if the women are not quarantined, they might choose to use such a place so as not to render their usual furniture unclean by sitting on it. The Babylonian Gemara says nothing about the passage. Yerushalmi covers only the first four chapters of *m. Nidda*. See also Milgrom's discussion Josephus, *Ant.* 3.261 and several Qumran scrolls on the possible isolation within the community (rather than banishment) of menstruants. Milgrom nevertheless concludes that the "lenient" rulings in the Babylonian Talmud are those consistent with Levitical legislation.

have touched a corpse, a menstruant, or even men and women with abnormal discharges. The Tosefta, *Ber.* 2:12, reads: "Men who have an abnormal sexual discharge (*zabim*), women who have an abnormal sexual discharge (*zabot*), menstruants, and parturients are permitted to read the Torah, and to study Mishnah, Midrash, laws, and homilies. But the ejaculant is prohibited from all these."[28] Boyarin remarks on *b. Ber.* 22a, which reads, "Gonnorheics and lepers and *those who have had intercourse with menstruants* are permitted to study Torah, but men who have had a seminal emission may not."[29] And thus, as Shaye Cohen concludes, the "Gospel story about the woman with a twelve-year discharge, clearly a case of *zabah*, does not give any indication that the woman was impure or suffered any degree of isolation as a result of her affliction (Matthew 9:18–26; Mark 5:21–43; Luke 8:40–56)."[30]

Finally, before we leave the Mishnah, we need to diagnose one other stain on the surface of the secondary sources. Davies and Allison also appeal to *m. Zabim* 5.1, 6 to indicate, correctly, that for the Tannaim the impurity of a menstruant can be transmitted through touch.[31] Whether Matthew followed Mishnaic rather than biblical rulings is an inevitable question; the Gospel itself provides no help concerning this specific pronouncement. What Davies and Allison do not mention, however, is that almost the entire Mishnaic tractate is dedicated to male discharges. These, too, are not mentioned explicitly in the Gospel of Matthew, yet surprisingly enough scholars have not attempted to read these into Jesus' contacts with men in various states of despair. If Peter's mother-in-law was in her "state of monthly uncleanness," then it seems likely that there would have been *Zabim*— men in states of Levitical impurity because of discharges—among all those who were sick and afflicted with various diseases and pains (4:24)

---

[28] Cited in Cohen, "Purity and Piety," 107. Cohen adds that while the Jerusalem Talmud is follows the Tosefta, *b. Ber.* 22a has been adapted to conform to the later view that menstruants are not permitted to read Torah. The *Bavli* also omits *zabot* and parturients, and substitutes "men who have intercourse with menstruants," for "menstruants." See *Ibid.*, 114 n. 8, as well as Cohen's "Menstruants and the Sacred," 283–84, where he concludes (284) that "neither Talmud raises any obstacle before a menstruant who wishes to pray, study Torah, or recite benedictions."

[29] Boyarin, *Carnal Israel,* 180 and discussion, 180–1 (emphasis his).

[30] Cohen, "Purity and Piety," 279, although as noted above, I question whether the Matthean woman is even a *zabah*.

[31] Davies and Allison, *Critical and Exegetical Commentary,* 128.

whom Jesus healed. Oddly enough, this possibility has not been raised.[32]

To be sure, the rabbinic sources do contain much that is oppressive concerning female sexuality and women's bodies in general, as well as vaginal bleeding and menstruation in particular. Nevertheless, the majority of Gospel commentators neither present a balanced treatment of these sources nor engage in detail the problems of their dating and their relevance for Matthew or Jesus. A late Talmudic gloss is given as much historical weight as an earlier Mishnaic pronouncement, and both are retrojected back to the first century.[33] The rabbinic sources then are seen as reflecting the practices of Matthew's Jewish social world (regardless of the setting of the Gospel, its Greek concerns, its particular form of "Judaism," etc.).

Moreover, the citation of Jewish sources that post-date the time of Jesus should be balanced by some discussion of contemporaneous Christian and pagan viewpoints. The gap in citation leads to the conclusion that Jews were the primary if not the only people in antiquity concerned with female discharges. As D'Angelo observes, "It is frequently assumed among interpreters of the NT, both scholarly and popular, that Purity is a Jewish concern of no real interest to either the Greeks or Romans."[34] Missing in most scholarship on the Gospels and menstruation are citations from, for example, Isidore of Seville, who records in his *Etimologias* xi.1.141 that menstrual blood causes fruits not to germinate, wine to sour, plants to parch, trees to

---

[32] Cohen, "Menstruants and the Sacred," 276, observes that "the biblical record as a whole shows much greater concern over the potential desecration of the sacred by an ejaculant than by a menstruant."

[33] Dating is often flagged as a problem, and then the Mishnah is cited anyway. Nor do the secondary sources do much in terms of distinguishing general concerns from specific laws. Cf. Wainwright, *Feminist Critical Reading*, 199 n. 53 on *m. Ohol.*, concerning corpse uncleanness and *m. Ned.* on menstruants, "both of which belong to the Order of Purities of which Neusner claims that 'the principal and generative ideas of the system as a whole are to be located at its very beginning, some time before the turn of the first century" (*Method and Meaning* 121 n. 2 2).

[34] D'Angelo, "Gender and Power," 4, citing as an example L. William Countryman, *Dirt Greed and Sex: Sexual Ethics in the New Testament and Their Implications for Today* (Philadelphia: Fortress, 1988), who treats purity as, in her words, a "Jewish preoccupation." D'Angelo provides the details of ancient Greek and Roman purity regulations, which are quite similar to those of Leviticus in their concern for the holiness of sanctuaries and for appropriate sexual intercourse. Ironically, as note 35 indicates, the Fathers on occasion followed Classical sources on the question of vaginal bleeding.

lose their fruit, iron to be corroded, bronze to turn black, and dogs to become rabid if they eat anything that has come into contact with it.[35] Omitted are the restrictions placed upon menstruants by ecclesiastics such as Hippolytus and Dionysius of Alexandria.[36]

Bad Theology

There is no indication in Matthew's account of the hemorrhaging woman and the dead girl that Jesus transgresses any sort of purity legislation and therefore that he breaks with Jewish tradition. To the contrary, both the placement and the content of the pericope reinforce the Matthean Jesus' conformity to the Law. Matthew 9:18–26 appears in the narrative portion of the Gospel that extends from 8:1 to 9:38. This section of the Gospel begins with an insistence on the Law: Jesus heals a leper and commands him: "See that you say nothing to anyone, but go, show yourself to the priest, and offer the gift that Moses commanded, as a testimony to them" (Matt 8:4).

Interest in practicing the Law reappears in the details of the pericope under discussion. In the account of the woman with the hemorrhage, Jesus does not touch the woman. Rather, she comes up from behind and touches him. Specifically, she touches *tou kraspeda tou himatiou* (Matt 9:20; cf. Luke 8:44), his *tzitzit* or fringes, those fringes Jewish men wore in compliance with Num 15:38–41, and Deut 22:12. Matthew brings together the *tzitzit* and healing again in 14:34–36, "When they had crossed over, they came to the land of Gennesaret. After the people of that place recognized him, they sent word throughout the region and brought all who were sick to him, and begged him that they might touch even the fringe of his cloak; all who touched it were healed" (cf. Mark 6:56). These fringes might then be related to those of the Pharisees and Scribes (cf. Matt 23:5), where the term is used in connection with ostentatious practices.

What tale then do these tassels tell? For Wainwright, the *tzitzit* do not have a relation to "ritual requirement connected to Mitzvot as is found in the Torah but rather is used in a worship context (Zech 8:20–

---

[35] Isidore is apparently following Pliny's *Natural History* 7.15.64.

[36] Hippolytus's *Apostolic Tradition* bars a catechumen from baptism should she be menstruating; Dionysius says the menstruant "would not dare in such a condition either to approach the holy table or touch the body and blood of Christ. For even the woman who had the twelve-year discharge and was eager for a cure touched not him but only his fringe." Citations from Cohen, "Menstruants and the Sacred," 288. See also his discussion, 289, of the *Didascalia*.

22) and it is the Gentiles . . . who take hold of the robe of a Jew . . . ."[37]
The Hebrew in Zechariah is *kanaf* not *tzitzit*, although the LXX does
read *kraspedou*. She goes on, "Well may the original storyteller have
used this same phrase for the action of the woman whose illness
rendered her an outsider . . . ."[38] Yet there is no fulfillment citation to
Zechariah here, and there is no indication that the woman is a Gentile
or an "outsider" because of her illness. In addition, given that Matt
23:5 explicitly uses the term *kraspeda* in relation to ritual requirements,
and given that Matthew does insist that the Law will not pass away, we
can at the very least see both the legal and the prophetic
interpretations as woven into to Jesus' clothing.[39]

Matthew's intercalated story does not present Jesus as abrogating
the law or as coming into contact with individuals marginalized
because of gender or ritual impurity. This pericope rather emphasizes
Jesus' conformity to the Law and his concern for healing those who
seek his power.

Healthy Readings

To concentrate on Levitical impurity, a point not mentioned by
the text, detracts from what is mentioned. First, only here does Jesus
"follow" (*akolouthein*) another person;[40] in the rest of the Gospel,
individuals and crowds follow Jesus. Since the term has connotations

---

[37] Wainwright, *Feminist Critical Reading*, 201. J. T. Cummings, "The Tassel of His
Cloak: Mark, Luke, Matthew—and Zechariah," in E. A. Livingston, ed., *Studia
Biblica 1978: II. Papers on the Gospels* (JSNTSup 2; Sheffield: JSOT, 1980) 51–52, also
proposes a connection to Zech 8:23.

[38] Wainwright, *Feminist Critical Reading*, 201.

[39] Geza Vermes, *The Religion of Jesus the Jew* (Minneapolis: Fortress, 1993) 16 n. 6
recounts the following anecdote: "The children requesting the charismatic
miracle-worker Hanan, grandson of Honi the circle-drawer, to end a drought,
seized the fringe of his mantle (*shippule gemileh*) and cried, 'Abba, Abba, give us
rain!'" (*b.Taan.* 23b). A rabbinic anecdote preserved in the Tannaitic midrash *Sifre*
on Numbers . . . and in the Talmud (*b. Men.* 44a), recounts how a young Jew,
getting ready to go to bed with a beautiful high-class prostitute, was prevented
from sinning by the miraculous intervention of the tassels on his garment." In
neither case is Zechariah relevant, but each case individually matches the
Matthean story: the first anecdote suggests the connection between imploring and
the tassels; the second suggests that the culture attributed magical power to the
tassels.

[40] As pointed out by Matthew Collins, whose insights into this section of the
pericope contributed substantially to the following discussion.

of discipleship for Matthew,[41] the pericope opens to the concerns of appropriate action. Second, the conjoined stories speak of bleeding and death followed by healing and resurrection; these motifs offer proleptic indicators of Jesus' own fate.

That Jesus "follows" is clear, but the implications of the term are not. It may well lack any technical indication in Matt 9:19. Kingsbury correctly argues that *akoluthein* can simply "signify accompaniment in the literal sense of the word," and he points to Matt 9:19 as the best example of this nontechnical use: "Now if Matthew had regarded *Akoluthein* exclusively as a *terminus technicus* connoting discipleship, obviously he could not have written these words, for he would thereby have made Jesus the disciple of the ruler."[42]

Nevertheless, the technical use of the term elsewhere encourages speculation about its import when ascribed to Jesus. At least two possible readings of "to follow" in 9:19 conform to themes located elsewhere in the Gospel: the reversal of status indicators and the proper use of authority, and Jesus as a model of discipleship. Particularly when read in the context of the other individuals with authority found described in Matthew's Gospel, the ruler of Matthew 9 emerges as an exemplar of discipleship as well as of church leadership. He would therefore be an appropriate person for members of Matthew's church to follow. Jesus already provides the model for the disciples in terms of healing, teaching, and suffering; he may here provide the model for following, which is something "leaders" in the Matthean community must also do.

The ruler of Chapter 9 finds a helpful comparison in the Centurion of Chapter 8. In both cases, Matthew presents a person in a position of authority who in turn places himself under the authority of Jesus. The centurion appeals to Jesus and expresses his humility by stating "I am not worthy to have you come under my roof" (8:9). The ruler "kneels" (*proskuneō*, with connotations of worshiping) before Jesus and expresses faith in his ability not simply to heal but to raise from the dead. Both men, identified not by names but only by titles that convey power,[43] are powerless to accomplish what they most want. Both implore Jesus to heal a younger and weaker person who cannot

---

[41] Jack Dean Kingsbury, "The Verb Akoluthein ('To Follow') as an Index of Matthew's View of His Community," *JBL* 97 (1978): 56–73.

[42] Ibid., 58.

[43] Contrast the parallels in both Mark and Luke, where the girl's father is named "Jairus" and where he is identified as a "synagogue" ruler.

make a personal supplication. Both are rewarded. The two accounts thus present the proper use of authority: a ruler or leader must be humble, must recognize the limitations of earthly authority, must make the effort to seek the sacred, must appeal on behalf of others.

Contrasted to the ruler and the centurion are other people in positions of authority. The Gentile Centurion finds his opposite in the Gentile Pilate and his soldiers, who use their authority to harm rather than to help. More striking, the Jewish "ruler"—and he is Jewish, since Matthew makes clear when characters are Gentile both through specific identification and through Jesus' hesitation to enter their homes or perform cures on their behalf[44]—may be compared to the other two "Jewish" rulers of the Gospel: Herod the Great and his son, Herod Antipas.

Herod the Great does not seek the life of a child; he seeks the death of the "child who has been born king of the Jews" (2:2). In his search, he causes the deaths of others. This Jewish ruler leaves only Rachel, "weeping for her children . . . because they are no more" (2:18). Complacent, entrenched in Jerusalem with his courtiers, removed from Jesus, he is a direct contrast to the "ruler" of chapter 9: active, in Galilee, unaccompanied, appearing at Jesus' feet.[45]

---

[44] Reading 8:7 as a question; comparing Matt 15:21–28 to the parallel in Mark 7:31–37; noting 10:5b-6 and 15:24, etc. See Amy-Jill Levine, *The Social and Ethnic Dimensions of Matthean Salvation History: "Go Nowhere Among the Gentiles" (Matt 10:5b)* (Studies in the Bible and Early Christianity 14; Lewiston/Queenston/Lampeter: Edwin Mellen, 1988).

[45] Almost all commentators note that the children killed in Bethlehem were boys. This view is based on the parallels in the Matthean infancy account to Exodus 1–2 and the notion that Herod would not fear a female rival or expect a female messiah. However, the terms used for the children who are slaughtered are *paidas* in 2:16 and *tekna* in 2:18. Both might include girls. Such a general reading (cf. the English "children") has much to commend it: it heightens the crime of which Herod and his soldiers are guilty, it fits in terms of verisimilitude the outrages of military brutality (i.e., if the soldiers will not take the time to distinguish between a newborn and a two-year-old, why would they take the time to distinguish girls from boys?), it conforms to Matthew's interest in women in general from the genealogy to the tomb as well as in particular to daughters, and it helps to explain both the shift from the LXX (Jer 38:15, cf. MT Jer 31:15), which reads *tois huiois autēs*, "for her *sons*" and Matthew's addition of *polus*, "much" in 2:18. If the dead children are to be seen as including daughters, then the connection of Herod the Great to the ruler of Matthew 9 is increased. My thanks to Alicia Erickson for suggesting the inclusive interpretation for the murdered children.

More closely related to the *archōn* of Matthew 9 is the depiction of Herod Antipas. Once again, a Jewish ruler is presented in relation to a child, and here the parallels are more extensive: both Matt 9:18–26 and Matt 14:1–12 depict rulers who cannot exercise their power (the ruler of Matt 9 cannot raise his daughter; Herod Antipas cannot retract his oaths or disappoint his guests); a young girl associated with death (*korasion*: 9:24–25; 14:11); a concern for resurrection (9:25; 14:2); a woman who interrupts the story (the woman with the hemorrhage, Herodias); music (from the flute players of 9 to the dance in 14); and a story that becomes well known. Yet the *archōn's* story ends with life restored while Herod Antipas's account ends with the beheading of John and the burying of his corpse.

These contrasts do much more than show Matthew's literary artistry. They indicate that the good and the bad, the saved and the damned, are not categorized according to social status, gender, or ethnic group. Leaders as well as followers may find themselves in the *Ekklesia* of disciples, provided those leaders appropriately perform their duty to serve others. Jews as well as Gentiles are welcome in the Matthean church, as are men and women. The issue is not who one is; the point for Matthew is what one does.

The ruler of Matthew 9 acts appropriately. It is therefore entirely fitting that Jesus, as a model for disciples as well as rulers, should follow such a leader. With some generosity, one can even locate the ruler's request as mirroring the technical aspects of the term *akoluthein*. According to Kingsbury, "following" has the connotations of discipleship when it involves personal commitment (one follows if one is summoned directly by Jesus) and cost (there is some personal sacrifice involved).[46] The pericope in question actually has both concerns: here Jesus is summoned by the *archōn*, and to comply with the ruler's demands, he must interrupt his missionary preaching.

Jesus therefore serves several functions in this pericope: he is both the miracle worker who recognizes the faith of those in need, and he is the exemplar who shows both by his healing and by his willingness to follow how other disciples are to behave. He is a ruler who can command the flute players and mourners to depart; he is a servant who can follow and acquiesce to a request when appropriate. More, Jesus shares much in common with both the woman and the child: his physicality is reflected in the depictions of their bodies. The woman,

---

46 Kingsbury, "Akoluthein," 58.

suffers, she bleeds, she acts in humility by coming up behind Jesus, she retains her faith but she does not speak. Jesus too will suffer, will bleed, will act in humility, will remain silent and yet retain his faith. Like the ruler's daughter, Jesus is a ruler's son. At the time of his death, he will be surrounded by a commotion, by people who laugh at or mock him. Like the girl, he will die. And, like the girl, he also will be raised from the dead. And the report of this resurrection too, will "spread throughout that district."

Women's bodies thus provide a model for the body of the Christ; women's suffering provides the model for the suffering of the Christ, and women's healing provides the model for the resurrection of the Christ. Matthew makes a Christological point not through negative contrast or devaluation of the Law, not through anti-Jewish pronouncements nor through appeals to marginalization or "female problems." The pericope depicts the healing of bodies from ailments that could affect anyone—bleeding and death—ailments that effect even the Christ. These are women's issues, yes, as are the diseases of sexism and anti-Semitism. But even more, they are human issues. Would that all such issues be discharged, and that the report of this healing be spread throughout the land.[47]

---

[47] My gratitude to Mary Rose D'Angelo and Shaye J. D. Cohen for providing copies of their articles, and to Matthew Collins, Kathleen Corley, Jay Geller, Nicole Kirk, and Adele Reinhartz for suggestions and criticisms.

Bibliography

Aarde, Andries G. Van. "The *Evangelium Infantium*, the Abandoment of Children, and the Infancy Narrative in Matthew 1 and 2 from a Social-Scientific Perspective." *SBLSP* 31 (1992): 435–53.

———. *God-With-Us The Dominant Perspective in Matthew's Story.* HTSsup 5. Pretoria: Hervormde Teologiese Studies, 1994.

———. "Matthew's Portrayal of the Disciples and the Structure of Matthew 13:53–17:27." *Neotestamentica* 16 (1982): 21–34.

Albright, William Foxwell and Charles S. Mann. *Matthew: Introduction, Translation, and Notes.* Anchor Bible. Garden City, NY: Doubleday, 1971.

Allen, Willoughby C. *A Critical and Exegetical Commentary on the Gospel According to Matthew.* International Critical Commentary. 3rd ed. Edinburgh: T. & T. Clark, 1912.

Allison, Dale C. "Divorce, Celibacy, and Joseph (Matthew 1.18–25 and 19.1–12)." *JSNT* 49: 3–10.

———. *The New Moses: A Matthean Typology.* Minneapolis: Fortress, 1993.

———. "The Structure of the Sermon on the Mount." *JBL* 106 (1987): 423–45.

Anderson, Janice Capel. "Double and Triple Stories, The Implied Reader, and Redundancy in Matthew." *Semeia* 31 (1985): 71–89.

———. "Mary's Difference: Gender and Patriarchy in the Birth Narratives." *JR* 67 (1987): 183–202.

———. "Matthew: Gender and Reading." *Semeia* 28 (1983): 3–27.

———. *Matthew's Narrative Web: Over, and Over, and Over Again.* JSNTSup 91. Sheffield: Sheffield Academic Press, 1994.

Anderson, Janice Capel, and Stephen D. Moore, eds. *Mark and Method: New Approaches in Biblical Studies.* Minneapolis: Fortress, 1992.

Aquinas, Thomas. *Super Evangelium S. Matthaei Lectura.* Ed. R. Cai. Torino: Marietti, 1951.

Argyle, Aubrey William. *The Gospel According to Matthew.* Cambridge Bible Commentary. Cambridge: Cambridge University Press, 1963.

Bacon, Benjamin Wisner. "Jesus and the Law: A Study of the First 'Book' of Matthew (Mt. 3–7)." *JBL* 47 (1928): 203–31.

———. "The 'Five Books' of Matthew Against the Jews." *Expositor* 15 (1918): 56–66.

———. *Studies in Matthew.* New York: Henry Holt & Co., 1930.

Balch, David L., ed. *Social History of the Matthean Community: Cross-Disciplinary Approaches.* Minneapolis: Fortress, 1991.

Barr, David L. "The Drama of Matthew's Gospel: A Reconsideration of Its Structure and Purpose." *TD* 24 (1976): 349–59.

Barta, Karen A. "Mission in Matthew: The Second Discourse as Narrative." *SBLSP 27 (1988): 527–35.*

Bauer, David R. "The Interpretation of Matthew's Gospel in the Twentieth Century." *ATLA Journal* (1988): 119–45.

———. "The Kingship of Jesus in the Matthean Infancy Narrative." *CBQ* 57 (1995): 306–23.

———. "The Major Characters of Matthew's Gospel." *Int* 46 (Oct. 1992): 357–67.

———. *The Structure of Matthew's Gospel: A Study in Literary Design.* JSNTSup 31. Sheffield: Almond, 1988.

Beare, Francis Wright. *The Gospel According to Matthew: Translation, Introduction and Commentary.* San Francisco: Harper & Row, 1981.

Becker, Jürgen. *Auf der Kathedra des Mose: Rabbinisch-theologisches Denken und antirabbinische Polemik in Matthäus 23,1–12.* Berlin: Institut Kirche und Judentum, 1990.

Bede, Venerable. *In Matthaei Evangelium expositio.* PL 92: 9–132.

Benoit, Pierre. *L'évangile selon Saint Matthieu.* La Sainte Bible 1. 2nd ed. Paris: Cert, 1953.

Betz, Hans Dieter. *Essays on the Sermon on the Mount.* Philadelphia: Fortress, 1985.

————. *The Sermon on the Mount: A Commentary on the Sermon on the Mount, Including the Sermon on the Plain (Matthew 5:3–7:27 and Luke 6:20–49).* Hermeneia: A Critical and Historical Commentary on the Bible. Minneapolis: Fortress, 1995.

Black, C. Clifton , III. "Depth of Characterization and Degrees of Faith in Matthew." *SBLSP* 28 (1989): 588–603.

Blomberg, Craig L. "The Liberation of Illegitimacy: Women and Rulers in Matthew 1–2." *BTB* 21 (1991): 145–50.

Boring, M. Eugene. "The Convergence of Source Analysis, Social History, and Literary Structure in the Gospel of Matthew." *SBLSP* 33 (1994): 587–611.

Bornhäuser, Karl. *Die Geburts - und Kindheitsgeschichte Jesu: Versuch einer zeitgenossischen Auslegung von Matthäus 1 und 2 und Lukas 1–3.* Gütersloh: Bertelsmann, 1930.

Bonnard, Pierre. *L' Évangile selon Saint Matthieu.* CNT. Geneva: Labor et Fides, 1982.

Bornkamm, Günther. "Der Auferstandene und der Irdische. Mt. 28, 16–20." In *Zeit und Geschichte: Dankesgabe an Rudolf Bultmann zum 80.* Ed. Erich Dinkler. Tübingen: J. C. B. Mohr, 1964.

————. "Die Binde- und Lösegewalt in der Kirche des Matthäus." In *Geschichte und Glaube.* BEvT 53. Munich: Kaiser, 1971.

Bornkamm, Günther, Gerhard Barth, and Heinz Joachim Held. *Tradition and Interpretation in Matthew.* New Testament Library. Philadelphia: Westminster, 1963.

Brandt, W. "Die geringsten Brüder: Aus dem Gesprach der Kirche mit Mt 25, 31–46." *JThSB* 8 (1937): 7.

Brooks, Oscar. "Matthew xxviii.16–20 and the Design of the First Gospel." *JSNT* 10 (1981): 2–18.

Brodie, T. "Fish, Temple Tithe, and Remission: The . . . of Matt 17:22–18:35." *RB* 99 (1992): 697–718.

Broer, Ingo. *Freiheit vom Gesetz und Radikalisierung des Gesetzes: Ein Beitrag zur Theologie des Evangelisten Matthäus.* Stuttgart: Katholisches Bibelwerk, 1980.

———. "Anmerkungen zum Gesetzesverständnis des Matthäus." In *Das Gesetz im neuen Testament.* Ed. Karl Kertelge. Freiburg: Herder, 1986.

Brown, Raymond E. *The Birth of the Messiah: A Commentary on the Infancy Narratives in Matthew and Luke.* Rev. ed. Anchor Bible Reference Library. New York: Doubleday, 1993.

———. "Gospel Infancy Narrative Research from 1976 to 1986: Part I (Matthew)." *CBQ* 48 (1986): 468–83.

Brown, Schuyler. "The Matthean Community and the Gentile Mission." *NovT* 22 (1980): 193–221.

———. "The Mission to Israel in Matthew's Central Section (Mt. 9.35–11.1)." *ZNW* 69 (1978): 73–90.

———. "The Two-fold Representation of the Mission in Matthew's Gospel." *ST* 31 (1977): 21–32.

———. "Universalism and Particularism in Matthew's Gospel: A Jungian Approach." *SBLSP* 28 (1989): 388–399.

Burger, Christoph. "Jesu Taten nach Matthäus 8 und 9." *ZTK* 70 (1973): 272–87.

———. *Jesus als Davidssohn: Eine traditionsgeschichtliche Untersuchung.* Göttingen: Vandenhoeck & Ruprecht, 1970.

Burnett, Fred W. "Characterization in Matthew: Reader Construction of the Disciple Peter." *McKendree Pastoral Review* 4 (1987): 13–43.

———. "Exposing the Anti-Jewish Ideology of Matthew's Implied Author: The Characterization of God as Father." *Semeia* 59 (1992): 155–91.

———. "Narrative Representation and Ideology in Matthew's 'Anti-Jewishness.'" Chicago: Society of Biblical Literature, 1994. Photocopy.

———. "Palingenesia in Matt 19:28: A Window on the Matthean Community?" *JSNT* 17 (1983): 60–72.

———. "Prolegomenon to Reading Matthew's Eschatological Discourse." *Semeia* 31 (1985): 91–109.

———. *The Testament of Jesus-Sophia: A Redaction-Critical Study of the Eschatological Discourse in Matthew.* Washington, D.C.: University Press of America, 1981.

———. "The Undecidability of the Proper Name 'Jesus' in Matthew." *Semeia* 54 (1991): 123–44.

Burton, E. D. "The Purpose and Plan of the Gospel of Matthew." *BW* 11 (1898): 37–44, 91–101.

Cargal, T. B. "His Blood Be Upon Us and Upon Our Children: A Matthean Double Entendre." *NTS* 37 (1991): 101–12.

Carr, A. *The Gospel according to St. Matthew: With Maps and Introduction.* Cambridge Bible for Schools. Cambridge: Cambridge University Press, 1878.

Carter, Warren J. "Challenging By Confirming, Renewing By Repeating: The Parables of "the Reign of the Heavens" as Embedded Narratives," *SBLSP* 34 (1995): 399–424.

———. "The Crowds in Matthew's Gospel." *CBQ* 55 (1993): 54–67.

———. "Kernels and Narrative Blocks: The Structure of Matthew's Gospel." *CBQ* 54 (1992): 463–81.

———. *Households and Discipleship: A Study of Matthew 19–20.* JSNTSup 103. Sheffield: JSOT, 1994.

Case, Shirley Jackson. "The Origin and Purpose of the Gospel of Matthew." *BW* 34 (1909): 391–403.

Cassidy, R. J. "Matthew 17:24–27–A Word on Civil Taxes." *CBQ* 41 (1979): 574.

Charette, Blaine. *The Theme of Recompense in Matthew's Gospel.* JSNTSup 79. Sheffield: JSOT, 1992.

———. "To Proclaim Liberty to the Captives: Matthew 11.28–30 in the Light of Old Testament Prophetic Expectation." *NTS* 38 (1992): 290–97.

Charles, J. Daryl. "The Greatest or the Least in the Kingdom?: The Disciple's Relationship to the Law (Matt 5:17–20)." *TrinJ* 13 (1992): 142–43.

Chilton, B. D. "A Coin of Three Realms (Matthew 17.24–27)." In *The Bible in Three Dimensions*. Eds. D. J. A. Clines, S. E. Fowl, and S. E. Porter. Sheffield: JSOT, 1990.

Chrysostom, John. *Commentarius in sanctum Matthaeum Evangelistam*. PG 57–58.

Clark, K. W. "The Gentile Bias in Matthew." *JBL* 66 (1947): 165–72.

Combrink, H. J. B. "Reference and Rhetoric in the Gospel of Matthew." *Scriptura* (1992): 1–17.

———. "The Structure of the Gospel of Matthew as Narrative." *TynBul* 34 (1983): 71–90.

Cook, M. J. "Interpreting 'Pro-Jewish' Passages in Matthew." *HUCA* 54 (1983): 135–46.

Cope, O. Lamar. *Matthew: A Scribe Trained for the Kingdom of Heaven*. CBQMS 5. Washington, DC: Catholic Biblical Association, 1976.

———. "Matthew 25: 31–46: 'The Sheep and the Goats' Reintepreted." *NovT* 11 (1969): 32–44.

Cox, George Ernest Pritchard. *The Gospel of St. Matthew*. Torch Bible Commentaries. London: SCM, 1952.

Crosby, M. H. *House of Disciples: Church, Economics, and Justice in Matthew*. New York: Orbis, 1988.

Davies, M. *Matthew: Readings, A New Biblical Commentary*. Sheffield: JSOT, 1992.

Davies, William D. *The Setting of the Sermon on the Mount*. Cambridge: Cambridge University Press, 1966.

———. *Torah in the Messanic Age and/or the Age to Come*. Philadelphia: Society of Biblical Literature, 1952.

Davies, William D., and Allison, Dale C. *A Critical and Exegetical Commentary on the Gospel According to St. Matthew*. 3 vols. International Critical Commentary. Edinburgh: T. & T. Clark, 1988.

Davis, Charles Thomas. "The Fulfillment of Creation: A Study of Matthew's Genealogy." *JAAR* 41 (1973): 520–35.

Davison, James. E. "Anomia and the Question of an Antinomian Polemic in Matthew." *JBL* 104 (1985): 617–35.

Dean, Margaret E. "Reading Matthew's Treasure Map: Territoriality in Matthew's Five Sermons." M.Div. thesis, Phillips Graduate Seminary, 1993.

Derrett, J. D. M. "Peter's Penny: Fresh Light on Matthew xvii 24–27." In *Law in the New Testament*. London: Darton, Longman & Todd, 1970.

Deutsch, Celia. *Hidden Wisdom and the Easy Yoke. Wisdom, Torah and Discipleship in Matthew 11.28–30.* JSNTSup 18. Sheffield: Sheffield Academic Press, 1987.

Dillersberger, J. *Matthäus: Das Evangelium des heiligen Matthäus in theologischer und heilsgeschichtler Schau. I: Sein Kommen in Vielfalt (die Vorgeschichte).* Salzburg: Otto Müller, 1953.

Donahue, John R. "The 'Parable' of the Sheep and the Goats: A Challenge to Christian Ethics." *TS* 47 (1986): 3–31.

Donaldson, Terry L. *Jesus on the Mountain: A Study in Matthean Theology.* JSNTSup 8; Sheffield: Sheffield Academic Press, 1985.

———. "The Law That 'Hangs' (Matt. 22:40): Rabbinic Formulation and the Matthean World." *SBLSP* 29 (1990): 14–33.

Duling, Dennis C. "Binding and Loosing: Matthew 6:19; Matthew 18:18; John 20:23." *Forum* 3 (1987): 3–31.

———. "[Do not swear . . .] by Jerusalem because it is the city of the great king (Matt. 5:35)." *JBL* 110 (1991): 291–309.

———. "Matthew and Marginality." *SBLSP* 32 (1993): 642–71.

———. "Matthew's Plurisignificant 'Son of David' in Social Science Perspective: Kinship, Kingship, Magic, and Miracle." *BTB* 22 (1992): 99–116.

Dumbrell, W. J. "The Logic of the Role of the Law in Matthew V. 1–20." *NovT* 23 (1981): 20.

Dupont, Jacques. "L'évangile de saint Matthieu: quelques clés de lecture." *CL* 57 (1975): 3–40.

———. *Les Beatitudes.* Louvain: E. Nauwelaerts, 1958.

Durand, A. *Evangile selon Saint Matthieu: Traduction et Commentaire.* Verbum Salutis: Commentaire de Nouveau Testament, 1. Paris: Beauchnesne, 1948.

Edwards, J. R. "The Use of *Proserchesthai* in the Gospel of Matthew." *JBL* 106 (1987): 65–74.

Edwards, Richard A. *Matthew's Story of Jesus.* Philadelphia: Fortress Press, 1985.

———. "Narrative Implications of *Gar* in Matthew." *CBQ* 52 (1990): 636–55.

Ellis, Peter F. *Matthew: His Mind and His Message.* Collegeville, MN: Liturgical, 1974.

Enslin, M. S. "'The Five Books of Matthew': Bacon on the Gospel of Matthew." *HTR* 24 (1931): 67–97.

Farmer, W. R. "Matthew and the Sermon on the Mount." *SBLASP* 25 (1986): 66.

———. "The Post-Sectarian Character of Matthew and Its Post-War Setting in Antioch of Syria." *Perspectives in Religious Studies* 3 (1976): 235–47.

Farrer, Austin. *St. Matthew and St. Mark.* London: Dacre, 1954.

Fenton, John C. "Inclusio and Chiasmus in Matthew." In *Studia Evangelica* 1. TU 73. Berlin: Akademie, 1959.

———. *Saint Matthew.* Westminster Pelican Commentaries. Philadelphia: Westminster, 1963.

Filson, Floyd V. *The Gospel According to St. Matthew.* Black's New Testament Commentaries. London: Adam and Charles Black, 1960.

Fitzmyer, Joseph A. "The Matthean Divorce Texts and Some New Palestinian Evidence." *TS* 37 (1976): 213–221.

Flusser, D. "Two Anti-Jewish Montages in Matthew." *Immanuel* 5 (1975): 37–45.

France, R. T. *Matthew.* TNTC. Grand Rapids: Eerdmans, 1985.

———. *Matthew: Evangelist and Teacher.* Grand Rapids: Zondervan, 1989.

Frankemölle, H. *Jahwebund und Kirche Christi: Studien zur Form- und Traditionsgeschichte des "Evangeliums" nach Matthäus.* NTAbh 10. Münster: Aschendorff, 1974.

———. "'Pharisäismus' in Judentum und Kirche. Zur Tradition und Redaktion in Matthäus 23." In *Gottesverächter und Menschenfeinde? Juden zwischen Jesus und frühchristlicher Kirche.* Ed. H. Goldstein. Düsseldorf: Patmos, 1979.

Friedrich, G. "Die formale Struktur von Mt. 28.18–20." *ZTK* 80 (1983): 137–83.

Fuchs, Ernst. "The Parable of the Unmerciful Servant (Matt. 18,23–25)." In *Studia Evangelica* I. Ed. Kurt Aland et al. Berlin: Akademie, 1959.

Gaechter, Paul. *Das Matthäus Evangelium: Ein Kommentar.* Inssbruch, Tyrolia, 1966.

———. *Die Literarische Kunst im Matthäus-Evangelium.* SB 7. Stuttgart: Katholisches Bibelwerk, 1955.

Garland, David E. *The Intention of Matthew 23.* NovTSup. Leiden: Brill, 1979.

———. *Reading Matthew: A Literary and Theological Commentary on the First Gospel.* New York: Crossroad, 1993.

Gaston, Lloyd. "The Messiah of Israel as Teacher of the Gentiles. The Setting of Matthew's Christology." *Int* 21 (1975): 24–40.

Gerhardsson, Birger. "The Hermeneutic Program in Matthew 22:37–40." In *Jews, Greeks, and Christians.* Ed. R. Hamerton-Kelly and R. Scroggs. Leiden: Brill, 1976.

———. *The Mighty Acts of Jesus According to Matthew.* Scripta Minora 5. Lund: GWK Gleerup, 1979.

Gewalt, D. "Matthäus 25,31–46 im Erwartungshorizont heutiger Exegese." *LB* 25/26 (1973): 9–21.

Gibbs, J. M. "Purpose and Pattern in Matthew's Use of the Title 'Son of David.'" *NTS* 10 (1963–64): 446–64.

—————. "The Son of God as the Torah Incarnate in Matthew." In *Studia Evangelica* IV. Ed. F. L. Cross. Berlin: Akademie, 1968.

Gnika, Joachim. *Das Matthäusevangelium.* 2 vols. HTKNT. Freiburg: Herder, 1988.

Gnuse, Robert K. "Dream Genre in the Matthean Infancy Narratives." *NovT* 32 (1990): 97–120.

Good, D. "The Verb *Anachōreō* in Matthew's Gospel." *NovT* 32 (1990): 1–12.

Goulder, M. D. *Midrash and Lection in Matthew.* London: SPCK, 1974.

Grassi, J. A. "Matthew as a Second Testament Deuteronomy." *BTB* 19 (1989):23–29.

Gray, Sherman W. *The Least of My Brothers: Matthew 25:31–46: A History of Interpretation.* SBLDS 114. Atlanta: Scholars Press, 1989.

Green, Frederick Wostie. *The Gospel According to St. Matthew: In the Revised Version with Introduction and Commentary.* The Clarendon Bible. Oxford: Clarendon, 1936.

Green, H. B. *The Gospel According to Matthew.* Oxford: Oxford University Press, 1975.

—————. "The Structure of St. Matthew's Gospel." In *Studia Evangelica* IV: Ed. Frank L. Cross. TU 102. Berlin: Akademie, 1968.

Grundmann, Walter. *Das Evangelium nach Matthäus.* THKNT. 5th ed. Berlin: Evangelische Verlagsanstalt, 1981.

Guelich, Robert. "The Matthean Beatitudes: 'Entrance Requirements' or Eschatological Blessings?" *JBL* 95 (1976): 415–34.

—————. *The Sermon on the Mount: A Foundation for Understanding.* Waco: Word, 1982.

Gundry, Robert H. *Matthew: A Commentary on His Handbook for a Mixed Church Under Persecution.* 2nd ed. Grand Rapids: Eerdmans, 1984.

Haenchen, Ernst. "Matthäus 23." *ZTK* 48 (1951): 38–63.

Häfner, G. "'Jene Tage' (Mt. 3:1) und der Umfang des Matthäischen 'Prologs': Ein Beitrag zur Frage nach der Struktur des Mt-Ev." *BZ* 37 (1993): 43–59.

Hagner, Donald A. "Apocalyptic Motifs in the Gospel of Matthew: Continuity and Discontinuity." *HBT* 7 (1985): 53–82.

———. "Imminence Delay and Parousia in Matthew." In *Texts and Contexts*. FS. Eds. L. Hartman, D. Hellholm and T. Fornberg. Oslo: Scandinavian University Press, 1995.

———. *Matthew 1–13*. WBC 33A. Dallas: Word, 1993.

———. "Matthew's Eschatology." In *To Tell the Mystery*. Ed. R. H. Gundry, M. Silva and T. E. Schmidt. Sheffield: JSOT, 1994.

———. "Righteousness in Matthew's Theology." In *Worship, Theology and Ministry In the Early Church*. Ed. M. J. Wilkins and T. Paige. Sheffield: JSOT, 1992.

Hahn, Ferdinand. "Mt 5,17 Anmerkungen zum Erfüllungsgedanken bei Matthus." In *Die Mitte des Neuens Testaments*. Ed. Ulrich Luz and Hans Weder. Göttingen: Vandenhoeck & Ruprecht, 1983.

Hamerton-Kelly, R. G. "Attitudes to the Law in Matthew's Gospel: A Discussion of Matthew 5:18." *BR* 17 (1972): 31–32.

Hare, Douglas R. A. *Matthew*. Interpretation: A Bible Commentary for Teaching and Preaching. Louisville: John Knox, 1993.

———. *The Theme of Jewish Persecution of Christians in the Gospel According to St. Matthew.* SNTSMS 6. Cambridge: Cambridge University Press, 1967.

Harless, C. A. "The Structure of the Gospel according to Matthew." *BS* 1 (1844): 86–97.

Harrington, Daniel J. *The Gospel of Matthew*. Sacra Pagina. Collegeville, MN: Michael Glazier, 1991.

———. "'Making Disciples of All the Gentiles' (Matt 28:19)." *CBQ* 37 (1975): 359–69.

———. "Matthean Studies Since Joachim Rohde." *HeyJ* 16 (1975): 375–88.

Heil, John P. *The Death and Resurrection of Jesus: A Narrative-Critical Reading of Matthew 26–28*. Minneapolis: Fortress Press, 1991.

———. "Ezekiel 34 and the Narrative Strategy of the Shepherd and Sheep Metaphor in Matthew." *CBQ* 55 (1993): 698–708.

———. "The Narrative Structure of Matthew 27:55–28:20." *JBL* 110 (1991): 419–38.

Heubült, Christine. "Mt 5:17–20: Ein Beitrag zur Theologie des Evangelisten Matthäus." *ZNW* 71 (1980): 145–49.

Hiers, R. H. "'Binding and Loosing': the Matthean Authorizations [Matt 16:19; 18:18]." *JBL* 104 (1985): 233–50.

Hill, David. "False Prophets and Charismatics: Structure and Interpretation in Matthew 7:15–23." *Biblica* 57 (1976): 327–348.

———. "The Figure of Jesus in Matthew's Story: A Response to Professor Kingsbury's Literary-Critical Probe [pp. 3–36]." *JSNT* 21 (1984): 37–52.

———. *The Gospel of Matthew*. NCBC. Grand Rapids, Eerdmans, 1972.

———. "Some Recent Trends in Matthean Studies." *IBS* 1 (1979): 139–49.

Hoffmann, P. "Die Bedeutung des Petrus für die Kirche des Matthäus. Redaktiongeschichtliche Beobachtungen zu Mt 16, 17–19." In *Dienst an der Einheit Zum Wesen und Auftrag des Petrusamtes*. Ed. J. Rateinger. Dusseldorf: Patmos, 1978.

Homeau, H. A. "On Fishing for Staters: Matthew 17,27." *ExpTim* 85 (1973–74): 340–42.

Honeyman, A. M. "Matthew V.18 and the Validity of the Law." *NTS* 1 (1954): 141–42.

Horton, Fred L., Jr. "Parenthetical Pregnancy: The Conception and Birth of Jesus in Matthew 1:18–25." *SBLSP* 26 (1987): 175–89.

Howell, David B. *Matthew's Inclusive Story: A Study in the Narrative Rhetoric of the First Gospel*. JSNTSup 42. Sheffield: JSOT, 1990.

Hubbard, Benjamin J. *The Matthean Redaction of a Primitive Apostolic Commissioning: An Exegesis of Matthew 28.16–20*. SBLDS 19. Missoula: Scholars, 1974.

Hummel, Reinhart. *Die Auseinandersetzung zwischen Kirche und Judentum im Matthäusevangelium.* 2nd ed. Munich: Kaiser, 1966.

Humphries-Brooks, Stephenson. "Indicators of Social Organization and Status in Matthew's Gospel." *SBLSP* 30 (1991): 31–49.

———. *Matthew's Community: The Evidence of his Special Sayings Material.* Sheffield: Sheffield Academic Press, 1987.

———. "Spatial Form and Plot Disruption in the Gospel of Matthew." *Essays in Literature* 20 (1993): 54–69.

Hutter, M. "Mt 25,31–46 in der Deutung Manis." *NovT* 33 (1991): 276–282.

Ingelaere, J. C. "La 'parabole' du jugement dernier (Mt 25,31–46)." *RHPR* 50 (1970): 37–56.

———. "Structure de Matthieu et histoire du Salut." *Foi et Vie* 78 (1979): 10–33.

Jerome. *Commentariourm in Matthaeum, libri IV.* CChr. SL 77.

Johnson, Marshall D. *The Purpose of Biblical Genealogies, With Special Reference to the Genealogies of Jesus.* SNTSMS 8. Cambridge: Cambridge University Press, 1969.

———. "Reflections on a Wisdom Approach to Matthew's Christology." *CBQ* 36 (1974): 44–64.

Jones, Alexander. *The Gospel According to St. Matthew: A Text and Commentary for Students.* New York: Sheed & Ward, 1964.

Kampen, John. "A Re-examination of the Relationship between Matthew 5:21–48 and the Dead Sea Scrolls." *SBLSP* 29 (1990): 34–59.

Kampling, R. *Das Blut Christi und die Juden. Mt 27, 25 bei den lateinisch-sprachigen christlichen Autoren bis zu Leo dem Grossen.* NTAbh N.F. 16 Münster: Aschendorff, 1984.

Kea, Perry V. "Writing a *bios*: Matthew's Genre Choices and Rhetorical Situation." *SBLSP* 33 (1994): 574–86.

Kilpatrick, George D. *The Origins of the Gospel of St. Matthew.* Oxford: Clarendon, 1946.

Kingsbury, Jack Dean. "The Developing Conflict between Jesus and the Jewish Leaders in Matthew's Gospel: A Literary-Critical Study." *CBQ* 49 (1987): 57–73.

————. "The Figure of Jesus in Matthew's Story: A Literary-Critical Probe." *JSNT* 21(1984):3–36.

————. "The Figure of Jesus in Matthew's Story: A Rejoinder to David Hill [No. 21, 37–52, 1984]." *JSNT* 25 (1985): 61–81.

————. "The Figure of Peter in Matthew's Gospel as a Theological Problem." *JBL* 98 (1979): 67–83.

————. "The Form and Message of Matthew." In *Interpreting the Gospels.* Ed. James Luther Mays. Philadelphia: Fortress, 1981.

————. *Jesus Christ in Matthew, Mark, and Luke.* Philadelphia: Fortress, 1981.

————. "The 'Jesus of History' and the 'Christ of Faith, in Relation to Matthew's View of Time—Reactions to a New Approach." *CTM* 37 (1966): 502–8.

————. *Matthew.* 2nd ed. Proclamation Commentaries. Philadelphia: Fortress, 1986.

————. *Matthew as Story.* 2nd. ed. Philadelphia: Fortress, 1988.

————. *Matthew: Structure. Christology. Kingdom.* Philadelphia: Fortress, 1975.

————. "The 'Miracle Chapters' of Matthew 8–9." *CBQ* 40 (1978): 559–73.

————. "On Following Jesus: the 'Eager' Scribe and the 'Reluctant' Disciple (Matthew 8:18–22)." *NTS* 34 (1988): 45–59.

————. "The Parable of the Wicked Husbandmen and the Secret of Jesus' Divine Sonship in Matthew: Some Literary-Critical Observations." *JBL* 105 (1986): 643–55.

————. *The Parables of Jesus in Matthew 13.* Richmond: John Knox, 1969.

————. "The Place, Structure, and Meaning of the Sermon on the Mount." *Int* 41 (1987): 136–42.

————. "The Plot of Matthew's Story." *Int* 46 (1992): 347–56.

————. "Reflections on the Reader of Matthew's Gospel." *NTS* 34 (1988): 442–60.

————. "The Title 'Son of David' in Matthew's Gospel." *JBL* 95 (1976): 591–602.

————. "The Verb *Akolouthein* ('To Follow') as an Index of Matthew's View of His Community." *JBL* 97 (1978): 56–73.

Klein, H. "Judenchristliche Frömmigkeit im Sondergut des Matthäus." *NTS* 35 (1989): 466–74.

Klostermann, Erich. *Das Matthäus-Evangelium.* HNT. 4th ed. Tübingen: J. C. B. Mohr, 1971.

Köhler, W. D. *Die Rezeption des Matthäusevangeliums in der Zeit vor Irenäus.* WUNT 2.24. Tübingen: Mohr, 1987.

Kornfeld, W. "Die Liebeswerke Mt 25,35f.42f in alttestamentlicher Überlieferung." In *Theologia scientia eminens practica: Festschrift für F. Zerbst.* Ed. H. C. Schmidt-Lauber. Vienna: Herder, 1979.

Krentz, Edgar. "Community and Character: Matthew's Vision of the Church." *SBLSP* 26 (1987): 565–73.

————. "The Extent of Matthew's Prologue: Toward the Structure of the First Gospel." *JBL* 83 (1964): 409–15.

Kürzinger, R. Riesner. "Der Aufbau der Redem im Matthäus-Evangelium." *TBei* 9 (1978): 173–76.

Lagrange, Marie-Joseph. *Évangile selon Saint Matthieu.* 7th ed. Paris: J. Gabalda, 1948.

Lambrecht, Jan. *The Sermon on the Mount.* Wilmington, DE: Michael Glazier, 1985.

Lapide, Cornelius à. *Commentarius in IV Evangelia: Argumentum in S. Matthaeum.* Antwerp: Meurstum, 1660.

Lee, G. M. "Matthew 17,24–27." *Theology* 68 (1965): 380–81.

Légasse, S. "Jesus et l'impôt de Temple (Matthieu 17,24–27)." *ScEs* 24 (1972): 376–77.

Levine, Amy-Jill. "Matthew." In *The Women's Bible Commentary*. Ed. C. Newsom and S. H. Ringe. Louisville: Westminster/John Knox, 1992.

———. *The Social and Ethnic Dimensions of Matthean Salvation History: "Go Nowhere Among the Gentiles . . ." (Matt. 10:56)*. SBEC 14. Lewiston, NY: Mellen, 1988.

Levison, Jack. "A Better Righteousness: The Character and Purpose of Matthew 5:21–48." *Studia Biblica et Theologia* 12 (1982): 171–194.

Lohmeyer, Ernst. *Das Evangelium des Matthäus*. Ed. W. Schmauch. KeK. 4th ed. Göttingen: Vandenhoeck and Ruprecht, 1956.

Lohr, Charles H. "Oral Techniques in the Gospel of Matthew." *CBQ* 23 (1961): 403–35.

Love, S. L. "The Household: A Major Social Component for Gender Analysis in the Gospel of Matthew." *BTB* 23 (1993): 21–31.

———. "The Place of Women in Public Settings in Matthew's Gospel: A Sociological Inquiry." *BTB* 24 (1994): 52–65.

Luck, U. *Das Evangelium nach Matthäus*. ZBKNT. Zurich: Theologischer Verlag, 1993.

Ludwig, J. *Die Primatswörte Mt 16, 18–19 in der altkirchlichen Exegese*. NTAbh 19.4. Münster: Aschendorff, 1952.

Lührmann, D. "Liebet eure Feinde (LK 6, 27–36/Mt 5, 37–48)." *ZTK* 69 (1972): 412–38.

Lund, Nils Wilhelm. "The Influence of Chiasmus Upon the Structure of the Gospel According to Matthew." *ATR* 13 (1931): 405–33.

Luz, Ulrich. *Das Evangelium nach Matthäus. 2 Teilband: Mt. 8–17*. EKKNT. GmbH, Zurich, and Braunschweig: Benziger Verlag; Neukirchen-Vluyn: Neukirchener Verlag, 1990.

———. "Das Primatwort Matthäus 16:17–19 aus wirkungsgeschichtlicher Sicht." *NTS* 37 (1991): 415–33.

———. "Die Erfüllung des Gesetzes bei Matthäus (Mt 5,17–20)." *ZTK* 75 (1978): 398–435.

———. "Die Jünger im Matthäusevangelium." *ZNW* 62 (1971): 141–71.

———. *Matthew in History: Interpretation, Influence, and Effects*. Minneapolis: Fortress, 1994.

———. *Matthew 1–7: A Commentary*. Minneapolis: Augsburg, 1989.

———. "Matthew's Anti-Judaism: Its Origin and Contemporary Significance." *CurTM* (1992): 405–14.

———. "The Son of Man in Matthew: Heavenly Judge or Human Christ?" *JSNT* 48 (1992): 3–21.

McConnell, Richard S. *Law and Prophecy in Matthew's Gospel*. Basel: Friedrich Reinhardt Kommissionsverlag, 1969.

McEleney, N. J. "The Beatitudes of the Sermon on the Mount/Plain." *CBQ* 43 (1981): 10–13.

———. "MT 17:24–27–Who Paid the Temple Tax? A Lesson in Avoiding Scandal." *CBQ* 38 (1976): 180–81.

McKee, Dean Greer. "Studia Biblica VI. The Gospel According to Matthew." *Int* 3 (1949): 194–205.

McKnight, Scot. "A Loyal Critic: Matthew's Polemic with Judaism in Theological Perspective." In *Anti-Semitism and Early Christianity. Issues of Polemic and Faith*. Ed. C. A. Evans and D. A. Hagner. Minneapolis: Fortress, 1993.

McNeile, Alan Hugh. *The Gospel According to Matthew: The Greek Text with Introduction, Notes, and Indices*. London: Macmillan, 1938.

Malina, Bruce J. "The Literary Structure and Form of Matt. xxviii.16–20." *NTS* 17 (1970): 87–103.

Malina, Bruce J. and Neyrey, Jerome H. *Calling Jesus Names: The Social Value of Labels in Matthew*. Sonoma, CA: Polebridge, 1988.

Margot, J. C. "Les Problèmes posés par la traduction de Matthieu 17.24–27." *Traduire sans trahir: la theorie de la traduction et son application aux textes bibliques*. Lausanne: Age d'homme, 1979.

Martin, Brice. "Matthew on Christ and the Law." *TS* 44 (1983): 54–70.

Matera, Frank J. "The Plot of Matthew's Gospel." *CBQ* 49 (1987): 233–53.

Massaux, E. *The Influence of theGospel of Saint Matthew on Christian Literature before Saint Irenaeus.* Leuven: Peeters, 1990.

Meier, John P. *Law and History in Matthew's Gospel.* Rome: Biblical Institute Press, 1976.

————. *A Marginal Jew. Re-thinking the Historical Jesus. Volume Two: Mentor, Message, and Miracles.* New York: Doubleday, 1994.

————. *Matthew.* New Testament Message 3. Wilmington, DE: Michael Glazier, 1980.

————. "Nations or Gentiles in Matthew 22:19?" *CBQ* 39 (1977): 94–102.

————. "Salvation History in Matthew: In Search of a Starting Point." *CBQ* 37 (1975): 203–13.

————. *The Vision of Matthew: Christ, Church, and Morality in the First Gospel.* New York: Paulist, 1979.

Menninger, R. E. *Israel and the Church in the Gospel of Matthew.* Theology and Religion 162. New York: Peter Lang, 1994.

Michaelis, Wilhelm. *Das Evangelium nach Matthäus.* Prophezei: Schweizerisches Bibelwerk für Gemeinde. Zürich: Zwingli, 1948.

Michaels, J. Ramsey. "Apostolic Hardships and Righteous Gentiles: A Study of Matthew 25:31–46." *JBL* 84 (1965): 27–37.

Minear, Paul S. *Matthew: The Teacher's Gospel.* New York: Pilgrim, 1982.

Mohrlang, Roger. *Matthew and Paul. A Comparison of Ethical Perspectives.* Cambridge: Cambridge University Press, 1984.

Morris, Leon. *The Gospel According to Matthew.* Pillar Commentary. Grand Rapids: Eerdmans, 1992.

Moule, C. F. D. "St. Matthew's Gospel: Some Neglected Features." In *Studia Evangelica* II. TU 87 (1964): 91–99.

Mounce, R. H. *Matthew.* NIBC. Peabody, MA: Hendrickson, 1991.

Mowery, Robert L. "The Activity of God in the Gospel of Matthew." *SBLSP* 28 (1989): 400–411.

————. "Rereading Matthew on Jerusalem and Judaism." *BTB* 19 (1990): 43–47.

Müller, Mogens. "The Gospel of Matthew and the Mosaic Law." *ST* 46 (1992): 109–120.

Musculus, W. *In Evangelistam Matthaeum commentarii.* Basel: Heruagius, 1561.

Neirynck, Franz. *"Apo Tote Erxato* and the Structure of Matthew." *ETL* 64 (1988): 21–59.

Nepper-Christensen, Paul. *Das Matthäusevangelium: Ein judenchristliches Evangelium.* Aarhus: Universitetsforlaget, 1958.

Nolan, Brian M. *The Royal Son of God: The Christology of Matthew 1–2 in the Setting of the Gospel.* Göttingen: Vandenhoeck and Ruprecht, 1979.

Oberlinner, L. and P. Fielder eds. *Salz der Erde—Licht der Welt: Exegetische Studien zum Matthäusevangelium: Festschrift für Anton Vögtle.* Stuttgart: Verlag Katholisches Bibelwerk, 1991.

Obrist, F. *Echtheitsfrager und Deutung der Primatstelle Mt 16,18f in der deutschen protestantischen Theolgie der letzten dreissig Jahre.* NTAbh 21.3–4. Münster: Aschendorff, 1961.

Ogawa, A. *L'histoire de Jesus chez Matthieu: La signification de l'histoire pour la théologie matthéenne.* Publications Universitaires Européennes, Europäische Hochschulschriften, 23/16. Frankfurt: Peter Lang, 1979.

Orton, David E. *The Understanding Scribe: Matthew and the Apocalyptic Ideal.* JSNTSup 25. Sheffield: Sheffield Academic Press, 1989.

Overman, J. Andrew. *Matthew's Gospel and Formative Judaism: The Social World of the Matthean Community.* Minneapolis: Fortress, 1990.

————. "Matthew's Parables and Roman Politics: The Imperial Setting of Matthew's Narrative with Special Reference to His Parables," *SBLSP* 34 (1995): 425–439.

Palmer, Caroline L. *Emmanuel: Studies in the Gospel by Matthew.* Atlanta: Committee on Women's Work, Presbyterian Church in the United States, 1947.

Patte, Daniel. "Anti-Semitism in the New Testament: Confronting the Dark Side of Paul's and Matthew's Teaching." *Chicago Theological Seminary Register* 78 (1988): 31–52.

————. *The Gospel According to Matthew: A Structural Commentary on Matthew's Faith*. Philadelphia: Fortress, 1987

Paul, Andre. *L'Évangile de l'énfance selon saint Matthieu*. New ed. Lire la Bible 17. Paris: Cerf, 1984.

Perkins, Pheme. "Matthew 28:16–20, Resurrection, Ecclesiology, and Mission." *SBLSP* 32 (1993): 574–88.

Pesch, Rudolph. "Der Gottessohn im matthäischen Evangelienprolog: Beobachtungen zu den Zitationsformeln der Reflexionszitate." *Biblica* 48 (1967): 395–420.

Pesch, W. *Matthäus der Seelsorger*. SBS 2. Stuttgart: Katholisches Bibelwerk, 1966.

Philips, Gary A. "History and Text: The Reader in Context in Matthew's Parables Discourse." *Semeia* 31 (1985): 415–37.

Pilch, J. J. "The Health Care System in Matthew: A Social Science Analysis." *BTB* 16 (1986): 102–106.

————. "Reading Matthew Anthropologically: Healing in Cultural Perspective." *Listening* 24 (1989): 278–89.

Plummer, Alfred. *An Exegetical Commentary on the Gospel According to Matthew*. London: Robert Scott, 1909.

Powell, Mark A. "Do and Keep What Moses Says (Matthew 23:2–7)." *JBL* 114 (1995): 419–35.

————. "Expected and Unexpected Readings of Matthew: What the Reader Knows." *ATJ* 48/2 (1993): 31–52.

————. *God With Us: A Pastoral Theology of Matthew's Gospel*. Minneapolis: Fortress, 1995.

————. "Matthew's Beatitudes: Reversals and Rewards of the Kingdom." *CBQ* (forthcoming).

————. "The Plot and Subplots of Matthew's Gospel." *NTS* 38 (1992): 187–204.

————. "The Plot to Kill Jesus from Three Different Perspectives: Point of View in Matthew." *SBLSP* 29 (1990): 603–13.

————. "Toward a Narrative-Critical Understanding of Matthew." *Int* 46 (1992): 341–46.

Pregeant, Russell. *Christology Beyond Dogma: Matthew's Christ in Process Hermeneutic.* SS 7 Philadelphia: Fortress; Missoula, MT: Scholars Press, 1978.

Przybylski, Benno. *Righteousness in Matthew and His World of Thought.* SNTSMS 41. Cambridge: Cambridge University Press, 1980.

————. "The Setting of Matthean Anti-Judaism." In *Anti-Judaism in Early Christianity. Vol 1, Paul and the Gospels.* Ed. P. Richardson and D. Granskou. Waterloo, Ontario: Wilfrid Laurier University Press, 1986.

Puzicha, M. *Christus Peregrinus: Die Fremdenaufnahme (Mt 25,35) als Werk der privaten Wohltatigkeit im Urteil der alten Kirche.* MBTh 47 (1980).

Radbertus, Paschasius. *Expositio in Evangelium Matthaei.* PL 120.

Radermakers, J. *Au fil de l'évangile selon saint Matthieu.* 2 vols. Louvain: Heverlee, 1972.

Rau, C. *Das Matthäus-Evangelium: Entstehung, Gestalt, Essenischer Einfluss.* Stuttgart: Urachhaus, 1976.

Reeves, Keith Howard. *The Resurrection Narrative in Matthew: A Literary-Critical Examination.* Lewiston, NY: Mellen, 1993.

Ridderbos, Herman. *Matthew's Witness to Jesus Christ: The King and the Kingdom.* New York: Association, 1958.

Rigaux, Beda. *The Testimony of St. Matthew.* Chicago: Franciscan Herald, 1968.

Robinson, J. A. T. "The 'Parable' of the Sheep and the Goats." *NTS* 2 (1955/56): 225–37.

Robinson, Theodore H. *The Gospel of Matthew.* Moffatt New Testament Commentary. London: Hodder and Stoughton, 1928.

Rothfuchs, W. *Die Erfüllungszitate des Matthäusevangeliums: Eine biblisch-theologische Untersuchung.* Stuttgart: Kohlhammer, 1969.

Roux, H. *L'Évangile du Royaume.* 2nd ed. Geneva: Labor et Fides, 1956.

Sabourin, Leopold. *L'Evangile selon Saint Matthieu et ses Principaux Paralleles.* Rome: Biblical Institute Press, 1978.

Saldarini, Anthony J. *Matthew's Christian-Jewish Community.* Chicago: University of Chicago Press, 1994.

Sand, Alexander. *Das Evangelium nach Matthäus.* RNT. Regensburg: Pustet, 1986.

——. *Das Gesetz und die Propheten. Untersuchungen zur Theologie des Evangeliums nach Matthäus.* Regensburg: Friedrich Pustet, 1974.

——. *Das Matthäus-Evangelium.* Erträge der Forschung 275. Darmstadt: Wissenschaftliche Buchgesellschaft, 1991.

Schenk, W. "Das 'Matthäusevangelium' als 'Petrusevangelium.'" *BZ* N.F. 27 (1983): 58–80.

Schlatter, Adolf. *Der Evangelist Matthäus. Seine Sprache, sein Ziel, seine Selbständigkeit.* 7th ed. Stuttgart: Calwer, 1982.

Schmid, J. *Das Evangelium nach Matthäus.* RNT 1. 3rd ed. Regensburg: Pustet, 1956.

Schnackenburg, Rudolf. "Großsein in Gottesreich. Zu Mt. 18, 1–5." In *Studien zum Matthäusevangelium: Festschrift für Wilhelm Pesch.* Ed. L. Schenke. Stuttgart: Katholisches Bibelwerk, 1988.

——. "Jeder Schriftgelehrte, der ein Jünge des Himmelreiches geworden ist (Mt 13, 52)." In *Wissenschaft und Kirche: Festschrift für Eduard Lohse.* Ed. K. Aland and S. Meurer. Bielefeld: Luther, 1989.

——. *Matthäusevangelium.* 2 vols. Die neue echter Bibel. Würzburg: Echter, 1987.

——. "Petrus im Matthäusevangelium." In *A cause de l' Evangile. Mélanges offerts à Dom J. Dupont.* LD 123. Paris: Cerf, 1985.

Schniewind, J. *Das Evangelium nach Matthäus.* NTD. Neues Göttinger Bibelwerk 2. 7th ed. Göttingen: Vandenhoeck & Ruprecht, 1954.

Schollig, Hugo. "Die Zählung der Generationen in Matthaischen Stammbaum." *ZNW* 59 (3–4, 1968): 261–66.

Schürmann, Heinz. "'Wer daher eines dieser geringsten Gebote auflöst . . .': Wo fand Matthäus das Logion Mt 5,19?" *BZ* 4 (1960): 241.

Schweizer, Eduard. *The Good News According to Matthew.* Atlanta: John Knox, 1975.

———. *Matthäus und Seine Gemeinde.* Stuttgart: Verlag Katholisches Bibelwerk, 1974.

———. "Observance of the Law and Charismatic Activity in Matthew." *NTS* 16 (1970): 216.

Segbroeck, F. van. et al., eds. *The Four Gospels 1992: Vol. 2.* Leuven: Leuven University, 1992.

Selvidge, M. J. "Violence, Woman, and the Future of the Matthean Community: A Redaction Critical Essay." *USQR* 39 (1984): 213–23.

Senior, Donald. *Invitation to Matthew: A Commentary on the Gospel of Matthew with Complete Text From the Jerusalem Bible.* Garden City, NY: Doubleday, 1977.

———. *The Passion of Jesus in the Gospel of Matthew.* Wilmington, DE: Michael Glazier, 1985.

———. *What Are They Saying About Matthew?* New York: Paulist, 1983.

Sigal, Phillip. *The Halakah of Jesus of Nazareth According to the Gospel of Matthew.* Lanham, MD: University Press of America, 1986.

Smith, B. T. D. *The Gospel according to St. Matthew: With Introduction and Notes.* Cambridge Bible for Schools and Colleges. Cambridge: Cambridge University Press, 1933.

Smith, Robert H. *Matthew.* ACNT. Minneapolis: Augsburg, 1989.

———. "Matthew 28:16–20, Anticlimax or Key to the Gospel?" *SBLSP* 32 (1993): 589–602.

Snodgrass, Klyne. "Matthew's Understanding of the Law." *Int* 46 (1992): 368–78.

Stanton, Graham. *A Gospel For a New People: Studies in Matthew.* Edinburgh: T. & T. Clark, 1992.

————. "The Origin and Purpose of Matthew's Gospel: Matthean Scholarship from 1945 to 1980." In *Aufstieg und Niedergang der römischen Welt.* Ed. W. Haase and H. Temporini. Berlin: de Gruyter, 1985.

————. "Revisiting Matthew's Communities." *SBLSP* 33 (1994): 9–23.

————, ed. *The Interpretation of Matthew.* IRT 3. Philadelphia: Fortress, 1983.

Stendahl, Krister. *The School of St. Matthew: And Its Use of the Old Testament.* 2nd ed. Philadelphia: Fortress, 1968.

Stock, Augustine. "Is Matthew's Presentation of Peter Ironic?" *BTB* 17 (1987): 64–69.

————. *The Method and Message of Matthew.* Collegeville, MN: The Liturgical Press, 1994.

Stonehouse, Ned B. *The Witness of Matthew and Mark to Christ.* Philadelphia: Presbyterian Guardian, 1944.

Strecker, Georg. "The Concept of History in Matthew." *JAAR* 35 (1967): 219–30.

————. *Der Weg der Gerechtigkeit.* FRLANT 82: Göttingen: Vandenhoeck and Ruprecht, 1962.

————. *The Sermon on the Mount: An Exegetical Commentary.* Nashville: Abingdon, 1988.

Suggs, M. Jack. *Wisdom, Christology, and Law in Matthew's Gospel.* Cambridge, MA: Harvard University Press, 1970.

Tagawa, K. "People and Community in the Gospel of Matthew." *NTS* 16 (1969–70): 149–62.

Tasker, Randolf Vincent Greenwood. *The Gospel According to Matthew: An Introduction and Commentary.* TNTC. Grand Rapids: Eerdmans, 1961.

Thomas, J. C. "The Kingdom of God in the Gospel According to Matthew." *NTS* 39 (1993): 136–46.

Thompson, William G. "An Historical Perspective on the Gospel of Matthew." *JBL* 93 (1974): 243–62.

———. *Matthew's Advice to a Divided Community: Mt. 17:22–18:35.* Analecta Biblica: Investigationes Scientificae in Res Biblicas 44. Rome: Biblical Institute Press, 1970.

———. "Reflections on the Composition of Matthew 8:1–9:34." *CBQ* 33 (1971): 365–88.

Tilborg, S. van. *The Jewish Leaders in Matthew.* Leiden: E. J. Brill, 1972.

Trilling, Wolfgang. "Amt und Amtsverständnis bei Matthäus." In *Mélanges Bibliques en hommage au R. P. Béda Rigaux.* Gembloux: Duculot, 1970.

———. *Das wahre Israel. Studien zur Theologie des Matthäus Evangeliums.* 3rd ed. Munich: Kösel, 1964.

———. *The Gospel According to Matthew.* 2 vols. New Testament for Spiritual Reading 2. London: Burns & Oates, 1981.

———. *Hausordnung Gottes. Eine Auslegung von Mt 18.* Düsseldorf: Patmos, 1960.

Valdes, J. de. *Commentary upon the Gospel of St. Matthew.* London: Trübner, 1882.

———. *The Sermon on the Mount as an Ideological Intervention.* Assen, Netherlands and Wolfeboro, NH: Van Gorcum, 1986.

Verseput, Donald J. "The Davidic Messiah and Matthew's Jewish Christianity" *SBLSP* 34 (1995): 102–116.

———. "The Faith of the Reader and the Narrative of Matthew 13.53–16.20." *JSNT* 46 (1992): 3–24.

Via, Dan. "Ethical Responsibility and Human Wholeness in Mt. 25:31–46." *HTR* 80 (1987): 79–100.

———. "The Gospel of Matthew: Hypocrisy as Self-Deception." *SBLSP* 27 (1988): 508–17.

———. *Self-Deception and Wholeness in Paul and Matthew.* Minneapolis: Fortress Press, 1990.

Vincent, Paul-Emile. *Les Généalogies de Jésus: Étude Critique de Matthieu I, 1–17, et de Luc III, 23–28.* Alencon: Guy, 1886.

Vischer, W. *Die evangelische Gemeindeordnung. Matthäus 16, 13–20, 28.* Zollikon/Zurich: Evangelische Verlag, 1946.

Viviano, Benedict Thomas. "Matthew, Master of Ecumenical Healing." *CurTM* 10 (1983): 325–32.

Vögtle, Anton. "Das christologische und ecclesiologische Anliegen von Mt. 22.18–20." In *Studia Evangelica* II. Ed. Frank L. Cross. TU 87. Berlin: Akademie, 1964.

————. "Die Genealogie Mt 1, 2–17 und die matthaische Kindheitsgeschichte." *BZ* 8 (1964): 45–58, 239–62.

————. "Die Genealogie Mt 1,2–17 . . . Kindheitsgeschichte." *BZ* 9 (1965): 32–49.

————. "Josias Zeugte den Jechonias und seine Brüder (Mt. 1, 11)." In *Lex Tua Veritas.* Ed. Heinrich Gross and Franz Mussner. Trier: Paulinus, 1961.

Waetjen, Herman C. "The Genealogy as the Key to the Gospel according to Matthew." *JBL* 95 (1976): 205–30.

————. *The Origin and Destiny of Humanness: An Interpretation of the Gospel According to Matthew.* San Rafael, CA: Crystal, 1976.

Wainwright, Elaine M. *Towards a Feminist Critical Reading of the Gospel according to Matthew.* New York: de Gruyter, 1991.

Walker, R. *Die Heilsgeschichte im ersten Evangelium.* FRLANT 91. Göttingen: Vandenhoeck & Ruprecht, 1967.

Watson, F. "Liberating the Reader: A Theological-Exegetical Study of the Parable of the Sheep and the Goats (Matt 25:31–46)." In *The Open Text.* Ed. F. Watson. London: SCM, 1993.

Weaver, Dorothy Jean. *Matthew's Missionary Discourse: A Literary Critical Analysis.* JSNTSup 38. Sheffield: Sheffield Academic Press, 1990.

Weiss, Bernhard. *Das Matthäus-Evangelium.* KeK I/1. 9th ed. Göttingen: Vandenhoeck, 1898.

Weiss, Johannes *Das Matthäus-Evangelium.* SNT I. 2nd ed. 1907.

Wengst, K. "Wie aus Böcken Ziegen Wurden (Mt 25,32f)." *EvT* 54 (1994): 493–97.

White, L. J. "Grid and Group in Matthew's Community: The Righteousness/Honor Code in the Sermon on the Mount." *Semeia* 35 (1986): 61–90.

Wikenhauser, A. "Die Liebeswerke in dem Gerichtsgemälde Mt 25,31–46." *BZ* 20 (1932): 366–69.

Wilckins, U. "Gottes geringste Brüder: zu Mt 25,31–46." In *Jesus und Paulus: Festschrift für W. G. Kümmel.* Ed. E. E. Ellis and E. Grässer. Göttingen: Vandenhoeck, 1975.

Wilhelms, E. *Die Tempelsteuerperikope Matthäus 17, 24–27 in der Exegese der griechischen Väter der Alten Kirche.* SFEG 34. Helsinki: Finnische Exegetische Gesellschaft, 1980.

Wilkens, W. "Die Komposition des Matthäus-Evangeliums." *NTS* 31 (1985): 24–38.

Wilkens, Michael J. *The Concept of Disciple in Matthew's Gospel.* NovTSup 59. Leiden: E. J. Brill, 1988.

———. "Named and Unnamed Disciples in Matthew: A Literary/Theological Study." *SBLSP* 30 (1991): 418–39

Winandy, J. "La scène du jugement dernier (Mt 25,31–46)." *ScEccl* 18 (1966): 178–186.

Witherup, Ronald D. "The Cross of Jesus: A Literary-Critical Study of Matthew 27." Ph.D. diss., Union Theological Seminary in Virginia, 1985.

———. "The Death of Jesus and the Raising of the Saints: Matthew 27:51–54 in Context." *SBLSP* 26 (1987): 574–85.

Wong, Eric Kun-Chun. "The Matthean Understanding of the Sabbath: A Response to Graham Stanton." *JSNT* 44 (1991): 3–18.

Yarnold, E. "*Teleios* in St. Matthew's Gospel." In *Studia Evangelica* IV. Ed. F. L. Cross. Berlin: Akademie, 1968.

Zahn, Theodor. *Das Evangelium des Matthäus.* 4th ed. Leipzig: Erlangen, 1922.

Index of Modern Authors

Index of the Bible